AMERICA'S
HISTORIC SITES

AMERICA'S HISTORIC SITES

VOLUME 1

ALABAMA—INDIANA

1-456

from **The Editors of Salem Press**

Managing Editor
Tracy Irons-Georges

SALEM PRESS, INC.

Pasadena, California   Hackensack, New Jersey

Editor in Chief: Dawn P. Dawson

Managing Editor: Tracy Irons-Georges *Acquisitions Editor:* Mark Rehn

Research Supervisor: Jeffry Jensen *Photo Editor:* Philip Bader

Research Assistant: Jeff Stephens *Layout:* Ross E. Castellano

Production Editor: Joyce I. Buchea *Design and Graphics:* James Hutson

Maps in this volume are adapted from Cartesia's MapArt™ Geopolitical Deluxe v2.0 (1998)

Library of Congress Cataloging-in-Publication Data

America's historic sites / the Editors of Salem Press; managing editor, Tracy Irons-Georges.
    p. cm.
  Vol. 1-3.
  Includes bibiographical references and index.
  ISBN 0-89356-122-3 (set : alk. paper) —ISBN 0-89356-123-1 (vol. 1 : alk. paper) — ISBN 0-89356-124-X (vol. 2 : alk. paper) — ISBN 0-89356-147-9 (vol. 3 : alk. paper)
  1. Historic sites—United States—Encyclopedias. 2. United States—History, Local—Encyclopedias. I. Irons-Georges, Tracy. II. Editors of Salem Press.

E159 .A45 2000
973'.03—dc21

00-056337

First Printing

Contents

Publisher's Note · · · · · · · · · · · · · · vii
Contributor List · · · · · · · · · · · · · ix

Alabama · · · · · · · · · · · · · · · · · · · 1
History of Alabama · · · · · · · · · · · · · 2
Montgomery · · · · · · · · · · · · · · · · · 4
Sixteenth Street Baptist Church,
    Birmingham · · · · · · · · · · · · · · · 8
Tuskegee Institute · · · · · · · · · · · 11
Other Historic Sites · · · · · · · · · · 15

Alaska · 17
History of Alaska · · · · · · · · · · · · · 18
Iditarod National Historic Trail · · · · · · · 20
Nome · 23
Sitka · · · · · · · · · · · · · · · · · · · 26
Skagway · · · · · · · · · · · · · · · · · · 29
Other Historic Sites · · · · · · · · · · · 33

Arizona · · · · · · · · · · · · · · · · · · 36
History of Arizona · · · · · · · · · · · · 37
Canyon de Chelly · · · · · · · · · · · · · 39
Casa Grande Ruins · · · · · · · · · · · · 44
Coronado National Memorial · · · · · · · · 48
Grand Canyon · · · · · · · · · · · · · · · 51
Navajo National Monument · · · · · · · · · 54
Taliesin West · · · · · · · · · · · · · · · 58
Tombstone · · · · · · · · · · · · · · · · · 62
Wupatki National Monument · · · · · · · · 65
Other Historic Sites · · · · · · · · · · · 70

Arkansas · · · · · · · · · · · · · · · · · 72
History of Arkansas · · · · · · · · · · · · 73
Arkansas Post · · · · · · · · · · · · · · · 75
Little Rock Central High School · · · · · · 80
Other Historic Sites · · · · · · · · · · · 83

California · · · · · · · · · · · · · · · · · 85
History of California · · · · · · · · · · · 86

Alcatraz Island · · · · · · · · · · · · · · 89
Angelus Temple, Los Angeles · · · · · · · 93
Chinatown, San Francisco · · · · · · · · · 95
Columbia · · · · · · · · · · · · · · · · · 102
Death Valley · · · · · · · · · · · · · · · 105
Donner Camp, Truckee · · · · · · · · · · 108
El Pueblo de Los Angeles · · · · · · · · · 111
Golden Gate Bridge · · · · · · · · · · · 115
Haight-Ashbury, San Francisco · · · · · · 119
Hearst Castle · · · · · · · · · · · · · · · 122
Hollywood · · · · · · · · · · · · · · · · · 125
John Muir National Historic Site · · · · · 130
Little Tokyo, Los Angeles · · · · · · · · · 133
Los Angeles Memorial Coliseum · · · · · · 136
Manzanar · · · · · · · · · · · · · · · · · 140
Mission Basilica San Diego de Alcalá · · · · 143
Mission San Gabriel Arcángel · · · · · · · 147
Mission San Juan Capistrano · · · · · · · 151
Monterey · · · · · · · · · · · · · · · · · 154
Nixon Birthplace, Yorba Linda · · · · · · 159
Presidio of San Francisco · · · · · · · · · 162
San Diego Presidio · · · · · · · · · · · · 165
Sonoma · · · · · · · · · · · · · · · · · · 169
Sutter's Fort · · · · · · · · · · · · · · · 173
Sutter's Mill · · · · · · · · · · · · · · · 178
Watts · · · · · · · · · · · · · · · · · · · 182
Other Historic Sites · · · · · · · · · · · 186

Colorado · · · · · · · · · · · · · · · · · 195
History of Colorado · · · · · · · · · · · · 196
Bent's Old Fort · · · · · · · · · · · · · · 198
Leadville · · · · · · · · · · · · · · · · · 203
Mesa Verde · · · · · · · · · · · · · · · · 209
Pikes Peak · · · · · · · · · · · · · · · · 213
Telluride · · · · · · · · · · · · · · · · · 216
Other Historic Sites · · · · · · · · · · · 220

Connecticut · · · · · · · · · · · · · · · 221
History of Connecticut · · · · · · · · · · 222
Mystic · · · · · · · · · · · · · · · · · · · 224
Nook Farm · · · · · · · · · · · · · · · · · 228
Old New-Gate Prison · · · · · · · · · · · 231
Other Historic Sites · · · · · · · · · · · 234

Delaware · · · · · · · · · · · · · 238
History of Delaware · · · · · · · · · 239
Eleutherian Mills · · · · · · · · · · 241
New Castle · · · · · · · · · · · · · · 243
Wilmington · · · · · · · · · · · · · 246
Other Historic Sites · · · · · · · · · 250

District of Columbia · · · · · · · · · · 251
History of the District of Columbia · · · · 252
The Capitol · · · · · · · · · · · · · 254
Ford's Theatre · · · · · · · · · · · · 259
Frederick Douglass National
  Historic Site · · · · · · · · · · · · 262
Gallaudet University · · · · · · · · · 266
Georgetown · · · · · · · · · · · · · 269
Lincoln Memorial · · · · · · · · · · 272
Mary McLeod Bethune Council House · · · 275
The National Mall · · · · · · · · · · 279
Sewall-Belmont House · · · · · · · · · 283
Smithsonian Institution · · · · · · · · 286
Thomas Jefferson Memorial · · · · · · · 290
Vietnam Veterans Memorial · · · · · · · 292
Washington Monument · · · · · · · · · 296
The White House · · · · · · · · · · · 299
Other Historic Sites · · · · · · · · · 304

Florida · · · · · · · · · · · · · · · 310
History of Florida · · · · · · · · · · 311
Cape Canaveral · · · · · · · · · · · 314
Key West · · · · · · · · · · · · · · 319
St. Augustine · · · · · · · · · · · · 326
Other Historic Sites · · · · · · · · · 331

Georgia · · · · · · · · · · · · · · 334
History of Georgia · · · · · · · · · · 335
Andersonville · · · · · · · · · · · · 337
Chickamauga and Chattanooga
  National Military Park · · · · · · · · 340
Fort Frederica · · · · · · · · · · · · 344
Martin Luther King, Jr., Historic
  District, Atlanta · · · · · · · · · · 349

Savannah · · · · · · · · · · · · · · 353
Stone Mountain · · · · · · · · · · · 356
Other Historic Sites · · · · · · · · · 359

Hawaii · · · · · · · · · · · · · · · 362
History of Hawaii · · · · · · · · · · 363
Iolani Palace, Honolulu · · · · · · · · 365
Kawaiahao Church and Mission
  Houses, Honolulu · · · · · · · · · 369
Lahaina · · · · · · · · · · · · · · · 371
Pearl Harbor · · · · · · · · · · · · 375
Other Historic Sites · · · · · · · · · 380

Idaho · · · · · · · · · · · · · · · 383
History of Idaho · · · · · · · · · · · 384
Lemhi Pass, Tendoy · · · · · · · · · 386
Nez Perce National Historical
  Park · · · · · · · · · · · · · · · · 388
Other Historic Sites · · · · · · · · · 394

Illinois · · · · · · · · · · · · · · · 396
History of Illinois · · · · · · · · · · 397
Cahokia · · · · · · · · · · · · · · · 399
Chicago Water Tower · · · · · · · · · 403
Haymarket Square, Chicago · · · · · · · 408
Hull-House, Chicago · · · · · · · · · 414
Museum of Science and Industry and
  Midway Plaisance, Chicago · · · · · · 419
New Salem · · · · · · · · · · · · · 425
Pullman · · · · · · · · · · · · · · · 429
Other Historic Sites · · · · · · · · · 433

Indiana · · · · · · · · · · · · · · · 438
History of Indiana · · · · · · · · · · 439
Columbus · · · · · · · · · · · · · · 441
New Harmony · · · · · · · · · · · · 445
Vincennes · · · · · · · · · · · · · · 450
Other Historic Sites · · · · · · · · · 454

Publisher's Note

Many of the greatest events in American history—both tragedies and triumphs—are intimately tied in the public consciousness to the places where they occurred: Valley Forge, Gettysburg, Tombstone, Little Bighorn, Pearl Harbor, Manzanar, Little Rock Central High School, Camp David. Other sites serve as reminders of the tremendous growth and progress of the United States from colonial times to the end of the twentieth century: Jamestown, Plymouth, Williamsburg, Wall Street, the Brooklyn Bridge, Harlem, Hollywood, Los Alamos. *America's Historic Sites* celebrates these places and many more that helped shape the nation. Its 237 site entries cover historic towns and districts, monuments to events and people, and the birthplaces and homes of noteworthy individuals in politics, the military, science, education, and the arts. Together, these places weave a rich tapestry representing the American experience.

Some of the material in *America's Historic Sites* first appeared in the *International Dictionary of Historic Places, Volume 1—Americas*, published by Fitzroy Dearborn in 1995. The entries on the United States were pulled, reformatted, and updated. New essays on 107 sites were added, as well as state histories and considerable public domain information on National Historic Landmarks. All the sites covered here are located in the United States.

This encyclopedia is arranged by state, including a chapter on the District of Columbia. Each of the fifty-one chapters begins with a history, first published in Salem Press's *The 50 States* (2000), that provides a broad outline of the state from its establishment to modern times. This section features a state map showing the locations of sites covered in the essays that follow.

Most site entries begin with a line for "Date." For towns or cities, the founding date is given. If the entry is an official National Historic Site, the date that it was established may be listed. Often, the dates of important events occurring at the site are provided. The "Relevant issues" heading identifies the subject matter associated with the site. In a few sentences, "Significance" explains why the site is important historically. "Location" provides a general sense of where the site can be found within its city or state. The official site office or the best contact for information on the site, such as a National Park Service office or chamber of commerce, is listed, including an address, phone number, and fax number, e-mail address, and Web site when available.

Each entry in *America's Historic Sites* discusses the earliest associated events, such as the founding of a town, and then traces the evolution of the site. Historical context is provided for the general reader, and all aspects of the site are considered. For example, although Salem, Massachusetts, is famous for its witch hunts in the late seventeenth century, the author also covers its other roles in American history, such as its status as a center for trade, its importance as a port, and the career and fictional works of native son Nathaniel Hawthorne. Most essays offer information about when the site can be visited and what is found there today. Many entries on cities conclude with a section describing various historic districts, homes, or other places of interest. An annotated bibliography of further sources concludes each site essay. All older essays have been updated with the latest editions and with recent popular and scholarly historical works.

Each chapter ends with a list of Other Historic Sites within the state, all of which are official National Historic Landmarks. Every site includes headings for "Relevant issues" and "Location." The "Statement of significance" is taken from the report submitted to the government when the site was first named a National Historic Landmark.

In the back of volume 3, a Category Index breaks down all sites in the encyclopedia—those covered in the essays and those listed as Other Historic Sites—into the twenty-nine subjects used for the "Relevant issues" heading: African American history, American Indian history, art and architecture, Asian American history, aviation history, business and industry, Civil War, colonial America, cultural history, disasters and tragedies, education, European settlement, health and medicine, Latino history, legal history, literary history, military history, naval history, political history, religion, Revolutionary War, science and technology, social reform, sports, Vietnam War, western expansion, women's history, World War I, World War II. The encyclopedia ends with a comprehensive subject Index that allows the reader to find sites by historical topic or personage.

The essays in *America's Historic Sites* are written by specialists in American history, most of whom are academicians; a list of their names and affiliations follows. Their invaluable contribution to this project was helping the past come alive for readers.

Contributor List

Patrick Adcock
Freelance writer

Richard Adler
Associate professor, University of Michigan-Dearborn

Craig W. Allin
Professor, Cornell College, Iowa

Eleanor B. Amico
Freelance writer and editor

Charles F. Bahmueller
Center for Civic Education, Calabasas, California

Sharon Bakos
Freelance writer and editor

Ann Stewart Balakier
Associate professor, University of South Dakota

Carl L. Bankston III
Tulane University, New Orleans

Alvin K. Benson
Professor, Brigham Young University, Utah

Cynthia A. Bily
Instructor, Adrian College, Michigan

Margaret Boe Birns
Adjunct assistant professor, New York University

Nicholas Birns
New School University, New York

Bernard A. Block
Freelance writer

Sarah Bremser
Curator, Honolulu Academy of Arts, Hawaii

Shawn Brennan
Editor, Gale Research Inc., Detroit

Elizabeth Brice
Special Collections librarian, Miami University, Oxford, Ohio

William S. Brockington
Professor, University of South Carolina at Aiken

Beverly A. Bunch-Lyons
Professor, Virginia Polytechnic Institute and State University

Joseph P. Byrne
Associate professor, Belmont University, Nashville, Tennessee

Douglas Campbell
Freelance writer

Edmund J. Campion
Professor, University of Tennessee, Knoxville

Ranès Chakrovorty, M.D.
Doctoral student, Virginia Polytechnic Institute and State University

Ron Chepesiuk
Associate professor/head of special collections, Winthrop University, South Carolina

Olive Classe
Freelance writer and translator

Carolyn J. Daily
Freelance writer

Bill Delaney
Freelance writer

Paul Demilio
Director of University Archives, Dusquesne University, Pennsylvania

Andy DeRoche
Front Range Community College, Longmont, Colorado

Elizabeth Devine
Professor, Salem State College, Massachusetts

Margaret A. Dodson
Freelance writer

Sina Dubovoy
Freelance writer

David Allen Duncan
Professor, Tennessee Wesleyan College

Laura Duncan
Reporter, Chicago Daily Law Bulletin

Robert P. Ellis
Freelance writer

Charles Endress
Professor, Angelo State University, Texas

Eric C. Ewert
Doctoral student, University of Idaho

Thomas H. Falk
Michigan State University

Jeffrey Felshman
Freelance writer

Edward Fiorelli
Associate professor, St. John's University, New York

John A. Flink
Freelance writer

Bonnie Ford
Sacramento City College, California

Thomas B. Ford
Reporter, Plastics News

John Franklin
Doctoral candidate, Texas Christian University

C. George Fry
*Winebrenner Theological Seminary, Ohio
University of Findlay, Ohio*

Steven P. Gietschier
Director of Historical Records, The Sporting News

Robert R. Gradie III
University of Connecticut

Richard Greb
Freelance writer

Irwin Halfond
Professor, McKendree College, Missouri

Sheldon Hanft
Appalachian State University, North Carolina

James C. Hart
Researcher, The Catholic Charities of the Archdiocese of Chicago

James Hayes-Bohanan
Assistant professor, Bridgewater State College, Massachusetts

Patrick Heenan
Research student, University of London

Michael R. Hill
University of Nebraska-Lincoln

Carl W. Hoagstrom
Professor, Ohio Northern University

Nika Hoffman
Crossroads School for Arts and Sciences, California

Ronald K. Huch
University of Papua New Guinea

Jeff W. Huebner
Freelance writer

Raymond Pierre Hylton
Assistant professor, Virginia Union University

John Quinn Imholte
Professor, University of Minnesota, Morris

Robert Jacobs
Professor, Central Washington University

Tony Jaros
Copy editor, Vegetarian Times

Joseph C. Jastrzembski
Minot State University, North Dakota

Albert C. Jensen
Central Florida Community College, Ocala

Gary A. Jones
Freelance editor

Jonathan M. Jones
Adjunct professor, University of Memphis, Tennessee

Kathleen Kadlec
Office of the State Archaeologist, University of Iowa

Leigh Husband Kimmel
Freelance writer

Linda J. King
Associate editor, American Dental Hygenists' Association

Andrew M. Kloak
Freelance writer

Christopher S. W. Koehler
Instructor, Sacramento City College, California

Gayla Koerting
Instructor, University of Missouri-Rolla

James Lahey
Freelance writer and editor, Jewel Editorial Services

Monique Lamontagne
Research student, University of London

Lyndall B. Landauer
Lake Tahoe Community College, California

Bob Lange
Freelance writer

Cynthia L. Langston
Strategic planning assistant, TBWA Advertising, New York

Eugene Larson
Professor, Los Angeles Pierce College

Sherry Crane LaRue
Teacher, Madison Metropolitan School District, Wisconsin

Gregory J. Ledger
Contributing writer, Windy City Times, Chicago

Van Michael Leslie
Professor, Union College, Kentucky

Thomas T. Lewis
Mount Senario College, Minnesota

Gina Macdonald
Instructor, Loyola University, New Orleans

Jane MacInnis
Freelance writer

Mary F. McNulty
Freelance writer and editor

Kim M. Magon
Freelance writer and editor

Rachel Maines
Maines & Associates, New York

Nancy Farm Männikkö
Historian, Walking into the Past, Michigan

Martin J. Manning
Office of International Programs, U.S. State Department, Washington, D.C.

Brent Marchant
Freelance writer and editor

Christine Walker Martin
Freelance writer and editor

Ruben G. Mendoza
Director, Institute of Archaeology, California State University, Monterey Bay

Linda K. Menton
University of Hawaii

Paul Merrion
Washington editor, Crain's Chicago Business

Kathleen M. Micham
Lexicographer, Dictionnaires le Robert, Paris

Phyllis R. Miller
Freelance writer and editor

Kevin M. Mitchell
Freelance writer

Lauren M. Mitchell
Copy editor, Salem Press, Pasadena, California

Bruce P. Montgomery
Curator/head of archives, University of Colorado at Boulder

Gail A. Moss
Contributing editor, Chicago Parent

Tabitha R. Oglesby
Freelance researcher

Keith W. Olson
Professor, University of Maryland

Lisa Collins Orman
Freelance consultant, writer, and editor

Steve Palmer
Sales representative and freelance writer

William A. Paquette
Professor, Tidewater Community College, Virginia

Robert J. Paradowski
Professor, Rochester Institute of Technology, New York

Robert L. Patterson
Emeritus professor, Armstrong Atlantic State University, South Carolina

Constance A. Pedoto
Miles College, Alabama

Nis Petersen
Professor, New Jersey City University

John R. Phillips
Associate professor, Purdue University Calumet, Indiana

Michael D. Phillips
Instructor, Brigham Young University, Utah

Erika E. Pilver
Professor, Westfield State College, Massachusetts

Marguerite R. Plummer
Assistant professor/director of Pioneer Heritage Center, Louisiana State University in Shreveport

S. Marshall Poindexter
Magazine writer and editor

Sharon M. Poindexter
Public administrator

Dorothy Potter
Assistant professor, Lynchburg College, Virginia

Tessa Powell
Freelance writer

Jenny Presnell
Humanities/Social Sciences librarian, Miami University, Oxford, Ohio

Cliff Prewencki
Freelance writer

P. S. Ramsey
Freelance writer

R. Kent Rasmussen
Editor, Salem Press, Pasadena, California

John David Rausch, Jr.
Assistant professor, West Texas A&M University

Thomas D. Reins
California State University, Fullerton

Trudy Ring
Commissioning editor, Fitzroy Dearborn Publishers, Chicago

Jonathan Rogers
Law student, DePaul University, Chicago

Roger W. Rouland
Freelance writer and editor

Terence J. Sacks
Freelance writer and editor

Robert M. Salkin
Commissioning editor, Fitzroy Dearborn Publishers, Chicago

Vicki A. Sanders
Freelance researcher

Paul R. Sando
Assistant professor, West Texas A&M University

June Skinner Sawyers
Associate editor, Loyola University Press, Chicago

Richard Sax
Dean, College of Arts and Humanities, Madonna University, Michigan

Helmut J. Schmeller
Emeritus professor, Fort Hays State University, Kansas

Roberta Schreyer
Associate professor, State University of New York, Potsdam

Rose Secrest
Freelance writer

Timothy J. Shannon
Assistant professor, State University of New York, Cortland

R. Baird Shuman
Emeritus professor, University of Illinois-Urbana

Michael W. Simpson
Bluefox Productions, Hawaii

Andrew C. Skinner
Professor, Brigham Young University, Utah

Jane Marie Smith
Slippery Rock University, Pennsylvania

Roger Smith
Freelance writer

Neva Jean Specht
Assistant professor, Appalachian State University, North Carolina

Roger J. Stilling
Professor, Appalachian State University, North Carolina

Leslie Stricker
Park College/Wright-Patterson Air Force Base, Ohio

America's Historic Sites

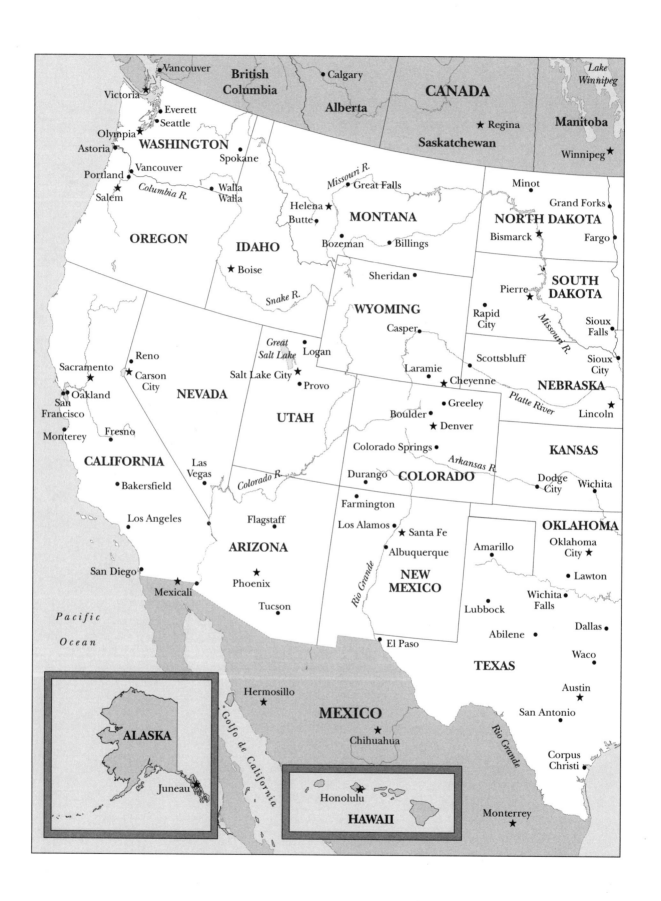

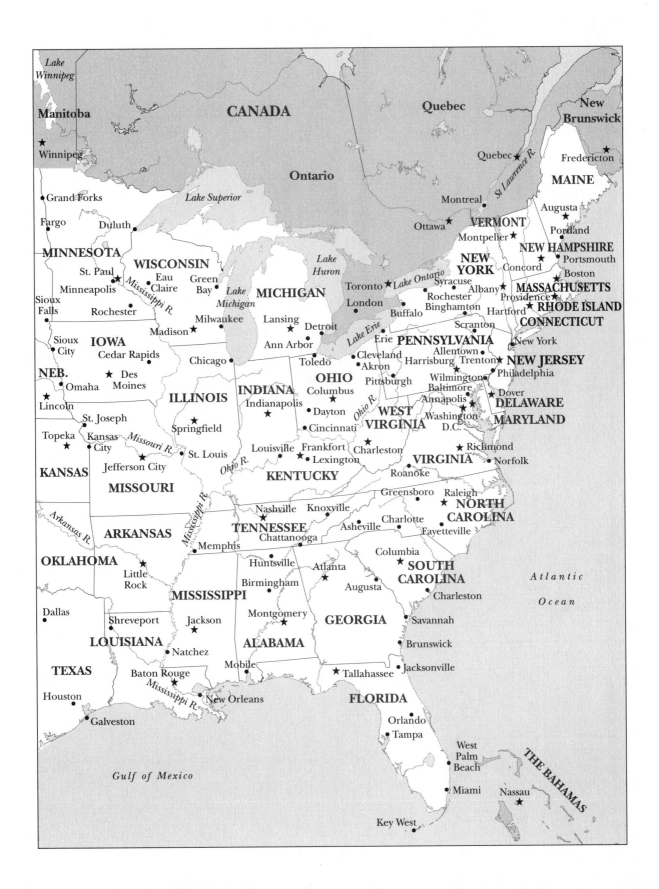

Alabama

History of Alabama 2

Montgomery 4

Sixteenth Street Baptist Church,
  Birmingham 8

Tuskegee Institute 11

Other Historic Sites 15

The State Capitol Building in Montgomery. (American Stock Photography)

History of Alabama

Alabama is in the southeastern part of the United States, between Mississippi to the west and Georgia and Florida to the east. Most of Alabama's southern border adjoins Florida, but a small portion of the state extends down to the Gulf of Mexico. The northern part of Alabama, just below Tennessee, is known as the Appalachian region. It is made up of high plateaus, ridges, valleys, and the high Talladega Mountains. The Piedmont Plateau, another rocky region, extends from the Talladega Mountains to the Georgia border. Until well into the twentieth century, many of the people in the highlands of Alabama lived the isolated lives of mountain and hill dwellers. The Interior Low Plateau region is the part of northern Alabama drained by the Tennessee River. Below the northern uplands, the Gulf Coastal Plains extend south to the Gulf of Mexico. The Gulf Coastal Plains include the Black Belt, a dark-soiled prairie.

The Tennessee River area and the Black Belt have rich soil. Together with Alabama's hot, humid climate, this has made these territories ideal for agriculture. As a result, agriculture tended to dominate the state's economic activities until the second half of the twentieth century. Worldwide demand for cotton in the nineteenth century led the state to specialize in cotton production. Since cotton was a crop that required a great deal of unskilled labor, this created a reliance on slavery that profoundly affected the state's history.

Early History

Before the arrival of the Europeans, Alabama was dominated by Native Americans known as the Mound Builders, after their ceremonial earth mounds. The best-known archaeological site of the Mound Builders in Alabama is at Moundville on the Black Warrior River in central Alabama. Moundville was a large and complex society, second in size and organization only to the Cahokia site of Mound Builder culture in Illinois. Both a populous town and a political and religious center, the Moundville community itself probably housed about one thousand people at its height and was surrounded by around ten thousand people living in the Black Warrior River Valley. This settlement lasted from about 1000 C.E. to about 1450.

In the eighteenth century, the Creek were one of the largest and predominant Native American groups in Alabama. The Creek, who lived in villages of log houses, sided with the British against the Americans in both the Revolutionary War and the War of 1812. At war with the Americans, they were defeated by General Andrew Jackson, and by 1828 they agreed to give up all of their lands and move to Indian Territory in modern Oklahoma. The Cherokee, who were spread throughout the Southeast, were also well represented in Alabama. In 1838 most of the Cherokee were also forced to relocate to Indian Territory. Similarly, most of the Choctaw and the Chickasaw were removed from Alabama and the adjacent states.

Exploration and Colonization

Spanish explorers reached Alabama around 1540. The Spanish attempted to establish a settlement at Mobile Bay but soon deserted it, leaving cattle, hogs, and horses behind, all of which became part of local Native American ways of life. The French claimed much of Alabama as part of their vast Louisiana territory, and they built forts and trading posts. After France and Great Britain fought the French and Indian Wars (1754-1763), Alabama fell under the control of the British. The coastal area, including Mobile Bay, became part of West Florida. North of West Florida, all of Alabama was reserved by the British for the Native Americans.

During the American Revolution, Spain captured Mobile from the British, shutting the British out of Alabama. After the Revolution, West Florida became Spanish land, and interior Alabama was turned over to the new United States. After several years of border disputes, the United States and Spain finally agreed in 1795 that 31 degrees north latitude would be the boundary between U.S. land and West Florida; this would continue to be the boundary between Alabama and the Florida Panhandle. In 1798 the U.S. Congress formed the Mississippi Territory, made up of modern Mississippi and Alabama. The portion of the territory along the Mississippi River became the state of Mississippi in 1817, and in 1819 Alabama was admitted to the Union as the twenty-second state.

Slavery and Civil War

Alabama's rich soil led to an influx of settlers. Worldwide demand for cotton made this crop enormously profitable for a few wealthy landowners. Black slaves worked the cotton plantations, and between 1830 and 1860 the state's slave population grew by 270 percent, while the white population grew by only 170 percent. Although the big plantation owners made up only about 6 to 7 percent of Alabama's population, they were enormously influential and dominated the state's society. The majority of white Alabamians, especially in the hills and mountains, were small subsistence farmers.

Slavery became a contentious issue in the United States in the first half of the nineteenth century. As new territories entered the United States, many northern leaders opposed the spread of slavery. The southern political leadership, dominated by the plantation owners, saw slavery as essential to the southern agricultural way of life and feared falling under the control of the populous north. In 1861 Alabama joined other southern states in seceding from the United States and forming the Confederate States of America. The bitter Civil War ensued. By 1865 Alabama and the other southern states were defeated and occupied by northern troops.

With the end of the Civil War, Alabama's slaves received freedom. However, there were few economic opportunities for them, and most had to take jobs working as low-income agricultural laborers for white landowners. The American Missionary Association and the Federal Freedmen's Bureau helped to establish schools that formed a basis for future African American education. Although African Americans received the right to vote during Reconstruction, the period from after the Civil War to 1877, when Union troops withdrew from the South, relatively few Alabamian blacks were able to take positions of political leadership because of the former slaves' lack of education and experience. By 1874, white southern Democrats managed to take control of the state government. Throughout the nineteenth century, the white state government established legal segregation and restricted the rights of African Americans.

The Civil Rights Era

During the 1950's and 1960's, African Americans in Alabama and other southern states began organizing to oppose segregation and racial discrimination. In 1955 Rosa Parks, a black citizen of Montgomery, Alabama, was arrested when she refused to give up her seat on a bus to a white passenger. In response, the African American residents of Montgomery, under the leadership of the clergyman Dr. Martin Luther King, Jr., organized a boycott of the city's public transportation system. The successful boycott made King a national civil rights leader, and he went on to advocate desegregation campaigns and marches throughout the South.

Alabama governor George Wallace, first elected in 1962, came to national prominence as a result of his opposition to integration. Wallace had experienced defeat in a first run for governor in 1959, when he refused the support of the Ku Klux Klan and ran a campaign of racial moderation. After that defeat, he became a staunch segregationist and attempted to block the integration of Alabama's schools and universities. On the basis of the national recognition brought by his segregationist policies, Wallace ran for president of the United States in 1968 as the candidate of the American Independent Party.

Although racial inequality continued to be a problem in Alabama, segregation became illegal, and black Alabamians achieved substantial social and political influence. From 1969 to 1970, the percentage of African American students attending integrated schools increased from 15 percent to 80 percent. In 1982, when George Wallace was elected to his third term as governor, he actively appealed to black voters and renounced his earlier racial positions.

Alabama's Industrialization

Alabama saw substantial industrialization over the course of the twentieth century. In 1907 United States Steel Corporation established a steel industry in Birmingham. Iron and steel became leading products of Alabama, concentrated mainly in the Birmingham area.

The port city of Mobile became a center of shipbuilding during World War I. Shipbuilding and ship repair continued to be important on the Alabama Gulf Coast, but the area around Mobile also began to produce paper and chemical products. The city of Huntsville became a focal point of U.S. government missile manufacturing and the aerospace industry after World War II. Cutbacks in federal government spending caused Huntsville to di-

versify its economy after the 1970's, and other high technology industries located there.

Despite the rapid industrialization, agriculture continued to be a major economic activity. However, most modern agricultural activities in Alabama are heavily mechanized and use relatively little labor. Cotton remains important, but many of the old cotton fields now produce peanuts, soybeans, corn, and other crops.

As Alabama has industrialized, its population has shifted from rural areas to urban areas. In 1990, 60 percent of the people in the state lived in places with more than 2,500 inhabitants. Birmingham had the largest concentration, with a population of 266,000. African Americans, who lived almost entirely in rural areas in the early twentieth century, were heavily concentrated in larger cities in the southern and central parts of the state by 1990.   —*Carl L. Bankston III*

Montgomery

Date: Founded in 1819

Relevant issues: African American history, Civil War, social reform

Significance: The city was the site of the Montgomery bus boycott that propelled Martin Luther King, Jr., into a position of civil rights leadership. It was also the first capital of the Confederate States of America.

Location: Central Alabama on the banks of the Alabama River, 90 miles south of Birmingham and 175 miles northeast of Mobile

Site Office:
Montgomery Area Chamber of Commerce
41 Commerce Street
P.O. Box 79
Montgomery, AL 36101
ph.: (334) 834-5200
fax: (334) 265-4745
Web site: www.montgomerychamber.org

As the capital of Alabama, Montgomery has been one of the leading cities of the South and southern culture. In its earliest days, Montgomery served as the economic hub of central Alabama's cotton plantations, and when the institution of slavery was threatened in the mid-nineteenth century, Montgomery's citizens became some of the

The Civil Rights Memorial in Montgomery, designed by Maya Lin, lists the names of those killed in the struggle for equality for African Americans. (Alabama Bureau of Tourism & Travel/Karim Shamsi Basha)

most vocal advocates of secession. So great was this opposition that Montgomery served as the capital of the Confederacy in the initial stages of the Civil War. Montgomery remained an important southern city after the war, and with the city's bus boycott of 1955-1956, it became an early center of the African American Civil Rights movement.

Founding

White immigrants first settled in the region that became Montgomery in the late eighteenth century. Originally they came to trade with Towasa and Ikantchati, two Alibamu villages in the region that were known to the Native Americans as Chunnanugga Chatty (high red bluff). However, the Alibamu evacuated the area following the defeat of the Creeks in 1814 by General Andrew Jackson in what has become known as the Creek War. Subsequently, the Mississippi territorial legislature created Montgomery County in 1816. The county was

named after Major Lemuel P. Montgomery, who was killed during the Creek War's Battle of Horseshoe Bend.

The county quickly became the center of land speculation as two men from the East—General John Scott and Andrew Dexter—and their financial supporters bought up the land in the region. Scott and Dexter both founded towns and competed for settlers until they merged their interests and founded Montgomery on December 3, 1819. The state of Alabama was admitted to the Union just eleven days later. Interestingly, the new town was not named for Lemuel Montgomery like the county but rather for Major General Richard Montgomery, a hero of the Revolutionary War who died in Benedict Arnold's expedition against Quebec.

In 1820, Montgomery was a struggling town on the frontier, but slaveholding families soon moved into the region and set up cotton plantations. Due to its location and easy access to the Alabama River, Montgomery became a center for cotton distribution. Cotton provided a basis of wealth for the town, and annual per capita income in the 1830's was slightly more than seven hundred dollars. The United States as a whole never reached such a high amount until after the Civil War.

Between 1830 and 1846, Montgomery's population grew 260 percent, and the town's wealth attracted settlers with greater affluence and social standing, such as doctors and lawyers, than did many other communities in Alabama. As a result, Montgomery soon became a political center in the state. By 1846, the town's political power was so great that the state legislature voted to move the capital from Tuscaloosa to Montgomery.

The state hired George Nichols, a Philadelphia architect, to design a building, and the legislature met for their first session in the new Greek Revival-style capitol on December 6, 1847. In just under thirty years, Montgomery had grown from a small frontier town into one of the most important cities in Alabama.

Civil War

As Montgomery grew in importance, the United States began to polarize along north-south lines over the issues of states' rights and slavery. As sectional tensions increased, Montgomery, led by the fiery orator William Lowndes Yancey, became a center of secessionist activity.

Following a vote in the state legislature on January 11, 1861, Alabama became the fourth state to secede from the union. The state legislature also issued an invitation to other seceding states for a conference to discuss the creation of a southern government. Six other states—South Carolina, Georgia, Mississippi, Florida, Louisiana, and Texas—accepted the invitation, and their representatives began to assemble in Montgomery on February 4, 1861.

The delegates created the government of the Confederate States of America, and they chose Montgomery as the provisional capital of the new government. After some discussion, the delegates also selected Jefferson Davis to be the Confederacy's president. Davis had been a United States senator from Mississippi and was on his plantation on the Mississippi River when he received word that he had been elected. Davis arrived in Montgomery on February 18, 1861, and he delivered his inaugural address from the balcony of the Exchange Hotel.

Despite its political importance to Alabama and the Confederacy, Montgomery was a relatively small town in 1861. The population was just under nine thousand, but the number of residents doubled almost overnight when the town became the Confederate capital. Overcrowding, coupled with a desire to improve communication with armies in the field, led the Confederate government to move the capital to Richmond, Virginia, in May, 1861. Montgomery only served as the capital for three months, but the town earned its nickname "The Cradle of the Confederacy."

After the capital moved to Richmond, the citizens of Montgomery remained ardent supporters of the Confederacy until the end of the war. Indeed, Montgomery was one of the last cities in the South to fall. Just before Union troops reached the town, the state legislators emptied the Capitol of all state records and moved to Eufala, Alabama. The citizens also burned 100,000 bales of cotton to keep the precious commodity out of Union hands.

General James Wilson and his raiders reached Montgomery on April 12, 1865, and they quickly occupied the town. Montgomery suffered for its defiance and its role in the creation of the Confederacy. Union soldiers first destroyed railroad tracks and cars and wrecked all the steamboats in the docks. Then they burned several outlying cotton plantations. Montgomery fought hard, but it was crushed along with the rest of the South.

Rebuilding

After the war, much of Montgomery's wealth had been stripped away. Its farms were gone, and its means of transport were destroyed. The process of reconstruction was slow. By the 1880's, the railroads were functioning again, and conditions steadily improved. Montgomery was rebuilt more quickly than many other southern cities because of its importance as Alabama's capital, its geographic location, and the fact that it was near some of the best farmland in the state.

Cotton remained important to Montgomery, but the city also placed more of an emphasis on industry following the Civil War. In 1890, the first large lumber mill went into operation, and by the beginning of the twentieth century, the city hosted textile and garment factories, cotton-processing plants, and fertilizer manufacturers.

The next major step in the town's development came in 1909 when Orville and Wilbur Wright opened a flight school just outside of Montgomery. They had their first flight there on August 26, 1910. Eventually, this flight school became Maxwell Air Force Base and the United States Air Force's most important teaching facility. The presence of the school at Maxwell proved to be of major importance to the growth of Montgomery.

The large number of state employees in Alabama's capital, coupled with the presence of the air base, kept the Great Depression from hitting Montgomery as hard as it did many other southern cities. Maxwell proved even more important to the city during World War II because the base served as a training center for over 100,000 pilots, navigators, and bombardiers by the end of the war. Maxwell played a major part in revitalizing Montgomery, and after the war, Maxwell remained a major training center.

Civil Rights

Montgomery made its most important contribution to twentieth century American history as an early center of the Civil Rights movement. On December 1, 1955, Rosa Parks, an African American seamstress at a local department store, was riding the bus home from work. The segregated bus was crowded, and Parks sat near the front of the black section. As the bus stopped to let on more passengers, the driver, James Blake, ordered Parks to vacate her seat for a boarding white passenger. Parks refused and was arrested for violating the city's segregation ordinance.

Certainly Parks was not the first African American arrested for refusing to give up a seat on the bus, but Parks served as the perfect focus for opposition to the segregation ordinance. Her husband was a barber at Maxwell. As a federal employee, he was immune to job threats. Additionally, Parks was well known and respected in the black community. E. D. Nixon, Montgomery's best-known advocate of civil rights, bailed Parks out of jail and encouraged black ministers to lead a boycott of the city buses. They agreed, and the boycott began on December 5, 1955.

Two ministers quickly came to the forefront of the protest movement: Ralph Abernathy, pastor of the largest black congregation in the city at First Baptist Church, and Dr. Martin Luther King, Jr., of Dexter Avenue Baptist Church. Abernathy initially proposed the creation of the Montgomery Improvement Association (MIA) as an organization to give the boycott structure, and King served as the MIA's president.

The boycott was well organized. Volunteers with cars ferried people to work, and many simply walked. The leaders also held frequent rallies at churches to keep up spirits, and the black community collectively refused to ride on the city buses. The boycott was so effective the bus company lost approximately six hundred dollars every day.

The boycott lasted 382 days until the Supreme Court overruled Montgomery's segregation ordinance in *Browder v. Gayle* and ordered the desegregation of Montgomery's buses on December 17, 1956. Four days later, King, Abernathy, and Nixon boarded a desegregated bus and ended the boycott.

Soon after the end of the boycott, King left Montgomery for Atlanta, where he took control of the Southern Christian Leadership Conference (SCLC), but he began his civil rights career and formed many of his opinions on nonviolent protest while in Montgomery.

Places to Visit

Many sites within Montgomery commemorate the city's history. The most prominent landmark is the state capitol at Bainbridge and Dexter. The building is one of the few state capitols which has been selected as a National Historic Landmark, due to Jefferson Davis's inauguration there.

The First White House of the Confederacy, where Jefferson Davis lived while in Montgomery, is located at 624 Washington Avenue. The building has been preserved and contains many of Davis's belongings.

Several sites display the city's civil rights heritage. One of the most important is the Civil Rights Memorial. The outdoor monument located on Washington Avenue features the names of forty people who were killed during the Civil Rights movement.

Visitors to Montgomery can also see Dexter Avenue King Memorial Baptist Church, King's first church. A mural of King inside the church features aspects of King's life from his Montgomery days to his death in Memphis.   *—John Franklin*

For Further Information:

Garrow, David, ed. *The Walking City*. New York: Carlson, 1989. Thirteen essays on a variety of aspects of the boycott by participants and historians.

King, Martin Luther, Jr. *Stride Toward Freedom*. New York: Harper & Row, 1958. King's personal account of the bus boycott.

Permaloff, Anne, and Carl Grafton. *Political Power in Alabama*. Athens: University of Georgia Press, 1995. Alabama politics from 1958 to 1970.

Rogers, William, Robert Ward, Leah Atkins, and Wayne Flynt. *Alabama: The History of a Deep South State*. Tuscaloosa: University of Alabama Press, 1994. Contains a great deal about Montgomery's history as it relates to the rest of the state.

Thornton, J. Mills, III. "Challenge and Response in the Montgomery Bus Boycott of 1955-1956." In *From Civil War to Civil Rights, Alabama 1860-1960*, edited by Sarah Wiggins. Tuscaloosa: University of Alabama Press, 1987. Discusses Montgomery city politics before and during the boycott.

Williams, Clanton. "Early Ante-Bellum Montgomery." *Journal of Southern History* 7, no. 4 (1941): 495-525. Economic, political, and social events prior to the Civil War.

Sixteenth Street Baptist Church, Birmingham

Date: Organized in 1873 as the First Colored Baptist Church of Birmingham, Alabama

Relevant issues: African American history, disasters and tragedies, political history, religion, social reform

Significance: This church is known worldwide for the September 15, 1963, bombing which killed four little girls (Denise McNair, Cynthia Wesley, Addie Mae Collins, and Carole Robertson) who were attending Sunday school. This senseless act of racial violence became the turning point in the struggle for civil rights in the city and the nation.

Location: Situated in the heart of downtown Birmingham; Kelly-Ingram Park is located diagonally across from the church, and a statue of the Reverend Martin Luther King, Jr., and the Birmingham Civil Rights Institute are nearby

Site Office:
Sixteenth Street Baptist Church
1530 Sixth Avenue North (corner of Sixteenth Street)
Birmingham, AL 35203
ph.: (205) 251-9402
fax: (205) 251-9811
Web site: www.16thstreet.org

The Sixteenth Street Baptist Church in Birmingham, Alabama, has been ensured a place in history due to its infamous bombing on September 15, 1963, in which four little black girls lost their lives. However, the church, placed in 1980 on the National Register of Historic Places by the National Trust for Historic Preservation, has had a rich church calling since its inception in 1873 as the First Colored Baptist Church of Birmingham. Its mission statement aims to advance the gospel, to serve the community at large, and to witness to the ends of the earth, according to the Reverend Dr. Christopher Hamlin in *Behind the Stained Glass* (1998). Also, this church was pivotal for the planning of civil rights activities and mass demonstrations that would impact future legislation and the national tone on desegregation. Furthermore, a proliferation of commemorative works of art resulted from the Sixteenth Street Baptist Church as a source of aesthetic and moral inspiration. This historic landmark, most important, has been a beacon of hope—racially, ethnically, socioeconomically, and gender-wise—for oppressed people throughout the world.

The History of the Church

The Elyton Land Company chartered Birmingham in December, 1871, and assisted in developing it as "the Magic City" with the construction of carefully planned rail lines in the heart of the city, which added to the natural coal-producing raw materials of limestone, coal, and iron, according to Hamlin's research. This company also donated land to industrial firms, the county and city for schools and parks, and white and black Christian religious sects. After the Civil War, the church was an important institution for combating mounting racial discrimination by creating community-family outreach programs for African Americans who worked in the mines. Therefore, on September 1, 1873, James R. Powell, president of the Elyton Land Company, received one dollar from the trustees of the First Colored Baptist Church for land for their building. As recorded in *Behind the Stained Glass,* the church later had to relinquish land in Birmingham city center—reserved for white denominations—but in July, 1882, the congregation purchased its known address at Sixth Avenue North and Sixteenth Street and later officially changed its name to Sixteenth Street Baptist Church (because a previous congregation established in 1881 assumed the name of the Sixth Ave-

The Sixteenth Street Baptist Church in Birmingham. (Library of Congress)

nue Baptist Church). By 1884, a beautiful building in the Gothic revival style was finalized to serve as both a church of worship and a facility for religious education.

However, in the early 1900's, the Sixteenth Street Baptist Church was considered structurally unsound. Trustees complied with the city's order to raze their building while simultaneously vowing to erect one of even greater stature. Therefore, in 1909, black architect Wallace Rayfield's design for a new facility was accepted, and Thomas Cornelius Windham, both a member of the church and a builder, constructed the new Sixteenth Street Baptist Church facility. It consisted of a Romanesque-Byzantine architectural design with twin towers and pointed domes, a cupola over the sanctuary, and a large auditorium with rooms in the basement. The new church was dedicated in 1911 and, according to the National Park Service's 1993 Historic American Buildings Survey, "The prominence of the structure—a reflection of the prominence of its congregation—coupled with its size and downtown location made Sixteenth Street Baptist Church a focal point for various activities in the black community." Throughout the twentieth century the church, under various pastors, became a stronghold for political debates, cultural activities, and diversified civic events, earning its nickname of "Everybody's Church."

Civil Rights Activities

Despite Birmingham's national and international reputation as "the Pittsburgh of the South" (symbolized by its mighty Vulcan statue), African Americans called their city "the Johannesburg of America," as quoted in George Cantor's *Historic Landmarks of Black America* (1991). In spite of the Sixteenth Street Baptist Church's concentration on youth programs and community outreach assistance, it could no longer evade racial disparities, such as Birmingham's segregated waiting rooms and lunch counters, white- and colored-labeled drinking fountains, frequent bombings of black homes in North Birmingham, and the racism of Birmingham Public Safety Commissioner Eugene "Bull" Connor and the Ku Klux Klan.

The Sixteenth Street Baptist Church opened its large doors for the mass meetings of the Civil Rights strategists and movement, especially for "Project C" (Confrontation)—a nonviolent approach that aggressively encouraged more all-public services and facilities to be open equally to blacks and whites. From the time of its earliest meetings in the 1960's organized by Dr. Martin Luther King, Jr., and the Reverend Fred Shuttlesworth, bomb threats ensued, marches in downtown Birmingham continued, and demands to open segregated businesses augmented. Reverend King's April 16, 1963, *Letter from Birmingham City*

Jail and ongoing mass demonstrations were assisted by the children's movement and freedom walks—the children receiving instruction from the church first. In May, tensions heightened in the city as the children's marches were met by Bull Connor's vicious dogs and water hoses. The homes of activists and the nearby Gaston Motel, which housed civil rights leaders, were bombed frequently, leading to Birmingham's pejorative nickname: "Bombingham." The Sixteenth Street Baptist Church was a definite contributor to the training and spirit of civil rights activism through voter registration clinics at the church, Dick Gregory's leading of children from the church, and even child pickets and incarceration, as Glenn T. Eskew describes vividly in *But for Birmingham: The Local and National Movements in the Civil Rights Struggle* (1997).

The September 15, 1963, Bombing

The moment in time most associated with the Sixteenth Street Baptist Church is 10:22 A.M. on September 15, 1963: the Sunday bombing of the church (under the exterior stairs) and the resulting tragic deaths of four little African American girls. Fourteen-year-old Addie Mae Collins, eleven-year-old Denise (Carol) McNair, fourteen-year-old Carole Robertson, and fourteen-year-old Cynthia Wesley were all pronounced dead on arrival at the hospital. Also, according to a 1963 *Washington Post* article, dozens of people were injured and twenty victims were treated at the hospital; two black teenagers, James Robinson and Virgil Ware, were also shot dead during the racial riots that followed. Ironically, according to authors William Rogers, Robert Ward, Leah Atkins, and Wayne Flynt in *Alabama: The History of a Deep South State* (1994), the bombing occurred on the church's annual Youth Day, and the earlier morning's sermon was entitled "The Love That Forgives." Furthermore, the only remaining stained glass window was one depicting Christ leading a group of children—with the face of Christ blown out.

Tensions that prefaced the horrific bombing had been mounting throughout the months of 1963 in Birmingham. In fact, Frank Sikora, in *Until Justice Rolls Down: The Birmingham Church Bombing Case* (1991), notes that the Reverend Martin Luther King, Jr., had highlighted segregated Birmingham for the Southern Christian Leadership Conference's attempt to overcome existing racial barriers. Shuttlesworth, who directed the Alabama Christian movement, joined with King and top aide Ralph Abernathy to stage marches, fight Commissioner Connor's police dogs and fire hoses, and denounce the continuous bombings of civil rights activists' homes. Victoriously, on May 9, 1963, an agreement was honored by Birmingham business leaders to desegregate rest rooms, drinking fountains, and lunch counters; then, on May 20, Bull Connor finally left office. After a brief calming of the city, tensions renewed when school desegregation issues flared in the late summer of 1963. In fact, the Sixteenth Street Baptist Church pastor and church members were uneasy and feared the worst due to numerous bomb threats.

At Carole Robertson's funeral on September 17, 1963, the eulogy emphasized not revenge but collaboration in God's love. On September 18, Reverend King's message at the service for Cynthia Wesley, Denise McNair, and Addie Mae Collins—echoing that of other Birmingham spiritual leaders—stressed nonviolence and hope for a new beginning. On November 18, 1977—fourteen years later—Robert Chambliss, a reported member of a Ku Klux Klan group called the "Cahaba Boys," was found guilty of the September, 1963, bombing and sentenced to life imprisonment for the death of one young girl, McNair. In 2000, two other men, Bobby Frank Cherry and Thomas E. Blanton, Jr., were indicted for the murders.

Resurgence of Commemorative Art

A resurgence of artistic works continues to commemorate the loss of the four little girls' lives. There is a memorable plaque (with victims' photographs) on the wall of the Memorial Nook in the lower auditorium of the Sixteenth Street Baptist Church that reminds visitors of the heinous act. Yet, the message of the last line exemplifies the spirit of the historic church: "May men learn to replace bitterness and violence with love and understanding."

Welsh stained-glass artist John Petts created, in his hometown Cardiff, the famous *Wales Window for Alabama*. According to Hamlin's interpretation, this work depicts a Jesus of African heritage with huge hands that illustrate a protesting, crucified Jesus (suggesting black protesters and racial injustice) and a Christ demonstrating a loving embrace.

Streams of water from the Birmingham Civil Rights movement and bullets on the cross's top beam suggesting the violence in South Africa combine to paint worldwide oppression; however, the multicolored background symbolizes God's everpresent love of all people—regardless of race, color, or creed.

Many poets and musicians wrote memorializing lyrics based on the Sixteenth Street Baptist Church bombing including Dudley Randall's "Ballad of Birmingham" and Joan Baez's recording of "Birmingham Sunday." Sculptor John Waddell's *That Which Might Have Been: Birmingham, 1963* (1964) in Phoenix, Arizona, depicts four large, lifelike nude girls facing four diverse directions. Imagery ranges from the lack of procreation and societal understanding of African Americans to acceptance of help, death, love, and hope (symbolized by an upraised hand inscribed with "prayer"). In 1992, John Rhoden gifted his native Birmingham and Sixteenth Street Baptist Church with a huge bronze plaque depicting events of 1963 centered around four dolls representing the four young bombing victims.

An Ameliorative Spirit
Following the turbulence and need for healing of the 1960's, the role of the Sixteenth Street Baptist Church is a positive, regenerative one. Out of the ashes, like a phoenix, the church has risen to a dominant role in the Birmingham community and beyond. It opened in June of 1964 for Sunday services; youth ministries and community outreach and educational programs have been instituted. It is a center of resource information about the Civil Rights movement and, concomitantly, a source of inspiration and reconciliation for all ethnic cultures and diverse creeds.

The church acts as a focal point for the Birmingham African American community. National and international figures speak at the church; workshops on women's rights and health issues such as acquired immunodeficiency syndrome (AIDS) are sponsored. Furthermore, the Sixteenth Street Baptist Church is a viable force for the arts with its collaborative liaison with the Onyx (Theater) Agency, Alabama Jazz Hall of Fame, and Operation New Birmingham. Mainly, this institution is a memorial house of worship where people from the community-at-large can be con-

tinually reminded of, touched and guided by, and delivered from the tragedy of September 15, 1963.
—*Constance A. Pedoto*

For Further Information:
Cantor, George. *Historic Landmarks of Black America.* Detroit: Gale Research, 1991. A scholarly national overview of major cities' historic landmarks. Short and concise entries with black-and-white photographs.

Eskew, Glenn T. *But for Birmingham: The Local and National Movements in the Civil Rights Struggle.* Chapel Hill: University of North Carolina Press, 1997. A comprehensive, well-documented anthology tracing Birmingham and national movements in the Civil Rights era. Details of leaders, events, and dates.

Hamlin, Reverend Dr. Christopher M. *Behind the Stained Glass: A History of Sixteenth Street Baptist Church.* Birmingham, Ala.: Crane Hill, 1998. A thorough historical text examining the church from its 1873 founding to the mid-1990's. Black-and-white photographs of major happenings.

"The History of 16th Street Baptist Church: Everybody's Church." www.16thstreet.org.

Rogers, William W., Robert D. Ward, Leah R. Atkins, and Wayne Flynt. *Alabama: The History of a Deep South State.* Tuscaloosa: University of Alabama Press, 1994. A detailed account of events leading up to and following the bombing of the Sixteenth Street Baptist Church.

Sikora, Frank. *Until Justice Rolls Down: The Birmingham Church Bombing Case.* Tuscaloosa: University of Alabama Press, 1991. A personal diary of the Sixteenth Street Baptist Church bombing victims and the subsequent investigation. With witness accounts, FBI depositions, and jury testimonies.

Tuskegee Institute

Date: Founded in 1881
Relevant issues: African American history, education, social reform
Significance: The Tuskegee Institute was the first college in the Deep South to offer educational opportunities for African Americans. Its founder, Booker T. Washington, is one of the most famous men in American history. The institute played a

notable role in the struggle for civil rights in the South.

Location: In Macon County, Alabama, thirty-five miles east of Montgomery and twenty miles west of Auburn

Site Office:
Tuskegee Institute National Historic Site
P.O. Drawer 10
Tuskegee Institute, AL 36087
ph.: (334) 727-3200
Web sites: www.nps.gov/tuin/; www.tusk.edu

Historically black colleges are now not the only educational options for African Americans, but they have played a crucial role in the black experience. Though not the first historically black college, Tuskegee is the most famous. For many years, it was associated with Booker T. Washington, one of the first African Americans to be respected nationwide. The history of Tuskegee is a microcosm of the history of race relations in the South.

Educating the Excluded

The Tuskegee Institute was formed as the result of a compromise. In the late 1870's, southern whites had once again succeeded in reestablishing political control after the brief window of black and Northern predominance in the aftermath of the Civil War. The whites, however, found they could not totally go back to the time of slavery. For one thing, African Americans now had the right to move, and many of them were migrating to the West. George Campbell, a former slave owner, realized that some sort of opportunity had to be given to local African Americans to keep them in Alabama. With input from James Adams, a former slave, Campbell and other Macon County whites decided to set up an educational institute that would give African Americans opportunity for education and training while carefully maintaining their second-class status.

Booker T. Washington's arrival at Tuskegee was not smooth. It was not expected that a black man would be the first head of the institution. Campbell asked Samuel Chapman Armstrong, the white, Hawaiian-born missionary who had founded America's first black college in 1866, the Hampton Institute, to recommend a candidate. Campbell had a white man in mind. Armstrong, however, insisted on recommending his most talented student—Booker T. Washington, a black man born in West Virginia. Armstrong did not back down, and in May, 1881, the trustees of the institute reluctantly accepted Washington.

The original physical plant of the institution was not imposing. The official founding of the school occurred on July 4, 1881, in Butler Chapel, a church set up for freed slaves some years before. The school started in a one-room shanty, but soon a full set of buildings was constructed, mostly built by the first group of students. Washington believed that manual labor was an important part of the sort of education he hoped to impart to his students. Thus, part of their education was building the college itself.

Washington had been thoroughly trained at Hampton and went immediately to work at fashioning the new school's curriculum. Washington shared Armstrong's view that the best sort of education for the African Americans of the postwar South was one that emphasized agricultural, industrial, and job-related skills. These skills, it was hoped, would raise the students above a subsistence level and enable them to provide for themselves and their families. Such abstract fields as poetry, philosophy, history, and the theoretical sciences were not taught at Tuskegee. The reason was partially because Washington genuinely did not think those were the highest priorities for the institution's students, and partially to reassure the whites of Macon County and Alabama as a whole that the black population was not receiving an education that would threaten white supremacy. Washington insisted that he did not mean to impose vocational education as the only possible training for African Americans.

The physical plant of the institute was decisively remodeled in 1895. The original buildings now seemed ramshackle and outdated. They were appropriate for a school desiring to impart the rudiments of vocational training to a poor and oppressed student body. However, they did not suit what Tuskegee was becoming: an institute for a center for advanced research in industrial and agricultural processes. Washington solicited a new wave of money from wealthy northern businessmen.

Tuskegee was not just a base for a black academic identity but a symbol of black social progress. Washington became the first national leader of the African American community. Politicians, especially Republicans such as President Theodore Roosevelt, treated Washington with respect and lauded him as an example for his people.

A Center for Black Self-Reliance

Robert Russa Moton succeeded Washington as president of Tuskegee in 1925. Moton was also a graduate of Hampton. Legend has it that his given name was Robert Russell Morton, but the northern whites in charge at Hampton found his southern accent so thick that they wrote down the name by which he was known throughout his career. Moton stressed that Tuskegee was different from other black colleges in that African Americans were in control at every level. Moton turned Tuskegee from a vocational institute into a full-fledged college offering a range of academic programs equivalent to those of most American universities. His biggest achievement was founding a veterans hospital to treat many of the black soldiers who had fought in World War I. The white community was fiercely opposed to this hospital and agitated against it for many years. The role of the federal government in funding the hospital, though, looked forward to the day when civil rights issues would be addressed on a national rather than a state level.

Scientific Advances, Military Valor

George Washington Carver came to Tuskegee in 1896. Hearing of Carver's expertise as an agricultural chemist, Washington hired him to head Tuskegee's Agriculture Program. With Carver, Tuskegee's academic mission went beyond vocational training. Carver was a scientist whose experiments in crop diversification meant a great deal to the entire American farm industry and probably helped it survive the Great Depression of the 1930's. A less spectacular event was the founding of a school of veterinary medicine in 1945. This was not only a necessary resource for farmers who needed their animals treated by trained professionals, but a way for African Americans to enter the field of medicine as a whole. It also offset the advantage of whites in the area who could draw on the expertise of nearby Auburn University's veterinary school.

Tuskegee's knowledge-intensive atmosphere (including its offering instruction in piloting) made it the obvious site when the government de-

cided to train black airmen for military service before and during World War II. The "Tuskegee Airmen" fought valiantly in the war and helped pave the way for the integration of the United States military. This, in turn, had a pivotal effect on the wider fight for civil rights and against racism.

Tuskegee itself was not immune to the changes that its research helped launch. After 1945, a new generation of Tuskegee faculty members such as Charles Gomillion were no longer content to accept second-class status. Gomillion was active in a campaign to secure African Americans the right to vote. Theoretically, everybody could vote in Macon County. In practice, however, a poll tax specifying literacy and property qualifications excluded almost all of the black community. Gomillion built a coalition of Tuskegee staff, working-class African

Charles Keck's sculpture of Booker T. Washington in Tuskegee. (Alabama Bureau of Tourism & Travel/ Dan Brothers)

Americans, and whites who accepted that segregation had to end. By the mid-1960's, these groups had enabled everybody to vote and had achieved integration of the public school system. In fact, the students at Tuskegee became so militant that older men such as Gomillion were sidelined. This ferment died down soon after, but the old racial rules were forever changed. The effect of this change was to make the Tuskegee area in the twenty-first century a place where racial differences mattered less than most ever thought they would.

New Generations, New Challenges

A hostile depiction of Tuskegee can be found in Ralph Ellison's great novel *Invisible Man* (1952). Ellison has his semiautobiographical protagonist go through a college much like Tuskegee (which Ellison himself attended in the 1930's). The college's goal of racial uplift is belied by the hypocrisy of its conformist president and its self-serving trustees. Ellison, an Oklahoman who lived most of his life in New York, did not like the southern ambience of Tuskegee, which he found backward and out-of-step with modern times. Though Tuskegee surely did not applaud the searing criticism from a famous alumnus, it eventually mentioned Ellison prominently on its Web page.

Tuskegee was also criticized from within over a long tradition of black radicalism. This began with William Edward Burghardt Du Bois (1868-1963), who called for a turning away from vocational education to an emphasis on the so-called talented tenth of African Americans who would serve as leaders for the other 90 percent of the race. It was assumed that the talented tenth would not attend historically black colleges such as Tuskegee but prestigious, traditionally white universities such as Harvard, from which W. E. B. Du Bois himself graduated. As more and more "mainstream" colleges opened their doors to African Americans in the decades after 1945, Tuskegee University (as, after several changes of name, it was now called) seemed to many more a part of history than of the present.

As African Americans became better educated and better off financially, Tuskegee's student body became more assertive. The students became less ready to accept the tight discipline and strict campus rules that had been in effect since the Washington era. Campus life at Tuskegee became much like that at any other college. Though Tuskegee still produces engineers and scientists, its graduates go on to careers of every sort, a good example being the comedian Keenen Ivory Wayans, star of the television show *In Living Color.*

Places to Visit

The National Historic Site itself was set up in 1974. It represents the recognition of African American experience within the history of Alabama. The site is centered on the George Washington Carver Museum and the Oaks, Booker T. Washington's former residence. Guided tours are available at the latter. The most visible symbol of Tuskegee, however, is the sculpture by Charles Keck of Booker T. Washington lifting the veil of ignorance from a freed slave. The freed slave is flanked by an anvil and a plow that recall the practical work that Washington advocated. The lifting of the veil represents Tuskegee's longtime goal of educating the dispossessed and downtrodden.

Tuskegee has made a palpable effort to preserve its historic buildings wherever possible. Buildings are demolished only when they cannot be saved. Band Cottage, the oldest building on the campus, was built in 1889. For many years, the cottage was the practice area for the university's bands. A building that has not survived is Huntington Hall, which succumbed in 1991 to a tragic fire whose effects are still visible. Rockefeller Hall was where Carver once resided and is still an operating dormitory. Tompkins Hall is architecturally notable as it has no sustaining steel support. The original campus buildings are part of the Historic Site and stand as a testimony to all that has been accomplished at this unique educational institution.

—*Nicholas Birns*

For Further Information:

Anderson, James. *The Education of Blacks in the South, 1865-1935.* Chapel Hill: University of North Carolina Press, 1988. On the origin and development of historically black colleges.

Elliott, Lawrence. *George Washington Carver.* Englewood Cliffs, N.J.: Prentice-Hall, 1966. An introduction to Tuskegee's great scientist.

Engs, Robert Francis. *Educating the Disfranchised and Dispossessed.* Knoxville: University of Tennessee Press, 1999. Focuses on the Hampton Institute, but also includes key information on Tuskegee.

Harlan, Louis. *Booker T. Washington: The Wizard of Tuskegee, 1901-1915.* New York: Oxford University Press, 1983. A good biographical work on Washington.

Murray, Albert. *South to a Very Old Place.* New York: Modern Library, 1985. Tuskegee's second most famous literary alumnus after Ellison tours his alma mater.

Norrell, Robert J. *Reaping The Whirlwind: The Civil Rights Movement in Tuskegee.* New York: Alfred A. Knopf, 1985. A history of not only the college but the town.

Washington, Booker T. *Up from Slavery.* New York: Dover, 1995. The great manifesto of Tuskegee's founder.

Other Historic Sites

Apalachicola Fort Site

Location: On the Chattachoochee River

Relevant issues: American Indian history, European settlement

Statement of significance: The northernmost Spanish outpost on the Chattachoochee River, the fort was completed in 1690 to prevent the English from gaining a foothold among the Lower Creek Indians, who had rejected Spanish missionaries and accepted English traders. Punative raids by the Spanish further alienated the Lower Creeks. In 1691, due to the threat from the British and their Native American allies, Fort Apalachicola was abandoned and destroyed by the Spanish, after being occupied for only a year.

Clayton House

Location: Clayton, Barbour County

Relevant issues: Business and industry, legal history

Statement of significance: From 1896 to 1929, this was the home of Henry D. Clayton, Jr. (1857-1929), author of the Clayton Anti-Trust Act (1914), which was designed to enumerate and outlaw a number of unfair trade practices and interlocking arrangements that had been the chief tools of monopolists. In 1914, Clayton was appointed a federal district judge, and he became recognized as an advocate of judicial reform.

Fort Morgan

Location: Gasque, Baldwin County

Relevant issues: Civil War, military history

Statement of significance: This fort was significant in Admiral David G. Farragut's 1864 naval battle that opened Mobile Bay to the Union Navy and sealed off the port of Mobile to Confederate shipping.

Ivy Green

Location: Tuscumbia, Colbert County

Relevant issues: Education, social reform

Statement of significance: This ten-acre site is associated with Helen Keller (1880-1968), author and lecturer. The property includes the cottage where Keller was born and the house where she spent her early childhood (1880-1888), and the water pump, site of the communication breakthrough for the blind and deaf Keller. With the aid of her teacher and constant companion, Anne Sullivan (Macy), Keller learned to communicate with the world outside of Ivy Green. This homestead was the location of the pivotal experiences which led to Keller's emergence in the forefront of the effort to provide better methods and facilities to educate the handicapped. Although Keller and Sullivan eventually left the homestead and resided in various locations throughout their lives together, they continued to return to Ivy Green.

Moundville Site

Location: Moundville, Hale County

Relevant issues: American Indian history

Statement of significance: Settled first in the tenth century, Moundville is situated on a level area overlooking the Black Warrior River and consists of thirty-four mounds, the largest of which is over fifty-eight feet high. The site represents a major period of Mississippian culture in the southern portion of its distribution and acted as the center for a southerly diffusion of this culture toward the Gulf Coast.

Saturn V Launch Vehicle

Location: Huntsville, Madison County

Relevant issues: Science and technology

Statement of significance: In July, 1969, a rocket of this type carried astronauts Neil A. Armstrong, Edwin E. (Buzz) Aldrin, and Michael Collins toward humankind's first expedition to the surface of the moon. Developed by the United States for the purpose of landing a man on the moon, this vehicle was the first Saturn V constructed by the Marshall Space Flight Center under the direction of Dr. Werner von Braun (1912-1977) and served as the test vehicle for all the Saturn support facilities at the Marshall Space Flight Center.

Sloss Blast Furnaces

Location: 1st Avenue and 32d Street, Birmingham, Jefferson County

Relevant issues: Business and industry

Web site: www.ci.bham.al/sloss/default.htm

Statement of significance: Erected in 1881-1882 by noted southern industrialist James Withers Sloss, this is the oldest remaining blast furnace in the area and represents Alabama's early twentieth century preeminence in the production of pig iron and cast iron pipe. The complex, which remained in operation until 1970, is an outstanding symbol of the post-Civil War efforts to industrialize the South and of the intense economic competition that existed between the predominantly agrarian region and the already-industrialized North.

Wilson Dam

Location: Florence, Colbert County

Relevant issues: Science and technology

Statement of significance: Constructed between 1918 and 1925 by the U.S. Army Corps of Engineers, this 4,535-foot-long concrete structure spanning the Tennessee River became the first hydroelectric operation to come under the Tennessee Valley Authority (TVA) in 1925. Today, Wilson Dam is one of thirty-three major TVA dams that provide flood control, regulate a 650-mile navigational channel, and provide over 100 billion kilowatt hours of electricity for the seven-state Tennessee Valley region.

Alaska

History of Alaska 18
Iditarod National Historic Trail 20
Nome 23

Sitka 26
Skagway 29
Other Historic Sites 33

Glacier Bay. (PhotoDisc)

History of Alaska

Alaska must be described in terms of absolutes and superlatives. When it was admitted to the Union in 1959, it became the first state outside the forty-eight contiguous states. It is the northernmost state, and remarkably, it is also the westernmost and easternmost state, extending from 130 degrees west longitude, across the 180 degree meridian, to 172 degrees east longitude. Its latitude runs from Barrow in the Arctic at 72 degrees north to the southernmost point in the Aleutian Islands, where its latitude is 52 degrees north, giving it a greater latitude span than the entire forty-eight contiguous states and almost as much longitude. Alaska lies geographically in four time zones, although, for practical purposes, two official time zones have been established.

Alaska is the only state that borders the Arctic Ocean and extends into the Arctic Circle. It lies closest to Asia of any of the states, its western extreme on Little Diomede Island being just two miles from the Russian island of Big Diomede. On the east and north, its border with Canada is the longest of any state. The shortest air routes between the United States and Asia are directly over Alaska, which has the largest oil and natural gas reserves in the United States. With a land mass of 570,374 square miles, it is the largest state, more than twice the size of Texas. Alaska has the largest glaciers and the most volcanoes of any U.S. state. With 1.1 persons per square mile, it has the lowest population density in the United States. Alaska's Mount McKinley, at 20,320 feet, is the highest point in the North American continent.

Early History

Alaska's earliest inhabitants were the Tingit-Haidas and members of the Athabascan Tribes. The Aleuts and Eskimos, or Inuits, crossed the Bering Strait from Russia more than four thousand years ago and settled along the coast, surviving largely by fishing and hunting. These migrants were likely Asians who came to the region when what is now Alaska was linked to mainland Asia by a land bridge. By 1750, some seventy thousand native Inuits lived in Alaska (that number has not significantly changed). Aleuts were driven from the Aleutian Islands by the Russians in the eighteenth and nineteenth centuries and by the American military forces during World War II.

The earliest incursions by westerners occurred in 1741, when Vitus Bering, a Dane supported in his ventures by Russia, sailed to Alaska and established the first settlement on Kodiak Island in 1784. The fur business, important and lucrative in early Alaska, thrived with the establishment in 1799 of the Russian-American Company. It controlled the fur trade from its headquarters in Archangel, present-day Sitka.

Russia owned Alaska until 1867, when President Andrew Johnson's secretary of state, William H. Seward, negotiated its purchase by the United States for $7.2 million. Although the U.S. Senate approved this purchase enthusiastically, buying this little-known area, which most people considered a frozen wasteland, the action was unpopular and known as "Seward's Folly." This "folly" paid off handsomely when a major gold strike was made near Juneau in 1880, unleashing a gold rush to the region and stimulating the exploration of Alaska for its mineral wealth.

In 1896 gold was discovered in Canada's Klondike, and, in 1898, at Fairbanks, causing another gold rush. Fish canneries built in the southeastern part of the area in the 1880's and 1890's imported workers from the United States. American traders moving to Alaska in search of riches established a route along the Yukon, the fourth longest river in the northern hemisphere.

Steps Toward Statehood

As Alaska became more viable economically, Congress viewed it with increased interest. In 1884, Alaska was made a judicial district, with Sitka as its capital. In 1906, it was permitted one elected delegate in the United States House of Representatives. The region was granted territorial status in 1912, and Juneau was declared its capital. Its political powers, however, were limited. Statehood was first proposed in Congress in 1916 but was rejected. In 1946, however, Alaskans, in a state referendum, approved statehood. Ten years later, a state constitution was adopted. On January 3, 1959, Alaska was admitted to the Union as the forty-ninth state.

When statehood was first proposed for Alaska in 1916, the state was extremely isolated from the rest of the country. Many U.S. citizens had gone there to work during last half of the nineteenth century, but communication and transportation were limited. With the advent of radios and telephones, these problems began to fade, although it was many years before telephone communication with the "lower 48" (the United States mainland) was perfected. Almost simultaneously with better telephone communication came the development of air transportation, which had evolved rapidly during World War I and was, by the 1920's, becoming a major factor in transportation worldwide.

Alaska's enormous spaces made it an ideal venue for private aircraft. During the late 1920's and the 1930's, many Alaskans owned private planes, shrinking perceptibly the time they needed to cover the state's huge expanses. Commercial aircraft began to serve Alaska's major cities, and An-

chorage became a refueling stop for planes flying from the United States and Canada to Asia.

These factors eliminated some of the earlier objections to statehood. Also, because the Japanese attacked and eventually occupied some of the Aleutian Islands during World War II, Americans became increasingly aware of Alaska's defensive importance.

Alaska's Economy

From its earliest days, Alaska had a stable economy. While mainland America struggled economically during the Great Depression of the 1930's, Alaska was undergoing an economic rebirth brought on largely by gold mining. Alaska had thriving copper mines as well. As revenues increased, the territorial government built much-needed roads, whose construction employed thousands of workers, many of whom came to Alaska and remained there as permanent residents.

World War II had a profound effect on the Alaskan economy. With Japan's invasion of the Aleutian Islands in 1942, the United States deployed about 200,000 military personnel to Alaska, where major military installations were built at Adak, An-

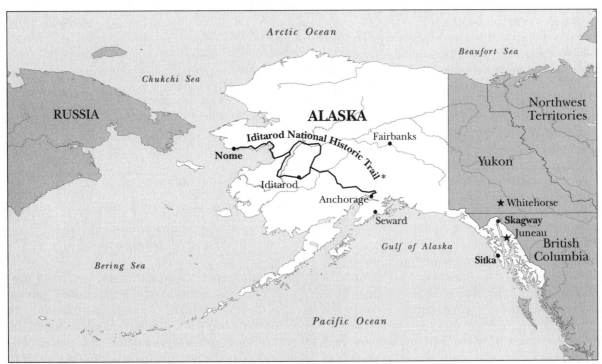

*Northern route run on even years; southern route run on odd years.

chorage, Fairbanks, Kodiak, and Sitka. The Alcan highway was completed, creating a road link among Alaska's major cities.

Throughout the 1950's, military construction in Alaska continued at a brisk pace. This activity brought both construction workers and military personnel to the area in large numbers. Many, impressed by Alaska's grandeur and economic opportunities, remained there when the work that originally brought them to Alaska was completed.

In 1957 huge oil deposits were discovered in Alaska's Kenai Peninsula, and shortly thereafter other vast fields were found at Prudhoe Bay. Despite the harsh climate and great distances involved, the eight hundred-mile-long Trans-Alaska Oil Pipeline was completed in 1977. Alaska became so oil rich that it was able to finance a giant expansion and still give each of its citizens more than one thousand dollars a year as a cash bonus for several years. It had no need for a state income tax.

The oil boom waned during the 1980's and by the mid-1980's was virtually over. The state by this time had attracted many new residents who viewed Alaska as the land of opportunity. Its population increased by 36.9 percent between 1980 and 1990, reaching just over 550,000 in 1990. The 1997 population registered a more than 10 percent increase, having grown to almost 610,000.

Following the oil boom, Alaska struggled to attract tourist dollars. It also began establishing trade with such Asian countries as South Korea, Taiwan, and Japan, although the slowing of the Asian economy in 1998 and 1999 temporarily stalled some of these efforts. Alaska's abundance of many resources that Asia does not have makes trade enviable. Natural gas development also became vigorously pursued within the state, which is also did a great deal to increase the amount of metal mining done within it boundaries. Alaska has deposits of every known mineral except bauxite.

The Threat of Oil Spills

Environmentalists were concerned about the building of the Trans-Alaska Oil Pipeline because portions of it were laid in areas with geological faults. However, the pipelines have been fashioned to resist the earthquakes that are common in fault areas. A severe earthquake in 1964, followed by a tsunami, a huge tidal wave, devastated much of coastal Alaska, doing considerable damage in An-

chorage, Kodiak, Seward, and Valdez. At this time, there was no pipeline that might rupture. The potential for destruction of the pipeline is slight, but still a cause for concern.

In 1989 a huge supertanker, the *Exxon Valdez*, foundered in Prince William Sound and spilled more than 240,000 barrels of oil into the surrounding water. The result was catastrophic: Commercial fishing was so negatively impacted that many who fished for a living were forced out of business. The area would take years to recover completely from the wholesale destruction of wildlife. If any good came out of the *Exxon Valdez* disaster, it is that the shipping of oil on supertankers became more strenuously regulated. Many new tankers have double hulls so that if the hull is punctured, the oil will not leak into the surrounding ocean.

—*R. Baird Shuman*

Iditarod National Historic Trail

Date: Established in 1978
Relevant issues: Cultural history, western expansion
Significance: The Iditarod Trail is a 2,450-mile historic trail and the site of the famous annual dogsled race.
Location: Runs from Seward in southeastern Alaska to Nome in the northwest
Site Offices:
Iditarod Trail Headquarters
Mile 2.2 Knik Road
Wasilla, AK 99654
ph.:(907) 376-5155

Iditarod Trail Committee
P.O. Box 870800
Wasilla, AK 99687
Web site: www.iditarod.com/
e-mail: iditarod@iditarod.com

The Iditarod National Historic Trail is a 2,450-mile trail across south-central Alaska. Visitors use the trail for hiking, cross-country skiing, and snowmobiling, but it is most famous as the site of the annual Iditarod Trail Sled Dog Race. The Iditarod race celebrates the 1925 "serum run" which brought life-saving diphtheria antitoxin to residents of Nome, but the Iditarod's importance as a key transportation route dates back much further.

Early Beginnings

The Iditarod National Historic Trail runs from Seward on the southern coast of Alaska north to Nome on Alaska's west coast. Centuries ago, portions of what would become the Iditarod Trail were initially blazed by caribou and other wildlife migrating from one part of the territory to another. They were followed by Athabaskan, Inuit, and northwest coastal Native Americans as they hunted and traded in the area. Native Alaskans improved transportation on the trail by introducing snowshoes and dogsleds.

In 1741, Russian explorers arrived on Alaskan shores from across the Bering Sea. Finding abundant supplies of natural resources there, they built forts and established settlements for trade. Russians dominated a profitable fur trade with local native Alaskans for over a century during which the Iditarod Trail was frequently used as a trade and transportation line. However, Russian interests dwindled when the fur trade became less lucrative, and Russia sold Alaskan territory to the United States in 1867.

Few Americans traveled to the remote new territory until gold was discovered in 1896 along the Yukon River. Word of the discovery spread quickly through the American press, and within months tens of thousands of hopeful miners flocked to Alaska seeking fortune and adventure. Alaska became the gateway to the Klondike and Yukon gold fields. The Iditarod Trail, then only a series of smaller connecting trails, became a vital and busy transportation and supply route.

Boomtowns such as Hope, Iditarod, and Ruby sprang up and grew quickly along sections of the Iditarod Trail. Travelers used horses, wagons, and snowshoes, but the most popular form of transportation was the dogsled. Teams of one to twenty-five dogs were leashed together to pull a sled and musher over the snow. In good weather, sled dogs could travel twenty to thirty miles per day. During the height of the gold rush, the United States Postal Service used dogsleds to establish and maintain weekly mail service. Roadhouses were built

The annual Iditarod Trail Sled Dog Race has become an international event. (AP/Wide World Photos)

one day's ride from one another to provide food and warm shelter for the night. These shelters, spaced approximately twenty miles apart, frequently made the difference between life and death in a region where nighttime temperatures could fall to minus 60 degrees Fahrenheit. Roadhouses kept lists of visitors so their positions could be tracked over the trail. Though the most popular form of transportation, dogsledding was still a difficult and expensive way to send parcels.

Mushers, their lead dogs, and teams became well known among boomtown residents, and a healthy competition rose among them. During the long, cold winter months when the mines closed down, mushers began racing their dogs to determine which team was the fastest. Residents cheered their favorite lead dogs and mushers, and sled dog racing became a very popular form of entertainment. The ten thousand-dollar Nome All-Alaska

Sweepstakes was the most prestigious and profitable race. The All-Alaska began in 1908 to settle a bet over who had the best lead sled dog. The course was 408 miles and encompassed a large portion of the Iditarod Trail. The All-Alaska did not survive World War I, but dogsled racing remained popular and became Alaska's official sport.

Nome, situated at the end of the Iditarod Trail, was a village of a few hundred people in 1890. Gold was discovered in the region in 1898. Within two years the village was a booming town of thirty thousand residents. When gold supplies dwindled a few years later, most of the miners left. Nome's population dropped to fewer than five thousand people by 1905, but the town survived and became one of Alaska's most popular trade centers. At the turn of the twentieth century, the Iditarod Trail—the only land route from Nome to the southern coast—facilitated transportation and communication. When the Bering Sea froze over between October and June, the Iditarod Trail was the only way in or out of Nome and residents' only access to the outside world.

In the early 1900's, Congress established the Alaska Road Commission to build and improve road systems connecting military outposts with local villages. The commission hired workers who marked and improved the Iditarod Trail during the winter of 1910-1911. The refurbished trail provided quicker access to outlying areas and less hazardous traveling conditions for local residents, the military, and suppliers.

Race for Life

The most famous "race" in the Iditarod Trail's history was the famous serum run of 1925, also known as the Great Race of Mercy. In January of that year, two young children died in Nome. Dr. Curtis Welch, Nome's only physician, identifying the disease as diphtheria, realized the threat it posed to the local population. An epidemic of diphtheria could kill hundreds or thousands of Alaskans if left untreated. Local native Alaskans were particularly susceptible because they had developed little resistance to European or American diseases. Dr. Curtis's scant five-year-old supply of antitoxin would inoculate only a few people, and its effectiveness was in question due to its age. After establishing a quarantine of the area, Curtis issued an emergency call for more serum.

An Anchorage physician who could send a million units of serum answered the call. How would it be transported, however, to far-off Nome in the middle of a forbidding Alaskan winter? Though railway transportation existed in some areas, the closest railhead to Nome was in Nenana, almost five hundred miles away. Airplane travel had been established but was extremely hazardous in winter weather: No one wanted to risk loss of both pilot and serum. It was decided the least risky way to get the serum to Nome was by dogsled.

Alaska's governor, Scott Bone, called for volunteer mushers to participate in a five hundred-mile dogsled relay. On January 26, 1925, a heavily insulated twenty-pound package of serum was loaded onto a train in Anchorage and transported 298 miles to Nanana. It arrived on January 27 and was passed to the first musher. Twenty dogsled teams transported the antitoxin 465 miles over harsh terrain and through frigid temperatures to Nome in only seventy-two hours, a trip that normally took at least a week to complete. Relay teams stopped at roadhouses along the trail to rest dogs, switch mushers, and warm the serum. The antitoxin arrived at 5:30 A.M. of February 2. With the serum in hand, Dr. Curtis was able to cure those already stricken and to prevent further spread of the disease. No additional deaths from diphtheria were reported. The twenty mushers who participated in the serum run were each awarded medals and certificates for their valiant efforts.

Over the next few decades, other faster forms of transportation replaced dogsledding as the primary source of conveyance over the Iditarod. In 1914, the Alaska Railroad built a line between Seward and Nenana, shortening the dogsled mail route by four hundred miles. Airplanes were added to the mail delivery service in 1920. By the 1930's, air service had replaced dogsleds on the trail, but the popularity of sled dog racing continued. In 1967, Alaska prepared for a centennial celebration of its purchase by America. As part of the celebration, local centennial committee chairperson Dorothy Page and kennel owner Joe Redington, Sr., proposed a fifty-six-mile dogsled race over the old Iditarod Trail. The idea was accepted, and the first Iditarod Trail Sled Dog Race was held in February, 1967, with a purse of twenty-five thousand dollars divided among the top winners. The first winner of the two-day, fifty-six-mile event was Isaac Okleasik from Teller, Alaska. The race was so popular it became an annual event.

Support of and participation in the Iditarod race waned over the next few years. In 1973, Joe Redington, Sr., proposed that the Iditarod race go all the way to Nome, a distance of over eleven hundred miles. A year earlier, the United States Army had cleared and marked the trail all the way to Nome. Though organizers were unsure mushers would sign up for such a grueling race, thirty-four of them lined up to participate. Twenty-two made it all the way to Nome and shared a fifty thousand dollar prize. Dick Wilmarth won the race, completing the course in twenty days.

Visiting the Iditarod Trail

In 1978, Congress made the Iditarod part of the National Historic Trail system. At the Iditarod Trail headquarters and visitors' center, visitors can view historical displays and videos and see an example of an Iditarod musher and dog team. The center houses a gift shop and offers a sample wheeled dogsled for visitor rides. Sections of the trail are open for hiking, skiing, and snowmobiling. The Iditarod Trail includes a large variety of changeable terrain. Thick forests, iced-over sections of lakes and rivers, open fields, and remote wildernesses offer beautiful scenery, but it is a difficult trail to traverse no matter what the season. Portions of the trail are very difficult to hike because of thick growths of tundra. In addition to below-freezing temperatures and chilling winds, there are hills, sea ice, and heavy snowfalls to conquer in winter. Tours and tour guides are available and a number of historic sites can be viewed along the trail, including prehistoric Native American, Inuit, and Athabaskan and villages, gold rush towns, and Russian Orthodox missions. The trail is divided into three sections. Each offers opportunities to view local wildlife including moose, wolves, walruses, caribou, beavers, foxes, bald eagles, and grizzly, polar, and black bears.

Travelers trekking the Iditarod Trail find it much the same as it was in the early part of the twentieth century. The trail can be viewed by airplane if visitors wish. The popularity of the Iditarod Trail Sled Dog Race continues to grow. The race runs annually in March from downtown Anchorage to Nome. The Iditarod race attracts mushers and spectators from around the world.

—*Leslie Stricker*

For Further Information:

Cordes, Kathleen Ann. *America's National Historic Trails.* Norman: University of Oklahoma Press, 1999. Lists and extensively describes each trail in the National Historic Trail system.

Jones, Tim. *The Last Great Race: The Iditarod Sled Dog Race.* Seattle: Madrona, 1982. Details the entire history of the Iditarod Trail Sled Dog Race.

Paulsen, Gary. *Winterdance: The Fine Madness of Running the Iditarod.* New York: Harcourt, Brace, 1994. Takes the reader along as Paulsen participates in the Iditarod race.

Riddles, Libby, and Tim Jones. *Race Across Alaska: First Woman to Win the Iditarod Tells Her Story.* Harrisburg, Pa.: Stackpole Books, 1988. The first female winner of the Iditarod Trail Sled Dog Race recounts her adventures.

Sherwonit, Bill. *Iditarod: The Great Race to Nome.* Anchorage: Alaska Northwest Books, 1991. Documents the history of the race and trail through text and photography.

Nome

Date: Incorporated in 1901

Relevant issues: Business and industry, western expansion, World War II

Significance: Founded during the last great American gold rush in 1898-1900, this town has persevered through a diphtheria epidemic, fires, and numerous floods and severe storms. It served as the last stop on the route ferrying American lend-lease aircraft to Russia during World War II. It is also the finish line of the famed Iditarod Dogsled Race.

Location: On the southern coast of the Seward Peninsula, 539 miles northwest of Anchorage, 150 miles south of the Arctic Circle, 161 miles from Russia

Site Office:
Nome Convention and Visitors Bureau
P.O. Box 240
Nome, AK 99762
ph.: (907) 443-5535
fax: (907) 443-2855
Web site: www.alaska.net/~nome

Nome began as a gold rush camp in 1898. The yellow metal discovered by three Swedes (Jafet

Lindeberg, Erik Lindblom, and John Brynteson) on the Anvil Creek caused thousands of prospectors to flock to the beach on the Bering Sea. By 1899, the tundra behind the beach was the site of a tent and log cabin city of twenty thousand prospectors, gamblers, claim jumpers, saloon keepers, and prostitutes, making Nome Alaska's largest city. By the time the rush quieted in 1901, the numerous mining camps had consolidated into a city and more permanent structures were constructed. Most of these structures were destroyed by a fire in 1934. St. Joseph's Catholic Church, one of the few buildings to survive the fire, was renovated in the mid-1990's in anticipation of the city's centennial and has since been used as a community center.

Gold on Anvil Creek

The founding of Nome began on Anvil Creek when the "Three Lucky Swedes" discovered gold in 1898. News spread to the Klondike, an area in northwest Canada also experiencing a gold rush, and by the winter of 1899, Anvil City's population reached ten thousand. In 1899, gold was discovered in the beach sands and the last gold rush in American history began as the outside world learned the news. Until shipments of finished lumber arrived during the summer of 1899, the thirty miles from Cape Nome to Cape Rodney was a tent city.

The naming of Nome is an interesting aspect of the city's history. Terrence Cole writes that in February, 1899, a group of forty-two men who had staked property and mining claims on the Snake River near Nome City officially agreed to change the name of the new mining camp to Anvil City. They did not want the new city to be confused with the Nome River, about four miles southeast of the city, and with Cape Nome, a point of land about twelve miles from the city. The town was known as Anvil City for most of 1899, but the United States Post Office officially called the community "Nome" because Anvil City could be confused with the village of Anvik on the lower Yukon. After a vote, city leaders reluctantly agreed to change the name of Anvil City to Nome.

Controversy surrounds the name of the city. One theory proposes that the name was the result of a spelling error. In the 1850's, an officer on a British ship off the coast of Alaska noted on a map that a nearby point was not identified. He wrote "? Name" next to the point. When the map was copied, another draftsman thought that the "?" was a "C" and that the "a" in "Name" was an "o." According to Terrence Cole, a mapmaker in the British Admiralty designated the point "Cape Nome." The second theory argues that Nome is derived from the Native American phrase *Ko-no-me*, meaning "I don't know," the natives' reply when asked the name of the place.

The Gold Conspiracy

The Nome gold rush attracted a large number of fortune seekers of questionable character to the

Nome is the site of the finish line for the Iditarod Trail Sled Dog Race. (AP/Wide World Photos)

tent city along the Bering Sea. Andrea Helms and Mary Mangusso argue that this gold rush was very similar to other rushes in the American West. Nome was a city in disorder with little governmental authority. While there was fraud, corruption, and some violence, the residents of Nome relied on legal process rather than action by local vigilantes. Nome residents regularly appealed to distant authorities to assist in settling disputes, particularly those involving the validity of land claims.

The "lucky Swedes" who initially found the gold sparking the rush were assumed to be aliens. Since many of the richest claims were held by foreigners, prospectors arriving later in 1899 questioned the legal rights of aliens to hold claims. Those who owned claims were forced to defend their property, often at gunpoint. By July, 1899, claim jumping had become violent enough that the United States Army sent Lieutenant Oliver J. Spaulding, Jr., to maintain the peace in Nome.

Lieutenant Spaulding was successful in keeping peace largely due to the discovery of gold on the Nome beaches. This new discovery allowed more prospectors to strike it rich without having to challenge the claims of those further inland. This discovery turned Nome into an even-larger boomtown. In 1900, the city's population grew from three thousand to twenty thousand. With the rapid increase in population, leading citizens called on the federal government to provide federal justice to the district. Federal judge Arthur H. Noyes of North Dakota was appointed to administer the newly formed judicial district created to settle the hundreds of claim disputes that plagued Nome. His first action was to put all contested claims into receivership. The judge, part of a "gold conspiracy," proceeded to exploit the claims, keeping miners from their claims, and benefiting Noyes's patrons in North Dakota and Washington, D.C. Two appeals to the Ninth Circuit Court in San Francisco and two U.S. marshals were required to jail Judge Noyes and his henchmen. Journalist Rex Beach dramatically recounts the conspiracy in his novel *The Spoilers* (1906).

Diphtheria, Disaster, and War

By the end of the first decade of the twentieth century, the gold rush in Nome had largely ended. Large mining companies replaced the independent prospectors. The large companies used dredging equipment to get at most of the gold. While Nome's founding was marked by drama, the current condition of the city has been shaped by a number of events. A diphtheria epidemic in 1925 required a serum run from Nenana, Alaska, that has been immortalized in the Iditarod Trail Sled Dog Race.

Much of the city's decline can be attributed to the weather. In October, 1913, one of the most destructive storms in the history of Nome pounded the city with wind and waves. Many buildings on Front Street were torn from their foundations while other structures were pummeled by the debris. Terrence Cole writes that the east end of the city and the business district were destroyed. Many of the survivors of the storm left Nome never to return. Other severe storms struck the city in 1945 and 1974. After the 1945 storm, Nome residents debated moving the city away from the coast. Instead of moving, city leaders decided to lobby the federal government to build a sea wall to protect the business district. The wall was completed in 1951 at a cost of approximately one million dollars. During the storm of 1974, the sea wall kept the city from being washed away. Despite damage estimated at thirty million dollars, residents of Nome rebuilt.

Fire also changed the face of Nome. The fire of 1934 destroyed most of the structures built during the Gold Rush. The cause of the disaster remains unclear. One legend holds that the fire started when a whiskey still exploded in the Golden Gate Hotel, a wooden structure in the central business district. The fire could not be contained to the hotel because twenty to thirty mile an hour winds carried embers to adjoining wooden structures. When the fire was brought under control after about four hours, almost all the gold rush buildings in downtown Nome were destroyed. Total damage was estimated at two to three million dollars, but no one was killed. Many of the persons left homeless by the fire decided to stay in Nome.

During World War II, Nome served as a base for the lend-lease aircraft ferried to the Soviet Union. American pilots flew the aircraft from Montana through Canada, stopping at newly constructed bases there and in Fairbanks, Alaska. Since the Soviet government would not allow American airmen to enter Siberia, Soviet pilots picked up the planes in Fairbanks, stopping in Nome for refueling before heading to Siberia. Nome's population increased during the war as more military personnel were stationed in the region to protect Alaska from potential Japanese attacks.

After the war, Nome returned to a state of relative peace. The city, being on the "frontlines" of the Cold War, was affected by a number of "red scares." The military maintained a presence in the region with several early-warning radar stations. Since the war, Nome rebuilt from the 1974 storm and worked to modernize a city located only 150 miles south of the Arctic Circle. At its centennial celebration, Nome's population was four thousand with an economy relying mainly on gold mining and tourism.

Places to Visit

Much of Nome's gold rush architecture was destroyed in the fire of 1934 or one of several violent storms. The Carrie McLain Memorial Museum on Front Street includes numerous photographs from the gold rush period in its collections. The museum also provides a self-guided walking tour of Nome; sites include famous homes, saloons, and the red-light district. One of the homes, a slightly run-down building on C Street north of Seppala Drive, is said to be the boyhood home of Jimmy Doolittle, the World War II general whose raid on Tokyo in April, 1942, made him a national hero. The city owns the building.

St. Joseph's Catholic Church, the first Catholic church in Nome, is the city's oldest building. It was established in 1901. Dogsledders used St. Joseph's lighted cross as an important navigational aid, known to the Eskimos as "white man's star." In 1946, the church was replaced by a newer version and the old church became a warehouse for a mining company. In the mid-1990's, the city, after a long debate, decided to renovate the old church. Townspeople worked to restore the building from the foundation to the rotting steeple. The church has become a community center and is used for business meetings, seminars, and weddings. It also has been nominated for inclusion in the National Register of Historic Places. The church's steeple remains the tallest point around.

While Nome is not connected to other Alaskan cities by a highway system, there are roads out of the city. The Dexter Roadhouse is about ten miles outside of town on the Kougarok Road. Wyatt Earp is said to have been an owner of the roadhouse at one time. Other roads take visitors to neighboring villages, native fishing camps, and gold mining areas. From Nome, visitors also may board flights to Siberia.

The Iditarod Trail Sled Dog Race ends in Nome every March. The competition starts in Anchorage on the first Saturday in March. The first musher arrives in Nome approximately nine to eleven days later. A number of activities keep Nome residents and visitors busy while awaiting the mushers. These activities include reindeer potluck dinners, arts and crafts shows, the Iditarod Basketball Tournament, and a winter golf tournament. Couples have been married under the arch that serves as the race's finish line.
                                    —*John David Rausch, Jr.*

For Further Information:

Beach, Rex. *The Spoilers*. Reprint. Upper Saddle River, N.J.: Literature House, 1969. Fictionalized account of the Nome gold conspiracy.

Bronson, William. "Nome." *The American West* 6, no. 4 (July, 1969): 20-31. Brief history of Nome, focusing largely on the development of the city, with illustrations.

Cole, Terrence, ed. "Nome: City of the Golden Beaches." *Alaska Geographic* 11, no. 1 (1984). Illustrated history of Nome with particular emphasis on the gold rush.

Helms, Andrea R. C., and Mary Childers Mangusso. "The Nome Gold Conspiracy." *Pacific Northwest Quarterly* 73, no. 1 (January, 1982): 10-19. Scholarly discussion of the Nome gold conspiracy.

"Nome Gold Rush Centennial." www.nome100 .com. Provides information on the centennial of the Nome gold rush as well as the city's history.

"Nome Homepage." www.alaska.net/~nome. The official Web site of the Nome Convention and Visitors Bureau.

Sitka

Date: Sold to the United States in 1867

Relevant issues: American Indian history, business and industry, European settlement, western expansion

Significance: Originally an Alaskan Indian village, Sitka was the center of the northwest international fur trade, the site of the first recorded contact between Eurasians and Alaskan Indians, and the site of several battles between Indians and Russians; the capital of Russian America, the first capital of Alaska under U.S. rule, and the site of transfer for Alaska's sale to the United States by Russia in 1867.

Location: The seaward side of Baranof Island, an extinct volcano in southeast Alaska's island chain; approximately one hundred miles from the coast of North America

Site Office:

Sitka Convention and Visitors Bureau
P.O. Box 1226
Sitka, AK 99835
ph.: (907) 747-5940
fax: (907) 747-3739
Web site: www.sitka.org
e-mail: scvb@sitka.org

Sitka, a small fishing and tourist village on the Pacific side of Baranof Island in southeastern Alaska, has had a past that belies its present-day tranquillity. One of the largest in a chain of islands dotting the northwest coast of North America, Baranof Island lies directly in the path of a nutrient-rich current of warm water from the Sea of Japan. The Japanese Current keeps Sitka's bays, straits, and channels at a near-constant temperature of fifty degrees. The warm water supports an incredibly diverse ecosystem, including wildflowers, giant cedars, plankton, crustaceans, sea otters, seals, eagles, bears, and whales.

In the early 1700's, European demand for furs sparked interest in southeastern Alaska, and by the middle of the eighteenth century the stage was set for a profitable and sometimes violent fur trade. Protected harbors, close proximity to open sea, and an abundance of wildlife made Sitka the perfect location for a fur trade seaport. Originally a Native American village and hot springs retreat,

Sitka was the site of several battles between natives and Russian traders. It became the seat of government for Russia in North America, and, under U.S. rule, the state capital.

The Arrival of Russian Traders

Sitka was originally inhabited by the Tlingit (pronounced KLIN-kit), a Native American tribe whose ancestors are presumed to have crossed the Bering Sea to mainland Alaska as early as eight thousand years ago. The Tlingit are known for their dramatic carved and painted totem poles and canoes, and for their rich and complex social structure. Totem poles function as heralds of family histories and popular myths, and are carved and displayed by the Tlingit to this day.

The first documented contact between Tlingits and the Old World took place on July 20, 1741. During an expedition sponsored by the Russian government to prove that Russia and North America were not connected by land, Aleksey Chirikov, captain of the *St. Paul*, sailed into Sitka Sound and sent ten well-armed men ashore to seek water. When the sailors did not return, Chirikov sent five more men to search for them. They did not return, either. After the boat had set several days in port, a group of Tlingits came to the shore shouting "*agai, agai*," which translates as "come here." Chirikov

The town of Sitka. (American Stock Photography)

did not attempt to discover the purpose of the natives' actions and left Sitka Sound.

According to Tlingit oral history of this first meeting, Chief Annahootz of the Sitka Tlingit disguised himself in bear skins and so artfully imitated the mannerisms of a bear that Chirikov's men, excited at the prospect of fresh game, followed Annahootz into the forest. Once in the woods, Chirikov's men were dispatched by several Tlingit warriors.

During the late 1700's, trade relations with the Tlingits were established by the English, Spanish, and Americans. Russia did not attempt to initiate contact with the Tlingits until the summer of 1796 when the Russian trading vessel *Severnyi Orel* sailed into Sitka sound.

From 1796 to 1798, a trading company backed by the Russian monarchy sent frequent, very successful hunting parties to Sitka. The general manager of the trading company, and a man who would shape the history of Sitka, was Aleksandr Andreyevich Baranov.

Baranov was impressed by Sitka's abundance of furs and its natural attributes as a port. It was large enough to contain an entire fleet, and ice-free year-round. He resolved to establish a permanent settlement on Sitka Island. During the winter of 1799-1800, Baranov and twenty men began the construction of the fort. They spent the winter in tents and poorly built shacks, and were frequently under attack by the Tlingits.

Baranov and his men had enjoyed friendly relations with the Aleuts, a northern Alaskan group of Indians, but not so with the Tlingits. In the spring of 1800 the fort was completed, and was christened Archangel Michael. (Baranov was religious and encouraged missionary efforts in Alaska.)

The Tlingits' attacks abated for a time, but they did not trade extensively with the Russians. The Tlingits preferred to trade with British and U.S. ships, which offered a larger selection of goods in exchange for furs supplied by the Indians.

War with the Tlinglits

In 1802, upon hearing a rumor of war between Britain and Russia, Baranov left Sitka to prepare a place of hiding for his store of furs. During his absence, Archangel Michael was attacked and taken by the Tlingits. British traders inspecting the scene afterward reported a smoldering ruin strewn with the mutilated bodies of Russian and Aleut trappers. According to survivors, a large group of Tlingits surrounded the barracks and began shooting into the windows and setting the buildings on fire. The occupants were killed as they fled the burning buildings.

In all, twenty Russians and one hundred thirty Aleut trappers were killed. The Tlingits stole three thousand otter pelts, burned a Russian ship, and took several prisoners. After the battle, the British captain Henry Barber intervened, harboring survivors of the attack. When a Tlingit chief boarded Barber's ship and demanded the survivors, he was put in irons and held for ransom against all those whom the Tlingits had captured. The Tlingits protested, but after a volley of English cannon fire, they conceded and released three Russian and five Aleut men, eighteen women, and six children.

When he returned to Sitka in 1804, Baranov tried to negotiate peace with the Tlingits, but the conditions of surrender he tried to impose infuriated them and they attacked. The battle lasted for seven days. Eventually the Tlingits surrendered and abandoned the fort, resettling about one hundred fifty miles from Sitka.

Baranov devoted his energy to building a new fort on Sitka Island, and chose a hilltop in the middle of an abandoned Tlingit village as the new location. He had initially wanted to build his first fort there but had decided against doing so, for fear of offending the Tlingits.

The second fort was named New Archangel, and was considered sufficient protection against any Indian attack. The structure was three stories high with a palisade extending to the shore, and was armed with 147 cannon. Most Tlingits avoided the fort, but parties going to and from it were often attacked, and required an escort of armed guards.

In 1818 Baranov, aging and in poor health, left his post as general manager. After twenty-seven years in Alaska, Baranov had earned a net profit of nearly thirty million rubles for the company. He was suspected of embezzling company funds, and was ordered to turn over his records as well as his post to his successor, Leonty Andreyevich Hagemeister.

An investigation revealed no discrepancies in the handling of funds, but even so Hagemeister recommended that Baranov's pension be denied. On November 27, 1818, Baranov boarded a ship for Russia. He died en route, on April 12, 1819, and was buried at sea in the Indian Ocean.

Twelve managers followed Baranov. Many of them shared his missionary zeal, and on November 20, 1848, Russian Bishop Ivan Veniaminov dedicated Sitka's first cathedral, Cathedral St. Michael. Relations between the Russians and Tlingits grew more peaceful, and by the mid-1800's many natives were living about the walls of the fort.

The Purchase of Alaska

In 1867 the United States bought Alaska from Russia for $7.2 million, against strong opposition in both countries. On October 18, 1867, in the presence of President Andrew Johnson, some 250 U.S. soldiers, the Russian Prince and Princess Maksontoff, and many Russians, Indians, and U.S. citizens, Sitka became the capital of the U.S. Territory of Alaska. Sitka remained the capital of Alaska for thirty-two years. In 1900, because of Sitka's weakening economic position, the capital of Alaska was moved to Juneau.

Today, the Castle Hill State Historic Site marks the spot where the transfer of Alaska to the United States occurred. The hillside site is dotted with interpretive plaques and Russian cannon. The Sitka National Historical Park is the site of the 1804 battle between the Tlingits and Russians. The 106-acre park contains several Tlingit totem poles. Also within the park is the Russian Bishop's House, built in 1842-1843. It is the only original Russian building remaining in Sitka. It served as the bishop's residence for 127 years and was in extremely poor condition when it closed, but it underwent extensive restoration beginning in 1973. Nearby is a faithful replica of Cathedral St. Michael; the original burned down in 1966, but the replica contains religious icons and other articles that were rescued from the fire. Just north of Sitka is the Old Sitka State Historic Site, at the location of the Russians' first fort, Archangel Michael.

—Jonathan Rogers

For Further Information:

Gunther, Erna, ed. *Indian Life on the Northwest Coast of North America*. Chicago: University of Chicago Press, 1972. For information on Native Americans of Southeast Alaska, this book is a revealing collection of notes, paintings, and diaries of explorers and fur traders in the late eighteenth century. Well balanced with Gunther's objective text, these records reveal as much about European attitudes toward Native Alaskans as about the Alaskans themselves.

Rennick, Penny. *Sitka*. Anchorage: Alaska Geographic Society, 1995. This travel guidebook for the Sitka region includes illustrations and maps.

Tikhmenev, Petr. *A History of the Russian-American Company*. Seattle: University of Washington Press, 1978. A helpful work on Sitka, originally published in Russian in 1888, that covers Russia's involvement in North America from 1741 to 1867.

Skagway

Date: Settled by whites in 1887; incorporated in 1900

Relevant issues: Business and industry, western expansion

Significance: Part of the Klondike Gold Rush National Park, Skagway was a popular stopping point for gold seekers on their way to the Klondike during the Alaskan gold rush at the end of the nineteenth century.

Location: The southeast corner of the Alaskan mainland, north of the Alexander Archipelago, and the last stop on the Alaskan State Ferry

Site Offices:
Skagway Convention and Visitors Bureau
P.O. Box 1025
Skagway, AK 99840
ph.: (907) 983-2854
fax: (907) 983-3854
Web site: www.skagway.org/

Klondike Gold Rush National Historical Park
P.O. Box 517
Skagway, AK 99840
ph.: (907) 983-2921
fax: (907) 983-9249
Web site: www.nps.gov/klgo/
e-mail: KLGORangerActivities@nps.gov

Located in a windswept valley at the northern end of southeast Alaska's Inside Passage, Skagway attracts thousands of visitors each year with its lures of natural beauty and its historical role in the Klondike gold rush.

Downtown Skagway in 1913. (University of Alaska at Fairbanks, Helen van Campen Collection)

The Gold Rush

During the late nineteenth century, Skagway played host to thousands of prospectors and stampeders (those eager to capitalize on the finds of prospectors) during their journey to Canada's Yukon Territory in search of gold. Although the Alaskan gold rush is generally thought to have begun in 1897, it actually comprised a series of strikes that occurred over several decades.

The earliest reported strike took place in 1865 when Daniel B. Libby found gold in Nome while digging post holes for the Western Union Telegraph Company. In 1878 American prospector Arthur Harper found gold in Canada's Yukon Territory, and in 1880 Fred Harris and Joe Juneau discovered Alaska's first big strike just outside of the city of Juneau, Alaska's present state capital.

It was not until 1896 that the rush for gold in Alaska reached legendary proportions. That year George Washington Carmack, an American of European parentage who had adopted the Native American way of life, found gold on a tributary of the Klondike River in the Yukon, starting one of the world's greatest stampedes for gold.

Although Alaska and the Yukon are distinct regions separated by an international boundary, prospectors used the names Alaska, Yukon, and Klondike interchangeably, not in reference to any specific location, but to represent the region and its fever for gold.

Skagway was only one of several routes to the gold fields. Prospectors also came to the Yukon and Klondike via the cities of Edmonton, Valdez, Dyea, and St. Michael. The merchants of these towns played an important role in the stampede for gold by providing the newcomers, or cheechakos, with much-needed supplies and information, as most stampeders seriously underestimated the difficulty of the journey that lay before them.

The merchants, eager to drum up business, touted their respective towns as the fastest and easiest way to the Klondike. Each route, however, was beset with its own travails and dangers. The Chilkoot Pass out of Dyea, a small town nine miles out of Skagway, was the most direct route, but it was also the most arduous. The thin, winding pass proved too steep for horses, and men had to carry supplies on their backs. More than three thousand pack animals died on the Chilkoot, many at a place known as Dead Horse Gulch. The White Pass trail out of Skagway was a less direct route than the Chilkoot, but the terrain proved to be more manageable, and gold seekers could use pack animals on the three-month journey.

Skagway was originally settled by former riverboat captain William Moore, who, with his daughter, worked his 160-acre homestead before the gold rush. By 1897, however, the word of gold had spread, and prospectors, speculators, and criminals poured into Skagway. With no regard for Moore's ownership rights, the new entrepreneurs built stores, streets, and docks to accommodate the masses.

During the first year of the gold rush more than ten thousand stampeders came through Skagway, and the town's population grew to more than twenty thousand. Ships from Seattle and San Francisco brought people from all over the world to Skagway's shores. People and supplies were hastily set ashore without regard for comfort or decorum so that the ship might return as quickly as possible for the next load of gold seekers. Many prospectors disembarked at Skagway only to find their stores and equipment lost or stolen. By 1898 Skagway was considered the largest if not the busiest city in Alaska. Banks, supply shops, saloons, hotels, and dance halls offered gold rush stampeders everything they might need for their arduous trip across the White Pass, as well as comforts and diversions not found on the trail.

The trails to the Klondike's gold fields were fraught with difficulty. With no waystations for food or supplies, stampeders had to carry every item that might be required for the journey. Cold, hunger, loneliness, wild animals, impassable terrain, and criminal activity were all a reality for the stampeder. A sense of rugged individualism was vital to the survival of those on the pass and was romanticized to heroic proportions in contemporary fiction and newsprint, but without an official peace-keeping force in Alaska, it fostered a decidedly lawless environment.

Soapy Smith's Swindles

This environment was convenient for those who would prey on the cheechakos, and Skagway gained a considerable reputation as a center for the "con" game. During the late 1890's Skagway was controlled by the most infamous of Alaska's criminals and con men: Jefferson Randolph "Soapy" Smith. Smith earned his nickname by running a confidence game involving the selling of bars of soap. Smith sold his soap for one dollar per bar on the pretext that a certain number of bars contained under their wrappers a five, ten, or twenty dollar bill. Smith maintained the confidence of Skagway's naive newcomers by employing alleged strangers to "find" one of the lucky bars.

From 1897 to 1898 Smith ran a gang that had a stranglehold on Skagway's economy. He placed members of his organization on nearly every ship bound for Skagway in order to discover how much money was aboard and to set up potential customers for his confidence games.

Having arrived in Skagway, a newcomer might be steered by one of Smith's men to the Reliable Packing Company to buy items needed for the remainder of the trip, or to the Skagway Information Agency for maps and advice. Once inside, someone would bump into the customer and steal his wallet. In his attempt to catch the thief, the customer would be knocked down by someone allegedly trying to help, and the doorway would be blocked by those in pursuit.

Smith ran Skagway's only army recruiting office, where applicants received a physical while in the next room their clothes were meticulously stripped of any valuables. Smith also ran Skagway's only telegraph office, where one could communicate with loved ones for five dollars per message, several years before telegraph service came to Alaska.

Smith argued that his treatment of the cheechakos was beneficial both to them and to the United States. He rationalized that anyone taken in by his simple swindles in the relative safety of Skagway would never survive the dangers and hardships of life on the trail. Smith also felt that by relieving cheechakos of their money, he was taking capital that was ultimately bound for Canada and keeping it in the United States.

Oddly enough, Soapy enjoyed a reputation as a philanthropist. He provided for the widows and children of those his men had killed and often paid the passage back to Seattle for those whom he had robbed. However, these displays of kindness might have been motivated less from pity than from a desire to rid Skagway of angry victims seeking revenge.

Smith's brazenness would eventually result in his demise. During Smith's reign, Skagway's legitimate businesses suffered a decline as gold seekers avoided the town for safer towns such as Dyea. On July 7, 1898, the residents of Skagway had taken their last insult from Soapy Smith.

On that morning, J. D. Stewart, a stampeder returning from the trail, was robbed of $2,670 in gold in broad daylight by three of Smith's men. If the merchants of Skagway could tolerate Smith's weeding out the weak cheechakos, they refused to tolerate the blatant robbery of a man who had braved and worked the Yukon. A committee of townsmen immediately approached Smith and informed him that the gold must be returned and that he and his men were no longer welcome in Skagway. Smith promised that if the incident were kept quiet, he would return the money by four o'clock that afternoon and see to it that his men ceased preying on those returning from the Klondike. Smith underestimated the mood of the townsfolk and, rather than resolving the matter, began to drink heavily and speak defiantly of the committee and its ultimatum. Four o'clock passed, and the townspeople became furious. At nine o'clock they held a meeting in Sylvester's Hall. The gathering soon grew too large for Sylvester's, and was moved to the docks.

At 9:30 P.M., Smith approached the dock carrying a rifle and encountered four men guarding the meeting. Smith walked up to one of the men, Frank H. Reid, the city surveyor, and swung his rifle at him. Reid caught the barrel of the rifle, drew his own revolver, and the two fired at each other almost simultaneously. Smith was killed instantly, shot through the heart, and Reid soon died of his injuries. A committee was formed to clean up Smith's gang, and eventually all were jailed or banished from Skagway. Although Skagway still suffered from the unchecked individualism of the frontier, after Smith's passing it became a safer and more law-abiding town.

Ma Pullen's Ingenuity

Not all of Skagway's well-remembered residents profited from criminal activity. Skagway also yielded profits to those with perseverance and an iron will. One of those countless pioneers was "Ma" Pullen. Widowed, destitute, and with four children left at home, Pullen arrived at Skagway in September, 1897.

She was hired as a cook and sold pies in her spare time. Her pie business became so successful that she was able to send for her three sons. With her substantial knowledge of horses and able to speak five Indian dialects, Pullen left her pie business to become the only woman packer on the trail.

Pullen proved to be a great entrepreneur. While on the trail, she opened a restaurant and hauled other miners' equipment along with her own. When Pullen reached Lake Bennet near the end of Whitehorse Pass, she showed great ingenuity by purchasing a large boat for one hundred dollars with a ten-dollar deposit, and then charging ten stampeders ten dollars each to cross the lake. Pullen recovered her initial investment and crossed the lake at no charge.

Pullen fell and broke her arm before she could begin mining herself. Injured, and realizing that the coming of the White Pass Railway would put an end to the days of packing, Pullen returned to Skagway to make a profit in the hotel business. She rented a building and bought furniture on credit and decorated the grounds with ornamental landscaping. Within a year the Pullen House was so successful that Ma Pullen owned the hotel outright.

By 1900, the days of crossing the White Pass trail on foot were over. In 1898, a group of English investors began construction on the White Pass and Yukon Railroad, a narrow gauge line connecting Skagway with the Yukon town of White Horse. Amazingly, after only two years of work on the precarious mountain passes and sheer cliffs, with men using only hand tools and blasting powder, the line was complete. Skagway was now the most important city in Alaska.

Places to Visit

Today, although a few hardy individuals still mine and pan the area for gold, most of Skagway's visitors arrive via cruise ship to see the town for a day. During the summer, Skagway's wooden sidewalks and false-fronted buildings delight visitors with a taste of gold rush history. The Corrington Museum of Alaska History and the Trail of '98 Museum both offer Skagway's visitors a chance to see relics and photographs of the town's past.

Although the White Pass and Yukon Railroad closed for business in 1982, it was resurrected in 1988 for the benefit of tourists. Departing from downtown Skagway, the railway winds along tracks built against near-vertical mountainsides. From the train one can still see the trail carved by the stampeders, by the passing of countless feet and pack animals. —*Jonathan Rogers*

For Further Information:
DuFresne, Jim. *Alaska: A Lonely Planet Travel Sur-*

vival Kit. 5th ed. Oakland, Calif.: Lonely Planet, 1997. Offers an excellent overview of present-day Skagway.

Wharton, David. *The Alaska Gold Rush.* Bloomington: Indiana University Press, 1972. This book offers an objective and thorough examination of the last great stampede for gold.

Other Historic Sites

Attu Battlefield and U.S. Army and Navy Airfields on Attu

Location: Aleutian Islands
Relevant issues: Aviation history, military history, World War II
Statement of significance: Attu was the site of the only World War II battle fought in North America. Its occupation by Japanese troops marked the peak of Japan's military expansion in the North Pacific. Its recapture by Americans in 1943 was costly for both sides. Afterward, Attu provided a base for bombing missions against Japanese territories.

Birnirk Site

Location: Barrow, North Slope County
Relevant issues: American Indian history
Statement of significance: Composed of a group of sixteen mounds arranged in rows roughly parallel to the beach, this site is associated with the Birnirk and Thule cultures, both belonging to the North Alaskan branch of the Northern Maritime tradition, the earliest manifestation of the Inuit (Eskimo) culture in North Alaska.

Brooks River Archaeological District

Location: Naknek, Bristol Bay
Relevant issues: American Indian history
Statement of significance: The district is located along the series of ancient beach ridges and river terraces associated with the 2.5 mile-long Brooks River. The twenty well-preserved sites which make up the district date from 2500 B.C.E. to historic times. The district has yielded and is expected to continue to yield data of major scientific importance; included in the district is the single area of greatest concentration of Arctic Small Tool Tradition artifacts known in Alaska

and possibly in North America. It is estimated that over 90 percent of all the archaeological properties remain intact.

Cape Field at Fort Glenn

Location: Fort Glenn, Aleutian Islands
Relevant issues: Military history, World War II
Statement of significance: Fort Glenn was the first Alaska project commissioned after the outbreak of war with Japan in 1941. Secretly built under the guise of a fish-processing plant, Fort Glenn provided aerial defensive cover for the Dutch Harbor Naval Operating Base and Fort Mears at Dutch Harbor in Unalaska Bay. During the Japanese bombing raid on Dutch Harbor on June 3-4, 1942, fighter pilots stationed at Fort Glenn led the counterattack. Fort Glenn served as the initial forward base to launch bombing attacks on Japanese installations at Attu and Kiska. Downgraded to caretaking status in 1945, and finally decommissioned in 1950, Fort Glenn is the most comprehensive and intact World War II base in the Aleutian Islands.

Cape Krusenstern Archaeological District

Location: Kotzebue, Northwest Arctic
Relevant issues: American Indian history
Statement of significance: A series of 114 marine beach ridges, formed at an average of perhaps sixty years each since the time of the highest postglacial sea level, the district contains the remains of peoples who have inhabited these beaches for five thousand or more years. Adjacent to the ridges on unglaciated uplands in the Iguchuk Hills are surface deposits that extend the record backward to the time of the end of the Pleistocene. Cape Krusenstern beach ridges

place in a broad, horizontal stratigraphy virtually all phases of cultural history known in northwest Alaska and have made possible the identification of several new phases previously unknown.

Chaluka Site

Location: Nikolski, Aleutian Islands
Relevant issues: American Indian history
Statement of significance: This site contains a large stratified village mound appearing to represent all the periods of culture identified in the Aleutians. The site has contributed significant data on the origins and evolution of the Aleut people and culture.

Dutch Harbor Naval Operating Base and Fort Mears, U.S. Army

Location: Unalaska, Aleutian Islands
Relevant issues: Military history, World War II
Statement of significance: This complex was the farthest west of the Navy's Alaska bases when the Japanese attacked the Aleutians in 1942. It was bombed for two days in the most serious air attack on North American territory during World War II. These bases were an important part of coastal defenses throughout the war.

Eagle Historic District

Location: Eagle, Southeast Fairbanks County
Relevant issues: Western expansion
Statement of significance: Eagle was a military, judicial, transportation, and communications hub for interior Alaska at the end of the nineteenth century. Fort Egbert was established here as a control station and headquarters for northern Alaska in 1889. In 1905, Roald Amundsen trekked to Eagle to announce to the world the completion of the first successful Northwest Passage. More than one hundred buildings from the historic era remain, including the federal courthouse and structures of Fort Egbert.

Fort William H. Seward

Location: Haines, Haines County
Relevant issues: Military history, western expansion
Statement of significance: Established by executive order on December 31, 1898, and first known as Hanies Mission, Fort Seward was the last of eleven military posts established in Alaska during the territory's gold rushes between 1897 and 1904. Founded for the purpose of preserving law and order among the gold seekers, the fort also provided a U.S. military presence in Alaska during boundary disputes with Canada. The only active military post in Alaska between 1925 and 1940, the fort was closed at the end of World War II.

Kennecott Mines

Location: Kennecott, Valdez-Cordova County
Relevant issues: Business and industry
Statement of significance: A vestige of an early twentieth century copper mining camp, Kennecott represents the mining techniques of the era. The mines here were among the nation's largest and contained the last of the great high-grade copper ore deposits of the American West. The world's first ammonia-leaching plant for extracting concentrations of ore from low-grade ores was designed and first successfully used on a commercial scale here. The camp is little changed since its 1938 closing.

Kodiak Naval Operating Base and Forts Greely and Abercrombie

Location: Kodiak, Kodiak Island
Relevant issues: Military history, World War II
Statement of significance: A joint operations center here directed Alaskan operations in 1942-1943. It was the principal advance naval base in Alaska and the North Pacific when World War II broke out. Kodiak's ships and submarines played a critical role in the Aleutian campaign. Fort Greely, with its coast artillery and infantry troops, stood ready to repel an invader, but in the end the enemy did not come. In April, 1943, the Army erected a permanent eight-inch gun battery north of Kodiak and established it as a subpost of Fort Greely, naming it Fort Abercrombie.

Onion Portage Archaeological District

Location: Kiana, Northwest Arctic
Relevant issues: American Indian history
Statement of significance: For thousands of years, vast numbers of caribou have passed through this area on their seasonal migrations between tundra and taiga; drawn by these herds, hunters both ancient and modern have stationed them-

selves at the vantage point afforded by the site's location to await their coming. Nine cultural complexes, ranging from Paleo-Indians of the Akmak Complex (c. 8000-6500 B.C.E.) to the Arctic Woodland Eskimo (c. 1000-1700 C.E.) have existed in this area, which includes Onion Portage site proper, a deeply stratified river-edge site, and a series of smaller sites representing individual settlements of each of the cultures isolated.

Wales Site

Location: Wales, Nome County
Relevant issues: American Indian history
Statement of significance: Located on Cape Prince of Wales, this site contains material that spans the period from the Birnirk culture, the earliest recognizable manifestation of modern Inuit (Eskimo) culture in Alaska (500-900 C.E.), to the present Inuit inhabitants of the modern settlement of Wales, or Kinigin. Wales Site includes mounds, a midden, a present-day Native Alaskan community, and the first spot in Alaska where archaeologists found evidence of Thule culture.

Yukon Island Main Site

Location: Yukon Island, Kenai Peninsula
Relevant issues: American Indian history
Statement of significance: This is the oldest and most continuously occupied archaeological site on Cook Inlet. Excavation here helped define the Kachemak Bay Culture, which is related to that of the Salish Indians to the south and to that of the Kamchatkans and Ainu of Asia.

Arizona

History of Arizona. 37

Canyon de Chelly 39

Casa Grande Ruins 44

Coronado National Memorial 48

Grand Canyon. 51

Navajo National Monument 54

Taliesin West. 58

Tombstone. 62

Wupatki National Monument 65

Other Historic Sites 70

Downtown Tucson. (Corbis)

History of Arizona

Arizona's arid climate and southwest location combined to play influential roles in its history. Lack of rain has placed water at the center of Arizona's concerns, because without water, economic development is impossible. In the 1850's, the federal government even imported camels for a route through Arizona. The state was later than others in developing, with a population of barely forty thousand in 1880. On the other hand, the completion of a number of significant dams before and after World War II provided copious water and electric power, and the state's warm winters attract millions of new arrivals.

Early History
American Indians are believed to have inhabited Arizona for thousands of years, probably as early as 25,000 B.C.E. First to have settled were the Anasazi, ancestors of today's Pueblo, Hohokam, and Mogollon peoples. Not long before the entrance of Europeans to the region, the Navajos and Apaches arrived. In the sixteenth century, Spanish and Native Americans came in contact with each other. A succession of Spanish expeditions arrived, headed by priests such as Franciscan friar Marcos de Niza, who came in 1539 searching for the fabled Seven Cities of Cíbola. Other adventurers arrived, such as Francisco Vásquez de Coronado, who explored the region from 1540 to 1542. More explorers entered the region later in the century searching for precious metals.

In the next century a number of priests came in search of American Indian souls to save and began erecting missions. Perhaps the most illustrious was Father Eusebio Francisco Kino, a Jesuit mathematics professor of German origin, who went to Mexico in 1680. Kino thoroughly explored the region, covering twenty thousand miles and finding an overland route to California. Kino also founded several missions, including San Xavier del Bac Mission, located near Tucson, established in 1692. It is the only surviving Mexican Baroque church in the United States.

In the eighteenth century, Spanish activity continued. In 1776, when the American colonies declared independence from Britain, Spanish cleric Father Francisco Silvestre Vélez de Escalante undertook important explorations of the Colorado River region. The previous year, Tucson had been founded when a fortress, Old Pueblo, was constructed there. In succeeding years, Spanish troops were busy dealing with hostile American Indians. In the 1780's they conquered the Yumas, and in 1790 negotiations with the Apaches resulted in a peace lasting until 1822. Peace with the Navajos after their military defeat in 1806 lasted thirteen years.

American involvement in the region began in the 1820's, when traders and trappers entered the territory. From 1828, trapper, scout, and soldier Kit Carson used Taos, New Mexico, as a base for expeditions, which in some cases traveled through Arizona. Another famous trapper and scout, Pauline Weaver, arrived in 1830 and was active more than thirty years later when he led gold-hunting parties. In these years modern Arizona was part of Mexico, which gained independence from Spain after its War of Independence, begun in 1810.

From Spanish to American Rule
Arizona passed from Mexican to American hands as a consequence of the Mexican-American War (1846-1848). The terms of the Treaty of Guadalupe Hidalgo called for Mexico to cede all lands north of the Gila River, which runs through southern Arizona. Thus Arizona became part of New Mexico, which became a territory after its annexation to the United States.

The Gila River border proved problematic, however, when plans for a transcontinental railroad were being drawn up, since the best route ran south of the river. Accordingly, an American diplomat, James Gadsden, American Minister to Mexico, negotiated transfer of the required land. In 1853, by the terms of the Gadsden Purchase, Mexico agreed to sell a strip of territory along its northern border between Texas and California for ten million dollars.

Arizona was still part of New Mexico when the Civil War broke out. In 1861, when Confederate

president Jefferson Davis declared New Mexico part of the
Confederacy, Kit Carson was
asked to raise a force to defend
the territory against invasion.
When the Confederacy sent
troops to the region in 1862,
the only Civil War battle on Arizona soil occurred, resulting in
Union victory. Thereafter,
claims of the Confederacy to
the region rang hollow. To ensure its status, however, Congress made Arizona a separate
territory in 1863. Prescott was
the new territory's first capital,
though the site changed from
one place to another until
Phoenix became permanent
capital in 1889.

Native American Relations

During the Civil War, the area
was nearly emptied of European settlers. Yet after the war,
when miners and ranchers re-
turned, American Indian attacks became a serious
matter. In 1864 Kit Carson led a successful campaign against the Navajos. The defeated Indians
were then required to trek, many of them on foot,
to Bosque Redondo, New Mexico, some four hundred miles away. The event became known as the
Long Walk. They remained there until 1868, when
they made the Long Walk Home. The Apaches,
however, remained hostile and active in Arizona.
With such leaders as Cochise, Mangas Coloradas,
and Geronimo, the Apaches were a formidable
threat, attacking not only ranches but also towns
and even forts. Not until 1886 did the last raiding
party led by Geronimo surrender to federal forces.

Despite problems with Native Americans, much
economic progress was made. Mining made great
strides in the 1870's, and after 1886 grazing prospered despite frequent range wars between cattle
and sheep ranchers. In the 1880's copper was discovered near Bisbee, in the southeast. Eventually
copper became an important state resource. Settlement of the territory was assisted by several congressional acts, such as the Homestead Act (1862),
which gave land to settlers but required them to develop it to make good their claims. A tremendous
boost to the state's development occurred when
the first transcontinental railroad appeared in
1877. Six years later, track for a second railroad was
laid in northern Arizona. Population, which was a
dismal 9,658 in 1870, jumped to more than 40,000
ten years later and reached 88,000 in 1890. At the
close of the century, it was 123,000, and in 1910,
just prior to statehood, it passed 200,000.

From Territory to Statehood

With the American Indian menace behind them,
Arizonans of the 1890's agitated for statehood. Not
until 1910, however, could Congress be persuaded
to pass enabling legislation. Accordingly, a constitution was adopted. Like those of other western
states, it provided for the initiative and referendum
and allowed recall of public officials. This provision included recall of judges by voters, but President William Howard Taft strongly objected and
refused to agree to Arizona statehood unless it was
removed. He believed that judicial independence,
essential for constitutional government, would be
fatally compromised by such a provision. The of-

fending provision was therefore deleted. Upon attaining statehood, however, voters restored the provision.

The constitution provides for a governor elected for no more than two four-year terms. Four other executive branch officials are elected—a secretary of state, attorney general, treasurer, and superintendent of public instruction. These officials form a line of succession if a governor dies, resigns, or is removed from office; they, too, are limited to two four-year terms. Members of the bicameral legislature can be elected to a maximum of four two-year terms. The state's supreme court justices are appointed by the governor to six-year terms, at the end of which voters decide whether to retain them. The recall provision was most notably used in 1988 to remove a sitting governor.

Social and Economic Progress
By the time Arizona achieved statehood, it had begun the process of advancing from an extraction to a manufacturing economy. With the emergence of labor unions in mines, labor strife became familiar. Among militant labor organizers were the Marxist International Workers of the World (IWW). A notorious event in the state's labor history involving the IWW was the "Bisbee deportation" of July 12, 1917, during World War I. In this incident, some two thousand persons, most of them copper miners called out on strike by the IWW, were arrested by armed civilians, headed by the sheriff. Those who refused to abandon the strike, nearly twelve hundred men, were loaded onto cattle cars and taken across the New Mexico border. There, they were unloaded in the desert, where they spent two unsheltered days before U.S. troops arrived. Hundreds of civil suits were filed afterward and settled out of court.

Along with neighboring states, the American entrance into World War I gave a significant, though temporary, boost to Arizona's economy, when the price of minerals skyrocketed. During the two decades following the war, the federal government continued planning and constructing a series of dams and reservoirs that eventually would be of tremendous value to the state's economy by allowing irrigation, cheap power, and flood control. The Roosevelt Dam had been constructed prior to statehood. After the war, further projects included the Coolidge Dam on the Upper Gila River in south central Arizona, other dams on the Verde and Salt Rivers, and the great Hoover Dam, one of the century's great engineering projects, on the Arizona-Nevada border. In 1922, the Colorado River Compact devised a scheme for water sharing among seven states, including Arizona. As further irrigation became possible, agriculture prospered. The 1930's Depression years, however, were as difficult for Arizona as for the rest of the nation.

World War II and Postwar Developments
The state's economy rebounded through federal spending during World War II, when numerous air bases were opened due to the state's ideal flying weather. After the war the boom continued. Between 1940 and 1960, population nearly tripled, reaching 1.3 million. Adequate water supplies allowed manufacturing to expand, especially after 1963, when the U.S. Supreme Court awarded the state rights to 2.8 million acre feet of water a year from the Colorado River. By then, Arizona's extraction economy had been transformed by industrialization.

By the 1990's the state had undergone a second transformation. Manufacturing accounted for only 12 percent of its income, though high-tech industries were making their mark. Agriculture was just 2 percent and mining a scant 1 percent of state income. The lion's share was now taken up by services, including a thriving tourist industry. Society had also been transformed by a postwar flight from the eastern and midwestern "rust belt" to the warmer climate and economic opportunities of the Southwest. From a raw frontier territory at the start of the century, Arizona had become a prosperous modern, postindustrial society, with a rich and colorful past and a confident future.

—*Charles F. Bahmueller*

Canyon de Chelly

Date: Indian villages from 350-1300 C.E.; monument authorized on February 14, 1931

Relevant issues: American Indian history, western expansion

Significance: This National Monument, currently inhabited by Navajo farmers, includes well-preserved ruins of Anasazi cliff dwellings in sandstone canyons.

Location: East of Chinle, on the Navajo reservation, in northeastern Arizona near the New Mexico border; ninety miles north of Interstate 40 on Arizona 191

Site Office:
Canyon de Chelly National Monument
P.O. Box 588
Chinle, AZ 86503
ph.: (520) 674-5500

Canyon de Chelly National Monument has the distinction of being the only federal park not owned by the U.S. government; under a 1931 agreement, it is administered by the National Park Service in cooperation with the Navajo Nation, which retains title and property rights to the land. The monument includes 131 square miles consisting of three major canyons: Canyon de Chelly and its two branches, Canyon del Muerto and Monument Canyon. In these canyons, some eight hundred archaeological sites and one thousand rock art sites offer compelling evidence of prehistoric and historic human habitation during the past eighteen hundred years.

The name "de Chelly" is a corruption of the Navajo word *tsegi*, meaning "rock canyon." Through modification first by the Spanish, who pronounced it "day SHAY-yee," and then by Americans, it has come to be pronounced "d'shay."

Geological History
The history of Canyon de Chelly began 230 million years ago, when vast inland seas covered much of the North American continent. By the end of this era, the Permian period, the seas had begun to dry up; as they receded they left layers of mud and sand in their wake. At the same time mountains were forming as land was pushed from beneath the surface. The new mountains blocked the prevailing winds, cutting off moisture from the eastern slopes and generating deserts and vast sand dunes. The rock layer known as the de Chelly sandstone is a product of one of these immense layers of sand; it is easily visible in the canyon walls, where it appears as a red band. On top of this, at the canyon rim, is the Shinarump conglomerate, a layer of gravel most probably compacted to rock by yet another layer now eroded away. The Shinarump was formed 170

Canyon de Chelly. (Arizona Office of Tourism/Chris Coe)

million years ago and is the youngest part of the canyon.

At the end of the Cretaceous period, some 50 million years ago, a violent uplifting of land occurred along what is now the border between Arizona and New Mexico. As the uplift developed, streams of water poured down from the Chuska Mountains and cut into the uplift, slicing through the layers of rock and sandstone and carving the canyons. Continuous action by water, ice, wind-blown sand, and tree roots has further sculpted the cliffs.

Resulting from these millennia of erosion is a spectacular series of red canyons with sheer vertical sides, dramatic formations, and many caves and overhangs washed out of the rock. Among the more striking features of the cliff faces at Canyon de Chelly is the "desert varnish," striking dark vertical streaks that look as though they were painted on the canyon walls. In fact they were caused by chemical deposits from oxidation of the minerals in the rock; the blue-black streaks resulted from manganese, the red ones from iron.

The First People in the Canyon

The first people to live permanently in the canyons were those known as the Anasazi, a Navajo name meaning "the ancient ones." The Anasazi were an agricultural people who occupied much of the vast plateau area of the Southwest, including the watersheds of the San Juan, Little Colorado, and Rio Grande Rivers, much of Utah, and part of eastern Nevada, from the first century of this era to around 1300 C.E. At the height of their civilization, they had major population centers in the Chaco Canyon area of modern New Mexico, at Mesa Verde in Colorado, and in the Kayenta region of Arizona, including Canyon de Chelly.

The Anasazi were the first in this region to live by agriculture, growing corn and squash to supplement the plentiful game and wild plants around them. They stored the surplus of their corn harvest for winter use, raised domesticated turkeys for food and feathers, and kept dogs, probably as hunting companions and camp scavengers, although possibly for supplemental food as well.

The Anasazi culture has been divided into four stages based on their cultural development as evidenced by their artifacts: early Basketmaker (until 450 C.E.); modified Basketmaker (450-700); devel-opmental Pueblo (700-1000); and great, or classical Pueblo (1100-1300). Some archaeologists break down these stages further, with minor variations in the time frames.

Basketmakers

The Basketmakers moved into the canyon region to farm the rich canyon bottoms, where the land was fertile and well watered by streams and springs. During the summer months they lived in simple brush huts near their fields. During the cold winter months, they moved into the shelter of the many caves higher up the canyon walls. Around 450 C.E. they began to construct more permanent homes, called pithouses. These were circular pits, some five feet deep and twenty feet in diameter, covered with a thatched framework. It is believed that this was the forerunner of the modern kiva, or ceremonial chamber, still used by the Pueblos.

The artifacts left by the Basketmakers earned them their name, for they produced many beautifully woven products including baskets, cordage, sandals, cradles, and clothing. Their baskets served as storage vessels, cooking pots, and even caskets. They made warm winter robes by weaving strips of rabbit fur around yucca cordage. Eventually they began to learn to make pottery. While their early attempts produced crude air-dried vessels, the Basketmakers eventually learned to fire and decorate their pots. This new craft gradually replaced their basketry.

Burial Sites

The ruins in Big Cave in Canyon del Muerto are among the earliest in the park, dating to 331-835 C.E. Among the evidences of Basketmaker life in this location are evidences of Basketmaker death: several burials were found in Big Cave, including that of an old man who had two broken legs. The fractures had been expertly set and the bones had healed cleanly. Archaeologists also found the remains of fourteen infants buried in an old storage bin, a common burial practice, and four other children buried in a large basket. Since there was no indication of violence, the burials probably indicate some epidemic that ravaged the community.

In another part of the cave is the site of the most famous and mysterious burial in the canyons, the "Burial of the Hands." A pair of arms and their hands were found lying on a bed of grass, in a position that makes it unlikely any body was ever attached. The wrists had been wrapped with shell necklaces, and a pair of finely-woven sandals and a small basket of shell beads had been placed next to the hands. A basket two feet in diameter covered the remains. No satisfactory explanation of the burial has been found.

Cliff Dwellers

Around 700 C.E. the Anasazi began to experiment with a new type of dwelling: the pueblo (Spanish for village). The first pueblos were long rows of flat-roofed rooms made of mud over a framework of poles, still built over a pit. The pithouse itself now took on a ceremonial function. Over the next four hundred years the pueblo evolved from its crude beginnings into a multistoried multifamily complex built of stone masonry.

Along with the change in building technique came a dramatic change in location. The Anasazi moved their dwellings from the canyon floors to the caves and recesses in its walls. There were several advantages to living in these seemingly inaccessible sites: the walls were above the flood plain, and so the Anasazi, their dwellings, and their stored food remained dry; the available bottom land could be reserved for food production; the caves and overhangs offered protection from the elements; and their food was safer from rodents and insects. Furthermore, the dwellings were not so inaccessible as they seem today. Canyon del Muerto alone contains more than forty hand-and-toe-hold trails permitting a healthy climber to traverse from the canyon floor to the rim in twenty minutes.

Trade was an important activity for the Pueblo Anasazi. Many changes in Anasazi culture were undoubtedly the result of contact with other peoples; parrots were obtained from Mexico for their feathers, ornamental shells from the Gulf of California. Pottery making and cotton were probably both imported from Mexico; the Anasazi of Canyon de Chelly became master weavers of cotton cloth and may well have traded it to other communities. Evidence points to the Anasazi community at Mesa Verde as a frequent trade partner.

The great pueblo period of the Anasazi began about 1100 C.E., and it was during this time that the most impressive of the cliff dwellings were built. One of the most accessible sites today is the White House, six miles up the main canyon from the current park headquarters. It was built in two sections, one against the base of the cliff on the canyon floor, and a second in the small cavern above it. At one time it may have contained as many as eighty rooms, but much of the lower structure has been washed away by the stream; about sixty rooms and four kivas remain in some form. Most of this lower part was built after 1070 C.E.

The cave containing the upper section is thirty-five feet above the canyon floor, but one of the buildings on the lower level came to within four feet of the cave floor. The upper site contains ten rooms, with one very large room in the center. The outer wall of this room, some twelve feet high, was coated with white gypsum clay plaster decorated with a yellow band.

The largest of the sites is located at Mummy Cave, in Canyon del Muerto, about twenty-one miles northeast of park headquarters. Here the structures were built in two adjacent caves three hundred feet above the streambed. The largest section is in the eastern cave, which accommodated fifty-five rooms and four kivas. Twenty more rooms in the western cave are now accessible only by a ledge from the eastern cave, but originally a hand-and-toe-hold trail, long eroded, led there from the talus below. No space was wasted here: There are fifteen more rooms along the ledge between the caves, including a square tower house, similar to the ones at Mesa Verde. Much of the original colored plaster work in the structures remains, including some decorated with an elaborate fretwork design in the large kiva.

The Anasazi Disappear

For about two hundred years the Anasazi were a successful, spiritual, artistic, and seemingly prosperous people, but then the Anasazi suddenly left Canyon de Chelly and indeed all of the plateau region.

The reason for the mass exodus of these people is not completely clear, but it was probably the result of severe drought. Between 1276 and 1299 C.E., drought gripped the plateau region, drying up water supplies, killing vegetation and the animals who fed on it, and making farming difficult if not impossible. The Anasazi left other sites like Mesa Verde first; it is possible that some of those refugees settled in Canyon de Chelly before the pueblos there were abandoned. It has been suggested that the square tower house in Mummy Cave points to the presence of Mesa Verde craftsmen. In any case, by 1300, all the cliff dwellings throughout the plateau had been abandoned.

Yet the Anasazi did not become extinct. They moved south to the Black Mesa region and southeast to the Rio Grande, and their descendents survive today: the people known today as the Pueblos.

In the centuries after the Anasazi had abandoned their homes in Canyon de Chelly, another people migrated southward from the northern plains, down the eastern slope of the Rocky Mountains, and into the mountains of northern New Mexico. The Dineh, as they called themselves, were constantly being joined by groups from other cultures, and the Dineh excelled at learning and assimilating the best of these cultures. They soon combined these various elements into a distinctive culture of their own, the culture known today as Navajo.

Europeans Arrive

As the Spanish began to settle in the lower Southwest, friction between the native and the European cultures grew. In 1690 the Pueblos in the south revolted against Spanish domination; their revolt was short lived and many sought refuge with the Navajo. The Pueblo brought to their new home centuries of agricultural expertise, their sheep, and their skill at weaving. The Navajo clan system and certain aspects of their religion also reflect the influence of the Pueblo refugees. As the refugees added to the population, the Navajo, now mobile thanks to the Spanish-introduced horses, began to move across the region searching for arable lands and pastures for their sheep. By the mid-1700's a small group had settled in Canyon de Chelly.

The Dineh were traditionally a warrior people, and their new agricultural skills did not cause them to abandon raids against the Spanish settlers, as well as their Hopi and Zuni neighbors. The Spanish retaliated frequently, enslaving prisoners whom they did not kill. During the winter of 1804-1805, a terrible battle took place in the canyon when Spanish cavalry found a group of Navajo hiding on a high ledge of the canyon wall; though secure from an enemy armed with bows and arrows, the position was all too vulnerable to rifles. The Spaniards took a position on the canyon rim where they could

fire directly down onto the ledge. During the ensuing carnage, 115 Navajo were killed, of whom 90 were warriors and the rest old men, women, and children; 33 more were taken prisoners. The site is popularly called Massacre Cave; the ricochet marks from the Spaniards' bullets are still visible.

Raiding and retaliation on both sides continued as the territory came first under Mexican rule and then was ceded to the U.S. at the end of the Mexican War. The arrival of American settlers offered new raiding targets to the Navajo. U.S. Army expeditions were undertaken and treaties signed, but since the Navajo society had no single chief, the treaties were largely useless.

During these sorties Canyon de Chelly became known as a shelter and hiding place for the Navajo. Army expeditions often approached it, but it contained too many twists and turns, too many ledges and caves from which troops on the canyon floor could be harassed.

Finally, in 1863, General James H. Carleton, military commander of New Mexico, appointed Kit Carson to deal with the "Navajo problem." Unlike Carson, Carleton had no sympathies for the Navajo; nor did the volunteers serving under Carson, many of whom had suffered from the Navajo raids. The campaign was merciless; after chasing the Navajo from their homes, the troops burned their dwellings, slaughtered their sheep, and destroyed their fields. A last few were flushed from the canyon. With nowhere else to turn, the Navajo surrendered and took refuge at Fort Defiance, where they had been offered food and protection. The Navajo Nation seemed broken; the army exiled them to southern New Mexico.

The Long Walk

The Navajo remember the exile as the Long Walk. In the spring of 1864, 8,500 of the Dineh were marched to Fort Summer in New Mexico and then resettled at a place called Bosque Redondo. The land could not be farmed, however, and there was no pasture for their sheep. There was no source of fuel or clean water. After four years, the army conceded that the plan had failed. A new treaty was negotiated, and at the Navajos' insistence, they were allowed to return to Canyon de Chelly. They have remained there ever since.

Relations between the Dineh and the American settlers were still difficult. It was the advent of the trading post that was to prove the necessary intermediary in the complex task of cultural interchange. Successful traders served as translators, mediators, and merchants. Lorenzo Hubbell was such a trader. He opened the first trading post at the canyon in 1886. The post is now a National Historic Site.

The first published descriptions of the ruins in the canyon appeared in 1850, based on the journal entries of Lieutenant J. H. Simpson, who had accompanied a U.S. Army expedition the previous year. The first archaeological expedition was made in 1882, led by James Stevenson for the Smithsonian Institution. Stevenson's group sketched, photographed and drew plans of forty-six ruins in the two main canyons. One of his staff, Cosmos Mindeleff, returned later that year for the first of three visits to map the canyons and some of the larger ruins. Mindeleff published a major architectural survey of the ruins in 1896.

In the 1920's many of the cave sites were excavated by Earl H. Morris of the American Museum of Natural History. Morris was one of the first genuine archaeologists to explore the ruins and collect artifacts. Scientific interest and publications led to growing tourism, and in 1931 the area was organized as a National Monument. Archaeological work has continued under the supervision of National Park Service authorities.

—*Elizabeth Brice*

For Further Information:

Bradley, Zorro A. *Canyon de Chelly: The Story of Its Ruins and People.* Washington, D.C.: National Park Service, 1973. One of several good introductions to the history of the canyon. It complements the titles by Noble and Supplee et al. listed below.

Houk, Rose. *Navajo of Canyon de Chelly: In Home Hod's Fields.* Tucson, Ariz.: Southwest Parks and Monuments Assocation, 1995. Examines the history and social life of the Navajo of Canyon de Chelly. Includes illustrations and maps of the area.

Hunter, Wilson. *In Pictures, Canyon de Chelly: The Continuing Story.* Las Vegas: KC, 1999. Mostly photographs of the canyon and the surrounding area, the ruins, and the current Navajo inhabitants.

Noble, David Grant, ed. *Houses Beneath the Rock: The Anasazi of Canyon de Chelly and Navajo National Monument.* Santa Fe, N.Mex.: Ancient City Press, 1986. Provides a greater focus on the ancient people of the region.

Supplee, Charles, Douglas Anderson, and Barbara Anderson. *Canyon de Chelly: The Story Behind the Scenery.* Edited by Gweneth Reed DenDooven. Rev. ed. Las Vegas: KC, 1981. Offers a thorough account of the monument's prehistory and history. Illustrated with color photographs.

Casa Grande Ruins

Date: Authorized as a Ruin Reservation on March 2, 1889; redesignated as a National Monument on August 3, 1918

Relevant issues: American Indian history

Significance: This is the site of a large, unusual multistoried structure, the Casa Grande, built by the Hohokam people around 1350 C.E. Now protected by a steel shelter, the thick walls of the Casa Grande are clearly visible in the distance as visitors approach the monument, which for centuries has been used by travelers as a landmark and meeting place. Surrounding the Casa Grande are the ruins of one or more Hohokam villages that are open to visitors. Park rangers are available on the site to answer questions about the monument and the daily lives and culture of the Hohokam.

Location: Approximately forty miles south of Phoenix on Highway 87 or U.S. Interstate 10; the monument is on Highway 87 about one mile north of Coolidge, approximately halfway between Phoenix and Tucson

Site Office:
Casa Grande Ruins National Monument
P.O. Box 518
1100 Ruins Drive
Coolidge, AZ 85228
ph.: (520) 723-3172
fax: (520) 723-7209
Web site: www.nps.gov./cagr/

Who were the people who constructed and then soon abandoned the Casa Grande? For what purpose did they build the unique structure? Despite the influence of Mexican peoples evident in their architecture, crafts, and irrigation techniques, the Hohokam (a Pima word meaning "those who have gone"), researchers believe, were descendants of the very early desert culture known as Cochise, and they shared ancestry with the Mogollon peoples, with whom they were closely linked in the beginning phases of their culture. Differences developed when the Mogollon moved into mountainous areas, but the two groups continued to interact and share cultural traits throughout the Hohokam's residence in the Gila River Valley.

Origins of the Hohokam

The Hohokam apparently moved into the Gila Valley between 200 and 300 C.E., and lived there successfully and peacefully for about eleven centuries. By 600 C.E., Hohokam culture was already highly developed, and, according to some researchers, possibly near its peak. The people were producing fine crafts from shell and stone, their irrigation systems were in place and extensive, they had built a number of ceremonial ball courts, and their red-on-buff pottery had already become quite specialized.

Until the twelfth century, at almost the end of their history in the area and around the time that they built Casa Grande, the Hohokam lived in huts made of mud and sticks. For hundreds of years the traditional Hohokam village consisted of clusters of two to six grass-roofed, pole-and-mud-walled houses, near a source of water. Adobe-style construction such as that found in the Casa Grande compound was a late development in Hohokam culture, one possibly introduced through contact with the Salado people who lived north of the Hohokam, near the Tonto Basin.

By the twelfth century Hohokam culture had already begun to decline. Around this time the Hohokam appear to have come into contact with pueblo-based people, with whom the Hohokam may actually have shared some of the same villages. The Hohokam apparently kept their own customs for a while, such as living in pit houses and cremating their dead, while the pueblo people lived alongside them in adobe compounds and buried their deceased. By the time of the building of Casa Grande, however, the Hohokam appear to have begun living in huts above the ground (as ruins around Casa Grande suggest) and burying their dead. Persons selected for burial may have been members of an elite or priestly group. Whatever the true explanation, Hohokam skeletons do exist.

Canals in the Desert

To survive in the desert, the Hohokam depended primarily on the extensive system of irrigation canals they constructed, a sophisticated system that was the first of its kind in the Southwest. From the top story of the Casa Grande, one can see, about sixteen miles away, the lower section of the main canal that sustained local residents.

Through satellite photographs, it is now known that in the Phoenix area alone the Hohokam built more than six hundred miles of canals that diverted water from the Gila and Salt Rivers. The design of the canals—deep and narrow to minimize evaporation—indicates a sophisticated understanding of the irrigation needs of their environment.

Irrigation enabled the Hohokam to grow corn, beans, squash, cotton, and pumpkins. The people also ate local animals such as fish, river clams, rabbits, deer, and probably small rodents. Corn prepared in a variety of ways was likely the mainstay of the Hohokam diet, and also the cause of some health problems. Researchers who studied Hohokam skeletons from a different site found that tooth and gum disease was common, probably due to grit from the stones used to grind corn that got stuck in the gums and around the teeth. They also found signs of osteoporosis in many of the older women, and a fair amount of arthritis throughout the population.

Appearance and Customs

Physically, the Hohokam men were athletically built, with strong upper torsos, as one might expect in a people who survived through manual labor. The skeletons showed that the women, who were probably the grinders of the corn, had especially well developed hands.

Clay figurines found at their dwellings give us some clues about the appearance of the Hohokam. Cheek and lip plugs were popular, as were body paint or tattoos, and they wore a great deal of jewelry, including earrings, hairpins, pendants, bracelets, and rings. The Hohokam clearly were an artistic people. They made exquisite jewelry from jet, shells from the Gulf of California, and turquoise, and developed a unique etching process that probably involved using acids fermented from cacti.

The Hohokam also excelled at chipped, ground, and carved stone work, which they used to create a wide variety of miniature animal figures, such as birds or frogs, from thin pieces of stone or shell, as well as rectangular flat palettes with decorative borders. Hohokam craftsmanship also shows itself in finely crafted, long-bitted axes made from hard black stone. The Hohokam are also known for their characteristic cream- or buff-colored pottery painted with red designs.

Sports, possibly with ritual or ceremonial significance, were also part of Hohokam culture; some two hundred ball courts have been found in Hohokam sites, including Casa Grande. These ball courts, sunken oval fields, are another indication of Mexican contact or influence, since similar courts existed throughout prehistoric Mexico. No one knows precisely how the game was played, but there is on a wall of each of these courts a high stone ring through which players probably tried to pass a ball. The Mexican version of the game apparently forbade players from using their hands or feet when handling the ball; these rules may have been true for the Hohokam games as well.

The Mysterious Casa Grande

The greatest mystery left behind by the Hohokam Indians, however, is Casa Grande itself, a structure quite unlike anything else in the Southwest. What was its function? What was its purpose? Constructed between 1320 and 1350 C.E., the edifice was already in ruins in 1694, when Father Eusebio Kino, a Jesuit missionary, came upon it while exploring areas visited by Coronado one hundred years previously. In his journal, Father Kino wrote,

> I went inland with my servants and some justices of this Pimeria, as far as the casa grande, as these Pimas call it, which is on the River of Hila that flows out of Nuevo, Mexico. . . . The casa grande is a four-story building as large as a castle and equal to the largest church in the lands of Sonora. . . . Close to this casa grande there are 13 smaller houses, somewhat more dilapidated, and the ruins of many others, which make it evident that in ancient times there had been a city here.

The unusual structure, which is more suggestive of Mexican than Southwestern architecture, sits in the midst of what appears to have been a Hohokam village, in a compound surrounded by an adobe wall approximately 420 feet long, 230 feet wide, and originally 7 or 8 feet high. The Casa Grande itself is about 40 feet long and 60 feet wide, with walls that are deeply trenched into the ground and taper from a base thickness of almost 5 feet to an upper thickness of about 1.5 feet.

The walls are made from caliche earth, a subsoil of the desert that has an especially high lime content. The mud for the walls was probably mixed by hand on site in a process similar to contemporary concrete mixing. The construction most likely involved the use of a framework, made of canes or poles and woven together with grass or reeds, that formed an open trough with two parallel surfaces. The workers would prepare the mud within these frameworks, which were about five feet long and three or four feet apart, and then remove the frames when the adobe was dry. The walls now look as if they were made of bricks, but the vertical lines in the surface are actually just cracks in the adobe.

Most of the Casa Grande structure is technically just two stories high. Yet the building sits on five feet of baseline fill, and this essentially adds an-

Casa Grande. (Diane C. Lyell)

other story to it. There are five rooms, with the central room reaching yet another story higher than the outside rooms. Thus the building varies in height from about twenty feet around the perimeter to at least thirty feet in the central tower.

The Casa Grande originally had a timbered ceiling built from more than six hundred roof beams of juniper, white fir, mesquite, and ponderosa pine. Since much of this wood was not available in the immediate area, the Hohokam must have transported it from more than fifty miles away.

The Casa Grande would have made an excellent sentry station, lookout tower, or possibly a fortress, although no signs of warfare exist in the area. Because there are even, round openings in the highest part of the building that provide specific views of constellations, the night sky, and the setting sun of the summer solstice, many people believe that Casa Grande functioned at least in part as an astrological observatory. Researchers are confident that all the early residents of the Southwest used some type of calendar, but are not sure whether these other cultures also erected structures such as Casa Grande to serve as observatories. Casa Grande could also have been an administrative facility, a palace, a large residence, a storage house, or a multipurpose facility.

The entire Casa Grande compound, like other Hohokam compounds, includes the remains of smaller structures of varying size, and thereby differs greatly from standard Southwestern pueblos. Pueblos are constructed in more egalitarian fashion, with rooms of equal size and no single large structure dominating the dwelling site. Since the physical design of the structure in which people live and work often reflects the nature of their society, the Hohokam may have had a more stratified or hierarchical society than other Indian peoples of the Southwest. Hohokam architecture also suggests an additional link to central Mexican peoples, who constructed similar compounds.

With its thick walls and solid construction, the Casa Grande was clearly built to be a permanent structure, and indeed it has withstood extreme variations in desert temperatures for nearly seven hundred years, most of the those years without protection. Unfortunately, Casa Grande far outlasted the Hohokam's need or use for it. Despite the great efforts it must have taken to build the Casa Grande, the Hohokam used it for only about one hundred years. By 1450 the Hohokam had left the area, abandoning the Casa Grande compound and other dwellings in the region.

Departure of the Hohokam

Experts speculate that, like other Indian peoples in the Southwest, the Hohokam left the area because the land could no longer sustain their population. Possibly, their complex irrigation system failed as a result of lateral erosion of the Gila River, or perhaps the land itself became salinized from the extended use of irrigation. The climate may also have changed. Regional evidence indicates that periods of drought seem to have alternated with severe flooding during the final years of Hohokam residence in the area.

No one knows where the Hohokam went after leaving the Gila River Valley, but some experts speculate that the Pima Indians, who still live near Casa Grande, may be their descendants.

A Landmark for Travelers

Following Father Kino's discovery of Casa Grande, the site quickly became known to westward-moving pioneers, soldiers, other explorers, and numerous tourists. Because it was easy to see from a distance, people used it as a landmark and meeting place. There was even a Southern Pacific Railway train station erected just twenty miles away from Casa Grande by 1880; it helped to increase tourism dramatically.

The popularity of Casa Grande had negative consequences. By the time archaeologists were able to study the structure and surrounding compound, numerous people had carved their names in the walls, vandalized and disturbed the site, and strewn the entire area with the remains of pots and other artifacts in their search for souvenirs. For this reason, it has not been possible to do an accurate study of the Casa Grande ruins.

Fortunately, the historical and archaeological significance of the site was recognized before it was damaged beyond repair. In 1887 to 1888 some of the most famous Southwestern archaeologists and explorers, including Frank H. Cushing, Jesse Walter Fewkes, Adolph F. Bandelier, and Frederick Webb Hodge, visited Casa Grande. Their attentions spurred efforts to designate the area as archaeologically significant, and in 1892 the federal government declared 480 acres around Casa

Grande a Federal Reserve under official protection. This made Casa Grande the first archaeological preserve in the United States.

During the previous year, 1891, the first clearing, excavation, and stabilization of the ruins were conducted by Cosmos Mindeleff under the auspices of the Smithsonian Institution. The Smithsonian also studied Casa Grande from 1906 to 1908. Other excavations have been conducted by the Southwest Museum, the Los Angeles County Museum, and the National Park Service. In 1918, Casa Grande became an official National Monument.

—*Gail A. Moss*

For Further Information:

Kidder, Alfred Vincent. *An Introduction to the Study of Southwestern Archaeology.* New Haven, Conn.: Yale University Press, 2000. This edition offers a new essay by Douglas W. Schwartz. Provides comprehensive information about the lower Gila Valley, with particular emphasis on the cultural wares of the people who inhabited the region. There is an excellent photograph of a model of the excavation of the complete Casa Grande ruin, which shows the structure in relation to the compound within which it sits.

McGregor, John C. *Southwestern Archaeology.* 2d ed. Urbana: University of Illinois Press, 1982. An in-depth chronological study of the major early cultures of the Southwest, with extensive information about the pottery and other artifacts the cultures left behind. Photographs, numerous illustrations, and maps add to this thorough history and reconstruction of prehistoric life in the Southwest.

Noble, David Grant. *Ancient Ruins of the Southwest: An Archaeological Guide.* 2d rev. ed. Flagstaff, Ariz.: Northland Press, 2000. Offers a thorough, yet concise look at the prehistoric cultures of the Southwest. Noble provides a brief history of each of the cultures, a short explanation of the significance of each historical site included in the book, and excellent photographs and simple maps.

Wilson, Josleen. *The Passionate Amateur's Guide to Archaeology in the United States.* New York: Macmillan, 1980. Offers brief descriptions, maps, and photographs of archaeological sites throughout the country.

Coronado National Memorial

Date: Established as a National Memorial in 1941
Relevant issues: American Indian history, European settlement, Latino history
Significance: This memorial commemorates Francisco Vásquez de Coronado's exploration of the United States Southwest (1540-1542). The memorial is located near his point of entry into the United States in his search for the Seven Cities of Cíbola. It was established four hundred years later.
Location: Twelve miles south of Sierra Vista
Site Office:
Superintendent
Coronado National Memorial
4101 East Montezuma Canyon Road
Hereford, AZ 85615
ph.: (520) 366-5515
Web site: www.nps.gov/coro/

In 1536, Álvar Nuñez Cabeza de Vaca, Estéban de Dorantes, and two other survivors of Pánfilo de Narváez's expedition from Cuba to the southeastern United States stumbled into Spanish Mexico with stories of rich cities located to the north. Antonio de Mendoza, first viceroy of New Spain, assigned Francisco Vásquez de Coronado to lead a Spanish expedition into the southwestern part of today's United States in search of those cities of gold.

The Coronado National Memorial sits in the Huachuca Mountains overlooking the San Pedro River Valley where Coronado may have left modern Mexico and entered Arizona. The expedition explored the southwestern part of the country, from Arizona's Colorado River to central Kansas. They found no gold, but were the first Europeans to view the Grand Canyon, explore the Great Plains and its bison herds, and contact the Indian tribes in the southwestern United States.

The Legends of the Seven Cities of Cíbola
Dorantes, Cabeza de Vaca, and their companions had not seen the cities of gold, but recounted legends heard from the Indians they contacted during their two-year wanderings through the southwestern United States and northern Mexico. They were

not the first to tell such tales; the stories were common among the Spaniards in Mexico. However, Cabeza de Vaca's report gave them credence and stimulated Mendoza to dispatch a party to explore the "northern mystery," as the Spanish in Mexico thought of those lands.

Cabeza de Vaca refused Mendoza's offer to lead a preliminary scouting party, so Mendoza bought Dorantes, a black man and a slave of one of Cabeza de Vaca's companions, to act as a guide. As the excursion approached Cíbola, Dorantes scouted ahead of the main party and was captured and killed by the natives. Before his misfortune, he sent word confirming the great riches of the cities that lay to the north.

Dorantes's message and the news of his death sent the main party scurrying back to Mexico. Marcos of Niza, a Franciscan friar and leader of the scouting expedition, reportedly led a small group north to view the southernmost city themselves before retreating to Mexico. However, some historians believe that the entire group returned directly to Mexico without further scouting. If so, the riches of the cities were again reported on the basis of hearsay, not direct observation. Whether he saw one of the cities or not, Marcos's report to Mendoza reinforced the legend of the Seven Cities of Cíbola and their great wealth.

Given the recent conquests of the fabulous cities of the Inca in Peru and the Aztecs in Mexico, it is not surprising that the Spanish authorities and adventurers accepted the legends as authentic. With these firsthand reports from his emissaries, Mendoza prepared to conquer the Seven Cities for Spain. Aware that Hernán Cortés, conqueror of the Aztecs, and Hernando de Soto, already involved in an expedition into Florida, were also planning explorations in the north, Mendoza rushed to establish a priority claim there.

North to Cíbola and the Colorado River

In response to Marcos's encouraging report and to the competitive threat of Cortés and de Soto, Mendoza placed Coronado at the head of a large expeditionary force and commissioned him to conquer the Seven Cities of Cíbola and anything else of worth in the north. In 1540, Coronado set out on that quest. After a challenging march through northern Mexico, Coronado's troops moved down the San Pedro River Valley in the southern Huachuca Mountains and crossed the imaginary line that today separates the Mexican state of Sonora from the state of Arizona in the United States. The Coronado National Memorial overlooks that part of Coronado's route.

For the next two years, Coronado's troops lived one of the grandest adventures in American history. They found and conquered the Seven Cities of Cíbola (actually Zuñi Indian villages), none of which was named Cíbola and none of which was rich in precious metals or in any way that the Spanish measured riches. Coronado dispensed exploratory parties in all directions from the center he set up at Cíbola.

One, under García López de Cárdenas, went northwest to the Grand Canyon of the Colorado River through the Hopi Indians' homeland, which proved to be without gold, as were the Zuñi cities. They are believed to be the first Europeans to view that magnificent chasm. Melchior Díaz led another group west in an attempt to make contact with Hernando de Alarcón, assigned the task of supplying the expedition by sea from the Gulf of California. Díaz and Alarcón never made direct contact, but both did find the lower reaches of the Colorado River. Díaz also found a group of letters buried by Alarcón before Alarcón realized that he had no way of reaching Coronado with supplies and returned to Mexico.

The Rio Grande and Pecos

Yet another exploratory group led by Hernando de Alvarado went east from Cíbola and discovered the Rio Grande River and a group of Pueblo Indian cities. These were impressive pueblos, but none contained the gold the Spaniards sought. The conditions seemed more pleasant than in the Zuñi region, however, and at Alvarado's suggestion, Coronado moved the bulk of his force to Tiguex in the Rio Grande Valley near today's Albuquerque, New Mexico. Meanwhile, Alvarado's group had explored east to the Pecos River and beyond to the *llano estacado* (staked plain), where they saw great herds of bison. Their guides were two Plains Indians—a member of the Wichita tribe named Ysopete, and a Pawnee called the Turk by the Spaniards because they thought he looked Turkish.

The Turk told stories of Quivira—cities of gold to the north— fueling the explorers' imaginations and raising hopes for the success of their journey.

Coronado was determined to explore farther north and east, to Quivira, the next spring. Meanwhile, the Spaniards prepared for winter on the Rio Grande.

Coronado was apparently more conscientious in following the Spanish government's dictate to treat the natives decently than were other Spanish conquistadors. He took no slaves and was apparently less rapacious than the average conquistador. However, his command seems benign only by comparison. His army took the food it needed from native stores with no consideration for the needs of the natives. They occupied an entire pueblo, displacing the natives at the beginning of winter, forcing them to find shelter in adjacent pueblos during the most trying time of the year.

Some pueblos resisted the Spaniards' requests for blankets, food, and other commodities probably because of their own needs. In response, the Spanish destroyed villages, killing many of the people who lived in them. Indians were burned at the stake and captive leaders from other pueblos as well as the Turk and Ysopete were forced to watch so that they would develop proper respect for the Spanish and pass on that respect to their villages. Coronado denied giving orders for such activities and was apparently not present at any of the most egregious butcheries, but as leader of the expedition, he must bear some responsibility.

Quivira

The next spring Coronado's band, with the Turk and Ysopete as guides, headed north and east to find Quivira and its riches. The Turk led them into the staked plain of the Texas Panhandle, then south and east, not north toward Kansas and the cities of Quivira. At least two explanations have been tendered for his action. He may have been trying to lead them to the cultural centers of the Mississippi Valley, the closest thing in the United States to the Aztec and Inca cities of gold. However, most Mississippian cities were abandoned or in decline by 1541. Alternatively, he may have tried to lose them in the vast, unmarked expanse of the *llano estacado*. If the second explanation is true, it may have been a suggestion of the Pueblo Indians, who were understandably angered by Spanish oppression and would surely have appreciated losing their visitors.

The Turk was put in chains and held as a captive for the rest of the journey, and Ysopete became their guide. Coronado sent the bulk of his army back to Tiguex in the Rio Grande Valley and continued the hunt for Quivira with a more mobile force of about forty men. Ysopete led them north to Kansas and Quivira, the land of the Wichita, but the twenty-plus Wichita villages they visited failed to live up to Spanish expectations: They were neither grand cities nor full of gold.

The Turk gave no acceptable account for his role in misleading the Spaniards and was strangled and buried. Coronado apparently issued the order, again suggesting that this benign hand of Spanish conquest was so only by comparison with others. Tired of following empty leads and convinced that the north held no cities of gold, Coronado returned to the Rio Grande Valley to spend another winter, after which he determined to return to Mexico.

A considerable number of the party, especially those who had not accompanied him to Quivira, remained convinced that the golden cities lay farther to the east or north and talked him into another trip north in the spring. However, Coronado suffered serious injuries in a riding accident during the winter. The accident restored the original plan, and he returned to Mexico the next spring.

In Mexico, he was tried for mistreatment of the Indians and for not continuing the search beyond Quivira. He was acquitted but lost much of his influence and position. His poor health worsened, and he died on September 22, 1554. He was forty-four years old.

Accomplishments of the Exploration

Coronado's expedition discovered the Grand Canyon of the Colorado River, explored the lower reaches of that great river, explored the southern Great Plains, witnessed the plains' great bison herds, contacted the Zuñi, Pueblo, Hopi, Apache, Wichita, and other Indian tribes, and pretty well determined that the "northern mystery" held no cities of gold. His reward was disgrace—in his own mind and in the minds of his superiors.

Only in retrospect, long after his death, was the enormity of the expedition's accomplishments appreciated. Much of that appreciation was possible because of the journals kept by various members of the expedition, especially Pedro de Castañeda, a soldier in Coronado's army. These sources led to a comprehension and appreciation of the expedition's central role in American history.

The Coronado National Memorial
The Memorial overlooks the San Pedro River Valley, which contained an ancient Indian trail, through which Coronado entered today's United States. It contains a museum with weapons, military dress, and other clothing of Coronado's time. History programs and a video covering the Coronado expedition are presented periodically. Hiking trails and roadways allow exploration of the Memorial, including a cave named for Coronado.

In addition to the historic significance of the Memorial, its Huachuca Mountain surroundings are among the best areas in the country for natural history observation, especially of birds. Adjacent areas famous for their bird-watching and other natural history include the San Pedro National Riparian Conservation Area, Miller Peak Wilderness, Coronado National Forest, and Ramsey Canyon Preserve. Several canyons scattered around the area—Ash, Carr, Garden, and Miller—are also known for the diversity of their bird life.

—*Carl W. Hoagstrom*

For Further Information:
Bolton, Herbert Eugene. *Coronado, Knight of Pueblos and Plains.* Albuquerque: University of New Mexico Press, 1990. First published in 1949, it is among the best available accounts of Coronado's expedition.

Day, Arthur Grove. *Coronado's Quest: The Discovery of the Southwestern States.* Berkeley: University of California Press, 1940. An interesting account of Coronado's life and journey.

Flint, Richard, and Shirley Cushing Flint, eds. *The Coronado Expedition to Tierra Nueva: The 1540-1542 Route Across the Southwest.* Niwot: University Press of Colorado, 1997. A wealth of scholarship on the Coronado expedition.

Hodge, Frederick W., and Theodore H. Lewis, eds. *Spanish Explorers in the Southern United States 1528-1543.* New York: Barnes & Noble, 1965. Includes a translation of Casteñeda's report on Coronado's expedition.

Lavender, David. *De Soto, Coronado, Cabrillo: Explorers of the Northern Mystery.* Washington, D.C.: U.S. Department of the Interior. National Park Service, 1992. Explains Coronado's expedition in the context of other Spanish expeditions to the southern United States and gives a brief description of the Coronado National Memorial.

Vigil, Ralph H., Frances W. Kaye, and John R. Wunder. *Spain and the Plains: Myths and Realities of Spanish Exploration and Settlement on the Great Plains.* Niwot: University Press of Colorado, 1994. Treats Coronado's journey to Kansas in the context of other Spanish activities in the Great Plains.

Grand Canyon

Date: February 26, 1919
Relevant issues: American Indian history, political history, western expansion
Significance: This National Park protects most of the Grand Canyon of the Colorado, a spectacular example of erosion that reveals the geological history of the Colorado Plateau. The human history surrounding the canyon reflects both nineteenth century expansionism and the more recent politics of preservation.
Location: Encompasses 178 miles of the Colorado River in northwestern Arizona
Site Office:
Grand Canyon National Park
P.O. Box 129
Grand Canyon, AZ 86023
ph.: (520) 638-7888; TDD: (520) 638-7805
Web sites: www.nps.gov/grca/; www.thecanyon.com/nps/

Grand Canyon National Park preserves 178 miles of the world-famous Grand Canyon of the Colorado. This enormous canyon is one of the most spectacular examples of erosion in the world, laying bare a geological record that spans perhaps half the age of planet Earth. Since 1540 the Grand Canyon has been discovered, ignored, explored, exploited, developed, and preserved. Since the late nineteenth century, the canyon has been prominent in the history of American conservation. Known for its magnificent views, Grand Canyon National Park annually attracts about five million visitors.

Early History
Geologists estimate that the Grand Canyon has

been eroded by the Colorado River over a period of two to six million years. During that time the Colorado Plateau, of which the Grand Canyon is a part, has been rising. The result is a spectacular canyon 277 miles long, averaging about 10 miles wide, and over 1 mile deep. The rock strata, through which the canyon has been cut, is far older than the canyon itself. The canyon walls contain distinct layers. The ancient igneous and metamorphic rock of the Inner Gorge is nearly 2 billion years old. It is covered by sedimentary and volcanic layers, the oldest and deepest of which are more than 1 billion years old. At the canyon's rim, the most recent layers date back about 250 million years.

There is evidence of human habitation in and around the Grand Canyon dating back about five thousand years. The early residents hunted large and small animals and gathered native plant foods in season. About two thousand years ago, they adopted maize and squash farming. In the Grand Canyon region these earliest farmers are called Anasazi from a Navajo word meaning "ancient ones." The early Anasazi are also known as Basketmakers for their very sophisticated and beautifully decorated grass baskets. Later Anasazi were known as Pueblo Indians after the communal structures in which they lived. The region's Pueblo Indians made pottery, grew cotton, traded over large distances, and practiced elaborate ceremonies. More than five hundred Pueblo ruins have been found in the vicinity of the Grand Canyon, but none is of the size or complexity of better-known ruins like those at Mesa Verde. The Pueblo Indians abandoned the Grand Canyon about 1200. Since then the canyon has been frequented by the Hopi, who are descended from the Pueblo Indians, and occupied by the Havasupai and Hualipai south of the river and the Paiute to the north. The most recent arrivals on the scene were the Navajo. In the twentieth century, Indian lands in and around the Grand Canyon have been reduced to designated reservations.

Exploration

European discovery of the Grand Canyon took place in 1540 when Garcúa López de Cárdenas and his Hopi guides arrived at the South Rim. The Cárdenas group was part of the larger Coronado Expedition of Spanish conquistadors out of Mexico exploring to the north. Having discovered the Grand Canyon, the Spanish ignored it for two hundred years until the arrival of missionary priests in the 1770's. The last major Spanish explorations took place in 1776 and included one by Francisco Tomás Garcés, a priest who visited the Havasupai settlement on the South Rim and gave the Colorado River its name.

The Grand Canyon region became part of the United States with the Treaty of Guadalupe Hidalgo in 1848. American mountain men may have visited in the preceding quarter century, but their experiences seem to have died with them. By the 1850's, the War Department was interested in mapping the new Arizona Territory, and it dispatched Lieutenant Joseph C. Ives to determine the navigability of the Colorado River by steamboat. Proceeding upstream, Ives got to Black Canyon before wrecking his boat. Continuing overland, his party was the first to bring back sketches and geological observations of the Grand Canyon.

The Grand Canyon attracts millions of tourists every year. Mule rides are a popular way to experience the canyon from the inside. (Diane C. Lyell)

Major John Wesley Powell, scientist and Civil War veteran, first traveled through the Grand Canyon by boat in 1869. His expedition studied and mapped the canyon, and his 1875 *Report on the Exploration of the Colorado River of the West and Its Tributaries* introduced the canyon to the American public and popularized use of the name "Grand Canyon." The Powell Expedition left Green River on May 24, 1869, on a journey made perilous by terrible rapids. By August 15, the expedition had reached the mouth of Bright Angel Creek in the heart of what is now Grand Canyon National Park. Two weeks later they had completed their journey. Powell continued his explorations in and around the Grand Canyon in the early 1870's, accompanied for a time by the artist, Thomas Moran, whose sketches and paintings of the canyon excited the American imagination. Powell's protégé, Clarence Edward Dutton of the United States Geological Survey, visited the canyon in 1880 and 1881. His report, *The Tertiary History of the Grand Cañon District, with Atlas* (1882), was the first important book on the canyon's geology.

Development and Preservation

The number of prospectors, miners, and settlers in the Grand Canyon area increased rapidly in the 1870's. North of the canyon, Mormon settlers grazed cattle and sheep and cut timber in the Kaibab Forest. Entrepreneurs established river ferries across the Colorado upstream of the Grand Canyon. The Atlantic and Pacific Railroad was constructed across northern Arizona, and by the 1880's tourists were visiting the canyon. Despite a minor "copper rush" in 1890, mining was rarely successful. Nevertheless, miners and prospectors left their legacy. In order to provide themselves with a supply of pack animals, prospectors released burros in the canyon, where they multiplied, wreaking environmental havoc. Miners and prospectors also pioneered the hospitality industry at the canyon, building trails, hiring out as guides, and providing bed, board, and transportation. Their era ended with the arrival of the railroad at Grand Canyon Village on the South Rim in September, 1901. By 1905, the El Tovar Hotel had been opened, and the Fred Harvey Company was engaged in a lucrative tourist trade. The railroad era lasted until 1925; thereafter the dominant mode of transportation was the automobile.

The Grand Canyon and its environs were proclaimed a Forest Reserve by President Benjamin Harrison in 1893. Ten years later, President Theodore Roosevelt visited the canyon and declared, "Leave it as it is. You cannot improve on it. The ages have been at work on it, and man can only mar it." In 1906, Roosevelt proclaimed the Grand Canyon Game Reserve, which protected deer but encouraged the slaughter of predators, whose important ecological role was not yet understood. Two years later he established a Grand Canyon National Monument under the authority of the Antiquities Act of 1906. Interest in establishing a National Park increased after 1912, when Arizona achieved statehood. An Act of Congress establishing Grand Canyon National Park was signed by President Woodrow Wilson on February 26, 1919, but the National Park Service did not commence management until August 15.

Under management by the National Park Service, roads and trails were built or improved, a number of private facilities within the National Park removed, and others built. With Park Service approval, the Fred Harvey Company built Phantom Ranch in 1922 to serve as an overnight stop for riders on mule trips down Bright Angel Trail. On the North Rim an alliance with the Union Pacific Railroad facilitated park development. The park's first ranger-naturalist was hired in 1925. Seven years later the Grand Canyon Natural History Association was founded to further visitor education. The park was expanded dramatically in 1975 and named a World Heritage Site in 1979. At the end of the twentieth century, 94 percent of the park's 1.2 million acres was managed as wilderness.

Since its establishment as a National Park, Grand Canyon has been a natural and historic site of international importance. Its management has occasioned controversies involving wildlife, air quality, water, and visitors. Early in the park's history, predator control led to an explosion of the deer population on the North Rim followed by mass starvation. More recently, the Park Service has worked to save endangered native species while eliminating exotics such as the wild burros left over from prospector days. In the 1970's, air quality became an issue in the Grand Canyon as pollution from cities, smelters, and a coal-fired electrical generating plant reduced visibility and impaired the experience of park visitors. The problem persists.

In the last half of the twentieth century, dams were built above and below the park, taming the free-flowing Colorado and creating major changes in canyon ecology. In 1995, the Interior Department executed a massive discharge of water through the canyon in an attempt to restore its ecological balance. A year later the interior secretary issued new rules to govern discharges from the Glen Canyon Dam just upstream from the park. Perhaps most intractable have been the issues of visitor management. The Park Service has begun replacing private automobile use on the crowded South Rim with various forms of mass transit. River running and canyon hiking are heavily regulated to preserve the canyon. River runners wait many years for a permit. Aircraft noise from tourist overflights became a significant intrusion on the wilderness experience of canyon visitors. Assisted by a 1987 law and a 1996 executive order, the National Park Service and the Federal Aviation Administration (FAA) have sought to restore quiet to the canyon through a series of overflight restrictions.

Places to Visit

Most park visitors experience the Grand Canyon by automobile from overlooks along the South Rim. Eighty miles northwest of Flagstaff, the South Rim, with its visitor center and museum, is the most accessible part of the park and is open all year. The North Rim is one thousand feet higher, closed by snow from October to May, and less frequently visited. More adventurous visitors hike into the canyon's depths, ride a mule down the Bright Angel Trail, retrace Powell's river journey through the canyon, or fly over it by airplane or helicopter. The popularity of these activities is so great that many require reservations months in advance.

—*Craig W. Allin*

For Further Information:

Anderson, Michael F. *Living at the Edge: Explorers, Exploiters, and Settlers of the Grand Canyon Region.* Grand Canyon, Ariz.: Grand Canyon Association, 1998. Almost two hundred historic photographs and accompanying text describe the pioneer history of the Grand Canyon region prior to establishment of the park.

Beus, Stanley S., and Michael Morales, eds. *Grand Canyon Geology.* New York: Oxford University Press, 1990. Twenty chapters by various scientists explore the geological history of the prominent strata, formations, and features of the park.

Fishbein, Seymour L. *Grand Canyon Country: Its Majesty and Its Lore.* Washington, D.C.: National Geographic Society, 1991. This introduction to Grand Canyon National Park and the surrounding lands contains about one hundred photographs of exceptional quality accompanied by an engaging text.

"Grand Canyon National Park: Official Park Information." www.thecanyon.com/nps/. This is the park's expanded Web site and the place to start for anyone planning to visit.

Hughes, J. Donald. *In the House of Stone and Light: A Human History of the Grand Canyon.* Grand Canyon, Ariz.: Grand Canyon Association, 1978. This illustrated volume chronicles the prehistory and early history of Grand Canyon National Park.

Morehouse, Barbara J. *A Place Called the Grand Canyon: Contested Geographies.* Tucson: University of Arizona Press, 1996. This history of the greater Grand Canyon region emphasizes the competition for control of the land and its resources.

Powell, John Wesley. *Exploration of the Colorado River and Its Canyons.* New York: Penguin Books, 1987. This is a reprint of Powell's original *Report on the Exploration of the Colorado River of the West and Its Tributaries.* Contains an introduction by Powell biographer Wallace Stegner.

Navajo National Monument

Date: Proclaimed a National Monument on March 20, 1909

Relevant issues: American Indian history

Significance: Site of Betatakin, Kiet Seel, and Inscription House, three Anasazi dwellings built between 1250 and 1280 and abandoned around 1300. The sites, in what is today Navajo land, were excavated in the early twentieth century and made a National Monument in 1909. The monument's visitors' center is open year round and offers cultural exhibits about Anasazi life; between late May and mid-September, the staff offers guided tours on foot and horseback (guides must accompany all visitors to the ruins). Because of its extreme fragility, Inscription House is no longer open to tourists.

Location: On the Navajo Reservation in northeastern Arizona, about fifty miles northeast of Tuba City and twenty-two miles southwest of Kayenta, off U.S. Interstate 160, via Route 564, a nine-mile paved road that leads to the visitors' center

Site Office:
Navajo National Monument
HC 71, Box 3
Tonalea, AZ 86044-9704
ph.: (520) 672-2366, 672-2367
fax: (520) 672-2345

The Navajo Reservation is a fifteen-million-acre tract on which about 100,000 Navajo people live, work, and raise livestock. Rugged terrain, rock-walled mesas, windy highlands, steep canyons, and broad valleys characterize this land. Within the borders of the reservation lie the main features of the Navajo National Monument—three seven-hundred-year-old cliff dwellings once inhabited by the Kayenta Anasazi. The Anasazi lived in the Southwest from approximately 600 to 1300 C.E., roughly the same time period that the Hopewell and Mississippian peoples were the dominant groups in the midwestern and eastern parts of the continent. Although these ruins rest on what is now Navajo land, the Navajo did not migrate to the area until a few hundred years ago. The Anasazi and the Navajo are not ancestrally related. It is more likely that the Anasazi were ancestors of the Hopi, who live on the mesa tops east of Kayenta and seem to demostrate many of the Anasazi's cultural traits.

The three cliff dwellings in the Navajo National Monument were the last places the Kayenta Anasazi inhabited before leaving the area completely. All were built between 1250 and 1280 C.E. Scholars generally consider Kiet Seel (alternately spelled Keet Seel), a 155-room dwelling located in Tsegi Canyon, to be the biggest cliff dwelling in Arizona. About eight miles away from Kiet Seel, in a smaller canyon, lies Betatakin, an impressive 135-room pueblo built under a massive natural stone arch that resembles an amphitheater. The third dwelling, Inscription House, sits farther away, in Navajo Canyon, near the Utah border. With just 74 rooms, Inscription House is the smallest of these three ruins.

The Anasazi People
The Anasazi people who inhabited Betatakin, Kiet Seel, and Inscription House were one of three major cultural groups living in the Southwest from about 600 to 1300 C.E. The Anasazi clustered primarily around the Four Corners area (where Utah, Arizona, Colorado, and New Mexico all meet), while the second major group, the Hohokam, occupied the mountainous region along the Arizona-New Mexico border. The third group, the Sinagua, lived in and near the Sonoran Desert in south central Arizona.

The Anasazi (a Navajo word that can mean either "ancient ones" or "enemy ancestors") actually lived in three different geographic areas. In addition to the Kayenta district, Anasazi "cousins" congregated around Chaco Canyon and Mesa Verde. Each of the three groups appears to have excelled in a different way, perhaps as the result of variations in the local resources and environments. The Kayenta Anasazi were the most artistic and created the most beautiful pottery. The Chaco Canyon Anasazi were the business people who excelled in trade, while the Mesa Verde group, living in the most fertile area, grew the most prolific crops.

The Anasazi in general are known for their beautiful black-on-white pottery, as well as for later oxidized red and orange ceramics. The shapes and designs of their pottery are elegant and often exquisite, and they differed in each of the Anasazi regions. This same love of beauty and design also appears in Anasazi fabric weaving and wall paintings.

The Kayenta Anasazi, like their kin at Chaco Canyon and Mesa Verde, developed into a highly successful culture skilled in farming, building, and crafts. In its heyday, from the eleventh to the early thirteenth centuries, Kayenta Anasazi culture reached as far north as southern Utah and as far west as the Grand Canyon.

Remains of food found at Anasazi dwellings indicate the people lived mainly on corn, beans, and squash. Women, working in communal groups, ground the food into flour or meal with stones called *manos*, after first processing it in large, side-by-side rock troughs call *metates*.

Burial findings reveal that the Anasazi had dark hair and brown skin. They resembled the southwestern Indians of today but were shorter; the average Anasazi man stood just over five feet. The Anasazi also deliberately flattened their skulls by strapping their infants to hard cradleboards. No one knows definitively why they did this, but researchers suggest the custom may have developed after contact with admired outsiders who had flattened heads, or possibly in imitation of a great leader.

Anasazi men kept their hair long, but the women cut their hair to weave into snares and nets and as an element in rope, using it as a kind of natural resource. Anasazi women may also have worked as the plasterers of their culture. Gustavus Nordenskiöld, an early researcher of the Southwest, suggested this after finding small fingerprints in the mortar of Anasazi ruins near Johnson Canyon. By 1200 C.E., the Anasazi had already been using the bow and arrow for quite some time, instead of the more primitive *atlatl* (spear throwing device) their ancestors had used in earlier centuries.

Scholars believe the Anasazi developed from an earlier southwestern culture known as the Basketmaker, a prepueblo group that occupied the area from about 200 to 500 C.E. The Basketmaker people lived in pit houses, and may themselves have descended from very early peoples who followed a simple hunting and gathering way of life in the area.

Kiet Seel

The largest of the Anasazi dwellings at Navajo National Monument is Kiet Seel, a seven-hundred-year-old, 155-room masonry pueblo. It rests under the shelter of a large natural alcove in the side of a cliff in Kiet Seel Canyon, a branch of the Tsegi Canyon system, and looks out onto groves of cottonwoods, meadows, and a stream in the valley below. Kiet Seel, which means "broken pottery" in Navajo, received its name from the hundreds of pottery shards that explorers found when they first came upon the site shortly after the turn of the twentieth century. Visitors can readily see the remains of living quarters, storage rooms, and six kivas (round, subterranean rooms used for religious and ceremonial purposes).

Kiet Seel's former inhabitants lived in rectangular rooms with ceilings supported by roof poles. Many of the rooms had recessed doorways designed to be closed with flat stones. The entire dwelling faces what was apparently the predominant kiva, the central, spiritual focus of the community.

Kivas are common features of both prehistoric and present-day southwestern pueblos. For example, kivas and the ceremonies that take place in them remain an integral aspect of pueblo life for the Hopi. Archaeologists, in fact, borrowed the word "kiva" from the Hopi, as well as the understanding that kivas served religious and ceremonial purposes. Early European American explorers of the sites thought the kivas were storage pits, until Nordenskiöld realized that these rooms were the same as the ceremonial chambers that the Hopis called kivas.

Although kivas were built almost completely underground, they were scarcely crude earthen pits. The walls, which often had special niches, were constructed of masonry, sometimes painted with murals, and lined with benches. Kivas had beamed roofs with an opening for ventilation and smoke. People (most likely initiated men and on special occasions women) entered and exited a kiva by means of a single ladder. Spirits of the dead were believed by the Anasazi to come and go via a sand-filled hole usually found in the kiva floor.

Richard Wetherill, a rancher from Mancos, Colorado, and one of three brothers who devoted themselves to finding and exploring prehistoric southwestern Indian sites around the turn of the twentieth century, came upon Kiet Seel in 1907. He also discovered other prehistoric Indian ruins, including Cliff Palace at Mesa Verde, another Anasazi dwelling.

Nearly twenty years passed before Kiet Seel was excavated, stabilized, and studied in 1933 and 1934, when it became a project of President Franklin D. Roosevelt's Civilian Works Administration (CWA) under the auspices of the National Park Service. Notes and artifacts from the excavation were sent to the Museum of Northern Arizona.

Using tree-ring dating methods, archaeologists have determined the building sequence of Kiet Seel room by room. Most of the site was constructed in the 1270's, but rather than following a preconceived architectural plan, the inhabitants apparently expanded the dwelling randomly as new arrivals created the need for additional living quarters. Researchers have also found some building materials on the site that predate the 1270's, and believe these materials were recycled from construction that took place at Kiet Seel as early as 950 C.E. The greatest number of people who ever lived there at one time was probably about one hundred fifty. Because Kiet Seel is so well preserved (even many of the wooden roof beams are still intact), visitors often find it hard to believe the site was abandoned seven hundred years ago. Despite its beautiful setting and well-preserved construction, however, scholars have observed that the quality of the masonry at Kiet Seel is less skilled than that of similar Anasazi dwellings farther east.

Betatakin

Betatakin, which means "ledge house" in Navajo, was discovered in 1907 on an expedition led by Byron Cummings and John Wetherill. Cummings, a professor at the University of Utah, was one of the first archaeologists to specialize in early cultures of the Southwest. Wetherill, a rancher, trader, and brother of Richard Wetherill, was an accomplished explorer of Indian ruins. In 1909 he also became the first custodian of the Navajo National Monument.

Betatakin is a 130-room pueblo built with six tiers and a balcony of apartments. The floors are steeply pitched. Slightly smaller than Kiet Seel, it rests under the arch of an immense natural rock shelter that is nearly five hundred feet high, four hundred feet across, and about one hundred fifty feet deep. In its heyday, the dwelling may have housed as many as 125 people.

Visitors are able to walk through the ruins. Numerous thin waterfalls still pour over the edge of the cliff above, providing a steady supply of fresh water, while keeping the pueblo completely dry in the rain.

When the Cummings-Wetherill expedition found Betatakin, it was heavily overgrown with brush and almost invisible to a casual passerby. After clearing the brush and excavating the site several months later, Cummings found hundreds of well-preserved artifacts—including pots, baskets, and items used in food preparation. These artifacts were transported to Salt Lake City for protection and preservation.

Repair and stabilization of Betatakin occurred under the direction of Neil Judd, a former assistant of Cummings, in 1917, after Congress appropriated funds for the task. Judd and his crew endured an unusually long and harsh winter with only rice

to live on because no other supplies could get through. The cold was so intense that the men had to abandon their tents and move into the rooms of the pueblo to survive. Several members of the crew were then drafted into World War I, but Judd and the few who remained stayed on to complete their work. Betatakin now stands pretty much as Judd left it in 1917.

Tourists have eagerly sought out Betatakin since it was first discovered. For many years John Wetherill brought visitors on horseback to Betatakin from Kayenta, and he built a campsite below the ruin where the visitors could spend the night. Wetherill's nephew Milton lived at the camp during the summers and conducted guided tours of the dwelling. Milton Wetherill also became the first official park ranger at Betatakin.

Betatakin is somewhat unusual because, unlike Kiet Seel and most other southwestern pueblos, it has no kivas. The site does possess several rectangular structures that may have served the same religious purposes, but no one knows for sure. It is possible that these differences reflect a religious split between the residents of Kiet Seel and Betatakin, but most other tangible aspects of the sites indicate that the people of both dwellings shared essentially the same culture. Researchers believe Betatakin was occupied by a single group of people, possibly an extended family.

Inscription House

Byron Cummings and John Wetherill found Inscription House, a 74-room Anasazi dwelling, on the same exploratory expedition on which they discovered Betatakin. The Cummings-Wetherill party was exploring the highlands and canyons south of Navajo Mountain, hoping to find a large natural bridge they had heard about from local Native American residents, when they unexpectedly came upon this beautiful cliff residence. They named the site Inscription House because someone, possibly a member of a Mormon party traveling through the area, had scratched the year 1861 or possibly 1881 (originally and mistakenly deciphered as 1661) into the plaster of one of its walls. The graffitti suggests that the site may have been one of the first large Anasazi ruins visited by European Americans. Tree-ring dating shows that the dwelling was built in 1274—contemporarily with Betatakin and Kiet Seel.

Inscription House has some unique architectural features—for example, t-shaped doorways and partial adobe construction—that distinguish it from the other two sites. It also lacks the natural shelter of the rock overhangs at Betatakin and Kiet Seel. As a result, it is more fragile and has been closed to visitors since 1968.

The Anasazi Abandon the Site

The Kayenta Anasazi dwellings were built between 1250 and 1280, but abandoned around 1300, just two decades later. Archaeologists speculate that significant changes in the climate gradually made it impossible for the approximately seven hundred residents of the Tsegi Canyon area to grow enough food to sustain them. The changes began when the patterns of precipitation changed from gentle winter snows and rains to fierce summer thunderstorms. The new pattern caused sheet erosion that affected previously fertile farming areas, led to extensive arroyo (gully or channel) cutting, and lowered water tables. A period of drought then followed these drastic changes.

The Kayenta Anasazi had thrived for several hundred years before this, living in small scattered communities throughout the Kayenta area. The move to building and inhabiting larger, more concentrated dwellings such as Betatakin and Kiet Seel marked a distinct change in traditional Anasazi lifestyle, and probably indicated that the people were already finding it difficult to sustain themselves in smaller groups. Concentrating the population in large, canyon-based pueblos would have enabled the Kayenta Anasazi to make the best use of limited resources, such as reliable sources of water.

More dense populations may also have hastened the general degradation of the environment. Feeding more people meant having to cut down many of the local trees to use for fuel, pottery firing, and building materials. Residents also had to clear land from the naturally forested mesa tops so they could grow additional crops. All these activities led to further soil erosion.

When life became too hard to sustain, the Kayenta Anasazi moved south. Some carried with them everything they could. Others left many possessions behind and simply sealed the doors of their homes as if they planned someday to return. They never did.   —*Gail A. Moss*

For Further Information:

Gaede, Marni, ed. *Camera, Spade, and Pen: An Inside View of Southwestern Archaeology.* Tucson: University of Arizona Press, 1980. Offers a unique view of prehistoric southwestern Indian cultures such as the Anasazi and Hohokam through personal interviews with people who investigated and studied the archaeological sites where these early peoples lived. Though not a comprehensive study, the book provides special insights into the process—both exciting and tedious—of excavating the ruins of the Southwest. The photographs by Marc Gaede that accompany the interviews are spectacular.

McGregor, John C. *Southwestern Archeology.* 2d ed. Urbana: University of Illinois Press, 1982. An in-depth, chronological study of the major early cultures of the Southwest with extensive information about the pottery and other artifacts the cultures left behind. Photographs, numerous illustrations, and maps add to this thorough history and reconstruction of prehistoric life in the Southwest.

Noble, David Grant. *Ancient Ruins of the Southwest: An Archaeological Guide.* 2d rev. ed. Flagstaff, Ariz.: Northland Press, 2000. Offers a thorough yet concise look at the prehistoric cultures of the southwest. Noble provides a brief history of each of the cultures, as well as a short explanation of the significance of each historical site included in the book. Excellent photographs and numerous simple maps add to the usefulness of this book.

Wilson, Josleen. *The Passionate Amateur's Guide to Archaeology in the United States.* New York: Collier Books, 1980. Offers brief descriptions of archaeological sites throughout the country. A helpful introduction takes a look at the early peoples who inhabited this continent.

Taliesin West

Date: Founded in 1937
Relevant issues: Art and architecture
Significance: Taliesin West was the winter home, and later permanent home, office, and architectural campus of Frank Lloyd Wright, considered by many to have been the greatest architect of the twentieth century. Today it serves as resi-

dence and headquarters of seventy professional architects and apprentices who are following in Wright's tradition. The collection of modernistic buildings, designed for living, working, teaching, assemblies, and recreation, comprises outstanding examples of Wright's innovative approach to architecture, art, and interior design.

Location: On six hundred acres of the beautiful Sonoran Desert at the foothills of the McDowell Mountains; the entrance is located at the intersection of Frank Lloyd Wright Boulevard (114th Street) and Cactus Road in Scottsdale, a suburb situated directly to the east of Phoenix

Site Office:

The Frank Lloyd Wright Foundation
Taliesin West
Scottsdale, AZ 85261-4430
ph.: (480) 860-2700
fax: (480) 391-4009
Web site: www.franklloydwright.org

Taliesin (pronounced TAH-lee EH-sen) West is a living memorial to Frank Lloyd Wright (1869-1959), the great American architect whose genius revolutionized residential, commercial, and institutional buildings worldwide. The most striking feature is that it was built out of the stones, sand, and other materials taken directly from the site; it is a prime example of Wright's architectural design concept that a structure should seem a natural part of its setting. The complex serves as a living, working, educational facility with an on-site architectural firm that has a distinguished worldwide reputation for creations following in the Frank Lloyd Wright tradition.

A Biography of Wright

Over a period of seventy years, Frank Lloyd Wright created designs for buildings and furnishings which revolutionized twentieth century architecture. During this time, he authored sixteen books and numerous magazine articles.

Wright was born in Wisconsin on June 8, 1867, just two years after the end of the Civil War. In 1887, after attending the University of Wisconsin in Madison for only a few semesters, he moved to Chicago and worked directly under the distinguished architect Louis Sullivan for seven years. In 1893, Wright set up his own practice in his home in Oak Park, Illinois. He became one of the leading members of the Prairie School of architects, who were creating distinctively American homes and deliberately departing from the ornate, "gingerbread" Victorian tradition. By this time, Wright had formulated his highly individualistic credo, expressed in the following quotation:

Down all the avenues of time architecture was an enclosure by nature, and the simplest form of enclosure was the box. The box was ornamented, they put columns in front of it, pilasters and cornices on it, but they always considered an enclosure in terms of the box. Now when Democracy became an establishment, as it is in America, that box-idea began to be irksome. As a young architect, I began to feel annoyed, held back, imposed upon by this sense of enclosure which you went into and there you were—boxed, crated. I tried to find out what was happening to me: I was the free son of a free people and I wanted to be free. I had to find out what was the cause of this imprisonment. So I began to investigate.

An interior view of Taliesin West. (©2000 Frank Lloyd Wright Foundation)

Wright's first revolutionary masterpiece was the Winslow House (1893). Other early creations, including the Robie House and Unity Temple in Oak Park and the Larkin Building in Buffalo, New York, had a profound influence on modern architecture.

Wright was married three times. In 1911, he built his first permanent home in Wisconsin and called it Taliesin, which means "shining brow" in Welsh. It is an excellent example of the integration of architecture and landscape.

Wright's modernistic ideas appealed to a minority and offended many. He endured many years of financial hardship before achieving the recognition he deserved. He never compromised his principles. His strength of character and dedication to his profession, along with his creative genius, are the theme and thesis of his long life.

During the 1920's, Wright was commissioned to design such modern masterpieces as the Midway Gardens in Chicago and the Imperial Hotel in Tokyo. In 1932, at the age of sixty-five, Wright founded an apprenticeship program called the Taliesin Fellowship. The program continues to this day as the accredited Frank Lloyd Wright School of Architecture and maintains campuses at the original Taliesin and at Taliesin West. In 1936, he received two of the most important commissions of his career: the Johnson Wax Administration Building in Racine, Wisconsin, and the famous Kaufman house, built over a waterfall in Pennsylvania. These made him world famous and are the works most frequently appearing in photographs to illustrate books and articles about him.

Wright started building Taliesin West in 1937 as a winter home for himself and his third wife, Olgivanna Lazovich. The complex of impressive buildings wedded to the desert landscape is considered one of his greatest masterpieces. It remained in a constant state of evolution as Wright experimented with various materials and designs throughout the ensuing years. Some of his best-known later works included the Price Tower in Bartlesville, Oklahoma, and the bold, functional, and highly controversial Solomon R. Guggenheim Museum in Manhattan.

At the end of his life, Wright had more commissions than he could handle, and he delegated much of the work to the assistants who lived and worked at Taliesin West. Wright died in Arizona on April 9, 1959, at the age of ninety-one. By then, he had designed 1,191 works, including buildings, furniture, lamps, fabrics, carpets, china, silver, and graphic designs. More than five hundred of his buildings had actually been erected.

The Founding of Taliesin West

Taliesin West was created "out of the desert," in accordance with Wright's principle of wedding the structure to the setting. Wright and his apprentices gathered rocks from the desert floor and sand from the washes to build a winter home, studio, and architectural campus. Wright proudly proclaimed: "Our new desert camp belonged to the Arizona desert as though it had stood there during creation."

Taliesin West includes a Cabaret Theater, a Pavilion Theater for the performing arts, a large drafting studio, Wright's former architectural office, the Kiva conference room, a workshop, and residences for the apprentices and staff of the School of Architecture. The living room, called the Garden Room, is the central showplace. Experimental residences, some very small and temporary, have been built by apprentices in the desert surrounding the complex.

Taliesin West is now the national headquarters for the Frank Lloyd Wright Foundation, which owns and operates Taliesin West; Taliesin in Spring Green, Wisconsin; The Frank Lloyd Wright School of Architecture, which uses both places as its campus; and The Frank Lloyd Wright Archives.

The Frank Lloyd Archives

The most comprehensive collection of Wright's work is preserved at Taliesin West. Included in the archives are twenty-two thousand original Wright drawings; Wright's correspondence file from 1887 to 1959; Wright's manuscripts, published and unpublished, from 1894 to 1959; seventeen thousand historic photographs dating back to 1893; more than seven hundred Japanese prints, ninety Japanese embroideries and textiles, fifty-five Japanese and Chinese folding screens, kakemonos (scrolls), and Asian paintings; Occidental art collections, including prints, lithographs, wood engravings, and etchings; films and interviews of Wright; and thousands of books, periodicals, journals, and other publications on Wright and his work.

To expand public access, the foundation has

added research study space in recent years. The goal of the archives is to preserve the materials, making them available for study and research by photographic and electronic means in order to ensure preservation of the originals.

Guided Tours of Taliesin West

Every day from 10 A.M. to 4 P.M., there is a one-hour Panorama Tour. Tours begin at least every half hour, and more often during the peak season in January through April. The fee covers the Cabaret Cinema, Music Pavilion, Seminar Theater, and Wright's private office, plus most terraces, gardens, and walkways overlooking the desert and valley. Every day at 9:00 A.M., 9:30 A.M., and 4:15 P.M., there is a ninety-minute Insights Tour. It includes elements of the Panorama Tour, and visitors can also sit in Wright-designed furniture in Wright's spectacular 56-foot-long by 34-foot-wide Garden Room. The three-hour Behind the Scenes Tour is offered on Tuesday and Thursday mornings beginning at 9 A.M. It includes all the spots on the Insights Tour plus refreshments in the Taliesin Fellowship dining room and a walk to the Sun Cottage or another unique desert site. This is the most comprehensive tour of Taliesin West.

The ninety-minute Desert Walk occurs every day from October 15 through April 15 at 11:15 A.M. This is a guided tour through the desert trails surrounding the Taliesin West buildings. It provides frequent sightings of javelina, tortoises, rattlesnakes, coyotes, and other wildlife. The Desert Walk may be combined with other tours for discounted admissions. In the two-hour Apprentice "Shelter" Tour, Frank Lloyd Wright School of Architecture apprentices show visitors their own self-designed and personally constructed desert dwellings. This tour also includes elements of the Desert Walk Tour.

The Night Lights on the Desert Tour is given Friday evenings only from April 16 through the summer months at 7:00 P.M. and 7:30 P.M. This tour includes everything on the Insights Tour plus light refreshments. It offers an opportunity to see Wright's masterpiece in a lighted nighttime setting.

Visitors should check in advance because tours and times offered may change and may vary with the seasons.

Other Places to Visit

Two Frank Lloyd Wright sites open to the public in Arizona within easy driving distance of Taliesin West are the Arizona Biltmore Resort and Villas, at 24th Street and Missouri Avenue, Phoenix, AZ 85016, at (602) 955-6600; and the Grady Gammage Memorial Auditorium, at the Arizona State University Campus, Gammage Parkway and Apache Boulevard, Tempe, AZ 85287, at (602) 965-4050.

Many people from all over the world make pilgrimages to Frank Lloyd Wright sites from California to New York. These include such famous buildings as the Guggenheim Museum in New York City; the Johnson Wax Administration Building in Racine, Wisconsin; Fallingwater in Mill Run, Pennsylvania; and Unity Temple in Oak Park, Illinois. A complete list of sites that are open to the public can be obtained from the Taliesin West site office.

—*Bill Delaney*

For Further Information:

Heinz, Thomas A. *The West.* Vol. 3 in *Frank Lloyd Wright Field Guide.* New York: John Wiley & Sons, 1999. Heinz, a Wright scholar and author of several other books on the architect, provides an illustrated overview of two hundred Wright buildings in the western United States, Central America, Japan, South Asia, and the Middle East.

Legler, Dixie. *Frank Lloyd Wright: The Western Work.* San Francisco: Chronicle Books, 1999. Features twenty-three Wright designs in Washington, Oregon, Utah, Idaho, New Mexico, Arizona, Montana, and Wyoming in color photographs and archival images.

_____. *Prairie Style: Houses and Gardens by Frank Lloyd Wright and the Prairie School.* New York: Stewart, Tabori & Chang, 1999. Depicts three dozen homes, gardens, and communities in more than two hundred full-color photographs. The text tells the history of the revolt of Wright and other members of the Prairie School against the "fussiness" of Victorian architectural concepts.

Marty, Myron A., and Shirley L. Marty. *Frank Lloyd Wright's Taliesin Fellowship.* Kirksville, Mo.: Truman State University Press, 1999. In 1932, Wright and his third wife, Olgivanna, created the Taliesin Fellowship as an apprenticeship program to train young architects. This book tells the entire story of this unique institution.

Pfeiffer, Bruce Brooks. *Treasures of Taliesin: Seventy-*

six Unbuilt Designs. Carbondale: Southern Illinois University Press, 1985. Contains 106 drawings of seventy-six designs from the Frank Lloyd Wright Archives at Taliesin, providing an idea of the riches of these archives and incredible scope of Wright's creative imagination.

Satler, Gail. *Frank Lloyd Wright's Living Space.* De Kalb: Northern Illinois University Press, 1999. A sociological analysis of Wright's architecture that examines the interaction between people and the spaces they create. Focuses on the Larkin Building (1904) and Unity Temple (1907).

Smith, Kathryn. *Frank Lloyd Wright's Taliesin and Taliesin West.* New York: Harry N. Abrams, 1997. Studies of Wright's homes in Spring Green, Wisconsin, and in Arizona. Beautifully illustrated with photographs by Judith Bromley. Useful bibliographical references and index.

Wright, Frank Lloyd. *Frank Lloyd Wright's Collected Writings.* Edited by Bruce Brooks Pfeiffer. New York: Rizzoli, 1992. A comprehensive collection of Wright's writings published throughout his lifetime. Volume 2 includes a reprint of his autobiography.

Tombstone

Date: Founded in 1878; shootout occurred on October 26, 1881; courthouse built in 1882

Relevant issues: Business and industry, cultural history, disasters and tragedies

Significance: This primarily residential town was founded by Ed Schieffelin to support the mining industry. It was the site of the famed shootout at the OK Corral and is now a popular tourist attraction.

Location: In southeastern Arizona, about sixty-nine miles southeast of Tucson

Site Offices:

Tombstone Courthouse State Historic Park
P.O. Box 216
Tombstone, AZ 85638
ph.: (520) 457-3311

Tombstone Tourism Association
P.O. Box 917
Tombstone, AZ 85638
ph.: (520) 457-2211

It has been called "The Town Too Tough to Die." Its story has been told and retold in dozens of novels and motion pictures. Its legend lingers in the minds of those who have imagined the Southwest in its famous days of wild cowboys, reckless shootouts, and final showdowns. Tombstone, a town founded in 1878 after the nearby discovery of silver, was built and populated by young miners. Almost overnight, the town was tainted with rumors, partially true, of uncontrolled drinking, gambling, prostitution, and violence—rumors that stuck throughout its short, prosperous mining history.

Eight years of long days and lawless nights finally came to an end in 1886 as the silver boom died and the town's mines gave in to recurrent flooding. Tombstone soon discovered its bad reputation to be a hidden treasure. By stirring up the myth surrounding the highly publicized shootout at the OK Corral, the citizens of Tombstone were able to cash in on the tourist industry and ultimately make Tombstone the most famous town of the western frontier.

Founding

In 1877, Arizona's economic growth was slow. Most of the state's mining efforts were declining, if not already shut down. Hostile Indians, especially the Chiricahua Apache, constantly threatened the safety of new towns. Arizona was in desperate need of something to reinvigorate its economy. Due to the persistence of a young prospector named Ed Schieffelin, that something was on its way. Born in Tioga County, Pennsylvania, in 1847, Schieffelin had spent the better part of his life wandering Oregon, Idaho, Nevada, Utah, and California as a prospector. Year after year he had been unsuccessful. In 1875, at twenty-six years old, Schieffelin decided to take his chances in Arizona, near the San Pedro Valley. As he departed, he was grimly told that all he would find in the area would be his "tombstone."

For almost three years, Schieffelin prospected the area, never making a significant discovery but consistently uncovering small silver bits that hinted at huge shares of ore nearby. He managed to convince his brother, Al Schieffelin, and an assayer from New York, Dick Gird, to form a partnership.

On February 26, 1878, the discovery was made. Ed Schieffelin stumbled upon a large outcropping of ore—almost entirely silver—that proved to be the first of many in the area. As the word spread, men started arriving in the San Pedro Valley to claim a share of the treasure or cash in on the high wages (four to six dollars a day) being paid to mine the ore. Mines sprung up everywhere, some of the most famous being the Tough Nut, the Contention, and the Grand Central. In less than a year, the area, formed into a town and christened "Tombstone" by Ed Schieffelin, had more than a hundred residents, with hundreds more flocking to the area. A stageline was built to run express from Tucson to Tombstone, most of its riders purchasing a one-way ticket. Little by little, general stores and other establishments were opened to cater to Tombstone's growing population.

Growth of the Town

After the Golden Eagle Brewery opened in 1879, other breweries, saloons, and gambling houses sprang up faster than men could spend their money. By 1881, there were 110 liquor licenses in effect. Along with its drinking establishments, Tombstone boasted a variety of fashionable shops, luxurious hotels, and restaurants with chefs from New York, St. Louis, and Chicago.

Tombstone was no stranger to modern technology. Along with building a hospital and water company, the city was soon using gas lamps, the telegraph, and a good number of telephones. The area even had its own newspapers. Competing for the front line were the weekly *Nugget* and the daily and weekly *Epitaph*.

On February 21, 1881, a bill was passed to "incorporate the City of Tombstone, to define its limits and rights, to specify its privileges and powers, and provide for an efficient government of the same." This government would consist of a mayor and a councilman for each ward. In addition, Tombstone was designated the county seat for all of Cochise County. By 1883, ten thousand people resided in the town and its surrounding countryside. In four short years, Tombstone had become an area of nonstop activity, healthy profit, and unbounded optimism. At its peak, the city had a population of almost twelve thousand. Investments rapidly poured in; mines and mills operated for miles in all directions; elaborate corporate structures abounded; wages were high.

The growth of schools in the town sparked a fresh interest in education and culture. This attention led to the birth of organizations such as the Tombstone City Band, the Tombstone Club (a literary group), and theaters such as the Sixth Street Opera House and Schieffelin Hall. However, theaters like the Bird Cage also sprang up and began advertising alcohol and not-so-tasteful entertainment.

Temptation and Trouble

Most of the population of Tombstone was made up of miners. The days were long and the toil was difficult. Men were left to entertain themselves any way they could, usually through card playing, drinking, gambling, and consorting with "loose women." Saloons and gambling houses, open twenty-four hours, roared with music and laughter all hours of the day and night. Every day, the town grew wilder and law enforcement became more difficult.

Prostitution was a booming business in Tombstone. Women flocked to town to prosper from the needs of the lonely miners. Although work was abundant, pay was low and living conditions were poor. Most prostitutes lived behind the saloons in cheap shacks where they entertained their clientele. There was no medical inspection of any kind, and venereal disease ran rampant.

Another favorite pastime among miners was gambling—usually mixed with drinking. In fact, drifters often traveled from miles around to collect an evening's winnings from those too drunk to spot a trick deck of cards. Without regulation, the games were usually crooked and often resulted in the drawing of pistols. Men displayed no fear of ending a dispute with a gunshot, despite the town's efforts to enforce a law prohibiting the visible carrying of weapons.

Methods of justice in Tombstone were not always traditional. When it was dealt, punishment was severe and often granted deputized officials the opportunity for personal revenge. Likewise, when regular authorities were unable to handle a situation, miners would often resort to vigilante justice. Fighting and feuding were often the result.

Gunfight at the OK Corral

As the silver boom moved along, Tombstone was the frequent target of criminal bands who lived to the south and southeast. These "cowboys" made their living stealing cattle and horses from the United States to sell to Mexico—a practice from which dishonest law officers could profit. One of the most famous gangs of smugglers was the Clanton brothers—Ike, Phineas, and William—from the Charleston area. Often, the trio was joined by Frank and Tom McLowry, who owned a ranch nearby.

Meanwhile in Tombstone, two factions had emerged from the contest for sheriff of Cochise County. Both factions claimed that the other was allied with the "cowboys." One of the contenders was Democrat John H. Behan, a stable owner and former sheriff from Pima County who was an acquaintance of the Clantons. The other was Republican Wyatt Earp, a peace officer who, until Behan mysteriously usurped his power, had himself been sheriff of Pima County. Now both men were settled in Tombstone, with more than a few bad feelings. When Behan won the seat again in Tombstone, Earp suspected it had something to do with Behan's association with the Clanton gang.

Along with Earp traveled his four brothers—Jim, Morgan, Virgil and Warren—and his best friends, John Henry "Doc" Holliday and William "Bat" Masterson. When Virgil was appointed city marshal in 1881 by reform mayor John P. Clum, the animosity grew between the Earp faction, supported by the *Nugget,* and the Behan-Clanton faction, supported by the *Epitaph.* These feelings were sharpened again when Wyatt Earp became involved with Behan's mistress, and yet again with the occurrence of two stagecoach robberies for which the factions blamed each other. Finally, on October 26, 1881, the feud came to a head with what is remembered today as the shoot-out at the OK Corral.

The night before the shoot-out, members of both factions were in a saloon where Ike Clanton and Virgil Earp got into a heated argument during a poker game. The next morning, Virgil deputized his brother Morgan, and they went after Clanton, arresting and fining him for carrying a weapon. That same morning, Wyatt Earp initiated a fight with an unarmed Tom McLowry and left him bleeding in the street. Later that day, the Earp

Modern visitors to Tombstone can get a glimpse of what life was like in the days of the Old West. (Arizona Office of Tourism/Chris Coe)

brothers, along with Doc Holliday, marched toward the Clanton's OK Corral to settle the score.

Having been told by Behan that their rivals were unarmed, the Earps rode up to the corral. They were met outside by the McLowry brothers and Ike and Billy Clanton. To the Earps' surprise, the Clantons and McLowrys reached for weapons; the Earps reacted quickly. Shots echoed through the town, and in twenty short seconds Billy Clanton and the McLowrys were all dead, Virgil and Morgan Earp were seriously wounded, and Doc Holliday was grazed by a bullet.

Warrants were obtained for the arrests of Doc Holliday and Wyatt, Virgil, and Morgan Earp. The trial lasted until December 1, when all four men were released due to insufficient evidence. However, Virgil was suspended from his office as marshal, and the town turned bitterly against the Earp family to support Sheriff Behan. Soon after, an ambush killed Morgan and crippled Virgil, causing him to return to his parents in Florida. Wyatt and Warren Earp, along with Holliday, headed north to Colorado.

A Town in Decline

Tombstone's glory was short-lived. By 1883, despite its prosperous appearance, the town had begun to decline. Although certain changes were not immediately apparent, they eventually affected Tombstone. The price of silver was going down, underground shafts began to flood, and the local cattlemen were joining forces to drive out the smugglers. As word reached Washington, D.C., of the violent behavior in the Southwest, the federal government began to enforce control over the area. Finally, national attention turned away from silver toward the copper industry. Tombstone locals soon began to take interest in mining camps in Colorado and Montana.

Citizens of Tombstone fought hard to bolster the town's economy, but the next fifteen years marked a steady decline. Severe shaft floods and fires eventually led to the closing of Tombstone's mines in late 1910. Most of its residents had packed up and followed their fortunes elsewhere. Fewer than a thousand people now populated Tombstone—all that was left were a few scattered ranches and fabricated legends of wild, lawless days.

Ironically, these legends would eventually lead to Tombstone's rebirth. As time passed, the town's tales grew tall enough to attract tourists from all over the country. In the 1920's, citizens of Tombstone built up this new tourist industry by renovating old buildings; staging reenactments of hangings, killings, shootouts, and battles with Indians; and putting on tame, theatrical versions of the old saloons' bawdy reviews.

Publishing houses and filmmakers also sought to profit from the interest in Tombstone's past. Fabrication laced almost every retelling: Characters were deemed either wholly good or purely evil, and the town's violent character was monstrously exaggerated.

Places to Visit

Today most of Tombstone's historic buildings still stand. One site that has attracted international interest is the home of the *Epitaph*, founded on May 1, 1880, by John P. Clum. One hundred years later, this daily newspaper was still published locally, along with a national monthly edition circulated in every state and many foreign countries. The Crystal Palace, Tombstone's first and most popular place of drinking, socializing, and gambling, is another tourist favorite. Finally, the Boothill Graveyard on the northwest corner of town is the resting place of Tombstone's pioneers and many of those who made the town famous. Because it lay neglected for many years, much of the cemetery has returned to nature. However, in 1923, the city conducted a search to discover who lay buried there and undertook a cleanup and restoration of the site. Gravestones reveal the names of Tom and Frank McLowry and Billy Clanton.

Many other historic buildings and sites, such as the Bird Cage theater, St. Paul's Episcopal Church, the Rose Tree Inn, Tombstone Courthouse, and the OK Corral still stand as well. Although much of Tombstone's past has been glamorized, its rich history cannot be denied.   —*Cynthia L. Langston*

For Further Information:

Dollar, Tom. *Tucson to Tombstone: A Guide to Southeastern Arizona*. Phoenix: Arizona Highways, 1998. A guidebook to Tombstone and the surrounding area accompanied by photographs and maps.

Faulk, Odie B. *Tombstone: Myth and Reality*. New York: Oxford University Press, 1972. A detailed account of what happened at Tombstone, including its ascent and decline and many of the myths that have grown to be believed about the town.

Lake, Stuart N. *The Life and Times of Wyatt Earp*. Boston: Houghton Mifflin, 1956. Gives a detailed biography of Earp, along with speculative dialogue.

Lavender, David. *The Southwest*. Reprint. New York: Harper, 1984. A briefer account that focuses on the story of the shootout at the OK Corral, but gives solid background information on the circumstances in Tombstone surrounding the event.

Shillingberg, William B. *Tombstone, A.T.: A History of Early Mining, Milling, and Mayhem*. Spokane, Wash.: Arthur H. Clark, 1999. A description of frontier and pioneer life in Tombstone.

Wupatki National Monument

Date: Proclaimed a National Monument on December 9, 1924

Relevant issues: American Indian history

Significance: The thirty-six-thousand-acre National Monument is the site of Indian ruins dating from the twelfth and thirteenth centuries. The most famous ruins are Wukoki, the Citadel, Lomaki, and Wupatki Pueblo. The structures were built after a nearby volcanic eruption blanketed the area with volcanic ash, attracting a variety of Indian groups—the Sinagua, Cohonino, Anasazi, Hohokam, Mogollon, and Cíbola—to the newly arable land. The site was abandoned in the thirteenth century. In the mid-nineteenth century, the site was inhabited by Navajo and Hopi Indians. By the turn of the century, archaeological excavations had begun there.

Location: Thirty-two miles north of Flagstaff, between Flagstaff and Cameron, off U.S. Interstate 89 via a thirty-six-mile driving loop that leads directly to Wupatki as well as to the adjacent Sunset Crater National Monument

Site Office:

Superintendent
Wupatki National Monument
HC33 Box 444A
Flagstaff, AZ 86004
ph.: (520) 679-2365
Web site: www.nps.gov/wupa/

Except for a short period of about one hundred years, the Wupatki basin was uninhabited by archaic peoples. High winds, extremely varied temperatures, lack of water, and poor soil made the region inhospitable to long-term settlement. Even now, depending on the season, temperatures range from near 0 to over 100 degrees Fahrenheit. Annual rainfall is minimal, vegetation is scant, and the area can appropriately be described as desolate. Archaeological evidence suggests that archaic peoples were familiar with the area, because stone tools have been found to the east of the basin, on alluvial terraces along the Little Colorado River, but it is unlikely that early peoples inhabited the Wupatki basin itself unless conditions there were very different from what they are today.

Earliest Inhabitants

In the eleventh century the closest inhabitants to the Wupatki basin were the Sinagua (Spanish for "without water"), who at that time had been living for about four hundred years in villages to the south and east, around the San Francisco Peaks. The Sinagua were known for their ability to survive in semidesert conditions, successfully living and farming with very little water. Besides farming, some Sinagua also apparently hunted and gathered in the Wupatki basin.

In the last months of 1064 C.E., the Sinagua no doubt experienced strange rumblings and shaking of the earth on which they were living and cultivating. Gases and molten rock were about to erupt in the nearby Wupatki basin, and to form the volcanic cone known as Sunset Crater. The Indians fled the area before the eruption, which, according to tree-ring dating methods, took place some time during the winter of 1064-1065.

The eruption must have been surprising to the Sinagua and any other people in the vicinity because it occurred in an unimposing stretch of rocky, dry land, rather than an obvious volcano. Molten rock and highly compressed gases, a combination known as magma, exploded through the earth's crust, blowing rock and cinders all around the point of the explosion. This debris formed a small, cone-shaped volcanic mountain. The explosion also scattered ash and cinders for hundreds of miles around the point of eruption.

Before long, the Sinagua realized that the dark, unusual-looking residue that remained on the soil after the volcanic explosion had actually enriched the land and made it more suitable for agriculture. The ash and cinders worked as a natural mulch that conserved moisture and made the ground more fertile. As a result, dry farming became possible in the Wupatki basin. During this same time period, rainfall in the area also increased. It is unclear whether the increased precipitation was directly related to the eruption, but the climatic change also improved the ability of the region to support farming. Nevertheless, experts believe that, while farming was now possible in the Wupatki basin, it was never exceedingly productive.

The Arrival of Other Tribes

The Sinagua returned to the area, but they were not the only people drawn to this newly fertile region. Indian peoples who lived nearby in all directions gradually began migrating to Wupatki basin. The Cohonino came first, followed by Anasazi from the Kayenta region to the north. Hohokam moved up from the Verde Valley to the south, Mogollon migrated from the southeast, and Cíbola peoples, who were closely related to the Mogollon, migrated from the east.

Within two generations, Wupatki basin, once

Wupatki. (National Park Service)

the Sinagua, from the Anasazi and the Hohokam. Because only the physical artifacts and ruins of the Wupatki community remain, no one knows if or to what extent they adapted beliefs, customs, or rituals from one another.

Pueblos

Until they moved to Wupatki basin, the Sinagua had traditionally been pithouse dwellers. They usually lived in underground rooms, with roofs supported by four poles and an entrance passage that also served as a ventilator. At Wupatki, however, the Sinagua built and occupied the largest pueblo, now known as Wupatki Pueblo, apparently using the Anasazi pueblo style as a model. Wupatki Pueblo, in front of which the monument's visitors' center was built, was the only major pueblo built by the Sinagua in the area. The residence, constructed from sandstone and limestone held together with clay mortar, was so soundly built that it still remains fairly intact, despite the passage of seven hundred years and the destruction caused by vandals throughout the centuries.

The dwelling appears to have been occupied as early as 1106, and during the twelfth century as many as three hundred people lived in it. The residential compound contained single-story, single-family houses as well as a multilevel highrise that probably had more than one hundred rooms.

The Anasazi apparently influenced the Sinagua in other ways besides architecturally. The Sinagua also built a circular amphitheater or "dance plaza" that resembles an Anasazi kiva. Kivas were round, mostly underground pit rooms that the Anasazi used for religious and ceremonial purposes. Although similar in shape to an Anasazi kiva, the Sinagua amphitheater did not have a roof, as kivas did, nor all the ceremonial trappings of a kiva. It is

nearly barren, was supporting a population of between four thousand and five thousand people. The basin rapidly developed into a multicultural area, a "melting pot" of different Indian peoples living near one another. Because each of these groups also had numerous trade contacts outside the Wupatki basin, the cultural mix was broadened even further.

The diverse Wupatki community was unusual in prehistoric southwestern life. Before and after Wupatki, tribal groups tended to stay in specific areas, among their own kind. They lived separately, although peacefully, for centuries, frequently relocating where they could find better conditions, but mostly remaining with people of their own culture and apart from other groups.

For more than one hundred years, however, the multicultural community of Wupatki apparently fared quite well. Despite the potential for conflict that might have been caused by the interaction of different cultures and customs, archaeological remains suggest that the groups coexisted harmoniously and productively. The peoples appear to have learned from one another. There is much evidence that architecture and certain types of physical structures were borrowed, particularly by

unclear whether the structure served the same purpose as a kiva, but most likely it was used for ceremonial gatherings of some kind.

Ball Courts

The Hohokam at Wupatki basin also appear to have influenced the Sinagua, because the Sinagua constructed an oval ball court at their pueblo. These courts, which are similar to others found in Mexico and Central America, were the signature structure of the Hohokam throughout the Southwest. Although the specifics of the game or games played in the ball courts are not known, it is likely that the courts were introduced to the Hohokam from Indian peoples living in what is now Mexico. To the Maya and Aztec peoples there, the game had religious or ritualistic overtones. Apparently, the goal of the game was to get a rubber ball through a stone ring without using hands or feet. Whether the game was changed when played by the Hohokam and others throughout the Southwest is unknown.

The unique aspect of the ball court at Wupatki is that it is made of masonry; typically these courts are constructed of adobe. The Wupatki ball court is also located near a blow hole, a crack in the earth through which air passes in and out. Since other communities in the Southwest were built near blow holes, it is likely that these holes had special or possibly sacred meaning to the Indians.

Other Ruins

Among the other accessible ruins in the Wupatki monument area are Wukoki, Lomaki, and the Citadel. Wukoki, a three-story pueblo constructed entirely of finished blocks of Moenkopi sandstone, was built on an outcropping of the same kind of sandstone. Lomaki, an exquisitely constructed pueblo (its name means "beautiful house"), sits near a collapsed crack in the earth that may have had a special meaning to the people. The Citadel, originally a two-story structure that included fifty rooms and may have housed as many as sixty people, resembles a fortress, even though there is no evidence of war or fighting in the area at that time. These were the dwellings of Kayenta Anasazi, a distinctive subgroup of the Anasazi, whose homelands were to the northeast of Wupatki, in the Four Corners area.

Influences in the Region

It is likely that the Anasazi were the dominant group in Wupatki basin. Theirs was a dynamic and expansive culture close to its height of development in the twelfth century, and they exerted the most apparent influences on architecture and possibly religious ritual of all the residents in Wupatki basin. The Anasazi, who had a long tradition of dwelling in pueblos, traced their roots to Basketmaker peoples, among the earliest farmers in the Southwest. Experts speculate that the development of pueblos may be related to the development of farming, since growing crops meant that the Anasazi had to stay in one place for extended periods of time.

The building of ball courts suggests that the Hohokam may have been the second most influential of the peoples in the multicultural Wupatki basin. The Hohokam, who lived primarily in the Salt and Gila River valleys, were also known for their engineering abilities, particularly for building extensive networks of irrigation canals that enabled them to survive in near-desert conditions from about 200 to 1450 C.E. Neither pithouse nor pueblo dwellers, the Hohokam usually lived in single-room, separate rectangular houses. They were also skilled artisans who created exceptionally fine jewelry.

The Mogollon and Cohonino, who migrated to Wupatki basin in smaller numbers than the Anasazi and Hohokam, were less advanced than the other cultures there. The Cohonino, for example, remained living in pithouses even at Wupatki. Consequently, very few of their cultural artifacts now remain. The Mogollon, whose culture during the eleventh century seems to have been influenced by the Anasazi's, are best known for their exquisite pottery. A Mogollon subgroup, for example, created the highly geometric, black-and-white pottery known as "Mimbres." With its detailed depictions of plants, animals, insects, and people, this pottery is among the most beautiful of the ancient Southwest. It is not clear how many Mogollon moved to the Wupatki basin, or whether they lived in pueblos there.

Abandonment

Like many other pre-Columbian dwelling places in the Southwest, the Wupatki basin was not long occupied. The drought that gripped the region during the thirteenth century affected the Wupatki basin as greatly as other areas. The volcanic ash that made the region arable was gradually dispersed by winds and time. It is also possible that soil depletion and disease affected the people's ability to remain in the area. By 1225 nearly all residents of the Wupatki basin had departed, leaving behind hundreds of pueblos.

Evidence suggests the Sinagua left initially in small groups and then in larger numbers for the Verde Valley, where the water supply was still ample and where related peoples also lived. The other residents may have returned to their homelands or migrated to new areas; no one knows for sure.

From the thirteenth to nineteenth centuries, the Wupatki basin was again largely uninhabited, although the Hopi, who trace their Parrot Clan to Wupatki Pueblo, apparently lived in the pueblo for a while, possibly half a century after the Sinagua left. In the mid-nineteenth century, Navajo people as well as some Hopi began living nearby.

Archaeological Expeditions

Although Spanish explorers traveled near the area in the sixteenth and eighteenth centuries, the first Anglo-American to document the existence of the Wupatki ruins was Lieutenant Lorenzo Sitgreaves. Sitgreaves came upon them in 1851 while searching for an overland route through New Mexico to the Little Colorado River. Eleven years later, Arizona became a U.S. territory separate from New Mexico, and shortly thereafter Wupatki was surveyed by archaeologist John Wesley Powell. Throughout the late 1800's, the Wupatki region began attracting more people. Both Navajo and Anglo-American ranchers grazed sheep in the area, and the newly constructed railroad brought settlers from the East. As a result of the growth of a new community around Flagstaff, many people visited the ruins and raided them of pottery and other artifacts.

The ruins at Wupatki were not systematically studied until the turn of the century, when archaeologist Jesse Walter Fewkes mapped and documented the area. The first custodian of Wupatki, J. C. Clarke, named the large pueblo Wupatki, changing it from Wukoki, the label Fewkes had given it. Wupatki was established as a National Monument in 1924. In 1933, it was studied and partially excavated by the Museum of Northern Arizona.

In 1933, when President Franklin D. Roosevelt established the jobs program known as the Civilian Works Administration (CWA), the Wupatki ruins were among several prehistoric Indian sites excavated and stabilized by workers in the National Park Service, under the auspices of the Southwestern Monument Service. Artifacts found during that excavation are housed at the Museum of Northern Arizona.

Many of the hundreds of pueblos and prehistoric sites on the thirty-six-thousand-acre National Monument have not been excavated. Exhibits at the visitors' center include a re-creation of a typical Wupatki room, a variety of crafts and artifacts characteristic of the peoples who lived in the area, and displays that explain the history of the region.

—*Gail A. Moss*

For Further Information:
Gaede, Marni, ed. *Camera, Spade, and Pen: An Inside View of Southwestern Archaeology.* Tucson: University of Arizona Press, 1980. Offers a unique view of prehistoric southwestern Indian cultures such as the Anasazi and Hohokam through personal interviews with people who investigated and studied the archaeological sites where these peoples lived. The photographs by Marc Gaede that accompany the interviews are spectacular.

McGregor, John C. *Southwestern Archaeology.* 2d ed. Urbana: University of Illinois Press, 1982. A helpful chronological study of the major early cultures of the Southwest, with extensive information about the pottery and other artifacts the cultures left behind. Photographs, numerous illustrations, and maps add to this thorough history of prehistoric life in the Southwest.

Noble, David Grant. *Ancient Ruins of the Southwest: An Archaeological Guide.* 2d rev. ed. Flagstaff, Ariz.: Northland Press, 2000. Offers a thorough yet concise look at the prehistoric cultures of the Southwest. Excellent photographs and numerous simple maps add to the book's usefulness.

Wilson, Josleen. *The Passionate Amateur's Guide to Archaeology in the United States.* New York: Collier Books, 1980. Offers brief descriptions of archaeological sites throughout the country. Entries include hours, phone numbers, addresses, admission fees, and directions.

Other Historic Sites

Awatovi Ruins

Location: Keams Canyon, Navajo County

Relevant issues: American Indian history, European settlement

Statement of significance: Located on the Hopi Indian Reservation, Awatovi Ruins is the site of one of the most important Hopi Indian villages encountered by Francisco Vásquez de Coronado's men in 1540. It contains the remains of a five-hundred-year-old pueblo and a seventeenth century Spanish mission complex. Excavations were conducted at the site by the Peabody Museum in the 1930's.

Casa Malpais Site

Location: Springerville, Apache County

Relevant issues: American Indian history

Statement of significance: Situated on terraces of a fallen basalt cliff along the upper Little Colorado River, the site dates from late Pueblo III to early Pueblo IV (1250-1325 C.E.) times. Casa Malpais appears to incorporate features of both early and late Mogollon culture settlement patterns.

Desert Laboratory

Location: Tucson, Pima County

Relevant issues: Science and technology

Statement of significance: Established in 1903 by the Carnegie Institution for the purpose of studying "the methods by which plants perform their functions under the extraordinary conditions existing in deserts," the Desert Laboratory was for over thirty-five years the center for the study of North American desert ecology. Much of the framework of plant ecology generally, and desert ecology in particular, was formulated here.

Gatlin Site

Location: Gila Bend, Maricopa County

Relevant issues: American Indian history

Statement of significance: Probably first occupied sometime before 900 C.E., the Gatlin Site contains one of the few documented Hohokam platform mounds. Associated with the mound are pit houses, ball courts, middens, and prehistoric canals. The mound is one of the only excavated and documented Sedentary Period platform mounds that is still relatively intact.

Hubbell Trading Post

Location: Ganado, Apache County

Relevant issues: American Indian history, western expansion

Statement of significance: This still-active trading post represents the varied interactions of Navajos and the white traders who ran trading posts on the Navajo Reservation in the late nineteenth and early twentieth centuries.

Jerome Historic District

Location: Jerome, Yavapai County

Relevant issues: Business and industry

Statement of significance: Jerome was one of the richest copper-producing areas in the United States in the late nineteenth and early twentieth centuries. The town and surrounding mining area illustrate the historic activities associated with copper production.

Kinishba Ruins

Location: Whiteriver, Gila County

Relevant issues: American Indian history

Statement of significance: This site contains the ruins of a pueblo capable of housing up to one thousand Indians that was abandoned about 1400 C.E. The culture of the inhabitants represented a blend of Mogollon and Anasazi ancestry.

Lowell Observatory

Location: Flagstaff, Coconino County

Relevant issues: Science and technology

Statement of significance: Founded in 1894 by Percival Lowell (1855-1916), this relatively small observatory was at the time the one significant center of pure scientific research in the Southwest. Here, Lowell studied Mars (and theorized that it was inhabited by intelligent beings) and performed the computations that led to the discovery of Pluto; A. E. Douglass (1867-1962) conducted research that led to the modern science of dendrochronology; and, in 1912, V. M. Slipher (1875-1969) discovered that the universe was expanding. The observatory is still in operation.

Old Oraibi

Location: Oraibi, Navajo County

Relevant issues: American Indian history

Statement of significance: Located on the westernmost of the Hopi mesas, this is probably the oldest continuously inhabited pueblo in the Southwest. Old Oraibi documents Hopi culture and history from before European contact to the present day. The village is on the present Hopi Indian Reservation.

Pueblo Grande Ruin and Irrigation Sites

Location: Pueblo Grande City Park, Phoenix, Maricopa County

Relevant issues: American Indian history

Web site: www.arizonaguide.com/pueblogrande

Statement of significance: The prehistoric platform mound and associated archaeological remains at Pueblo Grande represent one of the last surviving urban architectural sites of its kind in the southwestern United States. There is evidence that between 1100 and 1400 c.e., Pueblo Grande served as a Hohokam administration center for a major irrigation canal system. Due to its prehistoric significance, preeminent archaeologists have conducted research at Pueblo Grande since the 1880's.

Roosevelt Dam

Location: Globe, Gila County

Relevant issues: Science and technology

Statement of significance: Erected between 1906 and 1911, the world's highest masonry dam is acknowledged for its outstanding engineering. Roosevelt Dam was the first major public works project completed under the National Reclamation Act, which was enacted in 1902 during Theodore Roosevelt's administration. Roosevelt Dam was designed as a storage facility to increase the agricultural productivity of this arid region along the Salt River.

San Xavier Del Bac Mission

Location: Tucson, Pima County

Relevant issues: American Indian history, European settlement, religion

Statement of significance: Founded in 1700 by the Jesuits, Bac then formed the extreme northern thrust of Nueva España. The present structure is the third, perhaps the fourth, church on the site. Consecrated by Franciscans, it was begun in 1783 and completed in 1797. One of the finest Spanish Colonial churches in the country, it is a synthesis of Baroque design and the desert materials from which it was built by Papago Indian laborers supervised by Spanish-American master craftsmen.

Yuma Crossing and Associated Sites

Location: Yuma

Relevant issues: American Indian history, western expansion

Statement of significance: First used by Native Americans, this natural crossing served as a significant transportation gateway on the Colorado River during the Spanish Colonial and U.S. westward expansion periods. The surviving buildings of the Yuma Quartermaster Depot and Arizona Territorial Prison are the key features on the Arizona side of the border; across the river, in California, stand the surviving buildings of Fort Yuma, an Army outpost that guarded the crossing from 1850 to 1885.

Arkansas

History of Arkansas 73

Arkansas Post 75

Little Rock Central High School 80

Other Historic Sites 83

The State Capitol Building in Little Rock. (Arkansas Department of Parks & Tourism/A. C. Haralson)

History of Arkansas

The history of Arkansas was greatly influenced by the natural division of the area into northwestern highlands and southeastern lowlands. Running through these two regions as it flows in a southeasterly direction to meet the Mississippi River, the Arkansas River has also been of major importance in the area's history. As long as ten thousand years ago, hunters and gatherers wandered the land surrounding the Arkansas River, attracted by the abundant wildlife. About one thousand years ago, bluff dwellers and mound builders grew crops in the area's fertile soil. By the time Europeans arrived in the New World, the primary groups of Native Americans inhabiting the area were the Osage, in Missouri and northwestern Arkansas; the Caddo, in Louisiana and southwestern Arkansas; and the Quapaw, along the Arkansas River. All three groups had been forced into Oklahoma by the middle of the nineteenth century.

Exploration and Settlement

The first Europeans to reach the area were led northwest from Florida by Spanish explorer Hernando de Soto in 1541. A French expedition led by Jacques Marquette and Louis Jolliet reached the area in 1673 by traveling south from Michigan. In 1682, a similar expedition was led by René-Robert Cavelier, Sieur de La Salle. La Salle claimed the entire valley of the Mississippi River, including all of Arkansas, for France. This enormous area was named Louisiana in honor of King Louis XIV of France.

Despite La Salle's claim to the area, European settlement of the area began modestly. In 1686, French explorer Henry de Tonti established Arkansas Post, the first permanent European settlement in the area, near the point where the Arkansas River meets the Mississippi River. Starting with a population of six residents, Arkansas Post grew to become the largest city in Arkansas until the nineteenth century. In 1722, French explorer Bernard de la Harpe led an expedition along the Arkansas River and named a natural rock formation Little Rock. Nearly a century later, a city of the same name was founded there.

The Road to Statehood

Settlement of the area continued slowly throughout the eighteenth century. In 1762, France ceded Louisiana to Spain. In order to encourage settlers, Spain offered free land and freedom from taxes to all who chose to live there. In 1783, British forces attacked Arkansas Post but were defeated by the Spanish and Quapaw. By 1799, Arkansas had nearly four hundred European settlers.

In 1800, Louisiana was returned to France. Three years later, the United States purchased this vast area, doubling the size of the young nation, for a payment of more than twenty-seven million dollars. At first a part of the huge Louisiana Territory, in 1812 Arkansas became part of the newly created Missouri Territory, then became a separate territory in 1819. In 1824, the western section of the area became part of the Indian Territory (Oklahoma), giving Arkansas its modern boundaries. By 1836, Arkansas had the sixty thousand residents necessary for statehood, primarily settlers from eastern states, and it was admitted as the twenty-fifth state.

The Civil War

Along with those who arrived from the eastern United States, the 1840's and 1850's brought large numbers of Irish and German immigrants to the area. The mountains and plateaus of the northwest supported small farms, while the lowlands of the southeast developed large cotton plantations dependent on slaves. By 1860, the population of Arkansas reached 435,000. About one-quarter of the inhabitants were slaves.

Arkansas seceded from the Union on May 6, 1861, nearly a month after the Civil War broke out. The delay in joining the Confederacy may have been due to strong Union sympathies in the northwest part of the state. About six thousand residents of the state fought for the Union, while about fifty-eight thousand fought for the Confederacy. Several important Civil War battles were fought in northern Arkansas, near the border with Missouri. The Battle of Pea Ridge (March 7-8, 1862) led to heavy losses on both sides, as Union forces

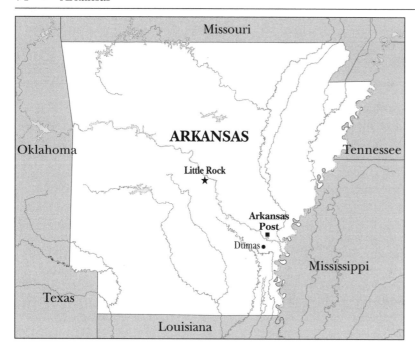

form of crops, usually cotton. The social and economic gap between the farmer and the landlord was often a large one.

An economic depression in the southern states in the late nineteenth century led to widespread poverty. The situation became even worse in 1885, when the state government defaulted on huge debts, including fourteen million dollars of interest payments. Race relations were a severe problem as well, with the state government completely controlled by the Democratic Party, which excluded African American citizens.

drove back an attack by the Confederates, ending the threat of a Confederate invasion of Missouri. In September of 1863, Union forces took control of Little Rock.

From the end of the war until the middle of the 1870's, a period known as Reconstruction, Arkansas and the other former Confederate states were occupied by federal troops and ruled by state governments dominated by the Republican Party. Arkansas was readmitted to the Union under Republican control in 1868. The Republican government, which attempted to win civil rights for freed slaves, was seen as an artificial structure imposed by the northern states. It was opposed, often violently, by many white Arkansans, leading to increased repression of African Americans after Reconstruction. After federal troops were withdrawn, the Democratic Party returned to power in 1874, completely dominating state politics for nearly a century.

After the War

Economic recovery after the devastation of the Civil War was difficult for Arkansans. The plantation system of the southeastern region of the state, which relied on slavery, was replaced with sharecropping. Under this system, tenants lived on and farmed a landowner's property, paying rent in the

The Twentieth Century

Along with the rest of the country, Arkansas experienced a large increase in the number of European immigrants at the end of the nineteenth century. Although the pace of economic growth remained slow, the state began to develop new resources in the early years of the twentieth century. Rice, which would later become a major crop, was first planted in 1904. With the rise of the automobile and the increasing industrialization of the United States, the discovery of oil and natural gas deposits in 1921 was an important boost to the economy. The many rivers in Arkansas became an important resource, and modern dams were built beginning in the 1920's.

Arkansas, along with the rest of the United States, suffered a severe economic setback with the Great Depression of the 1930's. Adding to the problem, years of drought forced many farmers to abandon their lands. The Southern Farm Tenants Union, created by Arkansas sharecroppers at this time, had an important influence on national farm policies. It was not until the United States entered World War II in 1941 that the economy began to recover. The enormous defense industry created by the war effort, as well as the technological and economic growth that followed the war, led to major changes in Arkansas society.

The number of Arkansans living in rural areas decreased, and many small family farms were replaced by large agricultural enterprises. Little Rock and other major cities experienced a rapid increase in population. Women entered the workplace in greater numbers. The most important social change in the middle of the twentieth century was the struggle to win civil rights for African Americans.

The attention of the world was focused on race relations in Arkansas in September of 1957. Three years earlier, the Supreme Court had declared public school segregation unconstitutional. To comply with the Court's decision, the school board of Little Rock created a plan to desegregate the city's schools. When nine African American students attempted to attend the city's Central High School, Governor Orval E. Faubus ordered the state militia to prevent them from entering. In response, President Dwight David Eisenhower sent federal troops to enforce the desegregation process.

Economic Growth
Economic development continued steadily throughout the second half of the twentieth century. In the 1960's, rice, soybeans, and poultry replaced cotton as the most important agricultural products. The McClellan-Kerr Arkansas River Navigation System, an ambitious project of building dams and locks, was completed after twenty-five years of work, in January of 1971. The project, the largest ever undertaken by the United States Army Corps of Engineers, made Little Rock an important river port and contributed greatly to the state's economy.

By the end of the twentieth century, important sources of income included fish farming, hydroelectric and nuclear power production, food processing, retail merchandising, computer software development, and financial services. The manufacturing sector of the economy produced clothing, furniture, machinery, electrical equipment, metal products, and electronic devices. With improvements in transportation, tourism became a particularly important source of revenue, with thousands of visitors traveling to attractions such as Hot Springs National Park and the Ozark Mountains each year. Despite this growth, Arkansas continued to have one of the lowest per-capita incomes in the United States.   —*Rose Secrest*

Arkansas Post

Date: Authorized as a National Memorial on July 6, 1960
Relevant issues: Civil War, European settlement
Significance: This National Memorial is the site of the first European settlement in the lower Mississippi Valley. It was founded for the French by Henry de Tonti in August, 1686; ceded to Spain in November, 1762; the site of a Revolutionary War skirmish on April 17, 1783; returned to French control in 1800; and taken over by the United States in 1804 following the Louisiana Purchase. It served as the capital of Arkansas Territory, was the place of publication of the *Arkansas Gazette* from 1819 to 1821, and was the site of a Civil War battle at Fort Hindman on January 10-11, 1863.
Location: Near the mouth of the Arkansas River, seven miles south of Gillett and twenty miles northeast of Dumas
Site Office:
Arkansas Post National Memorial
1741 Old Post Road
Gillett, AR 72055
ph.: (870) 548-2207
Web site: www.nps.gov/arpo/

Although little-known today, Arkansas Post was the first European settlement in the lower Mississippi River Valley. As its location shifted up and down the Arkansas River and its ownership passed back and forth between France, Spain, and the United States, Arkansas Post witnessed much of the early history of the North American frontier. Floods, wars, and soil erosion took their toll, however, and the Post slipped from prominence. Today it is home only to the Arkansas Post National Memorial.

Explorations
Arkansas Post was founded in August, 1686, by Henry de Tonti, the lieutenant of prominent explorer René-Robert Cavelier, Sieur de La Salle. Tonti, La Salle, and thirty French explorers had first come upon this spot four years earlier, on March 13, 1682, during their trip down the Mississippi River. Tonti was impressed with the area, located about thirty-five miles from the mouth of the Arkansas River, and was particularly taken with the

hospitality of the Quapaw Indians. He wrote in his journal, "we were well treated and given a cabin for our stay. . . . It can be said these savages were the best of all we had ever seen. . . . They had fish in abundance, roosters and chickens, and several kinds of unknown fruits." On their return up the river, La Salle granted Tonti several thousand acres in the area.

When La Salle returned to France to plan his next expedition, he left Tonti at Fort St. Louis, founded a year earlier near the site of present-day Peoria, Illinois. Tonti would never see La Salle again. Sailing back from France, La Salle's ship landed by mistake on the Texas coast. He was killed by his own men before he could find his way to the Mississippi. In the meantime, Tonti traveled south with his men to search for their missing commander. In August, 1686, he stopped once again near the mouth of the Arkansas River. Before moving on, Tonti settled six of his men there, near the Quapaw village of Osotouy. This was the first Poste de Arkansea, located approximately five miles from the site where the memorial stands today.

Developed, Then Deserted

While Tonti resumed his search for La Salle, the six men set to work building the Post. In the late spring of 1687, they received unexpected visitors: the bedraggled survivors of La Salle's expedition. Henri Joutel, leader of the expedition, described their discovery of the Post after traveling all the way from the Texas coast: "Looking over to the further side [of the Arkansas] we discovered a great cross, and at a small distance from it a house built after the French fashion. It is easy to imagine what inward joy we conceived at the sight of that emblem of our salvation." When Tonti returned he began developing the Post as a fur trading center.

Colonial Minister Jean-Baptiste Colbert had long opposed the fur trade in the area then known as Louisiana, however. To solidify the trade in Montreal and force the cultivation of Louisiana, he revoked the traders' licenses in 1694 and ordered all western forts to be abandoned, with the exception of Fort St. Louis. Tonti's protests bought a little time, but Arkansas Post was ultimately deserted by the French in 1699, possibly due to increased competition from English traders.

A Scheme for Settlement

The French returned to Arkansas Post after Scottish financier John Law acquired rights to the Louisiana concession in 1717. As part of the astoundingly ill conceived financial scheme known as the "Mississippi Bubble," Law proposed to settle six thousand colonists and three thousand African slaves in Louisiana. Countless shares in Law's Compagnie d'Occident were issued, and their price soon skyrocketed. In an effort to meet the demand, Law, who conveniently controlled the Banque Royale as well, simply printed more currency.

Using his newfound wealth, Law initiated plans to settle Louisiana, with the area around Arkansas Post to be his personal duchy. He sent eighty French workmen to begin construction at the abandoned site and gathered eight hundred Alsatian colonists and five hundred African slaves. By this time, however, the value of Law's stock had ballooned by 4,000 percent and the French currency was hopelessly unstable. The crash inevitably came, and both Law and the Compagnie d'Occident were discredited. The Alsatian colonists never reached the Post; they settled instead in New Orleans.

In March, 1722, Bertrand Dufresne, the new director for the Arkansas concession, arrived at the Post. A member of his party reported finding only forty-seven settlers (most likely the remaining workmen sent by Law), "twenty huts poorly arranged and three acres of cleared ground." There is no reason to accept later accounts that hundreds of Alsatian immigrants had settled near the Post and erected "pavilions" and "great storehouses." In 1723, a traveler to the settlement found only "three miserable shacks, fourteen Frenchmen, and six Negroes." The French had also established a small military outpost a few miles upriver, but they abandoned it in 1725. By the time Paul du Poisson, a Jesuit missionary, arrived at Arkansas Post in 1727, there were but thirty settlers. "Only the excellence of the soil and the climate have kept them, for in other respects they have received no assistance," he wrote.

Conflict with Local Tribes

In 1732, the French reestablished a military post on the shores of Lake Dumond, near several Quapaw villages. Within a few years they had constructed a barracks, a prison, a main house, a powder magazine, and possibly a stockade. These defenses would soon be put to the test. The Chickasaws, longtime enemies of the Quapaws, had begun raiding French shipping in the region. On May 10, 1749, one hundred fifty Chickasaws, Abekas, and possibly several Choctaws loyal to the English attacked Arkansas Post at dawn. The raiders easily outnumbered the twenty-odd settlers and the twelve soldiers under Ensign Louis-Xavier-Martin Delinó de Chalmette. To make matters worse, the Quapaws had moved upriver following the 1748 floods. The raiders took the French totally by surprise; fourteen settlers were captured outside the fort. The fort itself would have been overrun had the Chickasaw chief not been wounded and called a retreat. The male prisoners were killed, but the women and children were all eventually ransomed or released.

The visitors' center at Arkansas Post National Memorial. (Eastern National)

In response to the attack, the Post was moved upriver, near the new Quapaw villages at Écores Rouges (Red Bluffs). Today, this is the site of the National Memorial. After several false starts, the French deployed a full military company of fifty men to the Post and began work on large-scale fortifications, probably in the fall of 1751. The new fort was composed of seventeen buildings, was surrounded by a three-foot moat and an eleven-foot stockade, and was equipped with three cannon batteries and three sentry boxes. It was completed in 1755.

Despite the construction of these elaborate fortifications, Arkansas Post was moved again only a year later. The French wished the Post to be closer to the mouth of the Arkansas River, thereby offering greater protection and a more convenient trading center for their convoys on the Mississippi. The need to protect these convoys from the English and their allied Indian tribes was particularly urgent due to the start of the French and Indian War. The fort they constructed there greatly resembled the one completed the year before. Between 1756 and 1757, it was garrisoned by more than a hundred soldiers.

France and Spain at War

As a result of the war, France ceded its Louisiana holdings to Spain in November, 1762. About fifty French soldiers and forty settlers stayed on under Spanish rule. Like the French, the Spanish saw the area as a potential center of trade with the Indians. They also saw Louisiana in purely strategic terms, as a buffer zone between the English and Spain's more profitable colonies of Mexico. For both goals they needed the cooperation of the local Indian tribes. Because their colonial ambitions centered on Mexico, however, the Spanish wished to expend as few resources as possible in Louisiana. They therefore had great difficulty retaining the loyalty of the Quapaws. A series of Osage attacks, possibly instigated by the British, brought a tepid response from the Spanish governor. After several Quapaws engineered their own retaliatory raid, Fernando de Leyba, commandant of Arkansas Post, had to reward the Indians himself.

The British also used trade to weaken the Quapaws' alliance with the Spanish. In 1770, an Englishman settled on the Spanish side of the river, in the immediate vicinity of the Post. He soon opened a trading store and married the daughter of the Quapaws' great chief. When Leyba could not persuade the Quapaws to evict the Englishman, he invited tribal members to the fort and demonstrated its firepower. Whether Leyba meant to intimidate the Quapaws or prove his ability to protect them, it worked—they expelled the Englishman and closed his store.

British captain Philip Pittman described the Post in 1770 as a bustling military and trade center:

> The fort stands about 200 yards from the waterside and is garrisoned by a captain, a lieutenant, and 30 French soldiers, including sergeants and corporals. There are eight houses without the fort, occupied by as many families. . . . These people subsist mostly by hunting, and every season send to New Orleans great quantities of bear's oil, tallow, salted buffalo meat and a few skins.

In 1779, Commandant Balthazar de Villiers moved Arkansas Post back to Écores Rouges, probably because of the constant flooding at the mouth of the Arkansas River. The Post would remain at that location for the rest of its existence. According to de Villiers's 1779 map, there was no fort there, only thirty private dwellings: seventeen belonged to Frenchmen and thirteen to Americans who had fled the Revolution.

The American Revolution brought renewed strategic importance to Arkansas Post. The Spanish saw the Revolution as a means of recapturing their lost territory in west Florida and regaining ground with the local Indians. American forces in the area frequently rested and resupplied at the Post, even prior to Spain's declaration of war on Britain. The settlers at the Post grew increasingly wary of attacks by British-allied Chickasaws, but the Spanish had still not built a new fort. Finally, the settlers erected one themselves in 1781. De Villiers named the structure Fort Carlos III.

The attack the settlers had feared finally came on April 17, 1783, when James Colbert, a wealthy Scottish trader who had married into the Chickasaw tribe, led a party of eighty-one Chickasaws, African slaves, and European loyalists against the Post. While word of the recent peace treaty had not reached the frontier, all British troops in the area had surrendered in 1781. It is unlikely, therefore, that Colbert was acting under a British commission, as he later claimed.

Spanish authorities heard several months in advance that an attack was planned, and they increased the military presence at Fort Carlos III to two officers and sixty-seven soldiers. Although the Spanish were forewarned, Colbert's 2:30 A.M. assault caught them by surprise. The raiders killed three guards and captured several settlers outside the fort. After a lengthy battle at the walls of the stockade, ten Spanish soldiers and four Quapaws launched a counterattack meant to fool Colbert into believing that reinforcements had arrived. The bluff worked; Colbert called a retreat. According to American geographer Thomas Hutchins, who visited the following year, the raid left ten men dead and so shook the survivors that Commandant Jacobo Dubreuil was forced to buy "one cask of brandy to revive the troops [and] three rolls of tobacco to please the troops and volunteers who went in pursuit of the enemy." All the prisoners were rescued.

A Trading Center

The end of the Revolution began Arkansas Post's heyday as a trading center. In 1793 a visiting ship's captain reported that the town contained "about thirty houses with galleries around, covered with shingles, which form two streets." Just downriver the captain found an additional "dozen quite pretty houses." In 1796, a chapel was built in the town and a parish established there. By 1799, the European and African population had tripled to almost four hundred.

At the same time, the end of the war saw a decreased military presence at Fort Carlos III. The makeshift fort itself slid into the river in 1788 and needed to be rebuilt. Once again, the residents were forced to construct the fortification themselves. Raids by Osages and other tribes soon increased, however, as more American settlers began pushing into the frontier. In response, the Spanish built a new fort, called San Esteban, in the late 1790's.

Spain ceded Louisiana back to France in 1800, and the United States acquired it with the Louisiana Purchase of 1803. The U.S. Army took control of Fort San Esteban in 1804. Arkansas Post continued to grow as a trading center and frontier town. A post office was established in 1817, and the town was named the capital of the new Arkansas territory in 1819. On November 20 of that year, Post resident William Woodruff began printing the *Arkansas Gazette*, today the oldest surviving newspaper west of the Mississippi. The territory's first governor, war hero James Miller, arrived in December.

Thomas Nuttall, a naturalist who traveled down the Arkansas River in 1819, described the Post as follows:

> The town, or rather settlement of the Post of Arkansas, was somewhat dispersed over a prairie . . . and contain[ed] in all between 30 and 40 houses. The merchants, then transacting nearly all business of the Arkansas and White River . . . kept well-assorted stores of merchandize, supplied chiefly from New Orleans, with the exception of some heavy articles of domestic manufacture obtained from Pittsburgh. . . . I could not but now for awhile consider myself as once more introduced into the circle of civilization.

The Post's location, along with its floods, swampy ground, and swarms of mosquitoes, proved to be its undoing, however. Arkansas's first territorial legislature resolved that "the remoteness of this situation . . . together with its unhealthiness, forms a serious objection to the present location." Little Rock was chosen as the new capital, and the move was completed in 1821. The *Gazette* followed, an Arkansas Post began a period of decline from which it never recovered. William W. Pope, nephew and secretary to the territorial governor, surveyed the post in 1832 and found it had taken on "a very forlorn and desolate appearance . . . tall chimneys had fallen down and trees . . . were growing out through the roofs."

Role During the Civil War

Arkansas Post came to prominence for one final episode during the Civil War. In 1862, Confederate leaders saw that Little Rock was vulnerable to an advance up the Arkansas River. Arkansas Post, located on commanding bluffs, seemed an ideal spot to build defenses. Fortifications there could also harass Federal shipping on the Arkansas, White, and Mississippi Rivers. The Confederates therefore built Fort Hindman by the shores of the town. The fort was constructed as an eight-sided star, with each wall measuring three hundred feet. It was armed with three twelve-pound cannons and eight six-pounders on wheels. Approximately five thousand men garrisoned the fort, but only three thousand of these were armed and ready for battle. In

December, 1862, the fort was completed and Brigadier General Thomas J. Churchill took command. The men would not wait long to see action.

Since November, Federal forces had struggled to take Vicksburg, the last uncaptured city on the Mississippi. If they could take it, they would divide the South in two. The five thousand men at Fort Hindman posed a threat to the rear of any expedition travelling down the Mississippi toward Vicksburg. By capturing the fort, the Federals would not only eliminate this threat but would also boost troop morale, which was flagging since their early failures.

On January 4, 1863, Union general John A. McClernand issued orders to mount an assault on Fort Hindman. In addition to McClernand's force of thirty thousand men, the expedition was supported by Admiral David D. Porter's river fleet of nine gunboats. Churchill's pickets discovered the advance on the morning of January 9; he moved his three thousand effectives down to entrenchments and held the fort with his remaining men. Meanwhile, the Federals moved into position along the shore.

Around 9:00 A.M. on January 10, the Federal gunboats opened fire. Churchill soon found himself flanked by Federal cavalry and artillery, and at 2:00 he pulled back to his inner line of entrenchments. The Southerners managed to repulse a tentative ground assault that day and a combined ground and river assault that night. They inflicted heavy Federal casualties, but Fort Hindman was nearly destroyed.

When Churchill's superior, General Theophilus H. Holmes, learned of the attack, he apparently did not grasp the Federals' ten-to-one superiority. Rather than order a retreat, he sent a telegram on the night of January 10 instructing Churchill "to hold out till help arrived or until all dead." The latter seemed much more likely, especially since the main body of troops sent to reinforce Churchill was waylaid in the snow en route from Little Rock.

At 1:00 the following afternoon, January 11, 1863, Porter's gunboats and McClernand's artillery resumed fire. Half an hour later, the ground assault began. By 4:00 P.M., the Federals had destroyed all but one of the Confederates' heavy guns. Still, the Confederate ground forces held their positions, and Churchill planned to cut his way out that evening. Then, without any authorization, white flags began popping up in the Confederate ranks. The lines crumbled, and Churchill was forced to surrender the fort. In all, the Confederates counted 60 men killed, 75 or 80 wounded, and 4,791 captured; the Federals lost 134 killed, 898 wounded, and 29 missing. The battle destroyed not only Fort Hindman but most of the remaining buildings of Arkansas Post as well.

Arkansas Post Today

A tiny farming community existed here until the land was purchased by the state of Arkansas in 1929. A state park was created the following year, and in 1964 the federal government acquired the land and established the Arkansas Post National Memorial. Due to erosion from the Arkansas River, much of the original shoreline is now under water. Little remains, but visitors can follow paths marking the site where such buildings once stood. Two miles away from the memorial is the Arkansas Post County Museum, which displays artifacts from the Post's rich and varied history.   —*Robert M. Salkin*

For Further Information:

Arnold, Morris S. *Colonial Arkansas, 1686-1804: A Social and Cultural History.* Fayetteville: University of Arkansas Press, 1993. The fullest and most accurate exploration of the Post's early history.

Ashmore, Harry S. *Arkansas: A Bicentennial History.* New York: W. W. Norton, 1978. A good general history of the state and discusses most of the different phases of Arkansas Post.

Ferguson, John L., ed. *Arkansas and the Civil War.* Little Rock: Arkansas Historical Commission, 1962. For those interested in reading the actual reports submitted by the Union and Confederate commanders at the battle.

Paulson, Alan C. *Roadside History of Arkansas.* Missoula, Mont.: Mountain Press, 1998. A guidebook of historic sites and tours illustrated with photographs and maps. Includes a bibliography and an index.

Thomas, David Y. *Arkansas in War and Reconstruction, 1861-1874.* Little Rock, Ark.: United Daughters of the Confederacy, 1926. Presents a detailed, if pro-Confederate description of the Battle of Fort Hindman.

Work Projects Administration Writers' Program. *The WPA Guide to 1930's Arkansas.* Reprint. Lawrence: University Press of Kansas, 1987. Originally published in 1941 as *Arkansas: A Guide to the State*; this edition offers a new introduction by Elliott West. Contains many interesting quotations from primary sources.

Little Rock Central High School

Date: Established in 1953; previously Little Rock Senior High School

Relevant issues: African American history, cultural history, education, political history, social reform

Significance: This school was the site of early racial integration in the United States South. When the governor of Arkansas blocked the enrollment of nine black students in September, 1957, he precipitated a clash between states' rights and federal authority which attracted worldwide attention.

Location: As its name implies, in the central section of the city of Little Rock, itself located in the center of the state of Arkansas

Site Office:
Central High School
1500 Park Street
Little Rock, AR 72202
ph.: (501) 324-2300
Web site: www.lrsd.k12.ar.us/central.htm
e-mail: rxhowar@central.lrsd.k12.ar.us

Little Rock Central High School's place in United States history has been ensured by the racial crisis of 1957-1958; however, as Little Rock Senior High School, it had boasted a long and honorable tradition as one of the finest high schools in the South.

The Beginnings and Growth of Little Rock High School

The earliest schoolhouses in Little Rock were private homes converted into school buildings. After the Civil War (or the War Between the States, as it was known in Little Rock), the first schoolhouse constructed for that purpose was named Sherman School. It graduated its first class of four girls and one boy in 1873.

For a time, there was no high school separate

from the lower grades. However, a building on Capitol Avenue, constructed not long after the war on the site of an old cemetery, can be called Little Rock's first public high school. Before long, the Scott Street School was opened at Fourteenth and Scott Streets. It became the high school, and its predecessor was reduced in status to Peabody Grammar School. Throughout the remainder of the nineteenth century, the high school moved back and forth between the Scott Street and Peabody Schools as one or the other expanded its facilities. It was eventually settled at Fourteenth and Scott when, in 1905, a new one hundred thousand dollar high school was constructed on the site of the old Scott Street School. Little Rock Senior High School remained at this location for the next twenty-two years.

In 1927, Little Rock Senior (later to become Central) High School was opened at Fourteenth and Park Streets. The massive four-story building, its facade resembling a castle, was constructed at the cost of $1.5 million. It was at one time designated the most beautiful high school in America by the National Association of Architects. Its predecessor at Fourteenth and Scott became East Side Junior High School, and still later a trade school. Peabody School was eventually closed, demolished, and the Little Rock Federal Building was constructed on the site.

A Catholic high school for boys and a Catholic academy for girls had long existed in Little Rock. Dunbar High School, a high school for black students, and a small technical high school were a part of the Little Rock school system. However, until 1957, Little Rock Senior (Central) High School was the only public high school for whites in the city. By the mid-1950's, the enrollment was 2,400 students, making it by far the largest high school in Arkansas. It was also the best funded. It attracted an excellent faculty and dominated the state in athletics, especially football.

In 1953, however, plans were completed to build a second high school for whites in western Little Rock, the fastest-growing section of the city. Even though the second high school, Hall High, would not open its doors for another four years, the first high school could no longer retain the exclusive name. Little Rock Senior High School became Central High School, and the class of 1954 was the first to be graduated under that name. In time, fol-

lowing the racial integration of the schools, a third high school, Parkview, would be opened, and the former high school for black students would become an integrated junior high school. At the end of the twentieth century, Central remained the largest of the three high schools, though it would never again be so dominant as during the first half of the century.

The Crisis of 1957-1958

Five days after the United States Supreme Court ruled in 1954 that "separate but equal" public schools for black and white students were unconstitutional, the Little Rock School Board announced its intention to comply with the Court's mandate. The "Blossom Plan" (bearing the name of the district's superintendent, Virgil Blossom) was formulated, whereby the all-black schools would be continued, but grades ten through twelve would be open to black students beginning with the 1957-1958 school year. Then desegregation would proceed downward, year by year, through the junior high and elementary grades. The National Association for the Advancement of Colored People (NAACP) challenged this limited and gradual approach, but the courts ruled that it met the "deliberate speed" test enunciated by the Supreme Court.

Implementation of the plan was to begin with the opening of school on September 3, 1957. A small group of exemplary African American students was chosen by local civil rights activists to request admission to Central High School. By September 3, roughly half of those accepted had withdrawn their applications, unwilling to hazard the unknown risks of the historic enrollment. Those who remained would become famous as the "Little Rock Nine." Eight would finish the year. One, the most combative of the group, would be expelled for fighting back against harassment within the school. One, Ernest Green, would become the first black graduate of Little Rock Central High School.

When the nine appeared at Central High on the morning of September 3, they found the school closed and their way barred by Arkansas National Guardsmen. Orval Faubus, serving his second term as governor of Arkansas, went on statewide television announcing that he had taken these measures in order to protect life and property. He had, he said, received reports that a mob was going to assemble to prevent the integration of Central High by force. Federal Judge Ronald N. Davies accepted the governor's use of the National Guard, but only on the assumption that the guardsmen would protect the right of the nine to enter the high school without interference.

Three weeks passed, and Governor Faubus continued to use armed troops to prevent the black students from attending school. Unruly mobs did gather in front of the school, and several ugly incidents occurred, although no one was killed or seriously injured. Journalists from the major newspapers, news magazines, and television networks gathered in Little Rock to report on the conflict between the state power being asserted by the governor and the constitutional mandate he was opposing. On September 24, President Dwight D. Eisenhower responded. He called all members of the Arkansas National Guard to active duty; thus, they were immediately made members of the United States Army and were no longer under the governor's control. President Eisenhower also dispatched a detachment of the 101st Airborne Infantry to ensure the entry of the Little Rock Nine into Central High and to maintain order around the school. By early October, the paratroopers were withdrawn to nearby Camp Robinson to be replaced by national guardsmen.

The 1957-1958 academic year was the unhappiest in the history of the school. Governor Faubus claimed that the federal government was conducting a military occupation of Arkansas, and many segregationist sympathizers supported his claim. Little Rock Central High School, the community of Little Rock, and the state of Arkansas received negative publicity almost daily around the world. Recurring incidents of harassment of the black students—most verbal but some physical—were documented throughout the year. Still, eight of the nine finished the year, and racial integration had become a fact at Little Rock Central High School.

Little Rock Central High School. (Arkansas Department of Parks & Tourism/Tim Schick)

The Aftermath of the Crisis

All three Little Rock public high schools were closed from 1958-1959. Students were forced to gain admittance to a private school or move to another city to attend a public high school. Those who were to be seniors had to earn their diplomas somewhere else. The schools were reopened the following year, and two more African Americans were graduated from Central High in 1960. Only three of the Little Rock Nine completed their secondary education with their respective classes at Central High—the others went on to receive their high school diplomas elsewhere, and most earned university degrees.

Orval Faubus was reelected to a third two-year term as governor of Arkansas in 1958. He was subsequently reelected to three more terms, serving until January, 1967. Faubus's political opponents accused him of adopting his obstructionist stance at Central High School purely for short-term political advantage. He was for a time widely popular in the South but was generally viewed negatively outside the region. After leaving office, he spent the rest of his life attempting to rehabilitate his reputation, arguing, both in person and in print, that his actions in 1957-1958 were not racist but were principled given the circumstances he faced at the time. The *Arkansas Gazette*, which had supported the racial integration at Central High and had opposed the governor's actions throughout the crisis, was awarded the Pulitzer Prize for its coverage.

Under an order from the federal court, the Little Rock school district instituted a citywide busing program designed to achieve racial balance in every school and, by the 1970's, the district was largely integrated. In 1980, half the student body and a third of the faculty at Central High School were African American. By the 1990's, the enrollment featured a solid black majority. At the end of the twentieth century, the Central High School enrollment numbered 1,850 students, some 550 fewer than in the mid-1950's, but Central continued to lead all Arkansas high schools in scholastic honors, including National Merit Scholarships.

In 1977, Central High School marked the twentieth anniversary of its desegregation with an assembly at which the principal speaker was Ernest Green, its first black graduate. In 1997, on the occasion of the fortieth anniversary of the crisis, an elaborate ceremony was held on the school's front lawn. The president of the United States and the governor of Arkansas spoke, and several of the Little Rock Nine were in attendance. Across the street from Central High, on the site formerly occupied by a gasoline station where students often lounged before and after school, a small museum was established. The museum, dedicated to the desegregation crisis of 1957-1958, contains photographs and other memorabilia from that turbulent year.

—Patrick Adcock

For Further Information:

Bates, Daisy. *The Long Shadow of Little Rock: A Memoir.* New York: David McKay, 1962. The account of a civil rights leader intimately involved in the Central High crisis.

Faubus, Orval Eugene. *Down from the Hills.* Little Rock, Ark.: Pioneer, 1980. In his review of his six terms in office (spanning from 1955 to 1967), the former governor argues his side of the Central High crisis.

Graves, John William. *Town and Country: Race Relations in an Urban-Rural Context, Arkansas, 1865-1905.* Fayetteville: University of Arkansas Press, 1990. Examines the establishment and evolution of the segregation laws, most of which were still in effect in 1957. Argues that, ironically, Arkansas—especially in urban areas—had been one of the most progressive southern states in desegregating its people.

Huckaby, Elizabeth. *Crisis at Central High: Little Rock, 1957-58.* Baton Rouge: Louisiana State University Press, 1980. A memoir of the school year, written by the vice principal for girls.

Lester, Jim, and Judy Lester. *Greater Little Rock.* Norfolk, Va.: Donning, 1986. Central High appears throughout this history of the city, both in text and photographs.

Reed, Roy. *Faubus: The Life and Times of an American Prodigal.* Fayetteville: University of Arkansas Press, 1997. Chapters 16 through 20 deal specifically with the Central High crisis and its immediate aftermath.

Other Historic Sites

Bathhouse Row

Location: Hot Springs, Garland County

Relevant issues: Cultural history, health and medicine

Statement of significance: This, the largest grouping of bathhouses in the country, illustrates the popularity of the spa movement in the United States during the nineteenth and twentieth centuries. It is also an excellent collection of turn-of-the-century eclectic buildings in the Neoclassical, Renaissance Revival, Spanish, and Italianate styles. The hot springs are the resource for which the area was set aside as the first federal recreational reserve in 1832.

Camden Expedition Sites

Location: Little Rock, Pulaski County

Relevant issues: Civil War, military history

Statement of significance: The Camden expedition (March 23-May 2, 1864) involved Union forces stationed at Little Rock and Fort Smith under the command of Major General Frederick Steele. The plan called for Steele's force to march to Shreveport, Louisiana, where it would link up with an amphibious expedition led by Major General Nathaniel P. Banks and Rear Admiral David D. Porter, whose force was to advance up the Red River Valley; once joined, the Union force was to strike into Texas. The two pincers never converged, however, and Steele's columns suffered terrible losses in a series of battles with Confederate forces led by Major General Sterling Price and General Edmund Kirby Smith.

Fort Smith

Location: Fort Smith, Sebastian County

Relevant issues: Western expansion

Statement of significance: Established in 1817 near the confluence of the Arkansas and Poteau Rivers, the first fort at this site was among the earliest U.S. military posts in Missouri Territory. The fort's purpose was to control the encroachment into Osage lands by both the Cherokee and westward-moving American settlers. The second fort, begun in 1838 a short distance from the site of the first, was garrisoned until the U.S. District Court for the Western District of Arkansas moved to the town of Fort Smith in 1871.

Old State House, Little Rock

Location: 300 West Markham, Little Rock, Pulaski County

Relevant issues: Health and medicine, social reform

Statement of significance: From 1912 to 1916, the Arkansas State Board of Health, in partnership with the University of Arkansas Medical School, worked from this building on successful campaigns to control or eradicate hookworm, a scourge of the South, and malaria, a disease that plagued much of the planet. Arkansas's drive against malaria was a model of success, long acclaimed in the history of public health, which was used to eradicate malaria in the rest of the United States and the world. From the town of Crossett, Arkansas, the office of the surgeon general distributed nationwide a full report of the Crossett experiment as Public Health Bulletin No. 88, and this detailed description became the formula for sanitation workers around the world.

Rohwer Relocation Center Cemetery

Location: Rohwer, Desha County

Relevant issues: Asian American history, political history, World War II

Statement of significance: Rohwer Relocation Camp was constructed in the late summer and early fall of 1942 as a result of Executive Order 9066 (February 16, 1942). Under this order, over 110,000 Japanese aliens and Japanese Americans were relocated from the three Pacific coast states—California, Oregon, and Washington. In all, ten relocation camps were established in desolate sites, all chosen for their distance from the Pacific coast. Over ten thousand evacuees passed through Rohwer during its existence, and over two-thirds of these were American citizens. The monuments found within the camp's cemetery are perhaps the most poignant record of this time.

Toltec Mounds Site

Location: Scott, Lonoke County

Relevant issues: American Indian history

Statement of significance: A large ceremonial complex and village site, Toltec Mounds represents the northhernmost occupation during the Coles Creek Period (c. 700-1000 C.E.) and may yield information about the interaction between Lower and Central Mississippi Valley cultures. It is part of Toltec Mounds Archaeological State Park.

California

The State Capitol Building in Sacramento. (Digital Stock)

History of California. 86
Alcatraz Island 89
Angelus Temple, Los
    Angeles 93
Chinatown, San Francisco. . . . 95
Columbia 102
Death Valley. 105
Donner Camp, Truckee 108
El Pueblo de Los Angeles . . . 111
Golden Gate Bridge 115
Haight-Ashbury, San
    Francisco 119
Hearst Castle 122
Hollywood 125
John Muir National
    Historic Site. 130
Little Tokyo, Los Angeles . . . 133
Los Angeles Memorial
    Coliseum 136
Manzanar 140
Mission Basilica San Diego
    de Alcalá. 143
Mission San Gabriel
    Arcángel. 147
Mission San Juan
    Capistrano 151
Monterey 154
Nixon Birthplace,
    Yorba Linda 159
Presidio, San Francisco. 162
San Diego Presidio 165
Sonoma 169
Sutter's Fort. 173
Sutter's Mill 178
Watts 182
Other Historic Sites 186

History of California

To a much greater extent than in other states, California is a naturally defined region with a distinct history of its own. Its differences begin with its natural geography. Bounded by the Pacific Ocean on the west and the Sierra Madre range along the east, California had limited contacts with the outside world until the mid-nineteenth century. Until then, little was known about its abundant natural resources beyond the fact it had an equable climate and fertile land.

An estimated 300,000 Native Americans inhabited the region before Europeans arrived. Though they were among the most numerous and prosperous Indian societies in North America, most of them lived outside the main currents of Native American history. Compared to many cultures outside California, their culture was simple. Metallurgy, pottery, intensive cultivation, horses, and draft animals were all unknown to them. With economies based mostly on fishing, hunting, and gathering, they nevertheless achieved comparatively high levels of prosperity and lived largely peaceful lives.

Early Exploration

European contact with California began in 1542, when the Spanish navigator Juan Rodríguez Cabrillo found San Diego Bay. English navigator Francis Drake followed thirty-seven years later, when he reached Northern California. Little came out of these early explorations. Busy colonizing Mexico, Spain paid little attention to the California region over the next two centuries. Permanent European interest in the region finally began in the late eighteenth century, when Spain authorized members of the Franciscan order to build a chain of mission stations up the California coast. Father Junipero Serra founded California's first mission at San Diego in 1769; twenty other mission stations followed over the next fifty-four years.

During those years California was nominally a Spanish colony, but the government exercised only light control, and the burden of imposing European culture on California's peoples was left to the Franciscans. The missionaries began systematic agricultural development and gathered Indian communities around their mission stations. Meanwhile, Russian traders established posts north of the mission chain without interference. After a half century of formal Spanish colonization, the non-Indian residents of California numbered only about 3,300—a fraction of the number of Indians.

Mexican Rule

By this time, Spain was losing its hold on its New World empire and Mexico was in open revolt. When Mexico won its independence from Spain in 1821, and California's Spanish governor peacefully recognized Mexican rule, and California became a Mexican province. Mexico then followed Spain's example by taking little active interest in the region until the early 1830's, when it began secularizing California's mission stations and distributing titles to large blocs of land among favored families. In 1837 the Mexican government granted California's administration a large measure of autonomy, continuing California's tradition of comparative isolation.

Secularization was a disaster to the Indian communities attached to the former mission stations. The departure of the Franciscans left the Indians at the mercy of private landlords, who had little interest in their welfare. Most of the Indians left the missions for their original homes, where harsh economic conditions and European diseases reduced their numbers greatly. By the turn of the twentieth century their numbers fell to their lowest level ever—about fifteen thousand people, about one-twentieth their precolonial number.

By the early 1840's, Americans hungry for land and new opportunities were moving west and settling in California. Conflicts soon arose between these new, non-Spanish-speaking residents and the established Spanish and Mexican settlers, known as *Californios*. Soon, the U.S. government was taking an interest in the region, which it feared might be occupied by Great Britain or Russia. In 1845 it instructed its consul in Monterey to promote local interest in annexation to the United States. The following year, disgruntled American settlers in

Northern California found an excuse for rebelling against the Mexican regime and proclaimed an independent republic in Sonoma—a short-lived rebellion known as the Bear Flag Revolt, after the flag the rebels used.

For reasons largely unrelated to California, the United States declared war against Mexico in 1846. Placed under military rule by Mexico, California played a small role in the Mexican-American War. The Mexican government surrendered California to the United States when John C. Frémont arrived with an occupation force in 1847. In the peace accord that followed, Mexico formally ceded California, along with most of what became the American Southwest, to the United States. California officially became an American territory in early 1848;

however, its territorial status was short-lived. Two years later, before its territorial government was fully organized, California entered the Union as a state. Its rapid transition to statehood owed much to an unexpected and spectacular event that fundamentally changed the region's future: the discovery of gold near Sacramento.

The Gold Rush and Statehood

Scarcely a week before the treaty ending the Mexican-American War was signed, news of the discovery of gold in Northern California became public, and the seeds of one of the world's great gold rushes began. The effect the gold rush had on California would be difficult to overstate. Within a matter of only a few years, California was transformed from a sleepy backwater to perhaps the fastest-growing economy in the world. Hundreds of thousands of people poured into the state from the East and other parts of the world. Within ten years California's non-Indian population rose from less than ten thousand to several hundred thousands. Meanwhile, San Francisco grew from little more than a village to a booming metropolitan center offering virtually every service and amenity available in big eastern cities and controlling the commerce of the West Coast.

The multitudes who rushed to California dreamed of striking it rich from mineral wealth; however, the real fortunes made there grew mostly out of the many enterprises that arose to support the gold industry. Great profits were made in agriculture, retail trade, transportation, and countless other industries and services. For the first time, agriculture was undertaken on a large scale. As the gold rush made food production a critical priority, the agricultural potential of California's great Central Valley was finally recognized. Eventually, California's agricultural production would not only lead the nation but also reach a level exceeded by only a handful of nations in the world.

The gold rush peaked during the early 1850's; by 1861, when the Civil War began, the rush was essentially over. Nevertheless, California's economy continued to expand. The war interrupted commerce with the eastern United States but actually helped the local economy. Once again isolated from the East, California had to diversify its production to make up for what it could not import.

Pro-Unionists outnumbered Confederate sympathizers within California, but the state played no direct role in the war.

Communications

When California attained statehood in 1850, it was separated from the rest of the states by the Central Plains, Rocky Mountains, and arid Southwest. With people and goods arriving at increasing rates, cheaper and more rapid transportation became a paramount need. With overland travel slow and expensive, much of the goods and people reaching the state came by ship—by way of Central America. In 1860 the Pony Express was begun to speed mail service between California and the East. It lasted little more than a year—but only because it was displaced by transcontinental telegraph service. Completion of the first transcontinental railroad in 1869 linked California's capital, Sacramento, with St. Joseph, Missouri. These new links with the East were major steps in ending California's isolation.

With the building of the railway and the end of the Civil War, California settled down to a period of steady growth and development. Settlers continued to pour in from the East, doubling the state's population every decade—a rate of growth that continued through the twentieth century. As the proportion of European Americans rose, their tolerance for other immigrants diminished and racially discriminatory laws were passed. Particular targets of white intolerance were the thousands of Chinese workers who had come to California to help build the railroads. Most of these people stayed working at low-paying jobs shunned by whites, who pressed the state government to legislate against Asians.

Agricultural production grew and diversified until California led the nation in production in the late 1940's. Meanwhile, other industries arose to contribute to the state's growing economy. In 1895 oil was discovered in Southern California, just as the invention of motor-driven automobiles was creating new demand for petroleum products. Through the first four decades of the twentieth century, California led all states in oil production.

Most of California's early development occurred in the northern part of the state. During the twentieth century, the balance shifted to the south, where such new industries as petrochemicals, aeronautics, and entertainment attracted new immigrants from the East. By 1920 most of the state's residents lived in southern counties. However, its bicameral legislative system left the balance of political power in the north. With most water resources also in the north, supplying water to the largely arid south became a critical issue in state politics. Correction of the political imbalance finally came during the early 1960's, after a U.S. Supreme Court decision forced reapportionment of the state legislature. By this time, California ranked as the most populous state in the nation.

Over the next three decades, a central issue in state politics was the changing composition of the population. Opposition to immigrants of all kinds is an issue with roots going back to the late nineteenth century. During the Great Depression of the 1930's, for example, the state tried, unsuccessfully to keep out swarms of poor farmers fleeing the drought-stricken Midwest. After World War II, Californians became alarmed by the rising influx of Mexicans seeking higher-paying jobs—particularly in agriculture. Immigration from Asia, Mexico, and Central America grew through the rest of the twentieth century, making California the most multicultural state in the Union.

—*R. Kent Rasmussen*

Alcatraz Island

Date: Fort built in 1858
Relevant issues: American Indian history, cultural history
Significance: This was the site of the first U.S. fort on the Pacific coast. It was used as a federal maximum-security prison between 1934 and 1963, occupied repeatedly by Native American groups between 1964 and 1971, and absorbed into the Golden Gate National Recreation Area, a National Park, in 1972.
Location: An island one and a half miles from the city of San Francisco
Site Office:
Golden Gate National Recreation Area
Fort Mason, Building 201
San Francisco, CA 94123
ph.: (415) 556-0560
Web site: www.nps.gov/alcatraz/

It is nothing more than a desolate island, a chunk of rock jutting out of the San Francisco Bay. It is frequently shrouded in fog, buffeted by strong winds, and surrounded by icy water. For the most part, it is inhospitable to life, be it plant, animal, or human. Yet it has always been coveted by one group or another, serving as a fort, a military prison, a federal penitentiary, a haven for renegade Native Americans, and a National Park site. Known to all who have occupied it as the Rock, Alcatraz Island has played a significant and rich role in U.S. history.

Discovery
Who exactly discovered the island is a mystery, but it was named by a lieutenant in the Royal Spanish Navy. As he sailed into the bay, he observed that the island was covered with pelicans, so he aptly named it Isla de los Alcatraces (island of the pelicans).

The earliest American interest in the island came in 1853, when the U.S. Congress appropriated half a million dollars for the defense of the San Francisco Harbor. Despite the harsh conditions, Alcatraz was a natural harbor barrier and thus was chosen as the site for the first U.S. fort guarding the Pacific coast. During the fort's construction in 1854, a lighthouse was built to help ships navigating the dangerous waters. By 1858, the fort was completed, and although it was modern and strong for the times, it would never be needed to repel an enemy. Gradually, Alcatraz began receiving military prisoners, acting as a stockade and sometimes a sanitarium. It would serve as a military prison for many of the years from 1860 to 1933.

An Island Prison
During the 1930's, America was feeling the effects of a wave of gangster-run crime. Criminals such as Al Capone and George "Machine Gun" Kelly were at the height of their influence, and prison breaks were common and often deadly to guards and prisoners caught in the cross fire. U.S. Attorney General Homer Cummings needed a way to control the crime wave and the deteriorating conditions in the penal system. His solution came when he heard about Alcatraz.

Cummings believed that by converting the island into a maximum-security federal prison, he could move the worst of America's criminals out of other U.S. jails and right the failing system. So, the

Alcatraz. (Digital Stock)

good behavior merely returned them to the normal prison system. Alcatraz was truly a place for the hopeless.

The Inmates Arrive

Alcatraz was ready to receive prisoners by the late summer of 1934—among them were Al Capone and Machine Gun Kelly. Capone's arrival was eagerly awaited by the media, their interest fueled by stories that he ruled his notorious criminal empire from his cell at the Atlanta Penitentiary. In time, the papers would learn that the Rock could handle even Capone. He was relatively docile during his imprisonment there, in part, perhaps, because his syphilis had entered its final stages. He was transferred off the island in 1939.

When prisoners arrived, they found a fortress. There were three levels of singular cells, broken up into B, C, and D Blocks. (The fourth block of cells, A Block, was never renovated and was rarely used.) The prisoner rose at 6:30 A.M., and during the day ate three meals and served two work details. Lockdown occurred at 5:30 P.M., and lights-out was at 9:30. Monotony was the way of life.

Johnston did provide the convicts with one amenity: good food. The food at the Rock was known as the best in any prison. Johnston believed a well-fed convict was a good convict, less likely to stir up trouble. If a convict did misbehave, he would wind up in D Block, better known as the Hole, for a period of time determined by his offense. Each cell in the Hole was windowless, with nothing but four walls and a cold concrete floor to sleep on. If a convict was held there, he was given only four slices of bread per day and had no outside contact with anyone else for any reason. As elsewhere in the prison, offenders held in the Hole had to work their way back into normal prison life with good behavior.

The life of guards at Alcatraz was also difficult and monotonous. The prison was designed to be staffed by 110 people, but the figure was usually held to 100 to keep costs down. Because of other factors such as days off or sick days, only 75 men on average worked at any one time. To cover the nu-

Bureau of Prisons assumed command of the island and poured $260,000 into the renovation of the facility. Additional guard towers were built. Fences were erected and looped with barbed wire. Extra metal detectors, gun galleries, and checkpoints were added, making Alcatraz the most state-of-the-art prison of its day. Alcatraz's strategic position made it virtually escape-proof, according to new warden James A. Johnston. Even if a convict could make it through the fortress, swimming against the strong current in the ice-cold bay would be impossible. Escapees, if not caught, would either freeze or drown.

Johnston, a lifetime prison man who was known for his humanitarian side, did a complete about-face in his preparation of Alcatraz. The plan for prisoners' lives was extremely harsh. Convicts were not allowed newspapers, magazines, or radio. There was no prison store for candy, playing cards, or other diversions. Only one visitor was allowed per month, and that visit was limited to a two-hour phone conversation through a heavy pane of glass. Finally, an order of silence was imposed—convicts were not to speak to one another. (By 1939 the order of silence was repealed, as it was too difficult for guards to enforce.)

To land in Alcatraz, convicts had to earn it. No man could be sentenced directly to the Rock; only those who had caused trouble in other prisons were sent there as part of an additional sentence. Neither could prisoners be paroled from Alcatraz;

merous checkpoints, towers, and gun galleries, officials were forced to work long and lonely hours and make frequent counts and searches, which took place every time a large movement of prisoners occurred.

Escape Attempts

The prisoners' monotonous lives bred attempts at escape, while the guards became more lax, believing over time that no man could ever escape the confines. Prison rules eased as well; convicts were allowed to subscribe to magazines, see films four times a year, and check out books from a nine thousand-volume library. The relatively relaxed atmosphere spawned fifteen recorded escape attempts in the twenty-nine-year history of the prison. Of those, all ended with the convicts' deaths or their return for a long stay in the Hole, with the notable exception of one attempt that has become a legend.

Frank Lee Morris was a convicted bank robber who earned himself a place on the Rock with a series of unsuccessful escape attempts from the Atlanta Penitentiary. Brothers John and Clarence Anglin came to Alcatraz after stowing away in bakery boxes to be shipped out of Leavenworth, Kansas. With Morris's brains (he had a tested IQ of 133) and the Anglins' brawn, they devised and executed an escape that has never been solved.

The Morris-Anglin escape was the culmination of a year of planning involving many facets and the cooperation of other convicts. More notable was the lax security that allowed the three to smuggle tools past metal detectors to their cells. Spoons, files, and a sort of mechanical drill made out of a fan blade were all sneaked past the guards. The men used the tools to chip away at the concrete holding the air grates in their cells in place. To drown out the chipping sounds, other prisoners played their musical instruments; after the allotted one hour of instrument playing, the conspirators filled in their new holes with a plaster substitute made from wet cardboard.

On June 12, 1962, the full plan was ready for action. The grates had been removable for some time; roughly once a week, the three would leave their cells and climb up to the roof to prepare other necessary items. To fool the guards who walked past the cells hourly, they had made human-like heads out of papier-mâché with real hair collected by one of the Anglins, who worked in the barber shop. For flotation, they constructed water wings out of raincoats that the other Anglin had collected from his stint in the clothing shop.

Following the 9:30 P.M. guard check, the men left their cells for the final time. They made their way through the catwalks and up to the roof to get the rest of their gear. Somehow, they then avoided the searchlights and climbed two fences without being discovered. The men paddled away, never to be heard from again.

Their escape was not discovered until 7:15 the next morning. Their ten-hour head start was enough for them to reach shore, if they had not drowned. An area-wide manhunt began but yielded little in the way of hard evidence. Five days after the escape, an army boat found the only clue traceable to the trio, a small plastic bag containing photographs of Clarence Anglin and his relatives. Prison officials claimed the men must have drowned, but rumors circulated through the prison that they may have survived. No one is sure to this day.

Six months later, doubt about the security of the Rock again surfaced when two more convicts escaped out a basement window and walked across the island. One was recaptured immediately, but the other, using water wings made of rubber gloves, was able to paddle across the bay. Though he passed out from exhaustion upon reaching the shore near the Golden Gate Bridge and was also recaptured, his experience proved that someone could make it across the water to safety, fueling even more speculation about the possible success of the Morris-Anglin escape.

Alcatraz Prison Closes

Though no one could prove or deny that Morris or the Anglins survived, the Bureau of Prisons made it clear that their possible success signaled the end of Alcatraz as a prison. There had been rumors of the closing of Alcatraz for years due to the high cost of running the prison and its limited capacity. In January, 1962, it cost $5.27 per day to keep a prisoner in an average prison: In Alcatraz, that figure rose to $13.81. To guard a prisoner at an average prison ran $4.00; at Alcatraz, $9.69. Everything cost more at the Rock—food and even fresh water had to be brought in on a daily basis. The salty sea air had taken its toll on the prison's structural soundness as well. The diesel plant was giving out, the pipes were corroding, and the walls were crumbling—a factor that had contributed to the ease with which Morris and the Anglins chipped through. In 1961, the Bureau of Prisons spent $300,000 to do needed repairs, but a report said it would take nearly $4 million to restore the prison fully.

At the same time as Alcatraz's demise, a new maximum-security facility was being constructed at Marion, Illinois. The new prison would be less costly to run, hold more prisoners, and not involve the same day-to-day hassles of operation. Alcatraz was deemed a waste of money and time and was slated to close in December, 1963. Following the escapes in 1962 and 1963, the date was moved up; the last prisoners left the island on March 21, 1963, and the prison was officially closed and abandoned in June, ending more than one hundred years of prison history on the island.

American Indian Occupations

About a year after the abandonment of Alcatraz by the federal government, perhaps the most unusual period in the history of the island began. Local groups of various Native American tribes began landing on the Rock, trying to take it as their own in the hopes of constructing a cultural and learning center. Four landings in all took place, one resulting in the occupation of the island by "Indians of all Tribes" for nineteen months from 1969 to 1971.

The first landing was designed by a local group of Sioux Indians who primarily wanted to prove a political and legal point. In the 1860's, the Sioux had concluded a treaty with the American government that permitted nonreservation Native Americans to claim any land that the government had taken for its use and later abandoned. The treaty remained to that day, and local Native Americans wanted to see if it was still valid. A forty-person party set out for the island in 1964 by boat and landed on Alcatraz. Although the island's caretaker allowed them to land, the acting warden showed up soon after with federal marshals who escorted the Sioux off the island after only a four-hour stay. Some saw the landing as nothing more than a bizarre stunt, but it was covered by the local media as yet another example of broken promises by the government to the Native Americans. The Sioux had accomplished their goal.

No further landings were attempted by Native Americans until 1969, when the local Indian cultural center burned to the ground under mysterious circumstances. Without a home, the groups turned to Alcatraz as their new site, determined to make the government keep its promise. On November 9, 1969, a large group of Native Americans attempted to land on the island, but when the captain of the boat discovered their motive, he refused to approach the docks. A few tried to swim for it, and one actually made it, but all were picked up by the U.S. Coast Guard.

A second try was launched a few days later, with a little more success. Fourteen Native Americans were able to land on a night mission to the island and successfully hide from searches conducted by U.S. Coast Guard and other federal officials for nearly twenty-four hours. The visitors eventually surrendered and were returned to the mainland.

The third and final attempt on November 20 was the most successful. Nearly ninety Native Americans set sail for the island at 3 A.M. from Sausalito, California, and successfully reached the dock. Previous attempts had been covered extensively by the media, and by this time public sentiment had swung toward the side of the Native Americans. With a larger group landing this time, local officials were under pressure to find a good reason to remove them.

Over the next nineteen months, government officials tried everything they could to drive the Native Americans from the island. A water barge that traveled back and forth between the mainland and the island was taken out of service; with it went the largest source of fresh water for the residents. When electrical power failed, the U.S. Coast Guard sent men to fix the backup generators, but these men instead removed vital parts from the generators, rendering them useless. Another generator was supplied, but it burned to the ground mysteriously, with both residents and officials blaming each other. Still, the Native Americans would not leave.

The reason the government gave for finally ejecting the Native Americans was itself bizarre. Throughout the occupation, Federal Bureau of Investigation (FBI) agents kept the island under surveillance from the shore. When the Bureau of Prisons had abandoned the island, they removed everything of value, except for large bales of copper wire that were left buried. When the Native Americans found this wire, they dug it up and sold it as scrap to make six hundred dollars. Government officials classified this act as theft of federal property and sent armed marshals to the island to escort all residents off on June 11, 1971. The Native Americans would never return again.

Alcatraz Today

In 1972, the island was absorbed into the Golden Gate National Recreation Area, a National Park. Visitors ferried from the San Francisco shore can examine what remains of the old prison and grounds as well as learn about prison history and some of the famous convicts who lived in the cell blocks. The site is an extremely popular tourist attraction, continuing the mysterious fascination with what has always been so much more than just a forbidding chunk of rock.   —*Tony Jaros*

For Further Information:

Babjak, Jolene. *Eyewitness on Alcatraz.* Berkeley, Calif.: Ariel Vamp Press, 1988. Told from the point of view of a prison official's daughter living at the prison during its heyday.

Fortunate, Adam. *Eagle in Alcatraz! Alcatraz!* Berkeley, Calif.: Heyday Books, 1992. Examines the Native American occupation of 1969 to 1971 and other attempts.

Godwin, John. *Alcatraz, 1868-1963.* New York: Doubleday, 1961. An overview of prison history, paying special attention to the prisoners who were incarcerated at Alcatraz.

Presnall, Judith Janda. *Life on Alcatraz.* San Diego: Lucent Books, 2000. Discusses the prison on Alcatraz Island, otherwise known as "The Rock." Describes the cell house, the routine of prison life, inmates' leisure time, breaking prison rules, employee and family life, closing Alcatraz prison, and the island's future roles.

Angelus Temple, Los Angeles

Date: Opened on January 1, 1923
Relevant issues: Art and architecture, cultural history, religion, women's history

Significance: From 1923 until 1944, the Angelus Temple served as the international headquarters of the renowned evangelist Aimee Semple McPherson. Both her impressive preaching style and the stunning architecture of the edifice made the temple an instant tourist attraction.

Location: Eight miles from downtown Los Angeles, directly across from Echo Park at the northeast corner of Glendale Boulevard and Park Avenue

Site Office:
Angelus Temple
1100 Glendale Boulevard
Los Angeles, CA 90026
ph.: (213) 484-1000
fax: (213) 484-1703

The impressive Angelus Temple is both a monument to the United States' best-known female evangelist, Aimee Semple McPherson (1890-1944), and a major milestone in contemporary architecture.

An Evangelist

Born near Ingersoll, Ontario, Canada, on October 9, 1890, Aimee Elizabeth Kennedy was dramatically converted at age seventeen by a Pentecostal preacher, Robert James Semple. Aimee "shouted and sang and laughed and talked in tongues" and also married Semple. Ordained at Durham's North Avenue Mission in Chicago in 1909, Aimee left with her husband to evangelize China. Robert Semple died of malaria in Hong Kong in August, 1910. A month later their daughter, Roberta, was born. Ill and depressed, Aimee returned to America.

With the return of her health, Aimee Semple turned to revivalism. Within five years she toured the United States eight times, holding forty revivals in tents, tabernacles, and theaters. In Denver alone she drew twelve thousand auditors per night for a month to the coliseum. Her "old time religion" was joined with the newest technology. She rode in a "gospel automobile," preached from airplanes (which dropped tracts over the town), and spoke on the radio. A "woman preacher" at a time when few denominations ordained females (women gained the right to vote in 1920), Sister Aimee broke the gender barrier and also the racial barrier by holding integrated services in Key West, Florida. Her busy ministry led to the failure of her second

Angelus Temple. (Doug Long)

marriage to grocer Harold McPherson. From that union, which lasted from 1919 to 1921, Aimee's son and successor, Rolf, was born.

A Vision
Shortly after World War I, Sister Aimee settled in Southern California. Responding to a "vision," she selected a site eight miles from downtown Los Angeles for her Angelus Temple. Located at 1100 Glendale Boulevard at Park Avenue, it stood at the northwest end of famed Echo Park (where McPherson planted the lovely Oriental lotuses). Eleven mules, scrapers, and drivers joined her at the groundbreaking for what would become a very stunning building.

Critics contended it was a copy of the Mormon Tabernacle in Salt Lake City, Utah. McPherson maintained it was a "dream." Architect A. F. Leicht drew up the blueprints. Many were surprised that the building was not square (to match her Foursquare Gospel Church) but circular. The circle drew on primal symbolism for "inclusivity," "continuity," and "eternity." "Will the Circle Be Unbroken?" was one of Sister Aimee's favorite songs. The dome reminded one of classical temples such as the Pantheon and the Hagia Sophia and of such national monuments as the Capitol in Washington, D.C. When completed, the Angelus Temple was the largest unsupported dome in North America.

At an accessible location, with an aesthetically pleasing appearance, the temple was honest in the use of contemporary materials. Sister Aimee was persuaded that cement was the building material of the future. It was a stroke of genius to combine a modern medium (concrete) with an ancient symbol (the circle) to create one of America's greatest churches. It opened on January 1, 1923.

A Ministry
The Angelus Temple was an instant tourist attraction. Daily tours had to be offered from 9:30 A.M. until 4:30 P.M. Four thousand people visited each month. Many more came to worship at the four daily and three Sunday services. Though Sister Aimee never advertised, all fifty-three hundred seats were occupied long before she preached. Powerful music was provided by a massive organ that simulated the tones of forty musical instruments. Massed choirs, a brass band, and an orchestra (with marimba group) completed the ministry of music. The sanctuary was enhanced with a series of stained glass windows surveying the story of Jesus. Under a gigantic American flag was a mural of the Second Coming of Jesus, one of McPherson's "Four Points," the Returning King. Displays of discarded canes, crutches, and braces affirmed her doctrine of Jesus as the Healer. Eloquent preaching and reverent use of the ordinances showed Christ as Savior. Many marveled that Communion could be served to fifty-three hundred people at one sitting within fifteen minutes without any "semblance of haste or confusion." Some eight thousand people came to the altar during the temple's first eight months of operation. Christ as Baptizer was shown in the Thursday night immersion services and in the presence of "spiritual gifts."

A Fundamentalist reply to the "institutional church" of liberal Christianity, the temple never closed. "The lights never go out at the Angelus Temple," insisted Sister Aimee. A prayer tower, opened in 1923, offered intercessions without ceasing. The same year the Lighthouse of International Foursquare Evangelism (LIFE), a Bible school, began, as did the radio station Kall Foursquare Gospel (KFSG), the third-oldest in Los Angeles and the first operated by a church. There was also "children's church" (with youngsters both attending and leading), a music conservatory, an employment agency, and a commissary that fed and clothed a million people during the Great Depression. The temple grounds also had a publishing house (McPherson wrote eighty hymns and five sacred operas and edited two periodicals), Sister Aimee's home, and a bookstore with a roof garden. The complex also was the headquarters of the Foursquare Gospel denomination, which had a membership of two million people in 2000.

Conclusion

Sister Aimee's life was filled with controversy. A third marriage failed. At one time she faced forty-six lawsuits. During the 1920's, she disappeared for five weeks, allegedly "kidnapped." In the 1930's, there was a leadership struggle that pitted McPherson against her mother and daughter. By the 1940's, Sister Aimee had weathered the storm—and the temple ministry was vital. On September 27, 1944, while in Oakland, California, to dedicate a new church, the famed evangelist died of an accidental overdose of barbiturates. Services were held at the Angelus Temple with burial following in Forest Lawn Memorial Park, Glendale, California.

Though the founder died, the Angelus Temple's ministry remained vital and became a fundamental part of the religious community in Southern California, as well as a major tourist attraction.

—*C. George Fry*

For Further Information:

Blumhofer, Edith L. *The Assemblies of God: A Chapter in the Story of American Pentecostalism*. Springfield, Mo.: Gospel Publishing House, 1989. Volume 1, *To 1941*, offers an excellent account of McPherson's role within the broader Pentecostal movement.

Durasoff, Steve. *Bright Wind of the Spirit: Pentecostalism Today*. Englewood Cliffs, N.J.: Prentice Hall, 1972. A moving narrative of McPherson's public ministry.

Gebhard, David, and Robert Winter. *Architecture in Los Angeles: A Compleat Guide*. Layton, Utah: Peregrine Smith Bodes, 1985. A succinct, illustrated guide to the buildings of Los Angeles. The photographic consultant was Julius Shulman.

McLoughlin, William A. "Aimee Semple McPherson." In *Notable American Women: A Biographical Dictionary*, edited by Edward T. James. Vol. 2. Cambridge, Mass.: The Belknap Press of Harvard University Press, 1971. A concise and complete life of McPherson by a recognized authority on revivalism.

Moore, Charles, and Peter Becker. *The City Observed: Los Angeles, a Guide to Its Architecture and Landscape*. New York: Random House, 1984. Provides an excellent survey of the neighborhood in which the Angelus Temple is located. Photographs by Regula Campbell.

Rolle, Andrew. *Los Angeles: From Pueblo to City of the Future*. San Francisco: Boyd and Fraser Publishing Company, 1981. A brief but helpful introduction to the history of Los Angeles.

Weaver, John D. *Los Angeles: The Enormous Village, 1781-1981*. Santa Barbara, Calif.: Capra Press, 1980. Contains a fascinating view of McPherson's colorful career in Southern California.

The WPA Guide to California: The Federal Writers' Project Guide to 1930's California. 1939. Reprint. New York: Pantheon Books, 1984. Provides an outstanding description of the Angelus Temple during the Great Depression. This edition includes a new introduction by Gwendolyn Wright.

Chinatown, San Francisco

Date: Founded in the 1850's

Relevant issues: Asian American history, cultural history

Significance: San Francisco's Chinatown, with a 1990 population of more than eighty thousand, is the largest Chinese community outside Asia and the commercial center for Chinese Americans all over North America. The neighborhood, founded as Chinese immigrated to work in California's gold fields, includes shops, restaurants, bakeries, teahouses, food stalls, and markets. Stores offer a wide variety of goods from China, Taiwan, Hong Kong, Korea, and Japan, with the narrow, congested side streets offering a local flavor different from that on tourist-oriented Grant, which has been nicknamed the "Street of 25,000 Lanterns."

Location: Some twenty-four square blocks bounded roughly by Kearney, Broadway, Mason, and Bush Streets; most tourists are attracted to the eight-block stretch of Grant Avenue between Bush and Broadway, the main street of the community

Site Office:

Chinese Cultural Center
750 Kearney Street, 3d floor
San Francisco, CA 94108
ph.: (415) 986-1822
Web site: www.c-c-c.org/
e-mail: info@c-c-c.org

The Golden Gate to the Gold Mountain, San Francisco is to Chinese immigrants what New York is to those from Europe: the primary entry port to a new nation. Its Chinatown, which began to develop around 1850 to serve an influx of young men seeking their fortunes in the gold fields of California, remains the largest in the United States.

These emigrants were largely from the coastal provinces of Guongdong (Canton) and Fujian in southern China. More than 60 percent of the Chinese in America trace their ancestors to eight districts in Guongdong. Many were transients, so-called sojourners, who were lured to the "Gold Mountain" by the same hopes for riches and adventure that the discovery of gold inspired in immigrants from other countries. These hopes, at a time when natural disasters, population pressures, bureaucratic incompetence, and foreign invasions made life difficult at home, led them to risk the wrath of their government in an effort to improve economic conditions for their families. Those caught returning to the country were eligible for execution under the laws of the Manchu dynasty, which feared possible alliance between opposition forces at home and rebels abroad.

The Journey to America

The first Chinese settlers recorded in California were two men and a woman, probably servants of Charles Gillespies, who arrived in 1848. By 1850, the Chinese population of San Francisco had increased to 787 men and 2 women, and, by 1852, at least 20,000 men had arrived from China to seek their fortunes.

Over the following decades, tens of thousands of Chinese, most of them male peasants and workers between the ages of fifteen and forty, poured into America. The overwhelming majority of these immigrants settled on the West Coast. Unlike individuals from other countries who immigrated with the intention of bringing their families together again in a new land, the Chinese rarely abandoned their homeland. They frequently left behind a wife and children, and almost all hoped that, after a sojourn during which they would accumulate small fortunes of a few hundred dollars, they would return to their native villages to spend their remaining years in honor.

The Pacific crossing took two to three months aboard crowded ships with rationed supplies. After clearing the San Francisco customhouse, the immigrants registered their names with representatives of the Chinese community and were sent to boardinghouses with others from their home province. Each immigrant arranged for part of his wages to be sent to relatives and for his body to be returned to China for burial should he die in America, and then he left to work in the gold mine or on the railway.

Unlike the early nineteenth century "coolies," who were fraudulently or forcefully taken from China to the New World as virtual slaves, this later immigration was voluntary. The 1868 Supplementary Articles to the Sino-American Treaty of Tianjin ensured that the immigrants were independent and able to look after their arrangements whether paying their passage in cash or entering into credit ticket contracts, which were straightforward business deals with guarantees on both sides. The image of the coolie persisted in the American imagination, however, especially as anti-Chinese sentiment built in the 1860's and 1870's.

Initial Reception

In 1850, the Chinese were a welcome addition to the community. San Francisco's leaders gathered on August 25 of that year to honor, and attempt to convert to Christianity, a group of Chinese merchants. Led by mayor John Geary, speakers invited the "celestial men of commerce" to tell their friends in China "that in coming to this country they will find welcome and protection." The *California Courier* proclaimed, "We have never seen a finer-looking body of men collected together in San Francisco, in fact, this portion of our population is a pattern for sobriety, order and obedience to laws, not only to other foreign residents, but to Americans themselves. These Celestials make excellent citizens and we are pleased to notice their daily arrival in large numbers."

This sentiment would change, but in those days, the Chinese were supplying foodstuffs, tools, utensils, textiles, and clothing from across the Pacific to the gold miners of California. One miner wrote in his diaries, "Were it not for the Chinese, we might have starved the first year." Also welcomed were skilled craftsmen and technicians who passed through the city on the way to the gold camps.

Gold Mines and Railroads

The Chinese immigrants were among the first gold prospectors, with three of them arriving only one month after gold was found in Sutter's Mill. They brought with them knowledge of mining techniques in other lands and a sense of group cohesiveness. Thousands of Chinese dug in the mines over the next decades, many buying claims declared exhausted by former owners and extracting additional return through superior economy and patience.

Beginning in early 1865, Chinese were hired by the Central Pacific Railroad. Despite protests by white workers that these people (who had built the Great Wall of China and invented gunpowder) were too small and frail to take on heavy construction jobs, they proved at least as skilled as their white counterparts. Moreover, they proved more dedicated and less likely to malinger. By the time the Central Pacific and Union Pacific tracks were joined on May 10, 1869, in ceremonies from which Chinese participation was barred, news of the reliability of these workers had spread. It was a period of labor shortages and increasing wages, so even the most prejudiced employers were glad to use their skills.

Between 1868 and 1882, the peak of Chinese immigration, almost 80 percent of the Chinese resided in California, where they worked in the state's mining, manufacturing, farming, and fishing industries. As with most immigrant groups, the Chinese gathered together for the comfort of common language and customs. Being among the first to settle San Francisco, they congregated in a choice location at the heart of the city, on the slope facing the bay.

The Development of Chinatown

San Francisco became the unofficial capital of Chinese America. As early as 1854, the area from Washington Street to Sacramento along the east side of DuPont (now Grant) Street was called "Little China." By the late 1870's, between one-fifth and one-fourth of all Chinese in the United States, some thirty thousand people, resided in San Francisco, with most in the twelve-block area of Chinatown. Among the first Chinese businessmen in San Francisco were merchants and labor contractors who established stores, offices, and dormitories that became the nucleus of Chinatown and the source of traditional goods and services for Chinese throughout the country. The contractors served as the agents of the workers, who generally did not speak English. They would provide employers with relatives or fellow villagers and receive in return a lump-sum payment which they themselves distributed to their crews. They also provisioned the men, sometimes shipping supplies hundreds of miles to railroad construction or swamp reclamation sites.

Blood ties and common language and region of origin are the basis of Chinese society. Chinatown came to be governed by a group of organizations, called huiguan, which formed along these lines. A huiguan is a traditional and lawful association of fellow provincials away from home. Representatives of these associations, or of the labor contractors, were the agents who greeted newly arrived immigrants, got them settled, and found them jobs.

The first huiguan in San Francisco was formed in 1851. By 1862, after splintering and realignment, there had formed an umbrella group known in English as the Chinese Consolidated Benevolent Association, or the Six Companies. The Zhonghua Gongsuo, Congress of the Six Companies, was housed at 709 Commercial Street, from where it settled disputes, decided strategies for seeking relief from burdensome laws, devised ways to curb crime, and arranged for celebrations. During times of difficulty, such as the Great Depression of the 1930's, the Six Companies provided support so the Chinese people, in general, did not need to turn to federal relief agencies.

These were not the only organizations and associations the Chinese formed. In 1903, a Chinese scholar reported the existence in San Francisco's Chinatown of ten public Chinese organizations (including the Six Companies), two trade organizations, nine benevolent organizations, twenty-three clan organizations, nine combined clan organizations, twenty-five secret societies, and five cultural societies. Many were based in San Francisco and had operations in Chinatowns around the nation.

These organizations, referred to as tongs, meaning hall or parlor, met the needs and promoted the interests of Chinese residents. According to historian Shih-shan Henry Tsai, however, "their lofty effort to maintain Chinese heritage, language and religion in America retarded the acculturation of the first and second generations in the New World."

Chinatown, San Francisco. (American Stock Photography)

Manufacturing flourished in early San Francisco. In the 1860's and 1870's, between sixty and seventy Chinese merchants owned cigar factories, which required little capital investment. They employed 7,500 Chinese in 1876 and purchased two-thirds of the city's cigar revenue stamps. The Chinese ran more than seventy establishments to make shoes and boots, dominated clothing manufacture in the city, and made up one-quarter of the fishermen in the area.

They identified and provided needed services that elsewhere were the province of women, becoming houseboys, laundrymen, and restaurant owners. By 1876, San Francisco had three hundred Chinese laundries, each employing five men.

They started newspapers. The first Chinese language newspaper in America, the *Golden Hills News,* appeared in 1854. The first bilingual paper, the *Chinese World of San Francisco,* was published from 1891 until 1969.

Festivals and seasonal celebrations were important social events in Chinatown. Most important was the New Year, still a major celebration and tourist attraction each winter. The men also celebrated lesser festivals, enjoyed Chinese opera and other forms of Asian music, and played chess. As Chinatown grew, several theaters were built and traveling opera troupes were brought from China.

Crime and Isolation Within the Community

Tongs came to be thought of as illegal by most Americans, but only a small percentage were criminal. The illegal tongs grew from traditional Chinese secret societies but lost their religious and political significance in moving, becoming self-protection organizations that used violence and intimidation to punish enemies and accumulate wealth. Wars developed among the illegal societies in the 1880's, drawing the attention of officials from China who began jailing relatives in China for the crimes of members in America. Warfare declined after 1900 and, since the 1920's, tong wars have been practically nonexistent in American Chinese communities.

Chinatown did have a dark side, however. In 1876, there were an estimated two hundred Chinese gambling houses and two hundred opium dens operating in San Francisco. Gambling attracted many white Americans. Opium users were mostly Chinese and numbered more than three thousand. Opium was not illegal, although it was considered "special merchandise," subject to heavy import duties. Chinese prostitutes came mostly from Hong Kong, often under contracts rife with false promises. A Chinese official who visited California in 1876 reported there were some six thousand Chinese women in the United States and 80 to 90 percent were "daughters of joy." The Chinese community consistently denounced these high-profile vices that they knew gave Chinatown an unsavory reputation, despite their relatively low incidence.

This stereotype of evil was one of the factors that led to the isolation of the Chinese in Chinatowns. Perhaps the most basic was the sojourner mentality that led to a society composed almost entirely of young men who had no plans to buy property and settle permanently in America.

The process was circular. Isolated by language and custom and with no incentive to learn more about their host country, the Chinese were seen as an oddity. European settlers resented their industry and perceived them as haughty and standoffish. These perceptions led to negative stereotypes, which led to anti-Chinese rioting, random acts of violence, and discriminatory legislation, all of which drove the Chinese deeper into isolation.

Violence and Prejudice

While the most deadly mob activity was inflicted in other locations, San Francisco was not without hate-motivated violence. In one case, in the summer of 1868, the branded and mutilated body of a Chinese crab fisherman was found under a wharf. The murder was attributed by the *San Francisco Times* to young ruffians "eager to glut their cruelty on any Chinaman who must pass." In 1877, rioters burned down dozens of Chinese laundries.

Prejudice grew as the depression of the 1870's led to growing tension between labor and management. The Chinese workers who accepted wages lower than whites thought necessary for basic survival became the victims of anti-Chinese propaganda initiated by organized labor and political orators. They argued that the Chinese should be excluded from the United States altogether.

California, with the nation's largest Chinese population, was in the forefront of anti-Chinese activity. State law prohibited nonwhites from appearing in court to confront a white citizen. The state constitution was rewritten in 1879 to forbid anyone of "Chinese or Mongolian" ancestry from being employed by a white man, or from working on any public project except as punishment for a crime. It instructed the legislature to delegate municipalities all necessary power for the removal of Chinese and categorically declared the Chinese people "dangerous to the well being of the State." The rhetoric was a far cry from the compliments offered by the leaders of San Francisco twenty-nine years earlier.

Exclusion Laws

San Francisco, since 1865 a strong union city, endorsed these sentiments. The recently opened transcontinental railroad brought an influx of workers from the East, as well as the fifteen thousand to twenty thousand Chinese laborers who had returned from laying its track. By the 1870's, the surplus of labor led to the disintegration of the closed shop. The number of Chinese laborers soon approached that of white workers. While the Chinese accounted for only 10 percent of the city's population, the great majority were young men, making them far more than 10 percent of the labor force.

In 1876, Denis Kearney, a rabble-rousing San Francisco labor leader, offered the slogan "the Chinese Must Go" as the solution to "the Chinese Problem." Congress passed the first of a series of measures to prevent the entry of Chinese laborers into the United States in 1882. This exclusion law barred Chinese manual laborers from immigrating and disallowed Chinese residents of the United States from ever becoming citizens. This legislation and modifications that followed it also opened the way for widespread illegal immigration schemes. In the years that followed, the number of immigrants dropped even as resident Chinese who had achieved their financial goals retired to their native villages. The Chinese population of San Francisco dropped from 30,000 in the late 1870's to 7,744 by 1920. "The Chinese Problem" was no more.

Immigration officials received permission from the Supreme Court to enforce the exclusion laws in 1889. Thereafter, Chinese ship passengers arriving in San Francisco were detained in a two-story shed at a Pacific Steamship Company wharf until immigration officials could examine their papers. As many as five hundred people at a time were confined there, often for weeks. Newspaper reports described the treatment of the Chinese there as "worse than for jailed prisoners."

In 1910, the immigration department built an

immigration station on Angel Island in the middle of San Francisco Bay, where questionable Chinese arrivals were detained for anywhere from a few days to years. The station remained in use until 1940, processing more than 175,000 Chinese, of whom about 10 percent were deported. Detainees expressed their suffering in poems written on the walls of the detention building. Some 135 of these survived and have been translated by the Chinese Culture Foundation of San Francisco.

Discrimination

In addition to such restrictions and mistreatments applied to immigrants, the state and city continued to discriminate against the Chinese already residing in San Francisco. The Chinese were barred from city hospitals and subject to a series of head taxes, many of which had been declared unconstitutional. In the 1880's, California tried to outlaw Chinese shrimp fishing in the bay, and San Francisco sought to ban Chinese laundries and rooming houses. The city passed a cubic air law requiring lodging houses to provide at least five hundred cubic feet of clear atmosphere for each adult. When Chinese landlords and lodgers resisted, they were imprisoned en masse. San Francisco adopted an ordinance requiring every male prisoner to have his hair cut to a uniform length of one inch. This was aimed at the long braid, or queue, of the Chinese. In 1879, the Circuit Court of California ruled this unconstitutional and awarded a complainant ten thousand dollars in compensation. The city excluded Chinese children from its schools for nearly fifteen years and, when the courts ruled the practice unconstitutional, it established a segregated public school for them.

Barred from mining, railroading, fishing, and manufacturing, the Chinese concentrated in the fields of gardening, cooking, laundries, restaurants, and domestic work. The ratio of urban to rural Chinese increased substantially during the 1880's and 1890's. Lacking large amounts of capital, facing oppressive laws, and fearing racial violence, more and more people congregated in Chinatown.

Thus, for refuge, the Chinese withdrew behind the barriers white society erected around them. Once again, the larger society complained they were aloof. At the same time, society held tighter to its stereotypes of the mysteries and danger of Chinatown. The effect was both to cut the Chinese off from the opportunities of the larger society and to protect them from its blind excesses.

Americanization

Chinatown received a new face in 1906 when earthquake and fire ravaged San Francisco, allowing construction of what has been called the most charming Chinatown in the country. The Chinese turned to their history for inspiration, and their buildings began to resemble those of their homeland, though exaggerated and more ornate. They held onto their ties with their ancestral country and were often more involved with the massive changes taking place in China than with events in America.

Even with this involvement, however, Chinatown began picking up pieces of American culture. Western dress replaced traditional garb. A Young Men's Christian Association (YMCA) was established in 1912, a boy scout troop in 1914, and a Young Women's Christian Association (YWCA) in 1916.

At the forefront of the Americanization movement was the Chinese American Citizens Alliance (CACA), founded before World War I in San Francisco. It grew with the numbers of Chinese Americans born in the United States; they were only 10 percent of the Chinese American population in 1900 but a 52 percent majority by 1940. CACA built an elegant headquarters in San Francisco, started branches throughout the nation, established a life insurance fund, promulgated a constitution, and published a newspaper.

Gradually, America's perception of the Chinese changed. In the 1930's, with news of China's heroic resistance to Japan, and in the 1940's, as China became America's ally after Pearl Harbor, the Chinese were viewed more positively. Rather than a site of potential evil, Chinatown, with its exotic facade, became attractive. The Chinese population in the city expanded again; by 1940, it had rebounded to 17,782.

San Francisco hosted such wartime leaders as General Tsai Tingkai, who held off the Japanese for thirty-four days at Shanghai, and Madame Chiang Kai-shek. Following Madame Chiang's tour in 1943, the exclusion laws were lifted, making some 40,000 Chinese in America eligible for citizenship and increasing the number of Chinese immigrants permitted into the country. The repeal of the exclusion laws also increased immigration to the city: The number of Chinese living in San Francisco and Oakland had jumped to 50,000 by 1960, to 88,402 by 1970, and to 169,016 by 1980. Another effect of the exclusion laws' repeal was an increase in female Chinese immigrants entering the city. In 1910, 93.5 percent of the Chinese in San Francisco were male. This had fallen to only 74.1 percent in 1940, and it was not until 1970 that parity was approached, with 51.4 percent male.

The pace of acculturation increased markedly, including a significant movement of Chinese into previously restricted areas of employment. During the 1960's and 1970's, with the entry of more Chinese women into the United States, many people moved out of Chinatown, and the Chinatown itself changed flavor as Western furnishings, products, activities, and shops displaced more traditional elements. This led to predictions that all American Chinatowns would disappear.

In San Francisco, at least, these predictions have been countered by an influx of new immigrants from Hong Kong and Taiwan who do not speak English and start their lives as Americans in Chinatown, close to the moral and material support of relatives and friends. The previous few decades have also witnessed renewed interest among Chinese Americans in their ethnic heritage. The Chinese Historical Society of America was founded in 1963 and the Chinese Culture Foundation in 1967 to keep traditions alive.

Chinatown Today

Chinatown is today a major tourist attraction for visitors to San Francisco. Points of interest include St. Mary's Square and nearby Old St. Mary's Church, at Grant and California. The gothic church, dating from 1853, was built largely by Chinese laborers with granite from China and brick brought around Cape Horn from New England. The square features Beniamino Bufano's marble and stainless steel statue of Sun Yat-sen, founder of the Republic of China and short-term resident of Chinatown when he was building his revolution. On Waverly Place are some of Chinatown's colorful old buildings and remaining temples, including the Tien Hou Temple, dedicated to the protectress of travelers, on the third floor at 125 Waverly. The building at 743 Washington, now a branch of the

Bank of Canton, housed the Chinese Telephone Exchange from 1909 to 1949. Portsmouth Square, east of Grant between Washington and Clay, is a center of community activity, including early morning tai chi chuan exercises and afternoon chess matches.

More important than its attraction to tourists, however, Chinatown remains, in the words of writer Calvin Lee,

a place where Chinese live, work and play, a place which has a "lived-in" feel, adding to its culture and beauty. [It] feels the pulse of the metropolis. But, being on the Western shores and the largest port for newcomers to the New World from the Orient, it is always replenished with new immigrants and thus never completely loses the charm of the way of the Old Country.

—Richard Greb

For Further Information:

Fong-Torres, Shirley. *San Francisco Chinatown: A Walking Tour.* San Francisco: China Books and Periodicals, 1991. This guidebook includes a description of the history and social life of Chinese Americans in San Francisco.

Lee, Calvin. *Chinatown, U.S.A.* Garden City, N.Y.: Doubleday, 1965. Provides some history and a vivid description of San Francisco's Chinatown as it existed when the book was written.

Lee, Rose Hum. *The Chinese in the United States of America.* Hong Kong: Hong Kong University Press, 1960. Provides a more academic perspective on the development of the Chinese community in the United States and its interaction with American society at large.

Steiner, Stan. *Fusang: The Chinese Who Built America.* New York: Harper, 1979. Presents an interesting array of material and anecdotes supporting the premises that Chinese exploration of the Americas predated Europe's and that the Chinese played an integral role in winning the American West.

Tsai, Shih-shan Henry. *The Chinese Experience in America.* Bloomington: Indiana University Press, 1986. A solid and readable look at the history of the Chinese people in the United States.

Columbia

Date: Flourished from 1850 to 1870; State
   Historic Park established in 1945
Relevant issues: Business and industry, western
   expansion
Significance: A National Historic Landmark, this
   gold rush town, called the "Gem of the Southern Mines," yielded fifty million dollars in gold
   deposits between 1850 and 1870; during its
   boom in the 1850's, it was the second-largest city
   in California and narrowly missed selection as
   the state capital. The majority of the restored
   buildings can be found within Columbia State
   Historic Park.
Location: Four miles north of Sonora, near the
   foot of the Stanislaus National Forest in Tuolumne County in the Sierra Nevada of Central
   California; one hundred fifty miles east of San
   Francisco and thirty-five miles west of Yosemite
   National Park
Site Office:
Columbia State Historic Park
P.O. Box 151
Columbia, CA 95310
ph.: (209) 532-0150
fax: (209) 532-5064
e-mail: calaver@goldrush.com

Columbia had a meteoric rise after gold was
found in the dry Columbia Gulch by five miners in 1850. The relative accessibility, large amount,
and rich character of the gold extracted made the
settlement grow so quickly that within three years it
was one of the largest mining camps in California.
More gold was mined from gravel in the 640 acres
around Columbia than from any other equal area
in the Western Hemisphere. With the decline in
mining, Columbia's population diminished to a
few hundred by the late 1860's, but Columbia
never became a ghost town.

The town has been well preserved and resembles its gold rush-era prime of the 1850's and
1860's. It has an unparalleled collection of reconstructed buildings and mining artifacts. Many of
the early commercial buildings have been returned to operation as restaurants, hotels, and theaters. Once called the "Gem of the Southern Mines"
for its gold output, Columbia, during its peak, had
fifteen thousand miners working its gold fields.

Gold Is Discovered

Dr. Thaddeus Hildreth and a group of four other
prospectors that included his brother George, William Jones, John Walker, and Alexander Carson
discovered gold in Columbia on March 27, 1850.
Hildreth's party chose to camp for a night near the
spot that was to become Columbia's Main Street.
The next morning, after a rainstorm forced them
to wait and dry their blankets, John Walker went
prospecting and recovered an ounce of gold dust
in the Columbia Gulch. In the next two days, they
took out thirty pounds of gold, and news of the incredible strike spread to nearby Sonora.

After word reached the older Mother Lode mining camps, which had been established between
1848 and 1849, miners began to pour into the Columbia foothills. Within one month, five thousand
miners had pitched their tents in search of gold
near the gulch that led to the Kennebec Hill. The
spot was originally called Hildreth's Diggings, then
the name was changed to American Camp, and finally in 1851 to Columbia.

The stampede into Columbia was representative
of the phenomenal growth throughout the Sierra
foothills region. From 1848 to 1852, the population of the three-hundred-mile area from Downie-
ville in the north to Mariposa in the south exploded from 400 to 100,000 miners, and five
hundred new towns sprang up overnight. The early
miners who came to Columbia could be successful
at their trade with the simplest tools. A pan and
shovel were all that were necessary as the miners
frequently worked river and creek beds or dry ravines whose streams had changed course.

California was sweeping to the forefront of the
nation's mind. Armies of individuals and "California mining associations" quickly prepared to make
the trek west. Mail steamers via the Isthmus of Panama were the fastest way to get to the mines. While
moving across the jungles of Panama, the enthusiastic travelers taught the native canoemen the gold
rush song "O Susannah." When arriving by ship in
San Francisco, they fanned out to the booming
mining camps.

The geologic history of Columbia made the area
particularly well suited to become one of the richest districts in the Sierra Nevada. The town stands
in the center of a flat open valley underlain with
prevolcanic limestone deeply pitted with retentive
potholes. As the surrounding foothills began to

erode, gold fragments became lodged in crevices all across the two-mile-wide Columbia basin.

Rapid Growth of the Town

In the spring of 1851, Columbia continued to grow at an explosive rate. Main Street was home to forty saloons and gambling halls with a combined capital of two million dollars. According to historian Robert O'Brien, "there were seventeen general stores, eight hotels, three churches, three theatres, two fire companies, and four banks," all on land that one year before had been an open area surrounded by a forest of oak trees. By September, 1851, a citizens' committee was appointed to lay out the streets and lots.

Mail and newspapers were brought in daily by pony riders of the chain Lightning Express. Eight stagecoaches a day traveled between Columbia and Sonora, and supply wagons arrived around the clock bearing goods from nearby river ports. At its peak, Columbia's population was between fifteen and thirty thousand. Columbia had become the recognizable center for all the nearby southern mining camps, such as Gold Springs, Italian Bar, Yankee Hill, Martinez, Sawmill Flat, Squabbletown, Union Hill, and Springfield.

By the fall of 1851, families began to settle in Columbia. The four-mile road called Columbia Way that ran between Sonora and Columbia became lined with miners' cabins as the town overflowed with people. In the Columbia Gulch and the Kennebec Gulch, miners were finding twenty dollars of gold apiece every day. Gold dust began to hit the scales of the Wells Fargo office at the rate of $100,000 per week.

The Need for Water

As it always has been in California, water was a big issue in Columbia. Between 1850 and 1851, the first canals were capable of channeling water only a few miles. In June, 1851, the Tuolumne Water Company was formed to bring water to Columbia from Five Mile Creek, a distance of twenty miles. The project was completed in 1852. The miners grew resentful of the company's high rates, however, and three years later they entered into a deal with the rival Columbia and Stanislaus River Water Company. They were promised Stanislaus water at half the Tuolumne company's rates, provided that they help construct forty-four miles of water chan-

nels. Two hundred Columbia volunteers worked on Miners' Ditch, digging the canals by hand with picks and shovels. When ravines or canyons were crossed, they were forced to construct costly wooden aqueducts. Ridges of foothills were tunneled through. All told, the effort to bring water to Columbia took four years and cost a million dollars.

The demand for water in the settlement of Columbia was insatiable. While the local water companies had doubled the supply of water every year since the early 1850's, the demand was increasing even faster. For the first few years of the Columbia boom, prospectors needed to undertake the slow and laborious task of loading dirt into sacks, carrying it to streams or canals, and washing it to reveal gold.

A shift began in Columbia with the advent of hydraulic mining. Whole banks of earth that once would have taken hundreds of men several months to remove could now be removed by a handful of men in few weeks. Not only had the process been made quicker, but it also required greater resources of water.

Lobbying for State Capital

One of the most colorful characters to play a role in Columbia's early development was James W. Coffroth. When anything notable happened in Columbia, Coffroth would be on the scene. Soon after arriving in Columbia in late 1851, he became known as "Columbia's favorite son." His flair for publicity got him elected to the California Assembly and then to the Senate.

Coffroth indirectly played a role in Columbia's legendary bid to become the state capital of California. In November, 1853, Peter Nicholas murdered John Parrot in a Columbia store, and a band of agitated vigilantes demanded that Nicholas be hung. Coffroth, a friend of Nicholas, argued not to sully Columbia's reputation by an act of mob violence: "Let all things be done decently and in order. . . . As a matter of course Nicholas will be hanged. . . . but for the credit of Columbia give the man a trial." His strategy worked; the angered mob decided not to hang Nicholas on the spot. He was later found guilty.

While Nicholas was awaiting execution, his lawyer, Horace Bull, stole a petition that included ten thousand names about to be sent to the State Assembly in Benicia seeking the establishment of the state capital in Columbia. Bull is said to have clipped off the state capital petition and substituted a plea for commutation of his client's sentence above the signed names. He sent the names to Governor John Bigler, who was impressed by the ten thousand signatures and reduced Nicholas's sentence from death to ten years in San Quentin.

While the capital question never did get submitted to the ballot, Columbia got the popular reputation as the "town that came within two votes of being the capital of California." When Columbia was riding its golden wave in the 1850's, it ranked second in the state in population.

Fires and Recovery

The town was incorporated in 1854. At that time, its canvas and wood structures made it susceptible to fire. In July of that year a fire raced through the town and leveled the business district at a cost of half a million dollars. Columbia sprang back quickly; thirty new buildings were operational almost immediately after the fire. The reconstructed buildings were made larger and virtually fireproof with their brick and iron style.

Another fire hit Columbia in the summer of 1857 and raced out of control for two days. The efforts of volunteers firefighters were futile as the wells were dry. When the fire reached a town hardware store, forty kegs of blasting powder were ignited and five men were killed by the explosion. In a residential neighborhood, sixteen brick homes believed to be fireproof burned to the ground. Columbia's business district, valued at $700,000, was completely destroyed.

While the northern portion of Main Street was never rebuilt, the rest of Columbia worked hard to come back. Columbia went brick-crazy; fifty new houses were under construction within a month. The rebuilt town featured iron doors and shutters, thicker walls, and fire-resistant roofs. The response to the fire played a key role in protecting many of Columbia's finest buildings as historical landmarks up to the present day. A surprising number of the original red-brick and stone buildings have remained, including the Wells Fargo Building and the Saint Charles Saloon on Main Street.

Early on, entertainment in Columbia included liquor, gambling, and weekly bull-and-bear fights. Every Sunday afternoon thousands would flock to a ring outside town to watch these bloody contests. It has been suggested that after journalist Horace Greeley wrote about one of these competitions in Columbia, Wall Street began using the terms "bull" and "bear" to describe the outlook of the financial markets.

By 1856, the rough nature of the town began to shift, as more women and children arrived. The influence of family life on Columbia was soon reflected across its cultural landscape. A deepening sense of community developed as churches, schools, gardens, and homesteads were established.

Decline

In the early 1860's, Columbia started to decline, as it became obvious that the gold deposits were on the verge of being exhausted. Mining took place mostly on a limited, seasonal basis, depending on the availability of water. Excitement over new strikes at the Fraser River and Comstock Lode drained Columbia's resources and population.

The extensive use of hydraulic mining took its toll on Columbia as well. The process left the ground level at least ten feet lower than normal; in many places, deep pits and exposed boulders still scar the countryside. The remaining miners in Columbia began to work "city lots," tearing down structures to wash the gold underneath them or simply digging under their foundations.

By 1870, virtually the only plot of land that had not been washed and tunneled into rested atop Kennebec Hill. On that site stands St. Anne's Church and cemetery, built in 1856 with funds donated by Columbia miners. As the town's fortunes declined, miners were continually tempted to work the unviolated piece of land with their picks and shovels. Their digging encroached right to the edge of the cemetery, and it is said that on one occasion they went too far. As they worked near the edge of the cemetery, they dislodged a casket that opened to reveal the body of a richly dressed young woman. After carefully sealing the coffin, the stunned miners left, never to return.

As the legend goes, travelers passing by Columbia late at night have reported eerie organ music and flickering lights behind the Gothic windows at the abandoned St. Anne's. The church was rebuilt and rededicated in the late 1920's. It now offers visitors one of the most picturesque views of the once-booming Columbia countryside.

As the supply of gold dissipated, the excavation of high-quality marble, known for its even grain and adaptability, proved Columbia's most enduring form of mining. The white, rose, and gray marble from the Columbia Quarry was a valued source of building material. It was used in 1878 for the sidewalks around the Palace Hotel in San Francisco.

Columbia was in a rare state of preservation when Frederick Law Olmsted recommended in 1928 that the town become part of the California State Park system. Twenty to thirty of its buildings were in fair to excellent condition. In 1945 the state legislature passed an act to to preserve and rebuild the town as one of the best examples of a mining camp from the gold rush era.

—*Andrew M. Kloak*

For Further Information:

Kyle, Douglas E. *Historic Spots in California.* Stanford, Calif.: Stanford University Press, 1932. Rev. ed. 1990. A solid outline of the historical development and present-day landmarks of Columbia and Tuolumne County. Originally published in three volumes, the work provides a good overview of the town's preservation efforts.

Levy, Joann. *They Saw the Elephant: Women in the California Gold Rush.* Hamden, Conn.: Archon Press, 1990. Offers an interesting look into the often overlooked role of women in gold rush settlements like Columbia.

Meals, Hank. *Columbia Hill: Nevada County, California—An Interpretive History.* Nevada City, Calif.: S. Lamela, 1997. Maps and illustrations accompany this history of gold mines and mining in north Columbia.

O'Brien, Robert. *California Called Them: A Saga of Golden Days and Roaring Camps.* New York: McGraw-Hill, 1951. A sparkling, informative work on the Mother Lode Country and Columbia.

Death Valley

Date: National Monument proclaimed in 1933; National Park established in 1994

Relevant issues: American Indian history, business and industry, cultural history, western expansion

Significance: Death Valley has secured a place in American history for its active geology, delicate ecological systems, and the fascinating stories of miners and twenty-mule-team borax trains. Death Valley lays claim to having the lowest point in the Western Hemisphere (282 feet below sea level at Badwater basin) and to being the second hottest place on Earth (a surface temperature of 134 degrees Fahrenheit recorded on July 10, 1913, at Furnace Creek).

Location: Just west of the Nevada boundary in the Basin and Range district of the Mojave Desert of southeastern California

Site Office:
Death Valley National Park
P.O. Box 579
Death Valley, CA 92328-0579
ph.: (760) 786-2331
Web site: www.nps.gov/deva/

Death Valley National Park, established in 1994, encompasses over three million acres of spectacular desert scenery, interesting and rare desert wildlife, complex geology, undisturbed wilderness, and sites of historical and cultural interest. The presence of humans through hundreds of years can be found in almost every part of the valley. Rock drawings, ghost towns, and foot trails remain as traces of this historical development. The mystique, fascination, and long, rich history of Death Valley emerges through the lives of Native Americans, prospectors, and miners who lived in this geological wonderland.

Geological History and Development
Death Valley is best known for being the lowest elevation in North and South America. The valley is a deep trough, about 130 miles long and from 6 to 14 miles wide. The tectonic activity that produced this east-west extension and generated Death Valley may have begun as early as thirty million years ago and is continuing today as the basin is being pulled apart and offset along a number of faults. Faults occur when the earth's crust breaks and slips into various positions.

All the great divisions of geological time, the eras and most of their subdivisions, are represented in the rocks of the mountains that border Death Valley. These rocks and landforms tell a story of endless changes in the earth's crust—vast depositions, contortions, tiltings, alternate risings and lowerings, faultings, and intense heats and pressures that have changed the very nature of many of the rocks. In recent geological times, powerful forces of water, wind, and gravity have sculpted much of the scenery that is visible in Death Valley.

As dry as it is today, Death Valley has had periods in its history in which it was largely covered with water. During the last Ice Age, about ten thousand years ago, geological evidence indicates that there were several lakes, including one that was about six hundred feet deep. As recently as two thousand years ago, Death Valley contained a lake about thirty feet deep.

Death Valley is all but surrounded by mountain ranges. On the east side of the valley is the Amargosa Range, which is composed of the Grapevine Mountains, the Funeral Mountains, and the Black Mountains. The Owlshead Mountains lie in a circular position at the extreme south end of Death Valley. Located in the rain shadow of the Panamint Mountains that border the west, Death Valley receives an average annual precipitation of only 1.5 inches. Summer temperatures average about 100 degrees Fahrenheit for day and night combined, whereas winter temperatures average about 60 degrees Fahrenheit.

American Indians and Prospectors

The ancestors of the Timbisha and Panamint Shoshone tribes arrived in the Death Valley area sometime between 900 and 1000 C.E. The land provided them with plants, springs, and many kinds of wildlife, including bighorn sheep, rabbits, and lizards. These Native Americans ranged over the land in a seasonal pattern to harvest fruits, seeds, and plants and to hunt animals. Pinion pine nuts and mesquite beans formed a major part of their diet.

Evidence indicates that the native people were very close to one another. Tribe members gathered to listen to stories about the history of the world and to perform different religious dances for healing the sick and influencing the weather. People from different villages and districts frequently intermingled in group hunts, dances, games, and other social events.

The area was inhabited primarily by Panamint Indians when pioneer wagons brought the first white men into the valley on Christmas Day, 1849.

These so-called forty-niners were ill-advised emigrants from the east who were looking for a shortcut to the California gold fields. As hardships in the valley increased, twelve forty-niners in this thirty-member party died. The eighteen survivors who escaped named the valley for its desolate desert environment. Some of the forty-niners spread reports of silver deposits in Death Valley, and successive invasions of prospectors and miners sought to exploit the silver ore and other precious metals. Each ore strike gave birth to a new short-lived settlement in the valley. However, only the dreams of a few prospectors ever came true.

With the advent of mining and boomtowns in Death Valley, Native Americans could no longer pursue their traditional way of life. Watering areas became inhabited by white people, pinion pine trees were cut down for wood, and mesquite bushes disappeared. Eventually, the Panamints revolted, and hostilities surfaced during the 1860's that led to the deaths of both miners and Indians. In 1866, Congress ratified the Treaty of Ruby Valley, a statement of peace and friendship that granted the United States rights of way across western Shoshone territories.

In 1933, President Herbert Hoover signed a proclamation that set aside a reservation of 2,980 square miles of desert land as the Death Valley National Monument, thus assuring its continued use for public enjoyment. In 1936, the National Park Service set aside forty acres of the land for the residence of Native Americans. With help from Indian service funds, the Civilian Conservation Corps, and local Shoshone labor, a village of twelve small adobe structures was built. In October, 1994, Death Valley National Monument was expanded by 2,031 square miles and designated a National Park. In 1999, approximately sixty Native Americans were living in the Indian Village of Death Valley. Many members of the Shoshone tribe worked for local companies and organizations in Death Valley.

Mining and Twenty-Mule Teams

Since the discovery of gold in California in 1848, Death Valley has experienced over 150 years of boom-and-bust mining history. From the 1850's to the early 1900's, mining was limited and sporadic in the Death Valley region. Because of primitive and inefficient technological methods, scarcity of water and fuel, and the absence of nearby transpor-

Death Valley. (California Division of Tourism/Robert Holmes)

Upon creation of the Death Valley National Monument in 1933, Death Valley was closed to mining exploration. By prior agreement, however, the valley was quickly reopened to exploration by action of Congress in June, 1933. During World War II, the talc industry developed; it remained active until the 1980's, when declining markets made mining unprofitable. The National Park Service periodically reviews the status of over 140 active mining claims in Death Valley, determining their validity, ensuring that federal guidelines are being followed, and protecting the resources of Death Valley.

tation facilities, most of the early mining ventures met with little success. It was economically feasible to mine only the highest-grade ores.

One of the most notable but short-lived mines was the Harmony Borax Works, which was active from 1883 to 1888. Borax is used in soaps, medicines, and glass. William Tell Coleman built the Harmony plant, which produced three tons of borax daily during its peak years. This mine became famous not for its ore deposits, however, but for its twenty-mule-team wagon trains, as well as for the advertising campaigns in the 1950's for the radio and television series *Death Valley Days*. The twenty mule teams hauled loads of borax, up to forty-six thousand pounds at a time, a grueling 165 miles to the railroad in Mojave, California. In 1890, the operation was transferred to Daggett, in the Calico Mountains, which was closer to rail transportation.

With renewed interest in gold and silver mining during the early 1900's, many mines—particularly the Skidoo, Rhyolite, Keane Wonder, Radcliffe, and Eureka mines—became large-scale operations. The boomtowns that sprang up around these mines flourished until they were slowed down by the Panic of 1907. Besides gold and silver, prospectors scoured the valley for antimony, copper, lead, zinc, and tungsten. Prosperous, large-scale metallic mining in Death Valley ended around 1915.

Places to Visit

In the late 1990's, a yearly average of about one million tourists were attracted to Death Valley by the vastness of mountain panoramas, the pleasure of the winter climate, and the lore of past frontier life. Death Valley is generally sunny, dry, and clear throughout the year. The winters are mild, with occasional winter storms, but summers are extremely hot and dry. Death Valley National Park is open all year, but winter is the best time to visit the points of interest in the valley. The hot summer from May through October is only for the hardy and venturesome.

Located at the center of Death Valley is the Furnace Creek Visitors Center, which houses museum exhibits, a visitor information desk, and the Death Valley Natural History Association bookstore. California Highway 190, the Badwater Road, Scotty's Castle Road, and paved roads to Dante's View and Wildrose provide access to major scenic viewpoints and historic points of interest. More than 350 miles of unpaved and four-wheel-drive roads provide access to wilderness hiking, camping, scenery, and historical sites. From November through April, ranger-guided hikes, talks, and evening programs are presented.

Twenty-Mule Team Canyon, from which twenty-mule teams hauled borax in the 1880's, is a picturesque part of Death Valley to visit. A 4.5-mile un-paved road meanders through the mud hills, which have been strikingly sculpted by centuries of erosion. Still standing among the crumbling adobe are the old boiler and some of the vats of the borax works. Another spectacular tourist attraction is Scotty's Castle, the former dwelling place of one of the world's richest gold miners, Death Valley Scotty. On the way to or from the castle, a geological attraction to see at the northern end of the park is the Ubehebe Crater, an explosion crater that is a half a mile across the top and four hundred feet deep.

Rhyolite, the largest town in Death Valley during the mining boom of the early 1900's, is a visitors' attraction. Located near Beatty, Nevada, the ruins of Rhyolite include a house built completely of bottles, a train depot, a jail, a two-story schoolhouse, and a three-story bank building. Other places to visit and explore include Badwater, the lowest point in the Western Hemisphere; Devil's Golf Course, the most rugged surface on Earth; Stovepipe Wells, a rustic desert outpost; Death Valley Sand Dunes, some rising eighty feet high; Mosaic Canyon, full of naturally polished marble; and Artist's Drive, a traverse through the most colorful rocks on Earth in Artist's Palette. Another historical attraction is at the Manzanar National Historic Site, where the Manzanar Relocation Center was one of ten camps that interned Japanese American citizens and Japanese aliens during World War II.

—*Alvin K. Benson*

For Further Information:

Cronkhite, Daniel. *Death Valley's Victims: A Descriptive Chronology, 1849-1980.* Morongo Valley, Calif.: Sagebrush Press, 1981. Stories of the forty-niners, fabulous mining exploits, and men and women who braved some of the wildest, most remote, and desolate country east of the Sierra Nevada.

Digonnet, Michel. *Hiking Death Valley: A Guide to Its Natural Wonders and Mining Past.* Boston: Michel Digonnet, 1997. Well-organized, clearly written, and detailed maps showing a variety of one-day and multiple-day geological and historical excursions in Death Valley.

Greene, Linda W. *Scotty's Castle: An Interior History of Death Valley Ranch, Death Valley National Monument, California.* Harpers Ferry, Va.: National Park Service, U.S. Department of the Interior, 1991. Reviews the history of many intriguing sites in Death Valley. Includes many bibliographical references.

Laycock, George. *Death Valley.* New York: Four Winds Press, 1976. Traces the history of Death Valley and discusses the minerals, plants, and animals that are found there.

Lingenfelter, Richard E., and Richard A. Dwyer, eds. *Death Valley Lore: Classic Table of Fantasy, Adventure, and Mystery.* Reno: University of Nevada Press, 1988. Describes the historical development of Death Valley, including stories and folklore associated with the forty-niners, prospectors, and miners.

Nadeau, Remi. *Ghost Towns and Mining Camps of California.* Santa Barbara, Calif.: Crest, 1992. A historical look at the towns and mining camps of California, including Death Valley. For both the casual reader and the serious history buff.

Sharp, Robert P., and Allen F. Glazner. *Geology Underfoot in Death Valley and Owens Valley.* Missoula, Mont.: Mountain Press, 1997. Excellent overview of the geological history and formations in Death Valley, including mineral ore deposits.

Donner Camp, Truckee

Date: Winter of 1846-1847

Relevant issues: Disasters and tragedies, western expansion

Significance: The winter entrapment of the Donner Party as they tried to reach California was caused by bad advice, late arrival, and immense and heavy snowfall. Starvation led some of them to cannibalism and subsequent notoriety. Donner State Park is located at the main site of their ordeal.

Location: Donner Memorial State Park and Emigrant Trail Museum is on Donner Pass Road off Interstate 80 near Truckee

Site Office:

Donner Memorial State Park
12593 Donner Pass Road
Truckee, CA 96161
ph.: (530) 582-7892
Web site: www.cal-parks.ca.gov

In the nineteenth century, the Sierra Nevada were a massive barrier to anyone heading for California. Local native groups and mountain men traveled the rugged passes, though seldom in winter. In the 1830's, few tried it; some went around the north or south end.

The First Wagon Train Through the Sierra

The first wagon train to make its way through the seven thousand-foot-high Donner Pass was the Stephens-Murphy-Townsend group in 1844. They opened the Emigrant Trail that became one of the most traveled overland trails to California. Modern Interstate 80 follows the same path through the mountains.

This wagon train consisted of the Murphy and Townsend families of Missouri and a number of single men, among them Elisha Stephens. Selected as leader, Stephens was a quiet man with years of experience in the West. Caleb Greenwood, who had been in the west for thirty years, was their guide. Isaac Hitchcock also had lived in the West and brought his family. Most of the twenty-six men and eight women were between twenty and forty years old. There were sixteen children.

Arriving in the Sierra in winter, like the later Donner Party, the Stephens group did not know which way to go. At the confluence of two streams east of Donner Lake, they split up, each following one stream. Near Donner Lake, one group left four wagons and trekked onward. To guard the wagons, Moses Shallenberger spent the winter near the lake in a small cabin built by several of the men. He survived, and all of the Stephens group made it to Sutter's Fort. Two babies were born on the trail. The Stephens Party passage was successful but uneventful and was quickly overshadowed by the misfortunes of the Donner Party.

The Background of the Donner Party

The Donner Party did not exist until most members had reached Fort Bridger in the Wyoming Territory; it was among the last groups on the trail that year. Most were strangers with no loyalty outside their own families. The motive for combining forces was self-preservation. Everyone knew that group travel was the safest way.

The aged George Donner of Illinois was elected leader because he had prestige, wealth, and support from fifteen members of the Donner family on the train, including his frail elder brother. They had three wagons, twelve yoke of oxen, five saddle horses, cattle, servants, and a watchdog. John Reed, also prosperous, had traveled with his family from Ohio with the Donners. In Wyoming, ten families and sixteen single men decided to go on together. Ranging in age from twenty to sixty, they were from six different states and two foreign countries.

They intended to join a wagon train at Fort Bridger led by Lansford Hastings, but they were late and he did not wait for them. He left a note telling them to follow the tracks of the Harlan Young wagon train that he was leading. That company of sixty wagons made it safely to California in 1846, as did a number of other wagon trains.

Why Did They Suffer Such a Tragedy?

Most people in the Western world have heard what happened to the Donner Party, but why it happened is less well known. The Donner Party left Fort Bridger on July 31, 1846, one of the last trains to leave that year. They had twenty-four wagons; nearly ninety people; herds of oxen, horses, mules, and cattle; and a thousand miles to go to reach California. They knew they should arrive at the Sierra Nevada before winter set in, but they were slow and sometimes the wagons were strung out for miles. Few on the train knew how to hunt, and none had been on the trail or had wilderness survival skills.

On the advice of Lansford Hastings, they took a short cut that went south of the Great Salt Lake. It turned out to be miles longer and more difficult than the regular trail. To get their wagons through a rugged thirty-six-mile stretch of the Wasatch Mountains, they spent two weeks building a road, which made them later still. The men and animals were exhausted from the ordeal, but they slogged on. Then they came to the desert, which Hastings had said was only forty miles wide. It was eighty miles with no water. Many animals died, everyone got disoriented, and there were attacks by local natives. Four wagons were abandoned as too heavily loaded for tired animals to pull. Now they were two months late.

There was no cohesion between groups, and tension arose during the trip. Diseases and mishaps plagued them, but no more than on most wagon trains: This group was not prepared to handle them. Before they reached the Sierra Nevada, five

Bill Pugsley stands before a memorial at Donner Party State Park. In 1996, Pugsley and his dog Samantha walked nine hundred miles of the Donner Trail in honor of the 150th anniversary of the ill-fated expedition. (AP/ Wide World Photos)

men had died, only one from disease. At Truckee Meadows (current site of Reno, Nevada), they rested for nearly a week trying to decide whether to go ahead or wait where they were for the winter. They were out of food staples so several men walked to Sutter's Fort in California to bring back supplies. One man and two natives came back carrying food. It was all the help they received for months.

They decided to go ahead up the rugged mountain pass along the Truckee River. They traveled in separate groups, again days apart. The first wagons made it to a small lake, now called Donner Lake,

just before it began to snow. By November 6, they were unable to move forward or back, engulfed in five feet of snow. They were still a hundred miles northeast of Sutter's Fort with no hope of reaching it before the snow melted.

The Breen family arrived at the lake first and took over the small log cabin that the men of the Stephens Party had built two years before. It was only twelve feet wide and fourteen feet long, and its roof of hides and branches was gone. The Murphy family built another cabin several hundred yards away. The Reed and Graves families built a double cabin a half mile eastward. The Donners, with the slowest moving wagons, made it only as far as Alder Creek, five or six miles northeast of the lake. There were sixty people at the lake and twenty-one at Alder Creek. A series of storms, each lasting from three to ten days, raged for three months. By February, the snow was twenty-two to twenty-five feet deep.

Pushed to the Limit

Fifteen of the adults tried to make it out to bring back help. Later called the "Forlorn Hope," they were largely unsuccessful. Some reached Sutter's Fort, a few came back with food, and only half of them survived. Other unsuccessful attempts were made to get food to the starving party.

When the final rescue party arrived in April of 1847, what they found appalled them. This incident has been repeated and discussed for 150 years. The accounts vary widely, and not all are reliable. Even firsthand reports of the survivors do not agree in details because party members were in different places and had different experiences. However, the basic facts are clear. When they had consumed all the food, mules, horses, oxen, and dogs, they boiled blankets, boots, and hides to make soup. Families that still had food would not share it with outsiders. On December 16, when the first man died of starvation, some of his companions were driven to roasting his flesh for food. There was nothing else; cannibalism was the only way to survive. At first, they waited until a man died of starvation, and all agreed that no one ought to consume a relative. Then things got worse. There are unconfirmed reports that one young man and both natives were shot just for the food that their bodies provided.

While tales have gotten more lurid and graphic

over the years, they are generally true. Some writers have tried to downplay the horror, but it is clear that those who survived partook of human flesh at least part of the time. Some accounts by those who were there during the ordeal do not agree in detail, and some were eager to blunt the horror of the story.

The reasons for the tragedy are clear. Their late arrival in the mountains happened to come in a year of especially heavy snow in the Sierra. Leadership was nonexistent, no one had any knowledge of how to survive, and there was little cooperation outside family groups. Of the eighty-seven people trapped at the lake, almost half died. An interesting statistic shows that only half of the men made it through the ordeal, but nearly three-fourths of the women survived. Everyone over the age of fifty and under the age of five died of starvation. The Donner tragedy is a vivid example of the perils Western travelers of the nineteenth century faced in the rugged and formidable wilderness of California.

Reports on the fate of the Donner Party spread quickly, and many California-seekers avoided this trail because they feared being trapped like the Donner Party. When the gold rush began to bring thousands of people to California in 1849, fear faded. The passage became the Emigrant Trail, and hundreds of people used it. The first account of the Donner tragedy was sensational and horrifying. Writers then stressed the heroism and bravery of the survivors. In the 1880's, C. F. McGlashan of Truckee wrote a book restoring essential facts of the story that had been forgotten.

Donner State Memorial Park and the Donner Camp

Donner State Memorial Park, just east of the foot of Donner Lake, is situated on the site of the main Donner Camp. This California State Park presents dramatic reminders of the Donner Party's tragedy as well as other pioneers' triumphs. The Donner name abounds in the area. The most visible reminder is a monument to all pioneers who crossed the pass. Its base is twenty-two feet high, the depth of the 1846-1847 snow accumulation. It was erected in 1918 with some survivors present and stands on the site of the Shallenberger cabin. Another monument, dedicated in 1994, commemorates the first successful crossing made by the Stephens Party in

1844-1845. The Alder Creek campsite, six miles away, is operated by the United States Forest Service. Some archaeological work has been done in the area.

The visitors' center shows a film on the Donner Party daily and runs an excellent small museum that displays artifacts of the trek, from a large covered wagon to a tiny child's doll. There are many books and accounts of the story available, and brochures and maps list hikes and tours to various sites, as well as indigenous animals, plants, and trees. It is open all year, and a winter visit exhibits some of the problems faced by the Donner Party.

—*Lyndall B. Landauer*

For Further Information:

DeVoto, Bernard. *Year of Decision, 1846.* Boston: Little, Brown, 1943.

Houghton, Eliza P. Donner. *The Expedition of the Donner Party and Its Tragic Fate.* Chicago: A. C. McClurg, 1911. Reprint. Lincoln: University of Nebraska Press, 1997.

King, Joseph R. *Winter of Entrapment: A New Look at the Donner Party.* Lafayette, Calif.: K & K, 1992.

McGlashan, C. F. *The History of the Donner Party.* Reprint. Stanford, Calif.: Stanford University Press, 1940.

Mullen, Frank. *The Donner Party Chronicles.* Reno, Nev.: Humanities Committee, 1997.

Stewart, George R. *The California Trail.* Berkeley: University of California Press, 1953.

_____. *Ordeal by Hunger.* Boston: Houghton Mifflin, 1936.

Unruh, Jon D., Jr. *The Plains Across: The Overland Emigrants and the Trans-Mississippi West, 1840-1860.* Urbana: University of Illinois Press, 1979.

El Pueblo de Los Angeles

Date: Established in 1781
Relevant issues: Cultural history, Latino history
Significance: This ten-block area near the site of the original Spanish settlement contains a number of early Los Angeles buildings, which now serves as a monument to the early history of the city; it is jointly operated by the city, county, and state.

Location: Central Los Angeles; Ord Street (northern boundary) to Arcadia Street, adjoining the Hollywood/Santa Ana Freeway (southern boundary), and Alameda Street (eastern boundary) to Hill Street (western boundary)

Site Office:
El Pueblo de Los Angeles
125 Paseo de la Plaza, Suite 400
Los Angeles, CA 90012
ph.: (213) 625-5045

The sprawling metropolis laced with freeways that is modern Los Angeles began as a tiny farming village in Spanish California more than two hundred years ago. Those origins are memorialized in the state park established to protect the last few reminders of the old pueblo that remain in the heart of the great city. In 1981, Angelenos paused during the bicentennial of their city's founding to dedicate a bronze plaque to the memory of the original residents: forty-four *pobladores* (settlers)—some of Spanish ancestry, some Native American, some African—who journeyed from Mexico in 1781 to establish a *pueblo* (town) in the wilderness.

The Founding of Los Angeles

The site for the community was chosen by the Spanish governor of California, Felipe de Neve. It lay on the west bank of the Los Angeles River, not far from the Mission San Gabriel Arcángel, in the midst of a broad coastal plain between the Santa Monica, San Gabriel, and Santa Ana Mountains. Governor Neve also provided a name for the settlement: El Pueblo de Nuestra Señora la Reina de Los Angeles (the town of Our Lady the Queen of the Angels). A statue of Felipe de Neve stands watch today over the Plaza; it was a gift of the people of Chihuahua, Mexico, on the city's 150th birthday.

When the first settlers arrived, there were between five thousand and ten thousand Native Americans living in what is now Los Angeles County. The Yang-na, or Yabit, Indians were already familiar with the Spaniards from their mission contacts and made the newcomers welcome. Their village was near the pueblo's site, probably in the vicinity of the present City Hall; they survived by hunting the abundant wildlife and by gathering seeds, acorns, fruits, and shellfish from the fertile lands and seashore. After conversion to Catholi-cism by the mission priests, they were taught a variety of Hispanic agricultural and domestic skills and crafts.

The settlers Neve recruited were primarily farmers. Los Angeles was founded as a farming community to support the missions and the presidios, or garrisons, which protected them. The pueblos were part of Neve's plan to make California self-sufficient. Each family in the new pueblo received a house lot and a planting field nearby. Almost immediately the settlers dammed the river and built an irrigation canal. They grazed their cattle, horses, and mules on the common lands owned by the pueblo and raised corn, beans, and wheat in their fields. In their gardens they grew pumpkins, chiles, squash, melons, potatoes, and other vegetables. In the late 1790's, they began to grow grapes and olives, and for a time in the early 1800's, they grew hemp for export. Neve's plan succeeded, and by 1785 California no longer needed to import its grain.

A census taken in November, 1781, described the new pueblo as a village of earthen-roofed huts, made of willow branches laced with tule. They were quickly replaced by adobe houses, and a chapel was built, but the settlers still had to travel four leagues (about ten miles) to Mission San Gabriel for Mass. By 1790 the population of the pueblo had reached 139. In addition to the chapel there was a town hall, a barracks, a guardhouse, granaries, and twenty-nine adobe houses within the walls, and a few more buildings clustered outside. The town was run by a military liaison to the governor called a *comisionado*, who supervised the *alcalde* (mayor) and two councilmen who were elected by the people.

The Plaza

The heart of the old pueblo was the Plaza, the gathering place for trade, gossip, recreation, and religion. Here Angelenos gathered to exchange news, barter for goods, celebrate fiestas, gamble at cards, and enjoy their favorite sports, cockfighting and bullfighting. Bullfighting on horseback in Los Angeles was a game of skill; the rider's goal was to seize and twist the bull's tail, rolling him off his feet. The bulls were seldom killed, being too valuable to waste.

The Plaza had been part of the original layout of the town, when it was probably closer to the river, but its exact location is unknown. It was moved after the severe flood of 1815 to the corner northwest of its current site, and moved again for the last time about 1825. Originally a large rectangle, it has been modified through the years as the Pueblo grew and shifted. The plaza assumed its present circular form in the 1870's.

In 1818 Angelenos began to build a church of their own facing the Plaza, and from its dedication in 1822 to the present it has dominated Plaza life. Now called Our Lady Queen of Angels Catholic Church, it has served as the parish church for the Plaza

The Avila Adobe, the oldest house in Los Angeles. (Philip Bader)

neighborhood without interruption. Among those who labored on the church, in addition to many of the local Native Americans, was Joseph Chapman, the first Los Angeles resident to come from the United States. Chapman had been captured as a pirate and held a prisoner at the mission, but his skills won him the friendship of the priests, and he was pardoned. His experience as a logger proved useful in obtaining the lumber for the church roof.

The oldest existing residence in Los Angeles was built facing the second Plaza about 1818 and is now the centerpiece of Olvera Street. The Avila Adobe was built as a town house for Francisco Avila, at one time *alcalde*, or mayor, of the pueblo. The typical single-story structure was built of adobe brick, with three-foot-thick walls and a packed earth floor; the door and window frames were shipped from Boston. A planked floor was later added, among many modifications made over time.

Rancheros

The *rancho* period of El Pueblo de Los Angeles had its beginnings in 1784, when some retired soldiers received the governor's permission to graze their stock outside the pueblo's common lands. More of these grazing rights were granted from time to time, often to pensioned soldiers or as political favors, but during the Spanish period they were per-

mits only, subject to revocation. Only after 1822, when Mexico became independent of Spain, was legal title to the property included in the grants, and then ranching began in earnest. By the 1840's, with ranching at its height, the grassy hills around Los Angeles were dotted with the longhorn cattle of thirty-five ranchos. The *rancheros* raised cattle for their hides and for the fat, which was rendered into tallow for candles. Much of the labor was supplied by Native Americans who worked as *vaqueros* (cowboys) and servants for minimal wages.

The political struggles between Mexico and Spain during the early 1800's had little effect on Los Angeles, except indirectly by reducing the amount of available trade goods in the pueblo. Trade with foreign vessels, illegal under Spanish law, began to be tolerated as a necessity. In April, 1822, California became a territory of the newly independent Mexico, and Los Angeles accepted the transition without protest. An *ayuntomiento*, or city council, replaced the *comisionado*, and California was opened to foreign settlement, although with little immediate result.

Foreign trade was legalized, and the *rancheros* were quick to find new markets for their hides. A larger variety of trade goods became available in the pueblo, and many *rancheros* built comfortable town houses around the Plaza. One of the first was built by Jose Antonio Carillo, a *ranchero* and politician whose home boasted a red-tiled gable roof, a patio, and a ballroom. It was on the site now occupied by the Pico House. A house on the north side of the Plaza was acquired by Agustín Olvera, who arrived from Mexico in 1834. Olvera became the pueblo's first lawyer, and after California entered the United States, the first Los Angeles County judge. Olvera Street was named in his honor.

Conflict and Annexation

In 1835 Los Angeles was given status as a *ciudad* (city) and named the new capital of the territory by the Mexican government. Conflicts between California politicians and Mexico delayed the capital's move from Monterey for ten years. Los Angeles's new position as capital of the territory was short-lived, however.

The United States, eager for westward expansion, tried unsuccessfully to buy California from Mexico twice in the 1840's. The United States declared war on Mexico in 1846, and on August 13 of that year, U.S. troops under the command of Commodore Robert F. Stockton and Major John C. Frémont marched into Los Angeles. They met little resistance; the territorial governor, Pío de Jésus Pico, and his military commander, General José Castro, were both out of town. Stockton proclaimed himself commander in chief and governor of California.

After two weeks, Stockton and Frémont moved on and left Marine Lieutenant Archibald Gillespie in command of Los Angeles. Gillespie laid down many rules that Angelenos found unacceptable, and they organized an armed revolt that expelled Gillespie and his troops from Los Angeles. Several battles were fought around Southern California in the next few months, and U.S. forces retook Los Angeles on January 10, 1847. Mexico formally ceded California to the United States in 1848, as a condition of the Treaty of Guadalupe Hidalgo, which ended the Mexican War.

The U.S. annexation of California in itself had little immediate impact on life in the pueblo. At first the *ayuntimiento* continued to rule civilian affairs, and the social, business and religious affairs of the pueblo proceeded as before. On April 4, 1850, Los Angeles was incorporated as a U.S. city, and the *alcalde* and *ayuntimiento* were replaced by a mayor and city council. California became a state the following September 9.

Gold Brings a Ranching Boom

The real agent of change for Los Angeles was not political but economic. In 1848 gold discoveries in Northern California brought thousands of eager miners from Mexico and the eastern United States into Los Angeles on their way to the gold fields. Many stayed, including so many from the Sonora region of Mexico that the northern part of the pueblo acquired the name Sonoratown. Then, a U.S. military company that had occupied Los Angeles disbanded. Many of the former soldiers, without families or employment, roamed the streets, contributing to the growth of gambling, prostitution, and violent crime in the pueblo.

At the same time, the influx of miners into Northern California sent beef prices soaring, and the *rancheros* found themselves tremendously wealthy. Unheard-of sums were spent on costly furnishings and clothing, fancy parties, renovated homes, and heavy gambling. The fantastic wealth of the pueblo proved as irresistible as the gold rush to many fortune-seekers. In the Plaza outlaws, prostitutes, and gamblers rubbed shoulders with the *rancheros* in their expensive suits. Crime became rampant, and Los Angeles acquired a reputation as the most lawless city west of Santa Fe. In response to the escalating violence, a vigilante group calling itself the Los Angeles Rangers was formed in 1853. Its members were prominent Angelenos, and during the next two years they were credited with bringing about twenty-two executions.

The ranching boom continued through the 1850's, but it could not last. By 1857 the gold rush had dwindled in the north, and beef prices fell. The careless spending of boom days began to take its toll. Many of the *rancheros* had heavily mortgaged their lands and were deeply in debt. The U.S. government demanded proof of the *rancheros'* land ownership, and they found themselves involved in long, complicated, expensive, and alien legal entanglements. Devastating periods of drought during the 1860's dealt the fatal blow to the *rancheros*. Their property was sold to pay their debts and then broken up for farm land.

Attempts to Save the Plaza

The character of the Plaza had changed as well. By the 1870's the future of the city seemed to lie to the south, toward the bay of San Pedro. The Plaza was the old neighborhood now, a run-down remnant of the past. The barrio of Sonoratown on the north side and the growth of a Chinese community on the eastern side, along with some entrenched vice operations, had made it an undesirable area to the more prosperous Angelenos. The lynching of several innocent Chinese by an angry mob in the aftermath of a tong war in 1871 seemed to close the book on the Plaza, but it was not quite finished yet.

In 1869, Don Pío Pico, the former territorial governor, began building a palatial hotel at the intersection of Main Street and the Plaza. Named the Pico House, it was completed the following year, when William Abbot and his wife, Dona Merced Garcia, built the lavish Merced Theatre next to it. Built of brick and covered with painted stucco in imitation of marble, the Pico House was for a time the most celebrated hotel in Los Angeles and played host to a variety of famous visitors. Competition from newer hotels, Don Pío's financial troubles, and the continued deterioration of the neighborhood made its success short-lived; it was sold in 1880. The Merced Theatre did not enjoy long-term popularity, either. These and a few other efforts to revitalize the area were doomed when the city turned south. El Pueblo was forgotten.

The Rebirth of El Pueblo

When Christine Sterling, a native of San Francisco, became interested in the Plaza and its history in the 1920's, the area was in sorry condition. Only a few of the old buildings were left, and those were run-down and neglected. Olvera Street was an alley of slums, cluttered with garbage, distinguished by an open sewer. For two years her efforts to encourage renovation of the area met with only polite interest. Then in 1928 she learned that the Avila Adobe, the oldest building left in the city, had been condemned and was scheduled for demolition. This provided the leverage she needed. Armed with political encouragement and financial help, she leased the building and began renovating it. With contributions of family heirlooms from descendants of pueblo residents, Sterling refurbished the building to represent an early California home.

With this success Sterling convinced the city council to rescind the condemnation; further, the city provided prison labor to clean up Olvera Street. She encouraged the development there of a Mexican-style open-air market, bringing color, music, and income back to the pueblo. Her efforts were formalized through the incorporation of Plaza de Los Angeles, Inc. The group's purpose was "to preserve the Plaza as a monument to the founding of Los Angeles" and to create "an important Latin American trade and social center."

The ambiance created through the efforts of Christine Sterling and her group brought tourists and Angelenos alike back to the Plaza and paved the way for government assistance. In 1953, the city, county, and state reached an agreement cooperatively to acquire property and operate a park on the site of the old pueblo. El Pueblo de Los Angeles Historic Monument includes twenty-seven historic buildings; eleven are open to the public and four contain museums, including the Museum of Chinese American History. The staff of El Pueblo continues its efforts to acquire, preserve, and communicate the heritage of the old pueblo.

—*Elizabeth Brice*

For Further Information:

Grenier, Judson A., ed. *A Guide to Historic Places in Los Angeles County: Prepared Under the Auspices of the History Team of the City of Los Angeles American Revolution Bicentennial Committee.* Dubuque, Iowa: Kendall/Hunt, 1978. This useful guidebook includes introductory essays documenting the history of the city and concise, illustrated descriptions of historic sites, including the Plaza area.

Robinson, W. W., Jr. *Los Angeles from the Days of the Pueblo: A Brief History and Guide to the Plaza Area.* Revised with an introduction by Doyce B. Ninis. n.p.: California Historical Society, 1981. The standard history of El Pueblo. It is thorough, well-illustrated, and very readable.

Rolle, Andrew F. *Los Angeles: From Pueblo to City of the Future.* Expanded 2d ed. San Francisco: MTL, 1995. A history of Los Angeles with bibliographical references and an index.

Golden Gate Bridge

Date: Completed in 1937

Relevant issues: Art and architecture, science and technology

Significance: The Golden Gate Bridge, when built, was the longest single-span bridge in the world. Once considered impossible to build, it is now a major tourist attraction as well as a regular conduit for traffic between San Francisco and counties to the north.

Location: Highway 101 from San Francisco to Marin County, across the Golden Gate Strait

Site Office:
Public Information Director
Golden Gate Bridge, Highway and Transportation District
P.O. Box 9000, Presidio Station
San Francisco, CA 94129-0601
ph.: (415) 541-2000
Web site: www.goldengatebridge.org
e-mail: mcurrie@goldengate.org

The Golden Gate Bridge was a project that most people thought could not be completed. However, the determination and commitment of the people in nearby counties and the confidence and skill of its designer and chief engineer, Joseph Baermann Strauss, made the dream of spanning the Golden Gate Strait into a reality in 1937.

History of the Bridge

The entrance to San Francisco Bay, called the Golden Gate Strait, is a narrow strait about one mile wide, with currents from 4.5 to 7.5 knots. Often shrouded in fog and regularly subject to high winds of up to sixty miles per hour and strong ocean currents, the strait divides the peninsula of San Francisco from areas north. The strait was first given its name by Army captain John C. Frémont about 1846. Surrounded by water except to the south, San Francisco was isolated from areas across the bay to the east and the north until the building of the Golden Gate Bridge and the Oakland Bridge made motor traffic possible in these directions.

It was not until 1872 that a serious proposal was made to bridge the strait, by railroad entrepreneur Charles Crocker. Because of the seeming impossibility of the task, however, it was 1916 before the idea was seriously raised again, this time by James Wilkins, editor of the *San Francisco Call Bulletin*. He began an editorial campaign to build a bridge, and he was joined in his crusade by City Engineer Michael M. O'Shaughnessy, who polled engineers about the feasibility and cost of such a venture. Most said it could not be built, predicting costs of well over $100 million.

One man, however, an engineer who had many bridges to his credit, believed in the project and ultimately submitted a bid of $27 million. This was Strauss, who joined in the campaign to build the bridge. Because he was a respected and tested bridge-builder, his confidence in the project was taken seriously, and from that point on the idea of building a bridge across the Golden Gate Strait began to take shape.

On June 28, 1921, Strauss submitted preliminary sketches and his estimate, and he then proceeded to convince San Francisco's civic leaders not only that the bridge was feasible but also that it would pay for itself through tolls. In 1922, O'Shaughnessy, Strauss, and the secretary to San Francisco's mayor, Edward Rainey, proposed that a special district be formed to make construction of the bridge possible. Public response was positive, and on May 25, 1923, the Golden Gate Bridge and Highway District Act of California was enacted into law by the California legislature. This act allowed the six counties to borrow money, issue bonds, construct the bridge, and collect tolls. One hurdle remained. Only the War Department could authorize construc-

The Golden Gate Bridge. (California Division of Tourism/Robert Holmes)

tion, since it had jurisdiction over all harbor construction that might affect shipping traffic or military logistics, and it also owned the land on both sides of the strait. Application was made and on December 20, 1924, Secretary of War John Weeks issued a permit.

It was not until four years later, however, that the Golden Gate Bridge and Highway District was incorporated to design, construct, and finance the bridge. The board of directors first met in 1929, and Strauss was chosen as chief engineer. He submitted his final plans on August 27, 1930, and in November voters approved a thirty-five million dollar bond issue and also pledged the property of the six counties as security. This bridge, then, was the result not only of the dreams of a few men but also of the faith and confidence of the ordinary people of six counties in Northern California.

Work on the bridge began on January 5, 1933, and the project took four and a half years to complete. Strauss insisted on the most rigorous safety precautions in the history of bridge building, which included a prototype of today's hard hat for all workers to protect their heads, glarefree goggles, special hand and face cream to protect against the wind, and even special diets that would fight against dizziness. Probably the most dramatic precaution was an enormous safety net suspended under the bridge, a precaution that ended up saving the lives of nineteen men who would otherwise have fallen to their deaths in the water. These men became known as the "Halfway-to-Hell Club." During the first four years, only one man died in constructing the bridge, but on February 17, 1937, ten others were killed when a section of scaffolding fell through the net. Nevertheless, the low number of casualties was a major accomplishment; at that time, the norm was that one worker would die for every million dollars spent on a construction project.

In May, 1937, the bridge was opened, ahead of schedule and under budget. When his work was finished, Strauss penned an ode titled "The Mighty Task Is Done." It was to be his last mighty task, as he died the following year.

On May 27, the Golden Gate Bridge was opened to pedestrians, and 200,000 people walked across the bridge. A dedication ceremony was held the following morning, and then the first vehicular traffic crossed, a cavalcade of official cars. The rest of the day was again devoted to pedestrian traffic. It was not until the third day, May 29, that regular vehicular traffic began, paying tolls of fifty cents each way with a five-cent charge for more than three passengers.

Facts About the Bridge

The total length including the approaches is 1.7 miles, with the suspension span including both the main and side spans at 1.2 miles. The main suspension span, at 4,200 feet, was, when built, the longest in the world. This was surpassed in 1964 by New York City's Verrazano Narrows Bridge, and now there are others of greater length. However, the statistics about the bridge are still impressive.

The width of the bridge is 90 feet, and its height at midspan is 220 feet above the water. The bridge was designed to sway 27 feet in order to withstand winds up to one hundred miles per hour. The two great cables holding the bridge each contain enough strands of steel wire (eighty thousand miles) to circle the equator three times. Each cable is 36.5 inches in diameter, the largest bridge cables ever made. Each is 7,659 feet long and contains 27,572 individual wires, spun together using a loom-type shuttle. Each cable can hold 200 million pounds.

The two towers supporting the cables, at 746 feet, are the tallest bridge towers in the world. Although it is sometimes thought that the Golden Gate Bridge is named for its color, in fact it is named for the strait over which it passes. The color of the bridge is "International Orange," chosen to blend with its natural surroundings. The bridge has about nine million visitors each year, and as of November 1, 1998, the vehicles traveling across it numbered 1,578,652,981.

Recent History

In 1969, the state legislature authorized the Bridge and Highway District to formulate a plan for a mass transportation program in the Golden Gate Corridor, including ferry travel. This led to a change in the district's name to include the word "Transportation."

True to Strauss's promise and the belief of the people who supported it, by 1972 the debt for construction of the bridge had been retired, including thirty-five million dollars in principal and thirty-nine million dollars in interest, paid for entirely by tolls.

On May 24, 1987, in celebration of fifty years of existence, the first pedestrian walk was commemorated with "Bridgewalk 87," a parade of vintage cars, and suspension of toll collection for that day. That same year, tower lights, designed originally by consulting architect Irving F. Morrow but never implemented because of lack of sufficient funds, were installed on the bridge.

In 1994, the American Society of Civil Engineers named the Golden Gate Bridge one of the "Seven Wonders of the Modern World." In 1999, it was ranked second in the Top Ten Construction Achievements of the Twentieth Century.

Construction never ends, however. The bridge is undergoing a seismic retrofit to make it even more able to withstand earthquakes. Painting and maintenance are ongoing tasks. Seventeen ironworkers and thirty-eight painters work on maintenance on an ongoing basis.

Since the Bridge, Highway, and Transportation District cannot levy taxes, bridge tolls are the only way to finance the district, now including the public transportation section, the bus and ferry programs. In 2000, the toll was $3.00, collected only one way, upon entering San Francisco.

Enjoying the Bridge

Driving across the bridge is spectacular, but slower and more relaxed ways to enjoy it are also possible. Pedestrian sidewalks allow sightseers to enjoy the bridge on foot, and bicyclists are also allowed to use these walkways. However, rollerblades, skateboards, or skates are prohibited. Walkers are warned that the weather, even in the summer, can be windy, foggy, and cold, and warm clothing, in addition to comfortable shoes, is suggested. A walk across the bridge takes about an hour.

Near the San Francisco entrance to the bridge are a gift shop and a café, and nearby is a statue of Chief Engineer Joseph Baermann Strauss. Also on the grounds is a sample cross section of one of the main cables so visitors can see the strength that holds the bridge together.

The Golden Gate Bridge has been called the Colossus of the Pacific. Surrounded both to the north and to the south by the Golden Gate National Recreation Area, the largest urban park in the world, and leading directly to one of the most fascinating cities in the world, the Golden Gate Bridge has the reputation as the world's most spectacular bridge and one of the world's most visited sites.

—*Eleanor B. Amico*

For Further Information:

Doherty, Craig A., Katherine M. Doherty, and Bruce S. Glassman. *The Golden Gate Bridge.* Woodbridge, Conn.: Blackbirch Press, 1995. Written for young people, this book documents the building of the Golden Gate Bridge from inception to completion. Includes photographs.

"Golden Gate and San Francisco-Oakland Bay Bridge Construction, 1934-1936." www.sfmuseum.org/assoc/bridge00.html. Historical documents about the building of the bridge, including photographs from various stages of construction.

"Golden Gate Bridge." www.goldengatebridge.org. This comprehensive site maintained by the Bridge, Highway, and Transportation District is detailed and helpful, both for those wanting just to know more about the bridge and for those wishing to visit it.

Golden Gate Bridge: Chief Engineer's Report. San Francisco: Golden Gate Bridge, Highway, and Transportation District, 1970. Reprint of report number 456 of Chief Engineer Strauss to the board of directors. First published in September, 1937, this book presents the details of this engineering feat by the one who knew it best. Includes photographs.

Horton, Tom, and Baron Wolman. *Superspan: The Golden Gate Bridge.* San Francisco: Chronicle Books, 1998. Describes the history of the bridge, as well as information about the bridge today.

Pelta, Kathy. *Bridging the Gate.* Minneapolis: Lerner, 1987. Details the story of the bridge's construction.

Rigler, James. *San Francisco Moon: A Collection of Photography.* Berkeley, Calif.: Ten Speed Press, 1998. Night photographs of many San Francisco scenes, including the spectacularly photogenic Golden Gate Bridge.

Schock, James W. *The Bridge, a Celebration.* San Francisco: MacAdam/Cage, 1997. This large-scale book, filled with color photographs, tells the story of the bridge from the perspective of the people actually involved in its construction.

Haight-Ashbury, San Francisco

Date: Flourished from 1965 to 1970

Relevant issues: Cultural history, literary history, social reform

Significance: The name "Haight-Ashbury" became synonymous in the late 1960's with the counterculture in all areas of the arts and creative expression.

Location: Neighborhood in San Francisco taking its name from the intersection of Haight Street and Ashbury Avenue, four blocks east of Stanyan Street (the eastern terminus of Golden Gate Park) and two blocks south of the Panhandle (an area of green space eight blocks long and one block wide extending eastward from Golden Gate Park)

Site Office:

Haight-Ashbury Neighborhood Council
P.O. Box 170518
San Francisco, CA 94117
ph.: (415) 621-9553

The San Francisco neighborhood known as Haight-Ashbury takes its name from the intersection of Haight Street and Ashbury Avenue, immediately east of the Richmond district, north and south of the Panhandle, and east and southeast of Golden Gate Park. Affordable housing and proximity to Golden Gate Park apparently combined to make "the Haight" a desirable neighborhood and gathering point for the hippies of the 1960's who preferred the Haight to the more cramped and increasingly expensive North Beach district of San Francisco, which had been the locus of the beatnik activities of the 1950's.

The Human Be-In

Almost since the days of Father Junípero Serra and Captain John C. Frémont, San Francisco, the picturesque city of hills by the bay, has attracted artists and seekers of various sorts. Although North Beach had been the undisputed center of beatnik activity, the effect of the business activities of the so-called Hong Kong Mafia was the conversion of bistros and coffeehouses into sweatshops and noodle factories while rents increased in what had been a beatnik-Italian quarter near Broadway and Colum-

bus (site of Lawrence Ferlinghetti's City Lights Books). These pressures conspired to move hipsters south and west toward Haight-Ashbury (or "Hashbury," as some were soon to call it), for its cheap housing which ranged from Victorian-charming to contemporary-mundane but which had nice views of the Panhandle and Golden Gate Park and even of the Presidio and Golden Gate itself if one lived on the streets approaching Buena Vista Park.

Therefore, the neighborhood known as Haight-Ashbury was in many respects a fitting place to host a "Gathering of the Tribes," as the January 14, 1967, San Francisco Human Be-In was called. There was perhaps no more characteristic single event in the so-called hippie period of Haight history than the Human Be-In. Organized by Allen Cohen, an editor at *The San Francisco Oracle*, one of the first underground newspapers, the Be-In was

At the corner of Haight and Ashbury in 1970. (AP/ Wide World Photos)

intended as a "union of love and activism." Young people, poets, musicians, political operatives of the New Left, and college students converged at the Polo Grounds in one of the earliest examples of a mass gathering of young people for a nonpolitical cause. Although the antiwar movement had brought large numbers of young people together in the streets, organizing principles of the Human Be-In were very different. People came to "drop acid" (take LSD), listen to poetry and music, celebrate together their new religion of being in the countercultural congregation, enjoy the new-found sense of community, and celebrate the earth and themselves and each other.

Unlike rallies across the bay in Berkeley, there was nothing at all political at the Be-In. As the ingested LSD began to affect the collective consciousness, and the smells of marijuana and incense filled the air, a notable palette of San Francisco musicians and poets entertained the crowd in what became essentially the first major outdoor festival concert and happening—fully two and a half years before Woodstock and half a year before the notable 1967 Monterey Pop Festival. Timothy Leary, formerly a Harvard researcher, greeted the audience with what would later become his signature statement: "Tune in, turn on, drop out." The Grateful Dead, Jefferson Airplane, and Quicksilver Messenger Service played music throughout the afternoon. Poet Gary Snyder chanted the mantra of Maitreya, and poet Allen Ginsberg chanted the mantra of Shiva and danced in excitement as more and more people gathered. Other readings included those by poets Michael McClure, Ferlinghetti, and Lenore Kandel, all of whom were a part of the San Francisco literary community of the 1960's. The Diggers, a neosocialist community group familiarly known as the "hip Salvation Army," were very active, giving away slices of apple, turkey sandwiches, incense, and feathers. Although Jerry Rubin spoke briefly on behalf of the free speech and radical left movements of Berkeley, the events of the day were otherwise essentially apolitical. The crowd was estimated at anywhere from ten to twenty thousand, but the statistic is not as important as the effect: The music and poetry and drug-taking were no longer just occurring within the dark, evening confines of the Fillmore and Avalon Ballrooms—it was right out in the open, in daylight. There is perhaps no better musical evocation of the period than one-hit wonder Scott Mackenzie's song, "San Francisco," which includes the lyrical refrain, "If you're going to San Francisco,/ Be sure to wear some flowers in your hair."

The Free Clinic
What followed in Haight-Ashbury from the Human Be-In was the Summer of Love, 1967. With the lyrics of "San Francisco" as background, not only young adults but also teenagers, many of them runaways, converged in San Francisco, especially the Haight-Ashbury district, in the fabled summer of 1967. It remains a moot point whether the Haight at its countercultural zenith was populated with serious cultural radicals or merely with teenyboppers and runaways. What is undeniable, however, is that the medical needs of the community increased proportionally as the population—residential and street—swelled in the Haight during 1967 and 1968. Although the ethos of the Haight included freedom and openness, the presence of runaways and the active drug trafficking resulted in some community-wide paranoia. Countercultural journalist Hunter S. Thompson wrote, "Love is the password in the Haight-Ashbury, but paranoia is the style. Nobody wants to go to jail."

Although most of the inhabitants of the Haight did not have much money or personal possessions, their naturally passive attitudes as well as the effects of drugs rendered them easy targets of criminals. Hippie girls and women were especially vulnerable to attack, and such victims, due to their illegal drug usage, generally passive dispositions, and perhaps their status as runaways as well, were often reluctant to report crimes to the police or to seek legal redress.

In this context, affordable and universal health care was sorely needed. Dr. David Smith and his landmark Haight-Ashbury Free Clinic filled the vacuum in this regard. Located at 409 Clayton Avenue at the corner of Haight Street, the clinic was in the heart of the Haight-Ashbury neighborhood. It was founded on the belief that health care is a right, not a privilege. The health care administered by the Free Clinic was intended to be free, comprehensive, and nonjudgmental. Above all, it was to be humane. The history of the Haight-Ashbury Free Clinic remains one of the more positive legacies of the era.

The Summer of Love

In an April 5, 1967, press conference, *Oracle* editor and Be-In co-producer Allen Cohen announced that the summer of 1967 would be the "Summer of Love" in San Francisco. Coffeehouse owners and head shop owners, along with other small business-people in the Haight, combined to organize the Haight Independent Proprietors (HIP), a community and business organization. HIP subsequently formed the Council for the Summer of Love for the express purpose of directing Summer of Love activities. Although the Council was organized for what may seem to be valid purposes and objectives, the Diggers strenuously opposed what they perceived to be the increasing commercialization of the Haight. The Diggers would have preferred to keep media attention away from the Haight and the so-called hippie phenomenon, which even merited a *Time* magazine cover story for the July 7, 1967, issue: "The Hippies: The Philosophy of a Subculture." Many Haight residents grew bitter as their neighborhood was overrun with tourists, runaways, and increased police patrols while the rest of the country waxed nostalgic very quickly about what was perceived to be the charming countercultural community of Haight-Ashbury.

Death of the Hippie and Continuing Legacies

Police surveillance and media exposure combined with the natural, deleterious effects of a culture centered on drug-taking to doom the naïvely positive ethos that Haight-Ashbury had represented in 1965 and 1966. As early as October 6, 1967, a "Death of the Hippie" funeral service and parade was held, though the hippie ethos remained operative well into the 1970's. However, as marijuana was subsumed by cocaine, PCP (angel dust), STP, and even heroin as the Haight drugs of choice, the resulting human cost was proportionally higher as well. By the mid-1970's, many of the HIP storefronts were closed, and the crime rate soared in the Haight. A rejuvenated Haight developed in the mid- and late 1970's, largely through the gay pride movement and the political activism of supervisor Harvey Milk and others. Gay and lesbian store-owners started shops for cut and dried flowers, essential oils, and many of the types of arts and crafts that had been purveyed by the HIP storeowners one decade earlier. To this day, the Haight remains a countercultural mecca, the haven now for people informed and inspired by a gay and lesbian ethos rather than by the former hippie ethos.

Places to Visit

Any visit to the Haight should begin at the eastern terminus of Golden Gate Park at the so-called Hippie Hill. Proceed east along the eight blocks of the Panhandle, site of many impromptu concerts and Diggers free food giveaways. At 1748 Haight Street, the Straight Theater ("The Straight on the Haight")—site of a vaudeville movie theater that was renovated into a multimedia environmental theater which hosted the likes of the Grateful Dead, Janis Joplin with Big Brother and the Holding Company, Country Joe and the Fish, and Santana—was demolished in 1981. Many other sites of interest remain, however, including the Xanadu Leather Shop (1764 Haight Street), I/Thou Coffee Shop (1736 Haight Street), and the former site of the Diggers' Free Store (1090 Cole Street). —*Richard Sax*

For Further Information:

Gips, Elizabeth. *Scrapbook of a Haight-Ashbury Pilgrim: Spirit, Sacraments, and Sex in 1967-68.* San Francisco: Changes, 1994.

Harrison, Hank. *The Dead.* Millbrae, Calif.: Celestial Arts, 1980. This definitive history of the Grateful Dead through 1979 includes information on Haight-Ashbury as well as black-and-white photographs and several appendices, including five astrological charts for what Harrison considers to be the five watershed episodes in the development of San Francisco rock music culture.

Hoskyns, Barney. *Beneath the Diamond Sky: Haight-Ashbury, 1965-1970.* New York: Simon & Schuster, 1997. This is an evenhanded and accurate chronicle of the Haight during the psychedelic era with black-and-white photographs of significant musicians and other key figures.

Lurie, Toby. *Haight Street Blues.* San Francisco: Journeys I, 1988.

Obst, Linda, ed. *The Sixties.* New York: Random House/Rolling Stone Press, 1977. In a large-scale format reminiscent of *Life* magazine, this 315-page text is organized chronologically with five or six discrete articles on each year, including relevant material on San Francisco, the Haight, and the counterculture. There are large, museum-quality photographs.

O'Neill, William L. *Coming Apart: An Informal History of America in the 1960's.* New York: Quadrangle, 1971. A well-crafted combination of a scholarly and carefully researched text that is also very accessible reading. O'Neill, a history professor at Rutgers University, devotes a long chapter to the counterculture.

Pareles, Jon, and Patricia Romanowsky, eds. *The Rolling Stone Encyclopedia of Rock and Roll.* New York: Summit Books, 1983. This definitive rock and roll encyclopedia includes relevant articles on each of the San Francisco psychedelic groups that lived and played in the Haight during the mid-1960's.

Perry, Charles. *The Haight-Ashbury: A History.* New York: Random House, 1984. This text remains the definitive history of Haight-Ashbury.

Hearst Castle

Date: Built between 1919 and 1947

Relevant issues: Art and architecture

Significance: A California State Historical Monument that is also listed on the National Register of Historic Places, this 165-room, 127-acre estate was built by and for newspaper publisher William Randolph Hearst; the architect was Julia Morgan, and the landscape designer was Morgan, assisted by Orrin Peck, Gardner Daily, and Isabella Worn.

Location: At 750 Hearst Castle Road, on Highway 1, overlooking the Pacific Ocean in the Santa Lucia Mountains halfway between San Francisco and Los Angeles; about five miles inland from and 1,600 feet above San Simeon Bay

Site Office:
Hearst San Simeon State Historical Monument
P.O. Box 8
750 Hearst Castle Road
San Simeon, CA 93452
ph.: (800) 444-4445; (805) 927-2020

Hearst Castle is an appropriate monument to a man who did nothing in his life by half measures. William Randolph Hearst built a far-reaching publishing empire that influenced the news as well as reported it, amassed a huge collection of art and antiquities, produced (and in-

spired) motion pictures, socialized with the wealthiest and most famous people of his time, and presided over not one but several vast and luxurious homes, including a million-acre cattle ranch in Mexico, a castle in Wales, and numerous New York properties. Of all Hearst's homes, however, Hearst Castle at San Simeon is the most famous and is said to be where Hearst was happiest.

A Publishing and Motion-Picture Empire

When construction began at San Simeon in 1919, Hearst was fifty-six years old and had been in the newspaper business for thirty-two years. He began running his first newspaper, the *San Francisco Examiner,* in 1887. His father, George Hearst, who had made a fortune in mining and ranching, had ac-

La Casa del Sol guest house at Hearst Castle. (American Stock Photography)

quired the newspaper in 1880 as payment for a debt. William, having been expelled from Harvard University and looking for something to do with his life, decided he would like to take over the *Examiner*.

He invested in up-to-date printing technology, improved the newspaper's appearance, and began publishing the types of stories for which Hearst papers became famous—sensationalistic, often manufactured news, and investigative campaigns to expose various misdeeds. The *Examiner*'s circulation increased and its financial health improved, and Hearst soon added newspapers in New York, Chicago, and other cities. A measure of Hearst's influence was his *New York Journal*'s successful advocacy of war with Spain in 1898. His papers promoted numerous other causes; early in Hearst's career, he took markedly liberal stands, but he turned quite conservative as he grew older. He also became involved in politics more directly. He was elected to the U.S. Congress from New York in 1902 and 1904 but ran unsuccessfully for mayor of New York City and governor of New York State, and he lost his bid for the Democratic presidential nomination.

Hearst continued adding to his business ventures, going into magazine publishing in the early 1900's and film production in the teens. Films were a way for Hearst to promote the career of his mistress, actress Marion Davies, whom he met in 1916 when she was a performer in the Ziegfeld Follies stage show. Hearst's Cosmopolitan Productions starred Davies in forty-six films between 1917 and 1937. While Hearst's wife, Millicent, spent most of her time on the East Coast, Davies would become his hostess at San Simeon.

Designing a Castle in California

Hearst's family had owned property at San Simeon since 1865, when his father bought the Piedra Blanca ranch there. George Hearst subsequently added the adjacent Santa Rosa and San Simeon ranches. George Hearst died in 1891, leaving everything to his widow, Phoebe Apperson Hearst. When she died in 1918, she willed the land to her only child, William Randolph Hearst. He dubbed the hilltop property La Cuesta Encantada—The Enchanted Hill.

He initially envisioned a reasonably modest vacation home, along with some guest houses, on the San Simeon property. He, his wife, and five sons had made frequent camping trips there. In 1919, he retained Julia Morgan to begin designing the buildings. In 1894, Morgan had been one of the first women to receive a degree in civil engineering from the University of California at Berkeley, and in 1902 she became the first woman to receive a certificate in architecture from the École des Beaux Arts in Paris. She had worked on the design and construction of Phoebe Hearst's estate, Hacienda del Pozo de Verona in Pleasanton, California, from 1903 to 1910, and in 1915 she had designed the Spanish Mission-style headquarters for William Randolph Hearst's *Los Angeles Examiner* newspaper. Morgan received substantial input from her client on the design for the buildings at San Simeon, and the plans grew ever more elaborate. Hearst decided he wanted a complex of structures reminiscent of a hill town in Spain, and from this point his vision continued to evolve. As biographer W. A. Swanberg put it in *Citizen Hearst* (1961):

> San Simeon . . . was a mosaic of Hearst's memories, inspirations and possessions. In his card-index memory he had recollections of decorative schemes and arrangements he had seen in European castles and cathedrals, and which he wished to incorporate in his own palace. In his New York warehouse and in huge basement crypts at San Simeon he had the antique accumulation of years—entire gothic rooms, carved ceilings, choir stalls, paneling, staircases, corbels, stained glass, sarcophagi, mantels, columns, tapestries, a thousand other things—which he was determined to make a part of his castle. Thus, San Simeon was not only a vast construction project but also a complicated assembly job that kept Hearst and Miss Morgan in repeated sessions of close consultation. The castle was not so much a home as it was a museum, a setting for Hearst.

The first buildings to be completed were the three guest houses, set in a half-moon formation around the main building. Although Hearst's and Morgan's design plans referred to the guest houses as "cottages," each actually is a mansion. The houses were constructed in an Italian Renaissance style. La Casa del Mar (house of the sea), the largest of the three, was ready for occupancy by 1921. During most of the 1920's, Hearst spent his time at San Simeon in that house. La Casa del Monte (house of the mountain) and La Casa del Sol (house of the sun) were finished by 1924. Each of the houses was furnished with impressive collections of art and antiques, many between five hundred and one thousand years old.

Excavation for the Mediterranean Revival-style main building, La Casa Grande, began in 1922. The initial plan for the home called for one tower, but as the plans evolved Morgan and Hearst settled on the two-tower design that makes the 137-foot-high building so striking today. The white stone-and-concrete facade was decorated with carved teak, colored tiles, antique Spanish limestone figures, and cast-stone ornaments created by contemporary artisans. By 1926, enough of the house was finished that it was livable, but many sections were not completed until the 1930's, and it always remained a work in progress, as Hearst continued to come up with ideas. Hearst moved into La Casa Grande in 1928, and while he maintained other homes, it became his primary one.

Among the striking interior elements of La Casa Grande are the huge Assembly Room, a two-story, eighty-by-thirty-foot sitting room by which one enters the house; the Refectory, or dining room, containing a twenty-eight-foot stone mantel and life-size carved figures of saints; and the Doge's Suite, modeled after the Doge's Palace in Venice. The home also contains libraries, a theater (in which Hearst and Davies showed films), and a restaurant-size kitchen outfitted with the most up-to-date equipment of the time.

In all, La Casa Grande and the guest houses contain 165 rooms. La Casa Grande covers 60,645 square feet; La Casa del Mar, 5,875; La Casa del Monte, 2,291; and La Casa del Sol, 2,604. The complex contains many antique architectural fixtures obtained by Hearst during his travels and some reproductions. There also are numerous antique furnishings, including Egyptian and Renaissance sculptures, Roman sarcophagi, Chinese and Greek vases, Persian carpets, and clerical tapestries. Many other wealthy people of Hearst's time acquired huge and diverse collections of art and antiquities, but the Hearst collection at San Simeon is one of the largest that still exists.

The Estate Grounds

The grounds at San Simeon are as impressive as the buildings. The main outdoor pool, the Neptune Pool, is more than one hundred feet long and has a capacity of 345,000 gallons. It is surrounded by semicircular marble colonnades and a Greco-Roman temple facade. A terrace that overlooks the pool sits atop seventeen dressing rooms. The pool is notable for its engineering as well as its appearance. Set on a site excavated from the hillside, the pool is supported by reinforced concrete beams. Water from nearby natural springs is captured in two huge reservoirs, one holding up to 345,000 gallons, another able to contain 1.2 million gallons. Heating and filtration equipment are housed underneath the pool. An opulent indoor pool, the Roman Pool, lies beneath two tennis courts. The pool is lined with Venetian glass and gold.

The gardens on the castle grounds were designed to complement the buildings. Ornamented with statues, fountains, terraces, and walkways, the gardens are reminiscent of those in Spanish and Italian villas, with some American touches. Hearst gave instructions as to the types of flowers, shrubs, and trees to be planted, while Morgan designed the layout of the gardens, with assistance from Hearst's friend Orrin Peck, architect Gardner Daily, and horticulturalist Isabella Worn. The primary flowers planted were roses, azaleas, rhododendrons, fuchsias, and camellias, Hearst's favorite. Five greenhouses were built to supply the garden.

One of the more unusual features of Hearst's estate was a two thousand-acre zoo. The zoo was begun in late 1924 and for several years thereafter visitors could encounter wild animals including lions, bears, giraffes, and elephants, housed in spaces designed by Morgan to make the animals both visible and comfortable. By 1939, however, Hearst had given his animal collection to the San Diego and San Francisco zoos.

Citizen Hearst and the Final Years

Another kind of wildlife flourished at the Hearst estate, especially during the 1930's. Hearst and Davies entertained most of the established and rising stars of Hollywood during that period. Guests included motion-picture stars Clark Gable, Bette Davis, Gary Cooper, Cary Grant, Joan Crawford, and David Niven. The masquerade parties held on Hearst's birthday were particular highlights. Celebrities of the sports world visited San Simeon as well; tennis tournaments there featured such stars as Bill Tilden and Alice Marble.

One Hollywood celebrity who attracted Hearst's wrath instead of his hospitality was actor-director writer Orson Welles, who satirized Hearst in the classic 1941 motion picture *Citizen Kane*. The film told the story of ruthless newspaper magnate Charles Foster Kane, ending his life alone and unloved in a vast estate called Xanadu, after having tried to make an opera star of his talentless wife, Susan Alexander Kane. Hearst's newspapers refused to review the film and forbid any mention of Welles or of RKO Pictures, the studio that released it. Hearst was abetted in his campaign by Louella Parsons, who wrote a Hollywood gossip column for his papers; Hearst's son, William Randolph Hearst, Jr., contended, perhaps disingenuously, that the anti-Welles vendetta was all Parson's doing. The uproar over the film made it difficult for RKO to get it into theaters, but the few audiences it reached liked it, as did reviewers. Most critics and scholars continue to consider *Citizen Kane* one of the greatest films ever produced.

By the late 1930's Hearst's power was diminishing and his finances were shaky. He had earned a fortune, but his spending more than kept pace with his income; he was estimated to have spent between $30 million and $40 million on the San Simeon estate alone. In 1937, the Securities and Exchange Commission refused a Hearst Organization request to issue $35.5 million in debentures, noting that Hearst's companies already were under a staggering load of debt. Hearst turned financial control of his holdings over to lawyer Clarence Shearn, who appointed a committee of Hearst Organization executives, known as the Conservation Committee, to begin selling money-losing businesses as well as many of Hearst's art treasures, although the collection at San Simeon remained fantastic. The committee's efforts returned Hearst's corporate structure to some measure of health, helped along by improved newspaper circulation and advertising during World War II—a war that Hearst had urged the United States to avoid.

Hearst remained in reasonably good health well into his eighties. He attempted unsuccessfully to regain financial control of his publishing enterprises but continued to involve himself in editorial matters. He retained his enthusiasm for building as well, with additions to La Casa Grande going on until 1947. That year, Hearst suffered a serious heart seizure, and his doctors advised him to leave San Simeon so that he could have better access to medical care. Hearst and Davies moved to Beverly Hills.

When Hearst died in 1951, his heirs and executors donated the San Simeon estate to the state of California, and the state opened it to the public in 1958.

Hearst Castle is open for tours every day except Thanksgiving, Christmas, and New Year's Day. The site is so vast that there are separate tours for various portions of it. About 1.1 million visitors come to Hearst Castle every year.   —*Trudy Ring*

For Further Information:

Boutelle, Sara Holmes. *Julia Morgan, Architect.* Rev. and updated ed. New York: Abbeville Press, 1995. Provides many details on the architect's work at San Simeon and elsewhere. Informative and beautifully illustrated.

Hearst, William Randolph, Jr., with Jack Casserly. *The Hearsts: Father and Son.* Niwot, Colo.: Roberts Rinehart, 1991. Far less objective than Swanberg's biography listed below, but certainly intimate. Both biographies contain information about the development of the San Simeon estate and Hearst's life there.

Swanberg, W. A. *Citizen Hearst.* Reprint. New York: Galahad Books, 1996. One of the best biographies of William Randolph Hearst. Lively and comprehensive.

Hollywood

Date: Founded in 1888

Relevant issues: Business and industry, cultural history

Significance: This section of Los Angeles is considered the home of the U.S. motion-picture and television industry; although the industry has spread far beyond the boundaries of Hollywood, the name also is used to describe this business as a whole.

Location: In Los Angeles, northwest of the downtown area; roughly bounded by the Hollywood Hills on the north, Vermont Avenue on the east, Olympic Boulevard on the south, and Fairfax Avenue on the west

Site Office:
Hollywood Visitor Information Center
The Janes House
Janes Square
6541 Hollywood Boulevard
Hollywood, CA 90028
ph.: (213) 461-4213
Web site: chamber.hollywood.com

Hollywood is both a geographic area—a neighborhood of Los Angeles—and something more. The term "Hollywood" encompasses the entire industry of U.S. film and television production, although much of the activity takes place in such neighboring Los Angeles suburbs as Burbank and Culver City, and some even outside the Los Angeles area. During the twentieth century Hollywood has come to symbolize the glamour of show business and U.S. influence on popular culture worldwide. The most prosperous period for Hollywood filmmaking lasted roughly from 1920 to 1950. Major studios then turned to television production to supplement their big-screen output, and many of the studios became part of major corporate conglomerates. Most studios continue to maintain headquarters in the Los Angeles area.

The Advent of Film
Before the arrival of film studios in the early twentieth century, Hollywood was merely a small desert community. It had been part of a ranch in the 1850's, and in 1887 a man named Horace Wilcox gave the area the name of Hollywood and began selling lots for home building there. In 1910, when Hollywood's population was about four thousand, it was annexed to Los Angeles, primarily to gain access to the Los Angeles water supply. By then the filmmakers had begun arriving.

The U.S. film industry had originated on the East Coast. In the late 1880's and early 1890's, Thomas Alva Edison developed a motion-picture camera, as well as a machine called the Kinetoscope, which made it possible to view silent films through a peephole. The coin-operated Kinetoscopes were placed in penny arcades, where people could come to see the films. Arcade operators changed the films weekly, and this great demand for new films led Edison to create a studio in West Orange, New Jersey, in 1893. New York and Chicago were other centers of early film production.

Edison's company and others soon developed motion-picture projectors, which made it possible to show films to many people at once and made films more popular than ever.

As film technology developed and improved, patent infringement suits often resulted. In the early 1900's the Edison Company and another early film studio, Biograph, formed the Motion Picture Patents Company to control the licensure of patented technologies. Ten eastern and midwestern film production companies, including Edison and Biograph, were licensees. This was one factor that fueled the industry's migration to Los Angeles—producers who were not licensed by the patents company believed they might be able to evade lawsuits if they were located in Southern California, as it was not easily accessible from the East Coast and was close to the Mexican border.

Even some of the patents company's licensees, however, filmed in Los Angeles in the winter months, taking advantage of the area's climate and landscape, which in the long run were the most compelling reasons for film producers to locate there. Los Angeles's year-round warm weather and sunshine made for ideal filming conditions, and the desert, ocean, and mountains provided interesting locations. Another attraction of Los Angeles was that its labor force at the time was mostly nonunion; unionization would take hold in the 1930's.

The Birth of Studios
Most early film operations in Los Angeles were not in Hollywood proper. Late in 1907 the Chicago-based Selig Company set up a makeshift studio in downtown Los Angeles to shoot scenes for *The Count of Monte Cristo*. In 1909 Selig filmed *The Heart of a Racing Tout* in downtown Los Angeles; this was the first feature-length dramatic film to be shot entirely in California. Documentaries had been filmed in Los Angeles as early as 1903, but the concept of using film to tell a dramatic story was just beginning to develop then. *The Great Train Robbery*, produced by the Edison Company in 1903, is generally considered the first film with a plot.

Other filmmakers began wintering in Los Angeles, and the establishment of permanent studios quickly followed. D. W. Griffith, at the time with Biograph, filmed in Los Angeles in 1909 and 1910, mostly in the downtown area. Kalem and other eastern companies set up studios in the Los Angeles area around this time. The first studio in Hollywood proper was established in 1911 by the Nestor Film Corporation, formerly of Bayonne, New Jersey, in what had been a tavern at the corner of Sunset and Gower Streets. Carl Laemmle, founder of Universal Pictures, set up shop across the street in 1912. The number of film studios in this vicinity mushroomed, and the area was nicknamed "Gower Gulch." Short films, mostly comedies and westerns, dominated the studios' output; Hollywood's first feature-length film, *The Squaw Man*, was shot in a studio at Vine and Selma Streets in 1913. The film was produced by the Jesse L. Lasky Feature Play Company, founded by Lasky, a vaudeville manager, and his brother-in-law, Samuel Goldfish, who later changed his name to Goldwyn and became one of Hollywood's most successful independent film producers. Its director was Cecil B. DeMille, who later became famous for his spectacular biblical films.

Filmmaking was becoming more sophisticated. Motion-picture performers had once labored with some degree of anonymity, but certain ones became especially popular with audiences and were promoted by their studios as "stars." Florence Lawrence, whom Laemmle hired away from Biograph, is considered the first movie star; other performers who became stars in the 1910's and 1920's included Mary Pickford, Theda Bara, and Charlie Chaplin. Writing and directing techniques improved as well. One of the key developers of the art of filmmaking was Griffith, who left Biograph in 1912 and began producing and directing films independently. His 1915 release *The Birth of a Nation* is considered a landmark for its innovative camera work and sheer storytelling power, although it later was subject to much criticism because of the racist attitudes displayed in this melodramatic story of the U.S. Civil War and Reconstruction.

By the 1920's, the Hollywood film industry was in full bloom. Over the next three decades, the industry was dominated by the "big five" studios (MGM, Warner Bros., Paramount, RKO, and Twentieth Century-Fox), with significant contributions as well from the "little two" (Universal and Columbia). There were other companies that carved specialized niches—Republic, for instance, mostly made low-budget Western films, and Disney was the home of cartoons and family fare. There also were independent producers who did not work for any studio but arranged for the studios to distribute their films; the best known of these were David O. Selznick and Samuel Goldwyn. Hollywood films were the leading form of entertainment in the United States and served a substantial overseas market as well. Films from other countries, including France, Germany, and Russia, might have been considered more artistic, but the Hollywood product was the last word in popular entertainment.

Some of the major film studios were in Hollywood proper, such as Paramount, at Marathon Street and Bronson Avenue, and RKO, at Gower Street and Melrose Avenue. Warner Bros. and Universal originally had operations in Hollywood but soon moved to the San Fernando Valley north of the Santa Monica Mountains (of which the Hollywood Hills are a section), with Warners based in the community of Burbank and Universal in Universal City. Culver City, about six miles southwest of Hollywood, was home to the most prestigious studio, MGM, which claimed to have "more stars than there are in the heavens." Culver City differed from other film production centers in the Los Angeles area in that its developer, Harry H. Culver, had consciously set out to attract the film industry. Among those he attracted was pioneer producer Thomas Ince, who set up a studio in Culver City in 1915. After his business failed, the facility was used by Sam Goldwyn and finally, beginning in 1924, by MGM.

Effect on Los Angeles

The industry transformed Los Angeles. By the end of the 1920's, the city's population was nearly 1.25 million, up from 100,000 at the century's beginning. The Hollywood neighborhood had 150,000 residents. The film industry employed thousands of actors, writers, producers, directors, and technicians. Other entertainment businesses, such as recording and radio broadcasting, were important to Los Angeles as well. Many broadcast studios were in the area of Hollywood Boulevard and Vine Street, in the heart of Hollywood.

Residential and commercial development of the Los Angeles area were by-products of the booming film industry. Many early film stars and executives built homes in Los Feliz, a neighborhood lying between Hollywood and downtown Los Angeles. Eventually, the suburb of Beverly Hills supplanted Los Feliz as the most fashionable address for the show business set. Beverly Hills, once the site of unsuccessful oil exploration, was founded as a residential community by a real estate developer in 1907. It grew slowly until the movie-star couple of Douglas Fairbanks, Sr., and Mary Pickford built their mansion, Pickfair, in Beverly Hills in 1920. Others from the film industry quickly followed suit.

Fashionable shops, restaurants, and nightclubs also catered to the film community. Many of the nightclubs, including the Trocadero, Mocambo, and Ciro's, were on a stretch of Sunset Boulevard called the Sunset Strip, in West Hollywood. West Hollywood, originally called Sherman, had not been annexed to the city of Los Angeles as had Hollywood. It was under the jurisdiction of Los Angeles County authorities, who were said to be more lenient than their city counterparts, allowing nightlife to flourish.

Challenges for the Industry

During Hollywood's booming period, there still were challenges to be met. There was the conversion from silence to sound, with Warner Bros.'s release of *The Jazz Singer* in 1927; criticism of Hollywood by religious leaders and other moral guardians, with the industry eventually staving off outside censors by regulating itself; and the Great Depression of the 1930's, which forced many studios to cut their expenditures but saw the public continue to attend motion pictures, which provided an affordable means of entertainment and escapism.

As the war in Europe escalated in the late 1930's, the U.S. film industry lost some of its export markets, but for the most part business continued as usual. In 1939, the year that England declared war on Germany, the U.S. film community enjoyed what many consider to be its peak year, with the release of a huge number of classic motion pictures, including *Gone with the Wind*, *The Wizard of Oz*, *Stagecoach*, *Mr. Smith Goes to Washington*, *Ninotchka*, *Wuthering Heights*, and *Goodbye Mr. Chips*.

The war could not be held at bay indefinitely, however. After the Japanese attack on Pearl Harbor precipitated the United States' entry into World War II in 1941, films became important to the war effort. Films displayed much patriotic sentiment, mandated by the U.S. Office of War Information. The industry lost personnel to the armed forces and had trouble obtaining some needed materials,

but overall the war years were good to Hollywood. Americans had plenty of discretionary income, due to the wartime manufacturing boom, but few consumer goods to buy, due to wartime rationing; so many of them spent their money at the movies, which also provided a distraction from the problems of a world at war. The combined profits of the eight largest studios grew from $19.4 million in 1940 to $35 million in 1941; profits approached $50 million the following year and $60 million each of the next three years, surpassing pre-Depression levels. In 1946 the industry had a record $122 million profit—but major changes in the business were in the works.

The End of the Studio System

In the late 1930's the U.S. Department of Justice had brought an antitrust suit against eight major film studios. The suit was aimed at breaking the control that studios had over the distribution and exhibition of their films. This control was maintained through such practices as block booking (forcing theaters to commit to showing several mediocre films in order to obtain the most desirable ones) and studio ownership of theater chains. The war delayed action on the suit, but postwar rulings by a U.S. District Court (in 1946) and the U.S. Supreme Court (in 1948) found the studios in violation of antitrust laws and led to the divestiture of studio-owned theaters and an end to other monopolistic practices.

The major studios also saw their power over their employees diminish in the postwar years. Studios generally signed performers to seven-year contracts. During this period, if a performer refused any role, the studio could suspend the actor without pay and add suspension time to the end of the contract, thereby preventing the performer from seeking work elsewhere even at the end of the seven years. Actress Olivia de Havilland challenged this practice in a lawsuit filed in California in 1943, and the Superior Court of California ruled in her favor the following year. The decision was later upheld by the state appellate and supreme courts. A studio could no longer add suspension time to a performer's contract, and actors had more freedom to market their services. Performers began to work on a freelance basis. This increasing independence, plus tax considerations, led in the 1950's to the phenomenon of actors working for a percent-

The famous Hollywood sign. (Digital Stock)

age of their films' profits, rather than for upfront salaries. This practice proved lucrative for stars and their agents, and talent agents supplanted studios as the major force behind most performers' careers.

The Red Scare and Television

There were two other major developments in Hollywood in the late 1940's. One was the "Red Scare," which saw numerous actors, writers, and directors accused of being communists—a serious accusation in the anticommunist climate of the United States at the time—and prevented from obtaining work in Hollywood. A group known as the "Hollywood Ten" spent time in jail, on charges of contempt of the U.S. Congress. Others fled to Europe or worked in Hollywood under assumed names; some had their careers wrecked altogether.

The other development had an even greater impact. World War II had delayed the commercial exploitation of television technology, but with war's end television began its reach into almost every home in the United States. By 1948, 200,000 television sets were being sold each month, and theater attendance was dropping precipitously. The ascendancy of television destroyed the old Hollywood, with its focus on films for theatrical exhibition; but it gave birth to the new Hollywood, emphasizing production of television programs. By 1959, all the major Hollywood studios were making television series and specials, supplementing a greatly reduced output of theatrical films, which dealt with increasingly more adult themes. The studios thus remained a force in Hollywood, in their new role sharing power with television networks, talent agents, and independent filmmakers.

Hollywood Today

While the industry of Hollywood changed, the face of Hollywood changed as well, but some aspects of the glory years remain. Paramount is the last major studio in Hollywood proper; it offers only limited tours to the general public, but it is possible for visitors to get inside the Paramount lot by obtaining tickets to television programs taped there. In the San Fernando Valley, Universal and Warner Bros. offer more extensive tours.

On the Sunset Strip in West Hollywood, the nightclubs popular in the 1930's and 1940's have long since closed, but the Strip remains home to other, newer nightspots, as well as huge billboards promoting the latest efforts of film, television, and recording stars. West Hollywood, which became an independent municipality in 1984, also is the heart of the Los Angeles gay community.

Beverly Hills is still a wealthy community and home to many people in the entertainment business. It also is the site of the Academy of Motion Picture Arts and Sciences—best known for giving its annual awards, the Oscars—and the offices of leading talent agencies and other companies involved in various aspects of entertainment. Other suburban communities with numerous show-business residents include Bel Air and the beaches and canyons of Malibu. A variety of sightseeing tours to the homes of the stars are available in the Los Angeles area.

No visit to Hollywood would be complete without a look at Mann's (formerly Grauman's) Chinese Theatre, on Hollywood Boulevard, where stars have left their handprints and footprints in cement since 1927. Also on Hollywood Boulevard is the Hollywood Walk of Fame, a twelve-block stretch of star-shaped plaques, embedded in the sidewalk, bearing the names of show-business celebrities. Overlooking it all is the famed Hollywood sign. The sign, in the Hollywood Hills, originally read "Hollywoodland" when it was put up in 1923 to advertise a real estate development. With its last syllable removed, the sign stands as an emblem of Hollywood, the place, and Hollywood, the industry.

—*Trudy Ring*

For Further Information:

Alleman, Richard. *The Movie Lover's Guide to Hollywood.* New York: Harper, 1985. A detailed guide to historic places in Hollywood and greater Los Angeles. However, an updated edition is needed.

Clarke, Charles G. *Early Film Making in Los Angeles.* Los Angeles: Dawson's Book Shop, 1976. A slender volume containing the reminiscences of a veteran cinematographer; Clarke provides a rather quick overview, but his book contains several bits of information not available elsewhere.

Friedrich, Otto. *City of Nets: A Portrait of Hollywood in the 1940's.* London: Headline Books, 1987. Indispensable for readers whose primary interests are Hollywood personalities and studio politics in the golden era.

Mast, Gerald. *A Short History of the Movies.* 7th ed. Boston: Allyn & Bacon, 2000. A scholarly yet accessible exploration of the art of filmmaking, with some attention to the development of the industry.

Schatz, Thomas. *The Genius of the System.* New York: Pantheon, 1988. Views industry developments at four representative studios.

Stanley, Robert H. *The Celluloid Empire: A History of the American Movie Industry.* New York: Hastings House, 1978. Numerous books have been written about the careers of various Hollywood performers, directors, and studio executives, but this book is one of the few that traces the development of Hollywood as a whole. A thorough, informative, and readable account.

John Muir National Historic Site

Date: Established in 1964

Relevant issues: Cultural history, education, literary history, political history, social reform, western expansion

Significance: John Muir lived in the seventeen-room Victorian house at this site from 1890 until his death in 1914. In the upstairs "scribble den," he wrote books and articles to educate the American public on the importance of conserving wilderness. Muir helped to found the Sierra Club and served as its president. Historians often describe Muir as the "Father of National Parks."

Location: Fifty miles northeast of San Francisco in Contra Costa County near Martinez

Site Office:
John Muir National Historic Site
4202 Alhambra Avenue
Martinez, CA 94553
ph.: (925) 228-8860
fax: (925) 228-8192
Web site: www.npa.gov/jomu

Recognition of John Muir's influential role in American history increased as the environmental movement grew in the last half of the twentieth century. Muir had long been known as an adventurer, scientist, explorer, and naturalist. Renewed respect for his successes in persuading government to preserve Yosemite and a half dozen other sites as National Parks led to a reexamination of his writing. Adapting elements of his Scottish religious heritage to his own experiences in wild nature enabled Muir to portray vividly the sanctity and interrelatedness of all life-forms.

How Muir Came to Live in California

John Muir moved to California after an accident damaged his eyesight. His vision returned but during the recovery period he decided to leave his early vocation as an inventor, planning instead to travel and collect plant specimens.

Born in Dunbar, Scotland, on April 18, 1838, Muir had come with his family to the United States in 1849. They settled in Wisconsin where Muir lived and worked on the family farm. Although he was not allowed to attend school in America (mainly due to his father's extreme religious views), he did read and create mechanical devices by whittling. When he displayed his remarkable inventions at the state fair he won admiration and was soon invited to attend the University of Wisconsin. There he was introduced to the American philosophy of Transcendentalism and learned of the controversial scientific theory of glaciation introduced by Louis Agassiz in 1840. After two and a half years of study, Muir left school, going first to Canada and later to Indianapolis where the eye injury took place while he was working in a carriage factory.

Muir recovered his vision, but during his convalescence he decided to spend his life seeing the world instead of working in a factory. He left as soon as possible on a thousand-mile walk to the Gulf of Mexico. Journals from the trip record his joy at being immersed in nature even though he ran out of money and food and contracted malaria. He hoped to go on to South America but ended his trip after several weeks in Cuba. Attracted by a brochure on Yosemite, he decided to try California next.

Muir of the Mountains

Arriving in San Francisco in March of 1868, Muir went immediately to a rural area where he worked as a laborer and spent as much time as possible in the mountains. During his first summer in the Sierra Nevada, he was employed as a sheepherder. Returning to the lowlands, he lived nearby for several years while he worked, wrote, and guided visitors on trips into the mountains. Drawn by Muir's reputation for vision and intelligence, Ralph Waldo Emerson became one of many well-known visitors whom Muir guided. Through his scientific observations, Muir was able to prove that glaciers had formed Yosemite—a surprise to the experts who claimed that it had resulted from earthquakes.

Muir's writing campaign in favor of preserving the natural beauty of Yosemite began in the 1870's but was interrupted in 1880 by his marriage and the need to support his family. From 1880 to 1890 Muir, his wife Louie, and his growing family lived in the ranch house of the Strenzel Ranch, given to him along with twenty acres of the fruit ranch by his

John Muir National Historic Site. (National Park Service)

in-laws. Muir soon became responsible for the entire ranch and although his work there was highly profitable, he had little time to write, and his health suffered dramatically.

In 1889, Muir was enlisted to rejoin the wilderness preservation movement. Encouraged by Louie to renew his writing career, Muir took an apartment in San Francisco where he could focus on writing. There, Robert Underwood Johnson, an editor of the important magazine *The Century*, came to persuade Muir to write in Yosemite's defense. Johnson had not forgotten Muir's role as wilderness advocate and author in the 1870's. The two men went camping in areas that Muir had not seen for years. Undisciplined development had spoiled many of Muir's beloved areas: Meadows had been plowed, trees cut, and the forest floor eaten bare by sheep.

Johnson believed that if the American people learned of the tragedy of Yosemite through Muir's words, they would support the creation of a National Park. Yosemite would be the first National Park with the stated purpose of preserving wilderness. Muir agreed to write two articles. Then, when Muir's father-in-law, Dr. John Strenzel, died, the Muir family moved to the Victorian mansion that is the centerpiece of the John Muir Historical Site.

The two articles by Muir in *The Century* helped launch the Yosemite National Park campaign. The law creating the park passed in 1890, and three more National Parks were created in California soon after. In 1891, what is known as "The Enabling Act" was passed, allowing presidents to set aside lands for preservation. Heartened by success but aware of the need for continued vigilance, Muir and his conservation friends founded the Sierra Club in 1892 to protect the Sierra Nevada. Muir's book *The Mountains of California* (1894) increased his audience and heightened his reputation. President Theodore Roosevelt came to Yosemite to camp out with Muir and hear his views on wild nature. Roosevelt was impressed but later supported the multiple use practices advocated by the first chief of the Forest Service, Gifford Pinchot. These practices included ongoing or increased logging, grazing, and other development that preservationists opposed. Muir's worst setback came with the failure of Congress to save the Hetch Hetchy Valley, a part of Yosemite, from being flooded by a dam built to provide San Francisco with water. Muir had opposed the dam for years. The loss of Hetch Hetchy, however, solidified the preservationists, who redoubled their efforts to save wilderness reserves throughout the country.

Time to Revise

From 1890 until his death in 1914, Muir worked diligently at his writing. *Our National Parks* was published in 1901. He often drew from his journals, especially for *My First Summer in the Sierra* (1911) and *My Boyhood and Youth* (1913). Few who read him can forget his vigorous prose—his calling sheep "hoofed locusts" for the destruction they cause in forests and his saying about humans: "Any fool can destroy a tree." Most memorable is his unqualified love for nature. As he wrote in 1875, "No synonym for God is so perfect as Beauty. Whether it is seen as carving the lines of the mountains with glaciers, or gathering matter into stars, or planning the movements of water, or gardening—still all is Beauty."

The legacy of John Muir is remarkable. By the end of the twentieth century, the National Park Service administered over 350 parks, monuments, seashores, rivers, and preserves covering more than eighty million acres—sights visited by over 250 million people yearly. Further, over 650,000 people belong to the Sierra Club, a powerful environmental organization. As these examples indicate, it would be difficult to overestimate the importance of John Muir's leadership as the "Father of National Parks."

When to Visit and What to Do

The John Muir National Historic Site provides visitors with new insight into Muir's indoor life, his family, home, and writing career. The site may be reached by automobile or public transportation. Detailed directions are available from the National Park Service and the Sierra Club. The site is normally open several hours a day, five days per week. There is a small admission fee for adults to be paid at the visitor center, where a thirty-minute film about John Muir can be viewed along with exhibits.

The Muir House and the Martinez Adobe (where Muir's daughter Wanda and her husband lived) are open to visitors. In the Muir House, Victorian furnishings have been used to refurbish the house in the style of the period from 1906 to 1914 as based on descriptions given by Muir's daughters. Reproductions of landscapes by Muir's friend, William Keith, portray the natural scenes that especially inspired Muir, including Tuolumne Meadows and Yosemite Falls. Muir's upstairs bedroom windows have no curtains, as Muir liked to be awakened by the sun. His scribble den, the room in which he wrote his impassioned arguments in defense of wilderness, displays a disheveled authenticity.

Nine acres of the original orchards have been preserved and planted with fruit the Muir family cultivated. These species include plums, pears, apricots, cherries, pomegranates, oranges, and figs. The 1849 Martinez Adobe sits behind the orchards.

In 1988, the National Park Service added 325 acres to the site that were originally part of the Muir-Strentzel Ranch. The parcel includes a hill called Mount Wanda after Muir's oldest daughter, who accompanied him on walks in the surrounding hills. Visitors may also walk there. The area is connected to the original nine acres with a one-mile, self-guided loop trail and several additional miles of fire access roads.

There are numerous special events at the site including John Muir's birthday celebration and an annual celebration of Muir's Scottish heritage. In December, the traditional Mexican celebration of

Christmas, Las Posadas, is centered in the Martinez Adobe. Victorian Christmas decorations are displayed in the Muir house in accordance with the Muir family traditions. Included are pine boughs, red ribbon, and a big laurel branch hung with paper ornaments.

Other special programs at the site include bird walks, wildflower walks, monthly Victorian piano programs, and a junior ranger program. The National Park Service also owns the nearby John Muir gravesite.   —*Margaret A. Dodson*

For Further Information:

Cohen, Michael P. *The Pathless Way: John Muir and American Wilderness.* Madison: University of Wisconsin Press, 1984. Examines Muir's difficult decisions as he struggled to win protection for natural areas by increasing their popularity with the public at large.

"John Muir Exhibit." www.sierraclub.org. An informative site presenting an annotated bibliography of books by and about John Muir, further Internet resources, and information on the "John Muir Library Series" from Sierra Club Books—paperback reprints with introductions by modern writers. All of Muir's published books, now in the public domain, are reprinted at this site for reading online.

Kimes, William F., and Maymie B. Kimes. *John Muir: A Reading Bibliography.* 2d. ed. Davis, Calif.: Panorama West, 1986. A reference for Muir's published work beginning with his first letter on "The Calypso Borealis" in the December, 1866, *Boston Recorder* and concluding with the entry for the John Muir Papers.

Muir, John. *John Muir in His Own Words.* Edited by Peter Browning. Lafayette, Calif.: Great West Books, 1988. Thirteen chapters of quotations arranged in chronological order, including "Going to the Mountains" and "Tourists and Development." Includes detailed index.

Nash, Roderick. "John Muir: Publicizer." In *Wilderness and the American Mind.* 3d. ed. New Haven, Conn.: Yale University Press, 1982. A concise biography emphasizing Muir's role in the creation of national parks.

Wadsworth, Ginger. *John Muir: Wilderness Protector.* Minneapolis: Lerner, 1992. An easy-to-read biography of Muir's personal as well as professional life.

Wolfe, Linnie Marsh, ed. *John of the Mountains: The Unpublished Journals of John Muir.* Reprint. Madison: University of Wisconsin Press, 1979. Shows the journal base from which later works were written.

_____. *Son of the Wilderness: The Life of John Muir.* New York: Alfred A. Knopf, 1945. Reprint. Madison: University of Wisconsin Press, 1978. A well-researched and detailed biography of John Muir.

Little Tokyo, Los Angeles

Date: Founded in 1885
Relevant issues: Asian American history, business and industry, World War II
Significance: This district was the center of Japanese American life prior to World War II, and since the 1910's, home to more Japanese Americans than any other mainland city. The internment of over 100,000 Japanese Americans from the West Coast in 1942 reduced Little Tokyo to a ghost town.
Location: In downtown Los Angeles, bordered by East Los Angeles, Beverly Hills, and Glendale
Site Office:
Japanese American Cultural and Community Center
244 South San Pedro Street, Suite 505
Los Angeles, CA 90012
ph.: (213) 628-2725
fax: (213)617-8576
Web site: www.jaccc.org

Little Tokyo's founding can be traced back to the establishment of a small restaurant by a former seaman, Kame, whose formal name was Hamanosuke Shigeta, on the west side of Los Angeles Street in 1885. A handful of other Japanese men had trickled down from San Francisco by then looking for work. From the onset, there was racial tension between the Issei (first-generation Japanese) and Caucasians. In the ensuing twenty years, many more Japanese came to work on the railway and in farming in the San Gabriel Valley. In 1903, the first publication of the bilingual *Rafu Shimpo* appeared, and the East First Street area was referred to as "Little Tokyo."

The Early Years of Struggle

The year 1907 saw the greatest influx of Japanese at one time to come to the United States: over thirty thousand. A gentlemen's agreement was struck wherein no more unskilled laborers were allowed entry; however, professionals such as doctors and technicians were exempt. More than three hundred businesses in Los Angeles were Japanese-owned, of which forty occupied a mere two blocks of Little Tokyo. Because there were many more men than women, some men secured the assistance of a *haishakunin* (marriage broker) to bring brides from Japan. Between 1910 and 1924, over thirty thousand Japanese women came to America, but not all as a result of prearranged marriages. Some young girls were promised to a groom from the same village, and others joined relatives already in the United States.

The Japanese American National Museum in the Little Tokyo district of Los Angeles. (AP/Wide World Photos)

While anti-Japanese sentiment in San Francisco broke out into mob violence, Los Angeles had its share of racism. One Issei commented, "In those days, they insulted us at will. The best thing was not to go outside of Little Tokyo at all." Japanese immigrants continued undaunted. In 1909, a group of Issei produce vendors started their own market to sell the vegetables grown by Japanese farmers in outlying areas, eventually founding the City Market of Los Angeles at Ninth and Pedro Streets with other ethnic groups. Unfortunately, the success of Japanese agriculture and wholesale produce fanned the flames of an anti-Japanese fire. The California legislature introduced twenty-seven anti-Japanese resolutions in 1911.

In the years before 1924, Little Tokyo residents gathered forces to combat the rising tide of racism, building a hospital, Buddhist temples, the Shonien Japanese Children's Home, schools, and other cultural and educational organizations.

The Rise of the Nisei

By 1924, an immigration act was passed which limited immigration from other parts of the globe but ceased all movement from Japan. The birth of Nisei (first-generation American-born Japanese) helped establish some cultural affiliations with Caucasian Americans but did not stem the tide of hatred. As long as they stayed within "their town," Japanese Americans were relatively safe. However, as soon as they ventured into other parts of the city, landlords and neighbors met them with harsh rebuffs.

Kenjinkai (prefectural associations) acted as employment agencies and assisted families with their finances. Little Tokyo enjoyed lavish New Year's celebrations, annual sumo wrestling tournaments, and spiritually related events. In 1925, Nishi Hongwanji Temple was built, and it soon became a central meeting place for the community; later it was used as a storage facility for the many Japanese Americans forced into internment camps in 1942.

The economic solidarity of the Japanese community—from the abundant farms to the wholesale and retail markets—helped the Japanese through the Great Depression.

The Depression Years

Issei merchants, worried that the more Americanized Nisei were drifting away, collaborated with them in establishing a summer festival to attract people back to Little Tokyo. Kendo and judo (ancient forms of martial arts), as well as sumo, tournaments were held, and later street dances helped to revitalize interest in Little Tokyo.

Despite hard times, Japanese families pulled together to keep financially afloat, and Little Tokyo continued to attract Japanese American farmers from all over. The Yamato Club, later called the Tokyo Club, a famous gambling hall, was established to draw gamblers away from their sizable losses accrued in gambling in Chinatown. While it played host to the "seamier" side of life, the club was reputed to have served needy people with hot meals and even to have made loans to those with compromised credit.

The older generation may have had concerns about their offspring's adherence to Japanese customs, but they were nonetheless proud of the Nisei's accomplishments in an often-rancorous environment. The older and younger generations disagreed, however, on the issue of Japanese foreign policy as the commencement of World War II drew nearer.

By 1941, Japanese Americans were concerned that they would be caught between Japan and America as each country took opposing sides in what was to be a global war. Emissaries of goodwill traveled from Little Tokyo to Washington, D.C., but the Federal Bureau of Investigation (FBI) began investigating members of the Japanese American community anyway.

The Internment

On December 7, 1941, Japan launched a vigorous air raid attack on Pearl Harbor, swiftly sealing the fate of every Japanese American person in the western United States. FBI agents detained community members who had been under surveillance—for several years in some cases. Newspaper publishers and even Buddhist ministers were targeted. The Western Defense Command, helmed by Lieutenant General John L. DeWitt, moved into action, and General DeWitt urged Washington to "collect all alien subjects." Bank accounts were frozen, shops were shut down, and rumors ran rampant that Japanese Americans had sinister plans in store for their American "foes." Additionally, inflammatory news reports questioning Japanese American loyalty whipped up overwhelming hatred against them.

On February 19, 1942, President Franklin D. Roosevelt issued Executive Order 9066 giving the United States Army the authority forcibly to remove more than 110,000 Nikkei (people of Japanese ancestry). Within a month, the first Nisei group met at the Maryknoll Mission to begin the journey to Manzanar, an internment camp in Owens Valley. This marked the beginning of the removal of Japanese Americans from Little Tokyo and outlying areas, scattering them across ten far-flung relocation camps. Forced into selling all they owned except what they could carry, then corralled behind barbed wire, Japanese families made do under very cramped and inhospitable conditions. None knew if they would ever be allowed to return to their homes.

In their absence, African Americans moved into Little Tokyo, soon known as Bronzeville, in response to ship and aircraft building job opportunities. Four years later, the United States captured Saipan, the Marshall Islands, and the Philippines. It was not until 1945 that the Nikkei internees were freed to return to an uncertain future.

The Postwar Years

Although fearful that anti-Japanese sentiment was still present, Japanese Americans moved back to a changed Little Tokyo that now included the presence of another ethnicity. In excess of eighteen thousand former internment camp detainees settled in Illinois instead of going back to the West Coast, where memories of happier times were still painful. Thousands more moved to other parts of the United States.

While shops and restaurants reopened, the population of Japanese American farmers, fishermen, and wholesale produce sellers nevertheless had suffered great losses. Most of the prewar farmland had been converted for industrial usage or sectioned off for housing.

Another significant change occurred in the Nisei's realization of their rights. In 1948, the publisher of a Japanese newspaper challenged the 1920 Alien Land Law and won, purchasing property in Little Tokyo in his own name. Limited reparation was made on July 2, 1948, when President Harry S Truman signed the Japanese American Evacuation Claims Act, allowing some compensation for losses due to evacuation and imprisonment.

In 1950, the district suffered another great blow when the city planning commission decided to level the northwest part of Little Tokyo to make way for the new police headquarters. Over one thousand residents were forced to leave their homes, a disturbing echo of the prior, albeit larger, evacuation of Japanese Americans.

A decade later when plans were made public to widen First Street through the town's historic center, the community pulled together to establish the Little Tokyo Redevelopment Advisory Committee and other agencies. In 1986, thirteen of the original commercial buildings along the northern side of San Pedro Street were placed on the National Register of Historic Places.

Places to Visit

The Japanese American National Museum on East First Street is one of the finest of its kind in the country, with exhibits commemorating the 1940's internment camps as well as other cultural and historic events. It includes a museum shop, comprehensive resource center, and water garden. The museum is open year-round.

The original Nishi Hongwanji Temple, built in 1925 and located on North Central Street, is part of the older Japanese American National Museum structure. The temple is one of the most vital religious structures to have served the community. Its congregation, established in 1917, represented the merger of three Buddhist churches.

The Japanese Union Church on North San Pedro Street, now closed, was built in 1922. Japanese Americans awaiting processing for the internment camps went there.

Thirteen buildings (a few housing restaurants) as well as other businesses are still closed along East First Street, which forms the heart of Little Tokyo. A public artwork stretches along the sidewalk; it includes written memories, images, and a list of businesses that used to be in the area.

The Koyasan Buddhist Temple on East First Street, founded in 1912, has a main hall which serves multiple functions: It is a place of worship, a community meeting hall, an auditorium for judo and kendo, and the home to Boy Scouts of America Troop 379. Established in 1931, the troop has gained a national reputation. —*Nika Hoffman*

For Further Information:

Duus, Peter, ed. *Japanese Discovery of America: A Brief Biography with Documents.* Boston: Bedford Books, 1997. A very detailed collection of documents on everything from "A Black Ship Scroll with Dialogue" to "An Explanation of Twelve Western Words," this is a treasure trove for those interested in how both American and Japanese cultures historically viewed one another.

Hosokawa, Bill. *Out of the Frying Pan: Reflections of a Japanese American.* Niwot: University Press of Colorado, 1998. The author, who gained prominence as a reporter for the *Shanghai Herald*, chronicles life with his wife and infant child in a Wyoming internment camp.

"Japanese American National Museum." www.lausd.k12.ca.us/janm.

Maki, Mitchell T., Harry H. L. Kitano, S. Megan Berthold, and Roger Daniels. *Achieving the Impossible Dream: How Japanese Americans Obtained Redress.* Urbana: University of Illinois Press, 1999. Tells the story of how Japanese Americans received a written apology from the president of the United States and monetary compensation in accordance with the Civil Liberties Act of 1998.

Mike, Ichiro. *Little Tokyo: One Hundred Years in Pictures.* Los Angeles: Project of Visual Communications-Asian American Studies, 1983. With an extensive prologue about the history of the district and moving photographs of early Japanese American citizens.

Niiya, Brian, ed. *Japanese American History: An A-Z Reference from 1886 to the Present.* New York: Japanese American National Museum/Facts on File, 1993. Comprehensively compiled information on historical buildings, key personalities, and facts about internment camps.

Tunnel, Michael O., and George W. Chilcoat. *The Children of Topaz: The Story of a Japanese-American Internment Camp, Based on a Classroom Diary.* New York: Holiday House, 1996. Using a diary, teacher Lillian Yamauchi Hori recorded the moving experiences of her interred students. Includes photographs and a lengthy introduction by the authors.

Los Angeles Memorial Coliseum

Date: Construction completed in 1923

Relevant issues: Art and architecture, cultural history, sports

Significance: The Los Angeles Memorial Coliseum was the site of two Olympic Games, professional and college football, major league baseball, and even religious revivals. For much of the twentieth century, the coliseum was one of the city's most notable landmarks.

Location: Three miles south of the Los Angeles Civic Center off the Harbor Freeway

Site Office:
3911 South Figueroa Street
Los Angeles, CA 90037
ph.: (213) 748-6136
Web site: www.cityofla/coliseum

For much of the twentieth century, the Los Angeles Memorial Coliseum was perhaps the most recognizable structure in all of Southern California, being the venue of two Olympic Games as well as other athletic activities such as professional and collegiate football and professional baseball, political and religious assemblies, and numerous other events.

An Era of Growth

At the beginning of the twentieth century, Los Angeles, with a population of over 300,000 in 1910 (up from 50,000 in 1890) was, in the opinion of many, a poor second to San Francisco. Los Angeles, it was said, lacked culture, beauty, and the necessary elements to live a civilized life. There was some question whether Los Angeles was even a true city, and it became a widely repeated cliché that Los Angeles was best described as seventy suburbs in search of a city. What Los Angeles did have were blue skies and balmy temperatures for much of the year, as well as an avid booster mentality. The city was also notable for its public parks, particularly Griffith Park (the result of Colonel James Griffith's gift of thirty-five hundred acres to the city), as well as Hancock Park, Westlake Park, Echo Park, and Exposition Park, the latter becoming the location of one of the most famous stadiums in the world: the Los Angeles Memorial Coliseum.

The early twentieth century was an era of stadium building in Southern California. The Rose Bowl was constructed in Pasadena's Arroyo Seco, and the first New Year's Day football game was played there on January 1, 1923. In the city of Los Angeles, the one-time Agricultural Park became the focus of stadium hopes. South of Los Angeles's Civic Center, Agricultural Park was developed in 1876 to exhibit agricultural products. In 1880, the year that the University of Southern California (USC) was established immediately to the north of the park, the state took over the property. After numerous false starts, and under the leadership of William M. Bowen, a lawyer, and with the support of USC's President George Finley Bovard and other civic luminaries, the city, county, and state agreed to develop the land for public educational and recreational use. On November 13, 1913, the newly named Exposition Park was dedicated, which was to include a county Museum of History, Science, and Art and a state Exposition Building.

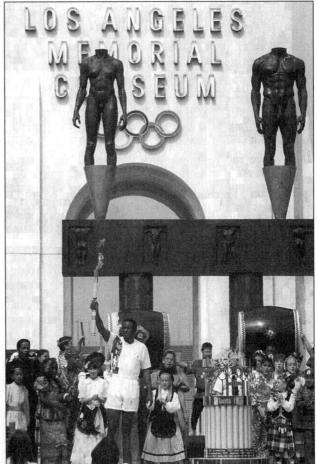

Champion Rafer Johnson, the first torchbearer on the trip to the 1996 Atlanta Games, holds up the Olympic flame in front of the Los Angeles Memorial Coliseum. (AP/Wide World Photos)

Next on Bowen's agenda for Exposition Park was an athletic stadium.

Construction

Bowen was not alone in advocating a stadium for the park. At the November 26, 1919, meeting of the California Fiesta Association, it was urged that a stadium be built in Exposition Park and named the Los Angeles Memorial Colosseum as a memorial to those who gave their lives in the recently concluded World War I. By the following July, "Colosseum" had been changed to "Coliseum." Partially in hopes of hosting the 1924 Olympic Games, and with the support the Community Development Association—a group of five Los Angeles newspaper publishers who guaranteed a loan of $800,000—the project proceeded, with the firm of Parkinson and Parkinson chosen to design the structure.

Born in England in 1861, John Parkinson had been a prominent Los Angeles architect since the 1890's. Among other structures, Parkinson had designed Los Angeles's first "skyscraper," the Braly Block at Fourth Street and Spring (1904), which remained Los Angeles's tallest building until the construction of City Hall in 1928. In 1920, Parkinson's son, Donald, joined his father's firm, and over the next two decades Parkinson and Parkinson designed many of Southern California's most famous architectural landmarks, including City Hall, the Bullocks-Wilshire department store (1929), and Union Station (1939). In 1919, USC's President Bovard chose John Parkinson to develop the university's master plan, and the Parkinson firm ultimately designed more than twenty university projects.

Bovard promised that if a stadium were built in nearby Exposition Park, USC would play its home football games there. With his status as one of Los Angeles's premier architects, including his participation in the design of a sunken garden within Exposition Park—later to be known as the Rose Garden—and given his USC project, Parkinson was a logical choice to design the proposed coliseum. Declining to make a profit on the project, Parkinson offered his firm's services at cost.

Plans for the stadium, with seating for seventy-five thousand, were approved by the Municipal Arts Commission and Allied Architects Association in August, 1921, with the final agreement signed in November. Construction began in December, 1921, and was completed on May 1, 1923, at a cost of $950,000. The first football game was played in the coliseum on October 6, 1923, between USC and Pomona College, with 12,863 in attendance to watch the USC Trojan victory.

Years of Fame and Fortune

Los Angeles was not awarded the 1924 Olympics, but it was chosen to host the Olympic Games in 1932. Modifications to the original structure were deemed necessary, and the Parkinson firm was again chosen to do the improvements, which included an additional thirty-five thousand seats as well as a new press box, a scoreboard, a four-hundred-meter running track, improved lighting, and the Eternal Flame Tripod at the peristyle. Although the 1932 Olympics took place during the height of the Great Depression, the Games were a great success, and the 1932 comedy film *Million Dollar Legs*, starring Jack Oakie and W. C. Fields, ostensibly featured the coliseum.

Nearly a half century later, the Los Angeles Memorial Coliseum would again host the Olympics, and although the 1984 Games were boycotted by the Soviet Union, a record 141 countries competed. In addition to the track and field events, both the opening and the closing ceremonies were held in the coliseum. The Games were privately financed, generating a profit of over $200 million, and the organizing president, Peter Ueberroth, was named *Time*'s Man of the Year.

The coliseum was long noted as a mecca for track and field, and during the middle decades of the twentieth century one of the premier world events was the annual Coliseum Relays. The coliseum was also the site of United States and Soviet track and field competitions, and United States Olympic trials were staged there. The stadium was used for other sporting events. In 1936, Sonja Henie even ice-skated in the coliseum, and motorcycle races and rodeos were held there. In the last decades of the twentieth century, as soccer increased in popularity, the coliseum was frequently the venue for soccer matches.

Major league baseball was played in the coliseum. In 1958, to the dismay of the people of Brooklyn, their Dodgers became the Los Angeles Dodgers, and the new Dodgers played in the coliseum from 1958 through the 1961 season. Baseball purists were disdainful of playing baseball in a football stadium, and because of the short dimensions in left field (250 feet), a high wire screen was added to keep at least a few ordinary fly balls from becoming home runs. Nevertheless, the Los Angeles fans fell in love with the Dodgers, and, playing in the coliseum, the team set baseball attendance records, with 92,706 at one World Series game in 1959.

Nevertheless, decade after decade football remained the major coliseum sport. USC continued to play all its home games at the facility, as did the University of California at Los Angeles (UCLA) before moving to the Rose Bowl. Through the decades a number of professional football teams also used the coliseum. The one-time Cleveland Rams, renamed the Los Angeles Rams, played their home games there from 1946 until 1979. The Los Angeles Chargers used the stadium a single season before relocating to San Diego. The former Oakland Raiders played there as the Los Angeles Raiders between 1982 and 1994, and two Super Bowls were held in the stadium. Through the years, thanks to television, the Los Angeles Memorial Coliseum became familiar to millions of football fans.

The coliseum was also a favored site for nonsporting events. Politicians and statesmen made regular appearances. Vice President Charles Curtis, substituting for President Herbert Hoover, opened the 1932 Olympic Games. President Franklin D. Roosevelt spoke there in 1935, and during the 1940 campaign his rival for the presidency, Wendell Wilkie, appeared there. In 1960, with Los Angeles the host city for the Democratic National Convention, presidential candidate John F. Kennedy delivered his nomination acceptance address in the stadium, as did the vice presidential nominee, Lyndon B. Johnson. Religious figures made use of the coliseum. It was a site of the evangelist Billy Graham's crusades, with a one-day record of 134,000 in attendance in 1963, and in 1987 Pope John Paul II performed a papal mass in the stadium. The 1988 Amnesty Tour also played there, and through the years there were many musical concerts. As recognition of the coliseum's significance, the state of California and the United States government declared it a State and National Historic Landmark in 1984.

By the last decade of the twentieth century, the coliseum was showing its age. Many new stadiums had been constructed with modern amenities, including luxury boxes. In 1993, at a cost of $15.5 million, the running track was eliminated, the floor was lowered eleven feet, and new seats were added which were closer to the field action. The 1994 Northridge earthquake caused considerable damage, necessitating $94.6 million in repairs, but in part because of the coliseum's remaining inadequacies as a state-of-the-art facility, the Raiders returned to Oakland after the 1994 season, and Los Angeles was left without a professional football team. Various plans were subsequently suggested to modernize the coliseum or, alternatively, to construct a new football stadium elsewhere in order to attract professional football back to Southern California, but at the close of the twentieth century neither proposal had been acted upon, and the future of the Los Angeles Memorial Coliseum remained unknown.

Places to Visit
In addition to the Memorial Coliseum, Exposition Park is the location of the Sports Arena, the Los Angeles County Natural History Museum, the California Science Center, the California African American Museum, and an Imax Theater. USC is just to the north, and UCLA is in Westwood. Downtown Los Angeles has several historic ethnic sites, such as El Pueblo de Los Angeles and Olvera Street, Little Tokyo, and Chinatown. The Los Angeles Civic Center has numerous architectural examples, ranging from the Bradbury Building (1893) to the Crocker Center (1983). Hollywood, with its film legacy—the Hollywood Bowl, Mann's Chinese Theater, and Griffith Observatory—is nearby, as are Beverly Hills, the Pacific Ocean, and the Getty Museums, old and new.

Southern California is the location of many Spanish missions, including Santa Barbara and San Juan Capistrano among others, and the region is notable for its domestic architecture, such as the craftsman houses of Green and Green (Pasadena's Gamble House) as well as homes designed by Frank Lloyd Wright (Barnsdall House) and Richard Neutra. To many, Southern California seems to have only a brief history, and thus even Disneyland, which opened in 1955, can be claimed to be historic in its own right. In spite of its relative youth, Southern California is a cornucopia of twentieth century history.

—*Eugene Larson*

For Further Information:

Field, William Scott. *Parkinson Centennial, 1894-1994.* Los Angeles: Los Angeles Conservancy, 1994. Historical summary of the Parkinson architectural firm.

Girvigian, Raymond. *Los Angeles Memorial Coliseum.* South Pasadena, Calif.: R. Girvigian, 1984. Materials regarding the dedication ceremonies for the State (California) and National Historic Landmark designations for the Coliseum in 1984.

Hoobing, Robert. *The 1984 Olympics: Sarajevo and Los Angeles.* Washington, D.C.: United States Postal Service, 1984. History of the 1984 Olympics, with numerous coliseum photographs.

"Los Angeles Memorial Coliseum." www.mediacity .com/~csuppes/NCAA/Pac10/usc/index .htm Brief history of the coliseum.

"The Parkinson Archives." www.parkives.com/ history.htm Parkinson firm Web site. Valuable for Parkinson contribution.

Starr, Kevin. *Inventing the Dream.* New York: Oxford University Press, 1985. The author, a premier historian of early twentieth century California, discusses aspects of Los Angeles.

Weaver, John. *Los Angeles: The Enormous Village.* Santa Barbara, Calif.: Capra Press, 1980. Weaver, a novelist and historian, gives an insightful and readable account of Los Angeles.

Manzanar

Date: Established in 1942; named a National Historic Site on March 3, 1992

Relevant issues: Asian American history, military history, political history, World War II

Significance: This was the site of an internment camp for Japanese Americans, many of whom were American citizens by birth, during World War II. It was the first, and the best known, of ten such relocation centers established in six western states. Located in eastern Owens Valley, the area was important to Native Americans (Paiute and Shoshone) for many centuries, and during the period from 1910 to 1935 it was a highly productive farming area for fruit—especially apples and pears. The area was dormant until the relocation center was established by presidential order early in 1942. During the war years, the center had a population of approximately ten thousand Japanese American detainees. The only remains of the camp are scattered foundation stones, some grave markers, and a few relic objects.

Location: Just off U.S. Route 395, twelve miles north of Lone Pine and five miles south of Independence

Site Office:
Manzanar National Historic Site
P.O. Box 426
Independence, CA 93526-0426
ph.: (760) 878-2932
fax: (760) 878-2949
Web site: www.nps.gov/manz/

The history of Manzanar—both written and unwritten—extends back some tens of thousands of years. The verdant valley was well supplied by local streams, and the lush grasses and other foliage attracted a variety of game animals. Hunter-gatherer Native Americans, mostly Paiute and Shoshone, used the area for a variety of food items and materials for making cordage, projectile points, and weapons. For reasons unknown, the natives moved elsewhere. The site was unoccupied for centuries until Europeans established settlements and began to raise agricultural crops, especially apples and pears. (*Manzanar* is the Spanish word for "apple orchard.")

Between 1910 and 1935, the thriving agricultural village of Manzanar shipped much fruit to California coastal cities. The demand for water from growing coastal cities like Los Angeles and San Francisco was partially met by diverting sources in Owens Valley. The productive orchards around Manzanar soon became unproductive, and the area began to undergo desertification. George Creek, named for Paiute chief George, no longer flowed, and cacti and other desert vegetation took over the land.

The Manzanar area lay under the hot California sun as a wasteland for the next decade. The Japanese attack on Pearl Harbor on December 7, 1941, was soon to change the dreary aspect of Manzanar.

The Internment of Japanese Americans

On February 14, 1942, the commanding general of U.S. Army forces in California wrote to the secretary of war requesting permission to evacuate Japanese and other "subversive" persons from the West Coast of the United States. Subversive persons included those of German and Italian extraction since the United States was at war with those nations as well as Japan.

Manzanar internment camp during World War II. (AP/Wide World Photos)

Five days later, President Franklin D. Roosevelt issued Executive Order 9066. This order gave permission to the secretary of war and any military commanders he designated to prescribe military areas in the nation. Any and all persons could be excluded from such areas. The main impact of the exclusion orders fell on the Japanese residing along the West Coast of the United States. Although the United States was at war with Germany and Italy as well as Japan, few persons of German or Italian descent were affected. The order soon came through to forcibly evacuate all persons of Japanese descent from the West Coast. This blanket order included Issei, Japanese who emigrated to the United States after 1907 and were not eligible at that time for American citizenship, and Nisei, persons of Japanese descent who were born in the United States and thus, under the U.S. Constitution, U.S. citizens by birth.

The decision was made to move all Japanese inland and away from the coastal areas. The orders to move in many cases gave the Japanese residents only a few days to settle their affairs and pack the few personal items they would be permitted to take with them. Homes were put up for sale at extremely low prices, and those that could not be sold were simply abandoned. The same was true for furniture, automobiles, and personal items including clothing. The first stops for many Japanese were temporary detainment centers including such places as Santa Anita Race Track.

Ten relocation centers were built. These were Manzanar and Tule Lake (California), Gila and Poston (Arizona), Minidoka (Idaho), Heart Mountain (Wyoming), Granada (Colorado), Topaz (Utah), and Rohwer and Jerome (Arkansas). At many of the relocation centers, it was a race to get the housing built before the first internees arrived. Too often it was a case of the evacuees being unloaded from buses onto the littered bare ground of construction sites still in progress. Trees and brush had been cleared and bulldozers and trucks raised clouds of dust as they moved about. The housing, actually barracks-like wood and tar-paper structures, was set up resembling a typical military base. The individual buildings were constructed of quarter-inch boards over a wooden frame, the whole then covered by tar paper (also called roofing felt) fastened with nailed boards. Each building was twenty feet wide and one hundred feet long, divided into four individual family units twenty feet wide and twenty-four feet long. The family unit, or apartment, was heated by an oil-burning stove. Each apartment was designed for a family of four; however, because of the shortage of space, sometimes as many as eleven evacuees (not necessarily related) found themselves sharing a single apartment.

Furnishings provided by the United States consisted of steel-framed army cots and blankets as well as mattress and pillow bags stuffed with straw, but nothing else. Electricity for lights was also provided but running water was not. Later, resourceful internees gathered scrap lumber and fashioned makeshift but serviceable tables and chairs, shelves, and bookcases.

Layout of the Camp

Manzanar, for example, was laid out in blocks, each with two rows of barracks, seven buildings in each row. The rows were separated by an open area in which laundry and ironing rooms were located as well as separate men's and women's lavatory buildings. Each block also included a dining building (mess hall) and a recreational hall. The dining halls were furnished with one-piece tables with attached benches. Some of the internees complained that being forced to eat with strangers made it difficult to perform any of the mealtime family social activities they were used to. Controlling the children was especially difficult.

The structures were not insulated and the summer sun beat down on the tar-paper buildings, sometimes raising the temperature to over 100 degrees Fahrenheit. In the winter, subzero temperatures made the little room heaters ineffectual against the cold. The floors were uncovered for a long time, and the wind blew dust up through the spaces between the floorboards. A common comment of internees at Manzanar concerned the grit in the bedding, in their clothes, and on everything in the apartment.

Despite the primitive conditions, the Japanese residents of Manzanar tried to make the best of it. They established both elementary-level schools and high schools and assembled orchestras and bands for dances and other entertainment. Churches were established and were apparently well attended. Eventually a newspaper was begun as well as a cooperative store to supply items not available from the government stores.

Jobs around the centers, including Manzanar, became available to the internees at a salary range of twelve to nineteen dollars per month. The jobs included carpentry, general cleanup, gardening, and farming in the communal fields. Many of the vegetables which fed the population of approximately ten thousand internees at Manzanar came from internees' own gardens.

The entire Manzanar detention facility consisted of about six thousand acres. The living area encompassed about 550 acres. All the living area was enclosed by barbed-wire fences and secured by guard towers and light towers. The internees were told the guard towers and wire fences were to protect them from anti-Japanese vigilantes. It was a common joke among the Japanese that if the guards and rifles were for their protection, how was it the guns pointed in and not out?

Vacating the Camps

As the war drew to a close, a trickle of Japanese detainees was allowed to leave the camp. The United States Supreme Court, in January of 1945, declared that the detaining of citizens in the relocation centers was unconstitutional. Peace came to Europe in May, 1945, and to Japan in August, 1945.

The imminent closing of the war relocation centers posed problems for both the United States government and the Japanese detainees. How would movement of the residents from the camps to the world they used to know be facilitated? What should be done with the camp infrastructure?

The resettlement of the Japanese and the dissolution of the camps started slowly and then took on the characteristics of a snowball rolling downhill. Some internees were released as early as 1944 and resumed life, not always in the coastal cities they had known but in Chicago and other Midwest cities. With the establishment of peace in 1945, the U.S. government was eager to relocate all the internees and close down the camps completely.

Curiously, many of the Japanese in the camps resisted leaving the homes they had known for over three years. At Manzanar, a model and plan for a resort-type community had been designed. Manzanar represented a form of security to the internees: They had created a community. Commonly, residents expressed in disbelief, "This is a town. You can't close a town!" Manzanar, however, and other war relocation centers were closed. With a train ticket and twenty-five dollars "pocket money," each of the internees was released. The buildings were sold at auction, and eventually all that remained were some of the stone and concrete foundations and a few scattered remnants of items left by former internees. The wind drifted the sandy soil over the site, and the desert reestablished itself.

—*Albert C. Jensen*

For Further Information:

Armor, John, and Peter Wright. *Manzanar.* New York: Random House, Vintage Books, 1988. Detailed examination, with photographs, of life in Manzanar as a typical war relocation camp.

Chang, Gordon H. "Witness and Victim." *The Humanist* 58 (January/February, 1998): 21-23. The strains of camp life on the internees and the United States quandary of what to do with them after the war was over.

Conrat, Maisie, and Richard Conrat. *Executive Order 9066: The Internment of 110,000 Japanese Americans.* Los Angeles: University of California, 1992. Photographs, accompanied by extensive captions, of Manzanar and other relocation centers.

Elton, Catherine. "The War away from Home." *Mother Jones* 23, no. 6 (November/December, 1998): 19. During the time Japanese civilians were interred in Manzanar and other relocation camps, the U.S. government secretly pressured thirteen Latin American nations to deport 2,264 of their citizens of Japanese descent to the U.S. for internment.

Gant-Wright, Iantha. "Breaking Barriers." *National Parks* 73, nos. 1-2 (January/February, 1999): 47-48. An African American woman relates the relocation of Japanese Americans during World War II to minority participation in U.S. National Parks.

Okihiro, Gary Y., and Joan Myers. *Whispered Silences: Japanese Americans and World War II.* Seattle: University of Washington Press, 1996. A professor of history and a photojournalist combine talents to produce a detailed story on the Japanese Americans and their lives in relocation centers.

Spicer, Edward H., Asael T. Hansen, Katherine Luomala, and Marvin K. Opler. *Impounded People: Japanese-Americans in the Relocation Centers.* Tucson: University of Arizona Press, 1969. Four anthropologists, all of whom were associated with the relocation centers, describe the rationale for the camps and the daily life of the internees before, during, and after the camps were in operation.

Mission Basilica San Diego de Alcalá

Date: Founded in 1769
Relevant issues: American Indian history, European settlement, Latino history, religion
Significance: This Franciscan mission in San Diego, founded by Father Junípero Serra, was relocated from Presidio Hill above Old Town to its present site, burned in an Indian attack, rebuilt, destroyed by earthquake, restored and enlarged, secularized, and sold. The mission was then returned to the Catholic Church, rebuilt, and named a minor basilica by Pope Paul VI.
Location: San Diego, five miles east of Interstate 5 in Mission Valley, off Interstate 8; on North San Diego Mission Road, between Mission Gorge Road on the east and Rancho Mission Road on the west, south of Friars Road
Site Office:
Mission Basilica San Diego de Alcalá
10818 San Diego Mission Road
San Diego, CA 92108-2498
ph.: (619) 281-8449

Mission Basilica San Diego de Alcalá, a simple, white adobe church with a five-bell tower and enclosed portico, stands on a small knoll overlooking Mission Valley in San Diego. The original mission, founded on July 16, 1769, by Spanish Franciscan missionary Junípero Serra, was a crude, thatch-roofed, brushwood hut that stood on Presidio Hill above Old Town, six miles up the San Diego River from its present site. It is the oldest mission in California, the first in a chain of twenty-one Franciscan missions that extended for 650 miles up El Camino Real (the king's highway) along the coast of Alta (Upper) California.

The original mission was moved to its present site in 1774, where it was burned in an Indian attack a year later. The mission was rebuilt in 1780 and destroyed again in 1803 by an earthquake. It was again restored and enlarged in 1813. The present structure is a 1931 restoration of the 1813 church. The church's sturdy facade, the only part of the structure still standing at the time of the 1931 restoration, is characterized by wide brick step and outspread walls on either side of the door. The church interior has been restored to its original form, the plastering applied unevenly in imitation of the original craftsmanship. The five bells, scattered during decades of neglect, were located and reassembled. The largest bell, the 1,200-pound Mater Dolorosa, was cast in San Diego in 1894 from five bells sent to the mission by the viceroy of New Spain (Mexico) in 1796.

Colonizing Alta California

Earliest interest in establishing a mission in San

Mission Basilica San Diego de Alcalá. (American Stock Photography)

Diego began soon after its port was discovered and mapped in 1542 by Juan Rodríguez Cabrillo. Spanish missionary orders sought government aid and permission to set up missions at Alta California's principal ports in San Diego and Monterey, but the viceroy of New Spain, responsible for the establishment of missions in California, was not interested at the time. It was not until after 1765, when news arrived in Madrid that Czarist Russian fur traders and explorers had been setting up temporary outposts in the Farollone Islands off San Francisco, that Spain revisited plans for colonizing Alta California.

Under Inspector General José de Galvéz, a high-ranking officer of the Spanish Council of the Indies and King Carlos III's personal agent in New Spain, plans were developed in 1768 for a settlement in Northern California to hold its frontier against Russian encroachment. Plans were worked out months in advance in Mexico City for two expeditions by land and two by sea from a base in Baja (Lower) California to colonize a port in Monterey in Alta California.

The port of San Diego was selected as a common intermediate stopping point between Baja California and Monterey for the four contingents of the expedition. Once the port of San Diego had been reached, three missions in Alta California were to

be established: one in San Diego, one in Monterey, and one at an intermediate point. Two presidios (military outposts) were also to be established.

Captain Gaspar de Portolá was assigned leadership of the project in 1768. One year previously, Portolá had been appointed governor of Baja California and ordered to supervise the transfer of Baja mission property to the Franciscans from the Jesuits, who has been banished from Spanish territories that year by King Charles III. Father Junípero Serra, who had been made president of the Baja missions in 1768, was ordered to turn over his presidency to the Dominican friars so that he could assist Portolá by supervising the missionaries in Alta California.

Born in Petra, Mallorca, Spain, in 1713, Serra had gained distinction as a brilliant professor of philosophy and theology, pulpit orator, skilled administrator, and devout missionary with thirty-five years of experience in the frontiers of New Spain. Although the padre stood only five feet, two inches tall and was fifty-five years old when he was named president of the mission in Alta California, Serra was known as a man of great energy, ambition, and religious zeal who, despite an infected leg, rode 750 miles on muleback leading a pack train up the California peninsula into San Diego.

The Voyage Begins

The first contingent in the packet, the *San Carlos*, sailed out of La Paz on January 7, 1769, with soldiers and supplies on board. A month later, the *San Antonio*, under Captain Juan Pérez, embarked for Alta California. The vessels were loaded with ornaments, sacred vases, church vestaments, household utensils, field implements, seeds, and other supplies needed for mission settlement. Both ships made landfalls near San Pedro. A supply ship, the *San José*, was dispatched in June, ran into problems and returned after three months, set sail again from La Paz the following spring loaded with food and supplies, and was never heard from again.

After the ships had left, the two land expeditions departed. In addition to the officers and cavalrymen, the expeditions included eighty-six Christianized Indians from the Baja missions for handling several hundred head of pack mules and beef cattle. The first land expedition, under Captain Fernando de Rivera and accompanied by Father Juan Crespi, diarist of the expedition, set out from El Rosario on Good Friday, 1769, driving a pack train of 180 mules and 500 domestic animals toward San Diego, 350 miles away. The party reached San Diego two months later.

In mid-May the final contingent, under Captain Portolá and Father Serra, departed, marching along an alternate route, also driving a herd of cattle. The party stopped along the way at the Baja mission settlements to pick up supplies for Alta California.

When Portolá and Serra reached San Diego on July 1, 1769, they learned that sixty of the ninety crewmen of both ships had died of scurvy. All but two of the crew of the *San Carlos*, which arrived April 29, had died; the ship had been at sea for 110 days after being blown two hundred leagues off course. The entire crew of the *San Antonio*, which arrived April 11, before the *San Carlos*, was ill. Of the 219 persons who had made up the original four contingents of the expedition, only half reached Alta California. A quarter of the entire expedition had died, and two-thirds of the Indians had died or deserted on the way.

Portolá ordered the remaining eight of the *San Antonio*'s original twenty-eight crewmen to return south to report on the conditions at San Diego and to bring back supplies, while he continued with a small company 450 miles northward to Monterey Bay to establish the capital of Alta California.

Shortly after Portolá's company had left, Serra ordered a small thatch-roofed chapel to be built on what is today Presidio Hill. On July 16, 1769, the padre raised a cross to dedicate formally the mission to Saint Didacus (San Diego) of Alcalá, a Franciscan friar sainted in 1588.

Conflict with Local Tribes

Converting the native Ipai-Tipai (Dieigueño) Indians proved to be a challenge for the padres. Friendly at first, the Indians accepted gifts of beads and clothing from the strangers. Once accustomed

to the settlers, they became bold and hostile and began stealing from the camp. Within a month of Portolá's departure, the natives attacked the camp with bows and arrows, attempting to drive the foreigners from their territory. The Spanish, defending the new settlement, opened fire with a musket volley. Two Spaniards died and three were wounded, and at least three Indians died during the attack. The Spanish soldiers built a stockade around the mission and forbade the Indians to enter, in an effort to protect the camp against a further attack. Although a temporary truce prevailed, the Indians continued to resist conversion, and it was two years before the mission baptized its first native.

By the time Portolá returned to San Diego from Monterey six months later, another nineteen men had died and mission supplies were running out. Portolá told Serra that if the relief ship *San Antonio* did not return by the Feast of St. Joseph (March 19), the mission, despite Serra's protests, would have to be abandoned.

On the evening of March 19, 1770, a ship was sighted, but it then disappeared from view for four days. The ship turned out to be the *San Antonio* on its way to Monterey with supplies. The ship had lost its anchor and had to backtrack to San Diego, where its shipload of supplies relieved the mission's crisis. The colonists erected a presidio and a temporary mission building of interlaced sticks fastened with mud.

Within a month, Portolá again headed north, this time to found a mission in Monterey. Serra, after turning the San Diego mission over to four padres, several dozen soldiers, and a few Christian Baja Indians, sailed aboard the *San Antonio*, which resumed its course up the California coast.

In August, 1774, the San Diego mission was moved from Presidio Hill to its present site six miles up the river. The garrison at the original site antagonized the Indians, and there was not enough arable land there to support the growing number of Christianized Indians. Thatch-roofed palisade buildings were soon completed at the new site, which was near Indian villages.

Although the new site was also chosen because it was believed to be a good source of water and land for farming, the padres soon discovered that there was not enough of either to produce sufficient crops for the growing population of Christianized

Indians. The Indians therefore stayed in their own villages and came to the mission only to work or attend services. The mission could only convert a few Indians at a time this way, and many of these converts reverted to their native religion.

On the night of November 5, 1775, under the leadership of ex-convert Francisco of the Cuiamac Rancheria, an army of eight hundred armed natives from seventy Indian villages united and attacked the mission. The Indians looted what they could and set fire to the buildings. Three Spaniards were killed in the attack: a carpenter, a blacksmith, and Father Luis Jaime, who was clubbed and shot with arrows when he tried to calm the Indians. Jaime thus became the first Christian martyr in California; he is buried under the altar of the mission sanctuary. (Four other padres are also now buried there.)

When the battle was over, it was discovered that the presidio garrison had slept through the entire attack. The mission's inhabitants moved back to the presidio, where they remained for several months. While the attack caused Governor Portolá to suspend the founding of additional missions without adequate military protection, the ultimate failure of the uprising served to discourage the Indians from attempting such an attack again.

Restoration

In 1776, eight months after the revolt, Serra returned to the burned-out site and began rebuilding the church and mission buildings. The church, shops, residences, storage areas, and other buildings were arranged in a full quadrangle, surrounding a 120-square-foot patio. The structures were footed in tile, and adobe was used to cover the walls to increase fire resistance in the event of another attack.

By 1780 the reconstruction was completed, and the mission was rededicated. Years of growth and prosperity for the mission began. In 1797, 565 Indians were baptized, bringing the number of converts to 1,405. The mission's landholdings had grown to fifty thousand acres on which wheat, barley, corn, and beans were grown. Vineyards, orchards, and vegetable gardens grew near the mission, which also owned 20,000 sheep, 10,000 head of cattle, and 1,250 horses. Barracks were erected for soldiers, corrals for the livestock, and dormitories for the converts.

The second church was destroyed by an earthquake in 1803, but by 1813, a restored, enlarged, adobe church was rededicated. A buttress-like structure, built onto the present structure, has withstood successive earthquakes.

Between 1807 and 1816, a 220-foot dam with a 12-foot-high center was designed by the padres and built by Indians six miles upriver. Stored water was brought to the mission through miles of cement flume aqueduct. Among the first irrigation systems in California, the dam outlasted the mission by several decades, surviving until a flood burst it open. Fragments of the dam, engulfed in silt, still stand and are visible in the river.

In 1830, having recovered from the damage of the earthquake, the mission owned more than sixteen thousand sheep, eight thousand head of cattle, and one thousand horses and mules.

In 1834, during the Mexican occupation of California, the Act of Secularization was passed, returning mission property to public use. After secularization, the mission declined rapidly.

From 1846 to 1862, the mission was occupied by the U.S. Cavalry, during which time the soldiers made some temporary repairs to the buildings. A second story was built inside, and horses were quartered on the ground level. Once the soldiers departed, the unoccupied mission gradually fell into ruin. In 1862, by order of President Abraham Lincoln, the U.S. Land Commission returned the twenty-two acres of mission grounds to the church.

By 1892, half of the mission had caved in. The roof tiles were used to cover Old Town homes, and most of the quadrangle had disintegrated into the soil. Neglect and weathering had reduced the structure to ruin. Only the facade, reinforced with heavy timbers, was still standing.

In 1915, fund-raising began to rebuild the mission; it took several years to raise the needed money. By 1931, after nearly a century of neglect, the mission was restored and rededicated. Original portions of the church's buttresses and walls were incorporated in the reconstruction.

On March 1 of the same year, a statue of Serra was unveiled in the Hall of Fame in Washington, D.C., in tribute to the pioneer missionary considered by some to be the founder of California. Other memorials are a bronze statue of the padre in Golden Gate Park in San Francisco and a granite monument at Monterey. During his fifteen years of service, Serra founded nine of the twenty-one California missions. In 1943, canonization proceedings began for Serra; they are still in process today.

The present mission church at San Diego was named a minor basilica by Pope Paul VI in 1976. Today, parochial school is conducted in the modern building beside the mission church, which serves as an active parish for the local Catholic community.   —*Shawn Brennan*

For Further Information:

Bates, Brian. *Along the King's Highway: The Missions of California.* Carmichael, Calif.: Wordwrights International, 1997. A guidebook that includes the history and descriptions of El Camino Real and mission buildings.

Heizer, Robert F., ed. *California.* Vol. 8 in *Handbook of North American Indians.* Washington, D.C.: Smithsonian Institution, 1978. Sympathetic to the Indian cause.

Johnson, Paul C., ed. *The California Missions: A Pictorial History.* Menlo Park, Calif.: Lane, 1964. An excellent, finely detailed, illustrated guide to the history of the mission chain.

Riesenberg, Felix, Jr. *The Golden Road: The Story of California's Spanish Mission Trail.* New York: McGraw-Hill, 1962. Another, less important guide to the California missions.

Wise, Winifred. *Fray Junípero Serra and the California Conquest.* New York: Charles Scribner's Sons, 1967. An account of Serra's life, detailed in notes from the writings and diaries of Serra and his contemporaries.

Mission San Gabriel Arcángel

Date: Founded on September 8, 1771

Relevant issues: American Indian history, art and architecture, European settlement, Latino history, religion

Significance: Heralded as the first European settlement of the Los Angeles basin, this mission was the most prosperous of the California missions and served as a way station for the colonization of Alta (Upper) California. In addition to its status as one of only two Spanish colonial-era stone churches of Alta California located south of

Monterey, the church is singularly unique for its Moorish-inspired architectural characteristics and its unique collection of *via cruces* paintings crafted by an Indian artisan of Mission San Fernando.

Location: Two miles north of the San Bernardino Freeway (Interstate 10) on South Mission Drive in the city of San Gabriel

Site Office:

Mission San Gabriel
428 South Mission Drive
San Gabriel, CA 91776-1299
ph.: (626) 457-3035
Web site: sangabrielmission.org/

Originally named La Mision del Santo Principe el Arcángel, San Gabriel de los Temblores (chief holy prince of archangels, Saint Gabriel of the earthquakes), this mission community was renowned for its prosperity and agricultural productivity. Despite its pivotal role in linking the missions of the Monterey Bay with that of San Diego de Alcalá, much of the early prosperity of Mission San Gabriel Arcángel was borne of a lucrative wine and brandy industry first introduced to early California by the padres of this Los Angeles basin mission community. Originally established by Fray (Father) Junípero Serra as the fourth in a chain of twenty-one early California Hispanic missions, San Gabriel's wealth led to its designation as the "Queen of the Missions," and subsequently to its acknowledgment as the "Mother of Agriculture in California."

The Mission's Founding

Like so many early mission communities, San Gabriel was founded, then moved, reestablished, and rebuilt as the result of tumultuous beginnings at another nearby site in the Los Angeles basin.

Originally founded under the directive of Serra on September 8, 1771, by Franciscan friars Pedro Benito Cambón and Angel Fernandez de la Somera, the mission was eventually relocated to a different site by Father Fermin Francisco de Lasuén in May, 1775. Accompanied by fourteen soldiers and four muleteers, Fathers Cambón and Somera set forth from Mission San Diego de Alcalá on August 6, 1771. Their objective was the region explored by Don Gaspar de Portolá during the previous year. The original site was selected by Serra at

The six bells in the campanile at the Mission San Gabriel Arcángel. (Ruben G. Mendoza)

the site of the Rio Santa Ana or Rio de los Temblores, so named because on the day the site was first explored, four severe earthquakes shook the area in a single day. Upon reaching the site, a sizable party of Shoshone confronted the padres, and in an effort to placate them, one of the padres unfurled a large banner of the Virgin Mary, and the natives are said to have been pacified. Despite this reception, the padres determined that the land was unsuitable for the founding of the mission and soon moved on to the Valle de San Miguel and ultimately erected a large wooden cross and celebrated the founding mass at the Shoshone Indian village of Shevaanga located at the foot of a hill and near a stream named San Miguel on September 8, 1771.

The new site was strategically important in that it was located at the intersection of three well-traveled trails, two from Mexico and the third from the distant East Coast of the United States. One of these trails linked the earliest California missions via El Camino Real. As such, the padres began the work of building the first mission structures and were assisted by the Shoshone or Gabrielino inhabitants of the region. Soon thereafter, they erected several temporary structures built of willow poles, tules, and timbers, including a palisaded chapel, padre's quarters, *monjerio* or nunnery, boy's dormi-

tory, storeroom for carpentry tools, various rooms, and corrals for sheep and cattle.

Shortly after the mission's founding in 1771, catastrophic floods and conflicts between the Shoshone and the Spanish guard led to the abandonment of the original site at Montebello. Tragically, as the result of inappropriate advances made by a soldier toward the wife of a Shoshone tribal leader, a conflict erupted in which the tribal leader was killed; his head was impaled on a pole by the Spanish guard in an effort to dissuade the Shoshone from furthering efforts at retaliation. In the end, this action only had the effect of keeping the otherwise peaceful Shoshone away from the mission, and in time, this early mission settlement was abandoned for a new one located at the Shoshone village of Iisanchanga. The present site was settled in May, 1775, and ultimately came to accommodate two large quadrangles and the stone church for which it is justly famous.

The Church and Its Architecture

Construction of the church was begun on March 11, 1795, under the direction of Father Antonio Cruzado. The architecture of the church is unique in the California missions for its stone and masonry construction, its Moorish or "Fortress style" architecture, and its long and narrow floor plan and windows. According to architectural historian Mardith Schuetz-Miller, journeyman mason Toribio Ruiz worked to build the foundations and raised the stone and adobe walls of the church to half height before departing the mission. As with Mission San Juan Capistrano, the loss of the stonemason resulted in unanticipated changes in the architectural plan. In this instance, the original vault began cracking, and the builders were forced to replace it with a flat brick and masonry roof in 1808. The Indian master mason Miguel Blanco of Mission San Ignacio, in Baja California, is thought to have constructed the vaults that were eventually replaced.

He was the master mason of San Gabriel from 1794 through 1801. Master carpenter Salvador Carabantes of Tepic, Nayarit, followed the efforts of Blanco in framing the doors and windows of the new church. It is also likely that Carabantes was involved in the construction of the timber roof that replaced the vaults installed by Blanco.

Perhaps the most distinctive feature of the mission church is its architectural layout and Moorish-inspired facade. The capped buttresses, or Fortress style facade, are characteristic of sixteenth century churches of the Valley of Mexico. These were in turn inspired by the architecture of the Moors or Arabs who ruled Spain for nearly seven hundred years. Other unique features include the floor plan and windows of the church. The long and narrow nave of the church measures one hundred fifty feet in length by thirty feet in width by thirty feet in height. The long and narrow windows are similarly unique, as is the massive staircase located at the exterior of the southeast corner of the southern facade that provides access to the choir loft. In addition, the church of 1805 boasted a massive bell tower at the east end of the north wall. Today, only the inaccessible second-story door and ruined walls bear witness to the existence of this bell tower, which collapsed in 1812. Although the main entrance to the church was designed to open to the east, the collapse of the bell tower resulted in the bell wall being relocated to the southwest corner of the southern facade. The long-overdue restoration of the church and reconstruction of the campanile damaged in 1812 took place in 1827-1828. Since 1908, the Claretian Missionary Fathers have lovingly preserved and maintained the old mission.

The six bells of the campanile represent an eclectic mix of peoples and cultures pertaining to the mission. Paul Ruelas cast the three oldest bells—those of circa 1795—in Mexico City, and two of the three bear his name, ornate cross elements, and a dedication to *Ave Maria Purisima* (hail Mary most pure). These bells, and the copper baptismal font of the baptistery, were presented to the mission by the king of Spain at the request of Father Serra. The remaining three bells vary in date and origin. The largest bell, which hangs from a crown-shaped top, weighs nearly a ton and was cast in 1830. This bell bears the Latin inscription *Fecit Benitves: Recibvs, Ano D 1830*. The other two bells were cast in Medford, Massachusetts, by Major

G. H. Holbrook, who learned his craft from colonial silversmith Paul Revere. The summit of the campanile bears a wrought-iron cross attached to a circular iron ring symbolizing the spread of Christianity over the world.

Prosperity and Decline

Mission San Gabriel was among the most prosperous of its time. Its agricultural base consisted of the cultivation of wheat, barley, maize, kidney beans, chickpeas, peas, and other beans and the harvesting and processing of olives, grapes, oranges, and other fruit. In the census of 1820, the mission reported ownership of 16,000 head of cattle, 13,000 sheep, 152 goats, 289 swine, 440 mares and colts, 448 tame horses, and 130 mules. Mission industries included carpentry, masonry, metalwork; a tannery and sawmill; and textile, oil, candle, and soap production. Evidence of large-scale olive oil, soap, and candle production and the tanning of hides remains in the form of massive fired brick boiling vats and tanning basins located just north of the main church in the area adjacent to the cemetery. So productive was this candle and soap processing facility that it is said that at one time San Gabriel produced these products for all the California missions.

Other indications of the mission's prosperity are evident in that Father José Zalvidea (1805-1825) undertook several construction projects, including the Church of Our Lady of the Angels, a horse-powered flour mill, a water-powered oil and flour mill near San Marino, a water-powered sawmill, several large granaries, Gabrielino Indian housing, and a mission hospital for the Indians of San Gabriel completed in 1814. One other distinctive mission project was the commission of a sixty-foot schooner, the *Guadalupe*, built by Boston boat builder Joseph Chapman. This was the second such vessel built in early California and as such represents but one more indication of the old mission's prosperity.

As with all the missions of Alta California, Mexican independence from Spain heralded a difficult and challenging period for San Gabriel. As a result of the Secularization Act of 1833, San Gabriel was divested of all of its holdings and Father Estenaga, who was then in charge of the mission, was forced to hand over all church properties to a civil administrator in 1834. The extent of the loss is made apparent by statistics that show that when the mission was secularized in 1834, it owned some 16,500 head of cattle and much of the land of the Los Angeles basin, whereas by 1840 less than 100 head of cattle could be accounted for. By the time that the Franciscans were permitted to return temporarily in 1843, virtually everything of any commercial value had been removed and the mission was left in ruins. In the interim, Governor Pío Pico took personal possession of all former land and stock holdings of San Gabriel. Those Franciscans who remained with the mission continued to care for those Gabrielinos who remained with the mission until 1852. The dismantling of the mission and the expropriation of its lands ultimately left the Gabrielinos, who were to have inherited the newly improved agricultural lands, all but destitute and subject to exploitation at the hands of the new landowners. In 1859, U.S. president James Buchanan restored the old mission to the Catholic Church.

California's Earliest Wine Industry

San Gabriel was the heart of the early California wine industry. At its height, the mission produced some five hundred barrels of wine per year from its four vineyards. In addition to fine wines and extensive vineyards, San Gabriel was noted for its production of brandy under the direction of Father Narciso Duran, whose brandy was described by wine connoisseur Fred McMillin as "double distilled and twice as strong as the good father's faith." In fact, the mission once boasted the oldest and largest winery in California and maintained three wine presses and eight stills for the production of brandy. So prosperous was the wine and brandy industry of Mission San Gabriel that between 1818 and 1822, it contributed seven barrels of brandy toward the establishment of the Church of Our Lady of the Angels some eight miles distant. Today, a single ancient grapevine bears witness to the vast wealth and great history of this mission's agricultural legacy.

Places to Visit

Because the mission is located in the heart of the Los Angeles basin, one need only travel a few miles in any direction to find sites of historic significance related to San Gabriel or its vicinity. Where San Gabriel is concerned, the must-see sites are located in the area of the mission proper and within a radius of two to three miles around the old mission itself.

The Spanish era, from 1771 to 1820, is best characterized by the San Gabriel mission complex itself, including the mission church of 1805, a museum room-block dating to 1812, a cemetery of 1778, the mission kitchen, four brick-lined soap and tallow cisterns or boilers, laundry or tanning tanks, an original water cistern, and brick-lined hearths and an aqueduct located at the center of the courtyard.

Plaza Park, which lies immediately south of the church, includes markers commemorating the 1774 land expedition of Juan Bautista de Anza and the 1776 overland trek that saw the arrival of two hundred settlers from Sonora, Mexico. Two blocks north of the mission is "The Old Grapevine," which represents the sole surviving strand of the mission mother vine used to plant the vineyards from which the mission's wine industry grew.

The Old Plaza Church, or Iglesia de Nuestra Señora de los Angeles, was an *assistencia* or religious outpost of San Gabriel founded in 1784 to serve the needs of the new pueblo of Los Angeles. The church is located in downtown Los Angeles on Main Street.

On a hillside two miles northwest of the mission, in the City of San Marino, is located El Molino Viejo, or the "Old Mill" of San Gabriel dating to 1816.

Representative of the Mexican-rancho period, from 1821 to 1847, San Bernardino de Sena is an *estancia* or ranching outpost of San Gabriel located some fifty miles southeast of the mission in the city of Redlands. Originally founded as a ranch in 1818,the outpost was relocated to its present site in 1830.

—*Ruben G. Mendoza*

For Further Information:

Bonestell, Chesley, and Paul Johnson. "San Gabriel Arcangel." In *The Golden Era of the Missions: 1769-1834*. San Francisco: Chronicle Books, 1974. With paintings by Bonestell.

City of San Gabriel Historical Walk.www.san gabrielcity.com/intrsite/histwalk/.

Krell, Dorothy, ed. "San Gabriel Arcangel." In *The California Missions: A Pictorial History*. Menlo Park, Calif.: Sunset, 1993.

La Fiesta de San Gabriel. sangabrielmission.org/ parish_fiesta.htm.

McMillin, Fred. "San Gabriel Rang the Bell." *Wine Day.* www.foodwine.com/food/wineday/1999/wd0599/wd051999.html.

Mendoza, Ruben G., and Kenneth D. Halla. "Mission Systems: Eighteenth and Nineteenth Centuries." In *The Encyclopedia of North American History.* Pasadena, Calif.: Salem Press/Marshall Cavendish, 1997. Reviews the mission system and the role of Serra in the founding of the California mission chain.

Ruscin, Terry. "San Gabriel, Arcangel." In *Mission Memoirs.* San Diego: Sunbelt, 1999.

Schuetz-Miller, Mardith K. *Building and Builders in Hispanic California, 1769-1850.* Santa Barbara, Calif.: Santa Barbara Trust for Historic Preservation, 1994. An excellent resource for the study of Hispanic architecture in early California.

Wright, Ralph B., ed. "San Gabriel Arcangel." In *California Missions.* Arroyo Grande, Calif.: Record Printing, 1980. A useful overview to the founding and development of the mission.

Mission San Juan Capistrano

Date: Founded November 1, 1776

Relevant issues: American Indian history, art and architecture, European settlement, Latino history, religion

Significance: This is the site of one of two remaining chapels in California used by Father Junípero Serra for religious services. It is also the site of the most catastrophic earthquake-related tragedy to befall the California missions. Today, the mission is famous for the migrating swallows that return each year to nest in the ruins of the Great Stone Church.

Location: North of San Diego and two miles north of Interstate 5 on Ortega Highway at Camino Capistrano, San Juan Capistrano

Site Office:
Mission San Juan Capistrano
31522 Camino Capistrano
P.O. Box 697
San Juan Capistrano, CA 92693
ph.: (949) 248-2000
Web site: www.missionsjc.com/

Named for the Italian crusader Saint John of Capistran, San Juan Capistrano has witnessed over two centuries of change, tragedy, and triumph. Established by Fray (Father) Junípero Serra as the seventh in a chain of twenty-one early California Hispanic missions, San Juan Capistrano is popularly known as the "Jewel of the Missions" and "America's acropolis." It has been heralded as singularly unique for the Great Stone Church that was once the largest European structure west of the Mississippi River. The church required nine years of construction and was completed in 1806, but it was reduced to rubble within seconds in the earthquake of 1812. In the catastrophe, some forty Acjachemem (ah-ha-SHAY-mem) or Juaneño Indian parishioners were killed, and to this day the church remains a sad but historic reminder of that fateful day in 1812.

In addition to its status as the largest California mission church, San Juan Capistrano is also unique in that it was one of only two stone churches constructed in the California mission chain—the other being San Carlos, or Carmel. In addition to the church, Serra's Chapel (the chapel of 1777) predates the main church by some twenty-nine years and is the oldest colonial church in all of Northern California. It is also distinguished as one of two surviving chapels used by Serra for religious services.

The Mission's Founding
Father Fermin Francisco de Lasuén established the first mission settlement with the erection of a large cross, the hanging of bells, and the building of temporary structures on October 30, 1775. Soon thereafter, a devastating Indian raid on Mission San Diego de Alcalá forced Lasuén and his companions to abandon the effort and return to San Diego. Formal dedication of the new mission necessarily awaited the return of the Franciscans under the leadership of Serra on November 1, 1776. The site was selected for its resources, arable land, water, and sizable Native American community of Luiseño and Gabrielino peoples. Serra first selected the site of Arroyo de la Quema for settlement. Due to the scarcity of water, the mission was moved to the present site of El Trabuco on October 4, 1778. Though hundreds of villages of Uto-Aztecan-speaking Shoshone tribal peoples inhabited the region, only the Acjachemem or

Juaneño-Luiseño and Gabrielinos were documented parishioners according to early mission records. Various estimates indicate that between five thousand and ten thousand Luiseño tribal peoples inhabited this portion of the California coast at first contact. The introduction of European diseases decimated whole villages and hastened the demise of the aboriginal populations of the region. Despite the documented presence of only five Europeans in the early mission period, in April of 1820, the padres baptized 3,731 Indians, married 985, buried 2,369, and counted 1,078 neophytes (converted) Indians among parish residents.

The Great Stone Church

Designed and constructed by architect and stonemason Isidro Aguilar of Culiacán, Mexico, the church was elaborately decorated. It measured 140 feet in length and 40 feet in width. The sanctuary incorporated nine *nichos* (niches) within the carved and plastered stone altar screen. The nichos once held the elaborately carved and painted *santos* (saints) hosted by the mission and its church. The church's bell tower, rising to a height of some 115 feet, was the largest bell tower west of the Mississippi River. Aguilar incorporated some six massive domes over the naves and transepts of the church and a lantern in the ceiling over the sanctuary; three domes survived the earthquake of 1812 but were subsequently demolished with dynamite by misguided historic preservationists in the 1860's.

Aguilar was summoned to the mission in 1796 for the purpose of building the church. Tragically, on February 21, 1803, Lasuén notes that Aguilar was killed in a mishap during construction; a seventh dome was added after his death to enclose the structure fully. Despite his death, Aguilar's refined masonry designs found their way into much of the architecture. Particularly notable are the many elaborately carved elements on the walls, doorways, and archways of the monastery. Today, only portions of the sidewalls and the main altar of the church remain intact.

The church was but one part of a mission complex consisting of an adobe chapel, soldiers' barracks, friars' quarters, workshops, kitchens, courtyards, an aqueduct system, gardens, a *campanario* (bell wall), and a cemetery. Industrial features included soap vats, tannery tanks, brick kilns, and

olive-milling areas. The architectural footprint of the great compound was drafted without the benefit of survey instruments, and according to legend, the old padres merely paced the area in order to determine its irregular architectural footprint. The builders also constructed an enclosed quadrangle measuring approximately 260 feet on each side. At the center of the quadrangle once stood a defensive tower that measured approximately eighteen to twenty-two feet in height. The east half of the courtyard was dominated by the original mission chapel (Serra's Chapel). Father John O'Sullivan restored the chapel and its early wall paintings in the 1920's. To this restoration was added the elaborately carved and gilt *reredos* (altar screen) from Spain that now dominates the chapel. The three hundred-year-old altar screen was obtained by Archbishop Cantwell of Los Angeles in 1906 and donated to the mission during the restoration.

Prosperity and the Mission's Decline

The mission prospered in the early days, and its agricultural base included the cultivation of wheat, barley, maize, kidney beans, chickpeas, peas, and beans, and the harvesting and processing of olives, grapes, and other varieties of fruit. Ranching included the raising of livestock, including Spanish cattle, horses, mares and colts, mules, sheep, swine, goats, and chickens. In its census of 1818, the mission reported that it owned 13,200 head of cattle, 15,300 sheep, 363 horses, 300 mares and colts, 200 swine, 195 goats, and 166 mules. Mission industries included carpentry, masonry, metalwork, textile production, tanning, and oil, candle, and soap production.

In the same year, the French-born privateer Hippolyte de Bouchard attacked the California coast on November 20. Bouchard—flying the flag of Buenos Aires and threatening insurgency against Spain—ransacked the mission and looted its wine reserves. Ultimately, the threat of insurgency against Spain spread fear throughout the colony. Resources sorely needed for continued development were then redirected to the defense of the fledgling settlements of Hispanic California. The Spanish crown ultimately lost the fight to Mexican insurgents.

Mexico's hard-fought independence from Spain heralded a difficult and challenging period

Several attempts were made to restore the church to its former glory; however, the only early successful effort was Father O'Sullivan's restoration of Serra's chapel. In the 1990's, the mission, through its Mission Preservation Fund, embarked on a twenty million-dollar preservation campaign to restore and protect this significant historical landmark.

The Swallows of Capistrano

Each spring, cliff swallows migrate to Southern California to nest, and the return of the swallows to Capistrano has become the stuff of legend and folklore. Made famous by Leon Rene's song "When the Swallows Come Back to Capistrano," the annual migration draws tourists and bird-watchers from around the world. The six thousand-mile migration of the swallows from Goya, Argentina, in March begets their return to Goya in October of each year.

The mission's agricultural fields and the availability of water, mud, grasses, and twigs originally drew the swallows; the decline of agricultural cropping in the area has resulted in the flight of the swallows to other areas of the coast and Orange County. Despite this fact, the legend of the swallows is central to the lore of the old mission.

Mission San Juan Capistrano. (American Stock Photography)

for the old mission. In 1821, the Mexican government began redistributing mission holdings to the aboriginal peoples of California. As a result of the Secularization Act of 1833, the Franciscans were divested of all mission properties. In 1841, the Mexican government declared the mission a *pueblo de indios* (an Indian town as opposed to a Catholic parish) for the purposes of emancipating the native peoples. The experiment proved a failure as land grantees moved in and rapidly expropriated mission Indian (neophyte) lands and reduced the Indians to a state of servitude. As a result, the native peoples abandoned the mission and resulting conflicts reduced the mission to a state of near abandonment and abject neglect. In 1845, just prior to the American conquest of California in 1846, the Mexican government sold the mission to Don Juan Forster for $710. Forster made the mission his home until President Abraham Lincoln deeded the mission back to the Catholic Church in 1865.

Places to Visit

No visit to the mission would be complete without consideration of the living history program and annual pageant. On the last Saturday of each month, volunteers reenact early life at the mission. Actors don historically accurate costumes ranging from Franciscan attire to Spanish soldiers' uniforms to American gunslingers' garb and provide demonstrations and reenactments of each period in the mission's history. The pageant, on the other hand, features a very popular outdoor living-history play entitled *Capistrano* that provides a colorful and historically accurate portrayal of life at the mission from 1776 to 1865.

In addition to the mission proper—including Serra's Chapel, the bell wall, the monastery, and the barracks buildings—the business and residential areas adjacent to the mission are historically significant. The few square blocks of the village core are included in the city's inventory of historic and cultural resources. The *Walking Tour Guide to Historic San Juan Capistrano* is available at City Hall, in dispensers attached to downtown street signs, or by calling the city at (714) 493-1171. The area includes buildings from several periods in the community's history.

Representing the Spanish era, from 1776 to 1820, beyond the mission proper the period structures include the Los Rios Historic District; the Rios, Montanez, Blas Aguilar, and Silvas adobes; the Historic Town Center Archaeological Park; and Stone Field. Each of these sites provides a glimpse into the art and architecture of Spanish colonial construction in adobe and related materials.

From the Mexican-rancho period, from 1821 to 1847, several significant structures may be visited within the village core. These include a number of houses within the "Little Hollywood" portion of the Los Rios District, and the Avila, Garcia, and Yorba Adobes. This last site constitutes the El Adobe Restaurant.

Historic structures in the village core from the statehood era, from 1850 to 1900, include the Capistrano Depot, several structures within "Little Hollywood," the O'Neill Museum, and the Egan House. In addition to the many historically significant buildings of the statehood era, visitors should visit the New Parish Church. Though modern, the stone church (located behind the mission compound) was intended to reproduce the appearance of the original Great Stone Church of San Juan Capistrano.   —*Ruben G. Mendoza*

For Further Information:

Bean, Lowell John, and Florence C. Shipek. "Luiseño." In *California*. Vol. 8 in *Handbook of North American Indians*, edited by Robert F. Heizer. Washington, D.C.: Smithsonian Institution, 1978. A detailed overview of the Luiseño Indian peoples.

"The Capistrano Pageant." www.capistranopageant.com/.

"Capistrano: San Juan Capistrano Chamber of Commerce." www.sjc.net/

Edgar, Kathleen J., and Susan E. Edgar. *Mission San Juan Capistrano*. New York: Rosen, 2000. An introduction to the mission for elementary school students.

Haas, Lisbeth. *Conquests and Historical Identities in California, 1769-1936*. Berkeley: University of California Press, 1996. A multiethnic history of San Juan Capistrano that explores Spanish and American social change, rural society, ethnicity, and race.

Hallan-Gibson, Pamela. *Two Hundred Years in San Juan Capistrano: A Pictorial History*. San Juan Capistrano, Calif.: City of San Juan Capistrano, 1990. A photographic overview of the community's history.

Mendoza, Ruben G., and Kenneth D. Halla. "Mission Systems: 18th and 19th Centuries." In *The Encyclopedia of North American History*, edited by John C. Super. Tarrytown, N.Y.: Marshall Cavendish, 1997. Reviews the mission system and the role of Serra in the founding of the California mission chain.

Schuetz-Miller, Mardith K. *Building and Builders in Hispanic California, 1769-1850*. Santa Barbara, Calif.: Santa Barbara Trust for Historic Preservation, 1994. An excellent resource for the study of Hispanic architecture in early California.

Wright, Ralph B., ed. "San Juan Capistrano." In *California Missions*. Arroyo Grande, Calif.: Record Printing, 1980. A useful overview of the founding and development of the mission.

Monterey

Date: Church built and consecrated by Spaniards on June 16, 1770

Relevant issues: Business and industry, European settlement, Latino history, literary history, western expansion

Significance: Monterey, a city of approximately thirty thousand people, was the capital of California under Spanish and Mexican rule, although it was never a capital of the state of California. It has many well-preserved buildings dating from the early to mid-nineteenth century. It was the site of California's first constitutional convention, played an important role in the fishing and canning industries, and attracted artists and writers including Robert Louis Stevenson and John Steinbeck.

Location: On the Pacific coast 125 miles south of San Francisco and 345 miles north of Los Angeles

Site Office:
Chamber of Commerce of the Monterey Peninsula
380 Alvarado Street
Monterey, CA 93940
ph.: (831) 649-1770

In November, 1542, Don Juan Rodríguez Cabrillo, a Portuguese captain sailing under the Spanish flag, explored and mapped the Pacific coast of North America, something unprecedented for Europeans. He had come from the port of Navidad in Colma, Mexico. He led two ships, the *San Salvador* and *La Vittoria*. *La Vittoria* was sailed by Don Bartolomé Ferrelo, assistant to Cabrillo. The water was too rough to land, so Cabrillo had to view the land from the sea. He claimed the land for Spain and named the place La Bohia de los Pinos (the point of the pines) for the pine forests that lined the coast.

The Second Expedition

A second expedition to the area took place in 1602 under the command of General Sebastian Vizcaino. At the time General Vizcaino was sailing for Viceroy Don Gaspar de Zuniga, Conde de Monte Rey of New Spain. He was looking for a safe harbor for Spanish galleons traveling the Pacific and trading in the Philippines. The expedition consisted of four ships, *La Capitana* (also known as *San Diego*), *La Almiranta* (also known as *Santo Tomas*), *Tres Reys*, and a long narrow boat. These boats held approximately two hundred men and three Carmelite friars. On December 16, they entered the bay area near the mouth of the river. Vizcaino named the river El Rio del Carmelo after the friars, and the bay El Puerto de Monte Rey in honor of the viceroy. Many of the sailors suffered from scurvy by the time they reached Monterey. Vizcaino continued his expedition and sent *La Almiranta* back to Mexico to return the sick men and to obtain additional provisions.

Vizcaino wrote to King Philip III of Spain telling him of the natural beauty of the Bay of Monterey and how it could offer protection and security to ships coming from the Philippines. He wrote of the abundance of oak and pine trees that would be available to provide lumber for ship repairs. He also mentioned the quality of the soil, climate, wild grain, and animals. Apparently, however, the rulers of Spain were not impressed, and so it was more than a century and a half before Monterey was settled by Europeans.

The Third Expedition

A third expedition reached the Bay of Monterey on November 27, 1769. This expedition was composed of two parts—one by land and the other by sea. Don Gaspar de Portolá, governor of Baja (Lower) California, led the land expedition. The sixty-six men failed to recognize Monterey from the descriptions left by General Vizcaino, who had described the area as viewed from the sea, which did not give a clear indication of the site's position to the land-based explorers.

The men were quite disappointed and low on supplies. The ship that was to meet them at Monterey had not arrived. On November 28 they moved their camp to the Carmel River and erected two crosses, one at the point that is now known as Mussel Rock and the other at the Punta de los Pinos. The expedition returned to San Diego on January 24, 1770. Many of the men were sick with scurvy.

In March, with many of the party still sick and supplies low, Portolá wanted to start the journey back to Baja California. Father Junípero Serra, a leading Franciscan priest, was able to persuade Portolá to stay a while longer and pray a novena (nine consecutive days of prayer). One day before the group was to continue the trip back to Baja California, a ship was spotted. Although the explorers had to wait several more days before it arrived at San Diego, when it did they obtained the supplies and provisions for which they had been waiting.

With the new supplies in hand they made another attempt to find the Bay of Monterey. By May 25 Governor Portolá and Father Juan Crespi had again reached the Punta de los Pinos. The *San Antonio* (also known as *El Principe*), the ship at the command of Captain Don Juan Perez with Father Serra aboard, arrived eight days later and recognized the Bay of Monterey from the sea. They found the two crosses that they had erected the previous autumn, proving that their earlier expedition was on target.

On June 3, in a small shelter under an oak tree, a mass was said and the land blessed. After the religious service, Portolá took formal control of the land in the name of King Charles III of Spain.

The Custom House in Monterey, the oldest government building in California. (American Stock Photography)

These events were recorded by Portolá, Perez, and Don Miguel del Pino, the ship's pilot.

A Church Is Built

At the site of the first mass, a church was erected, then consecrated on June 16, 1770. A presidio, or fort, was also established at the site. Barracks were erected for soldiers, as well as living quarters for the missionaries and officers. This was the first settlement by Europeans in the Monterey area and the northernmost settlement on the Pacific coast.

As was customary, priests accompanied soldiers in the settlement of new territory in order to establish the Catholic religion in the regions that Spain claimed. The missions were created to make converts of the Native Americans and teach them the ways of Spanish life. Sometimes there was a conflict between the military and religious leaders.

Father Serra founded the second mission of Alta (Upper) California, the Mission San Carlos de Borromeo, at Monterey in 1770. The mission at San Diego was the first mission, established in 1769. In 1771, Father Serra moved the San Carlos mission to Carmel, a fertile valley approximately five miles south of Monterey. A few reasons are cited for the move from Monterey. It is said that there was a dispute between Governor Pedro Fages, the military commander of the settlement,

and Father Serra. Fages would not subject his military command to the authority of the church. It is also said that the soldiers of Monterey constantly harassed and fought with the Native Americans. In order to concentrate on the purpose of the mission, Father Serra may have felt it necessary to move from the Monterey settlement to Carmel. The Carmel site was still close enough to Monterey to be protected by the military forces there.

Father Serra was considered the *Padre-Presidente* (father-president) of the California missions and presided over the nine missions he founded, including San Carlos de Borromeo. By 1773, the San Carlos mission is said to have had the most converts of any mission in Alta California. Father Serra prohibited many of the local Indians' traditional practices. The Indians attempted to rise in revolt but quieted down at the appearance of soldiers. Native Americans were put to work herding, making pottery, weaving baskets, and tanning hides.

Indians had lived at Monterey for about four millennia before the Spanish came. These people discovered the benefits of Monterey's mild climate and abundance of food well before the Europeans. The Native Americans present in Monterey at the time of the first European settlement were the Ohlone people. The Ohlone are said to have succeeded the Esselens, who had inhabited the area for more than two thousand years. The Ohlone were made up of about forty small tribes around the San Francisco and Monterey Bays. The name Ohlone is derived from one of their villages on the San Francisco Peninsula.

Independence from Spain

The Spanish settlement at Monterey continued to increase in importance. In 1776 Governor Felipe de Neve arrived in Monterey and Colonel Juan Bautista de Anza led 247 men, women, and children with more than five hundred head of livestock over one thousand miles by land from the Presidio of Tubac in Sonora to Monterey. The majority of these people remained in Monterey. In 1777, Monterey became the capital of both Alta and Baja California.

During the uprising against the Spanish and for Mexican independence, groups of privateers attempted to destroy Spanish shipping. In 1818, Hippolyte de Bouchard, a French mercenary flying the flag of Argentina, arrived in the ship *Argentina* to attack Monterey. He and his men demanded the surrender of Alta California and proceeded to sack and burn the city when their wish was not granted. Governor Pablo Vicente de Solá, the last governor of the Spanish period, ordered the women and children to the missions and, realizing that he was outnumbered, retreated with his soldiers to Rancho del Rey, today's Salinas. After the invaders left Monterey, the citizens had the task of rebuilding.

In 1822, Mexico raised its banner above Monterey, symbolizing the end of more than three hundred years of Spanish rule. Monterey was established as an official port of entry and the city's trading era began. In 1827, Monterey's Custom House was opened. Ships could not unload or sell their merchandise until duties were paid. The Custom House still stands today; it is California's oldest public building.

During Mexican rule, Monterey participated to a great extent in the hide and tallow trade. Fourteen ranches in the Monterey area raised herds of cattle and horses to supply English and American ships with tallow and leather. The animals were slaughtered and the hides were dried. The meat was cut in strips to dry and the fat was rendered and poured into hide bags or bladders to be floated out to trading ships. By the 1830's the missions had begun the process of secularization. They had become very important places in the six decades that they existed in California. The priests had become farm managers, merchants, and the rulers of the area in the eyes of the Native Americans. The missions furnished supplies to the presidios. Government officials increasingly believed that the missions were becoming too wealthy and powerful. The missions were ordered to dissolve, and the land was divided up and given back to the Indians. Private ranchers, however, eventually took over most of the Indians' holdings.

An American Possession

Another change was on its way. Thomas Larkin, the American consul in Alta California at Monterey, had urged the leaders in California to follow Texas's lead and secede from Mexico as early as 1840. On July 7, 1846, U.S. Marines and sailors commended by John Drake Sloat raised the American flag over the presidio. This bloodless coup started a period of U.S. military occupation that lasted for the two years of the Mexican-American War. When the war ended in 1848 with the signing of the Treaty of Guadalupe Hidalgo, upper California became a territory of the United States.

The Reverend Walter Colton, who came to Monterey as chaplain on one of Commodore Sloat's ships, became the settlement's first American *alcalde*, similar to a mayor. In 1846 he published, in conjunction with Robert Semple, California's first newspaper in Monterey. He also organized the first American jury on the West Coast. He put prisoners to work on public works projects, resulting in Colton Hall, California's first schoolhouse and town meeting place.

In 1848 gold was discovered in the American River near Sacramento. The whole social order in Monterey was turned upside down. People who were once servants returned from the mines with thousands of dollars worth of gold. Soldiers and sailors deserted the ranks in search of wealth. A successful miner could earn more in a day than a soldier could earn in a year. Thousands of people came from the East and thousands of others came from around the world in search of instantaneous wealth. California experienced an influx of a variety of people much sooner than anyone could have predicted.

Statehood for California

In 1849, California's first constitutional convention was held in Monterey. At this convention, the constitution of California was drafted, debated, and signed. The document was very progressive. It recognized property rights for married women, outlawed slavery, and banned state lotteries. At this convention the delegates also decided to move the capital of California to San Jose from Monterey. In November, the constitution was ratified by the voters of California, and in 1850 California became the thirty-first U.S. state and Monterey was incorporated as a city. Over a span of more than two de-

The Monterey Canning Company. (American Stock Photography)

Monterey in August, 1879, from Europe to wait for Fanny Osbourne to divorce her husband and marry him. The two had met in Europe at an artists' retreat. While he waited for his lover to sort out her personal affairs, Stevenson worked on stories and wrote articles for the Monterey newspaper.

In 1880, the first of the grand resort hotels in California opened in Monterey. At this time Monterey had fewer than four hundred residents. The Hotel Del Monte, built by Charles Crocker, transformed Monterey into an international destination point. The city also grew as a result of the railroad connecting it to San Francisco and other cities. The Hotel Del Monte could accommodate 750 guests and was surrounded by 126 acres of park. It was known as "The Queen of American Watering Places." Although the hotel burned to the ground in April, 1887, and again suffered a severe fire in the 1920's, each time it was rebuilt even more elaborately than before. In the 1890's, a golf course was added and guests were treated to horsedrawn carriage rides from the hotel around the tip of the peninsula, the famous Seventeen-Mile Drive. More than seventeen thousand visitors came to the resort each year.

In the early 1900's, entrepreneurs Frank E. Booth, Knute Hovden, and Pietro Ferrante worked together to transform Monterey into the "Sardine Capital of the World." With the introduction of the lampara net, fishing for sardines in the Monterey Bay area became a multimillion-dollar industry. By 1913 fishermen were catching 25 tons of sardines a night. By 1918 nine sardine canneries were built on Monterey's waterfront. In the 1930's and 1940's annual sardine catches were recorded at 200,000 tons a year. Unfortunately, overfishing led to the demise of the sardine industry by the 1950's. John Steinbeck, who grew up in Salinas and lived in Monterey during the Depression, wrote two books

cades (1850-1873), Monterey served as the county seat.

Many Monterey residents relocated to San Francisco because of the gold rush, but the development of the whaling and fishing industry in Monterey ushered in a new era of growth. A whaler from Cape Cod came to Monterey in 1845 to establish the Monterey Whaling Company and soon whaling on the Pacific became an important industry. By the 1860's there were four whaling companies, largely run by Portuguese immigrants. Unfortunately, the whales were hunted to near extinction by the late 1880's.

The Chinese came to California in the 1850's for gold, but many turned to squid fishing for their livelihood. The Chinese neighborhood of Monterey was just south of the area that became Cannery Row. When a fire destroyed the Chinese village in 1906, local landowners and authorities did not allow the Chinese to rebuild. The Japanese also immigrated to the area, and many made their livelihood diving for abalone.

In the late nineteenth century Monterey became a refuge for artists and a vacation spot for the well-to-do. Writer Robert Louis Stevenson came to

about the fishing industry of the area—*Cannery Row* (1945) and *Sweet Thursday* (1954). These stories helped to foster the tourist trade in Monterey and the surrounding area.

During World War II, the U.S. Navy became a significant presence in Monterey. The Navy leased the famous Hotel Del Monte, which was well past its heyday, and established the Naval Postgraduate School. The Defense Language Institute and the U.S. Coast Guard were also established in Monterey. The military therefore played an important part in the economy of Monterey and the Monterey peninsula.

Monterey Today
Today a leading industry in Monterey is tourism, helped by the many historic sites in the area. One of the most significant historic homes is that built in 1835 by Thomas Larkin, the American consul, who combined Spanish colonial architecture with that of New England to create what became known as the Monterey style. The style was limited almost exclusively to Monterey, as most of the Spanish and Mexican residents of California did not care for the New England influences. The boardinghouse where Robert Louis Stevenson stayed in 1879 is now a museum of Stevenson memorabilia. The Custom House and Colton Hall also have been preserved as museums.   —*Susen Taras*

For Further Information:
Abrahamson, Eric. *Historic Monterey.* Monterey: California Department of Parks and Recreation, 1989. A wonderful, well-illustrated history of Monterey, detailing the Native American, Spanish, Mexican, and U.S. history of the area.

Gordon, B. Le Roy. *Monterey Bay Area: Natural History and Cultural Imprints.* Pacific Grove, Calif.: Boxwood Press, 1996. Examines the natural and cultural history of the Monterey Bay region.

Newcomb, Rexford. *The Old Mission Churches and Historic Houses of California.* Philadelphia: J. P. Lippincott, 1925. Information on early settlement and the missions is contained in this book and in various histories of California.

Reese, Robert W. *A Brief History of Old Monterey.* Monterey, Calif.: City Planning Commission, 1969. Written in a more formal style. The information is concise yet gives details.

Nixon Birthplace, Yorba Linda
Date: Nixon born on January 9, 1913
Relevant issues: Political history
Significance: This settlement on the edge of the desert, originally a collection of avocado and citrus groves, was transformed into an actual farming town over the course of President Richard M. Nixon's youth until the family moved to Whittier in 1922.
Location: Thirty-five miles southeast of Los Angeles
Site Office:
Richard M. Nixon Presidential Library and Birthplace
18001 Yorba Linda Boulevard
Yorba Linda, CA 92886-3949
ph.: (714) 993-3393, 993-5075
Web site: www.nixonlibrary.org

Richard Milhous Nixon, the thirty-seventh president of the United States, was born on January 9, 1913, in Yorba Linda, California, the second of five sons of Frank and Hannah Milhous Nixon. Frank had migrated from Ohio several years earlier and met Hannah at a Quaker religious meeting. After the wedding, Frank borrowed money from his father-in-law in order to purchase twelve acres of land on which he planted lemon tree seedlings.

The Homestead of a Future President
In 1910, Frank built the Nixon homestead from an eight hundred-dollar building kit ordered from the Sears catalog. It is the same house, a one and one-half-story bungalow, which was restored and has been open to the public since 1990 as part of the Richard M. Nixon Presidential Library and Birthplace. There is a large brick fireplace on the ground floor around which Richard Nixon had long family talks about local affairs and state and national politics. Downstairs there was also a bedroom for the parents, living room, and kitchen. All the boys slept together in a single upstairs bedroom. There was an outside privy which the family shared. At the time of Richard Nixon's birth, the bungalow had no electricity or running water, either.

Hannah insisted on naming four of the five sons after early English kings (Harold, Richard, Arthur, and Edward). The other son, Francis Donald, was named after Frank, but the family always called him Donald. Frank's foray into citrus farming, however, never brought the affluence or even the sustenance that he sought. The lemon trees suffered blight due to a number of frosts, and the soil in which Frank Nixon planted the seedlings was too sandy and pebbly to produce good fruit. Throughout the nine years that Frank Nixon and his growing family lived in Yorba Linda, the family lived in working poverty, and Frank took outside jobs to supplement income from the lemon trees and food from the family garden.

A "Hard but Happy" Early Life

Nixon, in his memoirs, characterizes his early life in Yorba Linda as "hard but happy." His mother had taught him how to read at home, which helped make him a star student at Yorba Linda Elementary School, which he entered in 1919. He did so well in the first grade—there was no kindergarten at Yorba Linda Elementary at that time as universal kindergarten, originally conceived in Germany in the nineteenth century, did not become ubiquitous in the United States until later in the century—that the following fall, he skipped from first grade to third grade. Hannah also tutored Richard at home in French and German and introduced him to the plays and sonnets of William Shakespeare. There is a confirmed report that on young Nixon's first day of school, Hannah told Miss Mary George, his first grade teacher, "Please call my son Richard and never Dick. I named him Richard."

Richard was reported to be a quiet and studious boy with a great inclination toward reading and a memory that some teachers called "photographic." In the three years that Richard attended Yorba Linda Elementary, he was consistently at the top of his class. In the family papers, his first-year report card shows an "E" (Excellent) in every graded subject except handwriting, for which he received a "U" (Unsatisfactory). There are school exercise books that Nixon composed while at Yorba Linda Elementary that can be viewed in the Nixon Archives. The penmanship is indeed difficult to decipher in areas, but the content is redolent of the classical notions which dominated elementary in-

struction at the time: Nixon, like his schoolmates, copied out famous speeches in the Western rhetorical tradition from Marc Antony's funeral oration for Julius Caesar to Abraham Lincoln's Gettysburg Address. Nixon apparently had a remarkable memory, and his ability to memorize long passages from various poems and orations amazed his peers and pleased the four teachers who taught all levels at Yorba Linda Elementary. Contemporaries of Nixon recall that he and a Japanese American girl, Yoneko Dobashi, generally competed for top honors in successive academically competitive early-elementary classes that they shared. Indeed, the Yorba Linda community was remarkably multicultural, due in part to the job opportunities available in new oilfields nearby and the relatively low price of real estate. Yorba Linda had been founded by members of the Whittier Quaker community, but there were many Chinese American and Japanese American farming families, some of whom also worked in the oilfields, which drew African American and Latino families to the small village as well.

Quaker and Other Influences

The Friends Meeting of Yorba Linda was a continuing influence on Richard and the entire Nixon family and probably constituted a more comprehensive influence on him than even his public elementary school education. Richard was expected to follow the precepts of Quaker Christian practice as espoused by his father, who, having converted from Methodism, taught in the Friends Sunday School. Richard was expected to be in attendance at no less than four Sunday services. Yet Richard recalls reading, almost every evening, newspapers and periodicals that allowed him to develop his lifelong love of politics and his consideration of issues of civics and public affairs. Even given the financial straits of the Nixon family, they apparently always subscribed to the *Los Angeles Times*, *The Saturday Evening Post*, and the *Ladies' Home Journal*, all of which Nixon read voraciously. Nixon recalls enjoying visits with his Uncle Oscar and Aunt Olive Marshburn in Whittier because of their *National Geographic* collection, which they generously shared with their nephew. In his memoirs, Nixon calls that magazine the preferred reading choice of his youth while in Yorba Linda.

Other influences on the development of Richard Nixon's personality during the first nine years of his life in Yorba Linda include his older brother, Harold, and his maternal grandmother, Almira Milhous. Harold, four years older than Richard and blessed with an insouciant personality and athletic ability which Richard did not have, provided an ideal for Richard which he could not attain and perhaps helped to develop his sense of perseverance which later served him well. Yorba Linda contemporaries recall Harold's physical superiority but remember as well the determination of young Richard to try to keep up with his older, stronger, more self-assured sibling.

After the death of grandfather Franklin Milhous in 1919, his widow, Almira Milhous, became more a part of the Frank and Hannah Nixon Yorba Linda household. Although she was a strict Quaker, she still liked and presided over midsummer picnics and family gatherings at Thanksgiving and Christmas. Of her thirty-two grandchildren, Grandma Milhous seemed to have most favored Richard; she appreciated almost immediately the talent that her nervous and studious grandson had for absorbing knowledge. Many members of the family recall her frequent compliment to young Richard, "That boy will one day be a leader." Other family members noted, and sometimes complained about, the favoritism that she on occasion showed for Richard. Grandma Milhous's influence on Richard was to give him an appreciation and respect for both religious values and humanitarian ideals: to believe strongly in one's preferred understanding of religious concerns while showing respect for other traditions and opinions.

By the early 1920's, Frank Nixon had become fairly convinced that citrus farming was not going to support his family of six (youngest brother Edward was not born until 1930). Frank sold off single acres in parcels, with the local school system purchasing several of the lots (which the school owns to this day). Hannah had never liked the proximity of the Yorba Linda homestead to the Anaheim irrigation ditch, a dirty and dangerous temptation for her sons and their friends in the neighborhood. Frank and Hannah Nixon moved with their four sons to the larger town of Whittier, twenty miles northwest of Yorba Linda. There was a larger Quaker community there and more opportunities, Frank Nixon thought, to assure his family a reasonable middle-class living. Frank again borrowed money, this time to buy land on Whittier Boulevard, the main road between Whittier and La Habra. Nixon cleared the land and installed a tank and pump; his service station was the first one on the eight-mile stretch between Whittier and La Habra. Almost immediately, he started selling Hannah's home-baked pies and cakes, and as he added items for sale, the Nixon Market developed as an early iteration of that very American, automobile centered establishment, the convenience store attached to a service station. Thus, the Yorba Linda era ended, and the Whittier era of the Nixon family began.

Places to Visit
Metropolitan Los Angeles's fabled and at times troubled freeway system puts several other areas of interest for Nixon historians—professional and amateur—close enough to merge into a single day's agenda. Nixon Winter White House is in San Clemente, seventy miles south of Los Angeles via the

The Richard Nixon Library and Birthplace. (American Stock Photography)

91 West to the 55 South (Newport Freeway) to the I-5 South (the Santa Ana Freeway, then the San Diego Freeway). Whittier College, Nixon's undergraduate alma mater, is located on the east side of Painter Avenue in Whittier, north of Whittier Boulevard and the downtown area.

—Richard Sax

For Further Information

Aitken, Jonathan. *Nixon: A Life.* London: Weidenfeld & Nicolson, 1993. A definitive biography that is thoroughly annotated.

Ambrose, Stephen E. *Nixon: The Education of a Politician.* 3 vols. New York: Simon & Schuster, 1987. A well-researched and -documented three-volume biography with forty pages of notes in the first volume alone, as well as an extensive bibliography and index.

Costello, William. *The Facts About Nixon: An Unauthorized Biography.* New York: Viking Press, 1960. An objective biography written during the 1960 presidential election that makes extensive use of private papers including letters, telegrams, diaries, journals, and other memoranda.

Hughes, Arthur F. *Richard M. Nixon.* New York: Dodd, Mead, 1972. An accessible biography for scholastic audiences.

Morris, Roger. *Richard Milhous Nixon: The Rise of an American Politician.* New York: Henry Holt, 1991. This 1,005-page biography includes significant detail about Nixon's early life in the first 300 pages. This volume concludes with Nixon's ascent to the vice presidency after the 1952 campaign.

Nixon, Richard M. *The Memoirs of Richard Nixon.* New York: Grosset & Dunlap, 1978. Nixon's complete memoirs, published four years after he resigned from the presidency.

Stone, Oliver, ed. *Nixon: An Oliver Stone Film.* New York: Hyperion, 1995. This text describes the making of Stone's controversial film about Nixon and includes illustrations as well as insights concerning the production and direction of the film.

Volkan, Vamik D. *Richard Nixon: A Psychobiography.* New York: Columbia University Press, 1997. This text is an exemplary psychobiography that attempts to show the relationship between Nixon's inner psychological dynamics and his outward style of leadership.

Presidio of San Francisco

Date: Founded in 1776

Relevant issues: Art and architecture, European settlement, Latino history, military history, western expansion

Significance: The Presidio was a military base from 1776 to 1994 under three different national governments. Now a National Historic Park, it contains a number of architecturally important buildings.

Location: Northwest corner of San Francisco

Site Office:
Golden Gate National Recreation Area
Building 201, Fort Mason
San Francisco, CA 94123
ph.: (415) 561-4323; TDD (415) 561-4313
Web site: www.nps.gov/prsf/

The Presidio of San Francisco has a rich history stretching back more than a thousand years. Once a military outpost, it is now a National Historic Park.

Native American settlements in the region of the Presidio date to the early eighth century. The Ohlone (or Costanoan) people inhabited the San Francisco region south to Monterey. Archaeological evidence places the Ohlone at the Presidio site by at least 740 C.E.

The Spanish Period

In 1776, the Spanish arrived at the peninsula, which they renamed San Francisco in honor of Saint Francis. By 1810, the introduction of exotic diseases and forced labor to the missions established by the Spanish led to the destruction of Ohlone society. The Spaniards' settlement of the region was part of a larger movement. While Spanish sailors had explored the coast of what would come to be called Baja and Alta California since the early seventeenth century, serious settlement efforts did not begin until the later eighteenth century. In 1769, expeditions set out to build settlements in San Diego and Monterey.

After seven years and many abortive attempts to extend their reach into the San Francisco region, the Spanish arrived at the spurs of land called the Golden Gate on August 4, 1775. In July of 1776, a party settled in a clearing overlooking the bay.

By this point, the settlement of San Francisco

The archaeological excavation of the Presidio chapel. (Ruben G. Mendoza)

The Mexican Period

The Spanish presence in the Presidio of San Francisco came to an end in 1821. The colonial government in Mexico, taking advantage of the increased weakness of the Spanish empire, declared its independence and took possession of all Spanish lands in North America, including the Presidio of San Francisco.

Unfortunately for the San Francisco Presidio, the neglect with which the Spanish had treated it continued under the new regime, primarily due to the instability of the new government. Physically and conceptually, San Francisco was a long way away from Mexico City.

From the 1820's through the 1840's, various European powers eyed San Francisco and dreamed of the natural harbor and riches the Presidio guarded. The weak grip of the Mexican government inspired dreams of empire in other nations, but it was the Americans, under the influence of the doctrine of Manifest Destiny, who posed the greatest threat to Mexico's governance. Briefly, Manifest Destiny held that it was the special mission of white Americans to settle North America from coast to coast, and to that end, an increasing number of Americans settled in Alta California.

For its part, the Presidio of San Francisco suffered continuing neglect, and by 1835, it was no longer a militarily important garrison. Although it continued what operations it could, the Presidio was virtually abandoned by the Mexican government.

The Americans, however, had taken note of it. In 1835, the American president Andrew Jackson offered the Mexican government five million dollars for the San Francisco area. After some consideration, Mexico refused the offer. Despite the obvious interest of Americans, the Mexican government did not change its policies of neglect. The

followed a pattern that had developed for two centuries. Upon moving into a new area for colonization, the Spanish would establish three interdependent institutions—the pueblo, the mission, and the presidio. The pueblo was a civilian settlement whose goal was to establish as quickly as possible a Spanish population base. It was also to provide food, something that the mission, a religious settlement of Franciscan monks, assisted in by Christianizing the native Ohlone and forcing them to work.

The presidio, its name derived from the Latin term *presidium* (garrisoned fort), was the military part of the colonization effort. In addition to its military functions, the presidio also furnished governmental leadership for the region.

Throughout the late eighteenth and early nineteenth centuries, the Spanish enlarged their presence in San Francisco, although "enlarged" was a relative term. When the captain of the American frigate *Hazard* sailed into the San Francisco Bay in 1804 requesting repairs from winter storms, the garrison numbered only eight soldiers who were occupied primarily with keeping the Spanish peace in the surrounding settlements, including putting down Native American uprisings around other nearby missions.

Presidio was without troops or even basic resources. By 1846, most of its structures had fallen into disrepair.

The American Period
Conditions for the Presidio were to change, however. In 1846, the United States declared war on Mexico, and American naval forces under Captain John C. Frémont occupied the Presidio. On July 9, 1846, the Mexican flag was lowered for the last time, and the flag of the United States was raised over the Presidio. The neglected fort's fortunes were to change dramatically in the coming years.

Volunteers repaired the Presidio within a year of its possession. With the discovery of gold at Sutter's Mill in 1848, the Presidio went from being a scruffy garrison on the edge of the American empire to the gateway to untold riches as the world rushed in to take advantage of the discovery. In 1850, realizing the strategic value of the San Francisco Bay area, President Millard Fillmore reserved the Presidio to the United States government for military use. Beginning with the Civil War of 1861-1865, the importance of not only California with its untapped resources but also the Presidio to national security and prosperity became increasingly obvious. Wars against Native Americans throughout the later nineteenth century emphasized this, and soldiers stationed in San Francisco saw combat against the Modocs in Northern California, as well as the Apache of the Southwest.

By the end of the nineteenth century, the United States was entering its Gilded Age, an era of both urbanization and industrialization on one hand and conservation on the other. As the Western frontier shrank, an increasing number of people worried that open space would vanish forever. The soldiers of the United States cavalry at the Presidio were given another task, and that was to protect the new national parks in the Sierra Nevada. Soldiers from the San Francisco Presidio patrolled Yosemite, Sequoia, and other parks during the summer months until the start of World War I in 1914. In 1916, the federal government created the National Park Service.

The military role of the Presidio was enhanced as well. During the Spanish-American War of 1898, thousands of troops camped at the Presidio awaiting deployment to the Philippines. Wounded soldiers returned to the Army's first permanent general hospital. During the 1906 earthquake and fire, the Army supported the civilian government of the shattered city with protection, food, shelter, and clothing. During World War I, troops under General John Pershing, commander of the American Expeditionary Force, left the Presidio for Europe.

The view of the Presidio changed throughout the nineteenth and early twentieth centuries. It was still an active military base, but many urban reformers advocated the idea of the Presidio as a public park. Many parts of the military reservation had already become favored weekend and holiday spots. By the turn of the century, reformers, who felt that open space and fresh air were absolutely necessary to life in a city, embarked on a movement to have part of the Presidio set aside. While this plan to set aside four hundred acres died in the Senate, Golden Gate Park was established elsewhere in the city. Even so, the Presidio itself was improved, not only with fortifications but also with trees. Yet the idea was there that the Presidio might one day become a park. When the Golden Gate Bridge was built between 1933 and 1937, civilian use of the Presidio increased.

1941-1994
After the attack on Pearl Harbor, the Presidio's military role increased. The Presidio became the Western Defense Command Center, and soldiers dug foxholes on the beaches of San Francisco. During World War II, over 1.5 million soldiers and 23 million tons of war material passed through the Presidio.

From the time of the Spanish settlement, San Franciscans considered the Presidio an open post, and this attitude lasted through the early part of the war. Yet fears of submarine attack prompted the Army command to close the base for the first time in its history. There were barbed wire and anti-aircraft batteries on the golf course and the beaches.

Despite these changes, however, the Presidio played a much less important role than it had during World War I. It had become clear that the post was no longer critical to the United States military. Great changes awaited the Presidio in the postwar years.

Despite protests on the part of the Sixth Army, it

was increasingly clear that the Presidio's days as a military establishment were numbered. In 1962, San Francisco prevented an attempt to develop part of the Presidio, and the Department of the Interior was prevailed upon to declare it a National Historic Landmark in 1963, which indeed it was, with over 350 buildings of historic value. The military presence declined noticeably between 1945 and 1970.

In 1972, the Presidio was designated part of the new Golden Gate National Recreation Area, should the military ever close the base. During the rounds of base closures in the late 1980's and 1990's, that eventuality occurred, and in 1994, the Presidio changed hands once again.

1994 to the Present
On October 1, 1994, the Presidio of San Francisco was transferred to the National Park Service. When it closed, the Presidio was the oldest military base in continuing operation in the country. It became a National Historical Landmark, with hundreds of buildings having historic value.

In 1996, Congress created the Presidio Trust to turn the former post into a self-sufficient park by 2013 while preserving its wealth of scenic and historic resources. While this type of park management had not yet been tried, it was deemed the only way to generate the vast sums of money needed to maintain the historic post.

The Presidio is open to visitors year-round, although the William Penn Mott, Jr., Visitors Center and the Presidio Museum maintain different hours. The museum contains images and exhibits representing the Native American, Spanish, Mexican, and American eras of use. While rangers and docents give a variety of programs on most weekdays, visitors can also explore the Presidio on their own on eleven miles of hiking and fourteen miles of bicycle trails.

In addition to having over two hundred years of military history, the Presidio is an architecturally rich location that features buildings from the Spanish to the modern eras of its occupation. These buildings, embodying a variety of styles, range from bunkers and ordnance storage to housing for troops and officers. These buildings include the Fort Point National Historic Site, the San Francisco National Cemetery, Crissy Field, and Baker Beach.
—*Christopher S. W. Koehler*

For Further Information:
Benton, Lisa M. *The Presidio: From Army Post to National Park.* York, Pa.: Northeastern University Press, 1998. Cultural-historical study of the Presidio and its various uses. Particularly informative as to the transfer of the base to the National Park Service.

Duffus, James, III. *Transfer of the Presidio from the Army to the National Park Service.* Washington, D.C.: General Accounting Office, 1993. Contains the statement of the Director of National Resource Management Issues before a congressional committee about the transfer of the post.

Langellier, John Philip, and Daniel B. Rosen. *El Presidio de San Francisco: A History Under Spain and Mexico, 1776-1846.* Los Angeles: Los Angeles Corral of Westerners, 1996. Explores the early history of the Presidio with an emphasis on the people who were important to its founding and settlement.

"Presidio National Trust." www.presidiotrust.gov Web site of organization responsible for maintaining the Presidio. Contains a number of useful links with pictures and history of the post.

Presidio of San Francisco National Historic Landmark District: Historic American Buildings Survey Report. San Francisco: U.S. Department of the Interior, National Park Service and Department of Defense, Department of the Army, 1985. History of the Presidio with an emphasis on its changing architecture; contains a number of photographs and maps.

Thompson, Erwin N., and Sally B. Woodbridge. *Special History Study of the Presidio of San Francisco: An Outline of Its Evolution as a U.S. Army Post, 1847-1990.* Denver: U.S. Department of the Interior, National Park Service, 1992. Easy-to-read survey of the American period to 1990.

San Diego Presidio

Date: Founded on July 16, 1769

Relevant issues: American Indian history, European settlement, Latino history, military history, religion, western expansion

Significance: The San Diego Presidio is the site where Father Junípero Serra established the first of twenty-one Franciscan missions and the first military garrison that became the foundation of Western European colonization in California. The area, the size of a modern city block overlooking what is now called Old Town and Mission Valley, has become known as "The Plymouth Rock of the Pacific Coast."

Location: Immediately adjacent to Old Town, approximately 3.5 miles north of downtown San Diego

Site Offices:

Serra Museum
2727 Presidio Drive
Presidio Park
ph.: (619) 297-3258

Casa de Balboa
1649 El Prado
Balboa Park
San Diego, CA 92138
ph.: (619) 232-6203
Web site: sandiegohistory.org

Old Town San Diego State Historic Park
4002 Wallace Street
San Diego, CA 92110
ph.: (619) 220-5422
fax: (619) 220-5421
Web site: www.oldtownsd.com

On the spot where the first presidio and mission were established there now stands the Serra Cross. On it is a bronze tablet with the following inscription:

> Here the First Citizen, Fray Junípero Serra,
> Planted Civilization in California.
> Here he First Raised the Cross,
> Here Began the First Mission,
> Here Founded the First Town
> —San Diego, July 16, 1769

Modern Southern California had been visited and claimed by Spain more than two centuries before the arrival of the Franciscan missionaries and military representatives of the king of Spain. It was only in the late eighteenth century, when fear arose that the harbors might be lost to Russian encroachment from the north and English privateers off the coast, that the inspector general of Mexico, José de Gálvez, undertook to colonize the area.

"The Sacred Expedition of 1769" was under the command of Gaspar de Portolá (1723-1784), the first military governor of California. Junípero Serra (1713-1784) was to be the father-president of a chain of missions established in Alta (Upper) California. The plan called for five expeditions from Baja (Lower) California to settle the vast area of the north—three by sea and two by land. The first ship, the supply ship *San Carlos*, set sail on January 9, 1769, from the port of La Paz on the east coast of the Baja California peninsula. It was followed on February 15 by the *San Antonio* and, a month later, by the *San José*. The *San Antonio* arrived in San Diego Bay on April 29, the first Spanish vessel to visit the harbor in 167 years. The *San Carlos* arrived two weeks later, having sailed too far north. Two dozen members of its sixty-two-man crew had died of scurvy, leaving only four sailors well enough to work the ship. The third vessel, the *San José*, was lost at sea.

The first land party arrived in San Diego on May 14, 1769, under the command of Captain Fernando Rivera y Moncada. With him came Father Juan Crespi, whose diary is the major source of the history of the early years in California. The party had marched for fifty-one days from Velicatá, a mission in Baja California. Governor Portolá and a few of his men arrived June 29 and Father Serra, along with the rest of the second land expedition, arrived on July 1, 1769. Of over three hundred men who had made up the five companies in Baja California, only 126 survived the arduous journey to San Diego. The site of their landing is now identified as "Spanish Landing" on Harbor Drive in downtown San Diego.

Captain Rivera moved the encampment to a more suitable location along the banks of the San Diego River in the general area now known as Old Town. There they set up a hospital to care for the many ill sailors, corrals to safeguard the animals they had brought, and several brush huts that served as headquarters for all. Choosing this site determined the location for San Diego.

Father Serra was fifty-six years old when he arrived in San Diego. For a long time prior to this trip he had suffered from asthma and a chronic sore on his leg. Despite these infirmities he founded nine missions along El Camino Real (the king's highway), once more establishing Spain's control of California and converting thousands of Indians to Christianity.

On July 16, 1769, Father Serra founded the mission on the hill immediately north of the encampment, overlooking the river and the bay, a site now known as the Presidio San Diego. Accompanied by about three dozen men, Father Serra set up a cross, consecrated the primitive brushwood chapel, and christened the entire enterprise "San Diego de Alcalá" in honor of the fifteenth century Saint Didacus of Alcalá. This was the first mission in Alta California and is known as the "Mother of the Great California Missions."

In addition to the church, the Spanish soldiers built a garrison at the Presidio (the name originally used by the Spaniards to identify a military post or fortified settlement). The first structures were built of mere wood and brush, but their presence on the hill was designed to impress upon the local Indians, the Kumeyaay, that the Spanish were now in control of the entire region and that Spanish colonization and land management were to dominate all phases of their lives. The records indicate that Christianizing and subduing the Kumeyaay in the early days was not at all successful. Within a month after the Presidio was founded, the Kumeyaay staged their first attack on the fort; five Indian warriors were killed. By the end of the first year Father Serra had baptized only one child.

Relocation of the Mission

In 1774, five years after the founding, the mission church was moved about five miles northeast, where it remains to this day. The military, on one hand, was charged with securing the land and subduing the indigenous population. This frequently led to instances of soldiers brutalizing the Kumeyaay, especially the women. The Franciscan friars, on the other hand, sought to "civilize" and convert the Indians to a peaceful life of Christianity, establishing and working in a harmonious agrarian society. It was believed that the new site, removed from the Presidio, would offer the church not only more arable land and a better source of water but also greater success in fulfilling its missionary goals.

The Kumeyaay, however, failed to distinguish between the two groups of Spanish conquerors. After less than one year, in November 1775, they attacked, looted, and burned the new mission, wounding and killing many, including the head of the mission, Father Luis Jaime, the first martyr in San Diego de Alcalá. The church was rebuilt immediately and over the years withstood additional attacks and earthquakes.

The Presidio

After a perilous beginning the original Presidio flourished on its hilltop location. It served as the Spanish civil and political center for the entire San Diego area, which within two decades extended 100 miles south to Ensenada, Baja California, and 125 miles north to present-day

Cobble foundations uncovered at the dig site for the San Diego Presidio. (Ruben G. Mendoza)

Malibu. This prosperity, however, also created problems. By 1800, San Diego Bay was visited frequently by American and foreign ships trading with Pacific nations and other West Coast ports. This development placed Spain's control of the region in jeopardy.

In 1821, Mexican revolutionary forces overthrew the Spanish rulers, and the entire American Southwest was made a part of Mexico. The California missions were secularized, the Franciscans left Mexico, and on April 20, 1822, the representatives of Spain officially abandoned the Presidio. Mexico did not occupy the Presidio and the garrison, and all its buildings were left to crumble.

Within a few months after independence, the soldiers from the Presidio and new settlers to the area built their homes down the hill in Old Town. By 1835 San Diego became a civil "pueblo" with a population of over four hundred ranchers and townspeople engaged in various trades. The Mexican period, however, was short lived. By 1846 the Mexican-American War had commenced and Presidio Hill was briefly used once more as a garrison by Commodore Robert Stockton. Following California statehood in 1850 the Presidio was again abandoned, and Old Town gradually declined in favor of "New Town," the site of present-day San Diego.

The New Presidio

The current appearance of the Presidio dates to 1907, when the San Diego merchant and philanthropist George Marston (1850-1946) purchased a portion of the hill in order to establish a park displaying the first European settlement on the West Coast. Receiving little support from either the city or the business community, Marston devoted the next two decades to developing the project in the spirit of American historical site preservation customary in the early years of the twentieth century. Rather than allowing the Presidio its barren natural appearance of native scrub brush and wildlife, Marston wanted the site to resemble a northern European park. In one year over twenty thousand plants and trees were planted. It was a time when Southern California marketed itself as a romanticized image of a European landscape set in a tropical paradise with an ideal climate.

In 1913, a civic group called the Order of Panama dug up hundreds of tiles from the old garrison and constructed a huge cross—the Serra Cross—which was erected on the Presidio site where they believed the first mission church may have been. The major development project, however, was not to be completed for many years. The imposing building now on the Presidio is the Serra Museum, sometimes mistakenly identified as the San Diego Mission. It was designed by the distinguished San Diego architect William Templeton Johnson (1877-1957) in a style that combined southern European and Mediterranean architecture with the California mission style of simple lines, arches, and deep-set windows. It was intended not to replicate a church but to symbolize the conquest of Spain and to illustrate the realization of civilization and Christianity in the New World. The structure ignores any reference to either the Native American or the Mexican contribution to the history of the Presidio; indeed, not even the harsh reality of life during the years of the mission fathers and the garrison is included. The Serra Museum, with all of its splendor, represents not a historically accurate account of the past but an illusory re-creation of facts. The fine interior furnishings are magnificent antiques from fifteenth to seventeenth century ruling-class Spain, rather than from the late eighteenth century when Father Serra lived and worked in Alta California.

The Serra Museum was dedicated on July 16, 1929, the 160th anniversary of the founding of the Presidio. On that day, Marston, who had developed the entire project at his own expense, gave title to the park and the museum to the citizens of San Diego.

Places to Visit

In conjunction with California's bicentennial in 1969 the area at the foot of Presidio Hill was established as the State Historical Park at Old Town. Nineteen structures were identified as suitable for restoration, representing the era of Old Spain, Mexico, and the early years of California. Most of the houses had crumbled adobe walls; they are now faithful modern replicas. Of particular interest are the Estudillo adobe home originally built in 1827 by the commander of the Presidio, the Casa de Bandini dating from the 1820's, and the Mason Street School, erected in 1865 as Southern California's first publicly owned schoolhouse.

—*Thomas H. Falk*

For Further Information:

Hennessey, Gregg, ed. *Junipero Serra Museum.* San Diego: San Diego Historical Society, 1999. Includes essays on the building of the Museum and Park, on the architect Johnson, and the historical uses of Presidio Hill.

Jackson, Helen Hunt. *Glimpses of California and the Missions.* Boston: Little, Brown, 1992. Provides an excellent account of life at the missions, including the procedures used at the founding ceremonies.

Kyle, Douglas. *Historic Spots in California.* Stanford, Calif.: Stanford University Press, 1990. A project of the California Conference of the National Society, including descriptions of all State Registered Landmarks and most places on the National Register of Historic Places.

McKeever, Michael. *A Short History of San Diego.* San Francisco: Lexikos, 1985. An excellent popular history, with many photographs, that provides a fine introduction.

Mills, James. *San Diego—Where California Began.* San Diego: San Diego Historical Society, 1985. A well-researched narrative, including many fine photographs, written by a former curator of the Serra Museum.

Pourade, Richard. *The History of San Diego.* San Diego: Union-Tribune/Copley Press, 1960-1977. This seven-volume series on the "Historic Birthplace of California" is the most extensive and well-documented writing on all aspects of San Diego's history.

Sonoma

Date: Designated a National Historical Landmark in 1961

Relevant issues: Business and industry, European settlement, Latino history, religion

Significance: The plaza, a National Historic Landmark, was originally conceived in 1824 with the founding of the twenty-first mission, San Francisco Solano de Sonoma, by José Altimira. The original church was replaced by a larger one in 1827, and that one was replaced by the present chapel, built in 1840. The mission was secularized in 1834 and put in the charge of General Mariano Guadalupe Vallejo. It was sold in 1881, purchased by the Historical Landmarks League in 1903, and restored from 1911 to 1913. The plaza surrounding the mission contains historic monuments from the period of secularization.

Location: In Sonoma County, forty-five miles north of San Francisco; between Highway 12 (southern boundary) and Spain Street (northern boundary), First Street West (western boundary) and First Street East (eastern boundary)

Site Offices:

Sonoma State Historic Park
East Spain and First Streets
Sonoma, CA 95476
ph.: (707) 938-1519; 938-1578

Silverado District Headquarters
20 East Spain Street
Sonoma, CA 95476

The town of Sonoma is situated in the Sonoma Valley, about forty-five miles north of San Francisco. The valley is bordered by two mountain ranges, the Mayacamas to the east and the Sonoma Mountains to the west. Sonoma began with the founding of the twenty-first and last California mission, San Francisco Solano de Sonoma, in 1824. From the mission grew the surrounding pueblo, whose natural agricultural resources generated economic growth. The pueblo was secularized in 1834 by General Mariano Guadalupe Vallejo, and it witnessed the end of the Mexican era and California's entry into the United States in 1850. During the latter half of the nineteenth century Sonoma became a renowned center for grape growing and commercial winemaking, and today it is considered the birthplace of the California wine industry.

The Last California Mission

The notion of a mission north of San Francisco and San Rafael belonged to Father José Altimira and Governor Luis Antonio Argnello. Altimira came to Monterey from Spain in 1819 and was posted at Mission Dolores in San Francisco. Altimira found that the cold climate and difficult soil conditions made it a challenge to attract neophytes and cultivate crops. He wanted to leave the effort at Mission Dolores and open a new settlement north of San Rafael, in a warmer climate.

Instead of presenting his plan to church authorities, he appealed directly to the governor, who approved the plan in order to establish a northern

The vineyards of Sonoma. (AP/Wide World Photos)

settlement that would create a barrier to Russian expansion. (As the Spanish had moved into Upper California in the late eighteenth century, the Russians crossed the Bering Strait, moved into Alaska, and eventually made their way down the California coast, where in 1812 they built Fort Ross.)

The Territorial Assembly in Monterey approved the Sonoma site as a new location for Mission Dolores and recommended that it absorb the existing San Rafael mission. Altimira relocated to Sonoma and blessed the site on July 4, 1823. The padre named the area surrounding the future mission "the Valley of the Moon," after an Indian legend that claimed the moon appeared seven times in a row over the mountains each winter. He then began construction of the new mission, only to be intercepted by church authorities, angered at his circumvention of the proper channels. The church and Altimira reached a compromise that allowed him to build and govern the new mission but kept Mission Dolores and the San Rafael mission at their present locations.

The new Mission San Francisco Solano de Sonoma was dedicated on April 4, 1824. Altimira received supplies from Mission Dolores and a donation of bells from the Russian settlers at Fort Ross. The mission was composed of a long adobe

building, 120 by 30 feet. It also included a chapel and granary buildings. Altimira planted wheat and barley fields, grapevines, and fruit orchards—the beginning of Sonoma's commercial agriculture.

After only two years at the new mission, Altimira was forced out by an Indian rebellion in 1826, a result of his mistreatment of the Indian neophytes. He fled to the San Rafael Mission and then returned to Spain. Altimira's successor, Father Buenaventura Fortuni, spent the next seven years restoring the mission, including building a new church. Almost completed in 1833, the mission was weather damaged and was not fully repaired until the early 1840's, when its only function was as parish church.

During California's mission period, Americans settling the United States and the resident Californians saw the missions as potential economic opportunities, and the Americans in particular noticed that they were weakly defended. The resident Californians (the first descendants of Spanish and Mexican settlers) aimed to take over leadership from the padres and gain the missions' resources. As early as 1813, efforts from Mexico and the Californians were made to halt the existing mission system, but the padres managed to prevent passage of any law doing so. By 1833, pressure finally resulted in secularization, which broke up all the mission properties and left governing responsibilities to the Mexicans.

Founding of the Town

In 1834, Governor José Figueroa put General Mariano Guadalupe Vallejo in charge of California's northern frontier. The general had been commander at the Presidio in San Francisco. His new responsibilities included secularizing Mission San Francisco Solano de Sonoma. Vallejo developed the pueblo of Sonoma in the style typical of a Spanish town, around the plaza adjacent to the mission's church. Sonoma was California's last pueblo, the only province to be formed by the Mexican government. Vallejo served in both local and state government and was a member of the first Constitutional Convention of California. He and his family developed buildings that served as the religious and cultural centers of the pueblo and stand today as historic monuments. For example, the present church was built by Vallejo in 1840 for the soldiers of the pueblo and their families.

General Vallejo's first home, built in 1836, was called Casa Grande. It burned in 1867, leaving only the Indian servants' wing. Its site is at the northern end of the Sonoma plaza. His next home, the Gothic-inspired Lachryma Montis (tears of the mountain), was built in 1851 and 1852. It is located northwest of the plaza on West Spain Street. He lived at Lachryma Montis until his death in 1890. The building's storehouse, the "Swiss Chalet," is now a museum.

Next to Casa Grande is the Swiss Hotel, the first home of Captain Salvador Vallejo, the general's brother. Captain Vallejo constructed it in the late 1830's and lived in it for a short period. It was then used as a business center around 1836 and finally converted into a hotel in the late 1800's. In the early 1840's, Captain Vallejo built a home directly west of Lachryma Montis. From 1858 to 1867, this house was occupied by the Cumberland Presbyterian Church.

The Americans Arrive

Another important structure built by General Vallejo was the Sonoma Barracks, located in the eastern corner of the plaza. Built in 1836, this was the headquarters for the Bear Flag Party during its 1846 occupation of Sonoma, and in 1847 it housed U.S. troops.

On June 14, 1846, thirty American horsemen known as the Osos (bears) arrived in Sonoma, under the encouragement of General John C. Frémont. Americans had ventured into California in the early 1840's to obtain land, but the Mexican government would not allow them to own property or hold office. The Osos captured General Vallejo at the Sonoma Barracks without violence and proclaimed the California Republic by raising a flag depicting a bear. Thus, Sonoma was the capital of the Independent Republic of California for twenty-five days, and the Bear Flag Revolt was the origin for California's first state flag. The Bear Flag Party elected William Ide as leader of the republic. William Todd, a nephew of Mary Todd Lincoln, made the flag, which symbolized independence from the Mexicans.

The California Republic lasted briefly but heralded significant events. On July 7, 1846, an American ship captured the Mexican capital at Monterey and claimed all of California for the United States. Bear Flag Monument, a bronze figure holding the Bear Flag, was erected adjacent to the Sonoma Barracks. The original flag was brought to San Francisco but was destroyed in the fire following the 1906 earthquake. The Bear Flag became the official state flag of California in 1911.

After the American entry into Sonoma in 1846, the mission was no longer an extension of the Mexican government. The mission existed briefly as a parish church, and after it was sold in 1881 along with the padre's quarters, it was used mostly for winemaking and hay storage.

In 1903, the mission property was purchased by the Historic Landmarks League, with the goal of restoration. The San Francisco Earthquake of 1906 damaged the church, and the restoration project was put on hold until 1911, when it was resumed with the aid of state funds. The Historic Landmarks League deeded the church to the state in 1926, and it became part of the Division of Beaches and Parks. It underwent further restoration between 1943 and 1944. The mission is now known as the Sonoma Mission State Historic Park.

In the 1850's, after California was admitted into the Union, farming was a primary occupation in Sonoma. Hay, wheat, beef, potatoes, cheese, eggs, and milk were all shipped to market in San Francisco. The town of Petaluma supplied the Bay Area with produce during the 1850's, and in 1878 Lyman Rice introduced the incubator in Petaluma. This invention revolutionized the poultry and egg industries, and Petaluma became the egg capital of the world during this period. Another resource from Sonoma County was wood; its redwood trees were used to build a good part of the American West. The railroad was key to creating successful commercial enterprises from the county's natural resources. In 1870, the San Francisco and Northern Pacific Railroad laid tracks between Petaluma and Santa Rosa, later extending the line to Cloverdale. The population within Sonoma County increased notably, growing from one thousand to six thousand between 1870 and 1875.

The Wine Industry

Today, Sonoma's best-known export is quality wine. The county's grape-growing and winemaking history is rooted in the mission period and continues to flourish in the present. The mission grape was brought to California from Mexico by the padres in 1769, when the first mission was established in San Diego. When Mission San Francisco Solano de Sonoma was dedicated in 1824, the grape was brought to the settlement to produce wine for mass. The Russians at Fort Ross had cultivated vines in Sonoma as early as 1812.

In addition to the vineyard at the mission, Altimira planted one thousand vines in the eastern part of Sonoma, at a site named the Sonoma Vineyards. In 1825, mission padres also produced sacramental wine at the site, which later became Sebastiani Vineyards and Winery.

When General Vallejo presided over the secularization of the mission in 1835, he took over its vineyard, called Quirquiriqui, located off the plaza. His first vintage was 1841, yielding twenty barrels of wine, which he bottled and sold to the San Francisco market under the Lachryma Montis label. The general's brother, Captain Salvador Vallejo, started a vineyard in the old Sonoma Vineyards east of the pueblo; the site would soon become the Buena Vista Winery.

In 1856, a political exile from Hungary, Count Agoston Haraszthy, bought 560 acres of Sonoma property, northeast of town, including this Sonoma Vineyard. The property began in the Sonoma Valley and ended in the foothills of the Mayacamas Mountains. This property had most recently been owned by the Kelsey family, who produced wine. On a visit, Haraszthy was so impressed by their vintage that he purchased the land. Haraszthy was a tireless promoter of the potential for wine grown in California. He had lived in San Diego and then San Mateo, where he had tried to grow grapes in the Crystal Springs area. The cold climate did not give him much success and prompted his search for a region with better climate and soil conditions.

Haraszthy transplanted about thirteen thousand vine cuttings from Crystal Springs to Sonoma in 1856 and established the Buena Vista Winery, where he constructed Sonoma's first stone wine cellars. Haraszthy is credited with producing California's first zinfandel in 1862. While waiting for his first crops, he promoted the scientific study of winemaking and encouraged the growth of the industry in Sonoma. By the end of 1857, he and others had more than tripled the total grape acreage in the county and established the area as a center of information on grape growing and wine making.

During the 1850's and 1860's, both Haraszthy and General Vallejo won prizes for their wines. Their friendly competition and enthusiasm for producing original, quality wines motivated the quest for further knowledge, transforming the enterprise into a commercial industry. In 1860, at the Sonoma County Fair, Haraszthy requested that the state establish an agricultural school to educate farmers; the school became the forerunner to the renowned Department of Viticulture at the University of California, Davis.

That same year, Governor John G. Downey sent Haraszthy to Europe to gather new vine cuttings to introduce to California. He returned in 1861 with 200,000 vines of almost five hundred varieties, and he sold the cuttings to growers all over the state, giving birth to the California wine industry of today. Haraszthy was elected president of the State Agricultural Society in 1862 and helped form the California Winegrowers' Association.

Although Buena Vista's wines were acclaimed for their quality, Haraszthy had a difficult time making a profit. By 1866, his investors discontinued their support, and Haraszthy left the country for Nicaragua, where he died. Winemakers from outside the area (many foreign, impressed with the availability of grape varieties and soil and climate similar to those in Europe), had been inspired by the Haraszthy's success with growing so many varieties in Sonoma. They began coming to the valley between 1856 and 1862. In 1864, Sonoma had a population of only five hundred. By 1868, it was in excess of one thousand, and land values had in many cases risen from $6 to $135 per acre.

During the 1870's, after Haraszthy's departure, the phylloxera vine louse got into Buena Vista and other vineyards, and much recultivation was required. The tunnels at Buena Vista collapsed during the 1906 earthquake; by this time, the abandoned vineyards were decimated, and the winery was closed.

By 1890, Sonoma's vintages made it an outstanding wine district, recognized throughout the state and the nation. The Simi brothers established their Healdsburg Winery in 1881. In 1896, Samuel Sebastiani came to Sonoma from Tuscany. He bought the Milani Winery in 1904 and survived Prohibition by making sacramental wines. Sebastiani was a community leader, building some of Sonoma's streets and financing a parochial school. Still standing in Sonoma are the Sebastiani Theater and the Sebastiani Bus Depot.

Honoring Famous Sons

One of Sonoma's other notable citizens was writer Jack London, who lived on an eight-hundred-acre ranch above Glen Ellen called Beauty Ranch. Only twenty-nine years old, London was already famous as the author of *The Call of the Wild* (1903) and *Sea Wolf* (1904) when he and his wife Charmian settled on the ranch. In 1913, he wrote *The Valley of the Moon* in tribute to Sonoma. Beauty Ranch is today a State Historic Park.

Throughout Prohibition, Haraszthy's contributions to the building of the wine industry were forgotten. Then in 1941, a San Franciscan named Frank Bartholomew bought 435 acres of land in Sonoma for a country home. The property included two decrepit stone buildings—he had unwittingly purchased Buena Vista. Bartholomew restored Buena Vista's status as a winery, and by hiring expert winemakers and retelling the Haraszthy history, he gave his winery national prominence. In 1949, Sonoma winegrowers dedicated a memorial, located on the north side of the plaza, commemorating Agoston Haraszthy as "The Father of California Viticulture."

—*Jane MacInnis*

For Further Information:

Krell, Dorothy, Paul C. Johnson, and David E. Clark, eds. *The California Missions: A Complete Pictorial History and Visitor's Guide.* Menlo Park, Calif.: Sunset Books, 1979. Contains a good overview of the Sonoma Mission.

McCormack, Don, and Allen Kanda, eds. *Marin, Napa, and Sonoma.* Martinez, Calif.: McCormack's Guides, 1993. Gives a good deal of current statistical information as well as observations on the different communities throughout Sonoma County.

Pinney, Thomas. *A History of Wine in America: From the Beginnings to Prohibition.* Berkeley: University of California Press, 1989. Good reading for those interested in exploring the wine industry in depth. The section on Sonoma represents the players in the early wine industry in a fair, objective manner, without glorifying Haraszthy as a maverick. Pinney gives solid attention to the contributions of others.

Sutter's Fort

Date: Built from 1840 to 1844

Relevant issues: European settlement, military history, western expansion

Significance: A frontier settlement built by Swiss immigrant John Sutter in the 1840's, Sutter's Fort was the first European outpost in the California interior. The fort became a way station for westbound emigrants and figured in military actions in early California. After gold was discovered nearby in 1848, the ensuing gold rush depleted Sutter's operations of labor and resources. Sutter's financial problems eventually led him to sell the fort and the land surrounding it, and on this land the city of Sacramento was founded. The fort, acquired by the state of California in 1891, has been restored to its 1840's appearance.

Location: At 2701 L Street in central Sacramento

Site Office:

Sutter's Fort State Historic Park
c/o Sacramento District Office
111 I Street
Sacramento, CA 95814
ph.: (916) 445-7373

Challenged throughout his life by problems that would have daunted lesser men, John A. Sutter held steadfast to his ambitious and self-aggrandizing plans. His fort, which stands as a permanent symbol of his charisma and tenacity, was built in lush, virgin terrain. Today, it is surrounded on all sides by the city of Sacramento.

Born in 1803 of Swiss parents living in Kandern, Germany, Johann August Suter—whose name eventually was Anglicized to John Augustus Sutter—moved to Basel, Switzerland, in his mid-teens. Having served a printing apprenticeship, he abandoned that trade to work in an Aarburg drapery store. In 1826, at the age of twenty-three, Sutter married Annette Dubeld (also known as Anna), who was already pregnant with his son, Johann August, Jr. By this time the young couple had moved to Annette's home in Burgdorf, and with help from his mother-in-law, Sutter established a dry goods store. In 1828, Sutter joined the Swiss Army Guard.

By 1834, John and Annette had a family of five children and few prospects. Sutter fared well in the Swiss Guard and rose to the rank of lieutenant, but he was a poor retailer, and his business failed.

Sutter Comes to America

Faced with the possibility of debtor's prison, the thirty-one-year-old Sutter entrusted his family to the care of his mother-in-law and crossed the Atlantic on a ship bound for New York. It would be sixteen years before he saw his family again.

Joining a group of German emigrants, Sutter headed for the Midwest, then worked as a trader on the Santa Fe Trail until business plummeted. By this time, he had decided to journey to the Mexican territory of Alta California. With the help of a mule-skinner named Pablo Gutiérrez, he planned to create a settlement in the largely unexplored interior.

Penniless in Westport, Missouri, Sutter set about raising the money for his venture. As the self-styled "Captain Sutter," he used his charm and powers of persuasion to advantage. After just a few months, in the spring of 1838, Sutter and Gutiérrez, suitably equipped, headed west.

The two men joined a fur trappers' caravan bound for the Wind River Mountains in what is now Wyoming. On the arduous and often tedious journey, traveling on horses and mules between forts, outposts, missions, and other settlements, Sutter attracted a small band of followers. These footloose men had little to lose, and under his leadership they might find fortune.

In October, 1838, Sutter and his party reached Fort Vancouver on the Willamette River, close to what is now the southern border of Washington State. Too late to make the 250-mile journey south to the Siskiyou Mountains and cross them into Alta California before the onset of winter, and unwilling to bide his time until the spring, Sutter took a surprising, but fortuitous, detour.

Leaving most of his men behind, he boarded a trading ship, *Columbia*, and sailed through the Columbia basin and across the Pacific to Hawaii. From there, he planned to travel to California on another trading vessel. Forced to wait on the islands for a few months, Sutter socialized with the local merchants, purchased on credit equipment that he would need in California, and recruited eight native men and two native women, one of whom became his mistress. Eventually, a merchant commissioned Sutter to deliver goods to California on the brig *Clementine*, but by way of the Alaskan port of Sitka, then under Russian sovereignty.

Arrival in California

When the storm-wrecked *Clementine* arrived in San Francisco Bay, Sutter and his party of ten Hawaiians and three white men were not allowed to stay in Yerba Buena (now San Francisco), the only sizable settlement on the bay. After patching up the *Clementine*, the chagrined Sutter and his crew sailed down the coast to Monterey, the seat of the Mexican governor, Juan B. Alvarado.

Sutter presented the governor with letters of recommendation from Hudson's Bay Company officials and other merchants whom he had met along the way. While Alvarado was probably impressed by the articulate and multilingual visitor, he had more compelling reasons for consenting to Sutter's plans for an inland settlement. The governor needed better representation in the interior and felt that the bold European might contain the delta natives who regularly raided the coastal communities. Sutter, with every reason to keep on the right side of the authorities, agreed to protect the area and promised to return to Monterey and apply for Mexican citizenship as soon as he was properly established. At that time, the governor would

Sutter's Fort. (Stephen C. Prey, Sutter's Fort State Historical Park Volunteers)

grant him rights to the land surrounding his outpost.

Now allowed to spend some time at Yerba Buena, Sutter hired seamen and chartered two large boats and a scouting vessel to take his party and equipment up through San Pablo Bay and on toward the Sacramento River. They set sail in August, 1839, and stopped briefly along the Carquinez Strait to visit a rancher, Ygnacio Martinez. Recognizing Sutter's potential as a customer and fellow trader, Martinez agreed to deliver cattle, crop seed, and supplies when Sutter was settled.

Finally, a Settlement

After some minor skirmishes with delta Indians and a couple of excursions up the wrong rivers, Sutter found the mouth of the Sacramento and traveled up it until he turned east into the American River. He decided to anchor a few miles upstream. An oak tree-covered knoll just above the flood line seemed a promising location for his settlement. The area possessed fresh water, an ample supply of game, plenty of fish in the river, and a profusion of berries and wild grapes. It also had swarms of mosquitoes.

The seamen wasted no time in returning to the cooler coast, and Sutter set his party and some

friendly local Indians to work. Now at last he could create his "New Helvetia," as he liked to call it. Though willing to live under the Mexican flag, he would be master of his own little Switzerland and would build a fort to protect himself from native raiders and from ranchers who might wish to usurp him.

The Hawaiians built temporary grass huts, and the Indians made adobe bricks. Oak trees were felled for cutting into floorboards and rafters, bullrushes were gathered for use as thatch, and the buildings began to take shape. From the settlement, a road was built to a landing stage at the river. With the arrival of trading ships, Sutter was able to obtain much-needed metal tools and implements. Fields were cleared and cultivated, pastures fenced for the cattle, and orchards and vineyards established. Sutter paid his Indian workers with metal tags exchangeable for goods at his new store. This system of payment was used by the Mexican ranchers and by the Franciscan missionaries.

Although Sutter's relationships with neighboring Mexicans—Ygnacio Martinez, Antonio Sunol, and Mariano Guadalupe Vallejo—soon soured, he did maintain good relations with Governor Alvarado. After his first year the proud leader of New Helvetia, heavily in debt, visited Monterey and officially assumed Mexican citizenship. He also was named an *alcalde* (a magistrate and high-ranking law officer), a position that gave him the power he needed to rule his domain. A year later, documents granting him some fifty thousand acres were signed and sealed.

Construction of the Fort

The construction of Sutter's Fort began in 1840, and in 1841 Sutter formed an Indian musketeer guard unit. At that time, the dilapidated Russian trading post of Fort Ross was up for sale. This coastal unit had been established by the Russian

American Fur Company in 1812, and Sutter outbid Vallejo for its entire contents, pledging thirty thousand dollars. John Bidwell, a recent arrival from the east, was commissioned to dismantle the Fort Ross buildings and ship them to Sutter's Fort, along with horses, livestock, cannon, muskets, and other equipment, on the Russian schooner that was also part of the purchase.

When completed in the early summer of 1844, Sutter's Fort had eighteen-foot-high adobe walls with bulwarks at each corner. The walls enclosed a courtyard measuring one hundred fifty by five hundred feet. With twelve cannon installed, Sutter was ready for all comers.

A Center for Trade

Of more immediate concern, however, were Sutter's ever-rising debts. Always an entrepreneur, he was never an accomplished businessman, but while his settlement was underfunded, it was nevertheless an important asset and his creditors usually remained patient, expecting that Sutter would eventually strike it rich. In many efforts to pay off debts, Sutter hired artisans to make a wide variety of items, and he frequently organized trading trips to Yerba Buena. His main dealings were in leather goods, pelts and skins, Indian blankets, cured salmon, and brandy.

As a traveler, Sutter had often relied on the kindness of strangers, and a kind man himself, he was delighted to help others requiring rest and sustenance along their way. His New Helvetia, located on what was fast becoming a major trade route between Oregon and the east, was the only white settlement in the interior of Alta California. Fortunately, his fields and pastures, newly irrigated with water from the American River, were producing enough meat, grain, fruits, and vegetables to feed all of his workers as well as his visitors.

John Bidwell, who helped Sutter with the Fort Ross project in 1841, had arrived that same year as a member of the Bartleson-Bidwell Party. This was the first of many organized parties of American easterners who, having encountered the Midwest depression, were once again moving steadily westward in their covered wagons to the legendary land of opportunity.

In 1843, Sutter was generous host to Joseph B. Chiles and Joseph R. Walker and hired one of their party, Pierson Reading, to assist him with the ever-increasing administrative duties. Some months later in March, 1844, the army topographer and chart-maker John C. Frémont arrived at the nearly completed fort with his group of trailblazers, including Christopher "Kit" Carson and Thomas Fitzpatrick. They had made the first winter crossing of the Sierra Nevada and were in desperate need of food and supplies.

Mexican Politics

Political uncertainties in Alta California increased in 1844, when Governor Alvarado was displaced by General Manuel Micheltorena. Alvarado joined forces with other *Californios*, notably the Castro brothers (Manuel and José) and the Pico brothers (Andres and Pío) to fight Micheltorena and his crude army of former convicts. Micheltorena begged Sutter for help, promising him another major land grant.

On bad terms with a number of Alvarado's supporters, and ever interested in expanding his own little empire, Sutter agreed to help the new governor. With his friend Bidwell he quickly organized a volunteer army of his most loyal Indians and white immigrants who were suspicious of the rebellious Mexicans. Sutter also used his powers as an alcalde to draft those who were reluctant to join him. One disaffected draftee, Sutter's neighbor Dr. John Marsh, did his best to encourage revolt and succeeded in lowering the morale of Sutter's ragtag army.

The troops of Micheltorena and Sutter met near San José and together pushed south with little resistance, defeating some dissidents at Mission San Buenaventura. However, closer to Los Angeles, at Rancho Cahuenga, rebels under the the command of General José Castro were well prepared. With no casualties inflicted, Sutter and Bidwell were quickly arrested, and the defeated Micheltorena was sent back home.

Pío Pico, the new governor, moved his headquarters to Los Angeles and released the humiliated Sutter after he had solemnly pledged a new allegiance. Fortunately for Sutter, Pico recognized the importance of Sutter's Fort and, rather than have it fall into the hands of potential rivals, Pico allowed the chastened Sutter to keep both his fort and his original land grant.

When Sutter returned to his settlement he quickly reaffirmed his strength by paying soldiers to quell the protests of a growing number of Indian workers. For a brief time Sutter's Fort was a peaceful and productive hub where emigrants came and went. One of them, who came in July, 1845, and stayed to work for Sutter as a carpenter, was the millwright James Wilson Marshall, who would later make a historic discovery.

In November, 1845, a group of local Mexicans offered Sutter a good price for his lands and fort. These wealthy landowners were increasingly threatened by the numbers of travel-worn settlers straggling endlessly into California and hoped to stanch the flow. Naturally, Sutter dismissed their offer; he had not become a Californian pioneer simply to make money and depart.

American Control

Throughout the region, tensions were rising between the Mexicans and the European settlers. General John C. Frémont returned, ostensibly to lead yet another charting expedition, but in fact he had been sent back because war between the United States and Mexico was a virtual certainty.

An early skirmish, the Bear Flag Revolt, in June, 1846, resulted in the capture at Sonoma of General Mariano Vallejo. He and three associates were brought to Sutter's Fort and held there by Frémont. When war was officially declared the following month, a large part of Alta California, including San Francisco, was controlled by U.S. forces. Sutter, the former Swiss national and erstwhile Mexican, was now a U.S. citizen.

Under military rule, Sutter's Fort was renamed Fort Sacramento by Frémont. Most of Sutter's men enlisted in Frémont's California Battalion of Volunteers while Sutter stayed at home, second-in-command of his own fort. It was at this time that Sutter sent help to rescue the Donner Party, trapped in the snow-laden Sierras.

When the war ended with a U.S. victory in early 1847, Sutter's men returned, and once again the fort was under his leadership. Having weathered Indian uprisings, Mexican opposition, and U.S. military occupation, the middle-aged Sutter must have hoped for a more peaceful and prosperous future under U.S. jurisdiction. He could not foresee that a fabulous discovery, about to occur, would in his case prove more of a curse than a blessing.

Gold Leads to Ruin

In partnership with his carpenter James Marshall, Sutter planned to build two water-powered mills, one for grinding grain and the other for cutting timber. When construction of the gristmill was under way at Brighton on the American River, Marshall went looking for a suitable spot for the sawmill. He decided on a site in Cullomah (Coloma) Valley, some forty-five miles east of the fort along the southern fork of the American River. It was there, in a newly dug trench, that on January 24, 1848, Marshall struck gold.

Pocketing some of the gold fragments, Marshall cautioned his workers to say nothing about the find, then rode back to the fort to inform Sutter. When satisfied that the samples were genuine gold, Sutter kept the matter secret, fearing that his men would abandon their work and rush to Cullomah. Marshall returned to the sawmill and was visited there by Sutter a few days later. As they had hoped, the two men were able to keep the discovery quiet until shortly before before the sawmill began to operate in March.

A San Francisco newpaper publisher, Samuel Brannan, quickly took advantage of the news, publicized the find in his paper, and opened up supply stations to satisfy the prospectors' needs. He soon became the richest man in California.

Sutter was not so fortunate. He had negotiated with the Indians for the rights to operate his sawmill in Cullomah Valley, but he could not get his contract ratified by the occupying U.S. authorities. Meanwhile, the quest for the precious metal was quickly becoming a gold rush, and, as Sutter feared, all but his sickest and lamest workers left him by 1849 to become "forty-niners." His Brighton gristmill remained half built, his crops rotted in the fields, and hungry gold seekers squatted in his building and killed his cattle.

While Sutter did make investments in a Cullomah store and several prospecting expeditions, he never profited from these ventures. Indeed, he was beset by financial woes and was forced to sell not only his share of the sawmill but also his beloved fort. Sutter sent for his eldest son and, now drinking heavily, moved to his Hock Farm property on the Feather River. When John A. Sutter, Jr., known as August, arrived, he was immediately put to work as assistant to his father's real estate attorney, Peter H. Burnett. Their task was to sell off parcels of land.

For a brief period, Sutter prospered again. The California gold rush had driven up real estate prices, and a town named Sacramento was established. When Sutter found out that his son and Burnett had been selling parcels of building land on the river landing, he fired them both. He had instructed that this land must remain part of his own estate.

Final Days

The fort itself was sold in 1849, and the following year the rest of Sutter's family finally arrived at Hock Farm. At that time, Californians were preparing themselves for statehood, and Sutter decided to run for governor, but he was defeated by Peter Burnett, the man he had recently fired. In 1850, when statehood was ratified, Sutter received a consolation prize. He was named a general in the state militia, a post that carried a useful pension.

Sutter and his family remained at Hock Farm for the next fifteen years, living there in reasonable contentment. The comforts Sutter could provide were a far cry from the riches he had hoped to bestow upon his offspring. The final blow for Sutter came in 1865, when Hock Farm was destroyed by fire.

With his wife, Sutter retired to a Moravian community in Lititz, Pennsylvania. From there he petitioned the U.S. Congress to reimburse him for the losses incurred when Frémont's men commandeered his fort and for damages inflicted by gold rush squatters. However, it was not until Sutter was in his late seventies that passage of legislation to compensate him seemed likely.

Sutter went to Washington in June, 1880, and waited there in a hotel for news from Congress. When the congressmen adjourned on June 16 without enacting the necessary legislation, Sutter was mortified. He died in despair two days later. Anna Dubeld Sutter died the following January and was buried beside her husband in the Moravian cemetery at Lititz.

The Fort Today

Final destruction of Sutter's Fort, which had fallen into disrepair, was scheduled for 1889 when the city of Sacramento planned to run a street through the middle of it. Due largely to the efforts of General James G. Martine, the street was never built. The first real restorations at the fort began in 1891,

when it was acquired by the state of California.

Further work on the central building commenced in 1958, and today the monument features the much-restored two-story adobe fort. Various other buildings, such as artisans' studios, storage rooms, and living quarters have also been reconstructed. A museum displays many artifacts from the fort's heyday, and there is an important collection commemorating the rescue of the Donner Party, as well as much fascinating pioneer memorabilia, including early firefighting equipment, instruments, maps, furnishings, forty-niners' diaries, documents, rare photographs, prints, and paintings. Set in beautiful grounds, the reconstructed Sutter's Fort is a fitting monument to one of California's most remarkable men.

—*Roland Turner*

For Further Information:

Dana, Julian. *Sutter of California: A Biography*. New York: Press of the Pioneers, 1934. One of the older biographical works on Sutter.

Gudde, Erwin G. *Sutter's Own Story: The Life of General J. A. Sutter and the History of New Helvetia in the Sacramento Valley*. New York: G. P. Putnam's Sons, 1936. Another older biography.

Lewis, Donovan. *Pioneers of California*. San Francisco: Scottwall, 1993. One of the most helpful sources of information on John Sutter and his fort.

Sutter, John. *The Diary of Johann August Sutter*. San Francisco: Grabhorn, 1932. Includes an introduction by Douglas E. Watson.

Sutter's Fort State Historical Monument. Sacramento, Calif.: Division of Beaches and Parks, Department of Parks and Recreation, n.d. An excellent guide to the fort.

Sutter's Mill

Date: Built in 1847

Relevant issues: Business and industry, cultural history, western expansion

Significance: The mill was the site of the discovery of gold in California in 1848, which set off the gold rush and the immigration of unnumbered settlers from the East Coast to the American West. Built near the confluence of the Sacramento and American Rivers, it was meant to supply lumber to Sutter's Fort. The city of Sacramento grew up around the fort and became the western terminus of the Pony Express in 1860, as well as the starting point for the western section of the transcontinental railroad.

Location: Outside of historic Coloma, about one hour northwest of Sacramento

Site Office:

James Marshall Gold Discovery State Historic Park
P.O. Box 265
310 Back Street
Coloma, CA 95613
ph.: (916) 622-3470

On January 24, 1848, the builder of Sutter's Mill, James Wilson Marshall, discovered gold in the tailrace. He is said to have stated: "Hey boys, by God, I believe I've found a gold mine!" This momentous discovery was the beginning of the gold rush, which brought tens of thousands of settlers, or "forty-niners," to the West Coast of the North American continent.

Marshall's Story

In 1840, John Augustus Sutter (born Johann August Suter, 1803-1880) arrived in California and began to seek a place to build his fort. He was the first nonnative resident of this area of rolling grasslands in the Sacramento Valley of Northern California, which had been the ancestral home of the Nisenan people, also known as the southern Maidu, who had only recently been released from slavery under the Spanish.

In 1847, Captain John A. Sutter contracted with James Marshall, an itinerant loner, as his business partner for the task of building a lumber mill on the south fork of the American River at its confluence with the Sacramento River. The spot was called Cullomah (beautiful valley) by the local Indians. It was in the Sierra Nevada foothills and rich in acorns, lily bulbs, and, more important to Sutter, large stands of virgin pine. Sutter desperately needed the timber to build his colony and to pay off his many bad debts.

Marshall, originally from New Jersey, was a failed miner and a millwright by trade. He had come to Oregon in 1844 and then moved to California in 1845, at the age of thirty-four, and constructed a cabin at the lumber mill site in 1847. He lived in it while he built the mill and used it as a workshop where he built furniture and coffins. Outside he planted orchards, vineyards, and a garden.

Discovering gold at Sutter's Mill was disastrous for Marshall. He was soon pushed off his land, and he wandered and prospected about the state, but he never found another good strike. He went back to Sutter's Mill in 1857 and returned to agriculture, establishing a winery. After a time, economic conditions led to his eventual impoverishment, even after going on tour as a lecturer and being awarded a small pension in 1872 by the state. The pension was cut off in 1878 after he dropped a bottle of brandy from his pocket in the state assembly, where he had gone to renew the stipend.

Though he was known to be awkward, shabby, morose, moody, and embittered, he was also considered honest, kind, and faithful. After the discovery, he was also hounded by fortune hunters and gold seekers who thought him endowed with mystical powers and even forced him at gunpoint to show them where they could find the precious metal. He died in poverty on August 10, 1885, and was buried behind his old restored cabin underneath a bronze monument—atop of which he stands pointing at Sutter's Mill and the spot where he made the discovery that electrified the world but ruined his life—erected by the state of California in his honor in 1890. The site is now James Marshall Gold Discovery State Historic Park. The historic town of Coloma, which grew rapidly after the discovery of gold, is still situated nearby.

Sutter's Story

As with his partner, most of the ventures John A. Sutter embarked on ended in failure. His was a classic case of bad timing. He was born in Baden, Switzerland, in 1803. He came to America and settled for a time in Indiana, then moved to St. Louis where he invested his meager savings in merchandise he took to Santa Fe, New Mexico, where he operated as a profitable trader. After returning to Missouri, he joined with a trapping party, found his way down the Columbia River to Fort Vancouver, and there made a plan to move to central California (then a wild land held by Spain and populated only by Indians) to establish a colony.

To accomplish this task, he first needed colonists, so he set out by ship for the Sandwich Islands, where he found a small group of Kanaka supporters. As there was no ship going to California, he and his party caught a ride on a Russian ship that went by way of Sitka, Alaska. When he finally arrived in California in 1840, he interviewed Juan B. Alvarado, the Mexican governor, and obtained permission to find a place to establish his colony. He was granted nearly fifty thousand acres and was authorized to protect it by any means he saw fit. He procured a small boat in San Francisco and sailed up the biggest river he could find, which he followed to the site where he built his fort and where Sacramento now stands.

Sutter bought out the Russian fort at Bodega Bay (Fort Ross) when he was passing through the area, and though he took possession of its cattle, horses, a seagoing launch, and other property, he never honored the note for $100,000. He used the goods from Fort Ross to help build and furnish Fort Sutter. He gathered around him a dozen or so local Indians, who, along with the resident Hawaiians, helped him get the fort and mill built. Sutter felt he owned the land, but he was at odds with the Mexican authorities over title until a new governor was appointed, and he made a lasting peace.

After the building of the fort commenced, Sutter said he was "very much in need of a sawmill, to get lumber to finish my flouring mill . . . at Brighton . . . for the small village at Yerba Buena." Word got back to him it that this was viewed by those who knew him as "another folly of Sutter's."

Sutter's Fort became the terminus for settlers headed for the gold fields. The city of Sacramento, built around the fort, later became the starting point for the transcontinental railroad. Yet, due to his abundance of generosity, he made contracts he could not keep and ended up even further in debt. He was said to be too nice and too trusting for his own good and employed 100 to 150 men of all sorts working at every imaginable business and enterprise. Yet, he rarely turned a profit.

One of his few profitable enterprises was carrying passengers, hides, tallow, furs, and wheat to the Bay Area by boat and bringing back cut timber fresh from the coastal redwood groves. The trip took a month. As Sutter was somewhat insecure about his title to the land, he stayed close and built the fort into a major defensive establishment with cannons mounted and aimed through the embrasures in the walls and bastions. The fort was seen as a place of safety and refuge.

The fort was begun in 1842 and finished in 1844. It was a massive adobe structure, more than two hundred feet long and one hundred feet wide. The walls were eighteen feet high and three feet thick. The founding of Sacramento, laid out by Sutter and a friend named Hastings, two miles west of Sutter's Fort and four miles below the mouth of the American River, in 1846, came only after gold was discovered. The original city was built along the eastern bank of the river at a mean elevation of thirty feet. It was originally called Sutterville, then Sacramento City. Sutter himself always called his colony New Helvetia, in spite of what others called the place.

Sutter's Mill

By 1847, there was a growing demand for lumber, which Sutter sought to fill. There was nothing in the way of suitable timber near the fort, however. It was nearly impossible to raft logs through the mountain canyons at higher elevations, so he sent parties into the foothills to search for a closer site along the Sacramento River or its tributaries where he could build a lumber mill which would provide the means to cut timber he and Marshall could ship downriver.

The site Marshall found seemed to him the best place from which to send log rafts from the foothills to be cut into lumber, then sent down the American River to the Sacramento, and on through Suisun and San Pablo Bays to San Francisco markets. The idea was impractical at best and a wildly impossible scheme at worst. Yet, Sutter was so confident and credulous as to patronize Marshall and have him build the mill. As fate would have it, the mill was to have a short life.

In the fall of 1847, after the mill seat had been located, Sutter sent a number of workers under the oversight of P. L. Wimmer to help Marshall build the main double cabin, construct a dam across the river, and build the millrace—the narrow manmade ditch, or channel down which river water would be diverted to drive the waterwheel, which would then provide power for the saws. Some forty Indians excavated the millrace, but it was slow going. The wheel would not turn fast enough, so they did some additional boring and blasting. At night the workers would turn the water through the tailrace in order to widen and deepen it further. In the morning the water flow would be stopped and the ground investigated in preparation for the digging to be done next.

When Marshall went down below the partially finished mill early in the morning (as usual), he shut off the water and stepped into the race, "near the lower end, and there, upon the rock, about six inches beneath the surface of the water," he discovered gold. He picked up a couple of pieces, examined them, and took them to Sutter, who tested them further and found them to be twenty-three karat gold.

The Aftermath

Due to his insecurity about his title to the land, Sutter tried to suppress news of the discovery, but it quickly leaked out. On February, 20, 1848, Captain Sutter came to the mill site and consummated an agreement with the Indians of Coloma to live with them in peace and enjoy mutual use of the land. The mill started up operations in the middle of April, but after cutting only a few thousand board feet of lumber, the enterprise failed; everyone left to go dig for gold. The site was abandoned, and the milling equipment was later sold to a buyer from Oregon named Asa Simpson, who would then install it at his North Bend mill on Coos Bay and become one of the wealthiest lumber barons of his day. In December, Sutter sold his half of the interest in the mill to new owners, stayed on to manage the operation, and ended up cutting most of the timber from which the town of Coloma was built before he left the area for good.

For some time after the news of the discovery reached them, people in Monterey and farther south would not believe it and said it was only a ruse of Sutter to bring in more settlers. Those who did believe made tracks to El Dorado. In December of 1848, President James K. Polk delivered a message to the U.S. Congress in which he mentioned the possibility of untold wealth in California. For Sutter this was the greatest of misfortunes. His flour mill was sold after the stones were stolen. His leather tannery was abandoned by the workers, who left unfinished hides in the vats; a great number of raw hides became worthless. Such work, and its products, were viewed as "trash" by those who left. He was ruined.

Sacramento, by 1850, was primarily made up of endless rows of tents, with not a frame structure anywhere in sight. It was a terrifying and frighten-

ing place, with shouting, cursing, yelling, shooting, and gambling on all sides. The uproar was awful, and it drove Sutter away. By 1860, he felt the fort had turned into a human beehive, "just swarming with people . . . in the little rooms all about the court, and soldiers." Most of the Indians of the area moved farther from civilization and gradually disappeared.

After a time, he closed the fort and left for Amador County to reestablish his colony up on Sutter Creek. After a few weeks, so many camp followers and hungry miners showed up that it got too crowded, and he returned to Sutterville. The fort became a thriving center for trade; the city of Sacramento grew so fast it looked like a sea of tents to new arrivals. Sutter stayed a short time and moved with his Kanakas and Indians, some of whom had been with him since birth or childhood, to a place called Hock Farm, leaving the fort under the charge of a majordomo. He went back to farming during the late 1850's.

Sutter later sought relief for his losses from the state and federal governments. "By this sudden discovery of the gold, all my great plans were destroyed. Had I succeeded for a few years before the gold was discovered, I would have been the richest citizen on the Pacific shore; but it had to be different. Instead of being rich, I am ruined." It was on a trip to Washington, D.C., in 1880, to settle his suit, that he died.

Visiting Sutter's Mill

The mill site was restored in 1966, according to original plans and maps, and can be reached year-round by taking Highway 50 East or Interstate 80 North from Sacramento to Highway 49, which runs in part from Placerville to Auburn. Halfway along Highway 49, just outside of the town of Coloma, one can find the monument to Marshall, the restored Sutter's Mill, and other buildings at the 150 acre Marshall Gold Discovery State Historic Park.

—*Michael W. Simpson*

For Further Information:

Bidwell, John. "Life in California Before the Gold Discovery." *Century* 41, no. 2 (December, 1890).

Dillon, Richard H. *Captain John Sutter: Sacramento Valley's Sainted Sinner.* Santa Cruz, Calif.: Western Tanager Press, 1989.

Koeppel, Eliot. *The California Gold Country: Highway 49 Revisited*. La Habra, Calif.: Malakoff, 1999.

Norton, Henry, K. *The Story of California from the Earliest Days to the Present*. 7th ed. Chicago: A. C. McClurg, 1924.

Sutter, General John A. "The Discovery of Gold in California." *Hutchings' California Magazine*, November, 1857. This article is reprinted on the Museum of the City of San Francisco Web site at www.sfmuseum.org/hist2/gold.html

Watts

Date: Annexed by Los Angeles in 1927
Relevant issues: African American history, cultural history, disasters and tragedies, political history
Significance: The community of Watts is best known for a six-day uprising by African Americans in August, 1965, that resulted in the deaths of thirty-four people and injuries to another thousand. Officials placed the damage to property at $200 million.
Location: A community in Los Angeles approximately ten miles southeast of Hollywood and roughly fifteen miles northwest of Long Beach
Site Office:
Watts Labor Community Action Committee (WLCAC)
10950 South Central Avenue
Los Angeles, CA 90059
ph.: (213) 563-5642
fax: (213) 563-7307
Web site: www.wlcac.org

Rancho Tajuata was a Spanish holding located south of the pueblo of Los Angeles. Charles and Julia Watts purchased it in the late 1890's; in 1902, they donated land for a train station that was called Watts Junction. Land around the station was divided, a city grid laid, and farmland subdivided into narrow lots. Reasonable prices drew working-class African American, Mexican, Japanese, and Swedish immigrants to the area. The formation of racial enclaves was enforced by law, as title deeds to single-family dwellings often included "racial covenants" restricting the ability of minorities to purchase land. Along Main Street to the east, Japanese families combined tracts to establish farms and gardens. To the southwest, farm labor attracted Mexican immigrants to an enclave called El Jardin (the garden). By 1912, the intersection of Pacific Electric street railway lines at the train station provided transportation and jobs for African American men. The combination of jobs and unincorporated farmland to the southeast created opportunities for African American residents; this early colony was named Mudtown. Watts was annexed by the city of Los Angeles in 1927.

Racial Conflict in Watts

Watts was a community with a history of racial turmoil. In the early part of the twentieth century, it was a community in transition, with a rapidly growing population. Natural growth as well as growth through immigration and migration brought racial groups into direct contact with one another. Vying for political control, economic resources, and housing, African Americans, Mexicans, and Anglos frequently found themselves in competition that bred distrust and often open hostility. As the city continued to grow through World War I, southern black migrants increasingly began settling in Watts or in the Central Avenue area. The population remained fairly equally divided between African Americans, Mexicans, and Anglos during the period following World War I. During the 1920's, Ku Klux Klan activities increased in Watts, as was the case across the rest of the country. Heightened Klan activities only served to further divide an already racially divided community.

World War II witnessed dramatic increases in the population in Los Angeles. In search of jobs in the wartime industries, African Americans flooded Los Angeles and Watts, one result being increased housing shortages. As whites vacated areas and Japanese Americans were sent to internment camps, African Americans moved in, finding living quarters that were poorly maintained by absentee landlords. Unable to locate decent and affordable housing, others were forced to live in federal housing projects. These early projects, such as Hacienda Village, were created with the intent of housing racially and ethnically diverse populations; however, most were quickly occupied by African Americans. Several of these early projects were intended to serve as housing for war workers. Af-

In 1998, Watts was declared an "empowerment zone," giving tax breaks for companies hiring from and conducting business there. Such measures have led to some improvements, such as this housing development, but many vacant lots remain, reflecting the continuing poverty in this community. (AP/Wide World Photos)

As the 1950's approached, the Watts population steadily increased and economic conditions seemingly worsened. By the end of the 1950's, roughly one-third of Watts residents lived in the projects. That decade also witnessed a marked decline in the number of families owning their homes. A related issue was the fact that the average age of Watts residents was decreasing rather dramatically so that by the early 1960's, 60 percent of residents were less than twenty-five years old. Among this segment of the African American population, both underemployment and unemployment rates were high, which in part explains the decline in home ownership.

The production of housing, schools, and recreational facilities did not kept pace with the growing population. The result was overcrowded conditions in the schools, not enough space devoted to recreational facilities, and inadequate housing to meet the demands of a growing population.

By 1965, African American residents clearly had become disenchanted and dispossessed. Railroad tracks and the Harbor Freeway isolated the poorest residents, primarily those living in Watts, which is located east of the freeway. They were locked into a declining community where absentee landlords charged exorbitant rates for rent, where it was easier to buy liquor than to buy food, and where store owners charged outrageous prices for their merchandise and, for those without ready cash on hand, astronomical interest rates on merchandise that was financed.

History of the Uprising

Like many other cities around the country during the same time period, Watts was a city on the verge of explosion. In his 1963 work *The Fire Next Time*, writer James Baldwin poetically forewarns the na-

ter the war, most were converted into permanent dwellings.

By the time that World War II ended in 1945, African Americans made up two-thirds of the population in Watts. As their numbers increased, so did racial and class conflict. Racial conflicts arose as African American and Anglo students were encouraged to attend separate high schools to avoid intermingling. Class conflicts arose in Watts as African American natives tried to maintain their control of churches and recreational facilities against the barrage of southern blacks migrating to the area.

tion of the inevitable episodes of deadly racial violence that will take place across the country if African Americans continue to be disproportionately plagued by unemployment, poverty, illiteracy, and social inequality as a result of racism and discrimination.

The Watts uprising began during the summer of 1965, in the middle of a heat wave in which temperatures were recorded as high as 97 degrees Fahrenheit. The spark that set off the subsequent episodes of violence and arson came when two black men were arrested by white police officers for a traffic violation. The arresting police officers and their vehicle were attacked by the crowd for using excessive force against the men and their mother, who joined in the confrontation. In only a short time, local businesses were ablaze as residents wreaked havoc on the area by looting and setting fires.

Even though the immediate cause of the violence in Watts can be traced to the conflict with the police officers, this particular incident only added fuel to a fire that was already smoldering. A year earlier, in the summer of 1964, similar events took place in New York City and Rochester, New York; Jersey City, Paterson, and Elizabeth, New Jersey; Chicago; and Philadelphia. Although the precise factors leading to these uprisings differed, similiar circumstances linked them together.

According to the controversial McCone Commission, the official committee assigned to write the report on what was termed the Watts riots, three central factors were common in all these conflicts: first and foremost, a high rate of unemployment and underemployment; second, poor schools; and third, resentment toward white police officers patrolling black neighborhoods. Although the report from the McCone Commission has received much criticism from scholars for both its blatant racism and its racist overtures, it is worth discussing the problems in this community as officially recorded.

The lack of jobs and the unavailability of training for employment was a continuous problem for the residents of Watts. National efforts to alleviate joblessness and poverty, known as the War on Poverty, had done little to remedy this situation in Watts. Local welfare programs had also fallen short. Based on figures taken from the U.S. Census Bureau, the unemployment rate in South Central

Los Angeles in 1965 exceeded 10 percent. Aside from unemployment and underemployment, the residents of Watts also faced job shortages and low-wage employment. Even those with high school diplomas often faced grim possibilities in the employment arena. Nearly 25 percent of those with diplomas were unable to secure employment of any kind.

Census records and other government documents substantiate claims made in the McCone Report regarding unemployment and poverty rates in Watts; however, what was missing from the report was the role of racism and discrimination in perpetuating unemployment and poverty in Watts and similar areas.

The report also suggested that the lack of adequate public transportation served to isolate Watts residents, making it difficult to secure employment outside the community. Critics argue that this explanation is both an exaggeration of the transportation problem and an oversimplification of the causes of high unemployment rates among Watts residents. While the McCone Report argued that only 14 percent of residents in South Central Los Angeles owned one or more cars, the 1965 Census reports the figure to be 65 percent. Although a factor, clearly poor public transportation could not be used as a fundamental ingredient contributing to unemployment in the area.

One of the most controversial aspects of the McCone Report was the discussion regarding the relationship between white police officers and the black residents of Watts, which members of the committee characterized as antagonistic. It was argued that residents simply resented the fact that white officers patrolled their neighborhoods and possessed the legal authority to arrest black residents. Little was made of the role that these police officers played in creating the antagonistic relationship with the residents of Watts, or in the case of the actual uprising, how the use of excessive force by police officers served to exacerbate an already volatile situation. The report instead argued that in cases where excessive force was used, the police officers were provoked. The report acknowledged that complaints of police brutality were common in Watts but absolved white officers of any real guilt by suggesting that they used necessary force based on the particular situation.

Long before August, 1965, the relationship between Watts residents and the white police officers patrolling the area was strained. According to residents, white police officers were notorious for treating blacks with disdain, viewing most as the stereotypical criminal prone to violent behavior. Even William Parker, the chief of police at the time, held similar views of Watts residents, referring to participants in the uprising as "monkeys."

One of the primary questions posed by uninformed outsiders looking at the Watts situation was why the violence took place there and at that particular juncture. The McCone Report aside, why did residents in Watts participate in actions that would have a devastating impact on their community for years to come?

All these factors taken together, Watts was a community ripe for conflict. Poor Watts residents, seeing the lush lawns, tennis courts, and swimming pools of whites and some middle-class blacks in nearby neighborhoods, clearly understood that alternatives existed. The events of 1965 can therefore be viewed as an attempt by the residents of Watts to gain a sense of agency over their lives. Uprisings like the one in Watts have often been characterized by the media and onlookers as mass, unintelligible riots. More recently, scholars have begun to dispute such claims.

This revisionist literature frequently makes use of oral interviews and often incorporates race, class, and gender as critical modes of analysis. For example, early reports of the uprising in Watts—even official records such as the McCone Report—suggested that the rioters haphazardly destroyed property in the community with little regard to the owners or use of those buildings. In reassessing this point, scholars have noted that participants were selective in their destruction of property, choosing the businesses of merchants notorious for overcharging for their merchandise, businesses with owners or employees who were hostile or rude to black residents, and businesses viewed as detrimental to the community, such as liquor stores. Because of their own racism and class prejudice, many of the early reporters of the Watts uprising missed these not-so-subtle aspects of the violence.

Like the McCone Report, many of these early records also used inherently racist theories to explain the behavior of "rioters." The riffraff theory is one example. In applying this theory to Watts, the

McCone Commission suggested that the rioters represented only a small segment of Watts residents, those on the periphery of mainstream African American society, characterized as uneducated newcomers or juvenile delinquents. The assumption was that the vast majority of African Americans were not disgruntled. Clearly, however, most Watts residents were not content. Society had failed them on a variety of levels. In some ways, the uprising can be viewed as an attempt to draw national attention to the plight of those living in the area. Most residents recognized that filing formal grievances against police brutality or petitioning for more and better schools and programs to alleviate poverty carried little weight. These avenues had been taken, mostly to no avail.

Although lessons were learned from the violence in Watts, racial tensions remain. Nearly thirty years later, in 1992, the Los Angeles area would experience yet another violent racial uprising, this time revolving around the brutal beating of African American motorist Rodney King by white police officers. However, it is significant that South Central Los Angeles and other areas around Southern California, and not Watts, experienced the resulting anger and violence.

Watts Today

Everyday citizens, community leaders, politicians, and organizations rallied to help rebuild Watts. Many of the businesses and organizations that remain today were created immediately following the events of 1965, including the Watts Health Foundation, The King/Drew Medical Center, Drew University, the Bank of America, and the Watts Labor Community Action Committee (WLCAC), a nonprofit organization founded by Ted Watkins. Poverty remains, but some residents of Watts now seek to celebrate the diverse and colorful history of their community.

A popular tourist destination in Los Angeles is the Watts Towers. These nine sculptures, perhaps the nation's best-known work of folk art sculpture, were built by Italian immigrant Simon Rodia from 1921 to 1955 as a tribute to his adopted country. The towers, the tallest almost one hundred feet high, are made from steel pipes and rods wrapped with wire mesh, coated with mortar, and embedded with seventy thousand pieces of porcelain, tile, and glass. Rodia used simple hand tools and cast-off materials such as broken glass, sea shells, pottery, and ceramic tile. The Watts Towers, one of only nine works of folk art listed on the National Register of Historic Places, are located at 1765 East 107th Street.

The Watts Towers Art Center, often called simply the Center, sponsors exhibits, classes, and other cultural events. It is located next to the towers at 10950 South Central Avenue. This seven-acre enclosed site contains the bronze sculpture *The Mother of Humanity*, a facade depicting sites in old Los Angeles called Mudtown Flats, and the Ted Watkins Center for Communication, which includes the Civil Rights Museum.

—*Beverly A. Bunch-Lyons*

For Further Information:q

Baldassare, Mark, ed. *The Los Angeles Riots: Lessons for the Urban Future.* Boulder, Colo.: Westview Press, 1994.

Bontemps, Arna. *God Sends Sunday.* New York: Harcourt, Brace, 1931. Reprint. New York: AMS Press, 1972. In this novel, Harlem Renaissance artist and writer Bontemps wrote about the early colony of Mudtown: "The small group in Mudtown was exceptional. Here removed from the influences of white folks, they did not acquire the inhibitions of their city brothers. Mudtown was like a tiny section of the Deep South literally transplanted."

Bullock, Paul. *Watts: The Aftermath, an Inside View of the Ghetto by the People of Watts.* New York: Grove Press, 1969.

Fogelson, Robert M. *Mass Violence in America: The Los Angeles Riots.* New York: Arno Press/*The New York Times*, 1969.

Gooding-Williams, Robert, ed. *Reading Rodney King, Reading Urban Uprising.* New York: Routledge, 1993.

Horne, Gerald. *Fire This Time: The Watts Uprising and the 1960's.* Charlottesville: University Press of Virginia, 1995.

Ray, MaryEllen Bell. *The City of Watts, California, 1907 to 1926.* Los Angeles: Rising, 1985. This book, written for young people, traces the history of Watts from its origins as a small Spanish land grant to its consolidation with Los Angeles.

Sears, David. *The Politics of Violence: The New Urban Blacks and the Watts Riot.* Washington, D.C.: University Press of America, 1981.

Sonenshein, Raphael. *Politics in Black and White: Race and Power in Los Angeles.* Princeton, N.J.: Princeton University Press, 1993.

Other Historic Sites

Big and Little Petroglyph Canyons

Location: China Lake, Inyo County
Relevant issues: American Indian history
Statement of significance: First reported in 1938, this site deep within the Coso Mountains is one of the most spectacular petroglyph areas known in the western United States, exhibiting more than twenty thousand designs. It represents at least two cultural phases.

Big Four House

Location: Sacramento, California
Relevant issues: Business and industry
Statement of significance: Built in 1852, the Big Four House was named after the "big four"—Collis Huntington, Mark Hopkins, Leland Stanford, and Charles Crocker—who planned, financed, and built the western end of America's first transcontinental railway. It was in this structure that the four made their offices while organizing the Central Pacific (California to Utah) section of the railway and where subsequently they founded the Southern Pacific Railroad (to Southern California) in 1873.

Bodie Historic District

Location: Bridgeport, Mono County
Relevant issues: Business and industry
Statement of significance: In its location, setting, and total isolation, and in terms of the number of historic buildings and associated mining remains that have survived in unusually good condition, Bodie is probably the finest example of a mining "ghost town" in the West.

Bradbury Building

Location: Los Angeles, Los Angeles County
Relevant issues: Art and architecture
Statement of significance: Completed in 1893, this unique five-story office building was designed by George H. Wyman, who had no formal architectural or engineering training at the time. The heavy sandstone exterior leaves one unprepared for the cage of light-filled glass within; the whole is a cobweb of cast iron covered with delicate Art Nouveau ornamentation.

Burbank House and Garden

Location: 200 Santa Rosa Avenue, Santa Rosa, Sonoma County
Relevant issues: Science and technology
Statement of significance: For a half century before his death, this was the home of Luther Burbank (1849-1926), internationally known horticulturalist whose work produced many new plant varieties. Often called the "Plant Wizard," Burbank experimented with thousands of plants, his sole goal the production of more and better varieties of cultivated plants; he introduced over 250 varieties of fruit alone.

Carmel Mission

Location: 3080 Rio Road, Carmel, Monterey County
Relevant issues: European settlement, Latino history, religion
Statement of significance: Established in June, 1770, by Father Junípero Serra, the Mission San Carlos de Borromeo served as the headquarters for the *Padre-Presidente* and was thus the most important of the California missions. By 1852, it lay in ruins. Since that time, it has been restored and reconstructed, and today is as an excellent example of a California mission.

City of Oakland

Location: Oakland, Alameda County
Relevant issues: Military history, naval history, World War II
Statement of significance: The U.S. Navy yard tug *Hoga*, now the fireboat *City of Oakland*, is typical of hundreds of World War II-era naval service craft. A well-preserved, largely unaltered example of this once-common type craft, *City of Oakland* is the only known surviving yard craft that was present at Pearl Harbor during the Japanese attack on December 7, 1941. While not engaged in combatting the enemy, these craft performed heroic service, extinguishing fires on burning battleships and other vessels in the harbor and rescuing wounded seamen from the oily waters of Battleship Row. *Hoga* fought fires on Battleship Row for forty-eight hours, particulary working on the blazing hulk of USS *Arizona*. For its actions, *Hoga* was awarded with a meritorious citation.

Elmshaven

Location: St. Helena, Napa County
Relevant issues: Health and medicine, religion
Statement of significance: From 1900 to 1915, Elmshaven was the home of Ellen Gould White (1827-1915), a cofounder of the Seventh-day Adventist Church, one of the nation's largest indigenous denominations. Raised as a devout Methodist near Portland, Maine, young Ellen and her family were expelled from their congregation for following a millenialist preacher who predicted the Second Coming of Christ in 1843 or 1844. Soon after it became clear this prediction was a disappointment, the seventeen-year-old Ellen began having visions, which she related to others. Ellen White and her husband played a central role in the formation of the Western Health Reform Institute in Battle Creek, which became famous under the leadership of Dr. John Harvey Kellogg.

First Pacific Coast Salmon Cannery Site

Location: Broderick, Yolo County
Relevant issues: Business and industry
Statement of significance: Here, between 1864 and 1866, William and George Hume and Andrew Hapgood of Maine perfected the canning techniques that led to the development of the multi-million-dollar Pacific coast salmon canning industry. The Hapgood, Hume, and Company cannery was situated on a scow anchored in the Sacramento River.

Flood Mansion

Location: San Francisco, San Francisco County
Relevant issues: Business and industry
Statement of significance: This, the only Nob Hill mansion to survive the earthquake and fire of 1906, was the residence of one of the bonanza

kings of the Nevada Comstock Lode. James Clair Flood (1825-1889) operated a saloon when he came to San Francisco in 1849, but by shrewd dealing in the stock exchange and the judicious exploration and development of mines—the Comstock Mine in particular—he amassed a tremendous fortune.

Folsom Powerhouse

Location: Off Folsom Boulevard, Folsom State Recreation Area, Folsom, Sacramento County
Relevant issues: Science and technology
Statement of significance: In 1895, this hydroelectric generating plant sent high-voltage alternating current over long-distance lines for the first time, a major advance in the technology of electric power transmission and generation.

Gamble House

Location: 4 Westmoreland Place, Pasadena, Los Angeles County
Relevant issues: Art and architecture
Statement of significance: Constructed in 1908, this summer house in the California Bungalow style exemplifies the Arts and Crafts movement of the early twentieth century. Contemporary with Franklin Lloyd Wright's "Prairie Houses," this structure is the finest surviving example of the work of architects Charles S. and Henry M. Greene.

Gunther Island Site 67

Location: Eureka, Humboldt County
Relevant issues: American Indian history
Statement of significance: One of the largest Wiyot villages, this site (900 C.E.) typifies the late prehistoric period and was instrumental in outlining the prehistory of the Northern California coast. The site is a shell mound encompassing approximately six acres and attaining depths of up to fourteen feet.

Hale Solar Laboratory

Location: Pasadena, Los Angeles County
Relevant issues: Science and technology
Statement of significance: Completed in 1925, Hale Solar Laboratory is important for its association with George Ellery Hale (1868-1938), the person most responsible for the rise of the science of astrophysics in the United States. Hale's scientific contributions were numerous, especially in the area of astronomy. In the latter part of his life, this was Hale's office and workshop, where he studied the sun with instruments of his own design.

Hanna-Honeycomb House

Location: Palo Alto, Santa Clara County
Relevant issues: Art and architecture
Statement of significance: Begun in 1937 and added to and expanded over twenty-five years, the main house is the first and best example of Frank Lloyd Wright's innovative "hexagonal design," where rooms flow together and, except the kitchen and baths, every room opens to extensive terraces and the outdoors. Patterned after the honeycomb of the bee, the six-sided figure, with open 120-degree angles, appears not only in the layout of the house but also in the landscape and many of the built-in furnishings.

Harada House

Location: Riverside, Riverside County
Relevant issues: Asian American history, legal history
Statement of significance: An architecturally plain residence near downtown Riverside, the Harada House was the object of the first test of the constitutionality of an alien land law in the United States. In *California vs. Harada* (1916-1918), the right of native-born citizens of the United States, albeit minors, to own land was upheld. Directly associated with Japanese Americans, the case is important to all Americans of immigrant heritage. The internment of the Harada family during World War II illustrates another aspect of America's troubled dealings with its Japanese American citizens. The house is still owned by a member of the family.

Hoover House

Location: Stanford, Santa Clara County
Relevant issues: Political history
Statement of significance: Designed by Mrs. Lou Henry Hoover, this house strongly reflects the couple's character and tastes. Legal residence of the Hoovers when Herbert was elected president, the house also served as their retirement home from 1933 to 1944.

Hotel Del Coronado

Location: 1500 Orange Street, Coronado, San Diego County

Relevant issues: Cultural history

Statement of significance: Begun in March, 1877, and open for business February, 1878, this enormous timber structure, rising from the Coronado Peninsula like a castle, was one of the last of the extravagantly conceived resort hotels in Southern California. It was the first hotel in the world, and the largest building outside of New York City, to use electric lighting; the lighting system was installed under the direct supervision of Thomas A. Edison.

Hubble House

Location: San Marino, Los Angeles County

Relevant issues: Science and technology

Statement of significance: From 1925 to 1953, this two-story stucco structure was the home of Edwin Powell Hubble (1889-1953), one of America's greatest twentieth century astronomers who, among other accomplishments, discovered extragalactic nebulae and their recession from each other.

Jeremiah O'Brien

Location: Pier 3, Fort Mason Center, San Francisco Maritime National Historical Park, San Francisco, San Francisco County

Relevant issues: Military history, naval history, World War II

Statement of significance: Jeremiah O'Brien is the only operative unaltered survivor of the many Liberty ships built during World War II as an emergency response to a critical shortage of maritime cargo ships. It participated in the D day invasion of France in 1944. In 1984, it was made a National Historic Mechanical Engineering Landmark by the American Society of Mechanical Engineers.

Lane Victory

Location: San Pedro, Los Angeles County

Relevant issues: Military history, naval history, World War II

Statement of significance: The Victory ships entered World War II ferrying supplies and troops to European and Pacific theaters. As the last Victory ship to retain integrity of original design and as best representative of its class, *Lane Victory* has been designated a memorial to the merchant marine veterans of World War II.

Las Flores Adobe

Location: Camp Pendleton, San Diego County

Relevant issues: Art and architecture

Statement of significance: Erected 1867-1868, Las Flores Adobe is an example of a two-story nineteenth century Monterey Style residence. This building combined the traditional Spanish-Mexican adobe with elements of New England frame architecture, including a double veranda across the facade, to create a popular building type unique to California during the mid-nineteenth century. It is located on Camp Joseph H. Pendleton.

Locke Historic District

Location: Locke, Sacramento County

Relevant issues: Asian American history, cultural history

Statement of significance: Founded in 1915, Locke is the largest and most intact surviving example of a historic rural Chinese American community in the United States, including more than fifty commercial and residential frame buildings in simple but picturesque style. Locke is the only such community remaining in the Sacramento-San Joaquin River Delta, which was a particularly important area of rural Chinese settlement.

London Ranch

Location: Jack London Historical State Park, Glen Ellen, Sonoma County

Relevant issues: Literary history

Statement of significance: On this site stand the ruins of Wolf House (1913) and the House of Happy Walls (1919), as well as the graves of John Griffith London and his wife, Charmian. Jack London (1876-1916), the most popular novelist and short-story writer of his day, wrote passionately and prolifically, drawing from his firsthand experience at sea or in Alaska or in the fields and factories of Califoria; between 1900 and 1916, he completed fifty-one books, hundreds of short stories, and numerous articles on a wide range of topics.

Los Cerritos Ranch House

Location: Long Beach, Los Angeles County

Relevant issues: Art and architecture

Statement of significance: Erected in 1844, this two-story adobe ranchhouse is an excellent example of the application of Monterey Colonial Style to the traditional Spanish-Mexican hacienda plan. The house is built on the usual U-shaped plan around a large patio, enclosed on the fourth side by an adobe wall. The foundations are of baked red brick brought around the Horn by sailing ships; the hand-hewn beams in the house came from forests near Monterey; and the walls in the center section are three feet thick.

Mare Island Naval Shipyard

Location: Mare Island Vallejo, Solano County

Relevant issues: Military history, naval history

Statement of significance: The U.S. Navy's first permanent installation on the Pacific coast, Mare Island illustrates the nation's effort to extend its naval power into the Pacific Ocean. The first U.S. warship (1859) and first drydock (1872-1891) constructed on the West Coast were built here.

Miller House

Location: Joaquin Miller and Sanborn Drive, Oakland, Alameda County

Relevant issues: Literary history

Statement of significance: In 1886, Joaquin Miller (1837-1913), the first major poet of the far western frontier, moved to this property near Oakland and built a small, three-room house which he dubbed the Abbey. Known as the "Poet of the Sierras," Miller wrote largely about the exploits of pioneers, outlaws, and Indians of the Wild West. On this property, Miller also built stone monuments to Robert Browning, John C. Frémont, and Moses, as well as a funeral pyre for himself. The pyre was never used.

Mission Beach roller coaster

Location: San Diego, San Diego County

Relevant issues: Cultural history

Statement of significance: Constructed in 1925, this is one of two large, wooden-scaffolded roller coasters with structural integrity that remain on the West Coast. The "Earthquake" roller coaster, as it is also called, is the only one on the West Coast by noted coaster builders Prior and Church. It is the prime survivor and most visible symbol of the Mission Beach Amusement Center, the centerpiece of sugar heir John D. Spreckels's ambitious early twentieth century recreational development.

Mission Santa Ines

Location: South of State Highway 246, Solvang, Santa Barbara County

Relevant issues: American Indian history, European settlement, Latino history, religion

Statement of significance: Mission Santa Ines is one of the best-preserved Spanish mission complexes in the United States, containing an unrivaled combination of landscape setting, original buildings, extant collections of art and interior furnishings, water-related industrial structures, and archaeological remains. The property is also important as the location of the start of the Chumash Revolt of 1824, one of the largest and most successful revolts of Native American neophytes in the Spanish West, representing indigenous resistance to European colonization. The intact archaeological remains of the two mission wings, a portion of the convent, and the Native American village are rare survivors and have been demonstrated to contain the potential for exceptional information on the critical period of accommodation between native peoples and European colonial powers.

Modjeska House

Location: 29042 Modjeska Canyon Road, Modjeska, Orange County

Relevant issues: Cultural history

Statement of significance: Madame Helena Modjeska (1840-1909), the internationally renowned Shakespearean actress and Polish patriot, was one of the first "stars" to settle in Southern Calfornia. The Modjeska House, located on the ranch she dubbed "The Forest of Arden" (from William Shakespeare's *As You Like It*), was her most important home (1888-1906) during her long years of exile. Design of the house is attributed to her friend, architect Stanford White (1853-1906).

New Almaden

Location: Fourteen miles south of San Jose, Santa Clara County

Relevant issues: Business and industry, European settlement, Latino history

Statement of significance: Santa Clara Indians had used cinnabar from this site long before 1824, when information provided by them led Mexican settlers to the first quicksilver deposits identified in North America. Europeans used the mercury in the ore to facilitate the mining of gold and silver. The site was named after the world's greatest quicksilver mine, Almaden, in Spain. Mercury from New Almaden's mines was essential to the mining process during the gold rush.

Norris Cabin

Location: Gilroy, Santa Clara County

Relevant issues: Literary history

Statement of significance: A writer of the American naturalism school, Frank Norris (1870-1902) lived here before his death at the age of thirty-two. Surrounded by magnificent redwoods, the cabin is in its original condition.

Old Sacramento Historic District

Location: 111 I Street, Sacramento, Sacramento County

Relevant issues: Business and industry

Statement of significance: Situated on the lower Sacramento River, the Sacramento's river port emerged in 1849-1850 as the great interior distributing and transportation center for the Northern Mines in the mother lode country of the Sierra Nevada. A large number of buildings dating from the 1840's through 1870's remain in the original business district.

Old Scripps Building

Location: 8602 La Jolla Shores Drive, La Jolla, San Diego County

Relevant issues: Science and technology

Statement of significance: The oldest building in continuous use by a major oceanographic research institution in the country, this is the first permanent structure of the Scripps Institution, an early marine biological station that became the nation's first oceanographic institute in 1925. Designed by a noted California architect, it is an early example of reinforced concrete construction.

Old United States Mint

Location: San Francisco, San Francisco County

Relevant issues: Business and industry

Statement of significance: Constructed between 1869 and 1874, this Greek Revival building became one of the principal mints in the United States during the nineteenth century and chief federal depository for gold and silver mined in the West. Designed by Alfred B. Mullett, it is one of the few downtown buildings to survive the 1906 earthquake.

Paramount Theatre

Location: 2025 Broadway, Oakland, Alameda County

Relevant issues: Cultural history

Statement of significance: Built during the Depression and opened in December, 1931, this great Art Deco film palace was the largest auditorium on the West Coast, seating 3,476. Designed by Timothy Pflueger of San Francisco, the Paramount combines spectacular advertising with stark functionalism. With its 110-foot facade featuring a tile mosaic of two monumental figures, a stage 32 feet deep and 50 feet wide, a mechanically elevated orchestra pit, and twenty production and dressing rooms, it serves all the arts from symphony to dance to variety shows and films.

Potomac

Location: Oakland, Alameda County

Relevant issues: Naval history, political history

Web site: www.usspotomac.org

Statement of significance: One of three surviving major vessels used as presidential yachts, *Potomac* served only one president. It was used by President Franklin D. Roosevelt between 1936 and 1945 and was a major symbol of his presidency; briefings, meetings, and decisions were made on board, and it provided transportation to a rendezvous with Winson Churchill to arrange the Atlantic Charter in 1940. Restored to its 1939 appearance, it operates as a working museum vessel.

Rock Magnetics Laboratory

Location: Menlo Park, San Mateo County

Relevant issues: Science and technology

Statement of significance: In this unimposing structure, three U.S. Geological Survey geophysicists—Richard R. Doell, Brent Dalrymple, and Allan Cox—demonstrated that, contrary to what most scientists then believed, the earth's magnetic field had reversed its direction on numerous occasions over the last five million years. The time scale developed in this laboratory from 1957 to 1966 was the key to the interpretation of the striped magnetic anomalies on the deep ocean floor that were being discovered and mapped by marine geophysicists around the world; their interpretation of this phenomenon led to the development of the theory of plate tectonics, the major revolution in earth science in the twentieth century.

Rogers Dry Lake

Location: Mojave Desert, Kern County
Relevant issues: Aviation history, science and technology
Statement of significance: This dry lakebed provided a natural laboratory for flight testing of aircraft that were on the cutting edge of aerospace and aviation technology. It is the primary resource associated with establishment of Edwards Air Force Base, the world's premier flight testing and flight research center.

Rose Bowl

Location: 991 Rosemont Avenue, Brookside Park, Pasadena, Los Angeles County
Relevant issues: Cultural history, sports
Statement of significance: Since 1922, this has been the site of the earliest and most-renowned postseason college football "bowl" game. Held every New Year's Day since 1916, the Rose Bowl also commemorates the civic work of the Pasadena Tournament of Roses Association, the sponsor of the annual flower festival, parade, and bowl game. Additionally, this was one of the venues of the 1932 and 1984 Olympics.

San Francisco Cable Cars

Location: 1390 Washington Street, San Francisco, San Francisco County
Relevant issues: Cultural history
Statement of significance: These are the only cable cars still operating in an American city. Begun in August, 1873, this system of traction locomotion was designed to accommodate even the steepest

grades, which explains why ten miles of track are still in use in this very hilly "city by the Bay."

San Francisco Civic Center

Location: Near Van Ness Avenue and Market Street, San Francisco, San Francisco County
Relevant issues: Cultural history
Statement of significance: Of international importance as the scene of the founding of the United Nations and the drafting and signing of the post-World War II peace treaties with Japan, the Civic Center is also the finest and most complete manifestation of the City Beautiful movement in the country. It illustrates the era of turn-of-the-century municipal reform movements and early public and city planning. Exposition Auditorium, in the Civic Center, is the only surviving building of the Panama-Pacific International Exposition of 1915.

San Francisco Port of Embarkation, U.S. Army

Location: Fort Mason, Golden Gate National Recreation Area, San Francisco, San Francisco County
Relevant issues: Military history, World War II
Statement of significance: During World War II, this was the principal port on the West Coast for delivering personnel, materiel, weapons, and ammunition to the fighting fronts in the Pacific Theater.

San Juan Bautista Plaza Historic District

Location: San Juan Bautista State Historic Park, 2211 Garden Road, San Juan Bautista, San Benito County
Relevant issues: Art and architecture, European settlement, Latino history
Statement of significance: A striking example of a nineteenth century village built on a traditional Spanish-Mexican colonial plaza plan, the district is composed of five buildings, all facing the plaza and all completed between 1813 and 1874.

San Luis Rey Mission Church

Location: 4050 Mission Avenue, Oceanside, San Diego County
Relevant issues: European settlement, Latino history, religion
Statement of significance: The church at Mission San Luis Rey de Francia (1798) is perhaps the finest

existing example of a California mission church as well as a mission complex. This, the third church at the mission, was erected between 1811 and 1815. In 1893, the Catholic Church rededicated the mission as a Franciscan college, a function it continues to serve.

Santa Barbara Mission

Location: 2201 Laguna Street, Santa Barbara, Santa Barbara County

Relevant issues: European settlement, Latino history, religion

Statement of significance: Built from 1815 to 1820, this mission, architecturally probably the finest and most distinguished of the twenty-one California mission churches, is the only original mission church to survive unaltered and in good condition into the twentieth century. In 1842, California's first Roman Catholic bishop arrived at Santa Barbara to establish his see at the mission and to administer the affairs of his diocese, which included all of Alta and Baja California.

Santa Cruz Looff Carousel and Roller Coaster on the Beach Boardwalk

Location: Santa Cruz, Santa Cruz County

Relevant issues: Cultural history

Statement of significance: Built in 1911, this carousel is one of the six essentially intact Looff carousels in the United States. The Looff family was one of the major early manufacturers of carousels. The roller coaster (1924) is the older of the two large, wooden-scaffolded roller coasters remaining on the West Coast.

Santa Monica Looff Hippodrome

Location: 276 Santa Monica Pier, Santa Monica, Los Angeles County

Relevant issues: Cultural history

Statement of significance: The principal historic element of the formerly extensive collection of amusement facilities at the Santa Monica (Looff) Amusement Pier, this is a rare, intact example of an early shelter structure built (1916) to house a carousel in an amusement park and the better preserved of the two such structures that remain on the West Coast.

Sinclair House

Location: Monrovia, Los Angeles County

Relevant issues: Literary history

Statement of significance: From 1942 until 1966, this was the principal home of Upton Sinclair (1878-1968), one of the most influential American novelists in the area of social justice. Virtually all of Sinclair's later works were written in this neo-Mediterranean house.

Space Launch Complex 10

Location: Lompoc, Santa Barbara County

Relevant issues: Aviation history, science and technology

Statement of significance: Built in 1958 for the U.S. Air Force's Intermediate Range Ballistic Missile (IRBM) Testing Program, this complex was adapted for spaceflight purposes. The launch facility was first used on June 16, 1959. The blockhouse contains one of the best existing collections of the working electronics used to support launches of that era, and the entire complex is the best surviving example of a working launch complex built in the 1950's at the beginning of the American effort to explore space.

Stanford House

Location: Sacramento, Sacramento County

Relevant issues: Political history

Statement of significance: Built in 1857, this Renaissance Revival, two-story, square house was the residence of the two Civil War governors of California. Pro-Union Leland Stanford (1824-1893) was the first Republican to be elected governor of the state; his successor, Frederick F. Low (1828-1894), was elected under the banner of the Union Party, a coalition of Republicans and Northern Democrats. Their leadership from 1862 to 1870 ensured the state remained loyal to the Union. Stanford also served as president of the Central Pacific Railroad, which constructed the western portion of the transcontinental rail system.

Tao House

Location: Eugene O'Neill National Historic Site, 1000 Kuss Road, Danville, Contra Costa County

Relevant issues: Literary history

Statement of significance: Eugene O'Neill (1888-1953), winner of the Nobel Prize in Literature in 1936, wrote some of his most significant plays here, where he lived from 1937 to 1944.

United States Immigration Station, Angel Island

Location: Angel Island State Park, Tiburon, Marin County

Relevant issues: Asian American history, political history

Statement of significance: The U.S. immigration station at Angel Island was the major West Coast processing center for immigrants from 1910 to 1940. What Ellis Island symbolizes to Americans of European heritage who immigrated to the East Coast, Angel Island symbolizes to Americans of Asian heritage on the West Coast. The largest island in San Francisco Bay, Angel Island was used as a prisoner of war camp during World War II. It was declared surplus in 1946 and since 1963 has been a California State Park.

USS Hornet (Cvs-12)

Location: Alameda, Alameda County

Relevant issues: Aviation history, military history, naval history, World War II

Statement of significance: Launched in 1943, this Essex Class aircraft carrier was part of the wartime buildup of the U.S carrier force during World War II. *Hornet's* distinguished war career included participation in the invasion of Saipan and the Battle of the Puhilippine Sea; the amphibious landings on Palau, the Philippines, Iwo Jima, and Okinawa; and strikes against the Japanese home islands; later, it was reactivated for duty in both the Korean and Vietnam conflicts. *Hornet* also acted as the recovery vessel for the command modules and crews of the first two manned landings on the moon.

Wapama

Location: Sausalito, Marin County

Relevant issues: Business and industry, naval history

Statement of significance: Wapama is the last surviving example of more than two hundred steam schooners designed for use in the nineteenth and twentieth century Pacific Coast lumber trade and coastwide service. These vessels formed the backbone of maritime trade and commerce on the coast, ferrying lumber, general cargo, and passengers to and from urban centers and smaller coastal settlements. *Wapama* is the last oceangoing, wooden-hulled passenger and cargo-carrying steamer in the United States. It is included in the National Maritime Museum at Golden Gate National Recreation Area.

Warner's Ranch

Location: Warner Springs, San Diego County

Relevant issues: Business and industry, western expansion

Statement of significance: Established in 1831, Warner's Ranch was foremost a pioneering cattle ranch. From 1848 on, it was also a popular resting place for overland travelers entering California over the southern route and was perhaps best known as a Butterfield Overland Mail stage station from 1859 to 1861. Today, two adobe structures—a house and barn—remain, situated on 221 acres of rural grazing land.

Well No. 4, Pico Canyon Oil Field

Location: San Fernando, Los Angeles County

Relevant issues: Business and industry

Statement of significance: Dating from the 1870's and 1880's, this is the birthplace of California's petroleum industry and the first commercially successful well in the state. Because of training in the Pico Canyon field, oil industry pioneers made California the second oil-producing state in the United States in the first two decades of the twentieth century.

Colorado

The State Capitol Building in Denver. (Denver Metro Convention & Visitors Bureau)

History of
   Colorado 196
Bent's Old Fort 198
Leadville 203
Mesa Verde 209
Pikes Peak 213
Telluride 216
Other Historic
   Sites 220

History of Colorado

The history of Colorado is marked by its geographical features, divided as it is by the Rocky Mountains, with rugged territory lying to the west and agriculturally productive plains to the east. Mining in the central and western parts of the state was influential in its early history, while agriculture, and its thirst for water in the parched eastern plains, was influential in later decades. Colorado's mountainous terrain has attracted generations of tourists, who flock to winter and summer recreational attractions.

Colorado History

The earliest inhabitants of the area were nomadic hunters, around 10,000 B.C.E. About the first century C.E., the southwestern area of the state was populated by a people known as the Basketmakers. By 800, the Cliff Dwellers had established their civilization in the state's mesa country. From 1000, the civilization of the Cliff Dwellers flourished, but around 1300, for unknown reasons, it died out.

Though their origins are unknown, many other Native American peoples populated today's Colorado when whites arrived. A number of Apache bands raided Colorado territory, but only one such band, the Jicarilla, lived permanently in Colorado and its environs, mainly in the southeastern portion. Bannock and Shoshone Indians roamed over the northwest corner of the state. The Cheyenne, Arapaho, and Comanche tribes hunted and made war in eastern areas, as did the Kiowa and the Kiowa Apaches, who always accompanied them. The Navajos occasionally entered the state from New Mexico, but the Utes occupied the state's entire central and western portions. Most of the Pueblos inhabited the state's north, in Colorado's famous cliff ruins, sometimes intermarrying with the Utes.

Spanish Exploration

In the sixteenth century the Spanish became the area's first European explorers. Searching for rich cities of gold, Francisco Vásquez de Coronado arrived in 1541. During the next 250 years, a number of Spanish explorers traversed parts of what would become Colorado, among them Juan de Ulibarri, who claimed the territory for the Spanish crown.

American Exploration and Settlement

In 1803 parts of Colorado were sold to the United States when the administration of Thomas Jefferson concluded the Louisiana Purchase with France. Thereafter, the territory was explored by a series of American expeditions: in 1806 by Zebulon Pike, for whom Pikes Peak is named; in 1820 by Stephen Long; from 1842 to 1853 by John C. Frémont; and in 1853 by the Gunnison-Beckwith Expedition. In 1833 Bent's Fort, the first permanent American settlement in Colorado, was completed. The area was also inhabited by various nomadic Indian tribes, as well as by American "mountain men," who lived by trapping and fur trading. Among them were those who became the subjects of American folklore, such as Kit Carson and Jim Bridger.

From Territory to Statehood

In 1848, Mexico ceded part of Colorado to the United States with the Treaty of Guadalupe Hidalgo, which ended the Mexican War. Two years later, a portion of the western area of modern Colorado became part of Utah Territory. In 1854 some eastern areas were incorporated into Kansas and Nebraska Territories. In 1858, gold was found in Colorado, first at Cherry Creek, near Denver. The next year, a rich vein was discovered in Central City. These finds brought thousands of adventurers in search of a new life, who adopted the slogan Pikes Peak or Bust. The miners ignored the claims of Indians to the land that had been deeded to them in past treaties. In place of Indian lands, newcomers attempted to set up a new, so-called Jefferson Territory, which Congress did not approve. After Kansas became a state in 1861, Colorado Territory was organized, with much the same boundaries as the subsequent state.

Colorado entered the Civil War on the Union side in 1861 and was the scene of significant fighting in the western phases of the war. Other notable events of these early years were wars between whites

and American Indians, and a number of gold and silver strikes. By the late 1860's new mining methods brought both further prosperity and more immigration from the East. The increased population was a key factor in the territory's seeking statehood. After several failures, statehood was finally attained in 1876.

Economic and Social Development
The formation of modern Colorado was preceded by a society and economy dominated by decades of gold and silver mining followed by agricultural development. The same year statehood was achieved, the Leadville area began to surrender its millions of dollars of gold and silver ore. More than a decade later, Cripple Creek was the scene of another notable gold strike. This discovery was especially welcome, because the free coinage of silver sent silver mining into a tailspin that the Cripple Creek find helped to offset.

The last of the battles with Indian tribes came in 1879, when the Utes rebelled. In the last uprising by Native Americans in the American West, the Utes massacred Nathan Meeker, an Indian agent, and his workers in what would become the town of Meeker, in the White River Valley in northwestern Colorado. This massacre resulted in the Utes' forcible removal to eastern Utah. Some Indians, however, appear to have maintained their presence, though in modest numbers. For example, in 1845, the Jicarilla Apaches were said to number 800. According to the census of 1910, there were 694, and in 1937, the Report of the U.S. Indian Office said there were 714.

If Indian wars were at an end, other conflicts were not long in arriving. When a depression struck in 1893, serious labor problems erupted after the federal government canceled its agreement to purchase substantial amounts of silver. Silver miners were thrown out of work; strikes by miners, now employees of mining companies, not independent adventurers, occurred in silver mines in 1893-1894 and 1903-1904 and in coal mines in 1913-1914. These strikes were settled with military force, a graphic reminder that the days of the romantic West were over.

The Twentieth Century
The opening of the twentieth century saw the beginning of the natural conservation movement that attracted tourists. In 1906, Congress created Mesa Verde National Park to preserve the remains of ancient Indian culture, and nine years later Rocky Mountain National Park was established. During these years, the economy depended on agriculture, as Colorado became the most irrigated state in the Union. Canning and other industries grew along with agriculture. In 1899 Colorado's first sugar beet factory began operations at Grand Junction; seven years later the U.S. Mint opened in Denver.

The advent of another industry, however, augured well for the future, when oil production and refining became prominent sources of income. With the plentiful availability of oil throughout the nation came the advent of the automobile. America's love affair with the automobile, coupled with the unsurpassed beauty of western Colorado, gave rise to the state's considerable tourist industry, which developed rapidly after World War I. Colorado, moreover, has its own oil sources. Small amounts of oil had been discovered in the nineteenth century, when in 1862 the first oil well was drilled near Canon City. In the next century, however, more, and larger, fields were found. By the 1920's, the importance of oil surpassed all other minerals, though not until after World War II and the development of the Rangley oil field in 1946 in northwest Colorado did oil production approach its zenith. Oil production rose from 1.7 million barrels in 1940 to 23 million barrels in 1950.

Like the rest of the nation, Colorado suffered considerably during the Great Depression of the 1930's. World War II lifted the state from its doldrums, as its oil and minerals were in great demand. Military and other federal installations opened in several areas, especially around Denver, the state's capital.

Postwar Developments

Colorado's population, which had grown to 800,000 in 1910, grew swiftly after World War II. With population increase and demand for expansion of agriculture came the need for water. Irrigation had begun in the nineteenth century. Large irrigation projects existed from the 1860's, but after the war a series of irrigation projects were carried out. In 1947 the Alva B. Adams Tunnel, which carries water eastward through the Rocky Mountains, was completed. Two years later Cherry Creek Dam, near Denver, was finished. In 1959 the Colorado-Big Thompson Project, a series of dams, reservoirs, and tunnels, was completed, of which the Adams Tunnel is a part. More water-conservation projects were carried out between the 1950's and the 1980's, such as the Colorado River Storage Project, begun in 1956, and the Frying Pan-Arkansas project, begun in the early 1960's and completed in 1985.

Other significant postwar changes in the state's economy changed the complexion of its society. Manufacturing replaced agriculture in importance by the mid-1950's. Federal agencies sank important new roots in the state, opening the laboratory of the National Bureau of Standards in Boulder in 1954, the United States Air Force Academy in 1958, and the North American Air Defense Command (NORAD) in 1966, sunk some twelve hundred feet deep in Cheyenne Mountain.

By the 1990's, Colorado had emerged as both a significant area of urban development below the eastern slopes of the Rocky Mountains and one of the nation's most popular recreation areas. The upscale mountain community of Vail, for example,

serves as an icon of winter sports, and the state's National Parks and other scenic wonders draw millions of vacationers each year. At the same time, the nation's academic life benefited from its universities, and several of its political figures reached national stature. If in its early decades, Colorado, seemingly connected more to the West, felt marginal to powerful eastern states, a century after its admittance to the Union the state became fully integrated into the nation's life. Signs of this integration include its thriving urban life, especially in its capital and environs; its significant defense installations; and its sports teams, such as those in professional baseball, basketball, and football.

—*Charles F. Bahmueller*

Bent's Old Fort

Date: Authorized as a National Historic Site on June 3, 1960

Relevant issues: Business and industry, military history, western expansion

Significance: A National Historic Site, this adobe trading fort was built on the Santa Fe Trail by business partners Charles and William Bent and Ceran St. Vrain in 1833-1834. It served as a military outpost for the U.S. invasion of Mexico in 1846 and was abandoned in 1852.

Location: Eight miles east of La Junta and fifteen miles west of Las Animas on Highway 194

Site Office:

Bent's Old Fort National Historic Site
35110 Highway 194 East
La Junta, CO 81050-9523
ph.: (719) 383-5010
fax: (719) 383-5031
Web site: www.nps.gov/beol/

Bent's Old Fort was a crossroads of the West, located both on the north-south route between Platte River country and Santa Fe and the east-west path up the Arkansas River to the mountains. Its location along the Santa Fe Trail made the site a key trading center, a quasi-diplomatic mission, and later a military outpost for the Mexican War. As a trading establishment, the fort served fur trappers, traders, and caravans of frontiersmen bound for the Southwest; Mexicans who controlled the area south of the Arkansas; and various and often war-

Comet Hale-Bopp over Bent's Old Fort. (AP/Wide World Photos)

ring Indian tribes. With this mélange of interests, business partners Charles and William Bent and Ceran St. Vrain assumed an important diplomatic role, trying to establish and maintain a precarious peace among Indians, Mexicans, and Americans to further the fortunes of the trading post. In its military capacity, the fort served U.S. dragoon expeditions and topographical surveys, and became the advanced guard for the American conquest and settlement of the Southwest.

The Santa Fe Trail

Bent's Old Fort was built by the brothers Charles and William Bent and Ceran St. Vrain, who were business partners in the Indian and Santa Fe trade. In the 1820's and early 1830's, various competing companies with headquarters in St. Louis were staking claims to the profitable fur trade up the Missouri River and in the Rocky Mountain region. The ruinous competition and violent trade wars along the Missouri compelled Charles and William Bent to move southward in search of more lucrative areas. On the borderland of Mexico, they found a vast and as yet unexploited territory for the Indian and Santa Fe trade. American traders for

years had tried vainly to market manufactured goods in New Mexico, where foreign trade was prohibited under Spanish rule. With the declaration of Mexican independence in 1821, however, merchants soon established a vibrant trade with New Mexico, reaping handsome profits and drawing new venturers into the market. By 1824, the Santa Fe trade was flourishing, creating a well-worn trading route along the Arkansas River.

Traders traveled by one of two routes to Santa Fe, both of which started at Independence, Missouri, the major outfitting center for trader caravans on the Santa Fe Trail. From Independence, the trail crossed the Kansas plains to the Cimarron Crossing on the Arkansas River, where it forked into southern and mountain routes. Most used the southern route to the Cimarron Cutoff. After 1845, the preferred route for wagons was the mountain branch, which proceeded up the Arkansas River beyond the Purgatory River in Colorado and continued in a southwesterly direction across the mountains at Raton Pass. The mountain branch was longer but safer from Indian attack, and was better watered and pastured as well. The two routes joined near present-day Waltrous, New Mexico, and then ran south and west to Santa Fe. A side route led to Taos. The location on the mountain branch put Bent's Fort within easy reach of the southern plains Indians and the annual trading expeditions between Santa Fe and St. Louis.

Bent, St. Vrain and Company

In 1831, the Bent brothers with Ceran St. Vrain formed their mercantile firm, Bent, St. Vrain and Company, which became the largest trading enterprise in the Southwest, with stores in Taos and Santa Fe. Born of a prominent St. Louis family, the Bent brothers grew up in the great commercial center of the western United States. The river ports of St. Louis handled goods from all over the East and sent them toward the headwaters of the Missouri and Mississippi across the West, down to New Orleans, and to Mexico. It was also the outfitting center for government explorers and soldiers, hunters, trappers, naturalists, and traders. Charles, the elder son, became enamored of the expanding fur trade as a young man, joining the Missouri Fur Company in 1822 and becoming a partner in the firm Pilcher and Company in 1824. During this time, William Bent went to work for his brother in the Missouri fur trade. Like the Bent brothers, St. Vrain was also from St. Louis and entered the Missouri fur trade, but he quickly developed a special interest in the New Mexican market, organizing trading caravans and outfitting hunters and trappers in Taos and Santa Fe. The partners met either while growing up in St. Louis or while engaging in the burgeoning Missouri River trade. Experienced in both the Indian and New Mexican trade, the partners were ideally suited to launch their commercial enterprise. Upon the firm's founding, Charles Bent assumed responsibility for securing credit for the company in St. Louis and procuring and transporting goods to New Mexico, where St. Vrain marketed the merchandise. Not long after the partners arrived in the Arkansas Valley in the late 1820's, however, other traders and trappers began penetrating the area, posing a threat to the company's new-found business. To fend off competitors, Charles Bent conceived the idea of building a major trading post comparable to the big forts along the Missouri River.

On a scouting trip, the Bent brothers are said to have discussed the idea of building a trading fort with Yellow Wolf, chief of the Cheyenne of the Hairy Rope Clan, who advised that the fort be built in the Big Timbers, a stretch of cottonwoods twenty-five miles downstream from the mouth of the Purgatory River. Here there were shelter, grass for horses, plenty of firewood, and numerous buffalo, and it was a common camping site for the Cheyenne. In the end, the partners selected a location on the north side of the Arkansas (in American territory), about twelve miles upstream from the Purgatory. In contrast to the Big Timbers, the site was in harsh terrain with few trees or grass, but it was still in buffalo country. It was also located on the mountain branch of the Santa Fe Trail, and that allowed them to transport supplies and goods from the East to Mexican territory. Moreover, it was in border territory claimed by the Cheyenne, prairie Apache, Arapaho, Comanche, Ute, and Kiowa, and at times roamed by nomadic tribes of the Shoshone, Crow, Gros Ventre, and Pawnee. In 1826 the partners built a picket fort at the site, both for protection and as a headquarters from which to plan their operations. Soon afterward, they began building Bent's Fort.

Construction of the Fort

In Taos, William Bent and St. Vrain hired Mexican laborers to help build the post. William Bent undertook responsibility for supervising construction, which was completed sometime in 1833 or 1834. With the exception of a few second story rooms added to the fort's southern and western walls in later years, the post's essential features had been planned from the beginning. The massive adobe fort stood as the most imposing structure for nearly two thousand miles from the Mississippi to the Pacific, with the possible exceptions of the American Fur Company's Fort Pierre and Fort Union far to the north. Since William Bent supervised the post's construction, it was named "Fort William," but it later came to be called Bent's Fort among most trappers and traders who frequented the station.

When completed, the fort stood as a massive trapezoidal structure formed of adobe, or sundried brick. The tunnel-like main entry was secured by iron-sheathed outer gates and was large enough to admit freight wagons. Above the entryway rose a watchtower encompassing a swinging telescope. Defense towers stood at the northern and southeastern corners of the trapezoid, each equipped with field pieces and musketry. In case of attack, this arrangement allowed defenders to fire down along all four walls. The main entrance opened up onto the main plaza, measuring about eighty by one hundred feet, surrounded by trading rooms, living quarters, kitchen, pantry, cook's quarters, dining hall, wash house, warehouses, blacksmith and carpenter shops, and a council room where Indians and others could assemble for talks. In the center of the plaza was a large fur press for processing buffalo hides. Beyond the plaza stood an extensive corral, its walls only six to eight feet high, but along the coping grew cacti to keep raiders from scaling them. The second story consisted of another row of living quarters, perhaps added as the business and retinue grew, and a billiard room.

The Fur Trade

By the fall of 1833, the Bents and St. Vrain were ready to start business. Charles Bent returned east to apply for a U.S. government trading license, which was granted on December 18, 1833. The move came at a fortuitous time, coinciding with a precipitous drop in the market for beaver pelts. In 1832, John Jacob Astor, owner of the giant American Fur Company, noticed silk hats on British men and foresaw the end to the lucrative trade in beaver felt. Prices for beaver dropped from $6.00 a pound to $3.50, signaling a dying trade that was soon replaced by a booming market for buffalo robes.

The Bents and St. Vrain had adeptly positioned themselves to exploit the new market. Their license granted them trading rights with Indian tribes far up into Wyoming. Yet, only a year after it had opened for business, Bent's Fort faced an immediate threat from William Sublette's and Robert Campbell's new trading post on Wyoming's Laramie River, near the junction of the North Platte River. Fort Laramie became more imposing when the American Fur Company assumed ownership in 1836, rebuilt the post a mile upstream, and considerably expanded its trading operations. Concerned over destructive competition, the two firms made a cartel agreement in 1838 that carved up the West into two large trading domains. Bent, St. Vrain and Company guaranteed that it would not encroach on American Fur Company territory above the North Platte River; in return, the American Fur Company ceded the South Platte River to the Bents and St. Vrain. Despite occasional dis-

putes in the beginning, relations between the trading empires soon improved, and they began entering into joint business ventures. The Bents and St. Vrain also fended off smaller rivals seeking a toehold in the profitable Indian trade by establishing in 1837 a branch post, called Fort St. Vrain, on the South Platte. With the cartel agreement and the new trading post, the company expanded its extraordinary trading nexus and ensured its regional ascendancy.

During the winter trading season, expeditions ventured to Indian villages to exchange merchandise for buffalo hides. Traveling in groups of twos or threes, the traders brought an assortment of goods, including blankets, guns and ammunition, colored beads, brass wire, butcher knives, axes, and iron for making arrow heads. Coffee and sugar were used mainly as goodwill gifts. In the summer, the Indians often brought their furs to the fort as well as horses and mules to trade. The trade prospered so that by the early 1840's, the company's monopoly extended far up the South Platte. The firm employed over a hundred men from a variety of backgrounds—French, Mexicans, Spanish, Americans, and Indians. Many of those employed at Bent's Fort were trappers looking for work after the precipitous decline in the beaver trade, including Dick Wooten, Bill Mitchell, Bill New, Old Bill Williams, and Kit Carson. These men were employed intermittently as traders with the Indians and mainly as buffalo hunters helping to supply meat for the fort's large staff.

Relations with Local Tribes

Although the Bents and St. Vrain had established trading hegemony over a vast domain, the company's existence depended upon friendly relations with the Indians. Warfare was bad for business and the company operated with skill and subtlety to maintain a precarious peace among their client tribes. The Bents were the most adroit Indian negotiators in the history of the mountain trade and maintained unusual standards of honesty and equanimity in their dealings with the various tribes. They monopolized business with the southern Cheyenne and nearly did so with the Arapaho as well. The southern Cheyenne were the most important of the neighboring tribes because Bent's Fort stood amid their hunting grounds. In 1837, William Bent, the partner who dealt most directly with the Indians, cemented his alliance with the Cheyenne by marrying Owl Woman, daughter of Gray Thunder, a powerful tribal shaman.

Aside from their own subtle diplomacy with the Indians, the company offered their fort as a de facto government post for treaty making by the U.S. Army. In 1835, the army arranged a general peace among the tribes near Bent's Fort to end Indian forays against the Santa Fe Trail. Under Colonel Henry Dodge's command, an army delegation met with leaders of several tribes, but the truce proved short-lived. Throughout the late 1830's, the Cheyenne and Comanche waged bitter warfare against one another; in 1840 they finally made peace, three miles below Bent's Fort. As part of the peace ceremony they exchanged gifts purchased from William Bent. With the end of hostilities, William Bent was able to open up a cautious trade with the Comanche. In April, 1846, the government located the Upper Platte and Arkansas Agency at Bent's Fort to oversee the tribes along the foothills of the Rockies, a move that signaled the passing of an era of relative tranquility with the Indians. Prior to this point, the government had exercised little interest in the southern plains Indians. The growing government presence and the Mexican War, however, presaged more difficult times ahead for the company's Indian relations.

The Mexican-American War
Bent's Fort was soon transformed into an advance military outpost for the U.S. conquest of the Southwest. As the post began launching military mapping and exploring parties, New Mexican officials viewed it as an ominous threat. The successful Texan rebellion against Mexico and the extension of diplomatic recognition of the republic by the United States exacerbated already mounting tensions between the two countries. When the United States annexed Texas in 1845, Mexico viewed it as an act of war, casting Bent's Fort in the role of a strategic military supply depot and recruiting post. The Mexicans' fears proved justified; the fort became a major staging point for the invading U.S. Army of the West. In July, 1846, General Stephen Watts Kearny and an army of 1,650 dragoons and Missouri volunteers rested and resupplied at Bent's Fort before marching unopposed into Santa Fe. With the steady flow of soldiers bound for the Mexican War, Bent's Fort became a crowded depot, its yards filled with army wagon trains, teamsters, cavalry, and mounted infantry.

The Mexican-American War precipitated dramatic changes that ended the company's trading empire. The massive influx of government soldiers and emigrant wagon trains produced simmering resentment among the Indians, and in 1847 open hostilities erupted. With the frequent traffic along the Santa Fe Trail buffalo herds were slaughtered or driven away from common grazing grounds, and the sparse grasslands and cottonwoods that the Indians needed for fuel, shelter, shade, and bark for winter forage were destroyed. Bent, St. Vrain and Company, which for fifteen years had maintained a fragile peace with the Indians of the southern plains, now found itself caught between the pressures of Indian hostility and relentless U.S. expansionism. The U.S. preoccupation with the Mexican War left trading caravans on the Santa Fe Trail ill-guarded and vulnerable to Indian attack. During the summer of 1847, the Comanche, Kiowa, and Pawnee killed 47 Americans, destroyed 330 wagons, and made off with 6,500 animals.

Destruction of the Old Fort
The Mexican-American War and Indian hostilities all but destroyed the once profitable Indian and Santa Fe trade. Charles Bent, who had been appointed New Mexico's first territorial governor, was brutally murdered in an uprising in Taos. St. Vrain sold his interest in the firm to William Bent and departed for New Mexico. In 1849, the last vestiges of the once robust Indian trade ended with the outbreak among the Indians of cholera, most likely brought by emigrants. Embittered over his inability to sell the post to the government at a price he deemed fair, and with the business near collapse, William Bent set fire to it in 1852, leaving the fort in ruins.

Following the post's destruction, William Bent moved his operations thirty-eight miles east to the Big Timbers on the Arkansas River and built a new stone trading fort, known as Bent's New Fort. In 1860, the U.S. Army agreed to lease the post for sixty-five dollars a month but later refused to honor the agreement on the grounds that Bent held no title to the land. The army eventually built its own post downhill from Bent's New Fort on the Arkansas. The post was named Fort Wise, after the governor of Virginia, Henry A. Wise.

The original post, now known as Bent's Old Fort, remained unused until 1861, when the Barlow and Sanderson Stage Line operating between Kansas City and Santa Fe used it as a home station. The post served as general headquarters for agents, conductors, and drivers, accommodated overnight passengers, and maintained a general repair shop. When railroads replaced the stagecoach, the remaining buildings were used as cattle corrals by ranchers. The historic post gradually disintegrated until February 26, 1926, when the grounds and remains were turned over to the La Junta Chapter of the Daughters of the American Revolution (DAR). Under the auspices of the DAR, the effort was begun to preserve and rebuild the fort. In June, 1954, the Colorado State Historical Society assumed responsibility for Bent's Old Fort and subsequently turned it over to the National Park Service on June 3, 1960. By the summer of 1976, the National Park Service had completed the reconstruction of the historic fort. Today, Bent's Old Fort resembles the post as it stood during its heyday in the mid-1840's.   —*Bruce P. Montgomery*

For Further Information:

Brown, William E. *The Santa Fe Trail.* St. Louis: Patrice Press, 1982. A good source of information.

Colorado Magazine, Fall, 1977. This issue is entirely devoted to articles on various historical aspects of Bent's Old Fort. The issue contains five articles, including "Life in an Adobe Castle, 1833-1849" by Enid Thompson; "From Trading Post to Melted Adobe, 1849-1920" by Louisa Ward Arps; "From Ruin to Reconstruction, 1920-1976" by Merrill J. Mattes; and "Furnishing a Frontier Outpost" by Sarah M. Olson. The issue also contains a short section of biographical notes.

Comer, Douglas C. *Ritual Ground: Bent's Old Fort, World Formation, and the Annexation of the Southwest.* Berkeley: University of California Press, 1996. Addresses the history of Bent's Old Fort and frontier and pioneer life in Colorado. Includes illustrations and maps.

DeVoto, Bernard. *Across the Wide Missouri* Boston: Houghton Mifflin, 1947.

_____. *Bent's Old Fort: The Year of Decision, 1846.* Boston: Little, Brown, 1943. These two books contain highly readable accounts of the West.

History of the Arkansas Valley, Colorado. Chicago: O. L. Baskin, 1881. An older account of this region.

Lavender, David. *Bent's Fort.* New York: Doubleday, 1954. While offensive in its treatment of Native Americans, this book is the most comprehensive source on the history of the old trading post as well as the exploits of the Bent brothers, Ceran St. Vrain, and its other inhabitants.

Leadville

Date: Established in 1878; incorporated in 1879
Relevant issues: Business and industry, western expansion
Significance: This mining town, located at an altitude of 10,188 feet, became the silver capital of America with the discovery of huge beds of silver ore in 1877. After the silver panic of 1893, the mines surrounding Leadville continued in active operation by producing diverse minerals, including gold, silver, lead, copper, zinc, magnesium, iron, bismuth, and molybdenum, with the latter serving as the backbone of the Leadville economy from the 1930's until the collapse of the global molybdenum market in 1982. Leadville has been declared a National Historic District.
Location: 103 miles southwest of Denver via U.S. Interstate 70 west to Copper Mountain, and 24 miles south on Highway 91
Site Office:
Chamber of Commerce
809 Harrison Avenue
P.O. Box 861
Leadville, CO 80461
ph.: (719) 486-3900

The history of Leadville is one of the most extraordinary in the American West. It originated with gold mining in California Gulch and rose to fame and fortune with the discovery of massive deposits of silver ore in 1877. During its heyday as the silver capital of America in the late 1870's and 1880's, Leadville won worldwide notoriety as a place of booming economic opportunity. These heady times were numbered, however, and within a decade, the once thriving mining town gradually slipped into a long, steady decline. Unlike other mining areas that became ghost towns, Leadville survived many boom-and-bust cycles because of its diverse mineralization. From the 1930's onward, the mainstay of the Leadville economy was the growing worldwide molybdenum market until it collapsed in 1982, leaving the town in severe economic straights.

A Gold Rush

With the 1859 Pikes Peak gold rush, tens of thousands set off for Colorado to strike it rich. Prospectors struck gold at Cherry Creek near Denver and made greater discoveries in the mountains at Idaho Springs, Silver Plume, Georgetown, Central City, Fairplay, Black Hawk, and Breckenridge. In the spring of 1860, five prospectors crossed Mosquito Range and began working an area later named California Gulch, drilling holes in the bottom of the stream and then panning for gold. On April 26, 1860, one of the prospectors, Abe Lee, hit pay dirt.

Leadville's silver king, H. W. Tabor. (AP/Wide World Photos)

The sizable extent of Abe Lee's discovery went unknown until, with the use of ground sluicing and diversion techniques, the prospectors dug their way to bedrock and hit gold that exceeded all expectations. News of the find spread quickly to prospectors working other streams and trails, igniting a vast gold rush to the area. By May more than one thousand prospectors crowded into the gulch to stake claims. By June the number rose to about four thousand, and by summer's end the flood tide swelled to fully ten thousand. Prospectors formed a mining district, elected officers, adopted simple bylaws, and named the mining district after California for the riches it held. Abe Lee was elected as recorder of mining claims. In the furious hunt for gold, miners scarcely took time to build themselves houses or cabins, preferring at first to live in wagons, bough huts, or tents, which blanketed the hills. The settlement went initially by the name of Boughtown, and gold dust served as the medium of exchange in the few stores that sold supplies at inflated prices. Soon a more permanent settlement of log cabins, stores, gambling houses, and dance halls emerged, which subsequently became known as Oro City.

California Gulch yielded two million dollars in 1860, and by 1862, its last good year, the region produced another one million dollars in gold. Its treasure soon gave out, and with gold no longer to be found, Oro City collapsed as prospectors moved on in search of other discoveries. By 1865, fewer than four hundred remained in the vicinity of California Gulch, and by 1867, it was virtually deserted. In the summer of 1868, however, the gulch underwent a brief recovery with the development of the Printer Boy Lode. The site had been staked in 1861, but poor management and mining methods slowed its development. Jars of gold from the Printer Boy were displayed in the national banks of Denver, Philadelphia, and New York, attracting renewed interest among eastern capitalists. The activity prompted the miners and merchants to move Oro City two and a half miles up the gulch to be close to the Printer Boy, which continued to yield gold through 1869 before it gave out. By 1870, the area was again abandoned.

Silver Reigns

Unlike the flurry of activity and publicity surrounding the Pikes Peak gold rush, Leadville's silver era was born in secrecy. The discovery of silver had already occurred in many of Colorado's gold districts. The state's first silver boomtown was Caribou, but its fame proved fleeting when in 1874 mining interests struck rich deposits of silver ore in Georgetown. By 1877, Georgetown reigned as the undisputed silver capital of Colorado, producing an annual yield worth two million dollars. Other strikes were made at Alma in Park County, and in southwestern Colorado at Ouray, Silverton, and Lake City. The huge silver strikes near Oro City eclipsed all others, however, precipitating a stampede that dwarfed the previous gold rush.

Following the Printer Boy's collapse, a few prospectors remained behind in the vicinity of California Gulch, but mining proved increasingly difficult as mud and black rock repeatedly clogged sluicing operations. In 1874, with the arrival of William Stevens and Alvinus B. Wood, the mining district would soon become the grand new silver capital of America. Stevens was a mining promoter who had visited Oro City in 1865 at the end of the first gold rush. In 1872, after inspecting mining districts in Utah, he returned to Colorado and began mining in Alma. Following his return to Oro City in the summer of 1873, Stevens concluded that with a sufficient water supply to operate hydraulic and sluicing operations, significant quantities of gold could still be taken from the gulch. As a result, Stevens purchased claims and water rights from other miners, secured financing from eastern capitalists, and formed a partnership with Alvinus B. Wood, a mining technician. Their operation used powerful pumps and high-pressure water jets to wear away stream and alluvial banks, a process that yielded gold by passing large quantities of gravel and sand through sluices. The venture proved profitable for

several years, but as others had already discovered, the heavy, dark rock and sand significantly hindered operations. After careful investigation and testing of the mysterious black rock, the partners discovered that it was in fact lead carbonate containing large amounts of silver. For more than two years, the partners concealed their discovery as they bought out claims covering the richest deposits, including numerous properties on Rock and Iron Hills, giving them a near monopoly over both areas. In the summer of 1877, other prospectors began moving in to stake claims and the word was soon out.

The silver strike ignited a new stampede to Leadville. In a matter of months, swarms of prospectors were frantically staking and recording thousands of claims, producing in the process mass confusion and numerous disputes. The many claims and counterclaims were further complicated by questionable surveying procedures. Leadville soon became a mecca for the legal profession, with the largest population of lawyers in the state. The difference between success and failure often depended on luck, misrepresentation, and timing in buying and selling mining claims.

The classic story of luck, fortune, and fame was that of Horace Austin Warner Tabor, Leadville's legendary silver king. In 1877, H. W. Tabor moved to Leadville and soon emerged as one of its leaders even before he rose to millionaire status. He assisted in organizing the town's government and was elected its first mayor in 1878. A veteran prospector and storekeeper in California Gulch, Buckskin Joe, and Oro City, Tabor harbored ambitions beyond middle-class respectability. In 1878, after grubstaking two needy prospectors, August Rische and George Hook, who discovered the fabulous Little Pittsburgh Mine on Fryer Hill, Tabor quickly amassed one of the greatest and most fleeting fortunes in American history. As his wealth grew so did his political status: He became lieutenant governor of Colorado in 1878, and in 1883, U.S. senator for a brief thirty-day stint. For several years, Tabor's mining enterprises and investments earned him ever-growing riches. He built lavish opera houses in Leadville and Denver and erected Denver's first skyscraper, the Tabor Block. In the end, however, his financial exploits led to his ruin, and he disappeared along with Leadville's grand silver age.

Tabor was not the only one to win fabulous wealth. Others included Samuel Newhouse, later an important copper baron and financier of the famous Flatiron Building in New York City; John L. Routt, later a Colorado governor; and Meyer Guggenheim, the future smelter king. Still others found wealth on Iron, Long and Derry, Carbonate, Fryer, and Breece Hills. The mines yielded about two million dollars worth of lead and silver during 1878 and more than nine million dollars the following year. Between 1879 and 1889 total production exceeded eighty-two million dollars in ore. As many arriving in Leadville soon discovered, however, the days of the lone, self-employed miner were over. Riches were now to be found in deep-rock silver mining, which required considerable expertise and capital. With the discovery of silver came the age of bankers, mining engineers, and legions of poorly paid laborers.

Growth of the Town

Founded in 1877 and incorporated in 1878, Leadville saw its population skyrocket from about fifteen hundred in 1879 to more than thirty thousand by summer's end in 1880, making it the second-largest city in Colorado, after Denver. Leadville grew fast in the fashion of other boomtowns, but unlike Central City, Georgetown, or Silverton, its sudden explosive growth was so spectacular that it gained worldwide notoriety. Despite sitting at an altitude of more than ten thousand feet on the western slope of the Mosquito Range, Leadville itself was not particularly scenic. The surrounding hills had been denuded of pine forests to make charcoal for the fourteen smelting and ore reduction plants that cast a pall over the town, itself composed of ramshackle log huts, board shanties, tents, and kennels dug into hillsides. In time, the jerry-built town yielded to more permanent brick and frame construction. Although in the beginning all the amenities of civilized life went wanting, by 1878 Leadville claimed a city council, a mayor, and a city marshal. Yet the murders, robberies, lot jumping, and vice that ran throughout Leadville's early history made it one of the toughest towns in the West. In 1878, Leadville witnessed its first murder with the barroom killing of Marshal George O'Conner.

With expanding wealth and population also came culture, society, and religion. Religious orga-

nizations, churches, and public schools were established along with fancy hotels and a nationally renowned opera house in 1879. An upscale residential area grandly called Capitol Hill was established on the north end of town for the respectable middle class. Leadville's great building boom followed the big silver strikes at the New Discovery and Little Pittsburgh Mines in 1878. In the spring of 1879, a business census showed that Leadville accommodated thirty-one restaurants, seventeen barbershops, fifty-one groceries, four banks, and one hundred twenty saloons. Also to be found were lumber businesses, a laundry, drug store, brewery, and three vigorously competing newspapers—the *Herald*, the *Democrat*, and the *Chronicle*. The telegraph came to Leadville in 1879, and in the following year, the telephone, to handle growing business transactions between mining and smelting operations. Besides mining, the lure of riches offered other paths to wealth. Real estate speculation, the provision of supplies and services, the freighting of goods to the two-mile-high city up mountain roads, and the less legitimate enterprises of prostitution and gambling all provided a steady source of income. Indeed, Leadville also claimed the dubious distinction of being home to one of the country's finest redlight districts.

Labor Disputes and Stock Prices

The thousands of laborers who worked the mines and smelters under abject conditions were mostly newly arrived immigrants from southeastern Europe—Italians, Austrians, Croats, Serbs, and Slovenes. The vast disparity in wealth between the laborers and the corporate owners, together with the perilous working conditions, made for a volatile mixture. In late May, 1880, a strike over a wage dispute at the Chrysolite Mine quickly spread to other mines on Fryer, Carbonate, Breece, and Iron Hills and throughout Lake County. For the next three weeks, as the threat of strike violence mounted, the owners hired armed guards and exercised political pressure to call in the state militia. When the state government complied and declared martial law, the strike collapsed, compelling the miners to resume work under the old wage rate.

That same year, Leadville was hit with even more devastating developments. The failure of both the Little Pittsburgh and Chrysolite Mines ended an era of easy wealth. The Little Pittsburgh, which had ushered in Leadville's heyday, went bankrupt in February, 1880, amid charges of stock manipulation, mismanagement, and overpromotion. Tabor and his two partners, U.S. senator Jerome Chaffee and financier David Moffat, held a controlling interest in the Little Pittsburgh until its seemingly inexhaustible riches began dwindling at the close of 1879. The partners maintained a facade of confidence while selling out at a huge profit, leaving eastern speculators holding stocks that plummeted in value from $65 a share to just $6 in a matter of months. The Chrysolite, too, failed, causing its stock to drop from over $40 a share to $4. By 1881, Leadville's silver era was in slow decline as the rich ore began to run out. Several other large mines almost failed in early 1881.

Yet Leadville continued to prosper well into the decade as new mines opened, making up for the lag in production. H. W. Tabor opened his Tabor Grand Hotel, which drew immediate praise as one of the finest hotels in the West. The opening followed a national scandal over Tabor's leaving his wife, Augusta, for a divorcée from Central City named Elizabeth McCourt Doe (or, as she was soon dubbed "Baby Doe"). The Rio Grande Railway defeated two rivals, the Sante Fe and the Denver and South Park, for the right to service Leadville's transportation needs. As a result, on July 22, 1880, the Rio Grande's first train arrived in Leadville carrying a famous passenger, Ulysses S. Grant.

Following 1885, Leadville's silver mines produced approximately five million ounces annually, about half that of their peak year in 1880. In a harbinger of harder times to come, in 1890 silver prices fell from $1.16 to $1.00 per ounce. In a campaign to boost falling silver prices, Congress in 1890 passed the Sherman Silver Purchase Act, obligating the federal government to buy 4.5 million ounces of silver each month, but in 1893 the act was repealed, which contributed significantly to a nationwide silver panic that closed banks across the country. The repeal of the act dealt the final blow to Leadville's glittering prosperity, starting it down a long, steady road of decline. Between 1890 and 1893, the number of operating mines plunged from about one hundred to only twenty, closing smelters and throwing many laborers out of work. To prolong their employment, the miners agreed to a fifty-cent pay cut, which lowered their daily wage to a mere $2.50. Although the silver crisis forced other mining camps to close, Leadville's remaining mining operations underwent a recovery, increasing production levels significantly despite silver prices averaging sixty-three cents per ounce. The year 1895 almost matched that of 1880 in the extraction of ore. The mines produced nearly nine million ounces, but most of this production stemmed from just one mine, the Little Johnny, part of the Ibex Properties that became Leadville's leading gold and silver producer.

In the summer of 1896, sixteen years after the 1880 strike, the daily wages of miners still stood at only between $2.50 and $3.00. The mine owners remained as adamant as ever against the demands of labor and refused to recognize the miners' union, the Cloud City Miners Union. On June 19, 1896, Leadville's great strike erupted, which would adversely affect labor-management relations in the hard rock mines for decades. The owners quickly responded with a lockout, and in retaliation, miners reacted with violence, arson, even murder. Eventually, the state militia restored order with the imposition of martial law. The owners then hired scab labor to work the mines under armed guard, maintaining the lockout for a full nine months before breaking the strike in the spring of 1897.

With the strike's end another chapter in Leadville's history came to a close. The long lockout wreaked considerable damage on many mining operations—shafts flooded, timbers rotted, mine workings collapsed, and parts of others became silted in. As the price of silver continued to fall, mining faltered, layoffs became common, and the miners harbored bitter resentment over the strike's loss and their paltry wages. At the turn of the century, Leadville's gilded age was past. Some of the silver barons who rose to dizzying heights of wealth had lost everything in the 1893 silver crash, and none felt the sting of misfortune more than Tabor. Tabor's vast wealth evaporated with poor investments and the silver panic, and he died in poverty in Denver in 1899. His widow, Baby Doe, returned to Leadville where she spent her remaining years in poverty in a shack behind the Matchless Mine, where she was found frozen to death in March, 1937. In many ways, the fate of these two paralleled that of Leadville. The surrounding hills lay scarred and barren, mines were abandoned, and the once-frenetic town in the days of the silver rush was now being deserted. By 1900 Leadville's population stood at only twelve thousand, a precipitous drop from the more than thirty thousand during its heyday in 1880.

Leadville survived the economically depressed times of the early 1900's through its diversified mineralization; in 1905, its mines produced eleven million dollars. The district's most profitable metal was now zinc, accounting for 40 percent of total production. Gold amounted to 10 percent of production; copper, 6 percent; silver and lead, 22 percent; and iron and magnesium represented a tiny fraction of the total value. By 1910, Leadville was nothing more than an average mining town with a population of only seven thousand. It remained stagnant until the 1930's, when the molybdenum mines at nearby Climax were opened, beginning a new era in Leadville history.

The Discovery of Molybdenum

In 1879, the prospector Charles Senter discovered deposits of molybdenum near Leadville while mining his Bartlett Mountain claims. First identified as an element by Swedish chemist Carl Sheele in 1779, the mineral existed as a curiosity for more than a century before the French discovered that it could be used to create an extremely hard steel alloy. When the German army proved the superiority of molybdenum-steel alloys during World War I, a frantic rush ensued to gain control of Bartlett Mountain, the world's largest known deposit of molybdenite. The American Metals Company (AMCO), the Molybdenum Products Company, and interests represented by Otis Archie King battled fiercely for sole control of the deposits, with AMCO winning the contest. AMCO established the Climax Molybdenum Company in 1916 and briefly began full-scale production in 1918 to supply the war effort.

Following the war, a national labor shortage drew a large Mexican American population to Leadville, where they worked in the smelters and the Climax mines and settled on the south side of town. The immediate postwar years saw little demand for molybdenum, however, and the Climax mines closed down. They would briefly open and then close again repeatedly until the 1930's. In 1928, the Climax Molybdenum Company built a company town to help alleviate chronic labor problems and the highest turnover rate in American industry, and in 1930, the molybdenum mines produced about 5 percent of Colorado's total ore production. During the years of the Great Depression, Leadville endured hardship with the rest of the nation. With only twenty mines remaining in operation, excluding Climax, Leadville's population fell to just 3,400. On nearby Freemont Pass, however, the Climax Molybdenum Company prospered throughout the 1930's with expanding molybdenum markets in domestic and foreign industry. Once a mere curiosity, the mineral and its compounds were now used to produce alloy steels, stainless steels, cast irons, paints, lubricants, agricultural fertilizers, and chemicals. One of the largest markets for molybdenum was Germany's Weimar Republic, soon replaced by the Third Reich.

By the late 1930's, Leadville awoke from its economic slump as increased demand caused prices for silver, copper, and zinc to soar to historic highs. In 1939, the number of Leadville mines reached forty-nine, which doubled with the coming of the war. With World War II, the federal government declared molybdenum a strategic metal and the Climax mines operated at full capacity. The metals and mining boom continued until about 1953, when production dramatically declined, leaving Climax as the mainstay of Leadville's economy. Throughout the 1970's, the Leadville mines rode a booming molybdenum market and soaring gold and silver prices, which surged to record highs in January, 1980. In just three months, however, prices plummeted and in 1982 the global molybdenum market collapsed, forcing the Climax facilities to close down operations for the first time in more than fifty years. With the closing of Climax, Leadville saw 85 percent of its tax base and 3,500 jobs vanish, and its population fall from 8,500 to just 3,000. As of 1988, about two hundred miners were still employed at smaller opertions, producing gold, pyrite, silver, lead, and zinc; seven hundred were unemployed, and the overwhelming portion of the workforce—about 1,800 people—worked in the nearby ski resort towns of Vail and Copper Mountain in the service industry.

Leadville Today

Leadville may never again recover its prosperous mining economy. Climax no longer dominates the world molybdenum market; it faces stiff competition from newly developed domestic and foreign mining interests. Although Leadville has now become a tourist attraction, it still contains vast quantities of unmined gold, silver, zinc, and lead. The United States Department of Energy declared California Gulch a Federal Superfund clean-up site due to the acidic, metallic water running from a tunnel in the Arkansas River. Many of Leadville's historic buildings from the early boom years remain for visitors to see, including the famed Tabor Opera House, Augusta Tabor's house, and Baby Doe's Matchless Cabin.   —*Bruce P. Montgomery*

For Further Information:

Blair, Edward. *Leadville: Colorado's Magic City*. Boulder, Colo.: Pruett, 1980.

Buys, Christian J. *Historic Leadville in Rare Photographs and Drawings*. Ouray, Colo.: Western Reflections, 1997.

Griswold, Don, and Jean Griswold. *The Carbonate Camp Called Leadville*. Denver: University of Denver Press, 1951. Focuses on the boom years from 1878 to 1880.

Larsh, Ed B., and Robert Nichols. *Leadville USA*. Boulder, Colo.: Johnson Books, 1993.

Ubbelohde, Carl, Maxine Benson, and Duane A. Smith. *A Colorado Reader*. 2d ed. Boulder, Colo.: Pruett, 1982.

Voynick, Stephen M. *Leadville: A Miner's Epic*. Missoula, Mont.: Mountain Press, 1984. A readable history of Leadville covering the years up to the 1980's.

Mesa Verde

Date: Established as a National Park on June 29, 1906; named a World Heritage Site on September 6, 1978

Relevant issues: American Indian history

Significance: The first area in the United States to be declared a national treasure for the preservation of the works of humanity: the ruins of an ancient people referred to as Anasazi (from the Navajo, meaning "ancient ones"). Evidence of a civilization growing in complexity in its tool making, agriculture, and architecture is to be found at numerous sites in Mesa Verde—however, for a complete picture of the Anasazi, a survey of the entire Four Corners region is necessary.

Location: In the high plateau or mesa country of southwestern Colorado, in the Four Corners area where Colorado, Utah, Arizona, and New Mexico meet; the park entrance is midway between Cortez on the west and Mancos on the east on U.S. 160

Site Office:

Mesa Verde National Park
P.O. Box 8
Mesa Verde, CO 81330
ph.: (970) 529-4465
Web site: www.nps.gov/meve/

The story of Mesa Verde is the story of the Anasazi, an ancient people who began to populate the area of southwestern United States at about 42 C.E. and left the area by 1300, leaving no written record of their civilization. What is left are the artifacts of an agrarian culture, which built unique settlement facilities, including ceremonial buildings; their greatest legacy is the mystery of how they came there, what caused them to move to dwellings under cliffs in the 1200's, and where they went after abandoning their settlements in the late thirteenth century.

The story of the Anasazi, as pieced together by amateur and professional archaeologists, is not only the story of the Mesa Verde. One view holds that the Anasazi cannot be understood without the context of the entire northern San Juan River region; another stresses the coevolution of Anasazi with the neighboring civilizations of Mongollon and Hohokam. Each of these tribes had descended from the nomadic people of the Desert Culture Archaic. Because of the stature of the Mesa Verde excavation sites among the archaeological community, much of the research has been directed to the Mesa Verde as a locus of these historic peoples' activity.

Early Exploration

When, in 1765, Juan Maria Antonio Rivera explored what is now Colorado in his search for silver, he wrote in his diary that ruins from an ancient culture could be seen along several of the rivers. In 1776 Silvestre Vélez de Escalante and Antanasio Dominguez led an expedition through southwestern Colorado and noted several ancient sites, one of which, along the Dolores River, was eventually named for Escalante. Despite these citations, the

Cliff Palace, Mesa Verde National Park. (PhotoDisc)

ruins remained unexamined for another century. Then in the 1870's, the United States federal government, having purchased land from the Ute Indians, sent an expedition under the supervision of F. V. Hayden to explore the Four Corners area. In 1874 William Jackson, a photographer with the Hayden Survey, photographed and named Two Story House in Mancos Canyon, at the south end of Moccasin Mesa.

The Wetherills, a family of cattle ranchers who lived near Mancos, began to explore the ruins of the cliff-dwelling Anasazi, along and under the walls of the mesas. In 1888 Richard Wetherill and his brother-in-law Charles Mason discovered huge cliff dwellings on Chapin Mesa, naming the spectacular ruins there Cliff Palace. Baron Gustaf Nordenskiöld, a twenty-two-year-old scholar visiting from Sweden, came to the Wetherills' Alamo Ranch, seeking guides to the ruins, in 1891. During that summer he recorded twenty-two cliff dwellings and made several excavations, the artifacts of which he took back with him to Europe. His collection is now part of the Finland National Museum. In 1906, the area was proclaimed a National Park in conjunction with the passage of the Antiquities Act. This led to the end of excavation by the Wetherills and the beginning of serious archaeological explorations.

Archaeological Studies

In 1927, Alfred Vincent Kidder, an archaeologist specializing in pueblo culture, invited colleagues to Pecos Pueblo near Santa Fe, New Mexico, in order to form a synthesis of the various data being collected in the region and to formulate a chronologically based development scheme for the prehistoric cultures. Known as the Pecos scheme, it is still used today, with several alterations. The scheme can represent a time continuum or generalized stages of development.

The period of prehistory of the Anasazi falls within the continent-wide Formative Age. The lifestyle of the Anasazi was communal, sedentary, and agrarian, similar to that of groups living in the Mississippi Valley at about the same time. Kidder's Pecos classification distinguishes eight periods, Basketmaker I-III and Pueblo I-V, with Pueblo III being the stage just before the Anasazi abandoned their dwellings and emigrated from the area.

Basketmaskers

When he drew up the Pecos classification, Kidder assumed that a stage of development earlier than those known would be discovered. It became apparent later that the first group to settle Mesa Verde came there during the Basketmaker II period, and the Basketmaker I category is now called either Archaic or Pre-Basketmaker.

Basketmaker II remains are scarce. Only four sites have been excavated in Colorado, all outside Mesa Verde. Basketmaker II builders constructed shallow, round houses, with central heating pits, and slab-lined storage chambers. There is evidence that residents made periodic excursions for hunting, gathering, and perhaps trade. Burials took place in abandoned storage chambers, in cave crevices, beneath house floors, or in middens. The burial custom of folding arms and legs against the body, clothing and adorning the corpse, and interning utensils in the grave continued nearly unaltered throughout the life of the culture. Evidence shows that crude attempts at pottery were made, but the people of the period primarily utilized baskets for containers. Many of the artifacts associated with Basketmaker II persist though all five stages of Anasazi prehistory. They include atlatls (throwing spears), bone awls, bone hide scrapers, drills, and gaming pieces.

Very few sites exist to represent the period of transition from Basketmaker II to Basketmaker III. Basketmaker III began about 450. Current thought holds that most Basketmaker III people resided in small villages of between three and eight pithouses. Early pithouses were shallow structures supported by four main vertical posts. Later pithouses were deeper, with benches and crawl spaces. Shapes of the pithouses varied from circular to square with round corners; some had ventilation tunnels with vertical shafts; some had ladders giving access to a smokehole in the roof.

The Basketmakers were so called because of the skill of their weaving and because they did not use pottery until much later in their development. Decorated baskets of many shapes and sizes were used for carrying water, storing grain, and for cooking—baskets lined with pitch held water into which heated stones were placed. The craft declined after the introduction of pottery. Quality ceramics first appeared during Basketmaker III. These were generally gray and undecorated; however, the Basket-makers decorated some pottery by using a black mineral or vegetable dye on a white surface.

Pueblo Periods

In the transition between Basketmaker III and the Pueblo ages, a distinctive structure appeared. These were unusually large pithouses, which were perhaps the forerunner of kivas, ceremonial structures that became widespread throughout the Pueblo II and Pueblo III stages. Pueblo I began around 750.

Pueblo I residential structures were larger than those of the earlier sites and were laid out in a distinctive pattern. Villages consisted of arcing rows of apartment-like dwellings with smaller storage rooms behind. These dwellings flanked the north and west sides of rows of deep pit structures. The above-ground apartments had jacal—post and adobe—walls, many with upright stone slabs lining the interiors. In late Pueblo I, some crude stone masonry appeared. While most Pueblo I people lived in this type of settlement, with a dozen or more dwelling units, isolated ruins of between one and three units suggest there were a few rural hamlets. Limited activity sites and temporary camps indicate excursions away from home bases, as in Basketmaker periods. Pottery decoration, in the use of neck bands and greater decorative symmetry of painted surfaces, shows a great deal of experimentation and contact with southern peoples.

Masonry house construction marked the age of Pueblo II, especially in Mesa Verde, although jacal construction continued into early Pueblo II elsewhere. Pueblo II began about 900. The persistence of jacal construction is noted well into the eleventh century. Stone walls became more frequently used in the late tenth and early eleventh centuries.

Kivas, ceremonial and social centers of Pueblo culture, came into full use in Pueblo II, though the archaeological record is obscured by Pueblo III renovations. Kivas were constructed of earthen walls in a circular form with roof support posts. Generally, each kiva had a ventilation shaft, a southern recess used for an altar, a firepit with an associated deflector, benches, wall niches, and pilasters. Each had a sipapu, which was a hole in the floor symbolizing the entranceway into the spirit world. Kivas were located south of rectangular or curved room block arrangements in the "plaza" area of residential settlements.

Some students of the Anasazi have characterized each settlement as a self-contained community. Others, however, have detected clusters of such settlements and have suggested that there was extensive interaction between the clusters.

The typical Anasazi day took place in the open courtyards in front of the room blocks. Women worked on pottery; men made tools out of stone and bone. Fires built in the summers were used for cooking. In the cold, damp winters, fires were used for heat as well; smoke-blackened walls bear evidence. In the summer adults wore loin cloths and sandals; in the winter, they covered themselves with hides and with blankets woven of turkey feathers and robes made of rabbit fur. The Anasazi domesticated dogs and turkeys.

Pueblo III, often called the highest stage of Anasazi civilization, often obstructs or overlaps with the developments of the Pueblo II people. It began about 1100. The masonry from this period reflects the highest degree of artisanship. Residence units at this time became multistoried complexes. On the Mesa Verde, Pueblo III is known for the massive structures built beneath cliff overhangs, giving rise to the name "cliff-dwellers" for the inhabitants. It is speculated that climactic conditions played a role in the move from pueblos atop the mesa to cliff dwellings.

The kiva remained an important part of the pueblo unit. Circular towers were being built by early Pueblo III architects, often associated with kivas via connecting tunnels. In some instances, towers and kivas stood apart from residential structures. Sometimes towers were located near springs or man-made reservoirs, which were the centers of Pueblo III settlements.

Large ceremonial structures or "great kivas" were a feature of many of the larger settlements. On mesa tops, they were circular, while under the cliff overhangs they were shaped more rectangularly. Concentric wall structures of a circular or D-shaped design were also a feature of many large settlements. Buildings of the Pueblo III era tended to be built of flat-faced stone blocks. Stones were pecked and ground flat; such a consideration for the appearance of wall facings is a clear marker of Pueblo III architecture.

The Anasazi farmed the land atop the mesa.

Cliff-dwelling farmers had to climb the dangerous cliff walls to get to their crops. Most crops depended on rainfall; the Anasazi built small dams and large reservoirs to guarantee the survival of their crops.

Pueblo III Anasazi crafted a wide variety of ceramics. Corrugated ware was made by coiling clay into a form resembling a basket and indenting portions of the clay. Other pottery styles include black-on-white decoration of mugs, ladles, bowls, and pots.

Why the Anasazi completely abandoned the Four Corners region remains a mystery. Beginning about 1200, building activity decreased among the Mesa Verde Anasazi. Long House was the last construction to have taken place, about 1280. Possible explanations include the persistence of a great drought, a growing scarcity of resources, various socioeconomic and political developments, and overpopulation. Depopulation nevertheless occurred at a slow rate, but by 1300 the Anasazi were gone. Emigrés most likely settled in New Mexico, where they would have assimilated into the tribes already living there. The Pueblo Indians are believed to be Anasazi descendants.

Visiting the Site

Mesa Verde National Park occupies 50,036 acres of southwest Colorado. Mesa Verde runs fifteen miles long and two thousand feet above the valley to the north. The plateau is bounded by mountains to the east and desert to the west. Canyons are a feature of its southern end. Vegetation includes ponderosa pine forests and pinion and juniper forestations, whose appearance depends largely on elevation (and thus precipitation).

The ruins, however, are the most compelling feature of Mesa Verde. Some recent excavations may reflect Basketmaker II activity. Basketmaker III sites are located at Twin Trees, Chapin Mesa, and Wetherill Mesa. Pueblo I sites may be found at Chapin Mesa, Wetherill Mesa, and Morefield Canyon. The Mummylake settlement on Chapin Mesa is a Pueblo II site. Pueblo III sites, such as Cliff Palace and Balcony House, are by far the best known ruins of Anasazi culture. —*Gregory J. Ledger*

For Further Information:

Berry, Michael. *Time, Space, and Transition in Anasazi Prehistory.* Salt Lake City: University of

Utah Press, 1982. A doctoral work that disputes the received wisdom and insists that discontinuity (sudden, en masse shifts of behavior relating to climactic conditions) describes Anasazi history better than does the concept of developmental stages.

Cassells, E. Steve. *The Archaeology of Colorado.* Rev. ed. Boulder, Colo.: Johnson Books, 1997. A carefully researched yet accessible document covering not only the prehistory of Colorado, but also the history of archaeology in Colorado. Its many illustrations make clear what is too often unclear in the discourse on Anasazi culture.

Cordell, Linda S., and George J. Gummerman, eds. *Dynamics of Southwest Prehistory.* Washington, D.C.: Smithsonian Institution Press, 1989. A collection of essays by eleven of the most established experts in specific areas of the Southwest. Arthur Rohn's essay contains extensive information on Mesa Verde and the Anasazi.

Wenger, Gilbert R. *The Story of Mesa Verde National Park.* Mesa Verde National Park, Colo.: Mesa Verde Museum Association, 1999. Examines the history of the park and surrounding area and pueblo culture.

Pikes Peak

Date: First American exploration in 1806
Relevant issues: Business and industry, cultural history, western expansion
Significance: The Pikes Peak region contains a modern metropolis that was once a historic tourist destination, historic landmarks and districts, an old mining region, several modern tourist attractions, and a National Monument.
Location: In south-central Colorado, along the front range of mountains
Site Offices:

Pikes Peak, America's Mountain
P.O. Box 1575, Mail Code 060
Colorado Springs, CO 80901-1575
ph.: (719) 385-7325
fax: (719) 684-0942
Web site: www.pikes-peak.com

Colorado Springs Convention and Visitors Bureau

104 South Cascade Avenue
Colorado Springs, CO 80903
ph.: (719) 635-7506
Web site: www.coloradosprings-travel.com

Pikes Peak is a sprawling mountain 14,100 feet high just west of where the Colorado Rocky Mountains dramatically rise above Colorado's eastern plains. It does not have a dramatic profile. It has a broad peak above the timberline that has a squat, dome-shaped summit. It is named after Lieutenant Zebulon Pike, who tried but failed to scale the peak in 1806. Pike had been sent out to look for the boundaries of the Louisiana Purchase, which had been acquired from France in 1803. His expedition was similar to that of Meriwether Lewis and William Clark.

He came to what was a sacred area for Native Americans noted for a pass from the mountains to the plains, later called Ute Pass; a sacrosanct camping ground, later called the Garden of the Gods; and a number of healing springs, later the basis of the city of Manitou Springs. To the west, the Ute people lived in the mountains, and to the east, the allied Comanches and Arapahoe hunted buffalo on the plains. The Ute had frequently warred with the Comanches and Arapahoe over hunting grounds, but all the tribes behaved peacefully when they came together in the sacred grounds near the great mountain. After clashes with white settlers, all the tribes in the Pikes Peak area were removed to distant reservations.

Pikes Peak was scaled by another expedition in 1820, but the mountain was not open to easy access until an Eastern mining magnate, Spenser Penrose, built an automobile road to the summit in 1915. The next year he sponsored the first Pikes Peak Auto Hill Climb, an event that still takes place annually on the first Sunday after July 4.

Penrose did more for the area: He refurbished a famous hotel, the Broadmoor, and he built a cog railway to climb the summit in 1891 and created the Cheyenne Mountain Zoo, which is still celebrated as the highest zoo in the world. The cog railway is still in operation also, still running from Manitou Springs but refurbished with new Swiss railcars. The ascent for the railway is at a few miles per hour on a 25 percent grade that covers 3.25 miles.

A young Wellesley College professor, Katherine

Lee Bates, chose to take a leisurely wagon trip up Pikes Peak in 1893 instead of using the railway. The result of the journey was the inspiration for her famous song, "America the Beautiful."

Several historic places surround Pikes Peak. The White House Ranch Historic Site has interpreters in period clothing to portray life in the region from 1860 to 1910. Glen Eyrie is a sixty-seven-room Tudor-style Victorian mansion now a retreat center for a religious group but available for special visits.

The Garden of the Gods is southeast of Pikes Peak on the edge of the city of Colorado Springs. It is a dramatic setting consisting of slabs of slender stone pinnacles of a golden salmon color. According to legend, its name came from an argument between two friends. When one said it should be a beer garden, the other replied that it should be "a garden of the gods." It is a 1,350-acre city park and is utilized for various performances and ceremonies. Another special natural site nearby is the Florissant Fossil Beds National Monument, located northwest of Pikes Peak. Set aside in 1969, it protects giant petrified sequoia stumps and an area of considerable natural beauty.

Colorado Springs

Colorado Springs, a thriving city of over a third of a million people at the end of the twentieth century, sprawls across the plains directly to the east of Pikes Peak. The city had its origin in a scheme to create a town which would be the "Newport of the West," meaning that it would function in relation to Denver as Newport, Rhode Island, did to Boston—that is, as a resort and tourist city. Nearly all the other cities in Colorado were founded as military posts or commercial or mining centers.

There already was a nearby shabby settlement closer to Pikes Peak called "Old" Colorado City (to distinguish it from the newer Colorado City south of Pueblo). When it was founded in 1859 to serve as a supply base for mining communities, it did not have "old" as part of its name. Old Colorado City was in the wrong location for its role, and Denver monopolized trade with the boomtowns of the mountains. As Old Colorado City decayed, William Jackson Palmer, a former Civil War general and a railroad magnate, envisioned the creation of Colorado Springs along the route of his Denver and Rio Grande Railway as it passed Pikes Peak.

There are no springs in Colorado Springs. The name was applied as a lure for tourists, banking on the proximity to what became known as Manitou Springs, an area a few miles away that did have them. Even so, the scenery and good air made it attractive to affluent tourists and visitors. Non-drinking people of good moral character were offered lots for sale by the railroad and its land companies. The city grew rapidly. Six months after groundbreaking in 1871, there were eight hundred residents, fifteen hundred by the end of the next year, and three thousand by 1874.

A large number of wealthy Europeans arrived, particularly from Britain, which inspired the town's nickname of "Little London." The city advertised "Eastern life in a Western environment." It gained a reputation for its high cost of living and keen business practices and sharp advertising to draw tourists. It was proclaimed the golf, tennis, and polo capital of the world, and no opportunity was lost to photograph the many celebrities who visited.

More growth occurred as Colorado Springs became a haven for people suffering from tuberculosis (or, as it was popularly called, consumption). Resident invalids brought in outside income as they filled boardinghouses and resorts. For a time, the only treatment available for the disease was rest and good air. When the contagious nature of the disease became known through scientific research, landlords in the city began to close their doors to its victims. The new methods of treatment called for sanatoriums, and several were built nearby.

In the twentieth century, business, tourism, a new migration of people to the sunny Southwest, and strong connections with the Defense Department assured prosperous, generally attractive, and steady growth.

The city became the hub for Defense Department operations in Colorado when Colorado Springs was chosen as the site for the North American Air Defense Command (NORAD) in 1957, which created a huge base inside of Cheyenne Mountain. Simultaneously, the Air Force opened its academy just north of the city, and its striking chapel and massive steel and concrete campus draws a large number of visitors. Fort Carson occupies a large area south of the city. Partly as a result of these installations, substantial numbers of military personnel have retired in Colorado Springs.

Pikes Peak and the city of Colorado Springs. (AP/Wide World Photos)

There are numerous other attractions in the city: Once the seediest part of town, Old Colorado City has been annexed and developed into a gentrified area of an assortment of shops, galleries, and restaurants housed in restored buildings. The Colorado Springs Pioneer Museum has excellent exhibits and incorporates the old courtrooms that it once featured. The Colorado Fine Arts Center displays the art of Native Americans, Southwestern Hispanics, well-known Western American painters, as well as avant-garde works.

Colorado Springs and the Pikes Peak region in general are filled with hotels, motels, and commercial attractions for tourists, such as recently built ghost towns. Downtown is clean and spacious, laid out on a convenient grid of wide streets.

Manitou Springs
Manitou Springs is five miles closer to Pikes Peak, immediately west of Colorado Springs. It was founded in 1872 by General William Jackson Palmer and his English friend, Dr. William Bell. The name came from the suggestion of an English

investor who was likely to have been inspired by Henry Wadsworth Longfellow's poem *The Song of Hiawatha* (1855). It was a fashionable resort from the 1870's to the 1920's, advertised as the "Saratoga of the West." Its main attraction, besides air and scenery, was the water of its naturally carbonated springs, which was drunk to cure ailments, as well as bottled and shipped out. Hotels, boardinghouses, and villas clustered along a lengthy thoroughfare. Today a Historic District winds along Manitou Avenue.

One attraction consisted of the cliff dwellings of the mysterious ancient Native Americans in the region, the Anasazi. They were not originally found in Manitou Springs but removed from several locations in the Southwest and reassembled in Manitou Springs. In the mid-twentieth century Manitou Springs declined, but in the late twentieth century it experienced a dramatic revival as a tourist and art center.

Cripple Creek and Victor
Cripple Creek is on a high plateau just southwest of

Pikes Peak, and Victor is just a few miles farther south. Cripple Creek's name came from the injuries sustained by cows that fell in a local streambed. These gold-mining towns were founded in the winter of 1890-1891, marking the final spectacular mineral discovery and bonanza in the state. The first gold strike in Colorado had occurred in 1858.

As in other Colorado mining towns, the gold ore suddenly changed a barren area to the home of a thriving metropolis where everything was high-priced. Since it was so close to Colorado Springs, miners were spared most of the hardships of a raw frontier. In fact, Cripple Creek had electric lights and telephones along with the usual saloons and brothels. A devastating fire in 1896 destroyed most of the wooden town. It was rebuilt around the turn of the century out of red brick and stone, and the streets were paved. By 1900, the boomtown boasted fourteen newspapers, two opera houses, 139 saloons, and fifty thousand people. The Cripple Creek District Museum displays relics of the town's heyday.

Many of Cripple Creek's miners were commuters, coming to work from the nearby town of Victor over the same route now traveled by tourists in the summer over the Cripple Creek and Victor Narrow Gauge Railroad.

When the ore ran out, the towns decayed and shrank, and at one time the combined population dipped to little more than one thousand people. Cripple Creek sought a new bonanza in 1990 when limited stakes gambling was introduced. Over a dozen casinos and rapid, often thoughtless development have put its status as a National Historic Landmark in jeopardy. Victor, by contrast, retains its character as an old mining town, having a core of old streets and a scattering of diverse houses on steep dirt roads. The town is still framed by reminders of the boom years—slag heaps and mine shafts.

—*Henry Weisser*

For Further Information:

Abbott, Carl, Stephen J. Leonard, and David McComb. *Colorado: A History of the Centennial State.* Boulder: University Press of Colorado, 1994. Many parts of this readable textbook on Colorado are devoted to the region.

Loe, Nancy E. *Life in the Altitudes: An Illustrated History of Colorado Springs.* New York: Windsor, 1983.

This is another well-illustrated, modern treatment.

Scott, James A. *Pikes Peak Country.* Helena, Mont.: Falcon Press, 1987. This is a well-illustrated book geared toward tourism.

Sprague, Marshall. *Money Mountain: The Story of Cripple Creek Gold.* Boston: Little, Brown, 1953. This is a classic treatment, still regarded as the best book on the city although its prose is stilted.

_____. *Newport in the Rockies: The Life and Good Times of Colorado Springs.* Denver: Sage Books, 1961. The same can be said about this book by Sprague.

Storey, Brit Allan. "William Jackson Palmer: The Technique of a Pioneer Railroad Promoter in Colorado, 1871-1880." *Journal of the West* 5 (April, 1966): 263-274.

Telluride

Date: Named a National Historic Landmark in 1964

Relevant issues: Business and industry, western expansion

Significance: Prospectors first found gold and silver in the area around Telluride in 1875. Completion of a railroad in 1890 led to a rush of fortune seekers, and Telluride experienced a mining boom through most of the 1890's. Many of the buildings from Telluride's heyday remain, providing an attractive setting for tourists who visit for the skiing or summer festivals.

Location: In the San Juan Mountains of southwestern Colorado, 327 miles from Denver, 68 miles south of Montrose

Site Office:
Telluride Visitor Information Center
666 West Colorado Ave
Box 653
Telluride, CO 81435
ph.: (303) 728-3041

From the 1870's to the early 1900's, Telluride was a classic Western mining town, with a boom-and-bust economy and a rowdy nightlife of saloons and bordellos. Incredible profits (sixty million dollars in the first thirty years) from the rich gold and silver veins sparked construction of churches, banks, a school, a courthouse, and the New

Sheridan Hotel. Telluride featured immigrant workers from many nations, typical of mining towns. It also was the site of very violent labor disputes between the miners' union and the mine management.

This rich labor history is what earned Telluride an honored place in United States history, and the fact that many key buildings remain intact makes it a rewarding place to visit from an educational standpoint. In the late 1980's, moreover, Telluride emerged as a popular tourist destination for skiing in the winter and several world-famous festivals in the summer.

Founding and Naming the Town

The first prospector, John Fallon, set up camp in the mountains above the future site of Telluride in 1875. He established the first mine, the Sheridan, and hit pay dirt. Within a few years he sold the mine for forty thousand dollars. In 1883, the Sheridan again changed hands when it was purchased by Scottish bankers living in Shanghai. In addition to the Sheridan, other rich early mines included the Tomboy, the Pandora, and the Smuggler. The Smuggler had one gold vein over a mile long. News of such strikes attracted a steady stream of adventurers, necessitating the organization of a town.

Telluride, originally named Columbia, was incorporated as an eighty-acre town site in 1878. Problems with mail going to a town of the same name in California quickly prompted debate about changing the name. In 1880, someone suggested the name Telluride, and it was adopted by the post office. Townsfolk did not officially adopt the new name until 1887, however. "Telluride" was derived from tellurium, a rare sulfurous element sometimes found in gold ore. Strangely enough, it is not at all common in the Telluride area.

The name has also become associated with a legendary warning to visitors en route to Telluride: "To hell you ride." This phrase probably had nothing to do with the naming of the town, but may well have been uttered by train conductors or wagon operators. If it was not, it should have been, because life in Telluride during its wildest days really could be hellish.

Growth of the town remained slow through the 1880's due to the extremely high costs of transportation in and out of Telluride. Some key advances did occur, however, with a town hall being completed in 1883 and the San Miguel County Courthouse going up in 1887. The first newspaper was established in 1881, a weekly called the *San Miguel Examiner.*

Another early landmark, the San Miguel National Bank, gained notoriety on June 24, 1889. On that day Butch Cassidy pulled his first bank robbery, escaping with about twenty-four thousand dollars. Telluride's sheriff had no luck catching Cassidy, but he did capture his horse and proudly rode it around town for many years.

A Railroad Brings Prosperity

The boom days for Telluride began in 1890, when a brilliant Russian-born engineer named Otto Mears headed construction of a railroad line into town. Beginning in the spring, some fifteen hundred workers started building the main line of the Rio Grande Southern, which would link Ridgway to Durango. A branch line into Telluride was completed on November 23. The first train chugged into town three days later on Thanksgiving, met by a band and the cheers and toasts of local citizens. The train line was soon hauling 150 carloads of ore out of Telluride per month, and the Wild West had arrived in Telluride.

By 1891, the population jumped to four thousand and consisted of miners from Finland, Sweden, England, France, Ireland, Germany, and Italy. Two industrious Chinese men even opened up shops in town, one a laundry and the other a general store. The most notorious businesses were clustered on or near Pacific Avenue—some twenty-six saloons and twelve bordellos. The most popular of the houses of ill repute was the Pick and Gad. There and in other bordellos such as the Cozy Corner and the White House worked approximately 175 prostitutes, including the famous Diamond Tooth Leona. Miners from Scandinavia were in such a hurry to get to the excitement of Pacific Avenue on payday that they strapped boards on their feet and slid down the mountainside, thus becoming the earliest skiers in Telluride.

Saturday nights in the saloons could get rough, and legends abound, such as the story of a man who tried to start trouble and had his thumb shot off by a lawman. The most successful of Telluride's sheriffs was gigantic Jim Knous, who usually roughed up potential troublemakers with his fists and sent them home before guns were drawn. An-

Telluride National Historic District. (Telluride & Mountain Village Visitor Services)

other effective, if brutal, lawman was deputy marshal Jim Clark, who had previously been a member of Jesse James's gang.

Bars and brothels were not the only new buildings in the 1890's, however. A miners' hospital was completed in 1893, and the first schoolhouse appeared in 1895. That year also witnessed construction of the town's first luxury hotel, the New Sheridan. The hotel could claim a bar from Austria and a mirror from Paris and featured fine food and wine. Some of the more popular dishes included seafood, possum, and strawberries. Famous early guests at the New Sheridan included Lillian Gish and Sarah Bernhardt, and it was the scene of speeches by leading labor activists such as Eugene V. Debs and Big Bill Haywood. The most famous oration, though, was the "Cross of Gold" speech given there by William Jennings Bryan in 1903.

Impressive construction was not limited to the town itself in the roaring 1890's. Five miles up the mountainside at the prosperous Tomboy mine could be found a huge boarding house, a YMCA, tennis courts, and a bowling alley. The Tomboy attracted international attention and was purchased for two million dollars by the Rothschilds of London in 1897.

Labor Strife and Mining's Decline

In the spring of 1901, the mine owners announced a new contract that would effectively require more work for less money. Workers belonging to the Western Federation of Miners Union responded by going on strike. Violence soon broke out between union members and scabs, with three people being killed and six severely wounded. In July, the union won a victory, gaining recognition and negotiating an agreement guaranteeing the eight-hour day at the prevailing wage rate.

In 1902, some radicals, disgruntled with the settlement, assassinated the manager of the Smuggler Mine. His replacement was Harvard-educated Bulkeley Wells. Wells hated union radicalism as much as he enjoyed good food and fancy clothes, and the showdown came quickly. When one hundred workers at the Tomboy struck against the hiring of scabs in 1903, Wells and the mine owners called in the National Guard.

Five hundred troops arrived and enforced virtual martial law, closing bars and bordellos and instituting curfews and pass laws. The troops ejected all perceived agitators from Telluride and constructed Fort Peabody at the top of Imogene Pass to keep them out. The troops departed in 1904, but Wells carried on the fight. His efforts earned him the everlasting enmity of the miners, and in 1908, radicals attempted to assassinate him. A bomb exploded under his bed and blew him out the window, but he was not seriously harmed.

In spite of the strife, the Smuggler and the Tomboy remained incredibly productive and had their greatest years between 1905 and 1911, during which time over sixteen million dollars of gold and silver were taken from Telluride. Decline came quickly after that, however. Labor left to work in higher-paying war industries or to join the armed forces. Operational costs soared while the price of gold remained fixed by law. All the great mines closed, with the Smuggler holding out the longest, until 1928. By 1930, the banks had closed and the population dwindled to about five hundred.

Rebirth Through Tourism

A brief glimpse into Telluride's future prosperity came in 1945, when the first ski lift (a rope tow) was constructed. It lasted only two years, but another was built in 1958. The lift utilized an old car motor, and season passes that year cost five dollars. Thenceforth, skiing and the economy of Telluride were linked.

Skiing remained relatively small-scale through the 1960's, but in 1971, the modern era began with the opening of the Telluride Ski Area. The slopes boasted some of the best expert terrain in the United States, and the lift lines were relatively short. The 1970's also saw the beginning of some complementary summer attractions—the first film festival and the first bluegrass festival—both of which quickly became world famous. Several other festivals have been initiated that attract summer tourists, most notably a jazz festival and a mushroom festival.

Construction of an airport in the late 1980's opened the floodgates of high-priced development and brought wealthy vacationers from around the world. Real estate prices in Telluride rose drastically. Fortunately, Telluride's status as a National Historic Landmark provided some defense against the onslaught of development within the town itself. An architectural review committee closely monitors new building, and Telluride retained much of its nineteenth century character.

Places to Visit

A great number of buildings from the mining heyday remain in Telluride for the interested visitor, and a short walking tour of downtown encompasses them all. The courthouse, schoolhouse, the San Miguel Valley Bank (robbed by Cassidy), and the First National Bank (turned into an Elks Lodge) are still standing. The renowned Sheridan Hotel remains open for business, and the Senate saloon has been restored and reopened, featuring a bar from 1880 and a hole in the floor from a bullet that took off a sheriff's ear. Walking from Main Street over to Pacific Avenue, one can see what was once the notorious Pick and Gad brothel.

What was built as a miners' hospital in 1893 has been turned into the Telluride Historical Museum. Exhibits include many powerful old photographs, beer tokens, pool balls, and a barber's chair including hand straps that were used when the barber doubled as a dentist or surgeon. The museum is open year-round.

—*Andy DeRoche*

For Further Information:

Abbott, Carl, Stephen Leonard, and David McComb. *Colorado: A History of the Centennial State.* Niwot: University Press of Colorado, 1994. Contains some good discussion of the labor disputes in Telluride and puts them into the broader context of Colorado history.

Buys, Christian J. *Historic Telluride in Rare Photographs.* Ouray, Colo.: Western Reflections, 1998. In addition to the story of mining in Telluride, this book includes a chapter on the Utes who lived in the area before the arrival of prospectors.

Fetter, Richard, and Suzanne Fetter. *Telluride: From Pick to Powder.* Caldwell, Idaho: Caxton Printers, 1979. A nicely written account of the history of Telluride from mining to skiing, with an excellent final chapter describing a walking tour of the town.

Lavender, David. *The Telluride Story.* Ridgway, Colo.:

Wayfinder Press, 1987. An informative overview of Telluride's history.

Weber, Rose. *A Quick History of Telluride*. Colorado Springs: Little London Press, 1974. A very brief narrative with great photographs.

Wenger, Martin. *Recollections of Telluride, 1895-1920*. Mesa Verde, Colo.: Wenger Press, 1978. Interesting first-hand account of growing up during the boom days.

Other Historic Sites

Central City/Blackhawk Historic District

Location: Central City and Blackhawk, Gilpin County

Relevant issues: Business and industry

Statement of significance: The Central City/Black Hawk National Historic Landmark is at the heart of one of the richest mining areas of the Rocky Mountain West. It was the discovery of gold here, in 1859, that triggered the great Pikes Peak gold rush. The district encompasses hundreds of buildings, including rare examples of mining camp-era wooden structures and the famed Opera House.

Durango-Silverton Narrow-Gauge Railroad

Location: Durango, La Plata County

Relevant issues: Business and industry

Statement of significance: Completed in 1882, this railroad was built to haul ores from isolated areas to smelters. It was also the main source of transportation and support for the mining community of Silverton. It is one of the few passenger railroads of its kind still in operation in the United States.

Georgetown-Silver Plume Historic District

Location: Georgetown and Silver Plume, Clear Creek County

Relevant issues: Business and industry

Statement of significance: This area flourished originally because of gold and silver production. The two communities have retained much of their mid-nineteenth century boomtown atmosphere.

Lowry Ruin

Location: Pleasant View, Montezuma County

Relevant issues: American Indian history

Statement of significance: This pueblo (c. 1100 C.E.) of fifty rooms is unusual in that it has a great kiva, a large ceremonial structure more commonly found in Arizona and New Mexico.

Pike's Stockade

Location: Sanford, Conejos County

Relevant issues: Western expansion

Statement of significance: Zebulon Pike (1779-1813) raised the American flag over Spanish soil at the stockade after leading the second official U.S. expedition into the Louisiana Territory in 1807.

Silverton Historic District

Location: Silverton, San Juan County

Relevant issues: Business and industry

Statement of significance: This was one of the two principal mining towns in southwestern Colorado. It was important in the economic development of the Rocky Mountain area in the late nineteenth century.

Connecticut

History of Connecticut 222
Mystic 224
Nook Farm 228

Old New-Gate Prison 231
Other Historic Sites 234

Hartford. (John Muldoon)

History of Connecticut

Connecticut is the third smallest state in area in the Union, after Rhode Island and Delaware. It is also the fourth most densely populated state. Positioned at the southernmost part of New England, Connecticut is bordered by New York on the west, Rhode Island on the east, Massachusetts on the north, and Long Island Sound—an arm of the Atlantic Ocean—on the south. Like most New England states, Connecticut is shaped by its abundance of water. It has more than 1,000 lakes and 8,400 miles of rivers and streams. The three major rivers flowing through the state, the Connecticut, the Housatonic, and the Thames, provide ports, fishing, and power for industry.

The Connecticut River Valley has very fertile land; potatoes, corn, onions, lettuce, tobacco, and other crops are grown there. Forests cover 60 percent of the state, making Connecticut one of the most wooded states in the United States. Maple trees are used to supply sugar and syrup. Until the nineteenth century, salmon fishing was a highly profitable industry. After a dam was built on the Connecticut River, preventing salmon from reaching their spawning grounds, the salmon supply was depleted.

Early History

Connecticut was inhabited by American Indian tribes for thousands of years before the first Europeans came to North America. By the 1600's approximately twenty thousand Algonquian Indians lived in the region. The dominant tribe was the Pequot, a warrior group who conquered most of the Connecticut River Valley in the 1500's. Other tribes included the Narragansetts, Quinnipiacs, Mohegans, and Saukiogs, who hunted moose, deer, and bear and grew corn, beans, and squash.

Dutch explorer Adriaen Block sailed the Connecticut River in 1614, meeting friendly Podunk Indians. In 1633 Dutch settlers built the House of Good Hope trading post near modern Hartford, where they traded with the Native Americans. In the same year, English settlers founded Windsor. Violence erupted between the settlers and the Pequots in 1637 over land disputes. The Native Americans were defeated during the Pequot War, with losses of six hundred people. Many remaining Native Americans left the state, and by 1990, Indians made up only 0.2 percent of the population.

Colonization

In 1638, 250 Puritans from the Massachusetts Bay Colony established the New Haven Colony. The government was based on the Fundamental Agreement, which stated that the Bible was the supreme law. The colony was not inclusive; only Puritans were allowed to vote or hold office.

The residents of Wethersfield, Windsor, and Hartford joined to form the Colony of Connecticut in 1639. This colony's government was based on the teachings of Reverend Thomas Hooker, which were known as the Fundamental Orders. A Puritan preacher, Hooker believed that the right to vote should belong to all, regardless of their religion. The Fundamental Orders, which served as Connecticut's constitution for many years, were the first document in the New World to give the government its power from the "free consent of the people."

In 1643, the Connecticut, New Haven, Massachusetts, and Plymouth Colonies banded together, forming the Confederation of New England. The colonies stayed independent of each other but made a pact to act together in times of war. In 1662, the Connecticut Colony received a royal charter, allowing it self-rule. The charter was revoked, however, twenty-three years later by King James. Edmund Andros, acting for the duke of York, tried to claim the area west of the Connecticut River for the New York Colony. The residents of Connecticut refused to turn over their charter, supposedly hiding it in an oak tree, and they were able to resume self-rule in 1689. Connecticut became a state, the fifth in the Union, in 1788.

The American Revolution

Connecticut played a major role in the American Revolution. It sent thirty thousand soldiers into action—more, in relation to its population, than any other colony. These men included more than

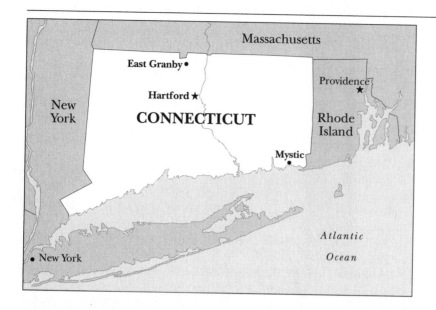

three hundred black soldiers. General George Washington called Connecticut the "Provisions State" because it sent so many supplies and munitions to the soldiers. The colony's navy captured more than forty British ships.

Connecticut produced both villains and heroes. One of its residents, Benedict Arnold, became a spy for the British, led English troops in an attack at Fort Griswold, and burned down the city of New London. Connecticut's Nathan Hale was a spy for the Union and became famous for the last words he uttered before the British hanged him: "I only regret that I have but one life to lose for my country."

Slavery in Connecticut

In the mid-1700's about three to five thousand blacks lived in the colony, most of them slaves. A law was passed in 1774 prohibiting residents from bringing in new slaves, and the 1784 Connecticut Emancipation Law allowed children born to slaves to be freed at the age of twenty-five. After the Revolution, all slaves who fought were freed.

A well-publicized Connecticut court case in 1839 brought the issue of slavery to national attention. Africans carried in the Spanish slave ship *Amistad* mutinied and tried to force the crew to turn the ship back to Africa. The crew instead secretly headed for Long Island, and the rebels, led by Joseph Cinqué, stood trial in Hartford for murder and piracy. In 1840 the U.S. Supreme Court ruled that the Africans were born free and taken as

slaves against their will, so they were returned home. Slavery was banished in Connecticut in 1848. Later, the antislavery state sent more than fifty-seven thousand men to fight in the Civil War on the Union side.

Industry

In its early days, Connecticut's economy depended on agriculture and fishing. Its economy grew during the early 1800's with the construction of cotton, wool, and paper mills. Samuel Colt invented the six-shooter, the first repeating pistol, and his factories boomed. A machine to remove seeds from cotton, the cotton gin, invented in 1793 by Eli Whitney, added to the growth of industry.

Connecticut was hit hard by the Great Depression of the 1930's, with 22 percent of its workers unemployed. However, the state's economy bounced back during World War II. Connecticut produced more war supplies per person than any other state. In the late 1940's, more than half of its adult population worked in factories. Most of the industry was centered in ten towns, especially New Haven, Bridgeport, and Danbury, and half of Connecticut residents lived in these factory towns.

After the 1950's, textile production and other factory work subsided, and service jobs grew. Most middle-class families left the cities, and poverty increased in urban areas. Urban renewal programs initiated in the 1950's to 1970's could not counter the riots that took place in poor areas in 1967.

Economy

By the end of the twentieth century, Hartford was the insurance capital of the world, a position it had held since the late 1700's. Groton was the submarine capital of the world in the early part of the century, but massive layoffs in the defense industry in the 1990's forced the closure of many shipyards and factories. Connecticut's population fell by several thousand during this period.

The state's economy was revitalized by the Mashantucket Pequot Indian Foxwoods Casino, which opened in 1993 as the largest casino in the

Western Hemisphere. Paying the state one-quarter of its earnings, the casino pumps about $1 billion per year into Connecticut's economy. Nevertheless, the state imposed its first income tax in 1993, to the dismay of many.

Politics

Connecticut traditionally has been a Republican state. In 1974, however, Ella T. Grasso, a Democrat and the first Connecticut governor of Italian descent, became the first female governor of a state elected in her own right. In 1981 Thirman Milner of Hartford became the first African American mayor of a New England city.

Crime rates fell in the 1990's, and efforts were being made to clean up Connecticut's deteriorating inner cities. The state government instituted a drug-policy reform in which drug addicts receive methadone (a heroin substitute) treatments and thereby possibly avoid long-term imprisonment. Connecticut was the first state to place drug courts in every jurisdiction. About 75 percent of the defendants stay in the program, compared to about 25 percent in regular drug-treatment programs.

—*Lauren M. Mitchell*

Mystic

Date: Pequot Indians expelled by English colonists in 1637; name officially granted in October, 1665

Relevant issues: American Indian history, business and industry, colonial America, naval history

Significance: This community on the Mystic River in southeastern Connecticut is composed of portions of the towns of Groton (west of the river) and Stonington (east of the river). The area was originally home to the Pequot Indians, who were expelled by English colonists in 1637. The English soon set up a small community at the site, which by the eighteenth century became a seaport and shipbuilding center. In the early nineteenth century, whaling became one of the seaport's major industries. The local shipyards flourished in the years leading up to and during the Civil War, but the postwar years saw a gradual decline in the industry. Today, Mystic is home to Mystic Seaport, a seventeen-acre indoor-outdoor museum featuring a re-creation of the seaport as it existed in the nineteenth century.

Location: Ten miles east of New London in southeastern Connecticut, on Route 27 approximately one mile south of U.S. Interstate 95

Site Office:
Mystic Seaport
75 Greenmanville Avenue
P.O. Box 6000
Mystic, CT 06355-0990
ph.: (888) 9SEAPORT (973-2767); (860) 572-5315
Web site: www.mysticseaport.org

In the early 1600's, the inhabitants of the area surrounding the Mystic River in southeast Connecticut were the Pequot Indians, a warlike people feared by all the surrounding tribes. Fittingly, the word Pequot means "destroyer." At that time, the Pequots possessed a forty-five-mile tract of land between the Connecticut River and the Weekapaug Creek, including the Mystic River area. One of the Pequots' primary territories was on Pequot Hill in the region that would become Mystic. The area's fertile soil allowed them to plant maize, beans, squash, pumpkins, and tobacco.

In 1631, English colonists in Boston and Plymouth became aware of this fruitful valley and wished to settle there. In May, 1637, Captain John Mason of Windsor and a group of seventy-seven Bostonians marched toward the area to invade the Pequots' territory. The English arrived during a boundary war between the Pequots and the Rhode Island Narragansett tribe. Although the Pequots were primed for battle, they were no match for the English, who, when they reached Pequot Hill, were joined by 160 Massachusetts men. The next morning, a bloody massacre took place on the hill; few Pequots escaped.

The English retreated, in the process having to cross more Pequot territory. By that time, word of the massacre had reached the other two Pequot fortifications. Although the Pequots were soon in close pursuit of Mason, the colonists arrived at Pequot Harbor on the Thames River to find vessels waiting to take them back to Boston.

A month later, Captain Isreal Stroughton and 120 more men joined Mason to pursue the remaining Pequots. After finding the tribe hidden in a

A replica of the Amistad *slave ship.* (PhotoDisc)

swamp, the English killed many of them and took the rest as prisoners in what is now known as the Great Swamp Fight.

English Settlement

After the massacre, Massachusetts claimed the right to settle the area. The Massachusetts General Court granted these rights in 1646, but they were soon transferred to Connecticut by the Commission of the United Colonies.

Housing development began in the area immediately after the Pequots' expulsion. The Magistrates of Connecticut divided the remaining Pequots into three groups and made them join other existing tribes in the surrounding areas. A treaty for perpetual peace was signed between the English and these tribes. Still, some Pequots were unhappy with their new tribes and tried to move back onto their original land. Because they were now becoming increasingly friendly with the English, they were permitted to stay.

In October, 1665, the General Session at Hartford decided to officially grant Mystic its name.

The name had already been given to the area by the Pequots in the form of *missi-tuk* or "great river." Also, the Mystic River was designated as the official boundary between the surrounding towns of Stonington and Groton.

When settlers first began to move into this area surrounding the Mystic River, they did not form any kind of common colony. They had mostly come by water and preferred to lay scattered holdings along the line of the river. From the beginning, Mystic saw a steady growth of small manufacturing, starting with the building of grist and saw mills that used waterpower from local brooks. To support the needs of the early shipyards, the colonists erected planing and lumber mills along with mills that manufactured cotton and wool fabrics, brass, iron and wooden tools, textiles, engines, and machines. Mystic's deep granite ledges and access to convenient transportation contributed to the success of granite quarrying.

Meanwhile, the colonists were also busy developing other aspects of their economy. Services were exchanged as each colonist became an expert at a particular trade: Coopers, yeomen, weavers, carpenters, and shoemakers were soon common. Usually, apprenticeships were granted to young men for the chance to master a trade.

During growing season, the settlers harvested Indian corn, peas, and wheat. Although some of the soil in the Mystic area was fertile, much of the area was hilly and rocky, leading some residents to make their livelihood by raising poultry. Within the area, barter was common, but when cash was necessary, Indian wampum was adopted as the major form of currency.

Shipbuilding

The settlers soon realized that they could make a more profitable living by fishing and shipbuilding. Construction of shipyards began all along the shore. The first shipyards were built around 1750 at the head of the river. By the early 1800's, shipbuilding was the primary source of wealth for most of Mystic's residents.

In 1812, the United States declared war on Great Britain. British ships appeared immediately offshore to blockade all ports. Terrified, citizens fled inland. The citizens of Mystic felt their town needed protection from the British fleet, so they built Fort Rachel on the granite crags forty feet above the shipping channel and stationed fifteen men there. Shortly after the fort was built, Captain Jessie Crary of Mystic and his sloop were taken hostage by the British. Crary escaped and enlisted several volunteers to help recapture his ship. About a month after they found the sloop, the men at Fort Rachel successfully fended off an armed British attack, despite the presence of traitors among the fortsmen. A year later, a regular guard was posted at the fort and he would remain there until the end of the war.

During the postwar years, life returned to normal and Mystic continued to grow. The shipbuilding industry resumed and built better and faster boats that increased the range and speed of trade. As residential areas began to expand, neighborhoods often took the form of block buildings, typically consisting of several houses, a bank, a drugstore, a grocery store, and a few other public services. Many ladies sewed "seaworthy" clothes at home, then exchanged them at stores for credit. The stores sold the garments to vessels, which carried "slop chests," or small stores, onboard that

sold personal items to sailors during voyages.

Until 1816, Mystic's boats were used for fishing, but soon the demand for whale oil, whalebone, sperm oil, and ambergris made whaling as profitable as fishing. Whaling became the principal activity for Mystic from 1830 to 1850.

In 1829, a group of public volunteers, including many seafaring men, came together to erect a church to be used by members of all denominations. In thanks for the large contribution made by local sailors, the church was named the Mariners Free Church.

Early trade with Boston provided household goods, military accoutrements, woolen clothing, powder and lead, and implements of husbandry. Trade with Virginia was unnecessary, as the Mystic harvest satisfied the local demand for tobacco and wheat. By the 1830's, regular voyages were being made to New Orleans and Galveston. Direct trade with the South was very prosperous. Representatives of Mystic shipowners were stationed all the way from Baltimore to Galveston. The range of Mystic's trade extended far out into the Atlantic, and included trade with the British West Indies and later with the Caribbean. Exports included pork, cheese, horses, lumber, and tallow, while imports were sugar, salt, molasses, and rum.

The earliest vessels were of simple structure, usually designed by the master carpenter and built of white pine, spruce, and tall white ash. From the beginning, however, demand for bigger and better craft constantly increased. From the 1840's to the 1860's, the shipyards turned their attention to whalers, coasters, carraway boats, fishing smacks, packet sloops, and round-sterned, lofty clippers. Several of the smaller shipyards suffered when the demand for wooden sailing vessels lessened as a result of the exhaustion of Mystic's timber supply and a newfound confidence in steam power. Steamboats were especially used to transport passengers between towns. New clipper ships that carried larger cargoes were being launched, and whaleships still plied the river.

Many shipyards were owned and operated by large families and were passed down through several generations. These sites proved through the decades to be the strongest and most successful shipyards in the area. One family operation, started by Robert Palmer in 1832, launched almost six hundred merchant, naval, sail, steam, and tow vessels in its 113 years of shipbuilding. Other famous family shipyards were the Greenmans, Irons and Grinnell, and Maxson and Fish. Perhaps the most famous family operation was built by Charles Mallory around 1836 and passed on to his son, C. H. Mallory. In addition to designing some of the largest and fastest vessels of the time, the Mallorys turned out many of the ships used in the Civil War.

The Civil War and Local Disasters

As the Civil War drew closer, the citizens of Mystic and its neighboring towns began to prepare themselves. In 1860, the towns united in a protest against slavery; many young volunteers joined to create a company that became part of the Fourth Regiment, and the Mallory family donated money and the use of a hundred-ton yacht to the Union. The ladies of the Baptist Church formed a Soldiers Aid Society to provide soldiers on the battle front with food and bandages.

In 1862, a call went out for men to serve in the Union army for nine months. Most of the enlisted men from the Mystic area spent that year defending the north side of New Orleans at Camp Parapet. Back home, Mystic continued to grow as more families were attracted to shipyard employment. The latest demand in shipbuilding was for war transports and gunboats. Between 1850 and 1870, fifty-six steamers were launched from Mystic's shipyards, and the population of the Mystic area increased threefold.

Around this time, Mystic suffered several serious fires. In 1858, a fire broke out in the Mallory store and spread to other stores and hotels in the neighborhood. There was no fire company in Mystic, and a bucket brigade from the river had to be formed until an old hand-pumped fire engine could arrive from the next town, though not in time to save blocks of buildings from being destroyed. Six years later, after another large fire demolished a house and carriage shed, two volunteer fire companies were formed, and they purchased an old hand-brake fire engine. Shortly after, another fire broke out in a local mill. When the second-hand engine proved gravely ineffective in combating the flames, the townspeople donated money for a brand-new engine. In 1881, however, an entire block was destroyed by yet another fire.

In many ways, the turn of the century was a lean time in maritime Mystic. Shipyard employment thinned after the Civil War, and diphtheria was rampant and infected many citizens. Despite these challenges, it was also a time of great change. New industries began to develop, including motor works. In 1899, telephones were installed in the Mystic area. The Mystic Light and Gas Company provided the area's first electricity in 1906, and soon after the Mystic Valley Water Company brought running water to homes. Other additions included a post office, a public library, a greenhouse, and a laundry. With the exception of some recreational vessels, the style of boats also changed. Gasoline engines and then diesel engines followed steamships in replacing the clipper ships of old.

Mystic Seaport

In order to preserve the memory of its maritime heritage, three men formed the Marine Historical Association in 1929. Now known as the Mystic Seaport—The Museum of America and the Sea, the institution encompasses over seventeen acres on the site of what was once the George Greenman and Company Shipyard, and operates as a "living history museum" where visitors can see exhibits of maritime crafts being practiced. The museum is home to three major vessels: the *Charles W. Morgan* (1841), America's last surviving nineteenth century wooden whale ship (today a National Historic Landmark), the training ship *Joseph Conrad* (1882), and the fishing schooner *L. A. Dutton* (1921). Its more than sixty buildings display maritime art and artifacts, ship models, scrimshaw, carvings, paintings, and photographs. The Coastal Life Area is a reconstruction of a nineteenth century seafaring community complete with a bank, schoolhouse, tavern, rigging loft, shipsmith, cooperage, and mast hoop shop. The Henry B. duPont Preservation Shipyard provides equipment and craftsmen to restore and preserve wooden vessels. Also featured at Mystic Seaport are a planetarium, a small boat shop, various educational programs, and a maritime history library.   —*Cynthia L. Langston*

For Further Information:

Anderson, Virginia B. *Maritime Mystic.* Mystic, Conn.: Marine Historical Association, 1962. Emphasizes the seaport's great shipbuilding period.

Greenhalgh, Kathleen. *A History of West Mystic.* Groton, Conn.: Groton Public Library and Information Center, 1986. Tells the history of the western part of modern-day Mystic and some of its surrounding communities.

Hauptman, Laurence M., and James D. Wherry, eds. *The Pequots in Southern New England.* Norman: University of Oklahoma Press, 1993. A collection of essays that explore Pequot history, culture, and identity.

Nook Farm

Date: A colonial farm tract, but after 1853 a closely knit neighborhood of distinguished people

Relevant issues: Cultural history, education, literary history, social reform, women's history

Significance: From the time John Hooker and Francis Gillette purchased the 140-acre tract of land in Hartford, Connecticut, long known as Nook Farm, in 1853, a remarkably able group of their relatives and friends established homes there, the best known of whom are Mark Twain and Harriet Beecher Stowe. Because the distinctive homes of these two writers have been restored and scrupulously maintained, and because a nearby site has been developed as a research center for the study of them and their neighborhood, Nook Farm is an invaluable destination for all those interested in Twain, Stowe, and the area's other prominent nineteenth century residents.

Location: A section of east-central Hartford, bordered by Farmington Avenue, Laurel Street, Hawthorn Street, and the north branch of the Park River, and centering on Forest Street

Site Office:
The Stowe-Day Foundation
77 Forest Street
Hartford, CT 06105
ph.: (860) 522-9258
fax: (860) 522-9259

Nook Farm was part of a tract of land granted to John Haynes, the first governor of Connecticut Colony, as his woodlot. The city of Hartford

Mark Twain's house in the Nook Farm area of Hartford in 1905. (Arkent Archives)

grew up around this tract, but the rolling 140 acres which two prominent Hartford brothers-in-law, John Hooker and Francis Gillette, purchased in 1853 remained largely tree-covered. Hooker opened Forest Street and built his home there in that year. Over the next twenty years, most of the people who made Nook Farm famous built or purchased houses nearby.

A Gathering of Relatives and Friends

John Hooker had married Isabella, one of the remarkable children of Lyman Beecher, a minister in Litchfield, Connecticut. Isabella, a tireless battler for woman suffrage, is the earliest of the Nook Farm residents to become known beyond the Hartford area. She served for nearly two decades as the president of the Connecticut Woman Suffrage Association. Also in 1853 was born the first Nook Farm native to attain fame. William, the sixth and last child of Francis and Elizabeth Gillette, would go on to a long career as an actor and playwright. William Gillette performed his most famous role, Sherlock Holmes, over thirteen hundred times, and in fact wrote the stage play based on Sir Arthur Conan Doyle's immortal detective stories. Not well remembered today, Gillette was highly enough regarded in his time to be awarded the gold medal of the National Institute of Arts and Letters, the previous recipient being Eugene O'Neill.

The best known of Isabella Hooker's siblings had been living in Brunswick, Maine, when she wrote the book that took America by storm in the decade before the outbreak of the Civil War. When Harriet Beecher Stowe and her husband Calvin built a house near, though not precisely within, the Nook Farm acreage in 1864, she was world-famous for *Uncle Tom's Cabin* (1852). She had gone on to write well-regarded novels with New England settings, such as *The Minister's Wooing* (1859) and *The Pearl of Orr's Island* (1862). After moving to Hartford, she published another New England novel, *Oldtown Folks* (1869), its setting patterned upon her husband's hometown of Natick, Massachusetts, while Calvin, a biblical scholar, brought out *Origin and History of the Books of the Bible* (1867). In 1871, the Stowes moved to Nook Farm proper, and it is this house that thousands of tourists visit each year.

One of the attractions of this house is its adherence to Catharine Beecher's principles of home functionality and decoration. Harriet's elder sister was never a Nook Farm resident, but she had a long association with Hartford, having established the Hartford Female Seminary in 1823, which earned a reputation as one of the best schools in the country for young women. Catharine Beecher was not a feminist like her half sister Isabella, but believing that young women needed more than a mere finishing school, she stressed domestic economy, the rearing of children, and women's role in improving the moral tone of society. After eight years at the school, Beecher moved to Cincinnati and spent much of her time lecturing and promoting the training of female teachers. After Harriet established a home in the Nook Farm neighborhood, Beecher was a frequent visitor there.

Yet another of the Beecher women, Mary, lived at Nook Farm. The house that she and her husband Thomas Clap Perkins occupied on Hawthorn Street from 1855 to 1866 later became the home of other prominent families. Charles Dudley Warner, a young newspaper editor when he arrived in Hartford in 1860, moved into the Perkins House in 1866 with his wife Susan. She was an accomplished woman: a concert pianist, a patron of music, and a skilled hostess. He began to write weekly newspaper pieces about his hobby, gardening. These articles became the basis of his first book, *My Summer in a Garden* (1870). There followed a succession of travel books and novels, one of which earned for him a small but secure place in literary history.

Susan Warner lived for twenty-one years after her husband's death in 1900. For twenty years she served as vice president of the Hartford Philharmonic Orchestra, and in her seventy-third year gave a piano concert at Carnegie Hall. At the outbreak of World War I, she performed benefit concerts for Polish and French relief funds. Neighbors, piano students, and illustrious guests—among them the grand old man of American letters in the early twentieth century, William Dean Howells, and the young Helen Keller—enjoyed the Warner hospitality.

A Westerner Comes to Nook Farm

The most illustrious of all the Nook Farmers, though, was the man who began his career as a novelist by coauthoring with Charles Dudley Warner

The Gilded Age (1873); its title furnished a lasting sobriquet for the last third of the nineteenth century in the United States. Warner's collaborator had already achieved major successes in the literary world for his story "The Celebrated Jumping Frog" (1865) and his own travel book, *The Innocents Abroad* (1869). Samuel Langhorne Clemens, or as the world better recognizes him, Mark Twain, was by far the greatest of the Nook Farm writers, and the only non-New Englander among them.

The first notable American writer to be born west of the Mississippi (in Florida, Missouri, in 1835), Twain had spent his early life in the West, but after the European trip which provoked *The Innocents Abroad*, he married Olivia Langdon of Elmira, New York, and settled in Hartford, temporarily renting the Hooker House. He employed Edward Tuckerman Potter, the designer of Twain's friend Warner's house, to design one for him on Farmington Avenue, just around the corner from the Stowes' home. Twain was Nook Farm's most spectacular personality, and his house became the area's most spectacular house. It had gables, turrets, and an extensive first-floor porch—in Twain's mind a deck (long before the word came into vogue as an outdoor attachment to a house)—and another smaller third-floor porch simulating a Mississippi riverboat pilot's bridge. Inside were nineteen rooms of Victorian extravagance, including a bedroom featuring a bed with elaborate carvings, which he had purchased in Venice, and a third-floor billiard room that eventually became his writing room as well. There he penned such works as the immortal *Adventures of Huckleberry Finn* (1884).

Later Residents and Restorations

In the 1890's, Mark Twain left Hartford and Harriet Beecher Stowe died. By the turn of the century, most of the noted Nook Farm residents were gone, but one family who later lived in the Perkins-Warner House deserves mention. In 1908, Dr. Thomas Hepburn and his young family moved in. He was the first New England doctor to specialize in urology. His wife, the former Katharine Houghton, assumed a role similar to that played earlier by Isabella Hooker. Shortly before the family settled on Hawthorn Street, Katharine had attended a lecture by the British suffragist Emmeline Pankhurst. Inspired by what she heard, she organized the Hartford Equal Franchise League, which became one of the strongest of the organizations whose relentless activity resulted eventually in the passage of the Nineteenth Amendment conferring voting rights to women in national elections. In 1916, she became associated with Margaret Sanger, the great advocate of birth control. She spoke at rallies of the American Birth Control League and before the United States Senate.

One of the six Hepburn children, born the year after the family settled on Hawthorn Street, grew up with the reputation of a tomboy. She graduated from Bryn Mawr like her mother, but her career path led in the direction of the stage. After a successful Broadway debut in 1932, the younger Katharine Hepburn went on to even greater fame as a Hollywood actor.

Being close to the city's center, the Nook Farm area became increasingly commercial as the twentieth century wore on. This was particularly true of the street where Twain had lived, Farmington Avenue. On Forest Street, where the Stowes had resided, a public high school and apartment buildings replaced the older homes. Nook Farm was fast becoming unrecognizable.

One of its rescuers was Katharine S. Day, a grandniece of Harriet Beecher Stowe and granddaughter of John and Isabella Hooker, who purchased the Stowe House in 1927 and then joined with others to save the Twain House. She served for several years thereafter on the Hartford City Planning Commission and in 1937 established her own foundation. When she died in 1964, her will provided for the restoration of the Stowe House. Simulations of porches, fireplaces, and moldings that a previous owner had removed returned the house to its nineteenth century appearance, and Stowe furniture was retrieved from various places. By 1968, it was open to the public.

The restoration of the Twain house also took many years. The Mark Twain Memorial Commission purchased the building and its grounds in 1929 for $155,000, but lack of further funds slowed work on the project to a standstill until the 1950's, when restoration had proceeded far enough to permit an influx of visitors. Not until 1974, the centennial of the house's construction, did it return to its full splendor. Along with his bed and billiard room, Twain's printing machine, one of his many failed business ventures, is a highlight.

Working together, the Stowe-Day Foundation and the Mark Twain Memorial established a visitors' center in the carriage house between the Twain house on Farmington Avenue and the Stowe house, around the corner on Forest Street. For a single admission charge, visitors may explore each of these two sharply contrasting but fascinating houses.

The nearby Stowe-Day Foundation welcomes visitors who wish to use its extensive library of materials relating to Nook Farm, its architecture and history, and the achievements of its residents, with emphasis on Stowe and Twain.   —*Robert P. Ellis*

For Further Information:

Andrews, Kenneth R. *Nook Farm: Mark Twain's Hartford Circle.* Cambridge, Mass.: Harvard University Press, 1950. The best source of information on the relationships of the writers who lived in the neighborhood.

DeLana, Alice, and Cynthia Reik. *On Common Ground: A Selection of Hartford Writers.* Hartford, Conn.: Stowe-Day Foundation, 1975. One of the most useful of the publications of a foundation dedicated to the preservation of Nook Farm and the study of its literary heritage.

Faude, Wilson H. *The Renaissance of Mark Twain's House: A Handbook for Restoration.* Larchmont, N.Y.: Queens House, 1978. An account of the development of a long-neglected mansion into one of the most popular of all American literary sites.

"In the City." www.hartnet.org. This portion of the Web site of Trinity College in Hartford furnishes pictures and historical background on the houses of Harriet Beecher Stowe and Mark Twain, as well as information for prospective visitors.

Salisbury, Edith. *Mark Twain's House in Hartford.* Hartford, Conn.: Mark Twain Library and Memorial Commission, n.d. Describes the results of the intersection of Victorian architectural principles and Mark Twain's whimsical domestic ambitions.

Van Why, Joseph S. *Nook Farm.* Hartford, Conn.: Stowe-Day Foundation, 1975. Traces the history of Nook Farm, profiles its most notable residents, and contains excellent photographs of them and their houses, as well as a map of the area.

Old New-Gate Prison

Date: First copper deposits found in 1705; prison built in 1773

Relevant issues: Business and industry, colonial America, social reform

Significance: This historic site has a three-hundred-year history as a mine, prison, and museum.

Location: On Newgate Road in the town of East Granby, on the western slope of the Metacomet Ridge—a low mountain overlooking the Farmington Valley in the central Connecticut lowlands

Site Office:

Connecticut Historical Commission
59 South Prospect Street
Hartford, CT 06106
ph.: (203) 566-3005

The Metacomet Ridge was created in the Late Triassic period by successive floods of molten basalt alternating with the deposition of thick layers of eroded sediments of mud and sand. Mineral-laden hot springs deposited copper-rich sediments in the marshes and riverbeds of this landscape. The combination of erosional deposition, lava flows, and metamorphic pressure created alternate strata of basalt and sandstone, embedded with a copper-rich rock called chalcocite. Tectonic processes (the movement of the earth's crust) tilted this landscape eastward at an angle of 23 degrees, projecting the western end of the strata upward, creating the Metacomet Ridge and exposing the copper-laden sandstone strata.

Early Mining

The copper deposits were discovered in 1705 in what was then the town of Simsbury. The town claimed ownership of the deposits, and in 1712 leased them to a partnership of Boston and New York merchants headed by Jonathan Belcher, who later became governor of Massachusetts. German miners were imported, a smelter and ore-crushing apparatus were constructed, and a mineshaft sloping downward at an angle of 23 degrees was dug 120 feet eastward into the side of the Metacomet Ridge. Ultimately, this shaft was expanded by ore removal to form a cavern 100 by 180 feet. The mine was entered and ore was removed through two vertical shafts, one twenty-five feet, the other approx-

A guard tower and perimeter wall at the Old New-Gate Prison. (AP/Wide World Photos)

Crime and the Construction of a Prison

Crime in eighteenth century Connecticut was punished in three ways: by fines, incarceration in county jails, or public execution. These punishments included such penalties as sitting in the stocks, whipping, branding, and, at the most extreme, hanging. County jails, for the most part wooden structures, were used for holding persons awaiting trial, debtors, and those convicted of minor misdemeanors, with most incarcerations lasting less than six months. The goal of the legal system was quick resolution of an indictment, and most punishments meant the threat of impoverishment or public shame. Long-term incarceration as a punishment was not used in eighteenth century Connecticut.

Although its official name, New-Gate Prison, was chosen in an apparent attempt to emulate the notorious Newgate Prison of London, England, the purpose of New-Gate was to provide an alternative to what the Connecticut general assembly considered "infamous punishments," such as branding. Crimes punishable by confinement included burglary, highway robbery, forgery, counterfeiting, rape, arson, and horse stealing. Most sentences were to be for a period of three years, or lifetime incarceration for a third offense. Criminals were to be "profitably" employed by working the mine; by housing them in cabins in the mine, it was thought it "would be next to impossible for any person to escape." However, the first prisoner, John Hinson, confined for burglary in 1773, successfully escaped after eighteen days with the help of his lover, who dropped a rope down an unsecured mine shaft. Of the next five prisoners committed to the mine, two were killed in a cave while attempting to dig themselves out, and the remaining three

imately seventy feet in depth. As flooding from water seepage was a constant problem, a three hundred-foot drainage tunnel was excavated westward through basalt rock exiting the side of the ridge.

The ore was excavated by pick and shovel and blasting; a sandstone stratum approximately six feet thick was removed from between two strata of basalt. The ore, between 2 and 5 percent copper with trace elements of silver and uranium, was broken with hammers into cobbles approximately six inches in diameter and then graded. Cobbles with sufficient copper content were crushed and shipped to smelters either at Simsbury or in Bristol, England. Chalcocite was a difficult ore to process given the smelting technologies of the eighteenth century. Disagreements among the partners made the mine unprofitable, and the mine—the earliest and largest copper mine in eighteenth century British North America—was closed in 1741. In 1755, the property was acquired by John Viets, who, after several unsuccessful attempts to revive the mine, leased it in 1773 to the colony of Connecticut for use as a prison.

escaped two weeks later. By May, 1774, all prisoners confined at the mine had either died or successfully absconded.

Efforts were made to improve security by constructing a wooden blockhouse over the mine entrance shaft, blocking the drainage tunnel and other shafts, and installing guards. Escapes and deaths continued, however, and little ore was mined. After 1775, Connecticut used the mine to confine political prisoners (Loyalists who opposed the American Revolution). These men, committed to a cause and more motivated than ordinary prisoners, proved dangerous: They rioted. Between 1775 and 1782, there were twelve riots, sixty-two escapes, and the prison buildings burned three times. The last riot, in November, 1782, resulted not only in the destruction of the blockhouse but also in the death of a guard. The prison was closed and all prisoners removed to county jails.

The prison, now surrounded by a wooden pale fence topped with iron spikes, was revived in 1790. As the lower (eastern) end of the mine cavern was flooded, cabins for housing prisoners were constructed only in the upper (western) end. A brick guardhouse was constructed over the mine entrance for housing guards, and a brick forge house with eight blacksmith forges built. The prisoners were now to be employed making nails. In 1802, the wooden pale fence was replaced with a twelve-foot-high wall of sandstone blocks, enclosing approximately three quarters of an acre. In 1805, a brick hospital building was erected inside the compound, followed in 1814 by an attached brick chapel.

Conditions in this prison, even by late eighteenth century standards, were abysmal. The prison was overcrowded, with the prisoner population ranging from forty-four to seventy-seven inmates, all male. The mine was cramped, constantly damp, and unlit; the prisoners lived in darkness. Brought aboveground during the day, prisoners were chained by neck and leg fetters to their forges and given a daily production quota of nine pounds of nails. Failing to produce the quota or committing an infraction of prison rules was punished by whipping. Prison food, which consisted mostly of beef and pork, was cooked by the prisoners at their forges after being tossed to them by the guards. Lacking bathing facilities, the prisoners were dirty and unkempt. Riots and escapes were frequent, re-

sulting in the death of several prisoners. Despite these conditions, the state opened the prison to tourists, attracting approximately five thousand visitors per year. In 1807, English visitor Edward Kendall observed of the prison: "If it be to reform, it is one of the weakest of all human projects; if to punish, it is one of the most barbarous." Others, such as John Pease and John Niles, defended the prison as "consistent with their [the prisoners] security and the economy of the public treasury."

In 1819, a legislative oversight committee found the prison "contracted, filthy, and wretched" and nail manufacturing unprofitable. Reforms were attempted, and nail making was replaced with boot and shoe making, coopering, basket weaving, and light smith work. Whipping as a punishment was replaced with a wheel that powered a gristmill used to supply the prison kitchen with flour. In 1824, a four-story stone cell block building was erected, and prisoners were removed from the mine. With these improved conditions, four women were incarcerated for adultery, but the prison still proved inadequate. The prisoner population grew to 124 inmates, sanitation was poor, the cells were small and overcrowded, and in 1827, the prison was abandoned and all prisoners removed.

At least twenty prisoners died and were buried in an unmarked burial ground in the fifty-four years New-Gate was used as a prison. The present location of this burial lot is unknown.

Nineteenth Century Mining and a Museum

In an attempt to revive the mine, the Phoenix Mining Company, under the leadership of Richard Bacon, purchased the property in 1830. The prison forge house was demolished, a steam engine and other equipment were installed in its place, and the flooded portions of the mine pumped out. Some working may have been done in the mine but most effort seems to have been directed at recovering unprocessed tailings left by the colonial miners. The company failed in 1837, and Bacon then used the mine to manufacture the Bickford Safety Fuse, the first reliable blasting fuse to be used by miners. This enterprise, predecessor to the Engsin Bickford Corporation, was moved to Avon, Connecticut. In 1855, one last attempt at mining was made, but it failed in the depression of 1859, and the mine was permanently closed.

With the cessation of mining, New-Gate again became a tourist attraction. In the later part of the nineteenth century, the guardhouse was used as a dwelling, and visitors, for a fee, were allowed to explore the mine and prison buildings unescorted. In 1891, the Viets family repurchased the property. Lawns and picnic tables were installed, an observation platform was constructed atop the four-story cell-block building for viewing the Farmington Valley, and the prison grounds were used for family reunions. Unfortunately, many of the prison buildings, including the cell block, were destroyed in a 1904 fire.

The property became a commercial tourist attraction in 1926 with the organization of the New-Gate Historical Corporation. Guided tours of the mine were offered, the guardhouse became a dance hall, other buildings housed a restaurant and antique shop, and a new observation tower was built. Added attractions to this eclectic mix included a caged bear, antique cars, a World War I tank, and a wax figure of Ruth Judd, strapped in an electric chair. Goats were allowed to roam the grounds freely. The state of Connecticut purchased the property in 1968, removed the shop, restaurant, extraneous exhibits, and the observation platform and restored the site as a museum. In 1973, New-Gate was designated a National Historic Landmark by the National Park Service.

New-Gate is historically significant for many reasons. The geology of the mine offers insight into the processes of mineral formation that accompany plate tectonics, and it has been extensively studied by geologists from the University of Connecticut. The mine is an important chapter in American engineering history, providing a record of colonial mining methods and technology. Recently, archaeological investigations have examined both the mining and penal history of the site. Its use as a historic place tracks the development of Americans' sense of, and the use of, history. In these many respects, New-Gate is a significant historical landmark, but as a prison, it represents one of the most appalling chapters in American penal history.   —*Robert R. Gradie III*

For Further Information:

Domonell, William G. *Newgate: From Copper Mine to State Prison*. Simsbury, Conn.: Simsbury Historical Society, 1998. Examines the recent history of the site. A more complete bibliography of sources can be found in this publication.

Kendall, Edward Augustus. *Travels Through the Northern Parts of the United States in the Years 1807 and 1808*. 3 vols. New York: I. Riley, 1809. Offers a contemporary description of the prison.

Pease, John C., and John M. Niles. *A Gazetteer of the States of Connecticut and Rhode-Island*. Hartford, Conn.: William S. Marsh, 1819. Contains a contemporary description of the prison.

Perrin, John. *Geology of the Newgate Prison Mine of East Granby, Connecticut*. Storrs: University of Connecticut, Department of Geology and Geophysics, 1967. A discussion of the geology of New-Gate can be found in this master's thesis.

Phelps, Richard H. *A History of Newgate of Connecticut*. Albany, N.Y.: J. Munsell, 1860. Reprint. New York: Arno Press, 1969.

_____. *Newgate of Connecticut: Its Origin and Early History, Being a Full Description of the Famous and Wonderful Simsbury Mines and Caverns, and the Prison Built over Them*. Hartford, Conn.: American, 1876. New and expanded ed. Camden, Maine: Picton Press, 1996. Two versions of Phelps's history of the prison.

Other Historic Sites

Cheney Brothers Historic District

Location: Manchester
Relevant issues: Business and industry
Statement of significance: This 175-acre milling community is little changed since the Cheney family achieved supremacy in silk manufacturing here in the nineteenth century with technical innovations in spinning machinery.

Colt Home

Location: Hartford, Hartford County
Relevant issues: Business and industry

Statement of significance: Armsmear, a large, rambling Italianate house that features a five-story tower, was built in 1855 by Samuel Colt (1814-1862), inventor of the Colt pistol and developer of mass production techniques. Colt's pistol became popular during the war with Mexico, when the federal government ordered one thousand of them.

Connecticut Hall, Yale University

Location: New Haven, New Haven County

Relevant issues: Art and architecture, colonial America, education

Statement of significance: Constructed from 1750 to 1752, this large Georgian structure was the first of Yale's brick buildings and for many years probably the handsomest building in the colony. The only pre-Revolutionary War building on the campus, this is the lone survivor of "Brick Row," a group of Georgian-style buildings built before 1820 and razed after the Civil War.

Deane House

Location: Wethersfield, Hartford County

Relevant issues: Colonial America, political history

Statement of significance: This large-frame two-story Georgian structure was built in 1766 by Silas Deane (1737-1789), a delegate to the first Continental Congress who in March, 1776, was selected as the first envoy of the United States abroad. His instructions were to secure military and financial assistance and to seek an alliance with the French government; Deane succeeded in sending eight shiploads of military supplies to America and enlisting the aid of European military officers. In September, Congress appointed Deane, Benjamin Franklin, and Arthur Lee as the first official commission to France; their negotiations led to two treaties.

Ellsworth Homestead

Location: Windsor, Hartford County

Relevant issues: Colonial America, political history

Statement of significance: From 1782 to 1807, Elmwood was the Connecticut home of Oliver Ellsworth (1745-1807), a framer of the United States Constitution, author of the Judiciary Act of 1789 establishing the federal court system, and the third chief justice of the United States. The house, an eighteenth century two-and-a-half-story clapboarded dwelling, is located a short distance back from the road in a residential area of modern homes in the northern part of Windsor and is owned and administered by the Connecticut chapter of the Daughters of the American Revolution.

Fort Shantok

Location: Montville, New London County

Relevant issues: American Indian history

Statement of significance: From 1636 to 1682, this was the site of the main Mohegan town and the home of Uncas, the most prominent and influential Mohegan leader and statesman of his era. Uncas was first noted in European records as the leader of a small Indian community at "Munhicke" in 1636; within a few years of this, Uncas had emerged as the most prominent Indian client of the Connecticut authorities at New Haven and Hartford. Attracted by his success and influential connections, substantial numbers of Connecticut Indian people joined his community.

Griswold House

Location: Old Lyme, New London County

Relevant issues: Art and architecture

Statement of significance: From 1900 to 1915, Florence Griswold's house was one of the country's most important art colonies and served as the center for American Impressionism. Among the many painters who stayed at the late-Georgian house were Henry Ward Ranger, Louis Paul Dresser, Carleton Wiggins, William Henry Howe, Bruce Crane, Frank Vincent DuMond, Clark Voorhees, Henry Rankin Poore, Allen B. Talcott, Lewis Cohen, and Henry C. White. Griswold, beginning a new life at age forty-nine, provided shelter and a social center for the painters, who enjoyed living at this boardinghouse famous for its good table and its good times. By use of the attic, accommodation could be provided for as many as fifteen artists at any given time.

Historic Ship Nautilus and the Submarine Force Museum

Location: Groton, New London County

Relevant issues: Naval history, science and technology

Statement of significance: The brainchild of Admiral Hyman G. Rickover, the USS *Nautilus* was the world's first nuclear-propelled submarine. Its propulsion system is a landmark in the history of naval engineering and submersible craft. *Nautilus's* nuclear plant enabled the boat to remain submerged for weeks, even months. *Nautilus* demonstrated its capabilities in 1958 when it sailed beneath the Arctic icepack to the North Pole to broadcast the famous message "*Nautilus* 90 North."

Huntington Birthplace

Location: Scotland, Windham County
Relevant issues: Colonial America, political history
Statement of significance: From 1731 to 1747, this large two-story frame saltbox structure was the home of Samuel Huntington (1731-1796), signer of the Declaration of Independence for Connecticut, lawyer, politician, jurist, President of the Continental Congress (1779-1781), and later governor of Connecticut.

Kimberly Mansion

Location: Glastonbury, Hartford County
Relevant issues: Social reform, women's history
Statement of significance: This was the home of Julia and Abby Smith, two elderly sisters who, in 1873, protested vigorously and articulately the inequitable tax assessment of their property, Kimberly Farm. At a time when women were denied the vote, the Smith sisters refused to pay a tax without some voice in the dispositon of their money. The Smiths waged a two-year battle with local authorities, secured a legal decision against the tax collector, and in the process attracted international attention for their stand on women's rights.

Litchfield Historic District

Location: Litchfield, Litchfield County
Relevant issues: Art and architecture, colonial America
Statement of significance: Probably the finest surviving example of a typical late eighteenth century New England town, Litchfield was settled in the 1720's and named for the cathedral city in Staffordshire, England. For much of the 1700's, Litchfield was an outpost and trading center for the northwest frontier. The town reflects architectural styles of the late eighteenth and early nineteenth centuries, as well as the Colonial Revival.

Mashantucket Pequot Reservation Archaeological District

Location: Ledyard, New London County
Relevant issues: American Indian history
Statement of significance: The Mashantucket Pequot Reservation Archaeological District comprises nearly 1,638 acres of archaeologically sensitive land in the northern portion of the uplands historically called Wawarramoreke by the Pequots, and within territory first chronicled as Pequot land in the earliest known surviving map (1614) of the region.

Monte Cristo Cottage

Location: New London, New London County
Relevant issues: Literary history
Statement of significance: For most of his first twenty-one years, this cottage is where Eugene O'Neill (1888-1953), one of America's outstanding dramatists, spent his summers. The house served as inspiration for several of O'Neill's plays, including *Long Day's Journey into Night* (1956).

Morley House

Location: West Hartford, Hartford County
Relevant issues: Science and technology
Statement of significance: From 1906 to 1923, this was the home of the chemist Edward W. Morley (1838-1923), who collaborated with Albert A. Michelson in measuring the speed of light (1887) and determined the atomic weights of hydrogen and oxygen.

New Haven Green Historic District

Location: New Haven, New Haven County
Relevant issues: Art and architecture
Statement of significance: New Haven Green is significant as the setting for three churches erected between 1812 and 1816, remarkable both for individual architectural merit and as an outstanding urban ensemble of the nineteenth century. Center Church and United Church (fine examples of the Federal Style) and Trinity Church (one of the first large Gothic Revival structures in America) stand on the east side of the Green.

Old Statehouse

Location: Hartford, Hartford County

Relevant issues: Art and architecture, political history

Statement of significance: Designed in 1792 and erected from 1793 to 1796, this is the first of the great public buildings attributed to Charles Bulfinch (1763-1844). Also, this was the site of the Hartford Convention (1814), which voiced New England's opposition to the War of 1812.

Prudence Crandall House

Location: Canterbury, Windham County

Relevant issues: African American history, education, social reform

Statement of significance: From 1831 to 1834, this was the residence of Prudence Crandall (1803-1890), American educator and reformer. In 1831, Crandall had been invited by the residents of Canterbury to open a school for young women in their community; however, Crandall immediately lost local support when in the fall of 1832 she admitted Sarah Harris, a young black girl who aspired to be a teacher. Parents were outraged; on September 9, 1834, an angry mob broke into and ransacked the school. The next morning, fearing for the safety of her students, Crandall closed her school.

Reeve House and Law School

Location: Litchfield, Litchfield County

Relevant issues: Legal history

Statement of significance: Founded in 1784 and in operation until 1833, this was the first proprietary law school in the country. Many of the approximately one thousand men who attended became prominent lawyers, judges, and politicians. Aaron Burr and John C. Calhoun were among the graduates.

Remington House

Location: Ridgefield, Fairfield County

Relevant issues: Art and architecture

Statement of significance: For a brief period before his death, this was the home of Frederic Remington (1861-1909), who realistically documented the life of the post-Civil War West in his artwork. Remington designed this fieldstone-and-shingle two-story house himself.

Tarbell House

Location: Easton, Fairfield County

Relevant issues: Literary history, social reform

Statement of significance: From 1906 to 1944, this was the home of Ida Tarbell (1857-1944), one of the pioneers of contemporary journalism and literary biography. Tarbell grew up in Pennsylvania oil towns, witnessing at first hand the corrupt practices of large corporations. As a journalist working for *McClure's Magazine*, Tarbell established her reputation through biographical series on Napoleon and Lincoln and sealed it with a series on the development of Standard Oil, which was later published as the two-volume *History of the Standard Oil Company* (1904). Tarbell and other journalists such as Lincoln Steffens and Upton Sinclair who set aside bland objectivity and focused on grave social problems from a stance of deep moral concern were termed "muckrakers" by President Theodore Roosevelt.

Webster Birthplace

Location: West Hartford, Hartford County

Relevant issues: Literary history

Statement of significance: This is the birthplace of Noah Webster (1758-1843), noted American lexicographer. Webster is most famous for the *American Dictionary of the English Language* (1828).

Delaware

History of Delaware 239
Eleutherian Mills 241
New Castle 243
Wilmington 246
Other Historic Sites 250

A full-size replica of the Kalmar Nyckel, *the ship that brought the first permanent New World settlers to the Delaware Valley in 1638 under the leadership of Peter Minuit.* (Greater Wilmington Convention & Visitors Bureau)

History of Delaware

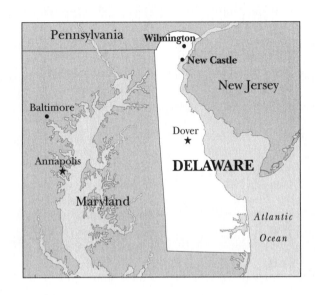

Of the fifty states, only Rhode Island is smaller in land mass than Delaware, which stretches one hundred miles from north to south and varies in width from ten to thirty-five miles. Bounded on the north by Pennsylvania, on the south and west by Maryland, and on the east by the Atlantic Ocean and the Delaware River, whose east bank is in New Jersey, this small state, with a land mass of 1,982 square miles, has just three counties, New Castle in the north, Kent in the middle, and Sussex in the south. The state's mean elevation is about sixty feet.

Early History

As early as 1609, English explorer Henry Hudson sailed on what became known as the Delaware River and the Delaware Bay. By 1631, the Dutch had established the first European settlement in the area around present-day Lewes, in the southeastern part of the state. Long before European settlement began in the region, prehistoric Indians occupied the area. Archaeological excavations at Island Field, twenty miles south of Dover, Delaware's capital, unearthed Indian graves that were close to one thousand years old. The Native Americans in this area are thought to have been the Owascos, a tribe related to the Iroquois, who inhabited the Finger Lakes region in New York.

Later Indian inhabitants in northern Delaware included the Lenni-Lenape Indians, also called the Delaware. Near the ocean and on the Delaware Bay lived the Nanticoke and Assateague Indians. These Indians massacred the first Dutch settlers in the area near Lewes. When more permanent settlement occurred with the arrival of the Swedes, these Indians disappeared from the area.

Permanent Settlements in Delaware

By 1638 a permanent Swedish settlement was established at Fort Christina, which is close to Wilmington on the Delaware River in the state's north. Peter Minuit, who had been colonial governor of New Amsterdam (present-day New York), helped create this settlement for the New Sweden Company, partly sponsored by the Dutch. They soon withdrew their support, leaving a hearty band of Swedes to manage as well as they could on their own. Their governor, Johan Printz, was an able leader who almost single-handedly sustained the beleaguered community.

This settlement, which eventually extended from below Wilmington to Philadelphia, had about one thousand inhabitants. It was eventually overcome in 1655 by Dutch forces sent from New Amsterdam. In 1664, however, the British, rankling at the inroads the Dutch were making on English trade, assaulted New Amsterdam and captured it, then, after a considerable battle, took the Dutch fort at New Castle. The whole of New York and Delaware became part of the province of New York. Delaware remained so until 1682, when the duke of York gave Delaware to William Penn, who owned Pennsylvania.

At first, Penn, whose colony needed more direct access to the ocean, tried to merge his two holdings, but the people in southern Delaware feared that their colony might in time be overwhelmed by Pennsylvania, many times its size. In 1704, Penn finally permitted the people of Delaware to form their own assembly and, although the area had the same governor as Pennsylvania, to make their own laws.

The Revolt Against England

Although sentiment about gaining independence from England was spreading, Delaware had many loyalists among its inhabitants. George Read, one of Delaware's three delegates to the Continental Congress in 1774, voted against the colonies' declaring independence from England. Had another delegate, Caesar Rodney, not ridden on horseback all night from Dover, Delaware, to Philadelphia to cast the deciding vote, Delaware might not have joined the twelve other colonies in supporting the Declaration of Independence.

In 1777, British forces making their way from the Chesapeake Bay to Philadelphia invaded Delaware. George Washington's army had dug in close to Wilmington, but the British troops cut into Pennsylvania south of Wilmington and finally met Washington's men at Brandywine. After the Battle of Brandywine, the British took Wilmington and controlled it until they gained complete control of the Delaware River in June, 1778.

After the Revolutionary War, Delaware, in 1787, became the first of the newly formed states to ratify the United States Constitution, thereby earning one of its nicknames, the First State. Because of its size, Delaware feared it would be viewed as politically inferior to larger states. During the Constitutional Convention in 1787, Delaware called for equal representation for all states. Finally, the Delaware delegation accepted a compromise whereby every state would have two senators but would have representation in the House of Representatives based on each state's population.

The War of 1812

Delaware, which was a Federalist state, opposed the War of 1812. Once the United States entered that war, however, Delaware gave its reluctant support. Residents of the state feared an invasion when the British took Washington, D.C., and, after burning the executive mansion, attacked Baltimore. Delaware was spared by the British, whose only assault on it was an abortive bombardment of Lewes in 1813.

The Du Pont Company

In 1802, Eleuthère Irénée Du Pont built a munitions factory on the Brandywine River. This marked the beginning of the highly influential enterprise E. I. Du Pont de Nemours and Company, which grew into one of the most important chemical companies in the world. The presence of this company in Delaware eventually attracted other corporations to the region.

In time changing its name to the Du Pont Company, having long since expanded from its original munitions manufacturing, it boasts a large nylon plant in Seaford, in the southwestern part of Delaware, and two major pigment factories in other parts of the state. Its home offices and laboratories are located in both Wilmington and Newark, Delaware. A large refinery in Delaware City drew many petrochemical companies to the state.

The Civil War

In 1790 Delaware had about nine thousand slaves, although the state was divided on the slavery issue and many abolitionists were active in helping African slaves escape from the South through Delaware. The state's first constitution, in 1776, made the further importation of slaves illegal. Because the state's tobacco industry was dependent upon slave labor, abolition bills introduced in the 1790's and again in 1847 were narrowly defeated. Nevertheless, by 1860, the slave population in the state had declined to about two thousand.

Although Delaware was staunchly opposed to secession, Abraham Lincoln won no electoral votes from the state in 1860 or in 1864. Delaware was more northern in its outlook and orientation than states in the Deep South. Some men from Delaware joined the Confederate forces, but most Delawareans fought on the Union side.

Despite its Union leanings, Delaware was occupied during the war by Union troops sent by President Lincoln to disarm some of the militia whose loyalty was suspect and to guard the polling places during elections. At war's end, many of the people in Delaware were so incensed by the federal government's punitive measures that the state became solidly Democrat, as did much of the Deep South.

Economy

Strategically situated on the Delaware River, Wilmington became a center of industrial activity in the state. In the city and its environs are textile mills, a steel foundry, automobile assembly operations, paper mills, and tanneries. Many large national corporations established their headquarters in Delaware, primarily in Wilmington, because of state's favorable business climate.

Because of its location near the point where the Delaware River flows into the Atlantic Ocean, Wilmington has proved an ideal location for shipbuilders, who built iron-hulled ships during the nineteenth century. During World War II, the largest employer in the state was a shipbuilding company based in Wilmington that produced ships for the U.S. Navy and Merchant Marine.

The Dover Air Force Base helped Delaware's economy substantially. The national headquarters of the International Reading Association in Newark, whose outreach is enormous, serves ninety thousand members in ninety-nine countries and employs more than eighty people in its headquarters. In 1998 nearly one-third of the people who worked in Delaware worked in the service sector, whereas slightly more than 20 percent were engaged in construction and about 15 percent in some aspect of manufacturing. The unemployment rate in that year was about 4 percent. The 1997 per-capita income was $29,022, up from $10,339 in 1980. The state had 2,667 federal employees in 1997 with average annual salaries of $40,159.

Despite its size, Delaware has a thriving agricultural industry that produces soybeans, lima beans, corn, potatoes, mushrooms, and various grains. It also produces considerable livestock, mainly chickens, hogs, and cattle. Its timber industry produced fifteen million board feet in 1998. Although it is not rich in minerals, Delaware produces magnesium, as well as sand, gravel, and gemstones.

Delaware's Population

A few of Delaware's Native American population, especially descendants of the Nanticoke and Moor Indians, remain in Kent and Sussex counties, although most of the native population was driven out or killed in combat with the Europeans who settled the state. In 1770, more than 20 percent of Delaware's population was African American; in 1998, 16.9 percent was black and less than 3 percent Hispanic.

During the mid-nineteenth century, many Germans and Irish came to Delaware. By the end of the century, southern and eastern Europeans began to arrive in large numbers, seeking work in the state's thriving industries. The first decades of the twentieth century saw the arrival of many Ukrainians and Greeks. As industry grew, many people arrived from other states to take advantage of Delaware's economic opportunities. In 1998 about 3 percent of the state's population was foreign-born.

Delaware, lying in the highly urbanized corridor that runs from Boston to Richmond, Virginia, experienced rapid population growth in the last third of the twentieth century. It population density of 340.8 people per square mile is among the greatest in the United States, and its population of three-quarters of a million should exceed the million mark well before 2010.   —R. Baird Shuman

Eleutherian Mills

Date: Established in 1802

Relevant issues: Business and industry, science and technology

Significance: This estate on the banks of the Brandywine River was the residence of Eleuthère Irénée Du Pont (1771-1834) and the site of his original black powder mills. Various grades of black powder—a mixture of sulfur, saltpeter, and charcoal—were used as explosives in the construction of roads, canals, and railroads, and in mining, farming, and war.

Location: Four miles north of downtown Wilmington on Route 141, near other Du Pont estates, including Longwood and Winterthur

Site Office:

Hagley Museum and Library
P.O. Box 3630
Wilmington, DE 19807-0630
ph.: (302) 658-2400
Web site: www.hagley.lib.de.us/

Eleutherian Mills, located in the Brandywine woods, encompasses the site of an early, successful industry in the young American republic and illustrates the use of water power to drive machinery. The Du Pont family, owner of the black powder works, helped stimulate the development of Wilmington, Delaware, as an industrial, shipping, and financial hub.

The Black Powder Company

In 1800, Eleuthère Irénée Du Pont, his brother Victor, and his parents emigrated to the United States from France. An avid hunter, Irénée was dismayed at the high price and poor quality of gunpowder. Resolved to start a business, he returned to France to gain expertise in the making of gunpowder and to buy equipment and raise capital. He founded E. I. Du Pont de Nemours and Company in 1802. A student of the great chemist Antoine-Laurent Lavoisier in the 1780's, Irénée had learned the importance of quality control and took great pains to purify sulfur (imported from Italy) and saltpeter (imported from India).

Irénée built the mills along the Brandywine River where a drop of more than 120 feet in only five miles supplied excellent waterpower. He had the mills constructed with safety in mind: They had three thick stone walls, with a wooden roof sloping toward the wooden fourth wall that faced the river. In the inevitable explosions, the wooden structures gave way, minimizing danger to workers and other buildings.

The first shipments of gunpowder were made in 1803, and the company prospered, aided soon by demands for black powder during the War of 1812. Irénée reinvested his share of the profit, thus enabling the company to grow.

During the history of Du Pont black powder manufacture, 288 explosions resulting in 228 deaths were documented. Though not required to do so by law, the Du Ponts gave pensions to widows and housing to families of workers who were killed. Irénée immediately rebuilt after each explosion and consequently remained in debt his entire life.

E. I. Du Pont, Botanist

Though Irénée worked in his family's printing firm in France, he listed his occupation as "botanist" in his emigration papers. His father—a Physiocrat and economist who believed that human well-being arose from the land—had taught him natural history on the family estate, Bois-des-Fossés. Irénée kept careful records of seeds that he brought to

Eleutherian Mills. (Kevin Fleming)

America and exchanged seeds with many people in France, including Joséphine, wife of Napoleon Bonaparte. In 1802, he began an orchard with fruit trees brought from France. The next year, he built a comfortable house overlooking the mills and planned its gardens in great detail.

Irénée utilized trees grown on his property to make the charcoal necessary for the black powder, to provide timber for dams, and to construct buildings and even waterwheel shafts and buckets. He also grew crops and had a sizable flock of Merino sheep, which provided wool for his brother Victor's woolen mill across the river.

Eleutherian Mills Today

The original sixty-five-acre site includes the house built by Irénée, a research library, and ruins of the black powder mills. After an explosion in the 1850's, the house was substantially enlarged. An 1890 explosion destroyed the mills for the last time and caused great damage to the house. It remained uninhabited for two years and was then turned into a club for workers. During World War I, troops were stationed at the house to guard against sabotage of other Du Pont mills added along the Brandywine River during the nineteenth century. An explosion in 1921 destroyed these mills.

In 1921 a grandson of Irénée, Colonel Henry A. Du Pont (1838-1926), bought the property for his daughter Louise Du Pont Crowninshield (1877-1958) and her husband. They remodeled the house, restored the first floor to appear as she remembered it from her childhood, and added a Renaissance garden in the mill ruins. In 1954, she gave the property to the Hagley Foundation, founded in 1952 to celebrate 150 years of the Du Pont Company. Archaeological excavations of the front lawn enabled the restoration of Irénée's original garden. *—Kristen L. Zacharias*

For Further Information:

Chandler, Alfred D., Jr., and Stephen Salsbury. *Pierre S. Du Pont and the Making of the Modern Corporation.* New York: Harper & Row, 1971. A biography of Pierre S. Du Pont (1870-1954) detailing diversification of the Du Pont Company. Includes discussions of the gunpowder industry.

Du Pont de Nemours, E. I. *Du Pont: The Autobiography of an American Enterprise.* New York: Charles Scribner's Sons, 1952. An account of the Du Pont Company in the context of American history and industry. Profusely illustrated with drawings and photographs.

Jolly, Pierre. *Apostle of Liberty and the Promised Land.* Translated and annotated by Elise Du Pont Elrick, Du Pont de Nemours. Wilmington, Del.: Brandywine, 1977. A biography of Pierre Samuel Du Pont de Nemours (1739-1817), Irénée's father. Discusses the relationships of Pierre with notable French personages and includes details about Irénée and the founding of the Du Pont Company.

Wall, Joseph Frazier. *Alfred I. du Pont: The Man and His Family.* New York: Oxford University Press. 1990. Biography of Alfred I. Du Pont (1864-1935). Provides a history of his ancestors and their business endeavors.

Wilkinson, Norman B. *E. I. Du Pont, Botaniste: The Beginning of a Tradition.* Charlottesville: University of Virginia Press. Published for the Eleutherian Mills-Hagley Foundation, 1972. Focuses on the botanical interests of Irénée and the history of the gardens at his and other Du Pont estates.

Winkler, John. *The Du Pont Dynasty.* New York: Reynal and Hitchcock, 1935. A history of the Du Pont family from their French origins to the early twentieth century.

New Castle

Date: Founded in 1655

Relevant issues: Colonial America, European settlement

Significance: The Dutch founded Fort Casimir in 1651 and the town of New Amstel in 1655 as a hub of the Dutch colony of New Netherland. The town became the capital of the English colony of Delaware and the seat of New Castle County. Architectural remnants survive from both the colonial and the Federal periods.

Location: About three miles south of Wilmington on the Delaware River

Site Office:
New Castle Court House Museum
211 Delaware Street
New Castle, DE 19720
ph.: (302) 323-4453
Web site: www.co.new-castle.de.us

The New Castle Historic District is a vestige of Delaware's colonial Dutch and English heritage, which began in the mid-seventeenth century as one of the earliest European settlements in North America. The city's surviving colonial and Federal-era architecture attests to its prominence as a vital part of the Dutch colony of New Netherland, the English colonial capital of Delaware, capital of the independent state of Delaware, and county seat.

Dutch Colony

The New Castle area was sighted by Dutch explorer Cornelis Hendricksen in 1614. Within a few years, the Dutch came to refer to the area as the *Santhoek* (Sand-hook). The "hook" was washed away by tides before the twentieth century. New Netherland director Peter Stuyvesant purchased the land from Minquas Indians in 1651 so the Dutch could dominate the confluence of the bay and the river, thereby blocking the colonial ambitions of their Swedish and English rivals. Stuyvesant established Fort Casimir on the site in 1651 (naming it after Count Ernst-Casimir, earl of Nassau-Dietz). The Minquas, however, had previously sold the Santhoek area to the Swedes in 1638, and the Swedes managed to capture Fort Casimir in 1654 (renaming it Fort Trinity). Stuyvesant struck back in 1655 and conquered the New Sweden colony.

He then laid out a Dutch colonial town called New Amstel in the vicinity of the fort. New Amstel consisted of a small urban core (originally about twenty houses) and surrounding lands called the "Colony of the City." The inhabitants bartered with the Indians for furs and sailed to New Amsterdam for firearms and alcohol. They also sold beer and slaves to the English colonists in Maryland in return for tobacco, which they shipped to the Netherlands. Only half of the town's inhabitants were Dutch; the rest were Swedish, Finnish, French, English, and Scottish (along with several dozen African slaves). The European population fluctuated between 130 and 200 residents and fell off in 1657 due to a disease that killed over one hundred residents.

English Conquest and American Revolution

The Anglo-Dutch rivalry erupted into war in 1664 when the duke of York fielded a campaign against Dutch positions on the Hudson and Delaware Rivers. Sir Robert Carr arrived on the Delaware with a force of over one hundred men aboard the HMS *Guinea* and stormed New Amstel on October 3, 1664, easily overwhelming its garrison of thirty Dutchmen. The Dutch who swore allegiance to the English crown kept their property. The English had been aware of the Delaware Bay area since Samuel Argall explored it in 1610 and named it after Lord de La Warre (hence, "Delaware"). The town was first referred to as "New Castle" in 1665, so named after the earl of New Castle, a friend of the duke.

In 1682, the duke of York transferred his Delaware holdings to William Penn, proprietor of Pennsylvania. Penn first came ashore in North America in New Castle on October 27, 1682. He organized New Castle as one of Pennsylvania's three "Lower Provinces," but many former Dutch colonists resented living under Penn's strict Quaker law, and Lord Baltimore questioned Penn's control over the area. Delaware formally separated from Pennsylvania in 1704, and New Castle was proclaimed the provincial capital. During the American Revolution, Pennsylvania and Maryland acknowledged Delaware's independence, but as New Castle was considered to be too exposed to the British, Dover was made the state capital.

Gradual Decline After the Revolution

New Castle became a commercial center again in the 1780's, aided by construction of a turnpike to the Chesapeake River. A devastating fire destroyed most of the old colonial wooden houses along the strand (near the waterfront) in 1824. The city saw trade diverted from it with the opening of the Delaware-Chesapeake Canal in 1828 and again in the 1840's, when Wilmington became the Delaware hub for rail lines connecting Philadelphia and Baltimore. In 1881, the seat of New Castle County was moved to Wilmington.

Places to Visit

There are only two Dutch colonial remnants in the town—the town green (perhaps laid out by Stuyvesant himself) and the so-called Dutch House located on Third Street. More buildings survive from the English colonial period, including two churches: Immanuel Episcopal Church located on Market Street (1703; tower dates from 1822), which was the first Anglican parish church in Dela-

Historic New Castle. (Greater Wilmington Convention & Visitors Bureau)

ware; and the Presbyterian Church on Second Street (formerly the Dutch Reformed Church of 1657, rebuilt in 1707). The Court House (1732) was Delaware's colonial capitol building from 1732 to 1777. It is located on Delaware Street. The palatial Amstel House (1738) is located at Fourth and Delaware Streets. There are several surviving old homes located on the strand which are now private residences, and the Rising Sun Tavern (1796), a famed early public meeting place on Harmony Street, is also now a private residence. Among the public Federal period sites is the restored George Read II House on the strand (original construction, 1801). The Old Town Hall (1823), located at Delaware and Market Streets, once served as the federal courthouse. —*William E. Watson*

For Further Information:

Eckman, Jeanette. *New Castle on the Delaware.* Wilmington, Del.: New Castle Historical Society, 1950. Reliable overview of the history of the town.

Myers, Albert Cook. *Narratives of Early Pennsylvania, West New Jersey, and Delaware.* New York: Charles Scribner's Sons, 1912. Compendium of early English, Dutch, and Swedish sources on the seventeenth and eighteenth century colonial history of the Delaware Valley.

Ward, Christopher. *The Dutch and Swedes on the Delaware, 1609-1664.* Philadelphia: University of Pennsylvania Press, 1930. Thorough assessment of Dutch and Swedish colonial activity in the Delaware Valley.

Weslager, C. A. *Dutch Explorers, Traders, and Settlers in the Delaware Valley.* Philadelphia: University of Pennsylvania Press, 1961. Authoritative study of Dutch colonial activity and concise explanations of Dutch motivations.

_____. *The English on the Delaware.* New Brunswick, N.J.: Rutgers University Press, 1967. Examines the causes, course, and consequences of the English successes along the river.

_____. *The Swedes and Dutch at New Castle.* Wilmington, Del.: Middle Atlantic Press, 1987.

Thorough examination of the early European presence at New Castle and useful assessment of the relevant Dutch and Swedish sources.

Wilmington

Date: Settled by Swedes, then taken over by English setters in 1664

Relevant issues: Colonial America, European settlement

Significance: Wilmington, the largest city in Delaware, has tswo downtown districts listed on the National Register of Historic Places: the Market Street Multiple Resource Area and the Lower Market Street Historic District. Greater Wilmington contains numerous important historic sites, such as the Hagley gunpowder mills and the historic homes of Odessa.

Location: Northern Delaware, on the Delaware River at the junction of the Brandywine and Christina Rivers, situated in New Castle County in Brandywine Valley

Site Office:
Greater Wilmington Convention and Visitors Bureau
1300 Market Street
Wilmington, DE 19801
ph.: (302) 652-4088
fax: (302) 652-4726
e-mail: info@wilmcvb.org

Inscribed on Delaware highway signs and in its information brochures is the state's apt motto, Small Wonder. One of the smallest states in the union, Delaware has a notable past, one predating even British colonial rule. Delaware's oldest city, Wilmington, and the surrounding Brandywine Valley contain much for the visitor to see—from a wonderfully preserved historic village outside the city limits, to landmarks of the Industrial Revolution, to a world class art museum. The city itself, one of the oldest in the United States, is situated at the confluence of two scenic rivers and boasts historic homes and a beautifully restored opera house.

Arrivals from Sweden and the Netherlands

Swedish settlers began arriving in what is now northern Delaware as far back as 1638. Their interest in North America was purely commercial, since land was abundant in Sweden and the country underpopulated. The fur trade was a highly lucrative one, and there were not enough fur-bearing animals in Western Europe to keep up with the demand for fur. A commercial venture in Sweden chartered two ships bound for North America, the *Kalmar Nyckel* and the *Vogel Grip*, which sailed up the river the Swedes would dub Christina (for Sweden's queen) to establish Fort Christina on its banks. This was the origin of future Wilmington, which would not adopt that name officially until 1740.

The Swedes, who immediately began trading with the neighboring Lenni-Lenape Indians for furs, were too few to withstand the aggressive, well-armed agents of the Dutch West India Company. They, too, were establishing commercial settlements along the Atlantic seaboard, as were the English. Fort Christina would fall to Dutch control, and then to the British, who asserted their ultimate authority over the colony in 1664. In that year, King Charles II of England granted all the territory between the Delaware and Connecticut Rivers to his brother James, oblivious to the fact that the area was populated by at least two Indian tribes, as well as by Swedish and Dutch settlers who had no desire to be subject to English rule. Charles subsequently ceded the territory to William Penn in 1682, and what is now Delaware—the name is not Indian, but rather, the name of a seventeenth century governor of Virginia, Lord De La Warr—became part of Pennsylvania. The three counties of Delaware gained their own legislature in 1704, but did not become completely separate from Pennsylvania until 1776.

The Swedes left their mark on early Wilmington. Holy Trinity Church (now known as Old Swedes Church), a Swedish Lutheran church until it was sold by the dwindling Swedish congregation to an English Anglican community in 1792, still stands with its original walls and pulpit, dating from 1698. The river Christina has retained its Swedish name to this day. The Swedish settlers also introduced log cabins into Delaware. The Dutch, who succeeded the Swedes, endowed early Wilmington with an important industry—brickmaking—which would play a major role in the city's economy until the coming of the Industrial Revolution in the 1840's.

English and Quaker Influence

White settlement increased rapidly in the Wilmington area after the English took possession in 1664. Slavery became important in the southern Delaware counties of Sussex and Kent, but not in New Castle County, where most blacks were free. These free blacks lived on the outskirts of Wilmington in the eighteenth century, on the least desirable land, and were restricted to casual day labor. Legal separation of the races in Wilmington was the norm until well into the twentieth century. African Americans did establish their own institutions, especially churches, some of which are still standing today.

Quakers from Pennsylvania played an important role in the history of Delaware and Wilmington. In the early eighteenth century one of them, Thomas Willing, inherited land bordering the original Swedish settlement on the Christina River. Aware of the rising value of land, he planned a town on a grid pattern much like that of Philadelphia and made the pragmatic decision to erect a market house that soon became a hub of commercial activity. In 1740, Willingtown, as the new hamlet was dubbed, was awarded borough status in a royal charter granted by King George II. He in turn insisted that the town adopt the name of a good friend of his, the first earl of Wilmington.

A steady stream of Quakers arrived in colonial Wilmington. They became leading businessmen, and were the owners of the many mills around the city. They built sturdy brick homes and a Friends Meeting House, one of the oldest structures in the city and still beautifully intact. They disdained slavery, drinking, gambling, dancing, and music, and were responsible for the first schools and charitable institutions in the city. The Quakers of Wilmington were recognized as conscientious objectors during the Revolutionary War and they inspired the establishment of the Delaware Abolition Society in the nineteenth century.

By 1739, more than six hundred people inhabited Wilmington. The influx of Quakers gave way in the mid-to-late eighteenth century to Scotch-Irish, who built the city's first Presbyterian church in 1740. The town's economy in that colonial era was diverse, based on agriculture but including important industries such as brickmaking and flour milling. Thousands of barrels of flour were shipped to the Philadelphia market each year. The city's main structures were its churches and market building. Its location on the confluence of two rivers, the Christina and the Brandywine, made the city an important locus of commercial activity. Artisans' shops proliferated, and the town was prosperous, socially stratified, and adverse to change.

Revolution, Political and Industrial

Anti-British sentiment predominated in the city before 1776, with the result that during the Revolutionary War, Wilmington was occupied for months by British Redcoats. Skirmishes took place outside of Wilmington, and war-weary citizens cheered the end of war and American victory with an outdoor party, complete with fireworks. In those days without the telegraph or electricity, an "express" horseman breathlessly announced the news of General Cornwallis's surrender at Yorktown, Virginia, and the town crier loudly proclaimed the victory in the streets of Wilmington. Delaware quickly became one of the original thirteen states, and tiny though it was, there was to be a marked difference between the two southern counties of Delaware, with their large estates and close ties and sympathies with the south, and the northern county of New Castle, with Wilmington the most rapidly developing economic area, closely linked to Philadelphia and New York. The construction in 1798 of Wilmington's beautiful Town Hall, still in use and wonderfully preserved, reflected not only civic pride but also the town's growing economic power.

At the start of the new century, a young Frenchman named Eleuthère Irénée Du Pont arrived in Delaware to escape the political turmoil of France. He brought with him his father and brother, and the three of them invested in a gunpowder mill a few miles outside of Wilmington, on the banks of the Brandywine River. This enterprise was an almost immediate success, and led to the creation of the famous Du Pont commercial empire, which in the twentieth century expanded into chemicals and related industries. The original gunpowder mill as well as the Du Pont estate and gardens have all been carefully restored and are open to the public.

The history of nineteenth century Wilmington is the story of the Industrial Revolution, beginning with the coming of the railroad to Wilmington in 1837. With the area rich in raw material and plentifully supplied with skilled labor, heavy industry in

Old Swedes Church in Wilmington. (Greater Wilmington Convention & Visitors Bureau)

the form of railroad and ship construction, carriage making, tanning, and foundry work, supplanted the original light industries of the late eighteenth and early nineteenth centuries. Delaware did not suffer the ravages of the Civil War as did neighboring states, but rather experienced an economic upswing because of huge government orders for goods of all kinds. The wealth of the city was reflected in the post-Civil War period with the construction in 1871 of the Grand Opera House, an elegant structure in popular baroque Second Empire style of the day. It was restored in the 1970's.

Free and newly freed blacks in the city, hovering around 10 percent of the population, saw their economic conditions worsen after the Civil War. Discrimination intensified—at least one electric trolley line instructed its conductors to ignore black passengers waiting on street corners—and with the advent of trade unions, which refused to accept blacks, skilled black workers found it nearly impossible to find employment in the city's many factories.

With the gradual decline of heavy manufacturing from the beginning of the twentieth century, Wilmington experienced a decline in wealth and population. The automobile enabled many to live outside the city, decreasing the city's tax base. The wealthy no longer preferred to live in the city, but in exclusive suburban enclaves. The presence of the Du Pont Company's headquarters in Wilmington was a stabilizing factor, however, and the downtown area experienced a renaissance in the 1980's. Downtown Wilmington now boasts two districts listed on the National Register of Historic Places: the Market Street Multiple Resource District and the Lower Market Street Historic District. The rejuvenation of the downtown area has attracted new businesses and increased tourism.

Places to Visit

Wilmington is nestled in the historic Brandywine Valley. Adjacent to Wilmington are New Castle, Hagley, and many other sites of interest. The Winterthur Museum and Gardens, six miles northwest of Wilmington, was the home of Henry Francis Du Pont, great-grandson of E. I. Du Pont, an avid art connoisseur and lover of gardens. In 1926 he inherited the estate, originally built in 1839, and transformed it into a showplace of American horticulture and decorative arts. Winterthur also operates another historic site, the Historic Houses of Odessa, a group of well-preserved eighteenth century homes in the town of Odessa, about twenty miles south of Wilmington. Another famous Du Pont family estate, in Wilmington itself, is the Nemours Mansion, a chateau in the style of Louis XVI, completed in 1910, with many original artifacts and lush flower gardens.

Just six miles south of Wilmington lies New Castle, a town of historical significance and beauty. New Castle was originally a Dutch village called New Amstel, established in 1651. When British forces wrested control of the Dutch settlements under their commander, Sir James, duke of York, in 1664, they changed the name of the settlement to New Castle. The village square had been laid out by Peter Stuyvesant in the 1650's. Around it arose a beautiful group of eighteenth century and, eventually, nineteenth century buildings.

Situated on the Delaware River, New Castle was the seat of Delaware's government until 1777. Because of its strategic importance and its antiroyalist inhabitants, it was bombarded during the Revolutionary War; its exposure to attack led to the capital's relocation to Dover. One can still visit the Old Court House, which was the home of the Delaware Assembly throughout most of the eighteenth century.

One of the most famous of the village's private homes is the beautifully preserved George Read II house and garden. Read, a lawyer and son of a signer of the Declaration of Independence, had the home built between 1797 and 1804. The house contains many original artifacts as well as the intricately carved woodwork that was at the height of fashion in the early years of the republic.

New Castle was at its zenith until the coming of the railroad in the 1830's, which lessened the strategic value of the town's location on the Delaware River. Consequently, there was little urban development and many of the historic houses and buildings were preserved, to be restored and renovated in the twentieth century.

In the small village of Hagley, three miles north of Wilmington, lies a charming and historically significant site, the first Du Pont gunpowder works, established in 1802. The Du Pont mills were almost immediately successful, and began to expand just before the War of 1812. The 230-acre, nineteenth century industrial site, now called the Hagley Museum, contains the original gunpowder mill, situated on the Brandywine River, which manufactured gunpowder until the end of World War I. Adjacent to the mill is Eleutherian Mills, the estate of E. I. Du Pont, a Georgian-style mansion with original furnishings intact and beautiful formal gardens open year-round to the public.

Wilmington and the surrounding area form a treasure trove of historic sites that reflect in microcosm four centuries of American history ranging from the original church of the early Swedish settlers, churches and buildings of the British colonial period, a beautifully preserved specimen of the Industrial Revolution in the Hagley gunpowder mills, and the growing affluence of the American business elite, reflected in the Grand Opera House in Wilmington as well as in the Du Pont estates.

—*Sina Dubovoy*

For Further Information:

Biggs, Michael. *Wilmington: The City and Beyond.* Wilmington, Del.: Jared, 1991. In a more popular mode is this beautifully illustrated work, with an excellent introduction to the history of Wilmington by Barbara Benson. This is a good book to take along on a historic walking tour of the city and its environs.

Hoffecker, Carol E. *Wilmington, Delaware: Portrait of an Industrial City, 1830-1910.* Charlottesville: University Press of Virginia, 1983. A more detailed, scholarly, but highly readable work focusing exclusively on Wilmington from earliest days to the early twentieth century. Urban, demographic, and economic trends are just some of the themes of this slender volume, replete with vintage photographs of old Wilmington.

Lincoln, Anna T. *Wilmington, Delaware: Three Centuries Under Four Flags, 1609-1937.* Port Washington, N.Y.: Kennikat Press, 1972. Also offers a detailed picture of Wilmington's early history.

McNinch, Marjorie G. *Festivals.* Wilmington, Del.: Cedar Tree Press, 1996. Covers the festivals and history of Wilmington, including ethnic festivals and social life.

Pearce, B. Ben. *Historical Vignettes of African American Churches in Wilmington, Delaware.* Wilmington, Del.: Chaconia Press, 1998.

Wamsley, James S. *Brandywine Valley: An Introduction to Its Treasures.* New York: Harry N. Abrams, 1992. The best one-volume, descriptive account of the major historic sites, museums, and gardens in this picturesque region surrounding Wilmington. Sites covered (and richly illustrated) include Winterthur and the Hagley gunpowder works.

Zilg, Gerard Colby. *Du Pont: Behind the Nylon Curtain.* Englewood Cliffs, N.J.: Prentice Hall, 1974. A compelling account of the Du Pont dynasty of Wilmington, and the evolution of the Du Pont Company from a humble gunpowder works on the banks of the Brandywine River to the largest chemical company in the world. It includes detailed descriptions of the Du Pont estates in and around Wilmington.

Other Historic Sites

Broom House

Location: Montchanin, New Castle County

Relevant issues: Colonial America, political history

Statement of significance: Jacob Broom (1752-1810), a signer of the U.S. Constitution, served in the Delaware legislature and attended the Annapolis Convention (1786). He lived in this house from 1795 to 1802.

Dickinson House

Location: Dover, Kent County

Relevant issues: Colonial America, political history

Statement of significance: John Dickinson (1732-1808) served in the Delaware and Pennsylvania legislatures. He was a member of the Stamp Act Congress, the First and Second Continental Congresses, and the Constitutional Convention. His political writings, such as *Letters from a Farmer in Pennsylvania* (1767-1768), were influential.

Fort Christina

Location: Wilmington, New Castle County

Relevant issues: European settlement, military history

Statement of significance: This was the site of the first Swedish military outpost (1638) in the Delaware Valley, which became the nucleus of the first Swedish settlement in North America and its trading and commercial center. It fell into disrepair after the English conquest in 1664, and the last vestiges of the fort disappeared.

Stonum

Location: New Castle, New Castle County

Relevant issues: Colonial America, political history

Statement of significance: This was the country home of George Read (1733-1798), signer of the U.S. Constitution, whose support led Delaware to become the first state to ratify the document.

District of Columbia

History of the District of Columbia 252
The Capitol 254
Ford's Theatre 259
Frederick Douglass National Historic Site . . . 262
Gallaudet University 266
Georgetown 269
Lincoln Memorial 272
Mary McLeod Bethune Council House 275

The National Mall 279
Sewall-Belmont House 283
Smithsonian Institution 286
Thomas Jefferson Memorial 290
Vietnam Veterans Memorial 292
Washington Monument 296
The White House 299
Other Historic Sites 304

The Supreme Court Building. (Digital Stock)

History of the District of Columbia

In 1783, the Congress of the United States of America determined that the newly independent country should have a permanent seat of government. Selection of the site was delayed as politicians argued, believing that prestige and wealth would flow to the area surrounding the new federal city. A compromise was reached in 1790 when northern leaders dropped their opposition to a southern site in return for political concessions. The following year President George Washington selected a ten-mile square of land along the Potomac for a new district in which the United States capital would be built. The area included land contributed by both Virginia and Maryland.

Washington hired Pierre Charles L'Enfant, a French architect and engineer, to design the layout for the new capital city. L'Enfant envisioned a city with massive public buildings, an array of open spaces, and a network of beautifully landscaped roads. L'Enfant was assisted by Andrew Ellicott, the chief surveyor, and Benjamin Banneker, a self-taught African American mathematician and surveyor. The engineers and architects working on the new capital named the city Washington, in honor of the president. Washington himself remained adamant in calling it "Federal City."

Construction and Early Growth

After a suggestion from Thomas Jefferson, L'Enfant designed the capital district in a diamond shape. At the heart of the design were the presidential mansion, which became known as the White House, the Capitol building, and Pennsylvania Avenue, the street connecting them. L'Enfant located the two buildings one mile apart—far enough for formal transportation between them, but near enough for the president to keep abreast of legislative activity. L'Enfant also planned a sweeping four hundred-foot-wide public walk from the Capitol to the Potomac, which would then angle to the president's house. The National Mall was designed as a place for museums, fountains, and monuments that would represent the heroes and ideals of the young republic.

When the federal government moved from Philadelphia in 1800, only the north wing of the Capitol building had been completed. It contained the House of Representatives, the Senate, the Library of Congress, and the Supreme Court. The Library of Congress was moved to a new building in 1897, and the Supreme Court in 1935. When Washington, D.C., was burned in 1814 by the British during the War of 1812, the White House and Capitol were rebuilt. The basic structure of the Capitol building, including the great dome, was completed in 1863.

Early predictions that Washington, D.C., would quickly grow into a commercial metropolis of more than 100,000 people were not realized. The established cities of Boston, New York, Philadelphia, Baltimore, and Charleston continued to dominate the coastal economy. By the 1840's, Washington, D.C., still had only 50,000 residents, leading Congress in 1846 to return land west of the Potomac to the states which had originally given it up when the federal district was authorized.

The secret to the city's eventual growth was crisis, not commerce. During the Civil War (1861-1865), the population of Washington, D.C., grew to 120,000, as troops, civilian planners, and freed slaves moved into the city. A housing shortage ensued, and the inadequacy of city services, already evident before the war, was further exacerbated. President Ulysses S. Grant implemented a hastily devised plan to expand and construct water, sewer, road, and sidewalk systems throughout the city. By 1873 a "new" and more functional Washington, D.C., had appeared, though the cumulative effect of building placement over the years and the installation of the new public works destroyed much of the aesthetic grandeur of L'Enfant's original city design.

Along with the city's new look came a new form of government. Congress had been empowered by

the Constitution to govern the federal district, but had by 1802 established a mayor and city council to help them govern. By 1820, citizens of Washington, D.C., were allowed to vote for council members and a mayor, though not for congressional representatives or the president. In 1871, Congress converted the district to territorial status, with an appointed governor, in order to facilitate the rebuilding of the city. Three years later, Congress established a local government comprising three commissioners appointed by the president. Washington, D.C., thus became the only American city which did not allow its people to elect local officials.

Social and Political Changes in the Twentieth Century

The next phase of rapid growth came after the United States entered World War I in 1917. In less than two years, the population rose from 350,000 to more than 450,000, once again straining city services. Much of the Mall was turned into a parking lot.

During the Great Depression of the 1930's, many Americans had trouble finding jobs. Jobs were plentiful in Washington, D.C., however, as the federal government organized and staffed many programs for ending the depression. As a result, the city's population grew from about 485,000 to 665,000 during the decade.

With the vast expansion of the federal government during World War II (1941-1945) and the Cold War (1945-1991), Washington, D.C., grew rapidly. Though the actual population of the city declined from its peak of more than 800,000 in 1950, the metropolitan area (including suburbs) grew faster than any other major city in the United

States. Between 1950 and 1980, the city's population doubled, from 1.5 million to more than 3 million.

Population growth brought dramatic social change. After World War II, whites steadily moved into the suburbs of neighboring Virginia and Maryland. African Americans thus became a majority of the population in Washington, D.C., beginning in the 1950's. At the time of the 1990 census, they composed more than 65 percent of the population.

The post-World War II period also saw increased public demand for political rights. The Twenty-third Amendment to the Constitution of the United States was passed in 1961, granting the presidential vote to the people of Washington, D.C., for the first time. The right to elect local government officials was restored by Congress in 1973.

Two movements for increased political power in Washington, D.C., failed during the last quarter of the twentieth century. A constitutional amendment that would have provided for the election of voting delegates to the U.S. House of Representatives and Senate was introduced in 1978, but failed to receive the approval of three-fourths of the states necessary for ratification. A movement in favor of statehood for the District of Columbia also began in the 1970's. Although a state constitution was drawn up in 1982 for the proposed fifty-first state of New Columbia, by the end of the century Congress had failed to act upon the measure.

The issue of political control was hotly debated throughout the 1990's as Washington, D.C., ranked high in virtually every negative category documenting quality of urban life, including infant mortality, crime, drug addiction, and school dropout rates. Facing bankruptcy and an erosion of city services, in 1995 Washington, D.C.'s finances were taken over by a control board appointed by Congress. In 1997, a bill was passed granting one billion dollars in federal aid to the District of Columbia over a five-year period. Though the aid provided a substantial boost to the economy, critics complained that the concurrent shift of control from the mayor's office to the appointed board was once again depriving citizens of their democratic rights.

Monuments and Marches

As the seat of American government, Washington, D.C., was the United States' preeminent city for monuments commemorating the democratic ideal and for marches demonstrating its flexibility. Memorials in honor of four of the United States' greatest presidents have been constructed there. The 555-foot-high Washington Monument is located on the National Mall, due south of the White House. It was begun in 1848 but not dedicated until 1885. The Lincoln Memorial, constructed in the style of an ancient Greek temple, was completed in 1922, at the west end of the Mall. The Thomas Jefferson Memorial, echoing Jefferson's own design for the rotunda at the University of Virginia, was finished in 1943. The Roosevelt Memorial, a 7.5-acre landscape of waterfalls and statuary partially enclosed by granite walls, was dedicated in 1997.

American soldiers have also been honored at several sites. The Arlington National Cemetery, including the Tomb of the Unknowns, and the Marine Corps War Memorial (Iwo Jima statue) are located just across the Potomac River in Virginia, on land that had once been part of the federal district. The Vietnam Veterans Memorial, two adjoining walls of black granite inscribed with the names of all Americans who died in Vietnam, was dedicated in 1982 and is located near the Lincoln Memorial at the west end of the Mall. In 1998, a design for a World War II Memorial was approved.

As a bastion of free speech, Washington, D.C., has been the site of many public demonstrations, including the famous civil rights march of August 28, 1963, led by the Reverend Martin Luther King, Jr. Standing on the steps of the Lincoln Memorial, King delivered his famous "I Have a Dream" speech to more than 200,000 marchers. Many major demonstrations protesting the Vietnam War were held in Washington, D.C., during the 1960's and 1970's. In 1995, the city was the site of the Million Man March, organized by Nation of Islam leader Louis Farrakhan. Promoted as a day of commitment and unity for African American men, the march was estimated to have drawn between 400,000 and 800,000 people.

Conclusion

Washington, D.C., was envisioned from the beginning as a great commercial and cultural center, as well as the seat of the American government. It was slow in developing. In 1842, English novelist Charles Dickens characterized it as a "city of magnificent intentions," with "broad avenues that be-

gin in nothing and lead nowhere." During the last half of the twentieth century, however, the city grew into its early promise. In 2000, Washington, D.C., boasted seventeen universities and colleges, including American University, George Washington University, Georgetown University, and Howard University. The Mall and nearby areas included great cultural centers such as the museums of the Smithsonian Institution, the National Gallery of Art, and the John F. Kennedy Center for the Performing Arts. Combined with the governing institutions of the American republic and the symbolic monuments to its growth, Washington, D.C., itself is one of the proudest monuments to the American way of life.
—*Tessa Powell*

The Capitol

Date: Construction began on September 18, 1793
Relevant issues: Political history
Significance: The second-oldest public structure in Washington, D.C., the Capitol houses the legislative branch of government, comprising the House of Representatives and the Senate. It contains 540 rooms and two wings (north and south), which intersect in the Rotunda, a room 180 feet high and 95 feet wide topped by a massive iron dome 135 feet in diameter and 218 feet in height that weighs nine million pounds. The entire Capitol complex (including office buildings) encompasses two hundred acres.
Location: Capitol Hill (until the early nineteenth century, Jenkins Hill) in the heart of Washington, D.C., overlooking the Mall on the west and the Library of Congress on the east
Site Office:
United States Capitol Historical Society
200 Maryland Avenue NE
Washington, DC 20002-5796
ph.: (202) 543-8919
fax: (202) 544-8244
Web site: www.uschs.org/
e-mail: uschs@uschs.org

George Washington ceremoniously laid the first stone of the Capitol on September 18, 1793, nearly a year after construction had commenced on the White House. Planning had been underway since 1790, when Congress, then located

The Capitol. (PhotoDisc)

in Philadelphia, approved an act to create a permanent "federal city" to be completed and ready for occupation in 1800. The project was overseen by three commissioners, Thomas Johnson, Daniel Carroll, and David Stuart. President George Washington was also given wide latitude over the construction of the first federal buildings. For the site of the Capitol, the city's chief architect, Captain Pierre Charles L'Enfant, chose Jenkins Hill, which he described as "a pedestal waiting for a monument." He could not have guessed that his "monument," the nation's Capitol, would take over seventy years to construct, by which time the name "Jenkins Hill" would have passed into oblivion.

A Design Competition

To obtain suitable designs for the Capitol and the presidential mansion, the commissioners announced architectural competitions, the winners of which would receive five hundred dollars each. Architects were few, undoubtedly the reason for canvassing the entire thirteen states. The commissioners congratulated themselves upon receiving an excellent proposal for the president's house by a professional architect, Irishman James Hoban. They were far less lucky with the competition for

the design of the nation's Capitol. None of the submissions was judged even passable. The least-objectionable entry belonged to Stephen Hallet, who was "strongly encouraged" to revise his plans and then resubmit them. Hence, when the future architect of the Capitol, Dr. William Thornton, sent in his submission three months past the deadline, he was not turned away. Thomas Jefferson expressed ill-concealed relief at a design, which was "simple, noble, beautiful, excellently distributed, and moderate in size." Most important, George Washington wholly approved of it.

William Thornton was a physician from the British Virgin Islands. In 1792, when he heard of the competition for a capitol building, he was living in Philadelphia and had become a naturalized citizen. His outstanding talent as an amateur architect had been established when he won first prize in a competition to design the Philadelphia library. The drawing that he submitted to a delighted Jefferson featured a building with a central rotunda flanked by a Senate (north) wing and a House of Representatives (south) wing. The design was in the popular neoclassical style, also featured in Hoban's plan for the White House.

Construction Begins

Because Thornton's entry to the competition was late, the commissioners informed him that Hallet was working on a revision of his first entry. Hallet's design was ultimately rejected, but he was given an award equivalent to Thornton's and was even made superintendent of the Capitol's construction, based on Thornton's plan. This was an ill-conceived gesture of goodwill on the part of the three commissioners; Hallet was intent on criticizing and obstructing Thornton's plan, the two got along poorly, and construction proceeded slowly.

Finally, a committee appointed to investigate the slow progress of the Capitol dismissed Hallet as superintendent and appointed James Hoban, architect of the White House, in his place. Thornton continued in his capacity as chief architect of the Capitol. By 1800, when the mandated ten-year period for readying the federal city had lapsed, only the north, or Senate, wing had been finished. It would take a little more than a decade to finish the south wing for the House of Representatives.

Succeeding Thornton as chief architect, or Capitol superintendent, was Benjamin Henry Latrobe, an Englishman whom Thomas Jefferson appointed in 1803. His job was to speed up the Capitol's construction. Under him, the interior of the House and Senate wings were beautifully furnished with velvet drapes and mahogany furniture; walls and ceilings were painted in blue and straw yellow; roofs were repaired; and the south wing was finally completed (and much admired by Jefferson) and decorated with elaborate carvings and columns. There were no skilled craftsmen in America capable of executing the intricate carvings, hence Latrobe wrote to an Italian friend of Thomas Jefferson's, asking him to recommend sculptors. He offered them three dollars a day to carve the tops (capitals) of twenty-four columns as well as a frieze (a carved band at the top of the walls) depicting an enormous eagle and allegorical figures of Liberty, Science, and Art. In 1806, two Italian sculptors braved the treacherous sea to begin work on the carvings.

Near Destruction

The beautiful frieze and carvings were all destroyed by the British on August 24, 1814; a contingent of redcoats under the command of Rear Admiral Sir George Cockburn fired cannon balls at the public buildings in Washington, D.C., in revenge for American troops' destruction of the Canadian town of York. Only a torrential rain that night extinguished the fires. The next day, the blackened walls of the Capitol alone remained standing. All the books in the Library of Congress, housed in one room in the Capitol, were casualties as well.

While President James Madison and his wife Dolley took refuge afterward in the Octagon, the private home of a friend, plans for the reconstruction of the federal city proceeded, thanks to the offer of generous loans from Washington, D.C., bankers and other businessmen. While the city had grown little in the decade and a half that it had been the nation's capital, many individuals of means had speculated in city land and were threatened with bankruptcy if Congress voted to abandon the district, which nearly happened. Instead, the swift promises of generous loans were accepted. The Capitol, President Madison believed, would take only two years to rebuild; in fact, it took decades.

Rebuilding

Once more, architect Benjamin Latrobe was appointed to supervise the construction. He was delighted to be recalled to service, especially since he was facing bankruptcy due to failed investments in steamboats. By 1817, only the north and south wings of the Capitol had been completed under Latrobe's supervision. There were labor disputes, work stoppages, and long delays. Because of mounting criticism, Latrobe resigned. The central portion of the building was still to be completed, but Latrobe left detailed sketches for its design.

A new architect, and the first to be an American-born citizen, became Capitol superintendent following Latrobe's resignation. Charles Bulfinch of Boston had previously been commissioned architect of Boston General Hospital. On a trip to Washington, D.C., he chanced to meet President-elect James Monroe, who was much taken by him. After he had assumed office, Monroe suggested that Bulfinch take on Latrobe's vacated position. At a salary of $2,500 plus moving expenses, he snapped up the prestigious post.

Bulfinch made an effort to win the favor of congressmen and the president, a tactic disdained by previous architects. For instance, realizing the difficulty the politicians had in understanding blueprints, he constructed small-scale wooden models of various Capitol designs. These models captured the Congress's imagination and actually speeded up the process of obtaining appropriations. One of the models, which Bulfinch personally did not favor, featured an immense dome over the Rotunda. To his dismay it became the favorite of Congress and the president. In fact, the politicians requested that Bulfinch enlarge the dome even further. When it was finally completed in 1830, the Capitol's central portion was capped by a dome larger than either Thornton, Latrobe, or Bulfinch had desired.

The Jackson Administration

By this time, Andrew Jackson was president. Although Jackson campaigned as a man of the people, he was in fact a person of refined taste who took a personal interest in both the White House and the Capitol. While Thomas Jefferson was the first president to take his oath of office in the Capitol, it was Jackson who, as the darling of plain and simple folk, insisted on taking his oath outdoors on the Capitol's east front, beginning a tradition that lasted for over a hundred years.

Jackson realized that the Capitol, finished in theory, was already too small to accommodate the increasing number of representatives from newly admitted states, as well as the Supreme Court, the Circuit Court, the Library of Congress, and, scarcely to be overlooked, the growing numbers of visitors, both native and foreign. After all, the Capitol housed at that time the only freely elected legislature in the world and consequently was on all visitors' itineraries. The visitors' gallery was always jammed, and from the beginning admitted both sexes, who mingled freely, to the shock of some visiting dignitaries. Crude behavior—hawkers selling fruit and candies in the galleries—and vulgar language flowed freely in those early decades.

Given the need for expansion, Andrew Jackson decided to reinstate the position of Capitol Architect, which had been abolished in 1829. In 1836 he appointed Robert Mills of South Carolina, who had recently won a five hundred-dollar prize for the design of the Washington Monument. While Mills's official title, Architect and Engineer of the Government, was broad, caring for the Capitol was his first priority.

Italian and American Artisans

Ever since the destruction of the Capitol in 1814, Italian craftsmen had continued their services to the building. Giovanni Andrei and his brother-in-law Giuseppe Franzoni, the two sculptors who had arrived at the behest of Thomas Jefferson and Benjamin Latrobe in 1806, saw their beautiful carvings go up in flames in 1814. Franzoni was instrumental in recommending other craftsmen from his native Italy to help in the Capitol's restoration and beautification. His brother Carlo created the

Chariot of History clock above the entrance of what would become Statuary Hall; Enrico Causici sculpted the Statue of Liberty that stands in the hall itself; Luigi Persico carved the figures of Peace and War that stand at the entrance to the Rotunda; and Antonio Capellano contributed the carved relief of George Washington in the Rotunda and the depiction of the rescue of John Smith by Pocahontas.

Yet few individuals' labor could match that of Constantino Brumidi, who for twenty-five years worked on the Capitol. Brumidi created the first real fresco in America, the canopy of the Rotunda (completed in 1855); he also painted, but never completed, the nine-foot-high frieze on the upper portion of the Rotunda, at some danger to himself (one day he slipped from his scaffold and was left dangling until rescued by fellow workmen). After his death in 1879, the work was continued by yet another Italian artist, Filippo Costanggini.

Gradually, American craftsmen replaced the Italians. One of these, Horatio Greenough, completed a statue of George Washington. At its unveiling in the Capitol in 1841, the statue embarrassed many people because it depicted a half-naked Washington, with only a cloth draped around his hips and thighs, in the classical Greek mode. It was considered too unseemly for public display in the Capitol and was eventually donated to the Smithsonian Institution, where it now stands proudly in public view. Thomas Crawford of New York, creator of the Statue of Freedom that has graced the Capitol dome since 1863, also designed the beautiful bronze doors of the House wing and carved the figures on the east pediment of the Senate wing.

Yet Another Architect

Robert Mills had planned to add new wings to the north and south of the Capitol building and suggested that the old chambers be used by the Supreme Court (which was housed in the Capitol until its own building was constructed in 1935) and for the display art and sculpture. Before these plans were executed, the new president, Millard Fillmore, replaced Mills with Thomas U. Walter in 1851, whose title was Capitol Architect. Walter is best remembered for his replacement of the Bulfinch dome with one of colossal proportions. Under Walter, who remained Capitol Architect until 1865, the Capitol tripled in size.

Walter hailed from Philadelphia and would become one of the founders of the American Institute of Architects. Walter saw the immediate need for carrying out the extensions that his predecessor Mills had proposed. Upon completion of the new wings in 1851, another cornerstone was laid and ceremonies performed. Four years later, Congress authorized the replacement of the wood and copper dome of Bulfinch's design by a magnificent iron dome, designed by Walter in the style of Saint Peter's in Rome. The need for a powerful symbol of national unity was felt by many. In 1862, with Civil War raging, the construction of the new dome was transferred to the domain of the Department of the Interior. Walter remained to oversee its building.

When completed in 1863, the dome, weighing nearly nine million pounds, had cost more than one million dollars. Building it in that day and age, without electricity and cranes, taxed Walter's ingenuity. It was his idea to extend supports through the Rotunda all the way through the eye of the dome. Scaffolding could raise and lower workmen, while a derrick, also constructed through the eye of the dome, hoisted the iron for the dome's casing. The derrick hoisted as well the nineteen-foot Statue of Freedom on December 2, 1863. The statue stands above a lantern that is fifty-two feet long. The colossal dome itself sits astride thirty-six corinthian columns, one for each state in the union at that time. When Abraham Lincoln took his second Oath of Office in March, 1865, with the completed dome in the background, it expressed more eloquently than words his hope for peace and national unity.

The Capitol Today
The Capitol still stands as a symbol of those aspirations. Many refinements have taken place within and outside the Capitol since 1863, including a thirty-two foot eastern extension of the Capitol's midsection, finished in 1961. Since 1908, six huge office buildings have been added as well. In 1800, Americans might well have been dumbfounded to learn that one day the Capitol would comprise 540 rooms, and the entire complex, grounds included, would encompass two hundred acres. Most of these rooms are used for offices or committee meetings. From the perspective of the visitor and outsider, the most notable chamber is the Rotunda, the Capitol's center, famed for its eight historical paintings by American artist John Trumbull and the remarkable statue of Abraham Lincoln, sculpted by the gifted, seventeen-year-old artist Vinnie Ream. Under the Rotunda dome is Brumidi's historic frieze and his fresco *The Apotheosis of George Washington.*

Off the Rotunda is Statuary Hall, which served as the chamber for the House of Representatives until 1857. Statues of notable men and women from each state fill the room. It was in this room in 1848 that former president John Quincy Adams died of a stroke. The two former Supreme Court chambers are also on view, both designed by architect Benjamin Latrobe in the form of classical amphitheaters. It was in the Old Supreme Court Chamber (used by the justices until 1860) that in 1844 Samuel F. B. Morse sent the world's first telegraph message.

The Old Senate Chamber was the assembly room for the senators until 1859. It witnessed dramatic scenes, largely revolving around the sectional conflicts of the pre-Civil War era. The Brumidi Corridor in the current Senate wing is named for and was decorated by the Italian artist who declared his aim in life "to make beautiful the Capitol of the one country on earth in which there is liberty."

The grounds outside the Capitol are a lush and beautifully landscaped counterpart to the classical embellishments within. Not until a decade after the Civil War was serious attention paid to the surrounding grounds. In the mid-1870's, the man who designed New York's Central Park, Frederick Law Olmsted, was commissioned to turn the Capitol grounds into a park. Thanks to his insistence, beautiful terraces were built on the Capitol's west side, facing the Mall. In the spring and summer months, amid the spacious lawns, appear a profusion of stately magnolias, brilliant azaleas, cherry trees, dogwood, and a multitude of foreign shrubs and plants.

—*Sina Dubovoy*

For Further Information:

Arnebeck, Bob. *Through a Fiery Trial: Building Washington, 1790-1800.* Lanham, Md.: Madison Books, 1991. Just as interesting as Herron's book below, but with an even greater wealth of detail.

Brown, Glenn. *Glenn Brown's History of the United States Capitol.* Washington, D.C.: Government

Printing Office, 1998. This annotated edition, published in commemoration of the bicentennial of the Capitol, is a history of the building by architect Brown (1854-1932).

Capitol Historical Society. *We, the People: The Story of the United States Capitol.* Washington, D.C.: Capitol Historical Society and the National Geographic Society, 1991. The standard, authoritative account of the Capitol, written in a highly readable style and richly illustrated. It is available in paperback and updated every two to three years.

Herron, Paul. *The Story of Capitol Hill.* New York: Van Rees Press, 1963. An informative work offering interesting anecdotes and a detailed account of the building of the Capitol and the formation of the surrounding neighborhood.

Ford's Theatre

Date: Completed in August, 1863

Relevant issues: Civil War, cultural history, disasters and tragedies, political history

Significance: Ford's Theatre is infamous in United States history as the place where President Abraham Lincoln was assassinated in 1865. Its restoration and reopening in 1968 put it back in its old place as a center for the performing arts in the U.S. capital.

Location: On Northwest Tenth Street in downtown Washington, D.C., two blocks off the National Mall and one block off Pennsylvania Avenue between the Capitol and the White House

Site Office:
Ford's Theatre National Historical Site
511 Tenth Street NW
Washington, DC 20004
ph.: (202) 426-6924
fax: (202) 347-6269
Web site: www.nps.gov/foth/

The significance of Ford's Theatre in American history was defined on the evening of April 14, 1865, when actor and Confederate sympathizer John Wilkes Booth fatally wounded President Abraham Lincoln as he watched a performance of Tom Taylor's popular comedy *Our American Cousin.* Founder John T. Ford undoubtedly had a high place in American theater history in mind when he

opened his venue in August, 1863, but no theater was performed in the building from the night of the assassination until the theater reopened in 1968, restored by private gifts and federal funding to replicate as closely as possible its appearance over a century before. Both an active performing arts center and a historical site, Ford's Theatre takes one back to its dramatic nineteenth century past by its careful restoration, associated museum exhibits, and the restored Petersen House across the street where Lincoln died, without recovering consciousness, at 7:22 A.M. on April 15, 1865.

Ford's New Theatre

The story of Ford's Theatre really begins with John T. Ford. A veteran manager and producer with experience in Philadelphia and Baltimore, Ford bought the former Tenth Street Baptist Church, remodeling it to become Ford's Atheneum, a popular music hall which he managed with the help of his brothers Harry and James. President Lincoln's first visit as a member of the audience came on May 28, 1862, when he and his party attended a concert by Claire Louise Kellogg. However, on the evening of December 30, a fire destroyed the converted church building, as well as the sets and costumes of the show scheduled to open the next night.

The determined Ford immediately began a new, larger, and more elaborate building. It would seat an audience of seventeen hundred in unusual comfort. Contemporary accounts stress excellent sight lines to the stage, modern ventilation and water circulation systems, and comfort of the seating. Of special interest were the boxes. The upper boxes, in particular, gave excellent views of both the stage and the audience. They were places to see and be seen, and boxes seven and eight, on stage left, were consolidated when needed into the "presidential" or "state" box. Ford's New Theatre soon established itself as one of the country's finest new theatrical venues. One highlight of the 1863 season was a two-week run in November with John Wilkes Booth, then regarded as one of America's most exciting young actors, appearing in both contemporary and Shakespearean roles. Though Lincoln was a lover of Shakespearean drama, he seems not to have attended any of Booth's Shakespeare performances. He did see Booth in the contemporary play *The Marble Heart.* In 1864, Booth had

The President's Box in Ford's Theatre. (Corbis)

ers. The surrender of General Lee negated the prisoner exchange idea, and Booth began plotting assassination. His motivations now became revenge against the North and the glorification of himself as the killer of a tyrant on the model of Brutus, the idealistic assassin in William Shakespeare's *Julius Caesar.*

Despite the failure of the kidnapping attempt, the core members of Booth's gang were still in touch with each other in the Washington, D.C., area. When the Fords received a request for tickets from the White House for President and Mrs. Lincoln and for General and Mrs. Grant, they made their attendance part of the advertising for the Good Friday performance of the English comedy *Our American Cousin,* with popular British actress Laura Keene in the lead role. Ticket sales soared when people realized they could see both Lincoln and Grant in person, and John Wilkes Booth, whose long friendship with John T. Ford gave him free and frequent access to the theater, immediately set a complex attack plan into action. Lewis Powell and David Herold would murder Secretary of State William Seward, who was bedridden at home from a carriage accident. George Atzerodt would kill Vice President Andrew Johnson in his hotel room, and Booth would end the life of President Lincoln with a theatrical flourish in front of a house packed with Lincoln admirers and, no doubt, many of his own.

Booth's part of the plan called for him to have a horse held for him in a public alleyway beside a door that exited from the backstage area of Ford's Theatre. Booth waited until President and Mrs. Lincoln were seated (the Grants declined at the last minute), and the play was well under way before he climbed the stairs from the orchestra, crossed the dress circle, and entered the presidential box quietly through a rear door and anteroom.

abandoned full-time performing to pursue business interests and secret activities in support of the Confederacy. The Fords, in the meantime, continued to run a successful theatrical enterprise until April 14, 1865, when the Lincoln assassination put an end to theater at Ford's Theatre for over a century.

The Assassination of Abraham Lincoln

By the spring of 1865, the tide of war had turned decisively in favor of the Union, and on April 9, Ulysses S. Grant accepted Robert E. Lee's surrender at the small town of Appomattox Courthouse, Virginia. With that event the Civil War was all but over.

During these events, Booth had remained an avid Lincoln-hater, putting together a loosely organized group of Southern sympathizers in an unsuccessful attempt to kidnap Lincoln, take him to Richmond, and trade him for Confederate prison-

Unchallenged by any security personnel, Booth fired a single shot from his .44-caliber Derringer pistol into the back of the president's head. After a brief but fierce struggle with Major Henry Rathbone, who, along with his fiancée Clara Harris, was a substitute guest for the Grants, Booth jumped to the stage, apparently stumbling as he landed, and faced the stunned audience to shout, "*Sic semper tyrannis!*" (Thus ever to tyrants!), a Revolutionary War rallying cry and the motto on the state flag of Virginia. In the confusion that followed, Booth escaped on his horse and left his pursuers behind.

Inside the theater, chaos ruled. Dr. Charles Leale was the first of three physicians who reached the presidential box. He located the bullet wound, which traversed Lincoln's skull from above and behind his left ear to its stopping place behind the right eye. Brain damage was substantial. Leale stabilized Lincoln's condition by using artificial respiration to restore his breathing, but the president never recovered consciousness.

Doctors and volunteers from the audience improvised a stretcher and slowly and painstakingly moved the comatose Lincoln out of the theater and into a second-floor bedroom of a boardinghouse across the street. This is the Petersen House, which has been restored to period condition and is administered by the National Park Service as part of the Ford's Theatre National Historic Site. At approximately 11 P.M., April 14, the president was stretched out diagonally on a bed too small for his lanky frame. For over eight hours, attended by doctors, government officials, his wife, and his eldest son, Lincoln remained alive but unconscious. Death was pronounced at 7:22 A.M. on April 15, 1865, ten days after Lee's surrender to Grant.

Secretary of War Edwin Stanton took immediate charge, launching a massive investigation and manhunt for Lincoln's killer, as well as for the assailants who nearly succeeded in taking Secretary of State Seward's life (George Atzerodt fled without making his attempt on Andrew Johnson). In succeeding days, the conspirators were rounded up and imprisoned to await trial. Booth, trapped by a force of army cavalry and police detectives at a farm in Virginia, was shot and killed resisting arrest.

All eight known conspirators who survived were convicted. Four were hanged, and the other four went to prison for varying lengths of time.

Immediate Aftermath for the Theater

In the wake of the assassinations, theatrical activity came to a halt at Ford's New Theatre, with the exception of several reenactments of the fatal scene of *Our American Cousin* for investigators attempting to reconstruct the details of the crime. Ford himself, and everybody involved in that night's production, fell under suspicion, and many went to jail until Stanton's investigators were confident they had all the conspirators in hand. As for Ford, it was his intention to reopen for business on July 7, 1865, less than three months after the assassination, but negative feelings still ran high and Stanton blocked the opening. The Stanton War Department first leased and then purchased the building, rebuilding its interior to house offices, a medical library, and the Army Medical Museum. In 1932, the War Department transferred the building to the National Park Service. Thirty-two years later, Congress authorized funding for the restoration of the theater to serve as both a historic monument to one of the most tumultuous events in American history and as a living theater once again.

Ford's Theatre Reborn

The nationally televised 1968 gala opening of Ford's Theatre brought this troubled location back into the mainstream of Washington, D.C.'s cultural life. The gala set a precedent that, since the "Tenth Anniversary Celebration" in 1978, became almost an annual event, first under the title "A Festival at Ford's," and during the Clinton administration as "A Gala for the President at Ford's Theatre."

The staple of performance activities at the reincarnated Ford's Theatre has been the presentation of musicals and plays. Many of these have been mounted by the Ford's Theatre Society, the production arm of the theater itself. These productions have included many world premieres—among them William Gibson's *John and Abigail*, Ed Bullins's *Storyville*, and Doug Marlette's *Kudzu: A Southern Musical*—as well as familiar favorites like Hal Holbrook's *Mark Twain Tonight*, Stephen Schwartz's *Godspell*, and Neil Simon's *Little Me*. The first Shakespeare play done was *The Comedy of Errors* in 1968, and the first American classic was also the new theater's first dramatic production, the historically relevant *John Brown's Body*. Visiting companies have presented classics from abroad such as Anton Chekhov's *Three Sisters* and John Gay's *Beg-*

gar's Opera, and American works by such playwrights as Eugene O'Neill, Arthur Miller, and Lorraine Hansberry. Nor has serious drama by contemporary writers been neglected, as the presence of challenging works such as Romulus Linney's *Holy Ghosts* and Anna Deavere Smith's *Twilight, Los Angeles, 1992* attest. After one hundred years of darkness, the stage of Ford's Theatre was alive and well again.

Visiting the Site

Ford's Theatre National Historic Site is administered by the National Park Service and is open every day from 9 A.M. to 5 P.M. except December 25. The theater itself may be visited except when rehearsals or performances are in progress. Periodic tours are given by National Park Service rangers. Within the theater building, there is also a Lincoln Museum, with memorabilia of Lincoln's life and death, and a bookstore with many items relating to President Lincoln and his life and times. Across the street, the Petersen House, where Lincoln was taken after being shot, has also been restored to its Civil War era look and welcomes visitors. Here one may see the room in which Lincoln died, as well as the rooms in which family waited and in which Secretary of War Stanton launched the manhunt that eventually brought the conspirators to justice.

Washington, D.C., is rich with visitor attractions. Within easy walking distance of Ford's Theatre are the Federal Bureau of Investigation Building, the National Portrait Gallery, and the National Mall with its striking views and plentiful places of interest.
—*Roger J. Stilling*

For Further Information:

Bishop, Jim. *The Day Lincoln Was Shot.* New York: Harper & Row, 1955. A best-selling page-turner that tracks the major figures in the story hour by hour through the fatal day.

Bryan, George S. *The Great American Myth.* New York: Carrick & Evans, 1940. Reprint. Chicago: Americana House, 1990. Many experts believe this to be the most authoritative general work on the subject.

Good, Timothy S., ed. *We Saw Lincoln Shot: One Hundred Eyewitness Accounts.* Jackson: University Press of Mississippi, 1995. Remarkable collection of accounts and reactions by people on the scene.

Kunhardt, Dorothy Meserve, and Philip B. Kunhardt, Jr. *Twenty Days: A Narrative in Text and Pictures of the Assassination of Abraham Lincoln.* New York: Harper & Row, 1965. A highly readable text with an amazing collection of photographs of the people and places in the story.

Reck, W. Emerson. *A. Lincoln: His Last Twenty-four Hours.* Jefferson, N.C.: McFarland, 1987. Thorough, factual, and detailed account based on recent research.

Smith, Gene. *American Gothic: The Story of America's Legendary Theatrical Family—Junius, Edwin, and John Wilkes Booth.* New York: Simon & Schuster, 1992. Places the assassination in the context of nineteenth century theatrical life.

Frederick Douglass National Historic Site

Date: Home built c. 1855-1859; Douglass's residence from 1877 to 1895

Relevant issues: African American history, Civil War, social reform

Significance: The house and grounds, which Frederick Douglass renamed Cedar Hill, served as the domicile and office for this former slave, author, orator, abolitionist, and political activist during the last years of his life.

Location: Washington, D.C.

Site Office:

Frederick Douglass National Historic Site
1411 W Street SE
Washington, DC 20020-4813
ph.: (202) 426-5961
Web site: www.nps.gov/frdo/

The original house was designed and constructed by an architect and contractor named John Van Hook between 1855 and 1859. The estate consisted of a large, whitewashed frame residence and seven outbuildings on nine acres, the residence being perched, facing the street, on a slight incline or "hill." The site was originally called Van Hook's Hill, but when Frederick Douglass purchased it in 1877 for $6,700, he changed its name to Cedar Hill, after the trees growing in the area. Apart from the time that he served as United States envoy to Haiti and the two years he spent on a

Frederick Douglass National Historic Site. (Washington, D.C., Convention & Visitors Association)

trip abroad, Cedar Hill would be his fixed residence.

Out of Bondage

Frederick Douglass was born Frederick Augustus Washington Bailey on the Lloyd Family Plantation in Talbot County, Maryland. The exact date is uncertain, and even the year, 1818, was not known until after his death—Douglass himself had always believed he was born in 1817. His mother, Harriet Bailey, was a slave; she died before Frederick reached the age of seven. The identity of Frederick's father remains unknown to this day, but it is generally suspected that he was the Lloyd Plantation's overseer, Aaron Anthony.

Until the age of seven, Frederick lived with his grandmother, Betsy Bailey; he rarely saw his mother, who worked on another plantation at the time. Then he was sent to work on the farm. After a year he was sent to Baltimore to serve Hugh and Sophia Auld, in-laws of Aaron Anthony. Sophia Auld began to teach Frederick to read and write until her husband ordered her to stop. By Frederick's own account, however, this incident awak-

ened in him a desire to complete his education and use it to become free; he built upon what he had been taught by Mrs. Auld secretly to advance his knowledge and skills.

In 1833, Frederick passed to Hugh Auld's brother Thomas, who sent him to a slave-breaker named Edward Covey so that any spark of independence in the young man would be destroyed and he would be prepared for life as a field hand. A lengthy battle between Douglass and Covey resulted in a physical struggle that neither man could win but ended with Douglass declaring that he would never again be beaten or broken. Covey concealed his failure by sending Douglass back to Thomas Auld without revealing the true outcome of the struggle. Douglass considered this incident to be one of his life's major turning points.

During the next few months, when Auld had Douglass "farmed out" to a small planter named William Freeland, he enjoyed a greater degree of latitude and less intensive supervision. His literate skills had developed to the extent that Douglass was able to teach other African Americans to read and write; he also held Sunday school sessions devoted to Bible studies. However, when he laid plans to escape and was discovered, Auld sent him back to Baltimore, where he was apprenticed to a ship-builder, William Gardner. Despite being kept on tighter reins, Douglass met a free black woman named Anna Murray; the two fell in love and plotted Frederick's escape. Since Auld had appropriated nearly all of Frederick's wages, Anna gave him money and, disguised as a sailor, he made good on his flight to New York City. Anna arrived later; they were married and soon moved to New Bedford, Massachusetts. As a symbol of his new life of freedom, Frederick changed his surname from Bailey to Douglass after a character in the popular novel *The Lady of the Lake* (1810) by Sir Walter Scott.

Early Activist Career
Just because Douglass had escaped from the South did not guarantee that he was safe. The Constitution of the United States contained a "fugitive slave" clause that legalized the pursuit and apprehension of escaped bondsmen no matter where they were within the United States. (This clause was contained in Article IV, Section 2, and has since been made null and void by the passage of the Thirteenth and Fourteenth Amendments to the Constitution.) Slave owners could and did hire bounty hunters to find and capture fugitives such as Douglass and transport them back to the South. In spite of this, Douglass's acute sense of justice and moral indignation over slavery and other inequities in American society led him to become active in the abolitionist movement and—in the larger context—sweeping social reform. To go public—to call attention to himself in that manner—was very dangerous, but Douglass chose to become that most visible of reformers: a charismatic orator who employed both moral biblical precepts and liberal constitutional principles to present the antislavery cause to diverse audiences throughout the North.

In 1841, at the request of abolitionist William Lloyd Garrison, Douglass went on a well-publicized speaking tour sponsored by the Massachusetts Anti-Slavery Society and immediately became a national figure. Stung by charges that he had lied about having been held in slavery, Douglass wrote his first autobiography: *Narrative of the Life of Frederick Douglass, an American Slave, Written by Himself* (1845). Learning of a conspiracy to kidnap him back into slavery, Douglass journeyed to England

to tour, speak, and agitate for the antislavery cause. On December 12, 1846, two British supporters, sisters Ellen and Anna Richardson, raised the money officially to buy Douglass his freedom.

In the years prior to the Civil War, Douglass became increasingly radical in his philosophy and firmly established himself as an independent voice. He broke with the predominately white mainstream of the abolitionist movement by founding his own newspaper, *The North Star*, in 1847 in Rochester, New York. Renamed *The Douglass Monthly*, the paper ran until 1863; within its pages Douglass advocated women's rights and Irish self-government and even justified revolution as a means of achieving emancipation.

A second autobiography, *My Bondage and My Freedom*, was published in 1855. His stance on violence and his association with John Brown (though he disapproved of Brown's uprising at Harpers Ferry in 1859 and took no part in it) put him under suspicion of treason, and he spent some time in exile in Canada and England until his name was cleared.

Civil War
Upon the outbreak of the Civil War, Douglass threw his efforts into supporting the struggle against the Confederacy. Though he had supported the Republican Party and the election of Abraham Lincoln for president, he often found himself at odds with the president over the final objectives and conduct of the war. Lincoln insisted that the struggle was only about saving the Union and remarked that if he could preserve the United States without freeing a single slave, he would do so. In the months between Lincoln's inauguration and the firing on Fort Sumter that began the war, Douglass had been deeply disappointed by the president's attitude and even considered immigrating to Haiti and urging African Americans to follow his example.

African Americans for the Union army came forward from the beginning, and units were actually formed in Albany, Ohio, and Pittsburgh, Pennsylvania. The president ordered that they be disbanded and consistently rejected the idea of African Americans officially serving in the U.S. armed forces. Lincoln's position initially revolved around the idea that, after the war, the slaves would be emancipated gradually, with compensation to their masters, and then be compelled to "resettle" in Africa or Latin America. When the president proposed this plan on August 14, 1862, Douglass led the opposition, emphatically rejecting the notion of colonization and charging Lincoln with hypocrisy.

Douglass himself urged Lincoln toward a policy of more immediate emancipation and the acceptance of African American recruits into the Union army, and Lincoln had relented on both issues by early 1863. Douglass himself was active in recruiting black soldiers for the Union cause, and his sons Charles and Lewis served in the famous Fifty-fourth Massachusetts Regiment.

Final Years

Following the war, with the collapse of the Confederacy and Reconstruction proving to be a failure, Douglass continued to battle for the guarantee of citizenship rights for African Americans, noting that despite the fact that slavery had been abolished, racism and discrimination were still very much in evidence throughout both the North and the South. Douglass viewed the beginnings of the Jim Crow system in "de-Reconstructed" Southern states as being especially alarming.

On June 2, 1872, the Douglass home in Rochester was gutted by a fire that many, at the time, believed had been deliberately set. The Douglass family moved to Washington, D.C., where Frederick resumed his journalistic work after being away from it for nine years by launching the "New National Era." With a loan from the Freedmens Savings and Trust Company, Douglass acquired Cedar Hill. Five years later Anna Murray Douglass died as the result of a stroke. Douglass sealed off his late wife's room. Douglass had five children by Anna; the eldest daughter, Rosetta, was followed by sons Lewis, Frederick, Jr., and Charles, and a second daughter, Annie.

While he served as recorder of deeds for the District of Columbia, Douglass hired, as a clerk, Helen Pitts from Holyoke, New York. In 1884, Douglass married Helen, who was white; the interracial marriage caused Douglass to be heavily criticized by many in both racial communities, and even by some of his children. Perhaps to escape the glare of publicity, the Douglasses took a lengthy honeymoon in Europe and Egypt from 1885 to 1887. An ardent supporter of the Republican Party—as were

the majority of African American voters until the mid-1930's—he secured a post as U.S. marshal for the District of Columbia from 1877 to 1881 before being recorder of deeds from 1881 to 1885. In 1889, President Benjamin Harrison appointed Douglass minister resident and consul general to the republic of Haiti; he served until 1891. In 1881, Douglass wrote his third autobiography, *Life and Times of Frederick Douglass, Written by Himself* (1881; rev. ed., 1892).

On February 20, 1895, Frederick Douglass died of a heart seizure. Helen Douglass deeded the property to the Frederick Douglass Memorial and Historical Association upon her death in 1903; the National Park Service took over the site's maintenance in 1962.

Visiting the Site

Cedar Hill itself, the gardens, the Growlery (outdoor study) outbuilding, and the visitors' center are open daily to the public except on January 1, Thanksgiving, and December 25. The hours are from 9:00 A.M. to 5:00 P.M. in the spring and summer and from 9:00 A.M. to 4:00 P.M. in the fall and winter.   —*Raymond Pierre Hylton*

For Further Information:

Andrews, William L., ed. *The Oxford Frederick Douglass Reader.* New York: Oxford University Press, 1996. Selected excerpts from all of Douglass's major literary works.

Chesebrough, David B. *Frederick Douglass: Oratory from Slavery.* Westport, Conn.: Greenwood Press, 1998. In three parts: The first contains sequential biography; the second analyzes Douglass's speaking techniques; the third is a representative sample of his speeches.

Foner, Philip, ed. *Frederick Douglass: My Bondage and My Freedom.* New York: Dover Publications, 1969. Douglass's own evaluation of his life and mission at the height of his career.

McFeely, William S. *Frederick Douglass.* New York: W. W. Norton, 1991. Popularized biography liberally illustrated with photographs and drawings. Focuses a great deal on his family life.

Quarles, Benjamin. *Frederick Douglass.* 1948. Reprint. New York: Da Capo Press, 1997. An early but balanced insight into Douglass's career, stressing the years of maturity and his interpersonal relationships.

Gallaudet University

Date: The parent institution, the Columbia Institution for the Instruction of the Deaf and Dumb and the Blind, started in 1857; blind students transferred and name changed to the Columbia Institution for the Deaf and Dumb in 1865. Renamed Gallaudet College in 1894 and Gallaudet University in 1986.

Relevant issues: Education, social reform

Significance: Gallaudet is the world's only university for undergraduates with programs designed exclusively for hard-of-hearing and deaf people. Its national and international students are trained to become fully functional members of their respective societies. The graduate program accepts hard-of-hearing, deaf, and hearing students and conducts research in deafness and educating the deaf.

Location: About two miles north and east of the Capitol

Site Office:

Gallaudet University
800 Florida Avenue NE
Washington, DC 20002-3695
ph.: (202) 651-5000
fax: (202) 651-5467
Web site: www.gallaudet.edu

The partial or complete loss of hearing is a major disadvantage in any human society. The deaf have always devised ways of communicating with others and among themselves by signs. In some countries, even today, the rights of the deaf are limited and they are severely restricted from joining the workforce. The history of Gallaudet University is the history of educating the deaf, and instructing the hearing about the deaf, not only in the United States but globally as well.

Formal training, and therefore education, for the deaf to communicate with others began in Europe. In the seventeenth century, a Spanish monk started training the deaf in sign language that was probably derived from the signs used by monks sworn to silence. His method was popularized by countryman Juan Pablo Bonet (who, however, recommended that the deaf be taught to speak and understand speech rather than to perform sign language). These two mainstreams of deaf communication are still current, although there are a number of variations.

While the oralist tradition was centered in Scotland, the Abbé l'Epée started a sign language school in Paris in 1760. His successor at the school was the Abbé Sicard, who made the Paris Royal Institute for the Deaf the preeminent institution for teaching the deaf in the Western world. A most successful student of this institution was Laurent Clerc. In one of their many lecture tours, the Abbé Sicard and Clerc met Thomas Gallaudet, an American, in London.

Gallaudet and Deaf Education in the United States

Thomas Hopkins Gallaudet (1787-1851), after whom Gallaudet University is named, had no direct relationship with the institution, as he died even before its the precursor was established in 1857. However, Gallaudet brought organized education for the deaf to the United States, and his family had a substantial, if not determinant, influence on the formation and development of the university.

Gallaudet was born in Philadelphia, although he moved to Hartford, Connecticut, with his family while quite young and spent most of his life there. A brilliant scholar, Gallaudet graduated, first in his class, from Yale in 1804 at the age of seventeen. He joined Andover Theological Seminary in 1812, graduating in 1814.

His interest in educating the deaf was initiated by an affluent neighbor, Dr. Mason Cogswell. Cogswell had a nine-year-old deaf daughter, Amy, whose education he wanted to entrust to Gallaudet. (A statue of Gallaudet teaching Amy Cogswell, by Daniel Chester French, can be found on the campus of Gallaudet University.) At the time, there were no suitable institutions in the country; in 1815, Cogswell and a number of other interested persons financed a trip to Europe for Gallaudet to study the methods of teaching the deaf. The Braidwood family of Scotland was well known at the time for having developed a method of educating the deaf to speak. Gallaudet first visited them but found that they were unwilling to share their secrets. Disappointed, he looked for other sources. Gallaudet met the Abbé Sicard, director of the Royal Institute for the Deaf in Paris, and his student Laurent Clerc in London. Impressed by their views and results, Gallaudet traveled to Paris to learn their techniques.

Having mastered their techniques, Gallaudet returned to Hartford in 1816 accompanied by Clerc. (Clerc spent the rest of his life in the United States helping Gallaudet and the cause of deaf education. The National Deaf Education Center at Gallaudet University is named for him.) They were able to raise some private and public money and in 1817 established the Connecticut Asylum for the Education of Deaf and Dumb Persons. This, the oldest institution of its kind, still exists as the American Institute for the Deaf in Hartford.

Gallaudet married one of his deaf students, Sophia Fowler. Both of their sons were actively involved in the cause of deaf education. The older son, Thomas Gallaudet, established churches for the deaf. The younger, Edward Miner Gallaudet, would become the first superintendent and his mother the first matron of the precursor institution. The education of the deaf was not the only interest of Thomas Hopkins Gallaudet. He helped establish public normal schools and was active in much less acceptable activities for the times, such as manual training in schools and the education and liberation of African Americans and women. Gallaudet is depicted on a green twenty-cent postage stamp issued by the U.S. Postal Service in 1983 in a series honoring Great Americans.

Origins of the Institution

The Gallaudet University of today started as the Columbia Institution for the Instruction of the Deaf and Dumb and the Blind in 1857. The moving force behind this institution was Amos Kendall (1789-1869), a rich philanthropist with a large estate in northeastern Washington, D.C. Born on a Massachusetts farm, Kendall graduated at the head of his class at Dartmouth in 1811. By 1829, he was a well-known newspaper editor in Georgetown, Kentucky, and he became a powerful political supporter of Andrew Jackson. With Jackson's election to the presidency, and the subsequent election of Martin Van Buren, Kendall became an important political figure in Washington, D.C. He was a principal member of Jackson's Kitchen Cabinet and held some consequential federal administrative jobs such as auditor of the Treasury and postmaster general. Later, he became very rich as the business manager of Samuel F. B. Morse, the inventor of the telegraph. A man of great probity and sincere religiousness—he established the Calvary Baptist Church of Washington—Kendall was appalled by the condition of some deaf, mute, and blind children who had been brought to Washington, D.C., by a man named P. H. Skinner. Kendall adopted them, donated two acres of land from his own estate to house them, and started a school for their education.

Edward Miner Gallaudet, the First President

Thomas Gallaudet had died, so Kendall invited the twenty-year-old Edward Miner Gallaudet to take over the superintendence of the new institution, with his mother as the first matron. Born in 1837, Edward had known the deaf since his birth. In fact, while he was a student at Trinity College, he also taught at the Hartford Institute for the Deaf-Mute. In 1857, Kendall helped persuade Congress to incorporate the new institution. In 1858, there were seventeen students; two years later, the number had increased to thirty as Maryland funded some of its deaf and blind students to be educated there. Under Gallaudet's leadership, the institution progressed well—by 1864, during the presidency of Abraham Lincoln, the institution, with Gallaudet as the president and Kendall as the chairman of the board of directors, was authorized to confer college degrees. The first college class had eight students. By 1865, the college was committed to educating only the deaf; the blind students were transferred and the institution changed its name to the more appropriate Columbia Institution for the Deaf and Dumb. The college section was now known as the National Deaf-Mute College.

In 1867, E. M. Gallaudet introduced speech training for suitable students; hitherto, only sign language had been taught. Kendall died in 1869, and eighty-one acres of his estate were sold to the college. The main campus and the primary school (moved to a new building in 1885) are named after him; a statue of Edward Miner Gallaudet can be seen on campus. Before his retirement in 1910, Gallaudet introduced many new activities. Women were admitted from 1887 to 1893, and Agatha Tiegel became the first woman to graduate with a bachelor of arts. A normal department was inaugurated in 1891 to educate hearing teachers of the deaf; in 2000, of a faculty of more than two hundred, about 34 percent were deaf or hard of hearing. In 1894, at the request of the alumni, the name of the graduate institution was changed to Gallaudet College.

The Years of Continued Expansion

Under the leadership of its presidents and faculty, Gallaudet College had a consistently progressive and expanding influence in global deaf education. During the first half of the twentieth century, technical courses were introduced so that students could take up manufacturing jobs. Many alumni and students participated in the war effort during World War II.

The curriculum was revised and expanded after the war. In 1954, the corporate name of the entire institution was changed to Gallaudet College, and the college sought and received full accreditation by the Middle States Association of Colleges and Secondary Schools, Commission on Institutions of Higher Education. Subsequent expansions have included the Model Secondary School for the Deaf (MSSD), which researches and tests new, innovative, and improved courses for deaf and hard-of-hearing high school students (1969); the Center for Continuing Education of Deaf Adults (1970); the International Center on Deafness (1974); the Gallaudet Research Institute (1978); the Laurent Clerc National Information Center on Deafness (1980); and a doctoral degree program in special education administration (1975).

Increased funding from the government and the public have allowed expanded physical facilities, barrier-free access for the physically disabled, and a larger number of national and international students. Gallaudet College had been a leader in deaf education for many years, and the enactment of the Education of All Handicapped Children Act (Public Law 94-142) in 1973 increased its activities, which are now facilitated through seven regional information centers.

Gallaudet University

During the presidency of Ronald Reagan, the Education of the Deaf Act (Public Law 99-371) was passed in 1986. Gallaudet College was simultaneously given university status and became a full member of the consortium of Universities of the Washington Metropolitan Area.

In 1988, a new, seventh president for the university had been selected. However, the alumni launched a strong movement called Deaf President Now (DPN). Their demands were met, and the eighth president was Dr. I. King Jordan, a graduate of the class of 1970 and the first deaf president of the institution. Philip Bravin, of the class of 1966, the chair of the board of trustees, is also deaf, and there is an ongoing effort to have 51 percent of the trustees to come from among the deaf or hard of hearing.

In 2000, Gallaudet University had more than two thousand students in more than fifty undergraduate and graduate programs in the College of Arts and Sciences and the Schools of Communication, Education, and Human Services and Management. The courses utilize the worldwide web and computer resources extensively. The University has an active and successful athletic program. It remains a leader in the education of the deaf and hard of hearing, allowing them to "mainstream" into society without losing their special identity nationally and globally. The university is one of the largest employers (and therefore an economic mainstay) of the region.

The extensive and beautifully landscaped physical plant is about two miles from the Capitol. Part of the campus (about seven acres of the original facilities) is listed on the National Register of Historic Places. In 2000, the university and the Laurent Clerc Deaf Education Center had 1,232 employees, of whom more than a third were partly or totally deaf. More than 750 were faculty members, and more than a tenth of this number were teachers. The university actively recruits deaf and hard-of-hearing students nationally and internationally. Staff and students regularly put out a number of publications, including the *Gallaudet University Link* for prospective students and *Research at Gallaudet* and *American Annals of the Deaf*, two specialist journals.

Housing for visitors is provided on campus, and there are many hotels and motels nearby. The visitors' center on campus offers guided tours at 10:00 A.M. and 1:00 P.M., Monday through Friday. There are open house programs for prospective students and deaf awareness sessions that provide basic information about deafness and Gallaudet programs. Special tours of specific facilities can be arranged. Visitors are advised to call the visitors' center two to three weeks in advance of a visit.

—*Ranès Chakrovorty*

For Further Information:

Cleve, John Van, ed. *Gallaudet Encyclopedia of Deaf People and Deafness.* New York: McGraw-Hill, 1987.

Hall, Percival. "Edward Minor Gallaudet." In *Dictionary of American Biography,* edited by Allen Johnson, Dumas Malone, and Harris Elwood Starr. Vol 7. New York: Charles Scribner's Sons. 1931.

_____. "Thomas Hopkins Gallaudet." in *Dictionary of American Biography,* edited by Allen Johnson, Dumas Malone, and Harris Elwood Starr. Vol 7. New York: Charles Scribner's Sons. 1931.

Lane, Harlan. *When the Mind Hears: A History of the Deaf.* New York: Random House, 1984. An excellent and detailed history of deaf education seen through the eyes of Laurent Clerc. Well documented with an extensive bibliography.

Georgetown

Date: Founded in 1751

Relevant issues: African American history, art and architecture, colonial America, political history

Significance: Washington, D.C.'s oldest and best-known neighborhood, Georgetown was once a separate town with a long and colorful history dating back to colonial times. Today it boasts a large number of historic residences and other buildings from many eras of American history.

Location: On the western edge of Washington, D.C.'s northwest quarter, bounded by Reservoir Road and Dumbarton Oaks Park on the north, Rock Creek Park on the east, the Potomac River on the south, and the Glover-Archbold Parkway on the west

Site Office:
District of Columbia Chamber of Commerce
1301 Pennsylvania Avenue NW
Washington, DC 20005
ph.: (202) 638-3222
Web site: www.dcchamber.org

Today an upscale shopping, restaurant, and entertainment district, Georgetown is also home to many historic buildings, and its narrow streets recall more than two centuries of colonial and American history and the people who lived it. Originally an independent town in Maryland,

Georgetown is now a part of Washington, D.C., and its history has blended with that of the federal city since Washington's inception at the end of the eighteenth century.

Georgetown Historic District

The entire neighborhood of Georgetown is included in the District of Columbia Inventory of Historic Sites, the official list of properties recognized and protected as part of the heritage of the nation's capital, made possible by the District of Columbia Historic Landmark and Historic District Protection Act of 1978.

Previously, however, the Old Georgetown Act of 1950 gave the U.S. Commission of Fine Arts the authority to review alterations to buildings in the district. The area became a District of Columbia landmark in 1964, was placed on the National Register of Historic Places in 1967, and became a National Historic Landmark in the same year.

Georgetown includes residential, commercial, institutional, and industrial buildings from all periods of U.S. history, including many of Washington's oldest buildings. There are houses of many types, from simple frame dwellings to richly built mansions and tightly spaced row houses. Architectural styles include Federal, Greek Revival, Italianate, Queen Anne, Romanesque, and Classical Revival, and there are about four thousand buildings that date from 1765 to 1940.

Georgetown's History

The first recorded inhabitants of the area now known as Georgetown were Native Americans, whose settlement was called Tahoga Village. In 1622 Captain Henry Fleet sailed up the Potomac and encountered this village. He set up a trading post and stayed for a period of twelve years.

Formal settlement began in the next century. The owner of Maryland, Lord Baltimore, granted 795 acres of land to a Scottish man named Colonel Ninian Beall in 1703. Beall called the area the Rock of Dunbarton, after a place near his boyhood home in Scotland, and it included much of the area that was to become Georgetown. At his death in 1717, his son George inherited the land.

A man named George Gordon also owned land nearby, and in 1751 the General Assembly authorized a new township on the banks of the Potomac.

Rowhouses in Georgetown. (Washington, D.C., Convention & Visitors Association)

Sixty acres of land were combined to form the town, originally called the Town of George.

Georgetown became a thriving colonial port, shipping Maryland farm products, especially tobacco, to Europe. There were several landing wharves on the Potomac, and commercial traffic was lively. In 1791, George Washington wrote that Georgetown ranked as the greatest tobacco market in Maryland if not the entire union.

After the Revolutionary War, the new nation needed a capital. After a great deal of controversy, it was decided to build a new federal city on the Potomac River, taking parts of the states of Virginia and Maryland. The area chosen was at the time made up of farms, forests, meadows, marshland,

and two towns, both ports on the Potomac: Alexandria, Virginia, and Georgetown. It was in Georgetown that the plans for this new city were drawn up and the negotiations were made for purchasing the needed property.

George Washington and a new board of commissioners met in 1794 at Suter's Tavern to work out the purchase of the property, signing agreements with the major landowners of the area to sell whatever land would be needed for the new city. The same location was later used as the meeting place for Washington and Pierre L'Enfant, who was hired to design the capital city.

Originally Georgetown was not part of the federal city, but many statesmen and politicians chose to live there, commuting to their work in what was then the raw, muddy town of Washington. Francis Scott Key also lived in Georgetown. His house was later used as a tourist attraction, but it has since been torn down to make way for the bridge that bears his name.

From the beginning Georgetown had, along with a slave population, a significant population of free African Americans who had their own businesses and churches and owned their own homes. Most of them lived in the section called Herring Hill, named for the most frequently caught fish in Rock Creek. The area was bounded by Rock Creek Park and 29th Street, north of P Street. During the Civil War, despite its proximity to the capital of the Union, Georgetown was a Confederate city. However, the strong presence of a black community made the city an important stop on the Underground Railroad, the system of safe houses that allowed many slaves to escape north to freedom.

In 1871 the city of Georgetown was annexed to Washington, D.C., and in 1895 many of the streets were renamed. In many cases picturesque and descriptive names were replaced by the lettered and numbered streets now used throughout Washington, with the result that old documents refer to street names no longer in use today.

In the 1930's, during the Great Depression, President Franklin D. Roosevelt's New Dealers began buying Georgetown townhouses, many of which were by this time owned by African Americans. The idea was to live in smaller homes to avoid the appearance of conspicuous consumption. This, however, ironically meant that the wealthy were now taking over neighborhoods that had been home to more middle-class people. This had the effect of squeezing the black population out of the area, although their historic black churches remain active.

Places to Visit

Most of Georgetown is made up of old, historic buildings, but only a few are open to the public. Many of the homes date back to very early in U.S. history, and at least one goes back to colonial times.

The Old Stone House (3051 M Street NW), built in 1765, is the oldest standing building in Georgetown. Cabinetmaker Christopher Layman built the house, which has been used through the years as a private residence, a boardinghouse, a tavern, a house of prostitution, a craft studio, and several shops. During the 1950's it was saved from destruction because it was mistakenly thought to have been the site of Suter's Tavern, where George Washington and Pierre L'Enfant's meetings took place. In 1972 the house was designated a historic site and placed in the care of the National Park Service. One intriguing fact about this house is that ghosts have frequently been sighted there, especially by staff members and visiting children. The ghosts are dressed in clothing from the various eras of the house's history, and are seen passing through the building.

The Halcyon House, now known as the Stoddert House for its original owners (3400 Prospect Street NW), was built in 1787 by Benjamin Stoddert, who became the first secretary of the navy in 1796 and the first secretary of war in 1800. A tunnel into the basement was used as a stop on the Underground Railroad, and this use has led to another case of ghost sightings. Although the escaping slaves were safe from slave hunters in the tunnel, several died in the dank basement from exposure and exhaus-

tion after swimming across the Potomac River, and their ghosts have been seen on occasion in the years since. This house is not open to the public.

Georgetown University also includes some of the oldest buildings in the district. Founded by John Carroll in 1789 and administered by Jesuits, it was the first Catholic institution of higher learning in the United States. Today it is Washington, D.C.'s oldest university and one of the top schools in the country, known especially for its School of Foreign Service. Some of the earliest buildings are still used, including the Old North Building, completed in 1792, which was the original main building.

Tudor Place (1644 31st Street NW), built in 1794, became a historic house museum in 1983. It was built for Thomas Peter and his wife, Martha Parke Custis, the granddaughter of Martha Washington.

Today at 3276 M Street NW is an old building that houses food stalls for people wanting a quick lunch. The building has been a market for a long time, having been built in 1860 of red brick on fieldstone foundations that had been used by an earlier market building since about 1795. Before the advent of the grocery store, merchants, farmers, butchers, and fishermen set up stalls in public markets like this building. The market was used for this purpose until 1945, when it became a warehouse, until it was declared a landmark in 1966; in the 1970's it turned into a market again.

Dumbarton Oaks (1703 32d Street NW) is another famous mansion open to the public. Built in 1801, the house was bought in 1920 by Robert Woods Bliss and his wife Mildred. They transformed the run-down mansion into a showplace of rare European and Byzantine art. The Blisses also created the gardens, which covered more than ten acres, and purposely left wild more acres at the back of the estate. In 1941, they gave the house and gardens to Harvard University, and in 1963 a modern gallery was attached with a collection of pre-Columbian art. The wild portion of the estate was given to the District of Columbia as a park.

The Bank of Columbia Building (3210 M Street NW) was built in 1796 and became the second-oldest bank in the District of Columbia. The bank moved its services in 1806 to another site, and the building was put to a series of other uses, including the Bureau of Indian Trade (1807-1822), Georgetown Town Hall and Mayor's Office (1823-1863), Lang's Hotel (1863-1870), District of Columbia government offices and storage (1871-1883), and a fire station (1883-1946). In 1981, it was remodeled into a Burger King restaurant.

Mount Zion Methodist Church (1334 29th Street NW) is the oldest known Washington church started by and for blacks, dating to 1816. Its cemetery is the oldest predominantly African American burial ground in Washington, and a vault there was a stop on the Underground Railroad.

In addition to these public buildings, Georgetown includes many other historic places, although most are not open to the public and can only be viewed from outside.
—*Eleanor B. Amico*

For Further Information:

Bergheim, Laura. *The Washington Historical Atlas*. Rockville, Md.: Woodbine House, 1992. Although only a few pages deal directly with Georgetown, those pages are immensely helpful in understanding the history and layout of the district, and many of Georgetown's important buildings.

"DCGenWeb." www.rootsweb.com/~dcgenweb/ This site offers not only genealogical tools, but also historical materials about Georgetown, including the old and new street names and the names of early Georgetown officials.

Durkin, Joseph T. *Georgetown University, First in the Nation's Capital*. 2 vols. Garden City, N.J.: Doubleday, 1964. Describes the history of Washington's first university and the nation's first Catholic university.

Ecker, Grace Dunlop. *A Portrait of Old George Town*. Richmond, Va.: Dietz Press, 1951. Written in sentimental style by a woman born and raised there, this history of Georgetown includes a detailed history of the district as a whole and each neighborhood.

Mitchell, Mary. *Chronicles of Georgetown Life, 1865-1900*. Cabin John, Md.: Seven Locks Press, 1986. Discusses one period of Georgetown life and the people involved in it.

Whitehill, Walter Muir. *Dumbarton Oaks: The History of a Georgetown House and Garden, 1800-1966*. Cambridge, Mass.: The Belknap Press of Harvard University Press, 1967. Details the history of Georgetown's perhaps most famous home.

Lincoln Memorial

Date: Dedicated in 1922

Relevant issues: Art and architecture, political history

Significance: This memorial honors Abraham Lincoln (1809-1865), the president during the Civil War (1861-1865) who fought to preserve the nation. His leadership contributed to the victory of the Union and the abolition of slavery. The memorial's construction took ten years, and it is considered an architectural masterpiece. The memorial has become a symbol for freedom, unification, and equality.

Location: The west end of the Mall in Washington, D.C.

Site Office:
National Capital Parks-Central
The National Mall
900 Ohio Drive SW
Washington, DC 20242
ph.: (202) 426-6841
Web site: www.nps.gov/linc/

Standing as a tribute to President Abraham Lincoln, the Lincoln Memorial was built as a permanent memory to the man who saved the Union and abolished slavery. As early as 1867, discussions began about a permanent memorial in memory of Lincoln to be located in the nation's capital. After years of debate as to the design of the memorial and its exact location, Henry Bacon was chosen as architect, and construction began in 1914. The memorial, located at the west end of the Mall in Washington, D.C., was dedicated in 1922 and is modeled after the Greek Parthenon.

Construction

Beginning in 1867, citizens and congressmen alike urged the construction of a shrine to honor the martyred president, Abraham Lincoln. Many ideas circulated about the appearance of the memorial and the best location for such a structure. Although some funds were raised for the construction, agreement on the style and location could not be reached. There was always agreement that some type of memorial should be constructed, but the ideas varied greatly.

Finally, on February 12, 1911, Lincoln's birthday, President William Howard Taft signed the bill that created a commission to choose a site and begin construction of a memorial to Lincoln. The Lincoln Memorial Commission decided that somewhere along the National Mall, a spacious expanse of grass and trees stretching from Capitol Hill to the Potomac River, would be appropriate. They decided that the ideal spot would be at the west end of the Mall, across from the Washington Monument. The commission selected Henry Bacon as architect of the monument. Bacon imagined a shining Greek temple of white marble containing a statue of Lincoln. Inside, Lincoln's Gettysburg Address, along with his second inaugural address, would be carved on opposite walls. The commission agreed with Bacon's ideas and on February 12, 1914, ground was broken for the Lincoln Memorial.

The building was to rest on what once was swampland. The land had earlier been drained and filled, but caution had to be taken when constructing such a massive structure. Therefore, a foundation had to be built. The foundation was completed in the spring of 1915, and work began on the main structure. With the United States' entry into World War I in April of 1917, construction on the memorial slowed due to shortages of material and labor. Work also began on the area surrounding the memorial, including landscape that consisted of roadways, walks, shrubs, and trees. Terraces surrounding the monument were built. The Reflecting Pool, which stretches between the Lincoln Memorial and the Washington Monument, was also constructed at this time.

The main structure was built in the form of a Greek temple, with openings in the sides and thirty-six fluted Doric columns around the perimeter. As a tribute to the Union that Lincoln helped preserve, the columns represent the thirty-six states that made up the nation at the time of Lincoln's death. The names of those states are listed

The Lincoln Memorial. (Arkent Archives)

on the frieze above the columns. Above those are listed the forty-eight states that made up the nation at the time the memorial was completed. Alaska and Hawaii, added to the union later, are represented by a plaque on the front steps.

The interior of the building is divided into three sections by fifty-foot-high columns. The center section contains the statue of Lincoln, and the two side sections contain murals created by Jules Guerin. On the left wall of the left section is the engraving of Lincoln's Gettysburg Address, and on the right wall of the right section is engraved his second inaugural address, just as Bacon originally envisioned. The two murals by Guerin were created to represent Lincoln's causes of unification and emancipation. The mural titled *Unification* hangs over the Inaugural Address, and *Emancipation* hangs over the Gettysburg Address.

The Statue

The Lincoln Memorial Commission selected Daniel Chester French in December of 1914 to design the statue of Lincoln for the memorial. French, who was chair of the Commission of Fine Arts at the time, resigned his position when he was appointed to create the statue. The Commission of Fine Arts would later have to approve French's design for the statue of Lincoln. French felt that a seated figure would be most appropriate, and he studied many photographs of Lincoln to find the exact features. He also studied the Volk Mask, a plaster impression that was made of Lincoln's face, hands, and torso by sculptor Leonard Volk in 1860. From these molds, French was able to learn many details of Lincoln's appearance that were not found in photographs.

French decided to depict Lincoln as he looked during his presidency. He felt that this would best capture the spirit of Lincoln during the Civil War. French and Bacon also decided that the statue should be ten feet tall. In June of 1915, French completed his first basic drawings of the statue. More detailed drawings to create Lincoln's exact positions were done in the following months. In 1916 the Commission of Fine Arts approved French's design.

French and Bacon later realized that the statue would be lost in the massive memorial and decided that a larger one would be needed. French designed a new statue to be nineteen feet high, nearly double the size of the original. Although the foundation of the memorial was completed by this time, it would now be necessary to reinforce the floor to accommodate the added weight of the larger statue. Steel struts were added beneath the floor to support the weight.

The stonecutting firm of Piccirilli Brothers was selected to carve the statue. The cost of the statue, made solely of Georgia white marble, would be $46,000, and the pedestal would cost another $15,000. The cutting of the marble began in the fall of 1918. Twenty-eight identical blocks would be needed to complete the statue. The carving was finished in November, 1919, and work immediately began on assembling the blocks. By May of 1920,

the statue was complete. For several more years, French worked on the exact lighting for the statue, which was accomplished by placing lights in the ceiling.

The statue depicts Lincoln seated in a throne-like chair that sits on top of a pedestal. He appears to be at rest, in a pensive pose. His coat is unbuttoned and his hands are resting on the arms of the chair. His facial expression is one of contemplation. He is calm, but his body is erect and his head held high. There is sorrow in his eyes, as if he is reflecting on the terrible tragedies of war. On the wall behind Lincoln, the following inscription appears: "In this Temple, as in the hearts of the people, for whom he saved the union, the memory of Abraham Lincoln is enshrined forever."

Dedication

The dedication of the Lincoln Memorial took place on Memorial Day, May 30, 1922, and it was a grand affair. Some 50,000 people attended the dedication, of whom 3,500 were invited guests. Robert Todd Lincoln, the only surviving child of Abraham Lincoln, was the guest of honor. Chief Justice William Howard Taft, who as president created the Lincoln Memorial Commission, was a notable guest. President Warren G. Harding was on hand formally to accept the memorial on behalf of the American people, and he delivered a speech praising the importance of the memorial not only for the people of the present but for future generations as well. A public address system was installed so that the large crowd could hear the proceedings. The ceremony was also broadcast nationally over radio, which was quite exciting because at that time radio was still in its infancy. Dr. Robert Russa Moton, president of Tuskegee Institute, presented the main address and spoke of the gratitude his fellow African Americans felt toward Lincoln, and of the responsibility that comes with freedom. Wallace Radcliffe, pastor of the New York Avenue Presbyterian Church—the church attended by Lincoln when he was president—delivered the invocation. Following the ceremonies the crowd flocked inside to marvel at the beautiful structure.

Materials and Size

The exterior of the building is made of Colorado Yule marble, while the interior walls and columns are Indiana limestone. The ceiling is Alabama marble, and the floor is Tennessee Pink marble. Tennessee marble was used for the pedestal and platform for the statue, and the statue itself is carved from white Georgia marble. The building is 188 feet high, 118 feet wide, and 99 feet tall. The height of the columns in the colonnade is forty-four feet, and their diameter is seven feet, five inches at the base. Each interior column is fifty feet high and five feet, six inches in diameter. The murals are each sixty feet long by twelve feet high. The total cost of constructing the Lincoln Memorial was $2.9 million.

After seventy-five years of exposure of the two murals by Guerin to the elements, work was begun in 1995 to restore their original vibrancy by slowly removing the buildup of dirt and by stabilizing cracked and flaking layers in the paintings. The National Park Service, which assumed jurisdiction over the memorial in 1933, sponsored the project. Because of fluctuations in temperature and moisture, the paintings, which were done in oil paint on canvas, began to show cracks. The cost of the restoration project was $407,000.

A Symbol for Freedom and Equality

Large numbers of people visit the Lincoln Memorial annually to reflect on the spirit of Lincoln and the ideals for which he stood. The memorial became a symbol for freedom and equality, especially for African Americans wishing to use Lincoln's memory in their pursuit of equality and civil rights. On Easter Sunday, 1939, Marian Anderson, a vocalist, used the Lincoln Memorial for a concert when she was denied use of Constitution Hall because she was black. It has been used more than one hundred times for various civil rights rallies, most notably in 1963 when Dr. Martin Luther King, Jr., gave his "I Have a Dream" speech from the steps of the monument. —*Paul Demilio*

For Further Information:

Alexander, C. F. "Memorials Pose Preservation Challenges (The Restoration of the Lincoln Memorial)." *Architecture* 83, no. 11 (November, 1994): 151. Discusses preservation needs of the Lincoln Monument.

Bodnar, John. *Remaking America.* Princeton, N.J.: Princeton University Press, 1992. Social history that explores public memory, commemoration, and patriotism in the twentieth century.

Goode, James M. *The Outdoor Sculpture of Washington, D.C.* Washington, D.C.: Smithsonian Institution Press, 1974. A comprehensive historical guide to the architecture and sculpture of Washington, D.C.

Redway, Maurine Whorton, and Dorothy Kendall Bracken. *Marks of Lincoln on Our Land.* New York: Hastings House, 1957. Describes the many monuments and shrines of Lincoln that have been erected across the United States.

Sandage, Scott A. "A Marble House Divided: The Lincoln Memorial, the Civil Rights Movement, and the Politics of Memory, 1939-1963." *Journal of American History* 80, no. 1 (June, 1993): 135-167.

Mary McLeod Bethune Council House

Date: Declared a National Historic Site in 1982

Relevant issues: African American history, education, social reform, women's history

Significance: This site was Mary McLeod Bethune's last official residence in Washington, D.C., and the first headquarters of the National Council of Negro Women. Now it is a National Historic Site where visitors may view exhibits, including special activities for children, interpreting Bethune's life and work. In addition, the National Archives for Black Women's History are housed there.

Location: Washington, D.C.

Site Office:
Mary McLeod Bethune Council House National Historic Site
1318 Vermont Avenue NW
Washington, DC 20005
ph.: (202) 673-2402
fax: (202) 673-2414
Web site: www.nps.gov/mamc/

The Mary McLeod Bethune Council House National Historic Site commemorates the life of Mary McLeod Bethune and the National Council of Negro Women, which she founded. At the end of the twentieth century, it was one of ten National Park Service sites commemorating African American history.

Mary McLeod Bethune. (Associated Publishers, Inc.)

The three-story, fifteen-room Victorian townhouse was used as the original headquarters for the National Council of Negro Women, and it was also Bethune's last official residence in Washington, D.C. Furnished originally with the help of individuals and various organizations that believed in the cause, the site was where Bethune gained her greatest national and international recognition and developed strategies and programs to advance the interests of African American women and the African American community.

The mission of the historic site is to interpret Bethune's life and legacy, to document and interpret the history of African American women in their struggle for civil rights, and to assure the preservation and restoration of the site from its most significant period, the years between 1943 and 1966.

Bethune's Life

Mary Bethune was born Mary Jane McLeod on July 10, 1875, in Mayesville, South Carolina. Her parents, Samuel and Patsy, had been slaves on the McLeod Plantation. Several of their children had also been born into slavery, and many had been sold off to other plantations. Her parents were able to keep track of the family, however, through a secret slave network, and after the end of the Civil War in 1865 they were reunited.

The family stayed on the McLeod Plantation for several years until they had saved enough money to buy a small farm of five acres nearby. There Mary was born, the fifteenth of seventeen children and the first to be born on her parents' farm. The McLeods were a devoutly religious family and generous to all.

In 1882 a black missionary named Emma Wilson began a school for black children in Mayesville, and Mary's parents immediately enrolled her. The seven-year-old girl walked five miles each day to the school. At the age of twelve she heard a black missionary speak about mission work in Africa and determined that this was her calling. Emma Wilson was able to get a scholarship for Mary to attend Scotia Seminary in Concord, North Carolina, where she graduated in 1893. She then went to Chicago, also on scholarship, to Moody Bible Institute, where she graduated in 1895.

That year she applied to the Presbyterian Board of Missions for an assignment to Africa, but she was told that there was no place in Africa for a black missionary. So she returned to the South, teaching at schools for African Americans in Georgia, South Carolina, and Florida. After teaching for a while, she realized that blacks in the United States needed education as much as Africans did, and her life's goal became to improve the education of young black Americans.

In 1898 she married another teacher, Albertus Bethune, and she had one son, Albert. However, the marriage did not last, and Albertus returned to South Carolina after six years and died in 1919.

In 1904 many African Americans were moving to Daytona Beach, Florida, to work on the new Florida East Coast Railway, and Mary moved there to start a school, a longtime goal of hers. With all the money she owned—$1.50—and packing crates for desks, she opened the Daytona Educational and Industrial School for Negro Girls on October 3, 1904, with five pupils aged eight to twelve.

She financed the school by selling homemade pies and ice cream to railroad construction workers, by soliciting funds from philanthropists and black organizations, and by staging concerts by her pupils. Although there was never enough money or resources, the school continued to grow, and in 1923 it merged with Cookman Institute, a school for males that was better endowed financially but whose student body was declining.

This merger saved both schools, and Bethune-Cookman Institute was founded. There was a faculty of twenty-five and a student body of three hundred. In 1929 it became a fully accredited college, and it awarded its first four-year degrees in 1943. That same year Bethune resigned as president of the college to devote more time to the national struggle for civil rights. By the end of the twentieth century, Bethune-Cookman College was enrolling about 2,300 students.

Bethune's influence extended far beyond Florida, however. In 1927 she was invited to meet the governor of New York, Franklin D. Roosevelt, and at that time she became friends with his wife Eleanor. The next year President Calvin Coolidge appointed her to the National Child Welfare Commission.

The next president, Herbert Hoover, appointed her to the Commission on Home Building and Home Ownership, and when Roosevelt became president he made her Special Advisor on Minority Affairs. He also appointed her Director of the Division of Negro Affairs of the National Youth Administration, making her the first African American woman to be placed in charge of a federal agency. There were also several black men who occupied administrative posts in Roosevelt's New Deal agencies, and together they formed an informal presidential advisory board known as the Black Cabinet.

Bethune continued to serve in a variety of governmental roles during and after World War II, but she was involved in other organizations at the same time. She became president of the National Association of Colored Women in 1924 and vice president of the National Association for the Advancement of Colored People (NAACP) in 1940. In 1935 she founded the National Council of Negro Women, uniting many major national black women's organizations. She was its president until 1949, living in the council's headquarters in Washington, D.C.

Bethune moved back to Daytona Beach in 1949 and lived the rest of her life there. In 1955 she wrote an article, published after her death in the August issue of *Ebony* magazine, called "My Last Will and Testament." Knowing that her life was drawing to a close, she outlined her legacy to the world. Realizing that her worldly possessions were few but her experiences were rich, Bethune wrote that she was leaving all African Americans the legacies of love, hope, the challenge of developing confidence in one another, thirst for education, respect for the uses of power, faith, racial dignity, desire to live harmoniously with others, and responsibility to young people. She died on May 18, 1955, and is buried on the campus of Bethune-Cookman College.

The Council House

The Mary McLeod Bethune Council House National Historic Site has exhibits on Bethune and the National Council of Negro Women, including original furnishings and historic photographs depicting the house during the 1940's. Park rangers give guided tours of the house, which include a video on Bethune's life.

For children and their families or small school groups, a treasure hunt through the house is available. This is an interactive tour using a series of questions and activities. There are other kinds of special programs for children and teachers as well, including workshops. There are also book signings, lectures, and changing exhibits, as well as year-round concert, lecture, and film series.

The Bethune Citizens Program provides students the opportunity to use Bethune's "Last Will and Testament" to make positive changes in their communities. This program is a youth volunteer initiative to enhance self-esteem, promote leadership, and support community service.

Rangers are also available to visit classrooms and talk about Bethune, the Council House, the National Park Service, or African American women's history. In addition, educational materials are available free to teachers, including copies of historic documents, posters, exhibit guides, and teacher's guides. These include packets on "A Week in the Life of Mary McLeod Bethune" and "Behind the Scenes in the Civil Rights Movement." The packets provide primary source materials that teachers can incorporate into their lesson plans, as well as activities and assignments.

The Archives
The site also houses the National Archives for Black Women's History, which are kept in the carriage house. This is the nation's largest repository of materials relating to black women, including correspondence, photographs, and speeches about Bethune, the National Council of Negro Women, and other black women and their organizations.

Collections in the archives cover a wide range of subjects: civil rights, consumer issues, education, employment, health, housing, international issues, religion, and women's issues. There are over six hundred linear feet of manuscripts, a small library and vertical file on African American women's history, and over four hundred photographs and other audiovisual materials.

Researchers of all ages can use the archives, but only by appointment. After a researcher submits a written request outlining the topic of research and naming the days he or she is available, the archivist sets up an appointment with the researcher.

History of the Council House
The Mary McLeod Bethune Council House National Historic Site is located in the Logan Circle Historic District. The Council House was built as a private residence in 1874 and went through several hands until it was sold to Bethune for $15,500 in 1943. The money for the purchase was raised through a large donation from Marshall Field and contributions from staff, sections, and affiliates of the National Council of Negro Women.

The conference room was the site of many meetings and the initiation of many programs to address problems of housing, racial discrimination, health care, employment, and the preservation of African American women's history. Eleanor Roosevelt was also a guest at the house, and in 1963 it was a rallying point for the March on Washington.

The building was damaged by fire in January, 1966, and the National Council of Negro Women relocated to another building. The house lay dormant for eleven years until 1975, when it was placed on the District of Columbia Register of Historic Sites and funds were raised to renovate and restore both the main and carriage houses.

In the fall of 1977 the Bethune Historical Development Project began, and in November, 1979, the house was opened to the public as a museum. It was declared a National Historic Site by act of Congress in 1982 and acquired by the National Park Service in 1994. The Council House is open from 10:00 A.M. to 4:00 P.M. Monday through Saturday except holidays. —*Eleanor B. Amico*

For Further Information:

Greene, Carol. *Mary McLeod Bethune: Champion for Education.* Chicago: Children's Press, 1993. A biography for young people.

Halasa, Malu. *Mary McLeod Bethune.* New York: Chelsea House, 1989. A detailed and helpful biography written for a young audience but informational for all readers.

Holt, Rackham. *Mary McLeod Bethune, a Biography.* New York: Doubleday, 1964. Tells and interprets Bethune's life, focusing on her educational and governmental work.

Peare, Catherine Owens. *Mary McLeod Bethune.* New York: Vanguard, 1951. Examines Bethune's life from her childhood to the 1940's, combining imagined dialogue with narrative to tell about her life.

Sitkoff, Harvard. *A New Deal for Blacks: The Emergence of Civil Rights as a National Issue.* New York: Oxford University Press, 1978. Examines Bethune's work during Roosevelt's New Deal and her campaigns for civil rights.

Sterne, Emma Geddes. *Mary McLeod Bethune.* New York: Alfred A. Knopf, 1957. A look at Bethune as a woman committed to improving the lives of African American women and unifying women across racial lines.

The National Mall

Date: Founded in 1790

Relevant issues: Art and architecture, cultural history, military history, political history

Significance: The National Mall was part of Pierre Charles L'Enfant's original plan for the city of Washington, D.C. L'Enfant designed the Mall as a promenade of green space in 1790. The Mall was to be a place where the nation remembered its heroes and preserved its culture. L'Enfant's original plan was never fully implemented, yet the 146-acre Mall contains some of the most important national monuments in the United States: the Washington Monument, the Lincoln Memorial, the Vietnam Veterans Memorial, the Korean War Memorial, and Constitution Gardens. Many of the Smithsonian Institution buildings also line the Mall.

Location: Downtown Washington, D.C.

Site Office:
National Capital Parks-Central
The National Mall
900 Ohio Drive SW
Washington, DC 20242
ph.: (202) 426-6841
Web site: www.nps.gov/nama/

Beginning at the United States Capitol Building and stretching eastward to the Lincoln Memorial, the National Mall contains some of the most important memorials in the United States. Pierre Charles L'Enfant designed the area as public space for the erection of monuments, as an arena for the presentation and preservation of culture, and for use by American citizens. Many well-known national memorials are located on the Mall, as is the Smithsonian Institution, the national guardian of our collective history. The Mall is also a place where Americans can gather for celebration, reflection, and protest. The Mall has been the site of demonstrations throughout its history.

The Creation of the National Mall

President George Washington chose the location for the nation's capital city in 1790 as part of the Residence Act. Washington chose Frenchman Pierre Charles L'Enfant, an engineer and architect, to perform a topographical survey of the town. Washington was acquainted with L'Enfant through L'Enfant's service to the American Continental Army in its fight against the British in the American Revolution. The choice of the site of the new capital for the nation had been a compromise; southerners in Congress had won a southern capital, while the federal government agreed to pay the debts owed by states and accumulated during the Revolutionary War. At the time that L'Enfant surveyed the ten-square-mile area, the United States government did not own the land. President Washington and Secretary of State Thomas Jefferson hoped that the landowners would donate portions of their land to the government with the knowledge that the value of their retained land would increase significantly.

L'Enfant was twenty-two years old when he volunteered for the Continental Army and received a commission as lieutenant of engineers. After the war L'Enfant settled in New York and began a career as an architect. When L'Enfant heard that a new capital was in the making, he wrote to Washington, saying that Washington, D.C., should be a great city, its plan "drawn to such a scale as to leave room for the aggrandizement and embellishment which the increase of the wealth of the nation will permit it to pursue at any period however remote."

L'Enfant's vision of the city informed his judgment, and what he produced was not what his employers thought necessary—a simple topographical survey—but rather a rough sketch of the city he envisioned. L'Enfant presented his ideas to Washington in March, 1791. Later that day Washington acquired the land, and L'Enfant was hired to plan the nation's capital.

The topography allowed L'Enfant to abandon the traditional grid pattern for a more diverse plan to highlight the scenic views within the new city. L'Enfant's plan called for a grand cascade coming from Capitol Hill ending in a canal that would empty into the Potomac River. This canal would assist the city to become a commercial center and increase the beauty of the area. Tiber Creek could be used as a forty-foot waterfall, with the water escaping through the canal. Parallel to this the National Mall would be developed as a grand avenue four hundred feet wide, beginning south of the president's house at a statue of Washington himself. L'Enfant hoped to see public buildings to house government offices, museums, theaters, and foreign embassies surrounding the Mall. L'Enfant envisioned the future Pennsylvania Avenue paved for carriages, lined with trees and theaters, academies, and other cultural attractions.

With Washington's approval, L'Enfant and his crews started work clearing the land and deciding on the quadrants of the city. Problems about financing L'Enfant's visionary city soon arose with the city commissioners. The commissioners, along with Jefferson and James Madison, decided to begin selling off city lots in order to increase revenue. L'Enfant disagreed with their strategy, thinking it better to secure loans for the public structures and sell lots as the land values increased. For L'Enfant the matter was more than just semantics. He did not wish to see the city develop in a piecemeal fashion and did not prepare a plan of the city to present at the sale. He then bragged to Washington's secretary, Tobias Lear, of his doings. Word of his misdeed was relayed to Jefferson, who became hostile, and Washington rebuked L'Enfant for his actions. Relations further declined when L'Enfant took it upon himself to raze a mansion that was being constructed inside the city by Daniel Carroll.

Legally at fault, Washington healed the rift this created between L'Enfant and the commissioners, but in 1792, relations between Jefferson and the commissioners on one side and L'Enfant and his engineers on the other had deteriorated dramatically. The major issue was control over the project; the commissioners and Jefferson believed their authority to be supreme, and L'Enfant believed that the commissioners and Jefferson could not appreciate the technical aspects of the project. All along, Washington tried to bridge the gap between the two parties, but when L'Enfant slighted the emissary Washington had sent to plead with L'Enfant to continue his work under the "full subordination" of the engineers, Washington had had enough and fired L'Enfant.

Washington, D.C., in the Early Nineteenth Century

Washington then commanded L'Enfant's subordinate, Andrew Ellicott, to amend L'Enfant's plan. In addition, in 1802, Congress reestablished the Army Corps of Engineers and created a military academy at West Point. Now president, Thomas Jefferson intended these two entities to complement one another, as he foresaw that the training of engineers was to be undertaken at the military school. Hence,

West Point graduates would not only defend the country but also build it. Threat of English attack in the first two decades of the nineteenth century prompted fortifications in the city, but very little construction along the Mall. Between 1800 and 1810, Congress spent money only on public buildings, leaving the rest of the city untouched. L'Enfant's plan had disappeared, and many visitors were appalled at living conditions in the nation's capital.

After the British burnt the city in 1814, the army began to rebuild not only the fortifications, but the city as well. The Army Corps of Engineers was soon transferred to Washington, D.C., by Secretary of War John C. Calhoun, and the city at last had a professional group of men trained to create a city out of forest and swamp.

The Smithsonian Institution and the Washington Monument

While the Army Corps of Engineers rebuilt Washington, D.C., L'Enfant's plan had not been entirely discarded by Congress. His concept of the Mall as a public space for monuments and American culture was slowly beginning to take hold. Two main additions were conceptualized in the first part of the nineteenth century: the Washington Monument and the Smithsonian Institution.

Congress had authorized a monument to George Washington in 1833, but construction did not begin until 1848. Originally funded privately by the Washington National Monument Society (WNMS), the monument was intended to be a colonnade, but financial considerations forced the abandonment of this plan. The Know-Nothing Party gained control of the WNMS in 1854, when contributions came to a halt, and construction was abandoned. After the Civil War, the Grant administration got the WNMS to donate the monument to the people of the United States, allowing Congress to appropriate funds. In 1885, the monument was completed and dedicated by President Chester A. Arthur. The Washington Monument is 555 feet tall and has 897 steps, which are now closed to the public except during tours led by the National Park Service.

In 1846, Congress had established the Smithsonian Institution to act as a repository and to "increase the diffusion of knowledge of men," a mission the Institution continues to serve to this day.

The National Mall. (Washington, D.C., Convention & Visitors Association)

British scientist James Smithson donated his fortune upon his death as seed money for the Institution. The same year that the Smithsonian Institution was established, it obtained its first building, the Smithsonian Castle, a twelfth century Normal Style building. The Smithsonian Castle is the oldest building on the Mall. James Smithson's body is entombed in a crypt within the building. The Smithsonian has grown to include many other museums that line the Mall: the Arthur M. Sackler Gallery, the Arts and Industries Building, the Freer Gallery of Art, the Hirshhorn Museum and Sculptor Garden, the National Air and Space Museum, the National Museum of African Art, the National Museum of American History, the National Museum of Natural History, and the National Gallery of Art.

The City Beautiful Movement

The early twentieth century saw the advent of the City Beautiful movement in urban planning, a response to the urban squalor that plagued American cities in the nineteenth century. Congress responded to this in 1902 by creating a park commission that would decide how to develop a District of Columbia park system. The commission consisted of Frederick Law Olmstead, the designer of New York's Central Park; architect Charles F. McKim; sculptor Augustus Saint-Gaudens; and the chair of the commission, Daniel H. Burnham.

The resulting McMillan Plan, named after Senator James McMillan, recommended basically a return to L'Enfant's original design. However, the plan called for extending L'Enfant's concept to include the new Potomac Park, as well as the Lincoln Memorial. The Commission decided to clear the Mall of existing structures, frame it with elm trees, and flank it with public buildings. Nothing was to obscure the view linking the Capitol and the future Lincoln Memorial. The McMillan Plan was not entirely adopted by both houses of Congress until 1929, seven years after the completion of the Lincoln Memorial.

The Lincoln Memorial

Congress authorized the building of the Lincoln Memorial, a tribute to Abraham Lincoln, president during the American Civil War (1860-1865), in

1911. Henry Bacon designed the building to resemble the Parthenon in Athens, and Daniel Chester French's statue of Lincoln sits inside the memorial, along with carved inscriptions of two of Lincoln's speeches. Thirty-six columns surround the building, representing the 36 states in the Union at the time of Lincoln's death. Above those states are the names of the 48 states in the Union when the memorial was constructed. President Warren G. Harding attended the 1922 dedication.

Constitution Gardens and Green Space

Constitution Gardens is not a traditional monument, yet recent additions have enhanced its function as "a living legacy to the founding of the republic as well as an oasis in the midst of a city landscape." The fifty-acre site of the park was originally beneath the Potomac River and was created by a U.S. Army Corps of Engineers dredging project at the turn of century.

President Richard M. Nixon, appalled by the temporary naval office buildings located here in the 1970's, began lobbying for their removal. After the Navy finally withdrew from the buildings, they were demolished in 1971. President Nixon ordered that a park be built on the land, leading to the creation of Constitution Gardens. The Gardens were dedicated in 1976 as a living legacy to the American Revolution. In July of 1982, a memorial to the fifty-six signers of the Declaration of Independence was dedicated on the small island in the lake. In 1986, President Ronald Reagan, in honor of the Bicentennial of the U.S. Constitution, issued a proclamation making Constitution Gardens a living legacy in tribute to the Constitution. Constitution Gardens has been a separate park unit since 1982.

The Vietnam Veterans and Korean War Memorials

Monument building on the Mall ceased after the construction of the Lincoln Memorial until, in 1980, Congress authorized the building of the Vietnam Veterans Memorial. By this time, the culture of memorializing great events in history had turned more toward remembering the individual sacrifices of Americans rather than erecting edifices for more prominent Americans, such as presidents. The contemporary "monuments" are no longer monuments, but memorials, which are more encompassing in their tributes. The Vietnam Veterans Memorial Commission specified that all of the American dead and missing be included and that the memorial harmonize with its surroundings.

Maya Ying Lin, then an architectural student at Harvard, designed the nontraditional wall, composed of seventy polished, black granite panels inscribed with fifty thousand names of those who lost their lives or are missing in action. The wall is located immediately northeast of the Lincoln Memorial, and the granite walls are imbedded into the gently elevated land of the Mall. When the design drew criticism from veterans' groups, a decision was made to add Frederick Hart's statue often called The Three Servicemen. The three soldiers represent different ethnic groups: Caucasian, Latino, and African American. In 1993, the Vietnam Women's Memorial was added to represent the work of women in the Vietnam War.

The next memorial on the Mall was a memorial to a war that began five years after the end of World War II. The Korean War began in 1950, as the communist government of North Korea invaded South Korea. The United States led a United Nations force to the remote Asian peninsula. The memorial to the 1.5 million men and women who fought in the Korean War was erected in 1995. Bringing together depictions of each branch of the armed forces, the Korean War Memorial consists of nineteen stainless steel statues representing a squad on patrol in a triangular "field of service." The statues are clothed in windblown ponchos depicting the harshness of the weather endured while on duty. A granite curb on the north side of the monument lists the twenty-two United Nations member countries that sent troops or provided support in defense of South Korea. On the south side stands a wall of California Academy black granite, with the etched images of more than 2,400 unnamed servicemen and women. The numbers of those killed, wounded, missing in action, and taken prisoner of war are etched into the curb. The message "Freedom Is Not Free" faces the counting of the war's toll. A "pool of remembrance," encircled by linden trees, stands adjacent to the mural.

Visiting the Mall

The memorials and monuments on the National Mall are open daily from 8:00 A.M. until 11:45 P.M., every day except Christmas Day. The Washington Monument is open daily from 8:00 A.M. until 11:45 P.M. from the first Sunday in April through Labor Day and the rest of the year from 9:00 A.M. until 4:45 P.M. It is also closed on Christmas Day. Most of the Smithsonian Institution museums are open daily from 10:00 A.M. to 5:30 P.M. and offer free admission.   —*Kathleen Kadlec*

For Further Information:

Cowdrey, Albert. *A City for the Nation: The Army Engineers and the Building of Washington, D.C., 1790-1967*. Washington, D.C.: Office of the Chief of Engineers, Department of the Army, Government Printing Office, 1979.

Green, Constance McLaughlin. *Washington: Capital City, 1879-1950*. Princeton, N.J.: Princeton University Press, 1963.

National Park Service. U.S. Department of the Interior. *Washington D.C.: A Traveler's Guide to the District of Columbia and Nearby Attractions*. Washington, D.C.: Author, 1989.

Penczer, Peter R. *Washington, D.C., Past and Present*. Arlington, Va.: Oneonta Press, 1998.

Sewall-Belmont House

Date: Designated a National Historic Site in 1974
Relevant issues: Political history, women's history
Significance: Built in 1800 and the oldest home on Capitol Hill, this house was sold to the National Woman's Party in 1929 and has been its headquarters ever since. It is also a museum of women's history.
Location: On Capitol Hill, near the Senate offices and the Capitol
Site Office:
Sewall-Belmont House National Historic Site
144 Constitution Avenue NE
Washington, DC 20002
ph.: (202) 546-3989, 546-1210
fax: (202) 546-3997
Web site: www.natwomanparty.org

The Sewall-Belmont House is the oldest residence on Capitol Hill, and that in itself makes it interesting, but it is also the working headquarters of the National Woman's Party (NWP) and a museum of women's rights. The building is named for its first owner, Robert Sewall, and for Alva Vanderbilt Belmont, who, with her wealth as part of the Vanderbilt family, purchased the house for the NWP in 1929. Curiously, the individual most closely connected with the site, Alice Paul, who founded and headed the NWP for over thirty years and lived in the house for many years as well, is not part of the name.

Early History of the House
The first structure on the site was a one-room farmhouse that dates, according to some sources, to 1680. This became the kitchen when a red brick Federal-period town house was built in 1799 by Robert Sewall, on land he had purchased from Daniel Carroll soon after the city of Washington, D.C., was laid out.

At about the same time, however, Sewall inherited his family's plantation in Maryland and wanted to live there. So he rented the house to Secretary of the Treasury Albert Gallatin, who served under Presidents Thomas Jefferson and James Madison from 1801 to 1813. Gallatin drafted and finalized the Louisiana Purchase in his front-parlor office, which is now preserved as the California Room. After Gallatin left, several American flotilla men were stationed at the house during the War of 1812, and because of several shots fired from there during the British invasion of Washington, D.C., it was the only residence burned by the British. These shots were, in fact, the only resistance that the British faced as they torched many public buildings in the new city.

Sewall had completely rebuilt the house by 1820, and from then on it was occupied by his family members and descendents until 1922, when it was purchased by Senator Porter H. Dale of Vermont. In 1929, Belmont bought it as headquarters for the NWP as a residence for the party's founder, Alice Paul.

Alice Paul and the National Woman's Party
Born January 11, 1885, in Moorestown, New Jersey, Alice Paul was graduated from Swarthmore College in 1905 and then went on to do graduate work at the New York School of Social Work. From there she went to England to continue her studies and do settlement work. While in England, she studied at the University of Birmingham and the University of London, earning a master's degree from the

Alice Paul (second from right) and the officers of the National Woman's Party stand in front of their headquarters in Washington, D.C. (Library of Congress)

University of Pennsylvania in absentia in 1907. On her return home, she earned her Ph.D. from the same school in 1913.

While in England, however, Paul did more than study and practice social work. She became involved in the radical, militant wing of the British suffrage movement, which was fighting for women's right to vote by staging marches and demonstrations. Three times, Paul was arrested and imprisoned in England.

Returning in 1910, Paul became involved in the struggle for suffrage in the United States. She began by joining the National American Woman Suffrage Association (NAWSA) and becoming, in 1912, the chair of the congressional committee of this organization, which had been working for many decades for women's right to vote.

NAWSA, however, continued to work as it always had, trying to convince one state after another to allow women to vote. The association, at this stage, was concerned about upsetting those in power and tried not to be too radical in its approach. Paul, used to radical and direct action in England, became frustrated with the slow movement she saw in

NAWSA, and in 1913 she formed a separate organization called the Congressional Union for Woman Suffrage. This would become the National Woman's Party in 1916.

Alice Paul used the ideas she had learned in England, and in 1913 she led the first picket of the White House. Women from all over the country chained themselves to the White House fence to symbolize their servitude since they could not participate in the country's government by voting. During World War I, the NWP used the rhetoric of the war to champion its cause, protesting a government that promised to make the world safe for democracy while denying the vote to half of its citizens.

With the country in a patriotic mood, the pickets, which continued, were threatened by hostile crowds and many women were arrested. Imprisoned three times for her actions, Paul waged hunger strikes. She was placed in solitary confinement and at one point was hospitalized in a mental institution, force-fed, and treated as insane. Her spirit, however, remained unbroken.

One dark mark on the NWP's actions at the time was its treatment of African American women. Alice Paul herself seemed ambivalent, expressing sympathy for black woman suffrage but in practice doing things that contradicted that conviction. She often refused to allow African American women to speak at NWP functions, and in the 1913 parade, Ida B. Wells, a prominent black woman of the time, was asked not to march with the Chicago delegation. It seemed expedient not to make an issue of black women's rights in order to avoid alienating white southern women, but the result was that African American women and men both continued to suffer for decades under racist state and local policies that prevented them from exercising their right to vote.

Paul's and the NWP's activism on behalf of woman suffrage, however, led to the passage of the Nineteenth Amendment and its addition to the Constitution on August 26, 1920. Shortly before her death, Alice Paul said that helping women gain the right to vote was the most useful thing she ever did.

Now that women had the vote, the NWP could perhaps have rested on its laurels, but Paul could see that without full equality under the law, just the right to vote did little to ensure that women would be treated fairly. So in 1923, she authored an Equal Rights Amendment (ERA), which stated that women and men should have equal treatment under the laws of the United States. This amendment did not pass Congress until 1972, and then it failed to receive enough state ratifications to be enacted and made part of the Constitution in the time span allowed. However, the struggle for ratification of the ERA remains the NWP's primary focus today.

After the ERA first failed to pass in the 1920's, Paul, while continuing her entire life to fight for the amendment, also turned her attention in other directions. She earned additional degrees, worked for the League of Nations, and lobbied for world peace. Alice Paul died July 9, 1977, at the height of the second wave of the women's movement, having spent her life in the cause of women's rights. The most well known organization that she founded, the National Woman's Party, remains active in the house where Paul spent so many years, the Sewall-Belmont House.

The Sewall-Belmont House Today

Although it is still an active headquarters, the house is also open today to the public as a museum. Most of its two floors are accessible to visitors, including Paul's bedroom on the second floor and the California Room, which commemorates an event in its earlier history, the Louisiana Purchase.

The house is filled with antique furniture, including Elizabeth Cady Stanton's chair, which she sat in at the first women's rights convention in 1848 in Seneca Falls, New York, and Susan B. Anthony's desk. There are also sculptures and portraits of many women in the suffrage and women's rights movements, such as Lucretia Mott, Stanton, and Alice Paul herself. In addition, there is a life-size statue of fifteenth century French martyr Joan of Arc.

Visitors can view scrapbooks, photographs, articles, early twentieth century newspapers and editorial cartoons, and rare archives about the struggle for women's rights. In the hallway hangs the gold-and-purple banner used during the first protests of the National Woman's Party, which says: "We demand an Amendment to the United States Constitution Enfranchising Women."

Tours are offered, which include a film about the history of woman suffrage and a narrated walking tour of the house. The site also offers internship programs, where young persons may gain knowledge and experience while working on projects from research to library skills. An indoor terrace and the garden are available to be rented for catered special events.

The Sewall-Belmont site also includes the oldest feminist library in the country. The library was set up in the former carriage house in 1940 to house the Alva Belmont Book Collection, which had been in storage since 1933. Opened in 1941, it was rededicated in 1943 as the Florence Bayard Hilles Library, after the woman who headed the project of creating the library. A restoration project was planned to return the library to its original state after years of neglect and make it accessible to researchers. In addition, the Sewall-Belmont House is also a center for work on ratification of the ERA and for women's rights activities.

The Sewall-Belmont House is easily found, next to the Senate office buildings and across the street from the U.S. Supreme Court building. It is four blocks from the Union Station metro stop. The house is open Tuesday through Friday from 9:00 A.M. through 5:00 P.M. and Saturdays from noon to 4:00 P.M. Tours take place at 11:00 A.M., noon, and 1:00 P.M. The site is closed on Mondays, Thanksgiving, Christmas, New Year's Day, and Sundays from November through March.

—*Eleanor B. Amico*

For Further Information:

Becker, Susan D. *The Origins of the Equal Rights Amendment.* Westport, Conn.: Greenwood Press, 1981. This book provides a history of the NWP and the ERA.

Ford, Linda G. *Iron-Jawed Angels: The Suffrage Militancy of the National Woman's Party, 1912-1920.* Lanham, Md.: University Press of America, 1991. Describes the radical tactics of the NWP and the result for many of its members—imprisonment. Like most of the books about Alice Paul and the NWP, this one is a scholarly study.

Gillmore, Inez Haynes. *The Story of the Woman's Party.* New York: Harcourt Brace, 1921. This book, written shortly after the passage of the Nineteenth Amendment, tells the story of the NWP from the perspective of its own times.

National Park Foundation. *Sewall-Belmont House National Historic Site.* www.nationalparks.org/ guide/parks/sewall-belmo-1727.htm. This Web page tells about the history of the house and provides information about visiting the site.

Rupp, Leila J., and Verta Taylor. *Survival in the Doldrums: The American Women's Rights Movement, 1945 to the 1960's.* New York: Oxford University Press, 1987. This book tells the rest of the story—the activity of the NWP in more recent years. The authors credit the party with keeping the women's movement alive until the 1960's.

Stevens, Doris. *Jailed for Freedom.* New York: Boni and Liveright, 1920. The story of the fight for woman suffrage told by one of the women who was imprisoned for civil disobedience and who also served an important role in the NWP.

Smithsonian Institution

Date: Founded in 1846

Relevant issues: African American history, American Indian history, art and architecture, business and industry, cultural history, education, literary history, military history, naval history, political history, science and technology, sports, women's history

Significance: The Smithsonian Institution is an independent trust instrumentality of the United States that fosters the increase and diffusion of knowledge. It is the world's largest museum complex that includes sixteen museums and galleries, the National Zoo, and research facilities in other states and in the Republic of Panama. The Smithsonian holds more than 140 million artifacts and specimens in its trust for the American people and it is a respected research center, dedicated to public education, national service, and scholarship in the arts, science, and history.

Location: Nine museums on the National Mall, between the Washington Monument and the Capitol, and five other museums and the National Zoo elsewhere in Washington, D.C.; both the Cooper-Hewitt National Design Museum and the National Museum of the American Indian Heye Center are in New York City, and numerous research facilities are located around the United States and abroad

Site Offices:

Smithsonian Institution
1000 Jefferson Drive SW
Washington, DC 20024

Visitor Information and Associates' Reception Center
Smithsonian Institution Building, Room 153
Washington, DC 20560-0010
ph.: (202) 357-2700; TTY (202) 357-1729
Web site: www.si.edu
e-mail: info@info.si.edu

The Smithsonian Institution is a trust establishment of the United States supported by federal appropriations and private trust funds. Under its founding legislation, it is controlled by a body called "the establishment" composed of the president, the vice president, and the cabinet. Actual oversight belongs to the Board of Regents, a body composed of the vice president, the chief justice of the United States (designated its chancellor), three members each from the Senate and the House of Representatives, and nine citizen members (two residents of the District of Columbia and seven from the states), all chosen by joint resolution of Congress. A secretary, who directs the Smithsonian and carries out its policies, is elected by the regents and serves at their pleasure.

An Unexpected Bequest

On August 10, 1846, President James K. Polk signed legislation (Smithsonian Act of Organization) that established the Smithsonian Institution as the culmination of more than a decade of debate among the general public and the Congress over a peculiar bequest.

English chemist and mineralogist James Smithson died in 1829 and left a will stating that if his heir died without heirs, his estate should go to the United States to found in Washington, D.C., an establishment, to be called the Smithsonian Institu-

The Smithsonian Institution. (PhotoDisc)

tion, for the "increase and diffusion of knowledge." When Smithson's sole heir died in 1835, the United States was notified of this bequest and President Andrew Jackson went to the U.S. Congress for permission to accept it. A controversy ensued between those who saw the gift as an example of British condescension, too demeaning for a sovereign state to accept, and others who wanted the bequest but could not decide on its proper use. Finally, in 1836, diplomat and lawyer Richard Rush went to London to file a claim for the Smithson estate in the British Court of Chancery. Rush won a judgment for the United States when the court awarded Smithson's properties, valued at the equivalent of $508,318, to the United States on May 9, 1838.

Almost a decade passed, however, before the Smithsonian Institution was actually created. Initially, most Americans assumed that Smithson intended to found a university. The debate centered on what type of school it should be, but other ideas were introduced, such as an observatory, a scien-tific research institute, a national library, a publishing house, and a museum. The final legislation included everything but the university. The Smithsonian Institution was created as a federal quasi agency, not part of the three branches of government, managed by a self-perpetuating Board of Regents.

Development of the "Museum on the Mall"

The new agency was housed in the Smithsonian Building, a Norman "castle" designed by architect James Renwick and finished in 1855, located on the National Mall in Washington, D.C. The first chief operating officer, or secretary, was Joseph Henry, a distinguished physicist. As secretary from 1846 to 1878, Henry focused on scientific research and established a national network of weather observers that became the National Weather Service.

The first objects donated to the institution were scientific apparatus, the gift of Robert Hare of the University of Pennsylvania, in 1848. In the same year the Smithsonian published its first book, *Smithsonian Contributions to Knowledge*. The next year it purchased art books and works collected by regent George Perkins Marsh and initiated the International Exchange Service for trading publications between the United States and interests abroad. In 1858 the Smithsonian was designated the National Museum of the United States. During the Civil War years programs were curtailed, and a fire in the castle in 1865 destroyed the central portion of the building and many of the early collections. Henry was opposed to the use of the Smithson fund for a national library or museum, so he transferred the art collection to the Library of Congress and to the Corcoran Gallery of Art. In 1866 he transferred the Smithsonian library to the Library of Congress and had the legislation providing for copyright deposit at the Smithsonian repealed.

Baird Years

To counter concerns about the expenses required to maintain collections and exhibits, in 1858 Congress began an annual appropriation to the Smithsonian for the care of its collections and exhibits. With this annual funding, Henry's successor, Spencer Fullerton Baird, was able to create a great national museum during his tenure (1878-1887). His goal was a comprehensive collection of all the natural resources of the continent in the United States National Museum.

He initiated this by transferring the government's collection of artworks, historical memorabilia, and scientific specimens from the patent office building to the Smithsonian and continued by preparing all of the U.S. government's exhibits for the international expositions, beginning with the 1876 Centennial Exposition in Philadelphia, which was a unique opportunity for the growing Smithsonian to publicize its expanding collections, to gain much-needed national visibility, and to provide more new displays for the Smithsonian through donations from other exhibitors. To house this expansion, Congress authorized funds to build a new National Museum building (Arts and Industries Building), which opened in 1881, two years after the Bureau of American Ethnology was added to the Smithsonian's programs to document rapidly vanishing Native American cultures.

Turn of the Century and Two World Wars

Under the third secretary, Samuel Pierpont Langley (1889-1906), the Smithsonian Astrophysical Observatory was created (1890) to facilitate research on solar phenomena, the National Zoological Park was founded (1891), a "Children's Room" opened (1901), and funding was secured for a new National Museum building. Langley's successor, Charles Doolittle Walcott (1907-1927), paleontologist and director of the United States Geological Survey, opened a new museum (now the National Museum of Natural History) in 1910 to house natural history and art collections. During World War I, this building was closed to become headquarters for the Bureau of War Risk Insurance. In 1920, a national gallery of art (now the National Museum of American Art) was created; it was followed three years later by the Freer Gallery of Art, which maintained industrialist Charles Lang Freer's collection of Oriental art and the works of James McNeill Whistler.

The fifth secretary, Charles Greeley Abbot (1928-1944), led the Smithsonian through the Great Depression and World War II. With assistance from the Works Progress Administration, National Zoo director William Mann installed new zoo buildings and created murals and backgrounds for animal displays. During World War II, the museum collections were moved to a warehouse in Shenandoah National Park, near Luray, Virginia, for safekeeping while the Smithsonian headquartered the Ethnogeographic Board, which provided the military with ethnographic and geographic information about little-known areas of the world, especially in the Pacific.

In the immediate post-World War II period, Alexander Wetmore, the sixth secretary (1945-1952), directed a program of modernization of exhibits, and in 1946 placed the Canal Zone Biological Area (now the Smithsonian Tropical Research Institute), a research station in Panama founded in 1923 to facilitate research on the tropics, under Smithsonian control. To house its growing aeronautical collection, which included Charles Lindbergh's *Spirit of St. Louis*, the National Air Museum was created (1946), and the Smithsonian Institution Traveling Exhibition Service (SITES) was inaugurated in 1952 to produce exhibits that could be displayed in locations outside the institution.

Museum Growth Spurt

Wetmore's successor, Leonard Carmichael (1953-1964), secured the appropriation for a new museum building for the history collections, which were scattered throughout the Smithsonian complex; the building (the National Museum of American History) opened in 1964. New wings had to be added to the Natural History Building throughout the 1960's to house additional collections. The patent office building was transferred to the Smithsonian in 1958 to house the national art collections, and a major capital improvement program was begun at the National Zoo. The Smithsonian Astrophysical Observatory was transferred to Cambridge, Massachusetts, in 1955, in time to track artificial satellites after the 1957 launching of *Sputnik.*

The building growth continued under the eighth secretary, S. Dillon Ripley (1964-1984), who supervised a major expansion in Smithsonian programs. The new additions included the Smithsonian Environmental Research Center (1965), the Anacostia Museum (1967), the Cooper-Hewitt National Design Museum in New York (1968), the National Museum of American Art and the National Portrait Gallery in the old patent office building (1968), the Archives of American Art (1970), the Renwick Gallery (1972), the Hirshhorn Museum and Sculpture Garden (1974), and the National Museum of African Art (1978). In the summer of 1967 the Smithsonian began one of its most popular annual events, the Festival of American Folklife, held on the National Mall, and on July 4, 1976, in celebration of the nation's Bicentennial, opened the National Air and Space Museum, which remains the most visited of all the Smithsonian museums.

The ninth secretary, Robert McCormick Adams (1984-1993), helmed the institution during a period of renewed emphasis on research, which included establishment of the International Center in 1987 and the opening of three museums: the Sackler Gallery (1983); the National Museum of the American Indian (1989), located in both New York and Washington, D.C.; and the National Postal Museum (1990). Several new scientific research programs focused on the role of humans in the environment, including the Biodiversity Program (1986), established in conjunction with the United Nations Educational, Scientific, and Cultural Organization's Man and the Biosphere Program; the Mpala Research Station (1992) in Kenya; the National Science Resource Center (1985), established in cooperation with the National Academy of Sciences; and a new observatory in Hawaii (1991).

End of the Millennium and New Beginnings

In the closing years of the twentieth century, the tenth secretary, L. Michael Heyman (1993-1999), the first nonscientist to hold the position, arrived in the middle of the controversy surrounding the *Enola Gay* exhibit, which war veterans and members of Congress saw as a cheap shot at those who fought World War II. Heyman revamped the exhibit, then oversaw new exhibit guidelines to prevent future problems. Heyman confronted the electronic dissemination of information with the initiation of the institution's Web site, and directed the major celebration of the 150th anniversary of the institution in 1996. By that year the Smithsonian had over 140 million artifacts and specimens in sixteen museums. Its endowment was over $378 million, and there was a staff of over 6,700 employees and some 5,200 volunteers to carry out its programs in museums and research centers, both in Washington, D.C., and around the world. The institution's influence and growth were expected to continue when Lawrence M. Small became the eleventh secretary in 2000.   —*Martin J. Manning*

For Further Information:

Field, Cynthia R., Richard E. Stamm, and Heather P. Ewing. *The Castle: An Illustrated History of the Smithsonian Building.* Washington, D.C.: Smithsonian Institution Press, 1993. A good history for the general reader with beautiful illustrations.

Hellman, Geoffrey. *The Smithsonian: Octopus on the Mall.* Westport, Conn.: Greenwood Press, 1978. Now outdated but good historical background.

Hinsley, Curtis M. *Savages and Scientists: The Smithsonian Institution and the Development of American Anthropology, 1846-1910.* Washington, D.C.: Smithsonian Institution Press, 1981. Comprehensive history of the establishment and early years of the Smithsonian.

Oehser, Paul H. *The Smithsonian Institution.* Boulder, Colo.: Westview Press, 1983. Good overall history.

Reingold, Nathan, ed. *The Papers of Joseph Henry.* Vols. 1-5. Washington, D.C.: Smithsonian Institution Press, 1972-1985. The official story of the Smithsonian's earliest days by its first secretary.

Rivinus, Edward F., and Elizabeth M. Youssef. *Spencer Baird of the Smithsonian.* Washington, D.C.: Smithsonian Institution Press, 1992. Long overdue biography of one of the most important Smithsonian secretaries and his many accomplishments, as both museum director and scientist.

Rothenberg, Marc, ed. *The Papers of Joseph Henry.* Vols. 6-7. Washington, D.C.: 1992, 1996. The continuation of the Smithsonian's beginnings as it struggled to define its mission.

Washburn, Wilcomb E. "Joseph Henry's Conception of the Purpose of the Smithsonian Institution." In *A Cabinet of Curiosities: Five Episodes in the Evolution of American Museums.* Charlottesville: University Press of Virginia, 1967. Lengthy chapter on the founding of the Smithsonian and its first secretary.

Thomas Jefferson Memorial

Date: Dedicated by Franklin D. Roosevelt on April 13, 1943, the bicentennial of Jefferson's birth

Relevant issues: Art and architecture, colonial America, cultural history, education, political history, science and technology, social reform

Significance: A prominent Virginia planter and politician, Jefferson was a key revolutionary leader who wrote the Declaration of Independence and was the chief rival of Alexander Hamilton. He defended individualism, states' rights, agrarian republicanism, and strict limits on federal power, and was the first secretary of state, the second vice president, and the nation's third president (1800-1808). His tenure featured the Louisiana Purchase, the Lewis and Clark Expedition, the Tripoli War, and an embargo act to avoid war with Great Britain. He has been praised as a model "enlightened man" for his pioneering work in architecture, education, botany, ethnology, music, and social reform and for his role in the creation of the University of Vir-

ginia. The Thomas Jefferson Memorial is one of the most striking structures in the heart of the nation's capital.

Location: To the south of the White House in the Tidal Basin of Potomac Park, bracketed by an orchard of Japanese cherry trees; the nearest metro station is Arlington Cemetery

Site Office:
National Capital Parks-Central
National Park Service
900 Ohio Drive SW
Washington, DC 20024-2000
ph.: (202) 326-6821
Web sites: www.nps.gov/thje/

Pierre Charles L'Enfant's initial idea for a cluster of monuments at the center of the nation's capital was enhanced by the McMillan Commission, which proposed in 1902 that the White House be the pivot for structures dedicated to George Washington, Abraham Lincoln, and Thomas Jefferson. When Franklin D. Roosevelt was elected in 1932 and the Democrats regained the White House, the new president led the call for building a monument to Jefferson, whom he considered the founder of his political party. In 1934 Congress appointed a Thomas Jefferson Memorial Commission chaired by Representative John J. Boylan of New York. The commission selected the Tidal Basin as the site for the memorial since it would close the cluster of monuments formed by the Mall, the White House, and the Lincoln and Washington Memorials. In 1937 the commission accepted a plan drawn by John Russell Pope, based on the Roman Pantheon, for a circular structure with a Greek facade, a Roman dome, and a bronze sculpture of Jefferson at its core.

While Congress quickly approved a three million-dollar allocation to begin the project, the design provoked controversy. Pope's design was opposed by some who thought it was too elitist or too expensive, or because they wanted a different style of building or a location where fewer cherry trees would be destroyed. The determination of both Pope's widow and the president brought the initial plans to actuality. Roosevelt held the groundbreaking celebration on December 15, 1938, and the cornerstone was laid eleven months later, after the granite steps and terraces were constructed. It took over two years to build the sides and rotunda and

The Thomas Jefferson Memorial. (Washington, D.C., Convention & Visitors Association)

two more years to complete the building. Vermont Imperial Danby marble was used for the exterior, while the interior walls were constructed of Georgia white marble on a flooring of pink Tennessee marble. The domed canopy was composed of Indiana limestone, featuring the Pantheon's lacunar pattern. A. A. Weinman's sculptural representation of the members of the Declaration Committee was placed on the facade above the entrance, and the four interior walls surrounding the giant sculpture of Jefferson were etched with quotations from his writings.

After a long competition, in October of 1941 the commission chose the design of Rudolph Evans for the Jefferson sculpture. While a plaster model was used during the dedication in 1943 due to a wartime shortage of metal, the five-ton, nineteen-foot statue (built by the Roman Bronze Company of New York) was installed on April 25, 1947, on a six-foot base of Minnesota granite. The exterior of the monument was restored in 2000.

The Life of the Third President

Born on April 13, 1743, in Shadwell, Virginia, Thomas Jefferson inherited five thousand acres and a workforce of slaves in 1757 before attending the College of William and Mary, where Dr. William Small introduced him to the ideas of the Enlightenment. At the age of twenty, he was admitted to the bar, and two years later he was elected to a seat in the House of Burgesses once held by his father. Using the writings of Renaissance architect Palladio, he redesigned his mansion at Monticello and later the Virginia capitol, an octagonal house called Poplar Forest in Lynchburg, and the University of Virginia.

As conflict between Britain and its colonies developed, Jefferson attacked parliamentary authority in a long pamphlet entitled *A Summary View of the Rights of British America* (1774) and later attended the Second Continental Congress. He wrote the Declaration of Independence that proclaimed human rights, political equality, popular sovereignty, and the right of revolution as universal principles. In 1779 he was elected Virginia's second governor, and soon afterward British forces attacked Monticello. In 1785, he was appointed to a commission that aggressively promoted American exports and published his only book, *Notes on the State of Virginia.* He also became ambassador to France. Jefferson obtained the passage of both the Virginia Statute for Religious Freedom and the Ordinance of 1784, which proposed that new states be given parity with the original states—a key feature of the Northwest Ordinance of 1787.

Jefferson opposed President John Adams's policies, and in the presidential election of 1800 he defeated Aaron Burr by eight electoral votes. His inauguration brought the first peaceful transfer of power from one political party to another through the ballot; it is often called the Revolution of 1800. During his tenure his followers—called "Republicans" and considered the founders of the present Democratic Party—replaced Federalist officeholders, an early example of the spoils system. Advocating democracy, he cut internal taxes, permitted the Alien and Sedition Acts to lapse, and tried to end the national debt. In 1803 he approved the Louisiana Purchase without a constitutional amendment. His reelection was supported by all states except Connecticut and Delaware.

His second term brought a successful conclusion to the Tripoli War (1801-1805) and the Lewis and Clark Expedition through the Louisiana Territory but was troubled by the mysterious Burr conspiracy, British and French violations of American sovereignty, and an Embargo Act that hurt foreign trade but promoted American industrial development. During Jefferson's second administration, the Twelfth Amendment to the U.S. Constitution was adopted, Robert Fulton invented the steamboat, and the importation of slaves to the United States was forbidden.

Jefferson's appraisal of his life is reflected in his own words, now written on his tombstone: "Here was buried Thomas Jefferson, author of the Declaration of Independence, of the Statute of Virginia for religious freedom, and Father of the University of Virginia."

—*Sheldon Hanft*

For Further Information:

Malone, Dumas. *Jefferson and His Times.* 6 vols. Boston: Little, Brown, 1948-1981. An exhaustive biography of the man and his many claims to greatness.

Peterson, Merrill D. *Jefferson Memorial: An Interpretive Guide to the Jefferson Memorial.* Washington, D.C.: National Park Service, 1998. A good illustrated introduction to both the man and the monument, by one of his major biographers.

Stein, Susan R. *The Worlds of Thomas Jefferson.* New York: Harry N. Abrams, 1993. A recent reassessment of Jefferson's place in history supported by the Thomas Jefferson Memorial Foundation.

Vietnam Veterans Memorial

Date: Dedicated on November 11, 1982

Relevant issues: Art and architecture, Asian American history, cultural history, military history, political history, Vietnam War

Significance: The Vietnam Veterans Memorial, commonly referred to as "The Wall," symbolizes America's attempt to come to terms with the Vietnam War.

Location: Constitution Gardens on the Mall, near the Lincoln Memorial

Site Office:
National Capital Parks-Central
The National Mall
900 Ohio Drive SW
Washington, DC 20242
ph.: (202) 426-6841
Web site: www.vvmf.org/wall/wall.htm

The Vietnam conflict was a battle in the larger Cold War, waged between 1945 and 1991, pitting the United States against the Soviet Union. It was fought to decide whether a pro-American or pro-Soviet government would ultimately govern that Southeast Asian nation, and after it began it almost immediately involved the United States as the nation attempted to contain the spread of communism. The U.S. commitment began with only advisers in the 1950's, but by 1964 President Lyndon B. Johnson committed American combat troops to Vietnam to support the government of South Vietnam in its struggle against Hanoi-led communist forces, which were drawn from both South and North Vietnam and backed by the Soviet bloc.

In less than four years, more than a half million American soldiers had been committed to the conflict that seemed less and less likely to be resolved by the presence of those servicemen. The war produced a deep cleavage among the people that eventually led to America's withdrawal in 1973 and a communist victory in 1975. It also led to the "Vietnam Syndrome," which associated the conflict there with, among other things, military defeat and tarnished veterans, who were often perceived as mentally unstable and drug-addicted. The Vietnam Veterans Memorial, called "The Wall," represents America's attempt to come to terms with the Vietnam War by at once honoring the war dead and repairing the rift among the disparate warring factions that did battle at home during the war.

The Inspiration and Struggle for a Memorial

The idea for a Vietnam Veterans Memorial likely originated independently in the minds of numerous American soldiers and civilians. However, Jan C. Scruggs, a combat veteran from Maryland, is probably the one who provided the inspiration and determination to make the idea a reality. After viewing the motion picture *The Deer Hunter* in March of 1979, he reflected on the meaning of the war. The principal characters in that early Hollywood dramatization of the Vietnam War came from a working-class background, and it occurred to Scruggs that the majority of America's casualties in fact were, like himself, ordinary young men who believed in their country and were asked to perform extraordinary tasks. Those who died doing their duty, as well as those who returned home, deserved to be recognized for their service instead of stigmatized for their participation in a war that had become unpopular and ended short of victory. Were these servicemen responsible for the war's unpopularity and lack of success?

Scruggs attended a meeting of Vietnam veterans who talked about organizing a victory parade and building a memorial. There he met Bob Doubek, a Vietnam veteran and lawyer who advised Scruggs to form a nonprofit organization to raise funds for the memorial. On May 28, 1979, Scruggs held a press conference designed to generate publicity and funds for the memorial project. When Washington, D.C., attorney and Vietnam veteran Jack Wheeler took interest in this fledgling project, the nucleus of the memorial organization emerged. The next stage of memorial realization was to convince Washington politicians and bureaucrats of the wisdom and feasibility of such a proposal.

This undertaking began when Scruggs contacted U.S. senator Charles Mathias from Maryland, a liberal who had opposed the Vietnam War but was sympathetic to a memorial. Meanwhile, Wheeler used his contacts in the Washington establishment to connect with the Veterans Administration, the National Park Service, and the Fine Arts Commission, all of which would need to approve the project. The Fine Arts Commission proposed a site across the Potomac River near Arlington National Cemetery, but the now-incorporated (as of April, 1979) Vietnam Veterans Memorial Fund demurred, insisting on a location central to Washington memorials, specifically Constitution Gardens adjacent to the Lincoln Memorial. The National Capital Memorial Advisory Committee, composed of a representative of each government agency involved in memorial projects, opposed any site-specific location. However, on Veterans Day, 1979, conservative Senator Barry Goldwater and liberal Senator George McGovern introduced legislation to give the Memorial Fund two acres next to the Lincoln Memorial, and similar legislation was introduced in the House of Representatives by John Hammerschmidt. After months of heated debate in Congress, both the House of Representatives and the Senate approved the Constitution Gardens site on June 24, 1980, and President Jimmy Carter signed the bill a week later.

Even as the politicians discussed the issues surrounding the Vietnam Veterans Memorial, the Memorial Fund launched a struggling but ultimately successful fund-raising campaign. Senator John Warner and his then-wife, Elizabeth Taylor, hosted a breakfast to raise contributions. A National Sponsoring Committee added luster to the memorial project with such patrons as Jimmy and Rosalynn Carter; entertainer Bob Hope; Nancy Reagan, wife of then-presidential candidate Ronald Reagan; and former prisoner of war Admiral James Stockdale. Billionaire H. Ross Perot made a substantial donation, veterans' organizations such as Veterans of Foreign Wars and the American Legion donated large sums, and tens of thousands of citizens sent in contributions. Thus, when the competition for the memorial's design began, the fund leadership had gained an elementary knowledge of how to maneuver around the political obstacles in government and how to raise cash to see the project through to completion.

What Kind of Memorial?

Perhaps it is fitting that, just as an ordinary citizen got the idea of a Vietnam Veterans Memorial off

The Vietnam Veterans Memorial lists the names of all American military personnel who died in the Vietnam War. (Digital Stock)

"make no political statement regarding the war or its conduct."

With these instructions, the jury proceeded to evaluate 1,421 entries, which eventually were narrowed to three, of which number 1,026 won unanimous approval. The winning design, announced on May 6, 1980, at a press conference at the American Institute of Architects in Washington, D.C., was submitted by Yale architecture student Maya Ying Lin, who was born in 1959, the year the first American soldier died in combat in Vietnam. However, the winning design still had to be approved by the Fine Arts Commission and, realistically, by veterans, politicians, and the public as well.

The Wall is actually two walls, each 246 feet long, that meet at an angle of 125 degrees, where the structure is ten feet high. The black granite used for the memorial came from Bangalore, India, and was cut in Barre, Vermont; the names and inscriptions were etched in Memphis, Tennessee. By Memorial Day, 1997, 58,208 names graced the memorial, listed in chronological order of death, beginning in 1959 and ending in 1975. When the design was made public it generated praise, condemnation, and a middle path of calls for alterations to a fundamentally solid project. Most major newspapers endorsed the design, as did most members of Congress, but Perot argued that the design honored only the dead; veteran Tom Carhard called it "a black gash of shame"; other veterans criticized it for various reasons; novelist Tom Wolfe labeled it "a tribute to Jane Fonda"; and influential journals such as *National Review* opposed it. Additionally, something of a generation gap existed between Lin and the older veterans that complicated discussions about the design.

Ultimately, and against the wishes of Lin, a sculpture of three combat infantrymen by Frederick Hart and an American flag were added to the

the ground, an unknown (but far from ordinary) twenty-one-year-old architecture student put the memorial into the ground. The process that produced the winning design first involved deciding how the memorial would be created: by fund members themselves, by architectural firms that would submit designs to the fund members, or by a competition judged by reputable architects and sculptors. The last approach won the day, the reasoning being that the fund members knew little about architecture, and that not much diversity of design would be achieved with only a few architectural firms submitting ideas. The jury was instructed by the fund that the memorial had to "recognize and honor those who served and died" in Vietnam and

memorial, a design approved by the National Capital Planning Commission and the National Park Service in March, 1982. Construction of the Wall commenced and was finished in time for the dedication on Veterans Day, 1982. Thousands of veterans, family members of the fallen soldiers, and other visitors gathered to listen to the dedication and hear the names of all killed in action read aloud. As the father of a fallen soldier put it, "It is important to have other people hear his name."

What Does the Memorial Symbolize?

The comments of columnist James J. Kirkpatrick probably best capture the significance of the Vietnam Veterans Memorial. After he viewed the design, but before it was built, he predicted that it would be "the most moving war memorial ever erected" and maintained that it would also signify whatever each visitor wanted it to express. The first forecast seems to have hit the mark. Each year more than two-and-a-half million sightseers view the Wall, making it the most-visited memorial in Washington, D.C. Testimony to its emotional impact on visitors can be seen in the assorted tributes they bring: a Hank Williams, Jr., tape, two shot glasses, photographs, a teddy bear, a mess kit with knife, a fishing rod, a rock "left by Jewish couple," an ace of diamonds, combat medals, walnuts, an ace of spades, and flags. According to a leading scholar of the Wall, the gifts serve as a reminder to the nation that it owes a debt to these forsaken soldiers and that the debt needs to be paid. One need only view the documentaries and photographs of the memorial, which contain vivid scenes of weeping veterans and nonparticipants in the war as well as the tributes left at the Wall, to realize that Maya Lin helped America begin to come to terms with the Vietnam War, if not its meaning. Lin, reflecting on her losing struggle to prevent the statue and flag from being included in the memorial, stated that "What is memorialized is also that people still cannot resolve the war, nor can they separate the issue, the politics from it." Indeed, her design elicited many different interpretations even as it was being constructed. Lin intended the "V" shape to symbolize an open book, whereas others interpreted the form to be a peace—that is, antiwar—sign. Lin utilized black granite to symbolize "the black earth, the earth polished," but many perceived the use of a black substance to signify evil or

shame. Whatever architect Lin wanted to convey in her creation, it is hard to argue that the Wall has become a sacred public space for most Americans.

—*Thomas D. Reins*

For Further Information:

Hass, Kristin Ann. *Carried to the Wall: American Memory and the Vietnam Veterans Memorial.* Berkeley: University of California Press, 1998. Studies the "offerings" or "gifts" which Americans brought to The Wall as a means of understanding America's continuing struggle to give meaning to the Vietnam War.

Katakis, Michael. *The Vietnam Veterans Memorial.* New York: Crown, 1988. Photographic impressions and commentary.

Maya Lin: A Strong Clear Vision. Directed by Freida Le Mock. Santa Monica, Calif.: Sanders & Mock Productions/Ocean Releasing, 1994. An excellent documentary exploring the role of architect Maya Lin in designing the Vietnam Veterans Memorial.

Palmer, Laura. *Shrapnel in the Heart: Letters and Remembrances from the Vietnam Memorial.* New York: Random House, 1987. Contains letters, poems, and other remembrances from the relatives and friends of those Americans who died in the Vietnam War.

Scruggs, Jan C., and Joel L. Swerdlow. *To Heal a Nation: The Vietnam Veterans Memorial.* New York: Harper & Row, 1985. Focuses on the political skirmishes involved in the creation of the Vietnam Veterans Memorial.

Smithsonian Institution. *Reflections on the Wall: The Vietnam Veterans Memorial.* Harrisburg, Pa.: Stackpole Books, 1987. An illustrated account of the Wall by four photographers who capture in faces and offerings the feelings of the visitors.

Strait, Jerry L., and Sandra S. Strait. *Vietnam War Memorials: An Illustrated Reference to Veterans Tributes Throughout the United States.* Jefferson, N.C.: McFarland, 1988. Discusses Vietnam War memorials throughout the United States, including the principal one in Washington, D.C.

Vietnam Memorial. Directed by Foster Wiley and Steve York. 1983. Alexandra, Va.: PBS Video, 1988. A PBS *Frontline* broadcast covering the events leading up to, and the dedication of, the Vietnam Veterans Memorial at Constitution Gardens.

Washington Monument

Date: Cornerstone laid in 1848
Relevant issues: Art and architecture, colonial America, political history, Revolutionary War
Significance: This 555-foot shaft honoring George Washington is the dominant landmark in the nation's capital and is considered the tallest freestanding masonry structure in the world. Each year, more than 1.2 million people visit this beloved national icon.
Location: The Mall, Potomac Park
Site Office:
Washington National Monument Association
5026 New Executive Office Building
726 Jackson Place NW
Washington, DC 20006
ph.: (202) 426-6841
Web site: www.nps.gov/wamo/

Just as the ancient Egyptians built obelisks to honor their pharaohs, the Washington Monument is designed as a classical Egyptian obelisk to honor the memory of the first president of the United States. Following the proportions of the classical obelisks, the monument is ten times as tall as it is wide at the base. It contains thirty-six thousand stones that together weigh 81,120 tons, and the foundation weighs another 36,910 tons. At the top of the structure, a pyramid occupies one-tenth of the height of the column. An observation room is located at the base of the pyramid, which is five hundred feet above ground level. An elevator and a flight of 898 steps lead visitors to the observation room. Standing straight and clean against the skyline, the white marble shaft rises above all other structures of the city, to be seen far away from any direction.

Early Projects to Honor Washington
Even when George Washington was alive, his contemporaries referred to him as the "father of the country." Soldier and politican Henry Lee (1756-1818), known as Light-Horse Harry Lee, described Washington as "First in war, first in peace, and first in the hearts of his countrymen." During the difficult days of the war for independence, Washington was a man of leadership abilities who inspired confidence. When the Constitution was written at the Great Convention in 1787, no other person was re-ally considered to preside over the occasion. The American presidency was created with Washington in mind, and twice he was elected to that office without opposition.

In 1783, just as the United States became an independent country, the Continental Congress resolved unanimously that "an equestrian statue of General Washington be erected at the place where the residence of the Congress shall be established." Later, when Congress voted to build the new capital on the Potomac River, city planner Pierre Charles L'Enfant decided that the statue should be situated on the National Mall at an intersection of lines south and west of the president's home and the Capitol. With more essential expenses taking priority, however, Congress failed to provide funding for the statue.

Washington's death in 1799 produced a multitude of sermons, speeches, and newspaper editorials expressing respect and affection for the man and his accomplishments. In response, Congress passed a bill authorizing a marble mausoleum as a memorial inside the Capitol, but Washington's descendants refused to allow his remains to be removed from Mount Vernon. In 1832, Congress authorized funds for a marble statue of Washington to be placed in the Capitol's Rotunda. When Horatio Greenough's bare-chested statue was completed, it was too controversial to be placed inside the Capitol, and it eventually found its place in the Smithsonian Institution.

Beginning of the Ambitious Project
In 1833 several prominent civic leaders of Washington, D.C., wanted more than a statue to honor the first president, and they organized the Washington National Monument Society with the goal of erecting a large and impressive memorial. George Witterston, former librarian of Congress, was the dominant force behind the organization, and Chief Justice John Marshall, at the age of seventy-eight, was elected its first president. In order to pay the estimated cost of a million dollars, the society launched a fund drive, appealing to Americans to contribute a limit of one dollar per person.

In 1836, having raised almost thirty thousand dollars, the society announced a public competition for the best design. Robert Mills, a former draftsman for Thomas Jefferson and an eminent architect of the time, was the winner. Mills believed that the architectural forms of the classical tradition were the most appropriate for a republican government. He had previously designed an acclaimed monument to Washington for the city of Baltimore, and he would soon be working on a number of famous public buildings in the nation's capital.

Mills's entry proposed a six-hundred-foot obelisk that was to be surrounded at the base by a circular Greek temple with large columns. The temple was to contain thirty statues of revolutionary heroes. At the top of the principal entrance there was to be a colossal statue of Washington driving a battle chariot drawn by six horses. The society was soon forced to discard the idea of an ornate temple because of a lack of funds. Mills estimated that the entire project, including the temple, would cost $1,250,000, but it turned out that the cost of constructing the obelisk alone was $1,187,710.

Construction of the Monument

The construction did not actually begin until 1848, after the federal government agreed to donate public land near the site originally chosen for Washington's equestrian statue. The cornerstone was laid on July 4 of that year, with a ceremony attended by more than fifteen thousand people. President James Polk was in attendance, as were three future presidents: James Buchanan, Abraham Lincoln, and Andrew Johnson.

Construction of the first 152 feet of the monument proceeded smoothly. The face of the shaft was covered with white marble from Maryland. The wall of the stairway was made of granite, 15 feet thick at the base and decreasing in thickness with ascending height. The society invited states, patriotic groups, and foreign countries to contribute stone blocks to decorate the interior walls. This resulted in 190 memorials, many quite ornate, which were placed at ten-foot intervals. Pope Pius IX contributed a marble slab from a Roman temple, but it was stolen and never recovered.

By 1854 the society was running out of funds. The Know-Nothing Party gained control of the project from 1855 to 1858, adding a few feet of inferior stonework that was later removed. As the Civil War approached, work on the monument stopped, and thereafter the Monument Society found it almost impossible to raise the money to resume construction. In 1867 Mark Twain wrote that the structure had "the aspect of a factory chimney with the top broken off." With the centennial of independence in 1876, Congress authorized public funding to complete and maintain the monument, and the title of ownership was transferred to the United States. The Army Corps of Engineers discovered that the foundation had to be strengthened with a deep concrete slab because of the spongy soil, and the projected height of the structure was reduced about five feet after Italian researchers published new information about the true dimensions of classical obelisks.

The Washington Monument. (Digital Stock)

Renewed construction began seriously after President Rutherford B. Hayes laid a second cornerstone in 1880. Thereafter the shaft grew an average of eighty feet annually. At first the builders used marble from Massachusetts, resulting in a slight color change, but the builders soon returned to using stone from Maryland, near the original quarry. Supervised by Colonel Thomas Casey of the Army Corps of Engineers, the work finally ended when a solid aluminum tip was placed on the capstone on December 6, 1884. The nine-inch aluminum tip, weighing one hundred ounces, was the largest such piece ever cast up to that time. The entire project had been completed without a single loss of life. The formal dedication of the monument took place on February 21, 1885.

Additions to the Monument

The Washington Monument has never been entirely finished. It was not until 1888 that the public was able to climb the stairs or take a twelve-minute ride on the steam lift in order to look through the eight windows in the observation room. In 1901 an electric elevator replaced the steam hoist, and the time of the ride was decreased to five minutes. The elevator was significantly improved in 1926 and again in 1959, cutting the ascent time to seventy seconds.

In 1901, a Senate committee recommended a landscaping project to make the National Mall more scenic. The plan envisioned that the area of the Mall should be divided into a series of terraced gardens, with trees, fountains, and a large, circular pool. Test borings in the ground, however, indicated that such alterations would undermine the foundation, perhaps producing a "Leaning Tower of Washington." The project was eventually abandoned.

The stairs for walking up the monument were closed to the general public in 1971, and the stairs for walking down were closed in 1976. They were closed in part because of the growing congestion at the top, and also because of problems of graffiti and exhausted visitors needing to be rescued. Bars were installed in the windows in 1926 after three men leaped out to commit suicide. Before safety glass was installed in 1961, many thoughtless visitors and pranksters enjoyed throwing things out the windows, which was sometimes dangerous to the people below.

It was not until 1994 that a statue of George Washington was installed in the monument. It is a bronze replica of Jean-Antoine Houdon's marble original, which is located in the state capitol of Virginia. Houdon had visited Mount Vernon in the 1780's in order to study the general and to get a plaster cast of his face.

Maintenance and Repair

Like all masonry structures, the Washington Monument must be periodically repaired because of the ravages of age and exposure to wind, rain, and frost. In 1934 and 1964, the marble shell of the structure was partially mended, and it was scrubbed from the base to the tip. For many years the large structure had produced water condensation, which precipitated indoor rain. This problem was mostly eliminated in 1959 when a giant humidifier was installed in the basement.

By the late 1990's, experts were concerned about a number of problems. The mortar joining the white marble and granite stones was loose, joints were leaking, large cracks could be seen near the top, and the exterior needed another cleaning. In February, 1999, the most extensive repair in the history of the obelisk began. The repair costs were estimated at $9.4 million, mostly supplied by Target Corporation and other business groups.

Damaged areas of stone were repaired using the "Dutchman" masonry method, whereby large sections are cut out and replaced by good pieces. In order to obtain a good match, stones were acquired from the original quarries in Maryland. The entire exterior was cleaned with steam at low pressure, without sand or detergents. Experts were especially concerned about the cracks at the top. It was uncertain how long the cracks had existed. If they were caused by heating and cooling, only sealing would be necessary. If tests revealed that the stone was pulling apart, however, it would be necessary to reinforce the structure with metal pins.

Architect Michael Graves was employed to design a functional scaffold that would respect the artistic integrity of the monument. Graves decided to taper the scaffold to conform to the shape of the obelisk. A blue screen netting around the monument was designed to imitate the stone block pattern of the exterior. In order to prevent damage, the scaffolding itself was not attached to the structure.

—*Thomas T. Lewis*

For Further Information:

Bryan, John, ed. *Robert Mills: Architect*. Washington, D.C.: American Institute of Art Press, 1989. A handsome volume with 115 illustrations, as well as a scholarly text.

Freidel, Frank, and Lonnelle Aikman. *George Washington: Man and Monument*. Washington, D.C.: Washington National Monument Association, 1973. The second half of the book provides an excellent summary of the monument's history. Highly recommended for the general reader.

Harvey, Frederick. *History of the Washington National Monument and Washington National Monument Society*. Washington, D.C.: Government Printing Office, 1903. A detailed historical account by the secretary of the society.

Liscombe, Rhodi W. *Altogether American: Robert Mills, Architectect and Engineer, 1781-1855*. New York: Oxford University Press, 1994. An interesting and scholarly treatment by an authority in architectural history.

Longstreth, Richard, ed. *The Mall in Washington, 1791-1991*. Washington, D.C.: National Gallery of Art, 1991. Provides perspective about the architectural development and historical preservation of the mall.

Washington National Monument Society. *A Brief History of the Washington National Monument Society*. Washington, D.C.: Author, 1953. A short summary from the society's point of view.

The White House

Date: Construction began in the fall of 1792; house transferred to the National Park Service on August 10, 1933

Relevant issues: Political history

Significance: This National Historic Landmark, the official residence of the president of the United States, has three stories and 132 rooms and is situated on eighteen acres. It was designed by architect James Hoban and constructed between 1792 and 1800. Though popularly known as the "White House" throughout the nineteenth century, its official title from 1818 to 1901 was the Executive Mansion; the name was changed by executive order in 1901 to the White House.

Location: 1600 Pennsylvania Avenue NW in the District of Columbia, opposite historic Lafayette Square, in the heart of downtown Washington, D.C.

Site Offices:

White House Historical Association
740 Jackson Place NW
Washington, DC 20503
ph.: (202) 737-8292

White House
c/o National Capital Region
National Park Service
1100 Ohio Drive SW
Washington, DC 20242
ph.: (202) 619-7222
Web site: www.nps.gov/whho/

The White House and the U.S. Capitol are the oldest public structures in Washington, D.C. Around this nucleus the city spanned out over time, and the U.S. presidency evolved into the most important and the highest office in the land—which few would have guessed at the outset. The story of the White House is far more than the story of a building, but of an institution and of a nation. The million and a half visitors to the White House each year enter a living museum of the presidency, carefully restored to its appearance in the early decades of the United States.

A Federal City

The history of this important national symbol began well before the first stone was ceremoniously laid by George Washington on October 13, 1792. The idea of having a new "federal city," carefully designed to reflect the separation of powers embodied in the new Constitution, was proposed and subsequently approved by an act of Congress in 1790. Three commissioners, Thomas Johnson, Daniel Carroll, and David Stuart, were appointed to oversee the transition to the permanent new capital from its temporary location, Philadelphia. Washington, already a revered hero, was president, and he was given wide latitude over the construction of the first federal buildings. In fact, while he never had a chance to live in the White House, he was intimately involved in all details of its design and construction, and even personally selected a site for the building, where it currently stands, on Pennsylvania Avenue.

The three commissioners set off for the new federal district in 1791. According to the act of Congress establishing the federal capital, they would have until 1800 to prepare the new capital to become the seat of government. Even in those days of poor transportation, ten years seemed more than enough time.

When the three commissioners arrived in the federal district, they found an unhealthy, unpopulated swampland. Only the chief architect of Washington, Captain Pierre Charles L'Enfant, saw the potential for a beautiful, graceful capital. Building this "Paris on the Potomac" would take careful planning, money, and plenty of workers. The three commissioners had the first, but little of the second and none of the last. Throughout the building of the capital, labor would be a problem. To resolve it, the commissioners sent letters to Europe, imploring skilled workers to come to the United States. Few of them did, particularly since it was a time of war in Europe and crossing the seas was especially treacherous. Another reason for their hesitancy was the existence of slavery in and around the federal city which skilled workers, in the U.S. as well as overseas, reasoned would keep wages low. Finally,

slaves from nearby plantations were procured. Some of them had to be trained on the spot.

Designing a House for Presidents

All three commissioners had a great deal of planning experience. To begin with, they decided upon a name for the new capital—after the hero of the Revolutionary War—with no objections from George Washington. Thomas Jefferson next suggested an architectural competition—the winner of which would receive five hundred dollars—to attract the best architect for the future home of the presidents. By then it was mid-March, 1792. The competition was widely advertised, and historians of the White House are almost certain that Jefferson himself entered the competition with an anonymously submitted proposal. If that was the case, he was undoubtedly chagrined when it was rejected in favor of James Hoban's plan.

Hoban was living in Charleston, South Carolina, when he saw an announcement of the competition in a city newspaper. While little is known of the future architect of the White House, much exhaustive scholarly research has revealed important fragments of this man's life and career. He was born in Ireland in 1758. As a native Irishman of the lower classes, he was legally barred from learning to read and write, but he learned anyway. When he entered the Dublin Royal Society's drawing school to become an architect, Hoban resented being excluded from architectural competitions in his own city, which were reserved for the British. When Hoban arrived in Philadelphia in 1785, he found that no commissions or competitions were barred to him, and he soon received important assignments, such as designing South Carolina's new state capitol at Charleston. Then, in the summer of 1792, he learned that he had come out the winner in the competition in Washington.

Present-day scholars of the White House agree that Hoban's plan for the Executive Mansion was not particularly

A view of the White House from the South Lawn. (Washington, D.C., Convention & Visitors Association)

original, but it was popular, conforming to the public's taste in those days for elegant neoclassical designs and clean, even austere lines. Especially important was the fact that George Washington liked it, and he had the ultimate say in selecting the winner. Washington was partial to spacious houses, but he asked the young architect to scale down his plan to a simpler version (two floors instead of three, for instance, and no added wings), reasoning that future generations could augment and embellish the mansion as they saw fit. Hence Hoban's final plan included a large but simple structure, containing those rooms that are accessible to the public today: the ground floor (basement) and first-floor rooms, including the celebrated East Room (the largest room in the White House), and the state dining room.

At last, after two years of agonizing over labor and money, George Washington laid the cornerstone of the future White House in the fall of 1792. Building the White House, however, took another eight years. The walls were made of sandstone, laboriously dragged to the site by slaves from a quarry near Aquia Creek, in Virginia. With much effort on Jefferson's part, Scottish skilled workers—never enough of them—became the stonemasons, responsible for the intricate carvings gracing windows and doorways. In those years the White House was a beehive of activity, all work being done by hand, with kilns and heaps of garbage still littering the grounds when the first occupants, John and Abigail Adams, moved into the drafty, unfinished house in 1800. It is unclear whether the term "White House" was in use by then. Officially, it was called "The President's House." When it was rebuilt after the British destroyed it in 1814, its official name became "The Executive Mansion." By then, however, the nickname "White House" was firmly entrenched in the public's vocabulary. No color of paint other than white ever appeared on the president's house.

Public Opinion and Presidential Styles
It is significant that the history of the White House's occupation began in 1800, the first year of the new century. Both Adams and Jefferson were impressed by the sheer size of the building (minus the East and West Wings that would be added decades later); for the vast majority of U.S. residents, it was the biggest house they had ever seen. It was

another hundred years, however, before the first perceptible signs of a kind of reverence for the White House began to emerge, as evidenced in the first major renovation of 1902.

It might surprise contemporary observers that in the nineteenth century, no president felt he must live there, although all of them did (Theodore Roosevelt ignored suggestions that he and his family live elsewhere). In fact, when the British destroyed the nation's capital in 1814, Congress narrowly voted to keep the District of Columbia as the capital only after local bankers and businessmen guaranteed a loan to help rebuild the infant city. Also surprising to modern sensibilities is the fact that a president with too many enemies in Congress could expect to receive little or no appropriations for the White House—yet Andrew Johnson, with nothing but enemies, paradoxically received a generous allotment for his home.

Last, there was no special role for the president's wife. Abigail Adams, wife of the first president to inhabit the White House, would have been astonished to hear herself called "First Lady." In the case of bachelor President James Buchanan, his youthful niece Harriet Lane served as White House hostess. The public's acceptance of the title "First Lady" by the end of the nineteenth century indicated that the White House had become a place where a woman also could leave her mark. The nineteenth century therefore defined the institution of the presidency and the character of the White House, and brought to the fore a special identity, if not yet a real role, for the president's spouse or hostess.

The first inhabitants of the White House, John and Abigail Adams, tended to be very formal in the four months that remained of Adams's presidency. The house was not open to the public, and Adams bowed stiffly to guests invited to formal dinner parties. Thomas Jefferson, the first president to spend both terms in the White House, antagonized many society matrons by often appearing at the White House door in his slippers, ignoring social rank at dinner parties, and shaking everyone's hand. In 1801 the White House's doors were thrown open to the public. While this was a democratic gesture, it became a nuisance for the president and his family, who inhabited the second floor, a favorite lounging area for lobbyists and job seekers. This remained the case until the Civil Service Act of 1883 turned many job appointments into civil service jobs, and definitely ended when the president finally established separate offices for himself and his staff in a new wing of the White House in 1902.

Until the Civil War the White House was considered merely a home for the president who, if he happened to wring sufficient funds out of Congress, could do what he wanted with it. The Adamses had brought their own furniture with them, at no expense to taxpayers. With a new president, Jefferson, to follow, improvements were made: The White House was fenced in for the first time, rubbish and decrepit laborers' huts were removed, and, in 1803, Jefferson designated an Englishman, Benjamin Henry Latrobe, to be the official architect of the White House, or Surveyor of Public Buildings. He installed a new roof, which had been badly leaking, and designed porticos for the north and south ends of the building, which remained incomplete, although he managed to add on a terrace and pavilions before the next president and his wife, James and Dolley Madison, moved in in 1809.

Destruction

The most notable happening in the tenure of James Madison was the War of 1812, which resulted in the torching of the entire capital by British troops under Rear Admiral Sir George Cockburn in August, 1814, during the hottest month in Washington. With the city open to invaders, thanks to the architectural plans of L'Enfant, and the president with his troops in Maryland, Dolley Madison could have fled immediately. Instead, she made a name for herself by rescuing a large portrait of George Washington by Gilbert Stuart and by ensuring that valuable Cabinet papers were carted off to safety before she left the White House.

After the fire, a disheartened Congress had decided to abandon the District of Columbia when area businessmen, fearful of losing their only good customer, lobbied successfully to retain Washington as the capital. The Madisons spent more than a year living in quarters close to the White House until it could be rebuilt. It had been gutted entirely by the fire on August 24, with only the blackened exterior walls left standing.

James Hoban was called upon to rebuild the structure he had designed. This time he had a freer hand, and went to work not only restoring the White House to its original appearance but also

eventually (in 1824 and 1829 respectively) overseeing the construction of the now-familiar north and south porticos. The White House was ready for occupancy again by September, 1817, and President James Monroe threw open the doors to the public in January, 1818.

Politics and Decor

President Monroe had used Congress's twenty-thousand-dollar appropriation to finance the purchase of costly material and Bellangé furnishings from France and elsewhere to decorate the White House. More than a century later, Monroe's acquisitions made up the core of the White House's antique collection.

Subsequent presidents, however, had little control over the fate of the White House, which was at the whim of congressional appropriations. John Quincy Adams, who followed Monroe, was castigated by his enemies on Capitol Hill for purchasing a billiard table—hence money for the White House's upkeep was meager. In contrast, the popular Andrew Jackson spent thousands of dollars on fine china, wine glasses, and elegant furniture. In the case of President John Tyler, however, Congress refused to appropriate a penny, and the White House interior rapidly went downhill. An observer complained that the once-elegant East Room was shabbier than the shabbiest bordello.

Abraham Lincoln had far weightier matters on his mind than furniture when he became president in 1861. While Mary Todd Lincoln overspent funds in her attempt to restore some semblance of dignity and beauty to the White House, her unpopularity combined with the exigencies of war made the task of keeping up the White House difficult. During the Civil War, Union troops were bivouacked on the White House lawn and bedded down in the East Room, which soon would witness the silent procession of mourners past Lincoln's coffin. After the president's assassination, Mary Lincoln's grief was so paralyzing that for the five weeks she spent mourning in the White House, she was oblivious to the intruders who openly pillaged furniture and goods, despite the existence of a White House police force since 1842.

Lincoln's death and the great Civil War drama that had unfolded in the White House seemed to put an end to congressional haggling over White House appropriations. Even the much-maligned

Andrew Johnson had no trouble drawing sufficient funds for the White House's upkeep. For the rest of the century, succeeding presidents and their wives refurbished the White House in the style of the day, auctioning off wagonloads of furniture regardless of its historical value, a practice that continued until well into the twentieth century.

Modern Conveniences

While the seeds of reverence for the White House were implanted by the end of the Civil War, the house was still in the main regarded as a building meant to be little more than functional—the seat of the executive branch—and livable. Presidents and their spouses throughout the nineteenth century were primarily interested in installing creature comforts, such as modern heating and plumbing (1850's), telephones (1879), the first elevator (1880), and electricity (1891). The First Ladies, although they were not called this until after 1900, began to make their mark in the nineteenth century. In addition to Dolley Madison, notable nineteenth century presidents' wives included Lucy Webb Hayes, who in 1879 began the annual Easter Egg Roll, and Caroline Harrison, who started the famous White House china collection in the 1890's.

When Theodore Roosevelt became president following William McKinley's assassination in 1901, he was reminded that he could live somewhere other than the White House. Instead, he hired the most prestigious architectural firm of the day, McKim, Mead, & White, to construct offices for himself and his staff in a separate wing of the White House, and to determine what needed renovation and alteration. The firm was renowned for its colonial-style buildings, and the three architects began the effort, which took decades to complete, of restoring the White House to its early nineteenth century appearance. The huge greenhouse on the White House lawn, in place since 1857, was ordered removed; an entire suite of presidential offices, the West Wing, was constructed; and other major repairs and restorations took place. The West Wing offices were enlarged in 1909. This process included the building of the Oval Office, which has been the president's office ever since. In late 1901, Roosevelt had signed an executive order declaring the "White House" the official name of the executive mansion.

First Ladies

Although the twentieth century started off with the president having a decisive impact on the future of the White House, First Ladies—the title was popularly accepted by Theodore Roosevelt's time—also would leave their mark in major ways. Thanks to President Woodrow Wilson's first wife, Ellen, the now-famous Rose Garden was born. Her successor, the second Mrs. Wilson, Edith, was much criticized for becoming a "president in petticoats" when Woodrow Wilson lay incapacitated by a major stroke. It was left to her to make important decisions; however, these decisions did not include major changes in the White House. Grace Coolidge took the restoration of the White House interior a step further when she persuaded Congress to provide funds for the acquisition of colonial-era and early nineteenth century antiques. A third floor was finally added in 1927, during the Coolidge administration.

Lou Henry Hoover continued the trend of restoring the White House interior by having copies made of President Monroe's early nineteenth century furniture. Eleanor Roosevelt, the most influential First Lady of the twentieth century, had little interest in interior decorating. Exigencies of war, however, demanded an expansion of the White House, and in 1942, the cornerstone for the new East Wing was laid in the presence of Franklin D. Roosevelt. President Roosevelt also enlarged the West Wing and installed the first heated, indoor swimming pool in the executive mansion.

Total Renovation

After Harry S Truman became president in 1945, he took an interest in the White House architecture, adding a controversial second-floor balcony, completed in 1948. By then, however, the White House showed conspicuous signs of structural damage. The extensive remodeling and rebuilding throughout the years had weakened the house's wooden beams and interior walls, but the full extent of the damage was not discovered until a thorough examination made during Truman's administration, prompting President Truman to appeal to Congress to establish a Commission on Renovation of the Executive Mansion.

The result of this study was the most important renovation of the White House since its rebuilding after the fire of 1814. In fact, the entire interior was demolished, with only the original sandstone walls left standing. The president and First Lady meanwhile moved to temporary quarters in Blair House across the street. By the spring of 1952, the rebuilding of the White House was completed. The entire interior had been restored, with many of the heavy decorative effects added in the late nineteenth century removed. A new, two-story basement was dug, a new foundation was laid, the original sandstone walls were girded by concrete and steel, and the interior was restored and refurbished with antiques, all interior details having been painstakingly catalogued before the demolition. A gymnasium, solarium, motion-picture theater, and air conditioning were installed. When it was all over, at a cost of nearly six million dollars, Truman became the first U.S. president to give a guided tour of the White House on television.

Ten years later, when John F. Kennedy was president, First Lady Jacqueline Kennedy took the initiative to preserve the executive mansion as a living national shrine for future generations. A Fine Arts Committee, appointed by her in 1961, conducted a nationwide search for antiques and White House furnishings that had been auctioned off in the nineteenth century. The Fine Arts Committee gave rise to the White House Historical Association, which raises funds for the preservation of the White House and the acquisition of historic furnishings, as well as disseminating knowledge about the history of this important structure through numerous publications. President Lyndon B. Johnson furthered this effort in 1964 by an executive order that established the Committee for the Preservation of the White House, which for the first time in White House history provided for a permanent curator. No longer could a president or First Lady sell White House furnishings at will; no one could ever doubt that the executive mansion was a historical monument that must be preserved for future generations. Since then, there have been further interior refurbishings and repaintings of the exterior walls, and serious scholarship has emerged on the history and architecture of the White House.

—*Sina Dubovoy*

For Further Information:

Freidel, Frank, and William Pencak, eds. *The White House: The First Two Hundred Years.* Boston: Northeastern University, 1994. A compendium of symposium papers commemorating the two hundredth anniversary of the White House. It is edited by two historians.

McCullough, David. *Truman.* New York: Simon & Schuster, 1992. A Pulitzer Prize-winning, readable, and fascinating biography of Harry S Truman. During Truman's tenure as president the most extensive renovation in the White House's history took place, requiring the President and First Lady to seek other living quarters.

Seale, William. *The President's House.* 2 vols. Washington, D.C.: White House Historical Association, 1986.

_____. *The White House: The History of an American Idea.* Washington, D.C.: American Institute of Architects Press, 1992. Both works are standard, authoritative histories of the White House. The most recent is a fully illustrated, portrait-like presentation of the White House since its inception; Seale's 1986 work is the most exhaustive account ever written of the history of America's most famous historic building.

White House Historical Association, with the cooperation of the National Geographic Society. *The White House: An Historic Guide.* 20th ed. Washington, D.C.: The Association, 1999. The official guide for the White House, updated annually. Beautifully illustrated, to the point and informative, especially for the would-be tourist.

Other Historic Sites

Abbe House

Location: Washington, D.C.
Relevant issues: Science and technology
Statement of significance: A handsome example of early nineteenth century Federal residential architecture, from 1877 to 1909 this was the home of Cleveland Abbe (1838-1916), a prominent meteorologist known as the father of the U.S.

Weather Service. The house is also associated with James Monroe and Charles Francis Adams.

American Federation of Labor Building

Location: Washington, D.C.

Relevant issues: Political history, social reform

Statement of significance: On July 4, 1916, at a site where a fine old mansion with a slave pen in the rear had once stood, the American Federation of Labor dedicated its new international headquarters (1916-1956). President Woodrow Wilson delivered the chief address. The imposing seven-story brick and limestone building served to symbolize the federation's growth from, in the words of its founder, Samuel Gompers, "a weakling into the strongest, best organized labor movement of all the world."

American Peace Society

Location: Washington, D.C.

Relevant issues: Political history, social reform

Statement of significance: From 1911 to 1948, this large Victorian town house served as the headquarters of the oldest organization in America dedicated solely to promoting international peace. The society was founded in 1828 by William Ladd (1778-1841), who sought to foster popular sentiment against war and attempted to persuade legislatures and individual leaders to organize an international court of arbitration as a logical alternative to war.

Ashburton House

Location: Washington, D.C.

Relevant issues: Political history

Statement of significance: For ten months in 1842, this was the scene of negotiations which resolved "one of the gravest and most inveterate diplomatic issues of the United States in the generation following the War of 1812": the long-standing dispute with Great Britain over major segments of the boundary with Canada. In addition, the Webster-Ashburton Treaty of 1842 saw the United States government protect and respect the rights of the states in international affairs and stand firm against British impressment of sailors aboard American ships.

Baker House

Location: Washington, D.C.

Relevant issues: Political history

Statement of significance: From 1916 to 1920, this was the residence of Newton Diehl Baker (1871-1937), one of the most notable secretaries of war. Baker presided over the nation's World War I mobilization. He continued to be a proponent of President Woodrow Wilson's concept of world involvement during the 1920's.

Blair House

Location: Washington, D.C.

Relevant issues: Political history

Statement of significance: Since 1942 the federal government's official guest residence, this house is significant for the great number of dignitaries who have resided or been received there. Previous residents have included Francis P. Blair, Sr., a member of Andrew Jackson's "Kitchen Cabinet," and George Bancroft.

Bruce House

Location: Washington, D.C.

Relevant issues: African American history, political history

Statement of significance: This was the residence of Blanche Kelso Bruce (1841-1898), the first black man to serve a full term in the U.S. Senate (1875-1881, representing Mississippi). Prior to serving in the Senate, Bruce had held various local elective and appointed offices; afterward, he remained in Washington and continued to serve both the district and the nation.

Cary House

Location: Washington, D.C.

Relevant issues: African American history, legal history, political history, women's history

Statement of significance: From 1881 to 1885, this was the residence of Mary Ann Shadd Cary (1823-1893), writer, journalist, educator, and abolitionist. Cary lectured widely in the cause of abolition and after the Civil War became one of the first black female lawyers.

Constitution Hall

Location: Washington, D.C.

Relevant issues: Art and architecture, cultural history

Statement of significance: Designed by John Russell Pope and begun in August, 1928, this great hall was built to accommodate the annual congresses of the National Society of the Daughters of the American Revolution, which are held during the week of April 19 (the anniversary of the Battle of Lexington and Concord). It has become a nationally known center for the performing arts.

Corcoran Gallery and School of Art
Location: Washington, D.C.
Relevant issues: Art and architecture, cultural history
Statement of significance: Chartered by Congress in 1870, this is one of the oldest museums in America. It was founded by merchant, businessman, and philanthropist William Wilson Corcoran (1798-1888), who contributed both his art collection and the building to house it; when the collection outgrew its first home, Corcoran gave funds for a new building and a school of design in connection with the museum. This new structure (1893), designed by Ernest Flagg in the the Beaux-Arts style, is identified as an early and integral part of the City Beautiful plan.

Coues House
Location: Washington, D.C.
Relevant issues: Science and technology
Statement of significance: From 1887 until his death, this was the residence of Elliot Coues (1842-1899), a leading nineteenth century ornithologist whose studies greatly expanded the knowledge of North American bird life. In 1883, Coues helped found the American Ornithologists Union. In addition, Coues edited approximately fifteen volumes of journals, memoirs, and diaries by famous Western explorers and fur traders.

Decatur House
Location: Washington, D.C.
Relevant issues: Art and architecture
Statement of significance: This house was designed by one of America's first professional architects for Commodore Stephen Decatur, suppressor of the Barbary pirates. Later residents included Henry Clay, Martin Van Buren, and Judah P. Benjamin.

Frances Perkins House
Location: Washington, D.C.
Relevant issues: Political history, women's history
Statement of significance: From 1937 to 1940, this was the residence of Frances Perkins (1882-1965), who was the nation's first female cabinet member. She served as secretary of labor (1932-1945) during the presidency of Franklin Delano Roosevelt. During her long tenure, particularly in the prewar New Deal years, Perkins was the prime mover on several pieces of legislation that are among the Democratic Party's most lasting achievements: the Social Security Act (Perkins chaired the committee which drafted the legislation) and the Fair Labor Standards Act, which created a minimum wage and restricted child labor nationwide.

Franklin School
Location: Washington, D.C.
Relevant issues: Education
Statement of significance: The Franklin School was the flagship building of a group of seven, modern urban public school buildings constructed between 1862 and 1875 to house, for the first time, a comprehensive system of free universal public education in the capital of the republic. It was hoped that this new public school system would serve as a model for the nation as the need to provide equal educational opportunities for all Americans was finally recognized as essential to the survival of a democratic society.

Gompers House
Location: Washington, D.C.
Relevant issues: Political history, social reform
Statement of significance: From 1902 to 1917, this narrow, three-story brick rowhouse was the home of Samuel Gompers (1850-1924), who from 1886 until his death served as president of the American Federation of Labor, an organization he had helped found. As president, Gompers directed all of his energies toward a realization of three goals for American workers: more wages, shorter hours, better working conditions.

Grimké House
Location: Washington, D.C.
Relevant issues: African American history, education, social reform, women's history

Statement of significance: From 1881 to 1886, this was the residence of Charlotte Forten Grimké (1838-1914), pioneer black female educator, early supporter of women's rights, writer, and active abolitionist. She was with the first group of Northern educators to enter the war-torn areas of the South, providing instruction to those slaves residing in Union-occupied territory. The journal she kept while at Port Royal, South Carolina, provides a vivid picture of her students' progress and growth; her activities encouraged other Northern African Americans to lend their skills in support of the newly freed black population throughout the South.

Howard House

Location: Washington, D.C.

Relevant issues: African American history, education, military history, social reform

Statement of significance: Completed in 1867, this was the private residence of Oliver Otis Howard (1830-1909), Union general, commissioner of the Bureau of Refugees, Freedmen, and Abandoned Lands, and the third president (1869-1874) of Howard University. Founded in 1866 by the church of which General Howard was a member, the university was dedicated to providing black men and women with an education that would prepare them for careers in the fields of law, medicine, dentistry, pharmacy, engineering, social work, teaching, the ministry, and the armed services.

Hughes House

Location: Washington, D.C.

Relevant issues: Legal history, political history

Statement of significance: From 1930 until his death, this was the residence of Charles Evans Hughes (1862-1948), a leader in the Progressive movement, the holder of important offices under several presidents, justice and chief justice of the U.S. Supreme Court, and Republican candidate for president in 1916.

Johnson House

Location: Washington, D.C.

Relevant issues: Political history

Statement of significance: From 1929 to 1945, this was the residence of Senator Hiram W. Johnson (1866-1945), a leading voice of the Progressive movement. Johnson called for the formation of the Progressive Party in 1912.

Lafayette Square Historic District

Location: Washington, D.C.

Relevant issues: Cultural history

Statement of significance: Lafayette Park, designated as the President's Park when Washington, D.C., became the capital in 1791, was renamed in 1824 to honor the visit of Marquis de Lafayette. Houses fronting the park have been residences of Washington's elite society.

Library of Congress

Location: Washington, D.C.

Web site: lcweb.loc.gov/homepage/about.html

Relevant issues: Education, literary history

Statement of significance: Established in 1800, the Library of Congress ranks as one of the largest and finest in the world. Although founded primarily to serve the Congress, its field of service gradually expanded to serve all government agencies, serious scholars, other libraries, and the general public. The library was originally located in the Capitol, but by 1881 it was apparent that a separate building was needed to house its expanding collections and activities. The Jefferson Building was constructed between 1888 and 1897.

Mellon Building

Location: Washington, D.C.

Relevant issues: Business and industry, political history

Statement of significance: From 1922 to 1937, this was the residence of Andrew Mellon (1855-1937), the millionaire industrialist who was secretary of the Treasury from 1921 to 1932, the longest tenure since Albert Gallatin. He authored the Mellon Plan, which stimulated the economic boom of the 1920's. It is now the headquarters of the National Trust for Historic Preservation.

Memorial Continental Hall

Location: Washington, D.C.

Relevant issues: Political history

Statement of significance: From November 12, 1921, to February 6, 1922, this was the site of the Washington Conference, a remarkable and significant attempt to reduce global tension. Delegates from nine nations, including Great Britain, France, Italy, the United States, and Japan, engaged in negotiation which resulted in three treaties. Though the results of this effort were fully discredited by the 1930's and 1940's, for a decade these pacts did stabilize the armaments race and establish an embryonic security system in the Pacific.

National War College

Location: Washington, D.C.

Relevant issues: Military history

Statement of significance: An adjunct to the General Staff established in 1903, the Army War College (at this site from 1907) was an expression of the "New Army" created by Elihu Root (1845-1937) and President Theodore Roosevelt at the turn of the twentieth century. Patterned after European prototypes, especially the Prussian system, the college offered a military graduate education in all phases of war-making: strategy, tactics, logistics, as well as training in the political economic, and social ramifications of the conduct of war. Since 1946, the college has been used as an interservice facility.

Octagon House

Location: 1799 New York Avenue NW, Washington, D.C.

Relevant issues: Political history

Statement of significance: Constructed in 1799-1800, this octagonal Federal-style town house, built by the architect who designed the U.S. Capitol, was occupied temporarily in 1814-1815 by President James Madison after the burning of the White House. The Treaty of Ghent, ending the War of 1812, was signed here.

Old Naval Observatory

Location: Washington, D.C.

Relevant issues: Naval history, science and technology

Statement of significance: Between 1844 and 1861, under the leadership of Matthew Fontaine Maury (1806-1873), the Naval Observatory became widely known as a world center for advances in oceanography and navigational information. Maury, considered the founder of modern oceanography, made his greatest contributions to science during these years.

Old Patent Office

Location: Washington, D.C.

Relevant issues: Art and architecture

Statement of significance: Constructed in four sections over a thirty-one-year period beginning in 1836, this is one of the largest Greek Revival buildings built by the U.S. government in the nineteenth century. Born of confused architectural parentage, this building nevertheless achieved a unity of design and boldly simple monumentality unsurpassed in American civil architecture. It now houses the National Portrait Gallery and National Museum of American Art.

Red Cross Headquarters

Location: Washington, D.C.

Web site: www.redcross.org/hec/1980-present/visitors.html

Relevant issues: Social reform

Statement of significance: Constructed between 1915 and 1917, this building houses the administration of the nation's official relief organization. The Red Cross was accepted in the United States about 1884, due largely to the efforts of Clara Barton (1821-1912).

Richards House

Location: Washington, D.C.

Relevant issues: Education

Statement of significance: From 1882 until his death, this was the home of Zalmon Richards (1811-1899), the founder and first president of the National Educational Association. Richards promoted the passage in 1867 of the bill establishing the Federal Office of Education.

St. Elizabeths Hospital

Location: Washington, D.C.

Relevant issues: Health and medicine, social reform

Statement of significance: Founded in 1852, St. Elizabeths Hospital was the federal government's first mental hospital designed to care for the nation's mentally ill military personnel. The first medical superintendent was Charles H. Nichols (1820-1889), who collaborated with the social reformer Dorothea Dix (1802-1887) to establish a model institution in the capital city.

St. Luke's Episcopal Church

Location: Washington, D.C.

Relevant issues: African American history, religion

Statement of significance: On Thanksgiving Day, 1879, the first services were held in this church, founded and led by the Reverend Dr. Alexander Crummell (1819-1898), founder of the American Negro Academy and one of the most talented and articulate black scholars of the nineteenth century. This edifice was a physical creation and embodiment of Crummell's belief in the role the church has played, historically, in the lives of African Americans as an advocate for social change, education, and self-help.

Supreme Court Building

Location: Washington, D.C.

Relevant issues: Legal history

Statement of significance: Although the Constitution provided, in Article III, for the creation of a national judiciary, it took 145 years for the Court to find a permanent residence devoted to its needs. The construction of a building exclusively for the use of the Supreme Court in 1935 was a reaffirmation of the nation's faith in the doctrine of judicial independence and separation of powers.

Terrell House

Location: Washington, D.C.

Relevant issues: African American history, education, social reform, women's history

Statement of significance: This was the residence of Mary Church Terrell (1863-1954), educator and civil rights leader. Terrell was the first president of the National Association of Colored Women (1896) and the first black woman to serve on an American school board (1895).

Tudor Place

Location: Washington, D.C.

Relevant issues: Art and architecture, cultural history

Statement of significance: Designed by Dr. William Thornton, architect of the Capitol, and completed about 1815, the house is a highly rational and sophisticated example of early nineteenth century domestic architecture. For many years, it was one of the centers of Georgetown society; guests at this fine early Federal house have included Robert E. Lee and the Marquis de Lafayette.

Volta Bureau

Location: Washington, D.C.

Relevant issues: Education, health and medicine

Statement of significance: In 1887, Alexander Graham Bell (1847-1922) founded the Volta Bureau as an instrument "for the increase and diffusion of knowledge relating to the Deaf." The bureau merged with the American Association for the Promotion and Teaching of Speech to the Deaf in 1908. The Volta Bureau continues its work in aiding the deaf.

Wilson House

Location: Washington, D.C.

Web site: sunsite.unc.edu/lia/president/pressites/wilson/WilsonH-brochure.html

Relevant issues: Political history

Statement of significance: Thomas Woodrow Wilson (1856-1924), the twenty-eighth president of the United States, spent his last years (1921-1924) here as a semi-invalid, weakened by a stroke and his fight for the League of Nations. The house contains memorabilia associated with the lives of the Wilsons.

Woodson House

Location: Washington, D.C.

Relevant issues: African American history, education

Statement of significance: From 1915 until his death, this was the home of Dr. Carter Godwin Woodson (1875-1950), the founder of black history studies in the United States. In an effort to correct the widespread ignorance and lack of information concerning black life and history in the country, Woodson established the Association for the Study of Negro Life and History (1915), the Associated Publishers (1920), *The Journal of Negro History* (1916), and *The Negro History Bulletin* (1937).

Florida

History of Florida 311
Cape Canaveral 314
Key West 319

St. Augustine 326
Other Historic Sites 331

The State Capitol Building in Tallahassee. (Visit Florida)

History of Florida

Although Florida has a long and varied history, many of the most important developments in the state, especially in terms of economic, political, and demographic changes, took place after the 1950's. Because of its geographic location, which promotes the influence of West Indian and Caribbean cultures, and its pleasant, tropical climate, which has attracted large numbers of residents from both the Northern and Southern Hemispheres, Florida developed a unique and distinctive character.

Early History
Native Americans arrived in Florida sometime around 10,000 B.C.E. and slowly made their way south, not reaching the southern tip of the peninsula until about 1400 B.C.E. Archaeological evidence from northeastern Florida and southeastern Georgia indicates that inhabitants of these areas invented pottery in the period around 2000 B.C.E. This would place their development of pottery approximately eight hundred years before other North American cultures.

Because of the abundance of game and marine life, early Native Americans in the Florida area were primarily hunters and fishers, rather than farmers. Great respect was paid to the dead, who were interred in large burial mounds. By 1500 C.E. a sun-worship cult, also centered around large earthen mounds, spread through the region. The tribes discovered agriculture and grew corn, beans, and squash, among other crops.

Along the northern Gulf coast lived the Panzacola, Chatot, and Apalachicola; farther west were the Apalachee. The lower part of the peninsula, from Tampa Bay extending south, was inhabited by the warrior Calusa, for whom warfare seemed to be part of their religious practice. In the north, the dominant group was the Timucua, who were the first Native Americans to encounter Europeans. By far the most famous of Florida tribes, however, were the Seminoles, who entered the state in 1750. The word *seminole* means "runaway" in the Creek language, and the people themselves were Creek Indians who came from Alabama and Georgia. At first scattered in small groups, the Seminoles united against those who wanted to remove them from Florida, first the Spanish and English and later the Americans.

Exploration and Colonization
The first European contact with Florida began in 1513, when Juan Ponce de León landed on the coast, claimed the land for Spain, and bestowed its current name, either because it was Easter (*Pascua Florida*, in Spanish) or because of the many flowering plants he discovered (*florida* also means "flowery" in Spanish). After Ponce de León's death during a battle with Native Americans in 1521, several other Spanish explorers, including Hernando de Soto, sought to establish a permanent presence in Florida. It was not until 1566, however, that a Spanish colony was founded at St. Augustine, becoming the first permanent European settlement in what is now the United States.

As they did elsewhere with their New World colonies, the Spanish implemented both imperial rule and the Catholic religion. Settlements and missions were established throughout Florida, but these were destroyed in the early 1700's in raids by Native Americans and British settlers from South Carolina. In 1763, as part of the treaties which ended the French and Indian War, Spain ceded Florida to the British in exchange for Cuba. The British divided the colony into East and West Florida.

Immigration increased the English population of Florida, and during the American Revolution the residents remained loyal to that crown. However, in 1778, Spain, which had become an American ally, seized West Florida. In 1783, at the end of the Revolution, Spain regained all of Florida. While many English settlers left for British possessions in the West Indies, others remained behind, stubbornly defiant to the Spanish and fearful of possible takeover by French forces.

Steps to Statehood
During the War of 1812 the British used Pensacola as a naval base, prompting its capture by American

forces under General Andrew Jackson. In 1819, Spain ceded Florida to the United States, and Jackson returned in 1822 as military governor of the new territory. The northwestern portion of the region, along the panhandle, became the site of numerous cotton plantations worked by slaves. Tallahassee was named the capital in 1823. In 1845 Florida was admitted to the Union.

Even before Florida officially became part of the United States, efforts had been underway to remove Native Americans from the territory. This ongoing conflict was concentrated on the Seminoles, who had formed a formidable presence against the threat from the Americans. From 1835 to 1842 the United States waged the Seminole War against the tribe. The war was begun when Osceola, a young Seminole chief, publicly rejected a harsh treaty with the United States by plunging his dagger through the document. Outnumbered by the Americans, Osceola led the Seminoles into the Everglades and conducted guerrilla warfare. He was captured while under a flag of truce and imprisoned in Fort Moultrie at Charleston, South Carolina; he died there in 1838. Without his lead-

ership, the tide turned against the Seminoles, and after their final defeat they were removed to lands in the western United States. Only a handful remained behind, hidden in the swamps and wilderness of Florida. The number of Seminoles increased in the state during the twentieth century, however.

Civil War and Reconstruction
In 1861 Florida joined other southern states in seceding from the Union. During the Civil War, Union naval forces quickly captured strong points along the coast, including Fernandina, Pensacola, and St. Augustine. However, when Union troops attempted an invasion of the interior, they were defeated at the battle of Olustee in 1864. A second Union attempt to capture Tallahassee failed in March, 1865; the Florida capital and Austin, Texas, were the only two Confederate capitals never captured during the war.

After being readmitted to the Union in 1868, Florida entered Reconstruction and began a period of transformation of the state's economic base. Citrus fruits replaced cotton as the major cash crop, and phosphate mining for fertilizer became a dominant industry. Tourism, almost unknown before the Civil War, began to become a key economic factor in the 1880's, especially with the development of railroads. Henry B. Plant completed the Kissimmee-Tampa cross-state railroad in 1884, and Henry M. Flagler inaugurated the Jacksonville-Miami Line in 1896. The two systems linked Florida and its produce to the rich markets of the Northeast and encouraged the growth of the tourism and retirement industries. Starting in the early 1900's, the state's population began to double approximately every twenty years.

The Florida real estate boom of the 1920's saw a dramatic increase in settlers, but by the middle of the decade the boom had ended. In addition, massive hurricanes in 1926 and 1928 further damaged the state's economy, which was severely affected by the Great Depression of 1929. President Franklin Roosevelt's New Deal brought relief and massive defense spending before and during World War II, helping bring the state into the modern age.

A Mixed Economy

Cape Canaveral on the east coast of Florida was one of the oldest sites to be named by Europeans on the North American continent. During the 1950's and 1960's it became the site of the nation's newest explorers, as the National Aeronautics and Space Administration (NASA) chose it for the site of the American space program. In 1958 it saw the launch of the first U.S. satellite, in 1961 and 1962 the first American manned spaceflight and orbital mission, and in 1969 the first lunar mission.

Modern Florida developed a mixed economy that depends upon traditional areas such as manufacturing and agriculture and also relies heavily on tourism. Companies that produce computer equipment and accessories have taken the lead in manufacturing. Citrus fruits, first introduced to Florida in the 1570's, are a strong staple, with Florida producing more than three-quarters of the total U.S. harvest of grapefruit and oranges. In addition, the state's pine forests are valuable sources of materials for pulp and paper, as well as turpentine and other products. The almost year-round growing season has made Florida a leader in truck-farming agriculture, shipping tomatoes, vegetables, and other produce throughout the nation.

A Multicultural State

The Cuban Revolution of 1959, which brought Fidel Castro and the Communist Party to power, saw a massive emigration from that island, largely among the professional, upper, and middle classes. Conservative in politics and religion, Cubans brought with them a tradition of respect for learning and for the free enterprise system. Although their initial plans had been for an early return to their home, these immigrants established themselves in south Florida, especially in the Miami area, where they developed a strong economy and thriving culture. By the late 1970's, south Florida had become a multicultural, bilingual area.

These developments were not without difficulty. In 1986 Bob Martinez became the first Hispanic to be elected governor of Florida. Significantly, he

won election as a Republican. However, many conservatives, disturbed at the increasing power of Hispanic voters, pushed hard to win approval in 1988 of an amendment to the state constitution that made English the official language of state government. Adding to the situation were sometimes tense relations between the white, Hispanic, and African American populations; in the early 1980's these tensions caused riots to flare in the Miami area.

Tourism and Nature

Tourism, long a staple of the modern Florida economy, received a major boost in 1971 with the opening of Walt Disney World near Orlando. Disney's Epcot Center followed in 1982. Soon, Disney World became the single most popular tourist destination in the United States. Other attractions, including Sea World, Universal Studios theme park, and Busch Gardens, increased Florida's appeal as a tourist destination. Added to these are the state's natural attractions, such as the Everglades, the Florida Keys, and the unique John Pennekamp Coral Reef State Park near Key Largo, which is entirely underwater and features living coral formations. In 1990, a record-breaking 41 million visitors from around the world visited Florida.

Although much of Florida's appeal rested upon its environment, much of that environment had been devastated by natural forces or harmed by human intervention. In 1992 the state was struck by Hurricane Andrew, at that time the costliest natural disaster in U.S. history. The storm raged through south Florida, ruining entire communities and causing more than $20 billion in damages.

As the state entered the twenty-first century, it began to address a potentially fatal threat to its environment. Decades of systematic draining of wetlands, including the vast expanse of the Everglades, to accommodate expanding human population and development seriously endangered the environment and wildlife. Finally realizing the seriousness of the situation, the U.S. Army Corps of Engineers and other organizations abandoned long-standing projects such as the Cross Florida Barge Canal and began efforts to reverse years of neglect and active damage. These efforts became critical for a state more dependent than most on its natural environment for its prosperity and continued growth. —*Michael Witkoski*

Cape Canaveral

Date: Constructed between 1961 and 1966

Relevant issues: Aviation history, disasters and tragedies, science and technology

Significance: Cape Canaveral is the term commonly used to refer to U.S. space exploration facilities on the cape and on Merritt Island, which lies between the cape and the mainland. Merritt Island is the site of the John F. Kennedy Space Center, which houses the National Aeronautics and Space Administration (NASA) Launch Operations Center, the central site of the U.S. space program. It was constructed as the launch center for missions to the Moon; since 1981 it has been the launch base for the Space Shuttle. On the cape itself is Cape Canaveral Air Force Station, site of the start of the space program, including the satellite projects Vanguard and Explorer, and all manned flight projects before Apollo. It remains active as a facility for launches of unmanned private payloads into Earth's orbit.

Location: On Florida's Atlantic coast, east of Titusville and Cocoa (both on U.S. Highway 1) and Merritt Island in Brevard County, east central Florida, 209 miles north of Miami and 45 miles east of Orlando

Site Office:

NASA Kennedy Space Center Spaceport USA
Route 405
NASA Causeway
Kennedy Space Center, FL 32899
ph.: (407) 452-2121
fax: (407) 452-3043
Web site: www.ksc.nasa.gov

The cape that was named *cañaveral* by the Spanish to describe its original appearance, a "place of reeds," or a reedbed, was little more than a stretch of uninhabited, barren scrubland until the middle of the twentieth century, when it quickly became the center for U.S. space program initiatives. Today it is home to a vast complex covering an area of 125 square miles that attracts more than two million visitors a year.

Early Development

The development of the cape is closely linked to the state of affairs between the two superpowers after World War II. The cape's original function had been military in nature. As in the case of the major launch centers of the former Soviet Union, the space vehicle launch sites at Cape Canaveral Air Force Station and the Kennedy Space Center are an extension of facilities built during the Cold War for the testing of long-range missiles.

At the end of World War II, the United States was conducting its long-range ballistic development out of five centers. Three of these, the Goldstone and Pendleton Ranges and the Naval Ordnance Test Station, were in California; the Hueco Range was in Texas, and the Allegheny Ballistics Laboratory in West Virginia. Missiles test-fired from these centers had a maximum range of not quite nine miles. The postwar period of wariness and hostility between the United States and the Soviet Union— an era known as the Cold War—called for missile capabilities of a longer range, and three new centers were constructed in the second half of 1945: Wallops Station in Virginia, Point Mugu in California, and the White Sands Proving Ground in New Mexico. White Sands benefited greatly from the work of Wernher von Braun and his team of German rocket experts, who had developed the original V-2 (also known as the A-4) in Germany during World War II. This rocket became the basis of modern U.S. and Soviet long-range missiles and space vehicles, and Braun figured prominently in the U.S. space program.

Maximum Missile Ranges

The maximum ranges of these new testing sites did not exceed one hundred miles. This meant that A-4/V-2 rockets, predecessors to the intercontinental ballistic missile (ICBM), had to be fired below their maximum range of around two hundred miles. The next generation of missiles was intended to have an intercontinental range, from five thousand to seven thousand miles. None of the three existing long-range facilities could cater to this expanding need. A new site had to be found, and this need for a longer-range missile launch site accounts for the initial development of Cape Canaveral.

Cape Canaveral was one of three potential facilities considered by the Committee on Long Range Missile Proving Grounds of the Joint Research and Development Board of the U.S. War Department. There were three requirements for the new site: favorable weather conditions, a seaside location, and a nearby, separate land mass, like a chain of islands. A coastal location meant that missiles of much longer range could be launched over the sea without compromising populated areas. Because the technology of the time did not allow the tracking of missiles from the moving decks of ships, tracking facilities had to be land-based.

One of the three sites, in Washington State with tracking stations along the Aleutian Islands, was eliminated because of its unfavorable climate. What had been the committee's first choice, El Centro Naval Air Station in California, was eliminated when sovereignty rights for tracking stations based in Mexico could not be secured. This left Cape Canaveral, which, with British agreement to allow tracking facilities on the British-ruled Bahamas, became the chosen site. The facility, named the Joint Long Range Proving Ground Base, was to be operated by the U.S. Air Force, Navy, and Army. The Air Force took on sole responsibility for the base in 1950, and the facility was renamed Patrick Air Force Base. Still operational today, it is located at the southern tip of the cape.

The First Launches

Missile launches from Cape Canaveral began in July, 1950, with the launch of an A-4/WAC-Corporal. In 1953 came the launch of the first Redstone missile, which was to play an important part in space vehicle propulsion. In that same year, Braun, at the time based with the U.S. Army Ballistic Missile Agency in Huntsville, Alabama, proposed the use of an enlarged version of the Redstone to place in orbit the first Earth satellite. The propulsion capability—needed after the initial liftoff stage—to make this possible became available in September, 1956, date of the first Jupiter launch. This was not going

to be the rocket, however, that would propel the first satellite into orbit; it was to remain dedicated to warhead testing. This was a decision based on policy.

Wernher von Braun's work was not with the Air Force, and it was the Air Force that was supposed to build missiles with intercontinental range. The Air Force's *Vanguard*, developed from a sounding rocket, was to make this first attempt into space. This choice resulted in the first-ever artificial satellite being Soviet. Its name was *Sputnik*, weighing 184 pounds and launched into orbit on October 4, 1957. Two weeks later *Sputnik II*, weighing 1,120

A space shuttle launch from Cape Canaveral. (PhotoDisc)

pounds and carrying a dog named Laika, also was orbited successfully. This second satellite was doubly ominous: The Soviets had developed large ballistic missiles and also had shown their intent to put humans in space vehicles.

Early Failures

The United States launched *Vanguard* on December 6, 1957. A live television audience watched the liftoff from Launch Complex 18 at the Cape: *Vanguard* rose four feet into the air, lost thrust, fell back onto the launch pad and exploded. The satellite it was carrying weighed 3.5 pounds. Wernher von Braun's team was given the go-ahead to proceed with preparations for a Redstone-propelled launch. This was *Explorer I*, which was successfully put into orbit January 31, 1958, from Launch Complex 26. This event established Canaveral's principal role in the U.S. space program. Although it had not been part of the selection criteria for Cape Canaveral a decade earlier, the site proved itself to be particularly well suited for satellite launches in that eastward launches could take advantage of the Earth's rotation to achieve orbit. This advantage had not been available at El Centro.

The failure of *Vanguard* was a major embarrassment to the administration of President Dwight D. Eisenhower. For the first time in the history of superpower rivalry, the Soviet Union had shown itself to be technologically superior. The administration's marginal interest in rocket technology quickly gained in intensity, which in turn led to the creation of the National Aeronautics and Space Administration (NASA) on October 1, 1958. On the day of its creation, Keith Glennan, NASA's first administrator, declared that the United States would put a man into space. This had been the Soviets' openly pursued aim, and the United States did not wish to be outdone again. A small task force was formed for this purpose on November 5, 1958, named the Space Task Group, made up of thirty-seven engineers and eight secretaries and led by Robert Gilruth. In the same year, NASA chose Cape Canaveral as the site for the U.S. space program.

NASA Begins Using the Cape

NASA's presence at the cape had a modest start. On June 9, 1959, a Space Task Group team arrived at the cape. Their project was to launch an Atlas missile carrying the first Mercury capsule, referred to as "Big Joe," with the purpose of establishing whether the heat shield could ensure bearable cabin temperatures during reentry into the atmosphere. Minimal resources had been allotted to the project. The Space Task Group did not yet have its own facilities at the Cape and had to rely on the Air Force to provide them. It was a rudimentary arrangement and a far cry from the sophisticated infrastructure in place today. The office space provided was a narrow area with one window in which the desks barely fitted end to end. Each time the draftsman had to get out from behind his desk by the window—he needed the light—all the other engineers had to get up, push their chairs into their desks and walk out into the corridor to let him pass. The team's work area was a roped-off section of Hangar S, which had to be shared with a team of Navy technicians working on its missiles. The Mercury capsule stood on the concrete floor while technicians in overalls worked on it.

When the time came to launch, the capsule was driven to the launch site in the back of a pickup truck on top of mattresses. "Big Joe" was launched, with accidental success, in September, 1959. Liftoff went well, but the second stage of the flight did not proceed as intended when the outboard booster engines did not separate from the rocket. As a result, the capsule was not released at the correct angle for reentry into the Earth's atmosphere. Despite this mishap, the heat shield experiment was concluded successfully. The design and center of gravity of "Big Joe" were such that the capsule eventually righted itself and reentered the atmosphere as originally planned. However, the haphazard aspects of this experiment had underlined the failure of the transporter rocket. Two months later, President Eisenhower signed an executive order to transfer Braun's team of rocket experts from Huntsville to NASA, greatly boosting the new agency's capabilities. He had not done so earlier because he had been determined to maintain NASA as an entirely civilian organization. Wernher von Braun's team, with its links to the U.S. Army, had not fulfilled this criterion.

The Moon Race

Following the world's first satellite launch in 1957, the two superpowers were racing each other to achieve the first manned space flight. On April 12,

1961, the Soviet Union beat the United States again with the successful launch and recovery of *Vostok I*, carrying cosmonaut Yuri Gagarin. This first perceived failure of President John F. Kennedy's administration was compounded a week later with the disastrous outcome of the Bay of Pigs invasion, in which a contingent of Cubans failed in their aim to overthrow Castro. On May 5, Alan Shepard was launched on a Mercury Redstone from Canaveral's Launch Complex 5. It was the first U.S. manned mission and it was concluded successfully with Shepard landing safely after a flight of fifteen minutes and twenty-two seconds. It was against this background that on May 25, encouraged by Shepard's success and driven by the need to correct recent failures, President Kennedy stood before Congress to request the provision of funds to carry out a manned lunar landing and safe return within the decade. NASA bought 125 square miles of land on Merritt Island adjacent to Cape Canaveral to develop a new space launch center.

Construction was under way by January, 1962. Two of the most remarkable structures erected were the Vehicle Assembly Building and the crawler spacecraft transporter. The construction of an assembly site for the Saturn rockets posed a number of problems. The size of the Saturn rocket, more than 360 feet long—the size of a Navy destroyer—meant that it could not be assembled in a horizontal position, as was the practice with the smaller V-2s and Redstones. In addition, the crane to be used for lifting hardware during assembly needed sufficient clearance. The elements at the cape, namely salt water and winds up to twenty-five knots, called for an enclosed building that offered shelter and allowed the performance of delicate technical work. Also, the president's declared goal of reaching the Moon by 1970 meant that the assembly site had to be large enough to enable the preparation of at least four Saturns at a time. These requirements were met in the huge Vehicle Assembly Building (VAB), which dwarfs all other facilities at the space center. The building is 525 feet high and its floor covers eight acres. Each of the four doors is 456 feet high, tall enough for the Statue of Liberty to pass through. One popular myth about the gigantic scale of the VAB was that it had to be air-conditioned to prevent clouds from forming inside.

Once assembled, the Saturn had to be transported to the launch site. The launcher was ninety-five feet above the ground and three miles from the VAB. The space vehicle had to be transported for these three miles, come to a five-degree slope and climb the ninety-five feet. As the Saturn climbed, its transportation platform had to be raised hydraulically so that the vehicle remained level throughout the climb. This was achieved by a giant transporter crawler that moved at a speed of twenty feet per minute along four tanklike tracks supporting a platform the size of a professional baseball diamond.

Kennedy and the Space Center

On November 16, 1963, part of the way through construction of the new complex, President Kennedy visited what was by then known as the Launch Operations Center on Merritt Island, where he inspected the construction sites for the VAB and Pad 39, to be used for the Apollo launches and later for those of the Space Shuttle. Six days later, President Kennedy was shot dead in Dallas. Six days after that, the center was renamed the John F. Kennedy Space Center. President Lyndon B. Johnson also extended the name change to Cape Canaveral itself, changing it to Cape Kennedy. The cape retained this name until 1973, when it returned to its original Spanish name, to the preference of Floridians. By May, 1966, the infrastructure needed for launching Apollo missions was in place.

First Americans in Space

Launches had continued during construction of the lunar mission facilities. Virgil "Gus" Grissom had replicated Shepard's success in 1961. Another milestone was reached on February 20, 1962, as John Glenn completed three Earth orbits during a flight lasting nearly five hours. This was followed by the Gemini project, which consisted of twelve two-man missions, primarily during 1965 and 1966. The project's aim was to gain knowledge regarding, among other things, long-duration flights, docking, and space rendezvous. These were highly successful missions that gave the United States a lead over the Soviet Union.

Use of the newly constructed facility began with the Apollo project in 1967. It was to use Saturn-propelled craft that could accommodate three astronauts over a two-week period. The project had a tragic start with Apollo 1. Gus Grissom, Edward White, and Roger Chaffee died as a result of a fire that broke out in the command module during a launch rehearsal. The project was resumed after a one-year moratorium, with the next major milestone being reached with Apollo 8 in December, 1968, when Frank Borman, James Lovell, and William Anders orbited the Moon ten times. Apollo 11, manned by Neil Armstrong, Michael Collins, and Edwin Aldrin, landed in the Moon's Sea of Tranquillity on July 20, 1969. This event more than any other made Cape Canaveral and the Kennedy Space Center into household names around the world.

Skylab

The cape has since been part of every major milestone in the history of U.S. space exploration. Skylab, the first U.S. space station, was launched unmanned May 14, 1973. Eleven days later, in another craft, its first crew—Charles Conrad, Dr. Joseph Kerwin, and Paul Weitz—made a rendezvous with the station. The first Skylab mission lasted twenty-eight days. The other two Skylab missions of July and November, 1973, lasted fifty-nine and eighty-four days, respectively.

After the last crew left in 1974, Skylab was to keep circling the Earth until the 1980's, when a Space Shuttle would meet it and either maneuver it into safe orbit or let it fall into the Indian Ocean. This was not to be. An expansion of the Earth's atmosphere, caused by sunspot activity during 1978-1979, meant that the gravitational pull on Skylab increased and dragged the station toward Earth. On July 11, 1979, after completing 34,981 orbits of the Earth, Skylab disintegrated over the Indian Ocean. Some debris landed in the Australian Outback without harming people or property.

The Space Shuttle

The next milestone of space exploration was the space shuttle program, which began in 1981 with the first orbital test flight of *Columbia*, manned by John Young and Robert Crippen. It lifted off from Launch Complex 39, which has been the launch site for all shuttle flights.

The space shuttle, known officially as the Space Transportation System (STS), is the first multipurpose reusable space vehicle. NASA engineers liken it to a truck, able to deliver satellites, pick them up

or repair them on-site. It can also serve as a space laboratory. The space shuttle orbiters *Columbia, Challenger, Discovery,* and *Atlantis* performed all these functions since the space shuttle program began. In June, 1983, the seventh shuttle mission, STS-7, on *Challenger,* lifted off. On board was Sally Ride, the first American woman in space. The tenth shuttle mission of February, 1984, also on *Challenger,* was remarkable for the first untethered spacewalk, performed by Bruce McCandless and Robert Stewart with the aid of manned maneuvering units (MMUs).

The *Challenger* Disaster

The twenty-fifth space shuttle mission of January 28, 1986, is remembered for its abrupt and tragic end. Mission objectives had included the Teacher-in-Space project, in which Christa McAuliffe was to conduct two lessons from space to millions of pupils across the country. Instead, Gregory Jarvis, McAuliffe, Ronald McNair, Ellison Onizuka, Judith Resnick, Francis Scobee, and Michael Smith lost their lives when the orbiter *Challenger* exploded seventy-three seconds after liftoff.

The flight took place in the middle of an unusual Florida cold snap. At liftoff, the temperature was 36 degrees Fahrenheit, 15 degrees colder than that of any previous launch. This cold temperature had affected the seals lining the joints between the rocket booster segments, which contain solid propellant. (The solid rocket boosters are placed on either side of the external tank. This is the large central cylindrical structure to which the shuttle remains attached during liftoff and which acts as a fuel tank to the shuttle's main engines.) The function of these seals is to prevent the escape of hot gases through the joint while the propellant is burning. An ill-fitting seal in the joint between the two lower segments of the right-hand booster rocket failed to contain these hot gases, which ignited as they escaped. This rapidly growing flame was aimed at the surface of the central, external tank, which quickly began to leak liquid hydrogen, further adding to the flame from the booster rocket. It was this leak that eventually developed into the massive explosion witnessed by national television audiences.

Spaceport USA

The NASA complex is a secured area, with public

access to the Kennedy Space Center restricted to Spaceport USA, the custom-built visitor center that stands on seventy acres within the complex. Visitors are taken around the facility by bus and are shown the Space Shuttle Launch Pads (Launch Complex 39, A and B), the Vehicle Assembly Building and a Saturn V rocket. An alternative tour takes visitors to the Cape Canaveral Air Force Station, where the U.S. space program began. Spaceport USA also includes a series of museums displaying objects of space exploration history. Two IMAX theaters show spaceflight films. An Astronauts Memorial stands at Spaceport USA consisting of a 42.5-foot-high by 50-foot-wide "Space Mirror" that tracks the movement of the Sun to illuminate the names of sixteen astronauts who died in the cause of space exploration.   *—Noel Sy-Quia*

For Further Information:

Bailey, John, ed. *Quest for Space*. Clearwater, Fla.: Belmont International, 1999. Recounts the history of NASA and the Kennedy Space Center, as well as the Goddard Space Flight Center and the Ames Research Center. Describes Project Apollo and spaceflight since then and offers astronaut biographies of such figures as Neil Armstrong, Buzz Aldrin, Sally Ride, Shannon Lucid, and Michael Collins.

Gaffney, Timothy R. *Kennedy Space Center.* Chicago: Childrens Press, 1985. A good introduction to the Kennedy Space Center for children, describing the surrounding area and history of the center with a concentration on the Space Shuttle program. Includes a glossary of common space travel terms.

Gatland, Kenneth. *The Illustrated Encyclopedia of Space Technology: A Comprehensive History of Space Exploration.* Rev. ed. New York: Harmony Books, 1984. An excellent factbook with illustrations explaining the events and technological developments of global space travel history. It includes a glossary and chronology of space travel events up to 1984.

Murray, Charles, and Catherine Bly Cox. *Apollo: The Race to the Moon.* New York: Simon & Schuster, 1989. An engaging account of the Apollo project told from a human-interest angle. It places the space program in its wider historical context and is full of entertaining anecdotes.

Key West

Date: First became a Spanish possession in 1565; sold to an American in 1822

Relevant issues: European settlement, Latino history, literary history, military history

Significance: Current seat of Monroe County, Florida, Key West has a long and colorful history of economic, demographic, and military importance. Today, the city is probably best known as the 1930's home of Ernest Hemingway, who used Key West and Key West-inspired tropical seaside cities as the backdrop for several of his novels and short stories. The city's population of approximately thirty thousand depends primarily upon fishing and tourism for economic sustenance. Key West's Old Town is a well-preserved historic district.

Location: The southernmost settlement in the continental United States, located approximately one hundred miles west-southwest from mainland Florida on a coral island slightly less than eight square miles in total area; often described as the westernmost of the chain of Florida Keys, but in reality only the westernmost inhabited island of the chain

Site Office:

Historic Florida Keys Preservation Board
510 Greene Street
Key West, FL 33040
ph.: (305) 292-6718
fax: (305) 293-6348

Due to its strategic location between the Gulf of Mexico and the Atlantic Ocean, only ninety miles from Cuba, Key West has seen more than its share of migrations, revolutions, conquests, and periods of prosperity. The city has lived under Spanish, British, and American flags, and its population and culture reflect a mix of Cuban, European, Caribbean, African, and mainstream American influences. Key West politics have run the gamut from socialist to libertarian and the city has been both the wealthiest and the poorest in Florida. Through it all, the residents of Key West—historic and modern—have earned a reputation for taking it all in stride.

The Old Town Historic District of Key West, a one-square-mile community located along Duval Street from the Atlantic to the Gulf, contains most of the city's historic sites. Fire destroyed approximately half of Key West in 1886, and serious efforts at historic preservation came in fits and starts between 1934 and the 1970's. A remarkably large portion of the city's history has been retained, however; 2,000 of the 3,100 buildings within the historic district are considered to be historically significant. Visitors to the city today will find plenty of important relics of Key West's freewheeling past tucked into the urban fabric amid the modern resorts and tourist traps that have become the island's economic lifeblood.

The Hemingway House in Key West. (Florida Keys & Key West TDC)

Early History

Key West was probably first sighted by Europeans in 1513 when Spanish explorer Juan Ponce de Léon landed at what is now St. Augustine, Florida, in his quest for the Fountain of Youth. Sailing southward along the Atlantic coast of Florida, Ponce de Léon recorded passing through the Straits of Florida between the Keys and Cuba, although he made no specific mention of Key West in his journals.

For the next 250 years, Spanish adventurers and entrepreneurs traded and traveled throughout mainland Florida and the Keys despite the territory's changes in ownership. Florida became a solid Spanish possession in 1565 after Spanish soldiers decimated a settlement of French Huguenots in northern Florida and established the city of St. Augustine, the oldest city in the United States. The Spanish named what is now Key West *Cayo Hueso*, meaning "island of bones" after the large quantity of human bones they found strewn about the island. Local legend says that they were the remains of the Calusa Indians, an unlucky tribe pursued by its enemies across the Keys and slaughtered when there was nowhere left to run.

Notoriety

Key West's rough-and-tumble reputation was born during this period. With treacherous coral reefs and unpredictable currents, the Keys provided both navigational hazards and plenty of places to hide. The thousands of islands in the 192-mile chain were favorites of the pirates who roamed the Straits of Florida in the eighteenth and early nineteenth centuries preying upon merchant ships or the Spanish fleet as it returned from South America, sometimes dangerously overladen with treasure. The pirates' practice of looting ships in trouble was eventually turned into a legitimate business by later generations of island-ers, who made "wrecking"—salvaging valuables from shipwrecks—a legal and lucrative enterprise. The legendary pirates Blackbeard and Jean Lafitte were among the motley crew who infested the Keys during this period.

Florida remained in Spanish hands until 1763, when British victory in the French and Indian War forced Spain to acquiesce to British demands for the territory. The territory once again found itself in Spanish hands in 1783, following the American Revolution, but continued to be used by Great Brit-ain for covert activities against the newly founded United States from 1783 through the War of 1812.

Cession to the United States

The king of Spain in 1815 granted Key West to a Spanish artillery officer named Juan Pablo Salas, whose service to the Crown at St. Augustine mer-ited a sizeable reward. Florida was ceded to the United States in 1819, but Salas managed to main-tain ownership of his island until 1822, when he sold it for two thousand dollars to an American named John W. Simonton, thereby making the is-land American territory.

Later that year the U.S. government sent Com-modore David D. Porter, with his famed "mosquito fleet" of the West Indies Squadron, to rid the Keys of the pirates who had held them for so long. Fol-lowing his mission a naval depot was established on Key West, beginning an American military pres-ence on the island that remained unbroken until 1974, when budget cutbacks forced closure of the naval base. A small naval air station is still based on a nearby Key.

The military was destined to play a major role in the growth of Key West. There are three fortifica-tions on the island alone, including Fort Zachary Taylor, East Martello Tower, and West Martello Tower. Located on the island's west side, Fort Tay-lor was constructed between 1854 and 1866 and served as an important naval base during the Civil War, when the Union navy, which controlled the is-land throughout the war, mounted a successful blockade of Confederate ships, which some say may have reduced the length of the war by as much as a year. The towers, begun in 1861, were never completed because advances in military equip-ment made them obsolete almost immediately. To-day, Fort Taylor is a National Park and the towers,

east and west, serve as home to an art gallery and the Key West Garden Club, respectively.

"Fort Forgotten"

Unused and buried under tons of sand, Fort Taylor was once dubbed "Fort Forgotten" by islanders and was once considered a possible site for a sewage treatment plant. In 1968, however, local resident Howard England, a historian and civil architect for the Key West naval base, waged a grassroots preser-vation campaign to save the historically important site. With the help of his sons and other volunteers, England began to dig, eventually uncovering most of the south side of the fort and excavating thou-sands of weapons and other artifacts from the Civil War. The fort is now considered to be one of the most important Civil War sites in the nation.

Although located in the Dry Tortugas, a small group of islands located seventy miles west of Key West at the very end of the Keys, Fort Jefferson, dubbed the "Gibraltar of the Gulf," was conceived as part of the same military buildup that had forti-fied Key West. Begun in 1846, Fort Jefferson was built on Garden Key and is well protected by a clus-ter of seven hazardous coral reefs and a large popu-lation of shark and barracuda. Intended for grand military purposes, Fort Jefferson managed only to serve as a prison during and immediately following the Civil War. Its most famous prisoner was Dr. Sam-uel Mudd, who treated Abraham Lincoln's assas-sin, John Wilkes Booth. The island is now a National Monument and a sanctuary for wild birds and a wide variety of marine life.

Early Nineteenth Century Growth

After Key West had been secured by Commodore Porter, it began to attract its unique population. Previously home to Spaniards, Britons, and (proba-bly) Indians, the island experienced unprece-dented growth in the 1820's and 1830's, bringing together the varied lot of entrepreneurs, pleasure-seekers, and eccentrics who continue to populate the island today.

First to settle in the new U.S. territory were New Englanders, Virginians, and South Carolinians in search of a new and different way of life. Joining them were pro-British Tories who had fled to the British-ruled Bahamas during the American Revo-lution. These settlers incorporated the modern city of Key West in 1828.

The "Conchs"

Along with these settlers of easily determined lineage came the people who came to be known as "conchs" (konks), after the large shellfish that forms an important part of the Key West diet. (Today, all Key Westers are known as conchs. Residents of the island not born there are known as "freshwater conchs" until they have lived there for seven years, at which time they become "honorary conchs.") The original conchs were descended from English Cockney fishermen who plied their trade throughout the American colonies and landed in Key West following the Revolutionary War.

The story of the conchs began in 1646 when Captain William Sayle, a British territorial governor from Bermuda, claimed to have been granted, by Parliament, no less, his very own island in the Bahamas. Although no record of this grant has ever been found, Sayle and a band of so-called Eleutheran Adventurers sailed to the Bahamas to found a colony "where every man might enjoy his own opinion or religion without control or question."

Their destination was an island named Segatoo by Christopher Columbus. They changed the name to Eleuthera, but the island eventually became known as Abaco. The island's politics were laissez-faire from the very beginning, and it soon became a haven for runaway slaves, revolutionaries, and religious zealots, all of whom found a niche on Abaco. One legend says that the conchs got their name when they said that they would rather "eat conchs" than pay the taxes levied against them by the British Crown. Why this was regarded as such an outlandish statement is not explained; conch has since become a staple of the Key West diet.

When Britain gained control of Florida in 1763, large numbers of Britons, largely Cockneys seeking a better life, moved to the new colony, only to be forced out in 1783 when Florida was returned to Spain. Having spent a generation in the tropics, most of the settlers moved to other parts of the West Indies, including Abaco. Eventually, many conchs came to the Florida Keys, and these settlers were to play a vital role in the development of Key West.

Wrecking

The first major industry established by the conchs on Key West was "wrecking," or salvaging ship-wrecks. The same navigational hazards that had given generations of pirates places to hide continued to wreak havoc on commercial shipping throughout the Keys and the Straits of Florida, creating a lucrative business out of the misfortune of others. In fact, some people believed that many a ship had been lured to its doom by overzealous wreckers eager to make some easy money.

Wrecking was fully sanctioned by law. In 1828 the United States established an official superior court on the island to handle the day-to-day legal affairs of the growing populace. One of the court's most prolific functions was issuing salvage licenses to professional wreckers. The court also ruled that salvage rights to the cargo of a wrecked ship belonged to whoever got there first. Therefore, competition was keen to be the first to reach a new wreck, leading many wreckers to head to sea in the same storms that had created the wrecks they intended to salvage. Such practices led to many disputes among the wreckers, which also had to be ironed out by the court.

Wrecking had always been a profitable business in the West Indies, but the rapid growth of Key West, not to mention its proximity to so many treacherous waterways, made the island the capital of the region's wrecking business almost overnight. Wreckers from Nassau and Havana set up shop in Key West. In particularly good years (or particularly bad, depending upon one's point of view), bidders spent more than $1 million on items salvaged by the wreckers. In 1846 alone, wreckers recovered $1.6 million worth of goods. Wrecking continued to be a major industry until 1852, when a system of lighthouses and blinking reef lights made sailing the Keys much safer.

Prosperity

In the 1830's Key West was the wealthiest city per capita in the United States. The sudden and massive influx of industrious entrepreneurs in the 1820's had created a boomtown on what had been an irregularly populated chunk of coral with no obvious natural resources. In fact, resources were there, but like wrecks they needed to be exploited properly.

One hidden resource was the vast quantity of natural sponge growing in the waters around the island. Conchs dominated this industry for decades, developing an ingenious method whereby they hooked sponges from depths of up to sixty feet without even venturing into the water. A small community of Greek spongers threatened the conchs' share of the trade by diving directly to the sponges, using weighted diving shoes that allowed them to stay longer on the bottom and harvest several sponges at once. The conchs clung to their old method, believing that the diving shoes worn by the Greeks harmed the sponge beds. At one point, conchs burned the boats of the Greek divers, and the Florida legislature eventually banned diving for sponges in the Keys, leaving the conchs to their tried-and-true method. A case of blight nearly destroyed the sponge beds in 1940 and several times thereafter, quickly shrinking the local sponging industry.

Civil War Years

Key West was held by Union forces for the duration of the Civil War, despite its claim as the southernmost city in the continental United States. Even so, sentiment among the islanders ran highly in favor of the Confederacy. The islanders' independent streak was thoroughly tested during this period, for Key West served as an important base for blockade runners loyal to the Confederacy. True, the presence of Union naval forces on the island made things difficult, but many of the conchs challenged the blockade anyway. Scores of blockade runners were captured and tried in Key West during the war.

The Civil War ended in 1865, but another war, the Cuban Revolution, began in 1868, sending a massive wave of Cuban immigrants into Key West, adding another layer to the Key West demographic. By 1868, Cubans were already a mixed lot, with Spanish, African, and indigenous influences. They brought with them their religions, their customs and cuisines, and, most importantly for Key West, their legendary love of good cigars.

Cigar Industry

The first cigar factory in Key West was established in 1831 by William H. Wall. In most cases, the term "factory" is misleading, as the *chinchares* (called "buckeyes" by Americans) were mostly small, home-based businesses. The first Cubans to come to Key West in 1868 established their own *chinchares*, and in 1869 a Spaniard named Vicente Martinez Ibor, owner of El Principe de Gales cigar factory in Havana, moved his operations to Key

West as a means of escaping persecution by Spanish authorities unhappy with his sympathy for the independence movement.

Ibor's move was followed by the influx of thousands of other cigar manufacturers from Cuba, and they soon turned Key West into one of the world's most important cigar manufacturing centers. At first, manufacturers returned to Cuba after making some money in Key West, but it did not take long for them to change their tactics and begin to return to Cuba only long enough to prepare to take their families back to Key West. In addition to the greater personal freedom gained by establishing residence in the United States, the Cubans also profited from not having to pay import duties on their cigars and from freedom from La Liga, the Cuban cigar manufacturing union.

The cigar workers, however, had different ideas about the desirability of unions. Shortly after the industry was established on the island, so were unions, becoming the first unions in the state of Florida. Inevitably, there was a major strike, called in 1889 to demand an increase in wages. The strikers won their raise early in 1890, but struck again in 1894 when their employers refused to stop importing labor from elsewhere. By the turn of the century the cigar business had almost ceased to exist in Key West, having transferred en masse to Tampa, a migration that had begun in 1886 following the devastating fire that destroyed almost half of the island and a large portion of the cigar industry. Still, the height of the Key West cigar business was achieved in 1890, when twelve thousand workers (of a total population of eighteen thousand) produced one hundred million cigars, making Key West the undisputed cigar manufacturing center of the United States.

Cuba's Revolutionary Movement

While the first Cuban revolutionary movement had been unsuccessful, Key West served as a handy staging area for the plotters of the subsequent War of Cuban Independence in the 1890's. The leader of the revolution, José Martí y Pérez, established residence on the island during the cigar industry boom. In conjunction with the Central Junta, based in New York, Martí planned the Patricio Revolucionario Cubano and on April 14, 1895, set forth from Key West to Cuba accompanied by Cuban General Máximo Gómez y Báez and a small army, beginning the revolution. During the fighting that followed, Key West provided a safe haven not only for refugees from the war but also for the obligatory horde of journalists assigned to cover it. When the Spanish-American War broke out in 1898, Key West served as an important U.S. naval base.

Building a Land Route
Key West's relative isolation and inaccessibility had always been its greatest blessing and its greatest curse. Isolation allowed the islanders to create a distinct society of their own with little interference from the outside, but the same isolation also forced islanders to take what they could get. Not just any industry could establish itself in Key West. All travel and commerce had to be done by boat, and relatively few people could get into Key West without booking passage with somebody else. As the island prospered, it became apparent that a land route to the island was needed.

In terms of turn-of-the-century technology, such an engineering feat was without peer, and it was left to a very wealthy visionary to make the dream a reality. Industrialist Henry M. Flagler, one of John D. Rockefeller's partners in Standard Oil, proposed extending the Florida East Coast Railway across the Keys from the mainland all the way to Key West. Skeptics immediately dubbed this plan "Flagler's Folly," to which Flagler responded "All you have to do is to build one concrete arch, and then another, and pretty soon you'll find yourself in Key West."

Construction on the railway began in 1906 and was quickly stalled by a hurricane that killed one hundred thirty workers. Flagler insisted that work continue, and in 1909 another hurricane destroyed forty miles of already-laid track. On January 22, 1912, the Overseas Extension finally opened. The railway stretched a full one hundred miles, hopping from Key to Key and covering twenty-five miles on land and seventy-five miles over water at a final cost of fifty million dollars and seven hundred lives.

World War I vastly increased the amount of military activity on the island, with surface ships, submarines and airplanes all stationed there. The island's strategic location on the Straits was crucial to the safety of the Gulf of Mexico. Inventor Thomas Edison carried out experiments with the first depth charges while in the Keys.

Prohibition and Depression
Prohibition, enacted in 1919, was roundly ignored in Key West. With Cuba, one of the world's largest producers of rum, only ninety miles away, illegal liquor was readily available on the island and restaurant and cafe owners made only the weakest of attempts to hide their patrons' activities from local authorities. Prohibition was still in force in 1931 when Ernest Hemingway, a notable drinker, first took up residence on the island. Rumrunning became something of a sport in Key West, with the activities of bootleggers and U.S. authorities adding still more color to the island's image.

The Great Depression took an especially heavy toll on Key West. In 1934, the city was officially bankrupt and approximately 80 percent of its residents were on some form of government relief. In July, 1934, the Key West City Council passed a resolution petitioning the governor of Florida to declare a state of emergency on the island. In response to this request, the Florida Emergency Relief Administration was instructed to find a way to assist the economically shattered community. As with most other ideas, the philosophy of the New Deal was destined to take a peculiar twist in Key West.

The answer to the problems of Key West, the state surmised, lay in its potential as an upscale resort town—a fitting rival to Havana, Nassau, and Bermuda. Buildings were renovated, beaches created, and hotels reopened. Residents contributed some two million hours of labor to clean and beautify the city's streets and public areas. As frivolous as it may have seemed initially, the experiment became a huge success, reinvigorating the local economy and paving the way for the tourist development that has grown on the island ever since. The program became regarded as one of the most interesting experiments in community planning ever devised, and the Florida Emergency Relief Administration quickly transplanted unemployed artists to the island and provided them with the funding necessary to further enhance Key West's appeal to tourists.

In 1935, disaster struck Key West when a Labor Day hurricane swept through the Keys, sparing Key West, but ruining much of the railroad that had done so much to broaden the nature of life on the small island. The railway company, already deeply in debt, abandoned what remained of the extension and moved its sea ferry operation to the Atlantic coast, near Fort Lauderdale. Key West's local fishing industry, lacking transportation to the markets of the mainland, was destroyed.

In 1936 the railway's right-of-way was taken over by the Monroe County Toll Bridge Commission and construction began on an extension of U.S. Route 1, to be called the Overseas Highway. Utilizing a combination of new bridges and some left over from the railroad, the highway opened to the public in 1938 and remains in service to this day.

World War II and the Conch Republic

World War II saw another military buildup on the island, when a seaplane base, Boca Chica Air Station, and a naval hospital were established at Key West. Key West's military history is reflected not only in the physical evidence of its former presence, but also by the presence of a large number of retired military personnel on the island—yet another demographic added to the Key West mix.

The peculiar character of the residents of Key West has been exaggerated, as with most such stereotypes, but they are undoubtedly the keepers of a genuinely distinctive lifestyle. For example, in 1982, when U.S. government authorities began a major campaign to curtail drug smuggling in the Straits of Florida, certain conchs responded by declaring Key West the "Conch Republic," and seceding from the Union. Naturally, the Conch Republic quickly collapsed, but not before making a last-minute plea for "foreign aid." Reminders of the short-lived republic can be seen in Key West today on such items as T-shirts and other souvenirs.

Architecture as a Key to History

Simply by looking at the architecture, visitors to Old Town will quickly understand the varied demographics that built the city. Primarily one-and-a-half- and two-and-a-half-story frame buildings called Conch houses, the structures drew their inspiration from Spanish, Victorian, and Creole designs. Very few of the older buildings on Key West were designed by trained architects, but were built by self-taught "carpenter architects" who adapted their designs to suit their own tastes. Many buildings are decorated with carved pieces of wood salvaged from wrecked ships, for example. Interior furnishings are equally eclectic, as everything in Key West came from somewhere else.

The Conch houses are ideally adapted to the rigors of life on Key West. Constructed entirely with such archaic techniques as dovetail joints, the fact that the buildings can withstand hurricane-force winds is borne out simply by the fact that so many of them have been standing since the early 1800's. Most buildings are equipped with extra-thick shutters to provide protection in high winds and all utilize cisterns in which to catch rainwater, usually from a pitched roof.

Literary Associations

Many notable writers have spent part of their careers in Key West, both deriving inspiration from and adding to the eccentric character of the island. The most famous of these was Ernest Hemingway, who wrote *A Farewell to Arms* and other works while in residence between 1931 and 1940. Key West also provided the setting for some of Hemingway's short stories and novels, including *To Have and Have Not*. Gore Vidal, Robert Frost, Wallace Stevens, and Kurt Vonnegut, Jr., are also associated with Key West, as is Tennessee Williams, who lived at 1431 Duncan Street from 1949 until his death in 1983. Hemingway's Spanish colonial house, at 907 Whitehead Street, has been declared a National Historic Landmark. The grounds are still home to many six-toed cats directly descended from Hemingway's pets.

Other notable historic buildings include Audubon House, located at 205 Whitehead Street. Built in the early 1800's for one of Key West's most prominent wreckers, Captain John H. Geiger, the house was restored in commemoration of its use in several portrayals of the gray kingbird and white-crowned pigeon painted by naturalist John James Audubon when he visited Key West in 1832.

Museums

Key West is also home to many fine museums dedicated to the preservation of the island's unique history. Among these are Mel Fisher Maritime Heritage Society, featuring artifacts salvaged from a Spanish treasure galleon that sank nearby in 1622; the Wrecker's Museum, featuring photographs and other artifacts from the wrecking era; the East Martello Gallery and Museum, located in the East Martello Tower and featuring information about the tower, the city's sponge and cigar industries, and an art gallery; the Key West Lighthouse Museum, specializing in lighthouses and offering a magnificent view from the top of its 110-foot tower, erected in 1847; Fort Zachary Taylor, a major repository of Civil War artifacts; Heritage House and Robert Frost Cottage, built on the site of the first freshwater well on the island, and the home of the late poet; and Curry Mansion, an elaborate 1905 home constructed by William Curry, a successful wrecker and Florida's first millionaire.

—*John A. Flink*

For Further Information:

In addition to the sources below, Key West is covered in most current Florida travel guides, and the Historic Florida Keys Preservation Board can provide even the most arcane information to determined researchers. The works of Key West's most famous resident, Ernest Hemingway, are available in various editions.

Federal Writers' Project. *Florida: A Guide to the Southernmost State.* New York: Oxford University Press, 1939. A product of the Works Progress Administration. The guide is a very well-researched, straightforward source. The WPA produced many such guides during the late 1930's, all of which, while somewhat dated, are excellent reference sources.

Kennedy, Stetson. *Palmetto Country.* New York: Duell, Sloan and Pearce, 1942. Provides a wealth of historical and anecdotal information on the entire region surrounding Key West, including mainland Florida, the Bahamas, and Cuba. It is short on hard facts but long on illuminating stories.

Langley, Wright. *Key West and the Spanish-American War.* Key West, Fla.: Langley Press, 1998. Describes the role of Key West and the rest of Florida of the Spanish-American War of 1898. Illustrated, including maps.

St. Augustine

Date: First colonized by Spain in 1565

Relevant issues: American Indian history, European settlement, military history

Significance: This resort and retirement town has a rich historic past as the oldest permanent white settlement in the United States. Historic points of interest include Castillo de San Marcos National Monument, which is the oldest standing fort in the United States, and the restored Spanish colonial historic district.

Location: On the Atlantic coast in northeastern Florida

Site Office:
St. Augustine Historical Society
271 Charlotte Street
St. Augustine, FL 32084
ph.: (904) 824-2872
Web site: www.oldcity.com/oldhouse/historical
.html

St. Augustine lays claim to being the oldest continuously settled city in the United States. During its turbulent history, St. Augustine has been under the jurisdiction of several governments—the first Spanish period (1565-1763), the British period (1763-1784), the second Spanish period (1784-1821), and, finally, the U.S. period (1821-present).

Peopling of Florida

The first people to settle in what is now Florida were Indians who arrived more than ten thousand years ago. The first Europeans did not arrive until the late fifteenth century. John Cabot, sailing under the English flag, was said to have reached these shores in the 1490's. Amerigo Vespucco, according to other accounts, also may have been an early visitor. Juan Ponce de León is credited, however, with being the official "discoverer" of Florida. Whether he was seeking his fortune in gold or the mythical "fountain of youth," which was said to possess miraculous powers of rejuvenation, is unclear, but he did name the peninsula Florida, claiming it for Spain.

Ponce de León left Puerto Rico with three ships on March 3, 1513. He sighted land on April 2, and named it La Florida. By all accounts, he seems to have landed somewhere between the mouth of the St. Johns River and Cape Canaveral. He made a second expedition to Florida in 1521. On this trip he met with hostile Indians and was mortally wounded when an arrow pierced through his protective cloak of armor. He died in Cuba shortly after the attack.

After other failed attempts at colonization, the Spanish government discontinued further expeditions. When the French began to express an inter-

The Castillo de San Marcos in St. Augustine. (Visit Florida)

est, however, the Spanish king, Philip II, reconsidered his decision. The news of a French settlement at Port Royal, in what is now South Carolina, persuaded Philip to order the Spanish naval commander, Pedro Menéndez de Avilés, to remove the French and establish a colony in Florida.

Spanish Occupation

On September 6, 1565, Menéndez arrived at the northeast coast of Florida. He called the port St. Augustine, in honor of the patron saint of his hometown. Two days later, on September 8, Menéndez claimed Florida under the banner of Spain. In less than three months, with help from bad weather, he rid Florida of the French presence. He also established the Ordinances of Governance, a code of laws designed to encourage the development and growth of towns. He also set up councils, or *cabildos*, to collect taxes.

Despite these efforts, St. Augustine was constantly assaulted by French privateers and faced perpetual threat of attack by Indians. It was not until the 1580's that conditions stabilized and the Spanish settlers' lives resumed a normal pattern. It was a short respite, however. In 1586, Englishman Sir Francis Drake attacked and burned the town. The Spaniards rebuilt, with assistance from other Spanish colonists who moved there from Santa Elena, Florida.

British Intrusion

In 1672 the settlers began construction of Castillo de San Marcos, a stone fort to provide protection against attack. In the 1680's periodic troubles with the Indians and the English placed the town on alert. In 1702, the situation came to a head when the English governor of Carolina, James Moore, assembled an Anglo-Indian army with plans to take

St. Augustine. By November of that year, the siege of St. Augustine was well under way. When four Spanish ships sent by the governor of Havana reached the shore, the English retreated. In their wake, they left behind a smoldering town. Buildings, homes, even the Governor's House were destroyed. Later, in 1740, and again in 1743, the British general James Edward Oglethorpe, founder of Georgia, led two unsuccessful assaults on the town.

During the 1750's, the French and Indian War erupted between France and Britain. Britain prohibited exports to all neutral ports, including St. Augustine. With trade between Spanish and British ports suspended, St. Augustinians faced the prospect of starvation. In 1760, the British captured Havana and exchanged Cuba for Florida. In February, 1763, Britain and Spain signed the Treaty of Paris, which made Florida a British possession. Britain then divided the territory into East and West Florida.

It would prove an important treaty with great consequences for the future of St. Augustine. Thousands of residents fled when they heard the news. Although the British encouraged the Spanish inhabitants to stay, many could not accept the change and decided to settle in Cuba or Mexico. Public officials, clergy, and ordinary citizens left. For all intents and purposes, the British assumed control of a ghost town.

British Administration

Gradually, the new owners began to put their stamp on the town. In August, 1764, Colonel James Grant, the first governor of British East Florida, arrived. The Scots-born Grant had fought against the Indians and the French in Ohio and Canada, and against the Cherokees in South Carolina. Prior to his assignment in East Florida, he had participated in the siege of Havana. Grant proved a popular governor. He was also one of the few colonial officials of that era to forge peaceful relations with the neighboring Indians. Further, he promoted the development of plantations in East Florida, leading to growth and a new era of prosperity.

During the Revolutionary War, St. Augustine remained loyal to the Crown and even enjoyed a period of calm and relative prosperity. Thousands of loyalists from neighboring Georgia and the Carolinas settled in the northern portion of Florida and made clear their feelings toward the "rebel" Americans by burning in effigy such prominent figures as John Hancock and Samuel Adams. The British used the Castillo, which they renamed Fort St. Mark, as a military base. Throughout the duration of the war, East Florida endured various invasion attempts from Georgia. In the summer of 1778, however, East Florida forces turned the tables, this time invading Georgia as far as Savannah. The northern frontier of Florida was, thus, protected.

Return of the Spanish

In the meantime, refugees continued to flood into St. Augustine. Carolina rebels, who had been imprisoned at St. Augustine and then paroled, further aggravated the housing shortage. Britain at this time was also involved in hostilities with Spain, and in May, 1781, neighboring West Florida fell to the Spanish. Five months later, George Washington defeated the British general Lord Cornwallis at the Battle of Yorktown, which effectively ended the Revolutionary War. While the Americans celebrated their victory, St. Augustinians shuddered, fearing an imminent attack.

In May of the following year, Sir Guy Carleton, the British commander, ordered the evacuation of both Savannah and St. Augustine. The news came as a crushing blow. Residents were devastated and felt betrayed. Two months later, Carleton changed his mind, instead claiming East Florida as a haven for refugees from Savannah and Charleston. Thousands came, many of them in ill-health and with no funds.

Despite the daily turmoil, living conditions continued to improve, and some semblance of a cultural life developed. St. Augustine's first theater opened in March, 1783, and its first newspaper, *The East-Florida Gazette*, had already began publishing one month earlier. Abruptly, everything changed in June, 1783, when East Florida was returned to Spain, under the terms of peace negotiated between the Spanish and British. With the return to Spanish authority, most of the British residents fled to the Bahamas, Jamaica, the West Indies, Bermuda, or the United States. Evacuations began almost immediately. Meanwhile, Americans flooded in, taking advantage of Spanish land grants.

The transition period was chaotic. Bands of outlaws raided the area, especially the plantations north of St. Augustine, looking for cattle, horses, and slaves. Some of the previous Spanish residents, who had fled when Britain assumed power, returned. A few Britons chose to stay, even though they were forced to take an oath of allegiance to the new government and convert to Catholicism. Later, they were allowed to remain Protestant, but the oath was still a requirement for residency.

Spanish-speaking settlers were encouraged to come to East Florida. Generous inducements were offered to residents of the first Spanish period to return, in the form of extra land, stipends, and compensation for former estates. Some accepted the offers, and some immigrants came directly from Spain.

American Intervention

In March, 1812, a plan to rid Florida of Spanish influence received the approval of U.S. president James Madison. Rebel forces, calling themselves "patriots," came to the outskirts of St. Augustine. Florida governor Juan José de Estrada refused to surrender. The following month about one hundred U.S. soldiers came to aid the rebels, but Madison soon withdrew support for their actions and the troops left.

Two years later, the Treaty of Ghent ended the War of 1812. The treaty allowed portions of West Florida that the U.S. had seized during the war to remain in that country's hands. Meanwhile, Spain's hold over the rest of Florida continued to deteriorate. The United States wanted to annex the rest of Florida, but negotiations dragged on for years. Finally, in March, 1821, President James Monroe appointed General Andrew Jackson the military governor of the entire territory of Florida. On July 21 of that year, the Spanish flag was lowered over Castillo de San Marcos and the American flag raised over Fort Marion, the fort's new name. Yet St. Augustine remained very much a cosmopolitan town with English, Spanish, and French as its languages.

The first assembly of the governing body, the Territorial Legislative Council, met in Pensacola in the early 1820's. Pensacola had been the capital of West Florida, St. Augustine of East Florida. One of the first decisions the council had to make was to select a more central location for the new territorial capital. Ultimately, Tallahassee, a former Indian site that consisted of little more than a few huts at the time, was chosen.

Seminole Wars

Meanwhile, relations between the United States and the Indians worsened, escalating into the Seminole War. Under the 1823 Treaty of Moultrie Creek, the Seminoles had exchanged all claims to Florida in exchange for four million acres in the central part of the territory. The treaty evaporated in a series of raids and retributions, and in late 1835 the situation erupted into open warfare. Despite the fighting, St. Augustine prospered during the war. Soldiers and refugees poured into St. Augustine, there was a building boom, and speculators looked at the town with promise. The war finally petered out in 1842.

In 1845, Florida entered the union as a slave state. Subsequently, it joined the Confederacy when the U.S. Civil War broke out. From 1862 to 1865, however, Union forces controlled St. Augustine.

Late Nineteenth Century Revival

Economic lethargy and decay in the immediate post-Civil War era gave way to a revival of sorts the following decade as the orange crop produced a short-lived boom. St. Augustine also had long been of interest to outsiders. Journalists and fiction writers frequently wrote about the city. The erection of the St. Augustine Hotel in 1869 foreshadowed the town's future role as a prominent tourist center, while the development of the railroad meant it would be easier for people to visit, especially northerners seeking a respite from the long and bitter winter months.

In 1884, one of the winter guests was Henry M. Flagler, a cofounder of Standard Oil Company and one of the richest men in the United States. He returned a year later with an ambitious plan to build the best and biggest resort hotel in Florida, one that would rival any hotel in the world.

In January, 1888, Flagler opened the Hotel Ponce de León. It was a lavish structure designed in a style that was called Spanish Renaissance but borrowed freely from other architectural styles and epochs—a dash of Roman motifs here, a smattering of medieval details there. Nearby, Flagler built a smaller hotel, the Alcazar, to handle overflow business. A winter resident from Boston, Franklin W. Smith, attempted to erect his own hotel, the Casa Monica, but the expenses proved too great, and he eventually sold out to Flagler. Flagler renamed it the Cordova.

In essence, Flagler was a one-man enterprise zone. He also purchased a railroad on the outskirts of town so that his guests would have easy access to the town. His other businesses in St. Augustine and vicinity included a baseball field, a laundry, and a dairy. He helped build four churches. In addition, he was the benefactor of a hospital, owned the building that housed the local government, built a wharf, operated a real estate firm, and established a residential subdivision near his hotels.

The townspeople had mixed feelings about Flagler. Some supported his wildly ambitious plans; others resented the presence of the opinionated, stubborn outsider who wanted everything done in his own fashion. St. Augustine's days as a mecca for the wealthy and elite were numbered, however. The development of other Florida resort towns soon undercut St. Augustine's status as the "Newport of the South." Ironically, it was Flagler himself who was partly to blame, for it was he who began to look elsewhere—to Palm Beach specifically—to establish a new dream town.

Rather than the flashy winter resort town that Flagler envisioned, St. Augustine soon settled into a considerably more sedate year-round community. For many it became the ideal retirement home. The Flagler era officially ended with the entrepreneur's death on May 20, 1913.

St. Augustinian History

St. Augustinians have always been aware of their town's rich historical associations. As early as the 1880's, the St. Augustine Historical Society was founded to preserve the town's historical sites and structures. In 1924, Fort Marion reverted to its original Spanish name and was designated a National Historic Landmark as Castillo de San Marcos National Monument. Fort Matanzas, which had been built south of St. Augustine as an outpost of the Castillo, also received National Historic Landmark status, as did the city gate. In the mid-1930's, there was talk of restoring the town to the glory of its Spanish days, using funds from the Washington, D.C.-based Carnegie Institution. The outbreak of World War II delayed plans, but on June 19, 1959, the St. Augustine Historical Restoration and Preservation Committee was established. It was later renamed the Historic St. Augustine Preservation Board.

Funded by a private organization, the commission focused its attention on physical restoration. It initially acquired thirty-four parcels of land and restored or reconstructed twenty-nine buildings. The second phase consisted of twenty restorations. The restored area is centered around St. George Street, and features tour guides costumed as early Spanish settlers. The hotels developed by Henry Flagler also have been preserved and put to new uses. In 1968, the former Hotel Ponce de León became Flagler College, and the former Cordova Hotel was transformed into the St. Johns County Court House. The Alcazar Hotel houses the Lightner Museum and the St. Augustine municipal offices. Another site of interest is the Fountain of Youth Park, north of St. Augustine. It features a well in a grottolike setting and is reputedly the "fountain of youth" sought by Ponce de León.

—*June Skinner Sawyers*

For Further Information:

Federal Writers' Project. *Florida: A Guide to the Southernmost State.* New York: Oxford University Press, 1939. A general history of the state.

Landers, Jane. *Gracia Real de Santa Teresa de Mose: A Free Black Town in Spanish Colonial Florida.* Washington, D.C.: American Historical Association, 1990. A history of African Americans in St. Augustine when it was a Spanish colony from 1784 to 1821.

Lyon, Eugene. *The Enterprise of Florida: Pedro Menéndez de Avilés and the Spanish Conquest of 1565-1568.* Gainesville: University Presses of Florida, 1976.

Martin, Sidney. *Florida's Flagler.* Athens: University of Georgia Press, 1949. For information on Flagler and his era.

TePaske, John Jay. *The Governorship of Spanish Florida, 1700-1763.* Durham, N.C.: Duke University Press, 1964.

Verrill, A. Hyatt. *Romantic and Historic Florida.* New York: Dodd Mead, 1936. Another general history of the state.

Waterbury, Jean Parker. *The Oldest City: St. Augustine Saga of Survival.* St. Augustine, Fla.: St. Augustine Historical Society, 1983. This anthology is the best and most comprehensive history of St. Augustine throughout all its various historical periods.

Wright, J. Leitch, Jr. *British St. Augustine.* St. Augustine, Fla.: Historic St. Augustine Preservation Board, 1975.

—————. *Florida in the American Revolution.* Gaines-ville: University Presses of Florida, 1975. More specialized studies of the town as well as the greater East Florida area.

Other Historic Sites

Bethune Home

Location: Daytona Beach, Volusia County

Relevant issues: African American history, education, social reform

Statement of significance: This two-story frame house belonged to Mary McLeod Bethune (1875-1955), the civil rights leader, administrator, educator, adviser to presidents, and consultant to the United Nations; it is on the campus of the school she established in 1904. This was her home from its construction in the 1920's until Bethune's death.

Bok Tower Gardens

Location: Lake Wales, Polk County

Relevant issues: Cultural history, literary history

Statement of significance: Edward Bok's Mountain Lake Sanctuary and Singing Tower were created as the ultimate gift he could present to the people of America, his adopted land. A native of the Netherlands, Bok came to fame as the editor of *The Ladies' Home Journal;* he was also a Pulitzer Prize-winning author, local and national civic leader, and philanthropist. The Sanctuary and Tower were dedicated, on Bok's behalf, for visitation by the American people by President Calvin Coolidge on February 1, 1929.

British Fort

Location: Sumatra, Franklin County

Relevant issues: African American history, American Indian history, military history

Statement of significance: This is the site of a fort established by the British in 1814 in conjunction with the War of 1812. After the war, the fort became known as "Negro Fort" because of the runaway slaves who occupied it. In 1816, the U.S. Army destroyed the fort, helping precipitate the First Seminole War. It also contains the site of Fort Gadsen, occupied by U.S. troops from 1818 to 1821.

Crystal River Site

Location: Crystal River, Citrus County

Relevant issues: American Indian history

Statement of significance: Consisting of ten temple, burial, shell, and sand mounds, Crystal River Site is a complex ceremonial center and burial site. Occupation at the site occurred during the Deptford, Weeden Island, and Safety Harbor prehistoric periods. This site has played a significant role in the development of archaeological method and theory by helping explain the relationship between early mound-building groups in the Gulf of Mexico coastal areas of Florida and the Hopewellian cultures in the Ohio River Valley. By focusing the debates in archaeological scholarship over the possibilities of direct communication between the Gulf Coast area of the Eastern United States and Mesoamerican cultures, Crystal River has also made significant contributions in the field of archaeology.

Dade Battlefield

Location: Bushnell, Sumter County

Relevant issues: American Indian history, military history

Statement of significance: This was the site of the first military confrontation of the Second Seminole War (1835-1842). It was symbolic of Chief Osceola's concerted plan of resistance to President Andrew Jackson's removal policies. It is now part of Dade Battlefield Memorial State Park.

Fort San Marcos De Apalache

Location: St. Marks, Wakulla County

Relevant issues: American Indian history, European settlement, military history

Statement of significance: This was the site of successive wooden and masonry fortifications occupied throughout the Spanish and British colonial periods, and by U.S. troops during the Second Seminole War. Capture of the Spanish fort by Andrew Jackson in 1818 was instrumental in events leading to the American acquisition of Florida in 1821.

Hurston House

Location: Fort Pierce, St. Lucie County

Relevant issues: African American history, literary history

Statement of significance: Zora Neale Hurston (1901-1960), writer, folklorist, and anthropologist, was the most noted black female writer of the mid-twentieth century. In addition to her four novels, two books of folklore, and an autobiography, Hurston wrote over fifty short stories and essays; her work, viewed by some as controversial, neither romanticized black folk life nor condemned it. Hurston lived in this little green house while working as a reporter and columnist for the *Fort Pierce Chronicle* in the final years of her life.

Maple Leaf

Location: Mandarin, Duval County

Relevant issues: Civil War, military history, naval history

Statement of significance: The sidewheeler *Maple Leaf* was designed and built in the Marine Railway Shipyard in Kingston, Ontario, and launched in 1851; it worked passenger routes on Lake Ontario prior to being chartered to the U.S. Army in 1862. As an Army transport, *Maple Leaf* steamed up and down the Eastern Seaboard from Virginia to Florida. Early on the morning of April 1, 1864, while returning to Jacksonville from Palatka, Florida, *Maple Leaf* struck a Confederate torpedo and sank quickly; five black crewmen sleeping on the foredeck above the explosion were killed instantly, but the remaining passengers and crew escaped into boats and were saved. During the day, Confederate artillery shelled the visible part of the wreck. After the war, the wreck was moved to deeper water, where it lay forgotten until 1984.

Mar-A-Lago

Location: Palm Beach, Palm Beach County

Relevant issues: Cultural history

Statement of significance: This sprawling, Mediterranean-style villa, home of Marjorie Merriweather Post, exemplifies the baronial way of life of the wealthy who built mansions in Florida during the Florida land boom of the 1920's.

Miami-Biltmore Hotel and Country Club

Location: Coral Gables, Dade County

Relevant issues: Cultural history

Statement of significance: The Miami-Biltmore Hotel and Country Club, one of the most luxurious and modern hotels of its time, opened on January 14, 1926. Designed by the prominent New York architectural firm of Schulze and Weaver, the Miami-Biltmore is Coral Gables' most notable reminder of the Florida land boom and is one of the most important monuments of this era in South Florida.

Okeechobee Battlefield

Location: Okeechobee, Okeechobee County

Relevant issues: American Indian history, military history

Statement of significance: Site of Zachary Taylor's decisive victory on December 25, 1837, which marked the turning point in the Second Seminole War.

Pensacola Naval Air Station Historic District

Location: Pensacola, Escambia County

Relevant issues: Aviation history, military history, naval history

Statement of significance: Established in January, 1914, this was the first permanent U.S. naval air station, first Navy pilot training center, and first U.S. naval installation to send pilots into combat.

Plaza Ferdinand VII

Location: Pensacola, Escambia County

Relevant issues: Political history

Statement of significance: Site of the completion of the formal transfer of Florida from Spain to the United States on July 17, 1821. Andrew Jackson, as newly appointed governor, officially proclaimed the establishment of the Florida Territory.

Ponce de Leon Inlet Light Station

Location: 4931 South Peninsula Drive, Ponce Inlet, Volusia County

Relevant issues: Naval history

Statement of significance: The nation's second-tallest

brick lighthouse, this 175-foot tower was begun in 1884 to mark Mosquito Inlet on the Atlantic coast of Florida. The light station is significant for its association with federal efforts to provide an integrated system of navigational aids to ensure safe maritime transportation. Ponce de Leon is one of the nation's best-preserved light stations, retaining not only its tower (complete with its original Fresnel first-order lens) but also its three keepers' dwellings, oil house, and combination woodshed/privies. The light station has been restored and open to the public since 1982.

Safety Harbor Site

Location: Safety Harbor, Pinellas County
Relevant issues: American Indian history
Statement of significance: This site depicts a late prehistoric and early historic period, representing the Gulf coast Timucua Indian culture at the time of European contact.

Vizcaya

Location: Miami, Dade County
Relevant issues: Business and industry, cultural history
Statement of significance: Vizcaya, which means "an elevated place" in Basque, was completed in 1916 as the winter home for the industrialist James Deering (1859-1925), who made this a showplace of personal fantasy. Deering's fortune was made in the production of farm machinery. A patron of the arts, Deering asked New York painter and designer Paul Chalfin to advise him on his plans for a Florida home; together, the two men created a mélange of Baroque, Rococco, Mannerist, and Louis XIV, adapted to a beach house in South Florida.

Ybor City Historic District

Location: Tampa, Hillsborough County
Relevant issues: Business and industry, Latino history
Statement of significance: Founded in 1886, Ybor City is significant in Spanish American and Cuban American immigration history. The district is also of importance in American industrial history, for it contains the largest collection of buildings related to the cigar industry in America and probably the world. In addition to factories, the district's buildings include workers' housing; the ethnic clubs organized by Ybor City's immigrants, who included Italians and Germans as well as Cubans and Spaniards; and the commercial buildings that served the community. Most buildings date to the first two decades of the twentieth century. Historically, Ybor City was a rare multiethnic and multiracial industrial community in the Deep South and is highly illustrative of manifold aspects of the history of ethnic and race relations.

Georgia

History of Georgia 335
Andersonville 337
Chickamauga and Chattanooga National
    Military Park 340
Fort Frederica 344

Martin Luther King, Jr., Historic District,
    Atlanta. 349
Savannah 353
Stone Mountain 356
Other Historic Sites 359

Atlanta. (Corbis)

History of Georgia

The last of the original thirteen English colonies to be founded, and the largest state east of the Mississippi River, Georgia has twice led its region in being the forerunner of the "New South," first following the Civil War and then during the second half of the twentieth century. A state of immense geographical variation, changing in height from one mile to sea level, it transformed itself from a primarily agricultural state to one that embraced modern manufacturing and technology. Its capital, Atlanta, is one of the largest and fastest-growing cities in the South and a metropolis of truly international distinction.

Early History

In approximately 12,000 B.C.E. the first inhabitants lived along the rivers and coasts of what would become Georgia with a diet of fish and shellfish. They were followed first by nomadic hunters and then by more settled residents who developed agriculture. When Europeans arrived during the mid-1500's, the Native American Cherokee and Creek tribes were dominant in the eastern and coastal areas. Along the coast the Yamacraw, a group of the Creek, were well established. The Chickasaw and Choctaw inhabited the western portion of the territory.

A Native American chief named Guale was the first to make lasting contact with the Europeans, meeting the Spanish soldier Pedro Menéndez de Avilés in 1566. As a result, for a time the entire coastal region was called Guale. British, French, and Spanish competed to make the Native American tribes their allies, with hopes of using them to defend their own colonies and eliminate those of their competitors. After the Yamasee War (1715-1728) nearly destroyed the British colony of Carolina, the British were determined to settle a buffer colony between themselves and the Spanish in Florida. That colony would become Georgia.

Exploration and Settlement

Spain, with strongholds established throughout the Caribbean and in Florida, sent the first European explorers into the area of Georgia. In 1540 Hernando de Soto passed through Georgia on his lengthy and difficult expedition in search of the fabled Seven Cities of Gold, which were rumored to possess wealth in excess of anything yet found in the New World. French Huguenots under Jean Ribaut landed along the coast in 1562, the same year Ribaut sought to colonize the Port Royal region to the north, in what is now South Carolina. Both attempts were failures. In order to strengthen its position and defend its Florida possessions, Spain established a string of missions and forts running along the coast from northern Florida to the sea islands.

The English responded by thrusting south, forcing the Spanish back to St. Augustine. To create a barrier between the Spanish and the rapidly growing colonies to the north, King George II granted a charter for a colony in 1732. General James Edward Oglethorpe, who wished to open the colony for debtors to give them a fresh start on life, was placed in command of the venture. In 1733, with just over one hundred colonists, Oglethorpe arrived at the bluffs of the Savannah River and struck a deal with Yamacraw chief Tomochichi for land along the river. Oglethorpe laid out the city of Savannah with a gridlike pattern of squares, which would remain.

The Spanish threat was effectively ended in 1742 with Oglethorpe's victory at the Battle of Bloody Marsh on Saint Simons Island. Georgia grew rapidly with an economy based on rice, indigo, and cotton. Slavery had been banned in the colony in 1735, but crops were grown best under the plantation system, and in 1749 the slave trade was legalized. The territory up the Savannah River was explored and settled; in 1753 the city of Augusta was founded. In 1754 Georgia became a royal colony.

Revolution and the New Nation

As the colonies moved toward independence, Georgia convened a Provincial Congress in 1775, and its Council of Safety sent delegates to the Continental Congress in Philadelphia. The year following the declaration of American independence,

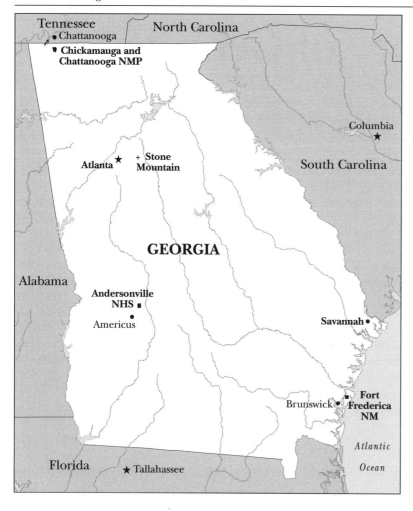

Tennessee
• Chattanooga
North Carolina
■ **Chickamauga and**
Chattanooga NMP

Columbia
★

Atlanta ★ + **Stone**
Mountain

South Carolina

GEORGIA

Alabama

Andersonville
NHS ■
•
Americus

Savannah •

Brunswick • ■ **Fort**
Frederica
NM

Atlantic

Florida ★ Tallahassee

Ocean

moval of the Cherokee and Creek Indians from Georgia. The Creek sold their lands in 1827 and moved to Arkansas. Although the Cherokee had tried to fashion a compromise with the European settlers, the discovery of gold on their territory doomed those efforts. Georgia ordered the removal of the Native Americans in 1832, and six years later the tribe began its Trail of Tears to Indian Territory, now the state of Oklahoma.

One of the most important developments in American history occurred near Savannah in 1793, when Eli Whitney invented the cotton gin. This device automatically separated cotton seed from cotton fiber, a time-consuming task which before had been done only by hand. The cotton gin made possible the booming growth of cotton farming in the South, including Georgia, where the rich soil in central part of the state made the crop highly profitable.

Georgia ratified its first state constitution. In 1778, as the British pursued a southern strategy to pacify the rebellion, their troops seized Savannah. American and French troops were repulsed in a bloody attempt to retake the city, which the British continued to hold until the end of the Revolution.

Georgia became the fourth state to ratify the Constitution, and it joined the Union in 1788, with Augusta, on the Savannah River, as its capital. Its western lands were rapidly developed, and this growth led to the Yazoo fraud, during which members of the state legislature sold 50 million acres to phantom land companies (most of which were owned by the legislators themselves), which resold them to the public. In the end, the federal government had to pay more than $4 million to settle claims from the incident.

The western movement also prompted the re-

Civil War and Reconstruction

In 1861 Georgia joined with seven other southern states and seceded from the Union. Later that year, in the temporary capital of Montgomery, Alabama, Alexander H. Stephens of Georgia was elected vice president of the Confederacy. While Georgia soldiers were fighting along the front lines in Tennessee and Virginia, Union forces bombarded and captured Fort Pulaski at the mouth of the Savannah River and clamped a tight blockade on the Georgia coastline. In 1863, after capturing Chattanooga, Tennessee, a Union army advancing into Georgia was surprised and overcome at the Battle of Chickamauga. The following year, the Federals returned under General William Tecumseh Sherman to strike at the strategic railroad center of Atlanta. After months of siege, Atlanta fell and was burned. Sherman then embarked on his March to the Sea, leaving a swath of destruction through Georgia sixty miles wide and capturing Savannah in December.

Following the war, Georgia, like the rest of the defeated South, entered a period of Reconstruction. The state attempted to rejoin the Union in 1868 but was refused reentry in 1869 because state leaders would not ratify the Fifteenth Amendment, which prohibits denying voting rights because of race. When Georgia complied with this amendment it was readmitted to the Union, in 1870.

During Reconstruction, Georgia began to rebuild its economy, repairing and expanding its railroad system, which had been largely destroyed during the Civil War, and diversifying its agricultural base to include corn, fruit—especially peaches—tobacco, and livestock. However, cotton, which had been a major crop before the Civil War, remained an essential part of the state's economy, and when a boll weevil infestation struck in the 1920's, it was a severe blow to Georgia's farmers and the entire state.

The state was making strides in other areas. In 1879, Henry Grady had become one of the owners of the Atlanta *Constitution*, the state's largest newspaper. As an unofficial spokesperson for Georgia, Grady prophesied the "New South," which would embrace progress, introduce industry and manufacturing, and move away from the wounds of the Civil War. Atlanta took as its symbol the phoenix, since the city had literally risen anew from the ashes of destruction. It became the headquarters of large regional companies, an economic powerhouse in the Southeast, and a literal symbol of Grady's New South. Among the local success stories was the rise of Coca-Cola, invented by pharmacist John Styth Pemberton in 1886 and, after a few years, the most popular soft drink in the nation.

The Modern Age

During the 1940's and 1950's, manufacturing in Georgia passed agriculture, forestry, and fishing as the major source of income. Textile mills, in particular, became a major force in the state's economy. Georgia became one of the world's largest sources of kaolin and fullers earth—the first used in producing paper and dishware, the second used for cat litter. High-quality granite was also mined in the upper portion of the state. Meanwhile, the growth of banking and financial institutions continued to

the point that Atlanta became known as the "Wall Street of the South," while businesses involved with modern technology also contributed to the growth of the state.

Georgia's passage through the civil rights era was aided by a tradition of moderation among its political leadership. From 1877 on, the state had only Democratic governors. Although Democrat Lester Maddox was elected governor in 1966 with an openly segregationist agenda, broad-minded Atlanta mayor Ivan Allen and progressive governors such as Ellis Arnall, Carl Sanders, and Jimmy Carter were more representative and helped bring the state through a potentially difficult period. Carter in 1976 was elected president of the United States. In 1972 Maynard Jackson was elected mayor of Atlanta, the first African American chosen to lead a large southern city. Also that year, Andrew Young became the first African American elected to Congress from Georgia since the end of Reconstruction. This period of Georgia's history is regarded as marking the birth of the second "New South," which combined economic development with racial progress.

Georgia's economy is strong, with its deep-water port of Savannah one of the most active on the East Coast. Atlanta's Hartsville International Airport is one of the largest and best equipped in the world. Natural resources contribute to the state's revenues.
—*Michael Witkoski*

Andersonville

Date: Established in 1864

Relevant issues: Civil War, disasters and tragedies, military history

Significance: Andersonville was an infamous prison camp during the Civil War. The site also includes the National Prisoner of War Museum, which displays artifacts and exhibits about prisoners of war in all American conflicts.

Location: Ten miles north of Americus and twenty miles from Plains

Site Office:

Andersonville National Historic Site
Route 1, Box 800
Andersonville, GA 31711
ph.: (912) 924-0343
Web site: www.nps.gov/ande/

In the last year of the Civil War, the Confederacy built a prison in Sumter County, Georgia. Between February, 1864, and April, 1865, a total of thirty thousand Union prisoners were confined in a twenty-six-acre stockade. The consequent overcrowding, inadequate supplies, and poor sanitary conditions resulted in widespread disease and a high mortality rate. More than twelve thousand federal prisoners perished over a thirteen-month period. The commandant of Andersonville, Major Henry Wirz, was taken into custody shortly after the conclusion of the war and tried before a military commission. The court found Wirz guilty of violating the laws and customs of war and sentenced him to death.

Establishment of Andersonville

Authorities established Fort Sumter, better known as Andersonville, because overcrowding continually plagued the prison system in Richmond, Virginia. The commanding general of the Army of Northern Virginia, Robert E. Lee, wanted the prison moved to another area because the 11,650 inmates caused a drain on the city's food supply. The already inadequate transportation system, according to Lee, should be devoted to the needs of the citizens and not federal prisoners. In November, 1863, Confederate secretary of war James A. Seddon ordered Brigadier General John H. Winder, the provost marshal for Confederate prisons east of the Mississippi, to locate a new site. Captain Richard Bayley Winder, the general's second cousin, selected an area near Americus, Georgia, as a possible location for a camp.

Union prisoners also proved to be a liability in case of an enemy attack. Lee believed the guard forces at Richmond were stretched beyond their limits, as the need for replacements at the front lines kept increasing every month. The threat to security seemed imminent as two Union columns, under the respective commands of General Judson Kilpatrick and Colonel Ulric Dahlgren, marched to Richmond from February 28 to March 4, 1864, for the purpose of freeing the prisoners at Libby Prison. The advance stopped, however, when Dahlgren died in an ambush, and the columns never united. The urgent need for a new prison was apparent after the failed raid, and Confederate officials pushed forward with construction.

Andersonville seemed the perfect spot for a prison because the location was far away from fighting lines and advancing federal armies. It was sixty miles from Macon and approximately one hundred miles from the Florida border. The first batch of five hundred prisoners arrived on February 25, 1864, while the stockade was still under construction. Building the stockade took another month because, although Captain Winder's superiors said he could get help with labor and supplies from farmers in the surrounding countryside, the rural population objected to the construction of a camp holding Yankees. Winder then received permission from Richmond authorities to obtain building supplies. The delay prevented work on the stockade until January, 1864. In order to thwart escape attempts, Winder placed artillery in an unfinished area of the stockade until its completion in late March.

Prison Stockade and the "Deadline"

The stockade of the prison, formed by pine logs twenty feet in height and shaped to a thickness of eight to twelve inches, enclosed sixteen acres of land (later enlarged to twenty-six). Platform walkways enabled guards to stand watch in waist-high boxes located at strategic points around the stockade.

Controlling inmates in this situation was impossible because the guards, armed with single-shot muskets, could not stop potential escapees. Instead, prison officials relied on a crude wooden fence fifteen feet within the stockade to mark the limit where prisoners could venture. The design of the "deadline" reduced escapes by keeping the prisoners away from the stockade wall. If prisoners approached the "deadline," guards warned them to leave the area; but if the inmates refused or failed to obey the order, they were shot by the sentries. Escaping from Andersonville was never a viable option for prisoners in any case, because it was so far from Union lines. Only 329 men successfully escaped from Andersonville. Even if the attempt was successful, the odds of being recaptured were great because guards used specially trained dogs to find fleeing inmates.

Overcrowding, Rations, and Lack of Supplies

Overcrowded conditions caused mortality rates to skyrocket within the stockade as the prison population grew dramatically over a six-month period.

When Andersonville began operations in March, the prison contained 7,500 enlisted Union soldiers. By August, 1864, the prison confined 31,678 men on 26 acres of land, or 35.7 square feet per man.

Congestion also adversely affected sanitation within the stockade. A small creek five feet in width flowed through the camp, and it eventually became a breeding ground for infectious diseases. A cookhouse built on the outer perimeter of the stockade in May, 1864, polluted the stream.

Originally the cookhouse satisfied the needs of ten thousand prisoners, but with the escalation in population, the facilities soon became inadequate. Refuse from the baking facility contaminated the only existing water supply in the camp. Furthermore, the absence of proper latrines along the banks led men to defecate in the stream, and the creek became an open cesspool, infested with vermin. At one point construction began on two dams across the stream to improve sanitary conditions within the compound. The upper dam would be utilized for drinking and cooking purposes while the lower would permit prisoners to bathe. The project stalled in May because the proper tools to finish construction never arrived at the prison. Both Winder and Wirz repeatedly reported difficulties in procuring such basic items as baking pans, padlocks, and shovels. Logistical problems increased after the winter of 1864 because the Union army successfully destroyed or cut off Southern supply lines.

Besides the basic problem of overcrowding, an improper diet contributed to the declining conditions within the stockade. The poor quality of rations caused health problems that exacerbated the occurrences of sickness. Doctors estimated that between the months of March and August diarrhea and dysentery caused 4,529 deaths. In May and June, hospital officials admitted 16,551 ill prisoners, of whom 1,909 (12 percent) died. The hospital consisted of twenty-nine small tents pitched one hundred yards outside the stockade. Bunks, beds, or blankets for sick inmates were never available, so men lay directly on the ground. Medical supplies, stored in Macon, were inefficiently routed to Atlanta for examination. Provisions required an inspector to check all medical requisitions before shipping them to their final destination.

The worst time for deaths occurred between June and October. The weather was extremely hot and humid during those months. The southern regions of the United States experienced very high humidity levels, and Northern enlisted men could not adjust to the changes in temperature. Furthermore, the mosquitoes were especially dangerous during the summer because the pests transmitted such contagious diseases as malaria and yellow fever.

Heat exhaustion raised mortality rates because the prisoners lacked adequate shade. Captain Winder planned to construct barracks for the prisoners, but the scarcity of lumber stopped the project. Although the area around Andersonville was woodlands, Winder decided that planks would cost less to use than logs. However, lumber could not be purchased for less than one hundred dollars for every one thousand linear feet, and the captain was limited to paying Georgia schedule prices of fifty dollars. With such prices, Winder could not procure lumber to build any type of shelter. After the first few months, men within the compound erected ramshackle tents from remnant cloth pieces on a first come, first served basis. There was never any internal organization for housing, and the haphazard living conditions contributed to more deaths.

When prisoners died, fellow inmates gathered the corpses on stretchers and carried them to the deadhouse located in the southwest corner of the stockade. The deadhouse was an unassuming structure that consisted of a wood frame covered by an old tent cloth. Sometimes the dead were so numerous that the disposal of bodies had to wait until the next day. The mass graves, which held over a hundred bodies, were a series of trenches dug eight feet wide and three feet deep, with planks reinforcing the sides. Once the corpses were placed in the trenches, loose dirt and branches were laid over the bodies to complete the burial process.

Northerners began placing the blame for increased overcrowding and the consequent high death toll at Andersonville on the termination of prisoner exchanges. During the first years of the war, the opposing governments operated exchanges on a man-for-man basis. However, the exchange system had already collapsed by 1863 when General Ulysses S. Grant took control of the Union forces. Grant contended that halting exchanges reduced the number of troops in the South. The general wanted total victory, and stopping the exchanges lessened available manpower for the Confederacy to continue fighting.

End of the War and Wirz's Trial

The number of deaths eventually dropped during the early months of 1865. The alleviation of the crowded conditions at Andersonville began when Union armies advanced into the lower Southern states. By September 2, 1864, General William Tecumseh Sherman's forces occupied the city of Atlanta. Southern officials decided it was no longer safe to hold prisoners at Andersonville and ordered them removed to camps in Charleston, South Carolina, and Savannah, Georgia. The prison continued to operate on a smaller scale until April 17, 1865, when a Union column under the command of General James H. Wilson captured Columbus. Within three weeks the liberation of Andersonville took place, and Wilson officially ordered the arrest of Wirz.

Henry Wirz awaited trial in Old Capitol Prison after being transferred to Washington, D.C. As commandant of Andersonville during its last months of existence, Wirz has had his name forever connected to crimes against humanity committed during the Civil War. He was hanged on November 10, 1865.

Places to Visit

The National Prisoner of War Museum opened at Andersonville in 1998. It is dedicated to prisoners of war from the American Revolution through the Gulf War. The 495-acre park is open year round, and walking trails and driving or ranger-led tours are available. Reservations for group or educational tours are welcome, but officials like one month's advance notice. Moreover, archaeological digs conducted between 1987 and 1990 revealed the location of the stockade walls and gates, and park authorities began a partial reconstruction of them.

—*Gayla Koerting*

For Further Information:

Blakely, Arch Frederic. *General John H. Winder, C.S.A.* Gainesville: University of Florida Press, 1990. Winder was the general in charge of the Confederate prison camp system and was Wirz's superior officer.

Futch, Ovid. *History of Andersonville Prison.* Gaines-ville: University of Florida Press, 1968. Scholarly treatment of conditions at Andersonville; argues "gross mismanagement" by southern officials caused supply shortages that affected the efficient administration of the prison.

Hesseltine, William Best. *Civil War Prisons: A Study in War Psychology.* Columbus: University of Ohio Press, 1930. Best-known work by historian regarding military prisons located in the North and South.

Laska, Lewis L., and James M. Smith. "'Hell and the Devil': Andersonville and the Trial of Henry Wirz, C.S.A." *Military Law Review* 68 (Spring, 1975): 77-132. The authors reiterate the argument of Wirz as scapegoat for all crimes against humanity committed during the war.

Marvel, William. *Andersonville: The Last Depot.* Chapel Hill: University of North Carolina Press, 1994. An excellent supplement to Futch's book on the prison. Marvel extensively uses published primary and secondary sources plus a variety of manuscript collections.

Rutman, Darrett B. "The War Crimes and Trial of Henry Wirz." *Civil War History* 6 (June, 1960): 117-133. Rutman concludes that Wirz was convicted of war crimes due to "post-war hysteria" and that the former commandant was a convenient scapegoat.

Chickamauga and Chattanooga National Military Park

Date: Officially dedicated September 18-20, 1895

Relevant issues: Civil War, military history

Significance: The largest and most visited national battlefield park in the United States. It was the site of two bloody Civil War battles that took place between September and November, 1863. Covering over eight thousand acres and with six hundred monuments and over seven hundred cast-iron plaques which describe the courses of the battles, the park attracts almost one million visitors per year.

Location: The main part of the park lies seven miles south of Chattanooga on U.S. Highway 27 in Fort Oglethorpe; satellite parks include areas

The Chattanooga Battlefield. (PhotoDisc)

at Lookout Mountain (Point Park), Orchard Knob, and Missionary Ridge, which can be reached by following Crest Road off U.S. 27 South (Rossville Road)

Site Office:

Superintendent

Chickamauga and Chattanooga National Military Park

P.O. Box 2128

Fort Oglethorpe, GA 30742

ph.: (706) 866-9241

fax: (423) 752-5215

Web site: www.nps.gov/chch/

The Battle of Chickamauga was fought on September 19 and 20, 1863. It was the culmination of a campaign begun four months earlier. On May 23, 1863, General William Rosecrans, commanding the Army of the Cumberland, began his invasion of Tennessee with a complex plan that completely confused the Confederate commander, General Braxton Bragg. Forcing Bragg to evacuate his prepared defenses along the Duck River and occupying Manchester, Tennessee, Rosecrans's army pushed south. Bragg's attempt to establish a defensive line at Tullahoma was also thwarted by Rosecrans's adroit maneuvers.

Failing to halt Rosecrans at Tullahoma, Bragg fell back to a strong defensive position at Chattanooga, intending to defend the city from the mountains surrounding it. Outmaneuvering Bragg, Rosecrans crossed the Tennessee River on pontoons near Bridgeport, twenty-five miles west of Chattanooga. In danger of being cut off from his supply lines running from Lafayette, Georgia, Bragg evacuated Chattanooga without a fight on September 8, 1863. In less than three months, Rosecrans had led the Army of the Cumberland over three mountain ranges and took one of the major cities of the Confederacy without fighting a battle.

Hoping to trap part of Bragg's force south of Chattanooga, Rosecrans divided his army. As the three corps of the Army of the Cumberland advanced into the wooded, mountainous terrain, they became separated. Seeing an opportunity to defeat the Union forces in detail, Bragg pretended to continue his retreat while consolidating his army near Lafayette, Georgia. At the same time, reinforcements were being rushed to support him (two divisions from the Mississippi department and General James Longstreet's corps from Virginia).

Ordering Generals D. H. Hill and Thomas Hindman to attack part of General George Henry Thomas's Fourteenth Corps at McLemore's Cove, Bragg hoped to turn the tide of the campaign. Slow to move and overcautious, the Confederate commanders allowed the Union units to escape. Warned, the already cautious Thomas began to consolidate his forces. Frustrated, yet still hopeful of victory, Bragg ordered a general attack on the dispersed Union forces on September 18.

The Battle of Chickamauga

Striking the Union forces at Reed's Bridge, General Bushrod Johnson's division spearheaded the attacks, but due to the confusion of the battle lines and the slowness of supporting forces, they quickly fell behind schedule. Bragg renewed the attack on September 19, attempting to flank the Union left. Anticipating Bragg's strategy, Rosecrans sent Thomas's corps to reinforce General Thomas L. Crittenden's Tenth Corps. As the day progressed, more and more units were thrown into the battle. Fighting continued until nightfall, when both sides began to dig in and prepare defensive positions.

While Bragg divided his command into two wings (General Leonidas Polk was placed in command of the right, and General Longstreet, who arrived at the battlefield at midnight, was to command the left) and ordered an attack to begin at dawn, the Union commanders met at Rosecrans's headquarters and prepared their defense. Concerned about the confusion in the battle lines, Thomas repeatedly warned of the possibility of gaps in the Union line and requested reinforcements. Thomas's Fourteenth Corps was protecting the only road capable of carrying the Union forces back to Chattanooga.

The Confederate attack was late on September 20—Polk had not been given written orders by Bragg and was slow in getting his units organized. As a result, his initial attacks were unsuccessful, but there were heavy casualties on both sides. At 11:00 A.M., as a result of a misunderstanding, General Thomas Wood was ordered to move his division to the left to cover a gap in the Union lines that was not there. As he was moving his unit out of the line, Longstreet launched his attack. Sweeping into the gap, the Confederates broke the Union line. The entire right flank (the Twentieth and Twenty-first Corps), along with Rosecrans and his headquarters, fled back to Chattanooga.

General George Henry Thomas, having been reinforced earlier in the day, was able to hold the high ground in Snodgrass Hill until nightfall. Thomas's gallant stand, earning him the title "The Rock of Chickamauga," allowed the Union army to retreat back to Chattanooga. It was a stunning victory for the Confederacy.

The Battle of Chattanooga

Rather than following up his victory quickly, Bragg opted to besiege Chattanooga, allowing the North time to collect reinforcements. Rosecrans was relieved of command and replaced by General Ulysses S. Grant, who immediately ordered General William Tecumseh Sherman to move his army east from the Mississippi. At the same time, General Joseph Hooker's corps was transferred from the East. Twenty-six thousand men and all their equipment were moved twelve hundred miles in nine days by rail to reinforce Grant.

Reestablishing his supply lines with what he called the "Cracker Line" and reorganizing his army, Grant was soon ready to break out of the siege. Meanwhile, Bragg spent his time drawing up charges against his willful subordinates and allowing Longstreet's corps to be sent to Knoxville, Tennessee.

On November 24, 1863, Grant ordered Hooker to assault Lookout Mountain and Sherman to flank the Confederate position on Missionary Ridge. Hooker was successful, forcing the Confederates to evacuate their positions on Lookout Mountain, but Sherman's attack was stalled. The next day, hoping to relieve the pressure on Sherman, Grant ordered Thomas to attack the Confederate positions at the base of Missionary Ridge. Coming under heavy fire, the Union troops continued up the ridge. There were only three Confederate divisions covering a four-mile front. The Union attack was successful, breaking the thinly held Confederate lines in several places. Only the stubborn resistance of General "Pat" Cleburne's division saved the Confederate army from destruction. The siege of Chattanooga was broken, the Confederate army was shattered and in retreat, and Ulysses Grant was promoted to the command of the Union army.

The Establishment of the Park

The Chickamauga and Chattanooga National Battlefield Park was the result of a series of newspaper articles that appeared in the *Cincinnati Commercial Gazette* in 1888 that suggested that the battlefield at Chickamauga be preserved like many of the Eastern battlefields. When the society of the Army of the Cumberland had its annual meeting, it created a committee to begin the process of purchasing the land where the Battle of Chickamauga was fought in order to create a memorial similar to the one at Gettysburg.

The first meeting of the committee was on February 13, 1889, and it was agreed that Confederate veterans of the battle would be invited to join what became the Joint Chickamauga Memorial Association. The stated objective of this group was "to mark and preserve the battlefield of Chickamauga." On September 19, 1889, the twenty-sixth anniversary of the battle, a joint meeting of the Union and Confederate veterans of the battle took place in Chattanooga to discuss the creation of the park. It was one of the largest barbeques ever held in the South. Over twelve thousand people attended, and a charter was drafted to create the park.

Seen as a gesture of reconciliation, the legislation to create the Chickamauga and Chattanooga National Military Park was passed by Congress without opposition. (It took only twenty-three minutes in the House and twenty minutes in the Senate.) The land for the park, with additional sites on Lookout Mountain and Missionary Ridge, was acquired at a cost of $400,000. Veterans of the battles visited the battlefield and designated where the markers were to be placed. Because the Southern states, in the aftermath of the Civil War, could not afford to erect many monuments, most of the monuments on the battlefield commemorate Northern

units. The state of Ohio appropriated ninety thousand dollars, and other Northern states spent almost as much. The Second Minnesota Regiment has four monuments in the park.

The park was officially dedicated on September 18-20, 1899. Ten thousand Northern veterans attended, and seventy special trains were used to bring visitors to Chattanooga. Vice President Adlai Stevenson made the opening remarks on September 19 after a forty-four-cannon salute. The ceremonies ended with a parade of the veterans.

To celebrate the park's one hundredth anniversary in 1989, Friends of the Park raised three million dollars to upgrade the facilities there. The additions were completed in August of 1990.

Places to Visit

The visitors' center at the Chickamauga Battlefield Park sits on the site of the McDonald family's log cabin. Built in 1935 and renovated in 1990, it provides an impressive twenty-four-minute multimedia presentation of the battle. The visitors' center also houses the Claude E. and Zenada O. Fuller Collection of American Military Shoulder Arms. One of the most extensive collections of its kind, it contains weapons dating from the colonial period of American history to World War I. Located at the main entrance, there is also a display of the different cannons used in the battle.

The battlefield is clearly marked with cast-iron plaques (blue for the Union and red for the Confederacy) that provide essential information about the battle and the various sites for visitors. A replica of the Brotherton Cabin stands where the Confederates, led by General Longstreet, broke through the Union lines. Wilder's Tower, which stands on the site of the Widow Glenn's home (which served as Rosecrans's headquarters during the battle), provides a panoramic view of the battlefield. It was dedicated in 1899 by veterans of John Thomas Wilder's brigade, who raised the money for its construction. (After the war, Wilder, who commanded a Union cavalry brigade at Chickamauga, moved to Chattanooga, started a business, and entered politics. He was elected mayor.) Snodgrass Hill, where General Thomas was able to hold back the Confederate attack, is located at the end of the driving tour of the battlefield.

Along Crest Road off Highway 27 there is a series of small enclaves (reservations), which commemorate the Battle of Missionary Ridge. The Bragg Reservation provides an excellent view of one of the places where the Union army broke through the Confederate lines on Missionary Ridge. Other points of interest include the Ohio, Turchin, Delong, and Sherman Reservations.

The most impressive view of the Chattanooga Battlefield can be seen from Point Park on Lookout Mountain. The visitors' center at Point Park provides a slide show, and next door, in the Lookout Mountain Museum, is a life-size diorama depicting the history of the area. There is also a large collection of Civil War weapons on display. Other sites of interest include the rebuilt and restored Cravens House, which served as the Confederate headquarters during the siege, and the Ochs Museum, which was opened on November 12, 1940, and contains exhibits that describe the battle for Chattanooga. Also on Lookout Mountain are three of the most impressive tourist attractions in the South—Ruby Falls, Rock City, and Cavern Castle.

A small outlying area of the park is the Signal Point Reservation, which overlooks the Tennessee River opposite Raccoon Mountain. It was the site of one of a series of signal stations set up by the Army of the Cumberland during the siege to maintain communication with their supply base in Bridgeport, Tennessee.   —*Jack Thacker*

For Further Information:

Connelly, Thomas L. *Autumn of Glory: The Army of Tennessee, 1862-1865.* Baton Rouge: Louisiana State University Press, 1971. Provides an excellent overview of the campaign and an understanding of the individuals involved.

Cozzens, Peter. *This Terrible Sound: The Battle of Chickamauga.* Urbana: University of Illinois Press, 1992. Provides an excellent in-depth narrative of the fighting at Chickamauga.

Downey, Fairfax. *Storming the Gateway: Chattanooga, 1863.* New York: David McKay Co., 1960. Well written and filled with interesting stories.

McDonough, James. *Chattanooga—A Death Grip on the Confederacy.* Knoxville: University of Tennessee Press, 1984. Probably the best overall study of the battle of Chattanooga.

Miles, Jim. *Paths to Glory: A History and Tour Guide of the Stone's River, Chickamauga, Chattanooga, Knoxville, and Nashville Campaigns.* Nashville, Tenn.: Ruthedge Hill Press, 1991. Presents an excellent guide for anyone seeking to follow the course of the campaign and battle. Maps, directions, and mileage, as well as details of all the major tour sites, are included. Contains forty-two maps and about one hundred illustrations.

Robertson, William G., et al. *Staff Ride Handbook for the Battle of Chickamauga: 18-20 September 1863.* Fort Leavenworth, Kans.: U.S. Army Command and General Staff College, 1992. Although prepared for army officers, it is the best guide to the Chickamauga Battlefield.

Tucker, Glenn. *Chickamauga: Bloody Battle in the West.* New York: Bobbs-Merrill, 1961. A lively but somewhat outdated study of the battle, it is still worth reading.

Woodworth, Steven E. *Six Armies in Tennessee: The Chickamauga and Chattanooga Campaigns.* Lincoln: University of Nebraska Press, 1998. Presents the best overall study of the campaign to date.

Fort Frederica

Date: Authorized as a National Monument on May 26, 1936

Relevant issues: Colonial America, European settlement, military history

Significance: National Monument; a three hundred-acre park surrounds Fort Frederica, which is primarily a series of archaeological sites founded in 1936 by an act of Congress. It is preserved and maintained by the U.S. Department of the Interior, National Park Service. The fort embraced military buildings and a small town and was laid out by James Edward Oglethorpe in 1736. Built along the lines of traditional early eighteenth century British military defense, most buildings were constructed of tabby and wood. The fort and town burned to the ground in 1758.

Location: Saint Simons Island, approximately the size of Manhattan, which lies off the Atlantic coast of Georgia, across a causeway five miles long; Fort Frederica's and its town's archaeological sites, covering forty acres, are situated on the western side of the island and slightly north, with one side bounded by marshland. The Bloody Marsh Memorial, located in an eight-acre park about six miles away, is on the southeastern side of the island. The nearest major city is Brunswick, and Interstate 95 is fifteen miles away.

Site Office:
National Park Service
Fort Frederica National Monument
Route 9, Box 286-C
Saint Simons Island, GA 31522
ph.: (912) 638-3639

Fort Frederica, located on Saint Simons Island off the coast of Georgia, played a critical role as a strategic military outpost for Britain during the colonial expansion of the mid-1700's. Fort Frederica marked the boundary of an area the British claimed as theirs, contesting Spanish claims to the land at a time when the British, French, and Spanish vied furiously for territories in what is today the U.S. southeast. Established in 1736 by James Edward Oglethorpe, Fort Frederica housed a military garrison and protected a small town inside its walls. It served as the launching point for Oglethorpe's unsuccessful assaults on the Spanish colony of St. Augustine, Florida, in 1740 and 1743. The Spanish counterattack was turned back at a pivotal encounter at Fort Frederica, the Battle of Bloody Marsh, in 1742, marking the end of the Spanish threat to Georgia and South Carolina.

Origins

Fort Frederica's existence dates back to a period when three European colonial empires—Britain, Spain, and France—held claims in the area that is now Georgia. The British North American colonies were in the ascendancy, their total population growing from 200,000 in 1689 to 400,000 in 1715. The colony of South Carolina, founded in 1670, was expanding to the south, in spite of skirmishes with the Spanish and their Indian allies. The Spanish, who first settled the area and claimed it as their own, were on the defensive by 1715. Although St. Augustine, Florida, established in 1565, was well fortified, the Spanish empire had been declining since about 1660. By 1715, only about two thousand Spanish inhabited Florida.

During the first two decades of the eighteenth century, the French strengthened relationships with southern Indian nations and built a fort in what is now Alabama. However, indiscipline and a series of political missteps left the French vulnerable overseas. The British colonists in South Carolina, feeling threatened by the Spanish and the French and their Indian allies, built and garrisoned a string of small forts along their southern frontier between 1716 and 1721. This incensed Spain, which vigorously protested the outposts. The British continued to claim that the border between Florida and South Carolina had never been clearly defined, and the matter remained unsettled.

Oglethorpe

In order fully to understand the colonization of Georgia and Fort Frederica, one must understand its founder and trustee, James Edward Oglethorpe, whose utopian and expansionist vision created Georgia. Born in 1696 into a well-to-do British family, he became a member of the British Parliament at a young age. Bright, energetic, and idealistic, although sometimes brash and autocratic, Oglethorpe was named chairman of a parliamentary committee formed to study the conditions of British jails, and in particular, the unfair and abusive conditions to which London's imprisoned debtors were exposed. The idea of creating a new colony in America, where debtors could have a fresh start in their lives, presented a creative solution to the problem for Oglethorpe and many of his colleagues.

A new province also meant further expansion of Britain's imperial domains, as well as a much-needed buffer between the fledgling colony of South Carolina and Spanish Florida and French Alabama Country. However, as the concept of establishing Georgia—named after reigning monarch King George II—took hold, the founding ideals changed. In fact, Georgia's board of ninety-six trustees marketed their new colony too brilliantly, creating an unrealistic image of contented prosperity. The result was that, upon setting sail for America in 1732 with his colony's recruits, Oglethorpe did not accompany a group of released and redeemable debtors, as originally planned. According to historians Phinizy Spalding and Edwin L. Jackson, he instead led a "cross-section of eighteenth century British society . . . including small businessmen, unemployed laborers, and a few from the upper middle classes and a sprinkling of adventurers."

To Oglethorpe, Georgia represented a new beginning that could be shaped with strong leadership. The trustees designed legislation to create a flourishing community of small businesses and, according to Spalding and Jackson, "make the province into a sort of idealized agrarian state." To accomplish this, they restricted land grants to male heirs, and rum and other hard alcohol were prohibited, as were slaves and servants. As the harsher realities of life and politics set in, these rules became difficult, if not impossible, to enforce. Oglethorpe arrived in Georgia and established Savannah in July, 1733. Politically astute, he immediately began cultivating supporters, first by opening his new colony to people suffering religious persecution.

A Jewish contingent and a community of Lutheran Salzburgers settled in and near Savannah early on, crediting Oglethorpe's involvement and paternalistic concern for their eventual success. Oglethorpe also made a point of befriending the Yamacraw Indian chief and of learning and openly admiring Indian customs and languages. He and the other trustees passed the Indian Act of 1735, which regulated the sometimes questionable practices of European traders by establishing a schedule of exchange rates for skins and pelts and requiring European traders to operate with proper licenses. Though this act strained relations with South Carolina, whose traders did not appreciate being curbed by upstarts, it gave Oglethorpe a solid foundation of Indian support.

Oglethorpe also earned the respect of his recruited settlers by disdaining creature comforts and living as his colonists did. A man of austere tastes, his home in Savannah was as plain and simple as the others around him. His habit of sleeping on floors or outdoors in his cloak whenever the occasion arose was favorably interpreted as an effort to share the experiences of his settlers. Frontier life was not easy, especially when colonists worked in the summer heat, swarmed by gnats and flies, and particularly when fever swept the settlements.

The Spanish Threat

In early 1735, a rising tide of fear of Spanish attack led Oglethorpe and other trustees to begin plans for a defensive fort on the west side of Saint Simons Island. The island had once served as a site for a Spanish mission. The planned site for Fort Frederica was well situated, close to both the mouth of the Altamaha River and to the mainland. It was named to commemorate the royal wedding of Frederick, Prince of Wales and George II's only son, to Augusta of Saxe Gotha in 1736. (Fort Augusta was built simultaneously along the Savannah River.) Oglethorpe returned to England to appeal for funding of the fort and to recruit new settlers. Both were easily forthcoming, the recruits in spite of Oglethorpe's honest warnings about discomforts of life on the frontier, especially for those doing double duty as laborer and fort guard. The 257 recruits departed England in December, 1735, aboard the *Symond*, after long delays due to foul weather. They arrived on the shores of Georgia in early February, 1736. Oglethorpe accompanied them on board, refusing the offer of passage on an escort ship that would have been uncrowded and quiet.

The compassion, fairness, and effective leadership Oglethorpe displayed throughout the arduous voyage won over his new group and no doubt contributed to their patience with him when, upon arrival at the mouth of the Savannah River, he stopped the journey for two weeks to attend to business in Savannah. The group waited and recuperated from the journey downriver at Tybee Roads. Then, Oglethorpe and his new settlers encountered a major obstacle to moving on to Saint Simons Island: The captains of the ship refused to sail further south into the uncharted waters of Jekyll Sound (present-day Saint Simons Sound). Likely, they were afraid of encountering Spanish warships. Eventually, Oglethorpe and a group of his men used a small scout boat to identify inland waterway (now Intracoastal Waterway) entrances to the island; the remainder of the Frederica group followed, rowing arduously in small, wooden open boats.

Finally, in March, 1736, after five days of rowing, all the settlers convened on Saint Simons Island and began construction of Fort Frederica. They started by building huts covered with palmetto fronds for shelter while assisting in the construction of the fortified town. Oglethorpe organized the group into parties, each with specific jobs, and he stayed on-site long enough to ensure that the town's streets were marked off, shelters provided, and the fort underway. According to historian Larry E. Ivers, "Fort Frederica was a square-shaped fortification, 124 by 125 feet on the inside with regular bastion at each corner and a spur battery that jutted beyond the fort on the river side. Sod-faced earthen walls and a row of palisades planted in a moat surrounded a storehouse, powder magazine, well and blacksmith ship." The main entrance opened onto the river. Broad Street, lined with Seville orange trees, divided the town into north and south halves.

An area of about thirty-five to forty acres was laid out in lots divided regularly by spacious streets. Garden plots were located about a half mile to the north, east, and south of town. Fifty-acre grants were situated on various parts of the island, and a large meadow near the town permitted settlers to graze cattle. The settlers planted potatoes, Indian corn, carrots, onions, peas, beans, flax, hemp, melons, and assorted squash, among other produce, and also hunted game and fished from the river or ocean. The first settlers numbered forty-four men and seventy-two women and children. Their early houses were rudimentary, like very large tents made from palmetto leaves. Later houses were more permanent, made of tabby or wood. Wealthier residents even imported brick and glass windows. Each freeholder had a lot approximately sixty by ninety feet for house and a garden, though the lots fronting the river were smaller.

Additional Fortification

In 1738, a regiment of foot soldiers arrived to protect against Spanish invasion, and in 1739 the town was further fortified with two gates, one at the land entrance on the east and the other at the water entrance on the west. The town also was encircled by a ten-foot-high fence of cedar stakes and a moat. A small fort with a watchtower, Fort Saint Simons, was constructed on the southern tip of the island, near the present-day lighthouse. It guarded the entrance to Saint Simons Sound and was connected to the main fort nine miles away by the Military Road. Civil government was administered by Frederica townspeople who served as bailiffs, constables, and tithingmen. A town court tried all civil and criminal cases. (Interestingly, no lawyers were allowed in the town, by decree.) By 1740, the main responsibility of the thousand Fort Frederica inhabitants was defense, and each kept firearms at home ready for use. Military training took place every day and discipline was strict. The stage was set for a confrontation with the Spanish, who were increasingly bothered by Britain's uninterrupted expansion.

The settlement and fortification of Fort Frederica had exacerbated tensions between the British and the Spanish, with the latter protesting vehemently. In late 1736, Oglethorpe and Governor Francisco Sanchez of Florida finally agreed on their common border, but their solution was not long lasting. Madrid, horrified by Sanchez's concessions, called him home and eventually hanged him. London, on the other hand, was so pleased with Oglethorpe's efforts that he was rewarded with a new infantry regiment, the Forty-second Regiment of Foot, and command of all forces in Georgia and South Carolina. For the time being, the Altamaha River remained the de facto boundary.

Asiento of 1713

Another important cause of friction between Britain and Spain surrounded the Asiento of 1713, which allowed the British to sell slaves and only one shipload of trade goods each year within the Spanish West Indies. Yet Britain violated the trade rules so flagrantly and Spain conducted its searches and seizures with such arrogance and cruelty that tensions increased between the two countries. Then, in the spring of 1738, Robert Jenkins, captain of a British merchant ship, fanned the flame of public resentment by displaying his severed ear before a parliamentary committee. Jenkins had saved the ear in his handkerchief after it had been cut off by the Spanish during a search and seizure seven years before in which Jenkins was caught smuggling. Parliament's ire was aroused, and the government protested to the Spanish, who in January, 1739, agreed to pay damages to British merchants. Because the Spaniards refused to punish their captains or stop their search practices, however, the British declared war; thus, the War of Jenkins's Ear began in October, 1739.

Oglethorpe was ready to take advantage of this turn of events, and by January, 1740, he had personally participated in two scouting trips to the St. Augustine area. During the second, he captured two small forts, isolating St. Augustine from Spanish settlements to the west. Oglethorpe felt that the Spanish had reacted to his incursions with timidity, and this fueled his ambition to attack St. Augustine directly while he had the chance. By May, 1740, he had raised a force, moved it from Fort Frederica to St. Augustine, and set up a naval blockade. He had hoped to maneuver the Spanish defenders away from heavily fortified Castillo de San Marcos and into the open. This strategy failed, however, and in mid-June he began a seige of the Spanish fort.

The seige did not go well for Oglethorpe and the British. In an effort to lure the Spanish out, he sent a decoy group of forty Indians and eighty-five Europeans to rove around the fort. The Spanish ambushed the party, killing fifty and capturing twenty. Also, British ships were too large to maneuver in shallow waters and could not support the ground troops or completely seal the port. Cannon shelled the fort for three weeks but had little effect on the reinforced structure. By early July, Oglethorpe's troops were becoming ill and starting to desert, and hurricane season was threatening. When three small Spanish ships slipped through the blockade and relieved the fort, it seemed clear that the campaign would not succeed, and Oglethorpe lifted the seige.

Collapse of the Defenses

After the failed campaign to take St. Augustine, Georgia lost all outside support to fend off the expected Spanish counterattack. South Carolina authorities, disappointed at the defeat, jealous of Oglethorpe, and frightened for their own safety, blamed Oglethorpe for the debacle and withdrew their forces from Georgia. Oglethorpe, who had been seriously ill following the Florida invasion, was depressed by the South Carolina accusations and the general lack of support from Parliament and his trustees. Momentum had shifted to Spain, which was also encouraged by a new alliance with France. By late 1741, they had developed a plan for a major expedition to destroy Georgia and all South Carolina settlements up to Port Royal, and then to incite South Carolina's slave population to revolt with offers of freedom and land in Florida. The Spanish force, including 1,950 troops from Spain, Cuba, and Florida, sailed from St. Augustine in June, 1742, under the command of Governor Manuel de Montiano of Florida. Oglethorpe's total force may have been as large as nine hundred, but only around five hundred were available to defend Saint Simons Island. When the Spanish arrived on Saint Simons Island, they captured Fort Saint Simons, which the British had hastily abandoned.

The fate of Fort Frederica was determined in two small but decisive battles that took place on July 7, 1742. On that day, Spanish parties numbering one hundred men were sent out to reconnoiter the island, coming to within a mile and a half of Fort Frederica before being detected by Oglethorpe's group. Oglethorpe collected what forces were immediately available and personally led them headlong into the advancing Spaniards. In a savage attack, the Spanish group was completely routed, while the British lost only one man. Oglethorpe, expecting the Spaniards to counterattack, established a defensive site about five miles away from Fort Frederica, on the western edge of what is now called Bloody Marsh. Oglethorpe deployed a group of rangers and Highlanders on one side of the path and regular troops on the other. By noon, retreating Spaniards from the mauled reconnaissance party returned to base camp and reported the clash.

Montiano responded by sending a larger group of troops back up the path. The British, concealed in woods along the path, opened fire on the approaching Spaniards, who responded in kind. Many of the British regulars became unnerved and fled north, back toward Fort Frederica. Those that remained held their ground. After an hour of exchanging fire across the marsh, and unaware that nearly half the British force had left the battlefield, the Spanish beat an orderly retreat south to Fort Saint Simons.

The battles on July 7 were important psychologically for the British. Although few troops were involved and the fights were little more than skirmishes, British forces had turned back the Spaniards twice in the same day and finally had the upper hand. The British also had full confidence in their strategies, while the Spanish were increasingly hesitant to leave the protective walls of Fort Saint Simons. From an escaped British prisoner, Oglethorpe learned how terrified the Spanish had become. To heighten Spanish anxiety, the British decided to hold a night raid on a Spanish camp. Just as the raid was about to take place, a Frenchman pressed into British service discharged his musket, alerting the Spaniards and spoiling the raid. The Frenchman then fled into the Spanish camp. Oglethorpe, concerned that the Frenchman would reveal how small British forces actually were, developed a clever ruse to confuse the Spanish. The next day, he freed a Spanish prisoner, giving him money to deliver a letter to the Frenchman.

The Spaniards, as expected, interrogated the freed prisoner and found the letter, which suggested a conspiracy between the Frenchman and the British. Oglethorpe's letter offered the Frenchman more money if he could lure the Spanish up the river to be ambushed by hidden British batteries and convince them to spend another few days on the island, until British reinforcements from Charleston could arrive. Montiano did not really believe the ruse, but he could not afford to dismiss it either, and when sails were sighted to the north later that same day, he and his expedition departed immediately for St. Augustine.

Waning Importance of Fort Frederica

The southern frontier of Georgia was never in question again. Correspondingly, Fort Frederica was destined to diminish in importance. Oglethorpe returned to Britain in 1743 to defend himself against the charges of a jealous fellow officer and to seek compensation from Parliament for the personal funds he had spent on Georgia's defense. The charges against him were dismissed, and he was reimbursed. Oglethorpe never returned to Georgia. Although the war continued until 1749, most of the Georgia forces were disbanded in 1747 because the border with Florida was relatively quiet and the British were trying to reduce military expenditures in North America. A skeleton garrison occupied Fort Frederica until 1758, when a mysterious fire burned the fort to the ground, never to be fully reoccupied as a military base or town again.

In 1936 the U.S. Congress established Fort Frederica National Monument, a three hundred-acre park surrounding the site where the fort once stood. Several of the fort's structures remain, including the soldiers' barracks and the magazine where ammunition was kept. Wayside exhibits use text illustrations and artifacts to describe the town and the lives of its inhabitants. A visitors' center houses a small museum and sponsors films about the history of the fort, as well as tours and living history presentations. Six miles from the fort, on the southern tip of the island, stands the Bloody Marsh Memorial, where the 1742 battle established Britain as the dominant colonial power of the southeastern region.

—*Christine Walker Martin*

For Further Information:

Inscoe, John C., ed. *James Edward Oglethorpe: New Perspectives on His Life and Legacy.* Savannah: Georgia Historical Society, 1997. A biography of Oglethorpe and a history of Georgia during the colonial period, circa 1600 to 1775.

Ivers, Larry E. *British Drums on the Southern Frontier.* Chapel Hill: University of North Carolina Press, 1974. An interesting, detailed, and very readable account of the military encounters between the British and Spanish during the colonization of Georgia in the 1730's and 1740's. Ivers includes colorful accounts of the battles around Fort Frederica.

Peckham, Howard H. *The Colonial Wars: 1698-1762.* Chicago: University of Chicago Press, 1964. Chronicles the geopolitical background of the big colonial powers—France, England, and Spain—and provides a sweeping view of the southeastern United States between 1689 and 1762.

Spalding, Phinizy. *Oglethorpe in America.* Chicago: University of Chicago Press, 1977. The definitive word on James Edward Oglethorpe and his influence on Georgia.

Spalding, Phinizy, and Edwin L. Jackson. *James Edward Oglethorpe: A New Look at Georgia's Founder.* Athens, University of Georgia, Carl Vinson Institute of Government, 1988. A broader, briefer outline of Oglethorpe's Georgia connection.

Spalding, Phinizy, and Harvey H. Jackson, eds. *Oglethorpe in Perspective: Georgia's Founder After Two Hundred Years.* Tuscaloosa: University of Alabama Press, 1989. A collection of essays by fellow historians to provide different views of Oglethorpe.

Martin Luther King, Jr., Historic District, Atlanta

Date: King born in the district on January 15, 1929

Relevant issues: African American history, social reform

Significance: This site, one of the country's most historic African American districts, is the place where civil rights leader Dr. Martin Luther King, Jr., was born in 1929 and where he often preached until his death in 1968. Historic sites in the area include King's childhood home, Ebenezer Baptist Church, the Southern Christian Leadership Conference (SCLC) headquarters, and the Martin Luther King, Jr., Center for Nonviolent Social Change.

Location: Roughly bounded by Irwin, Randolph, Elywood, Johnson, and Auburn Avenues in Atlanta

Site Offices:

Martin Luther King, Jr., National Historic Site
522 Auburn Avenue, NE
Atlanta, GA 30312
ph.: (404) 221-5190
Web site: www.nps.gov/malu/

Martin Luther King, Jr., Center for Nonviolent Social Change
449 Auburn Avenue
Atlanta, GA 30312
ph.: (404) 526-8900
Web site: www.thekingcenter.com

The Martin Luther King, Jr., National Historic Site and Preservation District in Atlanta is one the country's oldest and most significant African American historic districts. Within the area, several important institutions, organizations, and businesses were founded, including churches, retail stores, a trust company, and an insurance company. These historic institutions centered around Auburn Avenue, black Atlanta's most prominent thoroughfare.

African American Background

Early in the twentieth century, this area became predominantly African American. By the time Martin Luther King, Jr., was born on January 15, 1929, the district was thriving as a vital hub of commerce and social activity. Observing the successful businesses and houses of the black elite that lined Auburn Avenue, historian and journalist I. P. Reynolds gave the name of "Sweet Auburn" to the avenue.

Businessman Hemon E. Perry played an important role in making Auburn Avenue commercially viable. Perry founded Standard Life Insurance Company in 1913 and used the company to finance his other enterprises, which included dry cleaners, a drugstore, a construction company, a mortgage association, and a coal-mining concern. He eventually overextended his resources, however, and his empire collapsed in 1924.

By then other businesses had been established in the district. A barber named Alonzo F. Herndon started Atlanta Life Insurance Company in 1905; it remains in business today, the largest black-owned stock insurance company in the United States. Atlanta Mutual Building Loan and Savings Association, founded in 1920, and Citizens Trust Bank, established a few years later, became successful financial institutions. This section of Atlanta was (and still is) home to a black-owned newspaper, the

A marker at the Martin Luther King, Jr., National Historic Site in Atlanta. (AP/Wide World Photos)

Atlanta World, established in 1928, and the black-owned radio station WERD.

Birth and Childhood of Martin Luther King, Jr.

In this thriving Atlanta community, Martin Luther King, Jr., was born into a middle-class African American family. He grew up in a comfortable, thirteen-room, two-story house at 501 Auburn Avenue. His father, Martin Luther King, Sr., was a Baptist minister; his mother, Alberta Williams King, a schoolteacher.

From his father and grandfather, young Martin inherited the family's strong ties to the black Baptist church. His father was pastor of the Ebenezer Baptist Church, a large and prestigious church located a short distance from the family home. His maternal grandfather, A. D. Williams, had founded the church. Martin Luther King, Jr., eventually served as copastor of the church with his father.

King later recalled that his boyhood years were spent in "a very congenial home situation," and that his family was one "where love was central and where lovely relationships were ever present." The King family home was situated in the heart of Atlanta's thriving black middle class; as part of Atlanta's black bourgeoisie, the family did not suffer real deprivation during the Great Depression that devastated America in the 1930's.

In 1941 the King family moved to a larger home, a brick structure three blocks away at 193 Boulevard. This move happened at the same time as the completion of the new Ebenezer Baptist Church at its present site on Auburn Avenue. In September, 1944, after attending public elementary and high schools as well as the Laboratory High School of Atlanta University, young Martin entered Morehouse College as a special student. He was fifteen years old.

After receiving a bachelor's degree from Morehouse in 1948, King left Atlanta to attend Crozer Theological Seminary in Chester, Pennsylvania, where he graduated three years later with highest honors. He continued his education at Boston University, earning a doctorate in systematic theology in 1955. King remained away from Atlanta until 1960. During this time, he served as pastor of the Dexter Avenue Baptist Church in Montgomery, Alabama, and immersed himself in the civil rights struggle. King's leadership of the successful Mont-gomery bus boycott of 1955 thrust him into national prominence. The boycott was called to protest racially segregated seating on buses.

Rise of the Civil Rights Movement

By the 1950's, the South was afire with local civil rights movements. Leaders of these groups, including King, the Reverend Joseph Lowery of Mobile, Alabama, and the Reverend Fred Shuttlesworth of Birmingham, Alabama, began to meet informally. According to one participant, Stanley Levison, "If there was one individual who clarified and organized the discussion it was Dr. King."

Early in January, 1957, black civil rights leaders met at the Ebenezer Baptist Church to form an organization that would coordinate local activities. This organization became the Southern Christian Leadership Conference (SCLC), with headquarters on Auburn Avenue. In 1960 King became president of SCLC and returned to Atlanta. The SCLC planned many marches and activities for justice and freedom in the early 1960's.

King and the SCLC became involved in civil rights efforts all over the South and also lobbied for national support for the movement. King embraced the growing protest movement among black college students, and in 1960 he joined a group of students in demanding service at whites-only lunch-rooms in Atlanta department stores. King and numerous others were arrested. The incident may have helped sway the 1960 U.S. presidential election. Democratic candidate John F. Kennedy, initially reluctant about involvement with the case and rather noncommittal about the Civil Rights movement, eventually decided to telephone King's wife, Coretta Scott King, and offer his moral support. Kennedy's brother, Robert, phoned the judge in the case to protest the denial of bail to King. These actions undoubtedly won many black votes for John Kennedy. Previously, numerous black voters had been leaning toward his opponent, Richard M. Nixon.

King continued his involvement with desegregation, voting rights, and other civil rights causes in such cities as Albany, Georgia, and St. Augustine, Florida. Massive protests in Birmingham, Alabama, in 1963 led to more jail time for King, and the publication of his famous "Letter from a Birmingham Jail," in which he denounced not only the overt racist but the white moderate who is more devoted to "order" than to justice, who prefers a negative peace that is the absence of tension to a positive peace which is the presence of justice, who constantly says "I agree with you in the goal you seek, but I can't agree with your methods of direct action," who paternalistically believes that he can set the time-table for another man's freedom. . . .

On August 28, 1963, King led his famous March on Washington. Before 200,000 people, he shared his dream of America when he said: "I have a dream that one day every valley shall be exalted, every hill and mountain shall be made low, the rough places will be made plain, and the crooked places will be made straight, and the glory of the Lord shall be revealed, and all flesh shall see it together."

King's Later Career
King received many honors for his nonviolent brand of civil rights activism. In 1963 he received the Nobel Peace Prize, and early in the following year, *Time* magazine chose the young Baptist minister as "Man of the Year."

King continued to lead important civil rights campaigns before being killed by an assassin's bullet. The first of these campaigns was the dangerous Selma-to-Montgomery march, which took place from January to March, 1965. During the second campaign, the Civil Rights movement entered its "northern phase"; in the summer of 1966, King went to Chicago to attack the social and economic conditions that militated against the welfare of blacks.

The King-led campaign faced tough and angry opposition from local whites. For example, demonstrations launched by King in the southwest side of Chicago were met by jeering white marchers, who threw rocks and bottles. King left Chicago on August 6, 1966, vowing "to keep coming back until we are safe from harassment." After the Chicago campaign, some persons in the Civil Rights movement began questioning King's nonviolent methods, although his personal reputation remained unblemished.

After King
King was assassinated on April 4, 1968, in Memphis, Tennessee, where he had gone to show support for members of an all-black sanitation workers' union, on strike against the city. On April 6, King's body was put on public view at Ebenezer Baptist Church; three days later, he was buried in Atlanta's South View Cemetery. An eternal flame burns at the Martin Luther King, Jr., Center for Nonviolent Social Change, which is located at 449 Auburn Avenue. It symbolizes the ongoing effort to achieve King's dream of justice and brotherhood for all Americans. The center was established in 1969 to build on what the Civil Rights movement had accomplished under King's leadership. The center has organized programs that work to eliminate violence, poverty, racism, and war through peaceful means.

"All people are welcome here," said Coretta Scott King, the center's president and chief executive officer. "We want to be a place where people can come together. Hopefully, in the sharing process, we will all grow and understand and respect the dignity and worth of all human personalities."

Located on the third floor of the center's three-story red brick building is the heart of the institution: the archives and library. It was established soon after King's death, when his widow and other family members, as well as several friends, joined together to act to ensure the preservation and use of King's papers. Since those formative days, the archive has expanded its scope to become a repository of books, diaries, scrapbooks, newspaper clippings, photographs, films, tapes, phonograph recordings, and other records that total more than a million items and document the modern Civil Rights movement. Each year the library's small staff answers about five thousand research requests from all over the world.

Today, the King Library and Archives is the country's primary institution for preserving and documenting the pivotal period in U.S. history known as the Civil Rights movement. It tells the story of a movement that has its seeds in the Martin Luther King, Jr., Historic District—a movement that fundamentally altered the course of U.S. history. Within the historic district, other sites related to the Civil Rights movement and Atlanta's historic black community include King's birthplace; the Ebenezer Baptist Church; and the headquarters of various black-owned businesses that have operated there since early in the twentieth century.

—*Ron Chepesiuk*

For Further Information:

Several books have put the Martin Luther King, Jr., legacy, the Civil Rights movement, and the King Historic District's development in perspective. The following is a sampling of some of the best sources.

Branch, Taylor. *Parting the Waters: America in the King Years 1954-63*. New York: Simon & Schuster, 1988.

Garrow, David J. *Bearing the Cross: Martin Luther King, Jr., and the Southern Christian Leadership Conference*. New York: William Morrow, 1986.

Lewis, David Levering. *King: A Biography*. Urbana: University of Illnois Press, 1978.

Lincoln, C. Eric. *Martin Luther King, Jr.: A Profile*. New York: Hill & Wang, 1984.

Peck, Ira. *The Life and Words of Martin Luther King, Jr.* New York: Scholastic Book Services, 1999. A biography of King and a history of the Civil Rights movement.

Savannah

Date: Founded in 1733

Relevant issues: Civil War, colonial America

Significance: The oldest permanent settlement in Georgia and one of the most historic and picturesque cities in the United States. The city's history is commemorated by many monuments and buildings, indicative of Savannah's successful efforts to preserve and restore many fine examples of early nineteenth century architecture. Savannah was one of the first planned cities in the United States and was the chief city and capital of the Georgia colony until well after the ending of the Revolutionary War in 1783. Today, the city's history has made Savannah one of the most popular tourist attractions in the Southeast.

Location: On a bluff overlooking the Savannah River, in the eastern part of Georgia, about eighteen miles west of the mouth of the river

Site Office:

The Savannah Area Convention and Visitors Bureau

101 East Bay Street

Savannah, GA 31402

ph.: (877) SAVANNAH [728-2662]

Web site: www.savannah-visit.com

Savannah was founded in 1733 by General James Edward Oglethorpe, a philanthropist and military expert, and nineteen associates, when they received a charter from the British government empowering them to establish the colony of Georgia. The colonists had several reasons for wanting to establish a settlement there. The first was altruistic. Savannah was to be a settlement where the poor and persecuted might find refuge. The other reasons concerned economics and military defense. England hoped to strengthen the colonies, increase trade, and provide a buffer for Carolina against the Spanish, who had settled Florida.

Early Years

During its early years, Savannah became a haven for all kinds of religious groups experiencing persecution, including Methodists, Anglicans, Lutherans, Baptists, Presbyterians, and Jews. In 1734, just a few months after Georgia's colonization, Salzburger Lutherans fled Europe for Savannah, where they established a religious colony at nearby Ebeneezer. In July, 1733, Savannah became the home of the first Reform Jewish congregation in America. Today, its synagogue, Temple Mickve Israel, houses a museum with 1,790 historical books, as well as the oldest torah in America and letters to the congregation from U.S. presidents George Washington, Thomas Jefferson, and James Madison.

Early development also reflected Savannah's military importance. A strategic pattern was set when the entire city was walled against the Spanish. Later, fortifications were built to protect the city during the Revolutionary and Civil Wars. Today, Savannah has many reminders of its military history. Occupying a site fortified since colonial days is Fort Jackson, the oldest remaining brickwork fort in Savannah. Fort Pulaski, designed by Napoleon's military engineers and built between 1829 and 1847, is a National Monument maintained by the National Park Service. Fort Screven, built in 1875 and used during the Spanish-American War and World War I, is one of the last coastal artillery batteries erected along the East Coast of the United States.

The First Planned City

In the beginning, James Edward Oglethorpe gave order to Savannah's growth. The city, in fact, can lay claim to be America's first meticulously planned city. Oglethorpe's plan included twenty-four public squares designed to be meeting places as well as areas where local citizens could camp out and protect themselves against the Indians. Although some of the squares were built after Oglethorpe's time, his basic scheme remains in place today, with twenty-one of those public squares still in existence.

Many of these squares have strong associations with some of the most prominent names in U.S. and British history. Calhoun Square, which was laid out at Abercorn Street between Taylor and Gordon Streets, is named for South Carolina statesman John C. Calhoun. Chatham Square, created in 1847 at Barnard Street between Taylor and Gordon Streets, was named in 1851 after William Pitt, the earl of Chatham. Lafayette Square, at Abercorn Street between Harris and Charlton Streets, 1837, is named for the Marquis de Lafayette, the Frenchman who fought for the colonies in the Revolutionary War and who visited Savannah in 1825. Madison Square, between Harris and Charlton Streets, is named in honor of James Madison, fourth president of the United States.

Also in this area is the Trustees Garden, at East Broad near Bay Street, the site of an experimental garden planted by Oglethorpe in 1734. The peach trees planted here in the eighteenth century are believed to have marked the beginning of the Georgia peach industry. On the site is an herb house, from about 1734, that may be Georgia's oldest building.

Savannah "Firsts"

During the eighteenth century, Savannah established a number of firsts. In 1735, for example, the city exported the first silk from North America. A year later, John Wesley, the third rector of Savannah's Christ Episcopal Church, published the first hymnal in America and founded the world's first Sunday school. Later, Wesley returned to England and founded the Methodist Church. Savannah held its first horse race on June 26, 1740, and in 1763 established the colony's first newspaper, the *Georgia Gazette.*

Savannah grew rather slowly until after the Spanish left Florida in 1763. By the time of the Revolutionary War, Savannah had a population of between 2,000 and 2,500. During the last fifteen years of the colonial period. Savannah's export business

in rice, naval stores, lumber, and other items grew significantly.

Savannah During the Revolution

Savannah was caught up in the events leading to the independence of the thirteen colonies. The city was the site of the one of the Revolutionary War's most bloody battles when British troops arrived at Savannah in December, 1778, and captured the city. A combined force of Continental and French troops tried to dislodge the British on October 9, 1779, but the attack was poorly planned and did not succeed. The Continentals and French suffered more than a thousand dead and wounded. Among the dead was the famous Polish cavalry commander Count Casimir Pulaski. Today, a monument in one of Savannah's public squares honors him.

After the Revolution, Savannah grew and flourished. The city became an important cotton trade center, as cotton became the south's most important crop; Eli Whitney invented the cotton gin in 1793 on a plantation near Savannah. The introduction of steam navigation made possible the movement of goods by river to and from Augusta in 1817. Cotton planters in the Georgia interior would ship their crop to Savannah for export, rather than to Charleston as was their practice previously. Savannah's Cotton Exchange became the center of the world cotton market. During its period of post-Revolution growth, Savannah received a temporary setback in 1796 when two-thirds of the city was destroyed by fire, and another in 1820, when it experienced another fire as well as a yellow fever epidemic.

Historic Buildings

From 1830 until the onset of the Civil War the railroad increased Savannah's prosperity and created a cotton-merchant elite. Several significant Savannah buildings date from the first half of the nineteenth century. The Customs House, built between 1848 and 1853, remains the most important public building in Savannah. The 1819 William Scarborough House served as the center of festivities surrounding President James Monroe's visit to the city that year. The Owens-Thomas House, built during 1816-1819 at 126 Abercorn Street, is one of the country's finest examples of Regency architecture. The Telfair Academy, built in 1820 on Barnard Street, was the mansion of Alexander Telfair, a prominent local citizen. In 1875 it became the property of the Savannah Historical Society, and today is the oldest public art museum in the Southeast.

The Champion-McAlpin-Fowlker House, built in 1844 at 230 Barnard Street, is Savannah's greatest example of Greek Revival architecture. The Davenport House, built around 1820 by master builder Isiah Davenport on the northwest corner of State and Habersham Streets, is one of the country's best Georgian houses. The house was marked for demolition in 1955, but the Historic Savannah Foundation restored it and opened it as a museum.

The Mercer House in Monterey Square, Savannah. (American Stock Photography)

Several of Savannah's historic churches also were built in this period. The present structure of Christ Episcopal Church, the first church established in the colony in 1733, was erected in 1840. In the 1830's, the Cathedral of St. John the Baptist, the oldest Catholic church in Georgia, was moved from Liberty Square, its home since the late 1700's, to 222 East Harris Street, where a larger church was built. The First African Baptist Church at 23 Montgomery Street, completed in 1861, grew out of the first African American congregation in the United States, organized in 1788 at nearby Brampton Plantation. Other churches from this era include the Trinity United Methodist Church at 123 Bernard Street, the oldest Methodist church in Georgia, which was dedicated in 1848, and the Lutheran Church of Ascension at 21 East State Street, which German settlers had organized in 1741. The present church dates from 1844 and was enlarged in the 1870's.

The Civil War

Savannah's period of rapid growth ended with the Civil War. Savannah was an important Confederate blockade-running port during the war until its capture by Union general William Tecumseh Sherman's army, at the end of his March to the Sea. Instead of torching Savannah, Sherman decided to give the city as a gift to President Abraham Lincoln. On December 22, 1864, Sherman wrote a telegram to Lincoln from Savannah: "To his excellency President Lincoln, Washington, D.C.: I beg to present to you as a Christmas gift the city of Savannah, with 150 heavy guns and plenty of ammunition, also about 25,000 bales of cotton."

The occupation was peaceful and uneventful, perhaps because Sherman had taken a liking to the charming southern city. In his memoirs Sherman recalled that when he arrived in Savannah it was

an old place, and usually accounted a handsome one. . . . Its houses were brick and frame, with large yards, ornamented with shrubbery and flowers; its streets perfectly regular, crossing each other at right angles; and at many of the intersections were small closures in the nature of parks. These streets and parks were lined with the handsomest shade trees of which I have knowledge, viz, the willow-leaf live-oak, evergreens of exquisite beauty; and these certainly entitle Savannah to its reputation as a handsome town.

Postwar Recovery

After the Civil War, Savannah's economy weakened, for cotton was no longer king. Gradually, however, Savannah regained its position as an important port on the south Atlantic Coast. It began to take on the look of an industrial city as it spread out in all directions, attracted factories, and exhibited the characteristics of a busy manufacturing center. Today, the city serves the region as both a shipping and a manufacturing base for a wide variety of goods, including steel, chemicals, paper, and tractor trailers.

By the 1920's, Savannah's historic architecture had began to deteriorate, a decline that continued into the immediate post-World War II years. In the early 1950's, several important public buildings were demolished. Some historic preservation work, however, began in the 1940's when the city restored buildings in the Trustees Garden.

In 1955, residents created the Historic Savannah Foundation and began a project to restore old buildings in the historic center of town. The impetus for the foundation's creation was the threatened demolition of the Davenport House. Less than twenty-four hours before its scheduled demolition, the home was saved from the wrecker's ball by the foundation.

During the second half of the twentieth century, more than one thousand buildings were restored in the oldest section of Savannah, and the area became a popular tourist attraction. One of the foundation's major successes was the 1966 designation of the area from East Broad to West Broad (now Martin Luther King, Jr., Boulevard), from the River to Gaston Street, as a Landmark Historic District. It is one of the largest historic districts in the country. The foundation also established a revolving fund to buy historic properties, work for their preservation, and sell them to owners who had the desire to restore them. Today, few U.S. cities can claim such

a commendable record of historic preservation as can Savannah.   *—Ron Chepesiuk*

For Further Information:
Bell, Malcolm. *Savannah.* Savannah: Historic Savannah Foundation, 1977. Given Savannah's fascinating history and rich architectural heritage, numerous books have been written about the city. They include several fine illustrated works, such as this one. Includes photographs by Jane Iseley.

Mitchell, William Robert, Jr. *Classic Savannah.* New York: St. Martin's, 1991. Another fine illustrated work about Savannah. Includes photographs by Van Jones Martin.

Sieg, Chan. *The Squares of Savannah.* Savannah, Ga.: Savannah Area Chamber of Commerce, 1965. A worthwhile specialized book about Savannah.

Smith, Derek. *Civil War Savannah.* Savannah, Ga.: Frederic C. Beil, 1997. Examines the history of Savannah during the Civil War.

Stone Mountain

Relevant issues: American Indian history, art and architecture, Civil War, cultural history

Significance: Stone Mountain is the largest piece of exposed granite in North America and the anchor for an extensive park complex. The mountain also contains the largest work of sculpture in the world—a carving of three Confederate figures.

Location: Approximately sixteen miles east of Atlanta, in De Kalb County, Georgia

Site Office:
Stone Mountain Park Marketing Department
P.O. Box 778
Stone Mountain, GA 30086
ph.: (770) 498-5690
Web site: www.stonemountainpark.com

Stone Mountain is worthy of note for its geological significance alone; rising to 1,683 feet at its highest point, it dominates the terrain and can be seen from thirty miles away. Roughly four miles in circumference, it covers an area of over five hundred acres. It is the largest piece of exposed granite in North America, and for years was the site of extensive quarries; Stone Mountain granite is now found in important buildings throughout the world. However, it is now most well known for the large carving of three Confederate figures on its north face, a carving that constitutes the largest single sculpture in the world.

Earliest Known History

It is unclear when exactly Stone Mountain was formed, but geologists fix the date at approximately 200 million years ago, when underground molten stone bubbled up in a dome shape, forming layers of rock which later cooled very slowly to become dense, uniform crystals of granite. At the same time, the top of the structure began a continuing process of erosion, giving it a distinctive rounded or "bald" shape.

The earliest Europeans to see the mountain appear to have been Spanish soldiers, though early records are not absolutely definitive. When trappers, traders, and settlers inquired about the mountain, the local Native Americans informed them that they knew nothing of its origin, as it had been there before their own ancestors arrived.

Up until the early twentieth century, the remnants of a stone wall, several feet high, could still be seen on Stone Mountain's summit. A favorite pastime of early visitors was tossing the constituent rocks down the side of the mountain. While early visitors often mistakenly believed that this enclosure indicated an attempt to fortify by the early Spanish conquistadors, this was clearly not true, as the wall was apparently not high enough, and the lack of food and water at the site would make it indefensible in a protracted siege. Modern anthropologists believe that the wall, which is similar to many others found at ceremonial sites throughout the South, was used for religious ritual purposes by early Native Americans.

In fact, Stone Mountain is located within a neutral zone between early Native American nations within Georgia, and heads a crossroad of major trading routes of the Cherokee and Muskogee (commonly called Creek) nations. This location was important in one of the earliest known records of activity at the site—a meeting between Colonel Marinus Willett (an emissary of President Washington), Alexander McGillivray, and other representatives of the Muskogees—to begin a trip to New York for treaty talks.

Through various treaties and agreements, the land on which Stone Mountain sits was finally ceded to the state of Georgia in 1821 in a parcel that included the land on which Atlanta now sits. This opened the way to European settlement of the entire Stone Mountain area, and the Native Americans who had apparently once worshipped on the top of Stone Mountain were eventually removed by force from almost all of Georgia.

Early Settlements

Once the area near Stone Mountain—which was then often called Stoney Mountain or Rock Mountain—was opened to European settlement, a village quickly grew up at the base of the mountain, appropriately called New Gibraltar. The new town was incorporated in 1839, but in 1847 the name was changed to Stone Mountain to reflect the newly popular name for the granite structure. By the early nineteenth century, the mountain was a popular local tourist destination, and an observation tower was built on the summit called Cloud's Tower, which was later removed by a storm and replaced by a smaller structure. Other accidents were also distressingly common, and the people who have plummeted to their deaths from Stone Mountain may number in the hundreds. These mishaps, however, did not serve to discourage tourists.

During the Civil War, Stone Mountain was the site of numerous skirmishes and at least one full-scale battle just outside the town. During the Reconstruction period, the town of Stone Mountain grew rapidly, including a sizable settlement of freed slaves in the area called Shermantown. At this time the beginnings of a large quarrying industry began to grow up around the mountain, also. The industry was helped by the large demand for high-quality granite required to rebuild after the war; the newly repaired railroad which ran near the mountain was capable of transporting enormous stones off the summit. Beginning in 1869 and extending for almost a century, high-quality granite was blasted and cut from the mountain and sold for use in many prestigious building projects, including the locks of the Panama Canal, the Cuban capitol, and innumerable post offices and federal and state office buildings.

The Confederate Memorial Carving

The idea to use the granite of Stone Mountain as a canvas for a Confederate memorial was first proposed in print in an editorial in the *Atlanta Constitution* in June, 1914, by William H. Terrell. The call was soon taken up by others, but by none more enthusiastically than Helen Jemison Plane, honorary life president of the Georgia division of the United Daughters of the Confederacy (UDC). Plane conceived a bust carving of General Robert E. Lee on the face of Stone Mountain and asked the renowned sculptor Gutzon Borglum to come to Georgia and give his opinion as to the feasibility of the work; Borglum is now best known for his sculpture of four presidents on Mount Rushmore in South Dakota, which he began after his involvement with the Stone Mountain project. In August, 1915, Borglum arrived at Stone Mountain and, a few weeks later, presented his conception of the work to the UDC. He envisioned a huge carving of hundreds of figures in groups, representing political and military leaders of the Confederacy, as well as common soldiers of the cavalry and infantry.

While Plane and the UDC were enthusiastic about the plans, they were unable to secure adequate financing for such an enormous project. Additionally, many people doubted whether Borglum could accomplish the task, and whether the layered granite of the mountain could sustain such a carving without flaking away.

Further controversy was stirred in November, 1915, when the showing of D. W. Griffith's film *The Birth of a Nation* prompted William Simmons to organize a new Ku Klux Klan, and he chose Stone Mountain as the location for the first rally, which was accompanied by a cross-burning. However, despite such problems, Borglum began work on the project in May of 1916.

The onset of America's involvement in World War I halted the work for a time, however, and Borglum was not able to resume activities until 1921. The work then proceeded amid constant financial problems and conflicts between Borglum and the Stone Mountain Monumental Association, chaired by Hollins Randolph. In March, 1924, the United States Congress authorized the minting of a special half-dollar coin to commemorate the sculpture and raise funds for the project. Borglum's accusations that Randolph was mishandling the coin funds effectively ended Borglum's relationship with the project, and he left the state after destroying his original models.

Eventually, another sculptor, Augustus Lukeman, was chosen to complete the memorial. Lukeman's design was completely different from Borglum's, and vastly reduced in scale, from hundreds of figures in various groupings to three major figures seated on horseback—President of the Confederacy Jefferson Davis, General Robert E. Lee, and General Thomas Jonathan "Stonewall" Jackson. Nevertheless, though Lukeman began work on his plan

Stone Mountain. (Georgia Department of Industry, Trade & Tourism)

and completed substantial portions of it (blasting away Borglum's work in the process), he was unable to finish due to lack of funds and various disagreements with the association. After completing Lee's head and part of his body in 1927, Lukeman moved on to other projects.

Finally, in 1958, the Stone Mountain Memorial Association was formed by an act of the Georgia legislature. This body eventually acquired thirty-two hundred acres of land for the Stone Mountain Memorial Park. In 1963, Walker Kirtland Hancock was chosen to complete Lukeman's carving of Davis, Lee, and Jackson. Work officially resumed in July of 1964, and the finished sculpture was dedicated in May of 1970. Rising four hundred feet above the ground, the carving is approximately two hundred feet wide, ninety feet high, and reaches eleven feet deep into the mountain. It is the focal point for an extensive park complex that includes many recreation and historical opportunities for the more than one million tourists who visit annually.

Places to Visit
In addition to the enormous and impressive carving itself, Stone Mountain Park contains numerous square miles of protected wilderness area complete with hiking trails and other amenities. Naturalists often study the unique forms of flora and fauna found only in the area of the mountain, such as the Georgia oak. Further, there is a restored nineteenth century village, as well as a reproduction of an antebellum plantation, complete with actual historic buildings transported to the site from locations around Georgia; Memorial Hall contains various historic exhibits about the mountain and the Civil War in Georgia. The Stone Mountain Railroad and the sky lift transport visitors to the top of the mountain, and a traditional riverboat ride is also available. An extensive antique automobile and music museum displays some very fine examples of rare early automobiles and working versions of many early motion picture and music technologies. —*Vicki A. Sanders*

For Further Information:

Freeman, David B. *Carved in Stone: The History of Stone Mountain.* Macon, Ga.: Mercer UP, 1997. This book is the most comprehensive and detailed source of information on the mountain, the carving, and the towns associated with Stone Mountain.

Garrett, Franklin M. *Atlanta and Environs: A Chronicle of its People and Events.* 2 vols. Athens: University of Georgia Press, 1954. This two-volume history contains numerous references to Stone Mountain that help situate the monolith and its associated events in the context of other state places and incidents.

Hyder, William D., and R. W. Colbert. *The Selling of the Stone Mountain Half Dollar.* Colorado Springs: American Numismatic Association, n.d. Reprinted from *The Numismatist,* this short article reprint gives the most complete rendering of the coin controversy and the specifics of the various coins minted.

Morse, Minna. "The Changing Face of Stone Mountain." *Smithsonian* 29, no. 10 (January, 1999): 56-67. This lengthy article provides information about the inhabitants of the city of Stone Mountain and Shermantown, the early African American settlement.

Neal, Willard. *The Story of Stone Mountain.* Atlanta, Ga.: American Lithograph, 1963. This short volume provides an excellent overview of the history of the mountain and the sculpture.

"Stone Mountain Park." www.stonemountainpark .com. This site, maintained by the marketing organization of the state park at Stone Mountain, provides information about all the attractions and exhibits found at the park complex.

Other Historic Sites

Benét House
Location: Augusta, Richmond County
Relevant issues: Literary history

Statement of significance: Stephen Vincent Benét (1898-1943), known for his poetry and short stories, began his writing career in this two-story

Federal-style house after moving here in 1911. It now serves as the president's home for Augusta College.

Chieftains

Location: Rome, Floyd County
Web site: ngeorgia.com/site/chieftains.html
Relevant issues: American Indian history
Statement of significance: Built around 1794, this hand-hewn log cabin was purchased by Major Ridge (c. 1770-1839), a Cherokee leader, sometime before 1819 and is incorporated into the present larger house. Ridge himself made the first additions in 1827-1828. Ridge operated a ferry and trading post, was the speaker of the Cherokee National Council, and was a significant advocate of modifying Cherokee ways with Anglo-American culture.

Columbus Historic Riverfront Industrial District

Location: Columbus, Muscogee County
Relevant issues: Science and technology
Statement of significance: Dating from 1844 to 1900, this area physically documents the evolution of hydrotechnology and its contributions to the growth of an important southern textile center. Here is the best surviving concentration of nineteenth and early twentieth century hydromechanical and hydroelectrical engineering systems in the South.

Dixie Coca-Cola Bottling Company Plant

Location: Atlanta, Fulton County
Web site: www.atlanta.org/dept/urban/dixieco.htm#dixie
Relevant issues: Business and industry
Statement of significance: This small brick building served, in 1900-1901, as the headquarters of what has become the Coca-Cola Bottling Company.

Etowah Mounds

Location: Cartersville, Bartow County
Relevant issues: American Indian history
Statement of significance: This site is important as an expression of the eastern expansion of Mississippian culture, and of the forms Mississippian culture took as a result of interaction with other Southeastern cultural traditions (c. 1350). It

consists of three large platform mounds, a village area, and an encircling ditch or moat.

Governor's Mansion

Location: Milledgeville, Baldwin County
Relevant issues: Political history
Statement of significance: This was the home of Georgia governors when Milledgeville was the state capital from 1804 to 1868. It is distinguished by a Palladian facade with prostyle portico and a plan with round and octagonal rooms.

Harris House

Location: Atlanta, Fulton County
Relevant issues: Literary history
Statement of significance: Joel Chandler Harris (1848-1908), author of the Uncle Remus tales, lived here from 1881 until his death in 1908. The house contains many original furnishings.

Historic Augusta Canal and Industrial District

Location: Augusta, Richmond County
Relevant issues: Business and industry, science and technology
Statement of significance: This district contains an intact canal system and mills constructed from the 1840's to the 1880's representative of industrial aspects of the New South. It is the best surviving example of an engineering system singularly important to the southeastern United States.

Kolomoki Mounds

Location: Blakely, Early County
Relevant issues: American Indian history
Statement of significance: Excavations have revealed details of burial practices at this type site for the Kolomoki culture (c. 1400-1600). This site contains one of the largest mound groups on the southeastern coastal plain. It is now a state park.

Liberty Hall

Location: Crawfordville, Taliaferro County
Relevant issues: Political history
Statement of significance: Alexander Stephens (1812-1883), the vice president of the Confederate States of America, who also enjoyed a remarkable political career before and after the Civil War, lived at his Liberty Hall estate from 1834 until his death in 1883.

Low Birthplace

Location: Savannah, Chatham County

Relevant issues: Cultural history, women's history

Statement of significance: This is the birthplace and childhood home of Juliette Gordon Low (1860-1927), the founder of the Girl Scout movement in the United States. Low held the first meeting in her carriage house. She became the first president of the Girl Scouts after their incorporation in 1915. She lived here until she married William Mackay Low in 1886.

New Echota

Location: Calhoun, Gordon County

Web site: www.northga.net/gordon/echota.html

Relevant issues: American Indian history

Statement of significance: This was the first national capital of the Cherokees, established in 1825. It was here in 1835 that the Treaty of New Echota was signed, establishing the basic pretext for the final removal of the Cherokee to the West and the Trail of Tears.

Old Medical College

Location: Augusta, Richmond County

Relevant issues: Health and medicine

Statement of significance: The Old Medical College is nationally significant because of its impact on the medical instruction of physicians nationwide and its involvement in the establishment of the American Medical Association.

Ross House

Location: Rossville, Walker County

Relevant issues: American Indian history

Statement of significance: This square-timbered two-story log house was the home of John Ross (1790-1866), the Cherokees' most prominent leader who led his people for forty years as chief executive and primary diplomat. He became chief in 1828, led the delegations of protest and resistance to the policies of removal, and ultimately led the Cherokee Nation in exile beyond the Mississippi on the Trail of Tears.

Stallings Island

Location: Augusta, Columbia County

Relevant issues: American Indian history

Statement of significance: This is one of the most important shell mound sites in the Southeast, giving information on Archaic Indians who lived in the Savannah River drainage area.

Sweet Auburn Historic District

Location: Atlanta, Fulton County

Relevant issues: African American history

Statement of significance: This district was the center of black economic, social, and cultural activities in Atlanta from the 1890's to the 1930's. The Sweet Auburn District reflects an important element in the life of the African American community in a segregated South.

Walton House

Location: Augusta, Richmond County

Relevant issues: Political history

Statement of significance: This was the home of George Walton (1741-1804) from 1791 to 1804. Appointed to the Continental Congress in 1776, at twenty-six he was the youngest signer of the Declaration of Independence. After the war, he served as Georgia's governor and as a U.S. senator.

Warm Springs Historic District

Location: Warm Springs, Meriwether County

Relevant issues: Health and medicine, political history

Statement of significance: The district includes two vacation homes (1928-1932 and 1932-1945) of Franklin D. Roosevelt, who found relief from polio in the mineral springs of this small resort town, and the Warm Springs Hospital, founded by Roosevelt to aid fellow victims of the disease. Roosevelt's efforts led to the March of Dimes. He died at his "Little White House" in Warm Springs on April 12, 1945.

Hawaii

History of Hawaii 363
Iolani Palace, Honolulu 365
Kawaiahao Church and Mission Houses,
    Honolulu 369

Lahaina 371
Pearl Harbor 375
Other Historic Sites 380

Honolulu, on the island of Oahu. (Corbis)

History of Hawaii

Hawaii is unique in many ways. It is the only one of the fifty United States that lies outside the northern hemisphere and is, with Alaska, one of two states that is not part of the contiguous forty-eight states that, until 1959, constituted the United States of America. It is the only state that is composed of a group of islands, running from the big island of Hawaii to the islet of Kure at Hawaii's northwest extreme. Ka Lae, or South Cape, on the big island, is the southernmost point in the United States.

Hawaii is also the most multiethnic state in the Union. Some 40 percent of Hawaiian marriages are interracial. In this state of idyllic islands with inviting beaches, one can ascend the big island's Mauna Loa volcano in winter and, at an altitude of almost fourteen thousand feet, go skiing. Although 80 percent of its population lives in bustling, crowded cities, mainly Honolulu, Hawaiians are probably the most relaxed of all Americans.

Early History

As early as the middle of the eighth century, people sailed from the South Seas to Hawaii, presumably intent on colonizing some of its islands. Most of these people were southeast Asians who had made their arduous way to Tahiti and the Marquesa Islands. In time, sailing in large double-hulled canoes, they continued to Hawaii, carrying with them roots and seeds to plant, as well as animals, mostly pigs and chickens, to raise.

These seamen knew enough about sailing and about the currents of the Pacific Ocean, presumably, to make trips from Tahiti to Hawaii and safely back to Tahiti. Seemingly they did this regularly between 1100 and 1400. An influx of foreigners resumed, however, in the eighteenth century, this time from Europe as well as Asia. The native Hawaiian population, which exceeded 225,000 toward the end of that century, plummeted to about 50,000 one hundred years later, as many natives fell victim to diseases that visitors brought to the islands.

Although Spanish seamen sailed from Manila in the Philippines to the west coast of Mexico in the seventeenth century, they seem to have passed north of the Hawaiian archipelago and were unaware of this chain of volcanic islands. Captain James Cook, in January, 1778, was probably the first European to find the Hawaiian Islands, calling them the Sandwich Islands after the Earl of Sandwich, from whom he had financial support for his explorations. In February, 1779, Captain Cook was killed by natives on the big island of Hawaii in an argument over some thefts from his ship. In time, trade with white merchants began to flourish, Hawaii's chief export being sandalwood. As foreign merchants came to Hawaii to trade, the social structure of the islands began to change.

The Kingdom of Hawaii

In 1810, Kamehameha I, a warrior chief, founded the Kingdom of Hawaii after gaining the loyal support of Kauai's chieftain. Although a native Hawaiian gained political control, the islands had already been altered appreciably by the influx of people from the West who came there to do business. Upon the king's death in 1819, Kamehameha II, who welcomed traders from the West, was given the reins of power. Under his jurisdiction, the *kapu* system, based on the ancient laws and taboos that had long prevailed in the islands, began to give way to Western customs.

The following year, the first Christian missionaries arrived from New England. These Congregationalists were soon followed by Methodists from the United States, Roman Catholics from France, Anglicans from Britain, and Lutherans from Germany. Mormon missionaries arrived considerably later and had such great success in winning Hawaiians to Mormonism that they ultimately established a branch of Brigham Young University and a Mormon temple and information center on Oahu's northeast coast.

The pusillanimous Hawaiians, who were traditionally polytheistic, were easy to convert to Christianity, although they still preserved the myths of many of their deities, such as Pele and Maui. The arrival of the missionaries marked a wave of immigration to the islands and also heralded an era of

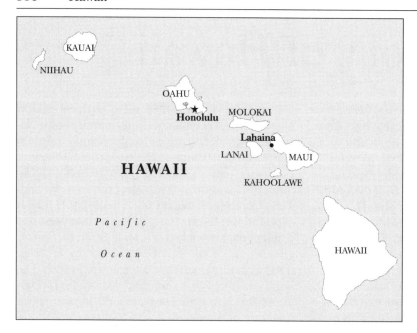

interracial interchanges and interracial marriage, thereby minimizing many of the ethnic divisions that characterize some societies.

The next wave of immigration came in the 1850's, when large numbers of Chinese immigrants arrived, drawn to Hawaii by its climate, its strategic location, and its commercial possibilities. The Chinese, many of whom initially worked on the sugar and pineapple plantations, soon gravitated to urban centers, mostly to Honolulu, to establish businesses. Soon they had the highest family income of all the ethnic groups in the islands.

During the nineteenth century, significant numbers of immigrants arrived, first from Japan around 1860, then from Scandinavia, Spain, Madeira, the Azores, Puerto Rico, and Germany. The overwhelming influx was from Asia. About half of Hawaii's population is of Asian ancestry. Intermarriage reduced the number of full-blooded Hawaiians from about 225,000 at the end of the eighteenth century to less that 10,000 at the end of the twentieth century.

Land Ownership
The king originally owned most of the state's land, held as crown lands. These properties, broken up in 1848, eventually reverted to the territorial government, which now owns about 40 percent of Hawaii's land. The federal government owns another 10 percent, and private land barons own all but about 3 percent of the remaining land. As a result, many people who own houses or other buildings in Hawaii built them on leased land. Long-term leases offer homeowners some protection, but when the leases come up for renewal, substantial increases are usually imposed.

The Bishop Estate is the largest private landowner in Hawaii, holding about 9 percent of all the land in the state. It uses the large income that these lands produce to fund the Kamehameha School, initially established to educate children of Hawaiian blood and thought to be the most affluent secondary school in the world.

The Annexation of Hawaii
By the middle of the nineteenth century, during the reign of Kamehameha III, the kingdom was increasingly influenced by American missionaries. Kamehameha III in 1843 ceded the islands to Britain, but within a few months, the United States had strongly protested this action, and, shortly thereafter, both Britain and France acknowledged Hawaii's independence. The kingdom was reformed under the Organic Acts of 1845-1847.

The reigns of Kamehameha IV and Kamehameha V witnessed the growth of huge sugar plantations owned mostly by Americans. U.S. financial interests in Hawaii grew before the reign of Queen Liliuokalani, who ascended to the throne in 1891. She showed signs of becoming a more absolute ruler than her predecessors, so in 1893 she was deposed, and a republic, whose president was American Sanford B. Dole, was soon created. Dole and his legislature requested that the United States annex Hawaii, which, after some hesitation, it did in 1898. It officially became a United States territory in 1900.

Moving Toward Statehood
With the advent of military aircraft during World

War I, Hawaii began to be viewed by military leaders as a first line of defense for the continental United States. With the bombing of Pearl Harbor on December 7, 1941, Americans soon realized how vulnerable Hawaii was to attack and how vital it was both as a line of defense and as a staging area for a Pacific war.

During the early days of World War II, Nisei Japanese who lived in Hawaii were viewed with a combination of distrust and contempt. They were barred from service in the U.S. armed forces, although they were not incarcerated in camps, as their counterparts on the mainland West Coast had been. Eventually they were admitted to the armed forces and, as members of the 100th Infantry Battalion and the 442d Regimental Combat Team, performed heroically in some of the most desperate battles of the conflict, proving their loyalty.

Shortly after the war, mainland labor unions called plantation strikes in Hawaii that paralyzed shipping in 1946, 1948, and 1958. The five business cartels that controlled a great deal of the islands' economy were forced to make substantial concessions to plantation workers. Many Japanese Americans rose to political power and did a great deal to reform state government. As the territory attracted large numbers of new inhabitants and gained considerable affluence, agitation for statehood grew. In 1959 statehood was conferred.

The Growth of Tourism

Hawaii's economy during the nineteenth century and the first half of the twentieth came largely from the sale of sandalwood, sugar, and pineapples, although the federal and territorial governments increasingly provided jobs that bolstered the economy. In 1970 seventy thousand of the islands' population of less than one million were employed in state and federal jobs. By 1997 the federal government employed only 20,221 people in Hawaii at an average salary of $39,984.

Although the federal government spends a billion dollars a year in Hawaii, its expenditures are far exceeded by the revenues generated for the state through tourism, which in 1996 amounted to more than fourteen billion dollars. The Hawaiian Chamber of Commerce is among the most efficient and accommodating in the United States. The five islands that are most often visited—Oahu, Maui, Hawaii, Molokai, and Kauai—have excellent tourist facilities and offer breathtaking beaches and waves that attract surfers from around the world. Of the inhabited islands, only Lanai, owned by the Dole Corporation, limits tourism.

Honolulu is Hawaii's most-visited city. Waikiki Beach, close to the main section of Honolulu, is lined with elegant hotels. Its beaches are filled with tourists and surfers throughout the year. Such natural attractions as the Haleakala volcano on Maui, the Mauna Loa and Mauna Kea volcanoes on Hawaii, Diamond Head on Oahu, and the Waimea Canyon on Kauai are popular among tourists.

—*R. Baird Shuman*

Iolani Palace, Honolulu

Date: Construction completed in 1882

Relevant issues: Art and architecture, cultural history, political history

Significance: Iolani Palace was the seat of government for the Kingdom of Hawaii from 1882 until the overthrow of the Hawaiian monarchy in 1893. It was the official residence of King Kalakaua and Queen Liliuokalani, the last monarchs of Hawaii. It then served as the capitol of the provisional government of Hawaii (1893-1894), the republic of Hawaii (1894-1900), the territory of Hawaii (1900-1959), and the state of Hawaii (1959-present) until a new state capitol building was ready for occupancy in 1969. The palace was reopened to the public as a historic museum in 1978 under the administration of the Friends of 'Iolani Palace, a nonprofit citizens' group established in 1966 to encourage the preservation and restoration of the palace.

Location: Historic Capitol District, downtown Honolulu, the island of Oahu

Site Office:
Friends of 'Iolani Palace
P.O. Box 2259
Honolulu, HI 96804
ph.: (808) 522-0822
Web site: www.openstudio.hawaii.edu/iolani

Iolani Palace was completed in 1882 under the sponsorship of Hawaii's last king, King Kalakaua. It occupies a site that has been sacred to Native Hawaiians, the indigenous people of the islands, for hundreds of years. It is the last in a series of royal palaces that were called '*iolani*, a reference to the high-flying Hawaiian hawk that once signified Hawaiian royalty.

The cornerstone of the present Iolani Palace was laid on December 31, 1879. It replaced an earlier palace of the same name near the same site that had been torn down because of termite damage. The new Iolani Palace was built at a cost to the Kingdom of Hawaii of approximately $360,000.

Iolani Palace is constructed of plastered brick and iron. It has four stories, including an attic and a basement. It has a square tower in the center of the front and back of the building and four smaller towers, one on each corner of the building. Verandas, supported by cast-iron Corinthian columns, run along all four sides of the building on both the first and second floors. Large glass windows line the verandas. The architectural style of the palace was dubbed American Florentine in an early newspaper article, a reference to its ornate exterior. However, the palace is surprisingly modest in size, measuring only 140 feet by 100 feet.

King Kalakaua took a lively interest in the construction of his palace. Consequently, it featured amenities that were decidedly modern for the time, including four full bathrooms on the second floor as well as two "water closets" for guests on the first floor. Even after he moved into the palace in late 1882, King Kalakaua continued to add innovations. For example, gas chandeliers initially lighted the building. After seeing electric lights in Paris in 1881, the king was determined to have them installed in the palace. By 1886 electric lights illuminated the palace verandas. In 1887 electricity was installed in the main rooms. A modern telephone, installed in 1883, allowed the king to talk to his household staff and to his friends who were connected to the city telephone system.

Inside Iolani Palace

During the eleven years that the palace served as the seat of government for Hawaii and home to Hawaiian royalty, the first floor was used for formal functions and the second floor provided living space for the royal family. The basement housed kitchens and storerooms, as well as offices for the household staff. The large attic was used principally as an airspace to keep the lower floors cool.

Guests invited to Iolani Palace almost always entered it through its main front doors. They then found themselves in the Grand Hall, an area constructed of polished wood lined with oil portraits of Hawaii's kings and queens. A magnificent staircase that leads to the second floor dominates the Grand Hall. There are three rooms on the first floor: the Throne Room, the State Dining Room, and the Blue Room.

The largest room on the first floor is the Throne Room; its predominant colors are maroon and gold. In King Kalakaua's day this ornate room, with its brilliant chandeliers and dazzling mirrors, was used to receive distinguished visitors. It was also the scene of magnificent dress balls, where guests danced until the wee hours to music provided by the Royal Hawaiian Band, which was stationed on the veranda immediately outside the Throne Room. Refreshments were served in the State Dining Room.

When the State Dining Room was used for official functions, as it often was, as many as forty guests could be seated at its long tables. Place settings included gold-rimmed Limoges china from France decorated with the Hawaiian coat of arms, crystal from Bohemia, and sterling silver from England, France, China, and the United States. Guests enjoyed elaborate meals that often included Hawaiian, European, and American dishes. The dining room was connected to the kitchen by two dumbwaiters.

The Blue Room, which, as its name indicates, is decorated predominantly in blue, is located immediately to the left of the main entrance to the palace. It was used for small receptions and informal gatherings.

The second floor of the palace held the private living quarters of the royal family. These consisted of three large rooms on each side of a large central hall. King Kalakaua's interconnected suite of rooms included a bedroom with a dressing room and bathroom, a library that served as his office, and a music room, sometimes called the Gold Room, where the family entertained informally. The suite of the king's consort, Queen Kapiolani, included her bedroom, with a dressing room and bathroom, and two guest bedrooms. Two sitting rooms were nestled under the front and rear corner towers of the palace on the queen's side of the hallway. The hallway itself served as a kind of sitting room. Here the royal family ate breakfast and entertained their intimate friends.

Iolani Palace. (Hawaii Visitors & Convention Bureau)

The Palace Grounds

Iolani Palace sits on a large, green, tree-shaded tract of land in what is now downtown Honolulu. It is surrounded by a stone wall topped by a decorative iron fence. There are four gates, each with its own name; during the monarchy era, each had a distinctive use. Several structures can be found on the palace grounds, including the Coronation Pavilion, which King Kalakaua built in 1883 to celebrate his long-postponed coronation. The octagonal pavilion, which is used today as a bandstand by the Royal Hawaiian Band, is also used for the inauguration of the governors of the state of Hawaii. Another structure, Iolani Barracks, was built in 1871 to house the Royal Guard. In 1965 this building was moved, stone by stone, from a nearby site and reassembled. It now serves as the palace shop and ticket office. A fenced-in mound of grass on the palace grounds marks the site of the former Royal Tomb. Although the remains of Hawaiian royalty were moved in 1865 to a new site, the Royal

Mausoleum, some accounts state that the bones of certain chiefs remain on the site. King Kalakaua raised a mound over this spot and had it planted with ferns and flowers. A fence and marker were erected in 1930.

Iolani Palace and Queen Liliuokalani

When King Kalakaua died in 1891, his body lay in state in the Throne Room for two weeks. He was succeeded by his sister, Queen Liliuokalani, who used the palace as her royal residence until she was forced to abdicate in 1893 under threat of force by American troops. The queen then moved back to her own residence, Washington Place, now the home of Hawaii's governors. The palace was renamed the Executive Building and became the seat of the provisional government.

In 1895 a group of supporters loyal to the queen initiated a revolt. Officials of what was then the Republic of Hawaii arrested the rebels and accused the queen of fomenting the rebellion. The queen was tried in her former Throne Room and found guilty. Sentenced to five years in prison, she was held in one of the former guest bedrooms on the second floor of the palace for eight months. After she was pardoned, the queen traveled to the United States to plead the cause of the Hawaiian kingdom, but to no avail. On August 12, 1898, Hawaii was officially annexed to the United States. The Hawaiian flag was lowered from the central flagpole atop the palace and the American flag was raised in its place. Two years later Hawaii officially became an American territory when President William McKinley signed the Organic Act.

Iolani Palace, 1900-1969

After the overthrow of the monarchy, most of the palace's furnishings were dispersed. Some remained in the royal family, some were moved to Washington Place, but most were sold at auction. The royal thrones were placed at the Bernice Pauahi Bishop Museum.

The building underwent a metamorphosis. The State Dining Room became the chamber for the Territorial Senate. The Territorial House of Representatives occupied the Throne Room. King Kalakaua's bedroom and library served as the executive chamber for territorial governors. Later, after statehood in 1959, the legislative and executive branches of the Hawaii state government continued to occupy the building.

The name "Iolani Palace" was restored in 1935, and the Throne Room was restored in 1938. A full-scale restoration of the palace began in 1969, when a new state capitol building was ready for occupancy. Then the dream of restoring Iolani Palace to its former glory became a reality. Under the leadership of the Friends of 'Iolani Palace, led by descendants of Hawaiian royalty, the palace was restored, inch by painstaking inch. Temporary additions to the exterior of the building and partitions that had been added to the interior were removed. Termite damage was repaired. Furnishings were recovered from all over the world. Carpets, draperies, and fabrics were re-created. Today Iolani Palace is open for guided tours. It offers the visitor an authentic glimpse of Hawaii's royal heritage.

Iolani Palace was declared a National Historic Landmark in 1962. It was placed on the National Register of Historic Places in 1978.

—*Linda K. Menton*

For Further Information:

Allen, Gwenfread. *Hawaii's Iolani Palace and Its Kings and Queens.* Honolulu: Aloha Graphics and Sales, 1978. Recounts the history of the current palace as well as those that preceded it. Includes information about the royal personages who lived in the palace and the many historic ceremonies and events that took place there.

Du Pont, Keoni. *A Walking Tour of 'Iolani Palace Grounds: A Guide for Teachers.* Honolulu: Friends of 'Iolani Palace, 1995. Includes historical information on sites and buildings on the palace grounds. Although the tour is designed for secondary students, this source contains excellent historical information for adult readers.

Hackler, Rhoda E. A. *'Iolani Palace: Hawai'i's Royal Palace, Official Residence of King Kalākaua and Queen Lili'uokalani, the Last Monarchs of Hawai'i, 1882-1893.* Rev. ed. Honolulu: Friends of 'Iolani Palace, 1993. Detailed history of the palace with information about it many rooms and historic furnishings, as well as its grounds. Illustrated with excellent color photographs. Includes bibliographical references.

Iolani Palace Restoration Project Staff. *Iolani Palace Restoration.* Honolulu: Friends of 'Iolani Palace, 1970. Describes tasks accomplished and outlines further work needed for restoration of palace as of 1970. Includes archival photos, photos of interior and exterior aspects of the palace in the late 1960's, floor plans, and architectural drawings.

Old Honolulu: A Guide to Oahu's Historic Buildings. Honolulu: Mayor's Historic Buildings Task Force, 1969. Contains brief descriptions of historic buildings on the island of Oahu, including Iolani Palace and other nearby structures such as Washington Place. Includes maps and photographs.

Peek, Jeannette Murray. *Stepping into Time: A Guide to Honolulu's Historic Landmarks.* Honolulu: Mutual, 1994. Includes information about the palace, the Coronation Pavilion, and Iolani Barracks. Illustrated with pen-and-ink drawings by the author.

U.S. Department of the Interior, National Park Service. *National Register of Historic Places.* Teaneck, N.J.: Chadwyck Healey, 1982. Includes Inventory and Nomination Forms and photographs of historic properties, arranged by state, county, and vicinity. Hawaii entry includes extensive information about the palace and other structures on the grounds.

Kawaiahao Church and Mission Houses, Honolulu

Date: Church completed in 1842; three adjoining mission houses built in 1821, 1831, and 1841

Relevant issues: Art and architecture, cultural history, education, European settlement, religion

Significance: Kawaiahao Church, still active in the Hawaiian community and offering Sunday worship in the Hawaiian language, is the first permanent house of worship in the Hawaiian Islands. The mission houses, preserved as a museum, reflect the daily life and work of the early Puritan missionaries and their successors.

Location: Central Honolulu, the island of Oahu

Site Offices:

Kawaiahao Church
957 Punchbowl
Honolulu, HI 96813
ph.: (808) 522-1333

Mission Houses Museum
5535 South King Street
Honolulu, HI 96826
ph.: (808) 531-0481
fax: (808) 545-2280
Web site: www.lava.net/-mhm/main.htm

The first ship of Puritan missionaries arrived in Hawaii from Boston in 1820 at an opportune time, when the established Hawaiian religion had lost power among the ruling class after the death of King Kamehameha I. King Kamehameha II accepted Christianity and donated land and labor to construct a church and a home for the Reverend Hiram Bingham and his family. The monarchs and their families were baptized, married, coronated, and laid in state in the church. The acceptance and sponsorship of this Congregationalist church by Hawaiian royalty gave it a reputation as the West-minster Abbey of Hawaii. The adjoining mission buildings housed missionaries and a printing center.

Establishment of Christianity in Hawaii

Reverend Bingham led the Congregationalist missionaries sent out on the brig *Thaddeus* from the Park Street Church in Boston. King Kamehameha I, who had united the Hawaiian Islands and started a ruling dynasty, had just died, and his favorite wife, Kaahumanu, had led the overthrow of the *kapu* system of forbidden practices that held together the traditional Hawaiian religion.

In this religious vacuum, Bingham was popular and influential with the *alii* (ruling class). Kamehameha II gave him land in 1820 and workers to build the first of four thatched churches at the site in 1821. He also allowed Bingham to ship a precut New England-style clapboard home as a rectory. In addition, an adobe schoolhouse, Likeke Hale, was built in 1835 to teach *palapala* (the Bible) and paper learning in general. Built of mud, limestone, and coral fragments, it is the only surviving adobe structure built in Hawaii in the early 1800's. It is still used for Sunday school classes and smaller church meetings.

Bingham worked with Elisha Loomis to develop the printing trade in Hawaii. He wrote down the oral Hawaiian language, establishing the seventeen-letter alphabet (which was later changed to eleven letters). The first edition of the New Testament in Hawaiian was completed in 1832, and the entire Bible in 1839. Bingham had five hundred adult students from the upper class of Hawaii; the education of children came later.

Kawaiahao Church

Construction of the existing building began in 1837 and took five years to complete. Bingham designed the church from memories of churches in his native New England. The severe Puritan lines are softened by the use of coral blocks as building material. King Kamehameha III formally deeded the land in 1840 and supervised the construction, ordering more than a thousand of his people to work on it. They quarried fourteen thousand one thousand-pound coral blocks from underwater offshore reefs cut with blunt axes by men diving ten to twenty feet. Logs cut from the forest on the windward side of the island were brought by canoe and

Kawaiahao Church. (Hawaii Visitors & Convention Bureau)

hauled over the *pali* (cliffs). The church was dedicated in 1842, two years after the Binghams and their seven children returned to New England due to the failing health of Mrs. Sybil Bingham.

The interior of the church has simple Puritan lines and can accommodate fifteen hundred people. From the choir loft with its large pipe organ extend two long upper galleries displaying twenty-one portraits of Hawaiian monarchs and their families.

In Puritan fashion, the church has served as a meeting place and political center. King Kamehameha III spoke in 1843 after the restoration of the Hawaiian sovereignty following a brief British takeover of the island, intoning what is now the motto of the state of Hawaii: *Ua mau ke ea o ka aina i ka pono* (the life of the land is preserved in righteousness). It holds Hawaiian-language services on Sundays at 10:30 A.M.

The grounds include two cemeteries. The missionaries and their descendants are buried at the back of the church. Native Hawaiians are buried on the harbor side, an estimated two thousand in the

1800's, many victims of diseases introduced by early sailors and settlers. King William Lunalilo is buried to the right of the churchyard's main entrance in a Gothic mausoleum.

The name *Ka-wai-a-Hao* means "the water used by Hao," a chief who was carried frequently from her home in Moiliili for ceremonial bathing and purification in a spring located perhaps near the present News Building on King Street. A stone was moved from the spring to the churchyard and set in the present artificial pool supplied by piped water.

The Mission Houses

The three restored and refurnished early nineteenth century buildings comprise the Mission Houses Museum. Frame House, built in 1821, a rectory for Kawaiahao Church, is the oldest wooden house in Hawaii. The precut timber for this two-story white frame house was shipped around Cape Horn from Boston. Chamberlain House, completed in 1831, is a more elegant, large coral house that initially served as the residence for the family of Levi Chamberlain, the mission's purchasing agent. Coral House, built in 1841, was used as a printing office and storehouse.

—*Joanna Yin*

For Further Information:

Damon, Ethel M. *The Stone Church at Kawaiahao.* Honolulu: Honolulu Star-Bulletin Press, 1945. Offers photographs, drawings, documents, and excerpts from missionaries' diaries.

Gowans, Alan, and Daina Penkiunas. *Fruitful Fields: American Missionary Churches in Hawaii.* Honolulu: Department of Land and Natural Resources, 1993. Gives historical and architectural contexts of Hawaiian churches.

Scott, Edward B. *The Saga of the Sandwich Islands.* Lake Tahoe, Nev.: Sierra-Tahoe, 1968. Traces the development of Honolulu and Oahu. Many old photographs.

Lahaina

Date: Palace built by Kamehameha the Great in the early nineteenth century; became a National Historic District in 1962

Relevant issues: Business and industry, European settlement, political history

Significance: This was the former capital of Hawaiian kingdom during the first half of the nineteenth century. Lahaina's harbor and businesses also played an important role in the booming whaling industry from the 1820's through the 1860's.

Location: On the island of Maui, from Honoapiilani Highway (northern border) to one mile out to sea (southern border), just east of Panaewa Street (western border) and west of Shaw Street (eastern border); historic district extends from Shaw Street to the north edge of Lahaina Center, one hundred feet from the mountain curb of Front Street and a hundred feet out from the shoreline

Site Office:

Lahaina Restoration Foundation
P.O. Box 338
Lahaina, Maui, HI 96761
ph.: (808) 661-3262
Web site: www.maui.net/~lrf

Lahaina's most prominent founder was Kamehameha I, called Kamehameha the Great, a Hawaiian king who unified the Hawaiian Islands at the end of the eighteenth century. Kamehameha gained control of the island of Maui in 1790, following a victorious battle at Iao Valley, just east of Lahaina in West Maui. In 1802, the king returned to Lahaina to plan an attack on neighboring Kauai, the final island outside his control. Though the attack was ultimately aborted, he built a palace in Lahaina and eventually made it the capital of his monarchy. It would also serve as the seat of government under his sons Liholiho, who ruled as King Kamehameha II from his father's death in 1819 until 1824, when he and his wife died of measles on a trip to London; and Kauikeaouli, who ruled as King Kamehameha III from 1832 (when he turned eighteen) until 1854. In 1845, midway through Kamehameha III's reign, the capital was shifted to Honolulu.

Outside Influences

In 1819, whalers discovered Lahaina and introduced the industry that would dominate Hawaii's economy until the 1860's. The whalers were soon followed to the area by Christian missionaries. In 1823, the Reverends Charles Stewart and William Richards came to Lahaina at the invitation of Queen Keopuolani, a wife of Kamehameha the Great and mother of Liholiho, Kauikeaouli, and their sister Nahienaena. Keopuolani was the first Hawaiian to be baptized as Protestant and helped the missionaries build a small grass church at Wainee.

Another Wainee Church, the first stone church constructed in the islands, was built for the Protestant mission and would literally come and go from the time it was founded in the late 1820's or early 1830's. In 1858, a strong Kauaula Valley wind blew both the belfry and the roof from the church. The church was burned down in 1894 by royalists protesting Hawaii's annexation by the United States. It was rebuilt, only to be burned down again in 1947. Four years later, the church fell victim to another Kauaula windstorm. When it was again rebuilt, it was redesigned so the front door faced the Kauaula Valley, rather than being at a right angle to the West Maui Mountains. The change seems to have done the trick. The Wainee Church was renamed the Waiola Church, meaning "water of life," at its dedication in 1953, and still stands today.

One of the first pastors of Wainee Church was the Reverend Dwight Baldwin, a missionary and Harvard-trained physician who arrived in Hawaii in 1830 from Durham, Connecticut. Baldwin served initially in Waimea before settling in Lahaina. In 1834 a new house was built for the pastor. It was constructed to last, with thick walls of coral, stone, and hand-hewn timbers, and today it is the oldest standing building in Lahaina. The Baldwin House served as the reverend's home from 1838 until 1871, and also as a medical office and a center for the missionaries. It has been restored by the Lahaina Restoration Foundation and is today a museum.

Westernization

In 1831, the missionaries opened the Lahainaluna Seminary, initially established to teach general academic classes to adults. Gradually it changed its offerings to focus on elementary and secondary students. The seminary was also the focal point of efforts to created a phonetic standard for writing the Hawaiian language. Hawaii's first newspaper, *Ka Lama Hawaii*, was published in 1834 at the Hale Pai (house of printing) on the seminary's campus. Following the California gold rush of 1849, many Californians sent their children overseas to school at the mission. They believed the voyage to be safer than the trek across Indiana Territory and the mainland wilderness to the schools of the East Coast. Today the school remains one of the most respected educational institutions in Hawaii and is the oldest American high school west of Colorado's Rocky Mountains. It became a public institution in 1923.

In their struggle to convert the people of Lahaina, the missionaries found themselves in conflict not only with the native traditions but with the representatives of the American and European governments, as well. Men such as British consul Richard Charlton saw more profit in encouraging prostitution and the sale of liquor than in restricting it. Two factions soon formed. On the one side were the missionaries, led by William Richards, and the converted Christian chiefs; on the other side were foreign representatives and the visiting whalers. In 1820, Richards worked vigorously to pass laws prohibiting local women from swimming out to greet the incoming whaling vessels. His success

can be measured by the violent reaction of the whalers. More than once they came ashore to attack him and had to be repulsed by Richards's Hawaiian allies. In 1827 the American whaling ship *John Palmer* actually fired its cannon directly at the mission house.

These events led to the creation of Lahaina Fort, which was completed in 1832. Constructed of coral blocks, it covered one acre, was enclosed by twenty-foot walls, and even featured at various times between twenty-one and thirty cannon. The original structure was taken down in 1854 to build the walls of a whaler's prison called Hale Paahao, or "place of confinement." It still stands today, on the corner of Wainee and Prison Streets.

Missionary Conflicts with the Kings

The missionaries had a turbulent relationship with Kamehameha III. Upon the death of Kamehameha II in 1824, a regency was established until the young king was old enough to rule. During that time, Kaahumanu, another wife of Kamehameha the Great, held sway. Kaahumanu was a devout Christian and had worked tirelessly with missionary Hiram Bingham to entrench Protestant education in Hawaii and to drive off French Catholics, who had arrived in July, 1827. With Kaahumanu's death on June 5, 1832, and the regency's end, the missionaries and the Christian chiefs lost their main advocate. Like his elder brother, Kamehameha III had never been comfortable with the Christian restrictions on sexual relations, or with the other foreign rules of conduct. He took up with a group of young men calling themselves the "Hulumanus," or bird feathers, who demanded that the foreign codes be abandoned. Kamehameha III proclaimed that the Christian laws established under Kaahumanu were revoked; only the penalties for theft and murder were to remain. The king also seized power from the ruling chiefs and declared that all authority now rested with him alone.

One of Kamehameha III's most flagrant violations of Christian morality was his relationship with his sister, Princess Nahienaena. The pair made no secret of their sexual relations, and eventually the outraged Christian chiefs forced the couple apart. Nahienaena was kept under the close scrutiny of William Richards and the other missionaries. She died in December, 1836, at the age of twenty. At her

Lahaina has become a popular tourist destination on the island of Maui. (Hawaii Visitors & Convention Bureau)

The same 1858 windstorm that damaged the Wainee Church and more than twenty buildings in Lahaina also destroyed Hale Piula. The courthouse would be rebuilt that same year using stones from the original structure; it still stands today by the Lahaina waterfront.

In Lahaina in 1840, the king proclaimed Hawaii's first constitution, which William Richards helped compose. The constitution allowed for representational government and a national legislature, which met for the first time in Lahaina that same year. Among the more notable authors of the constitution was David Malo, one of the first adults educated at the Lahainaluna Seminary. Malo is known as Hawaii's first modern native scholar and was the author of *Hawaiian Antiquities*, which is still consulted today.

Throughout his career, Malo was torn between Hawaii's ancient traditions and the changes brought by contact with Europeans. While he himself was a product of the new educational system and helped to forge the new political system, he feared that the foreigners would push aside the native culture and even the natives themselves. In 1837 he wrote,

> If a big wave comes in, large and unfamiliar fishes will come from the dark ocean, and when they see the small fishes of the shallows they will eat them up. The white man's ships have arrived with clever men from big countries, they know our people are few in number and our country is small, they will devour us.

When Malo died, he was buried, according to his wishes, on Mount Ball, a hill overlooking Lahainaluna Seminary.

funeral, grieving Hawaiians compared her death to a sacrifice to the ancient gods. During the funeral procession, they cleared a path through breadfruit trees, then named the new street Luakini, which denotes a temple where chiefs prayed and offered human sacrifices. The princess was buried in Wainee Cemetery, which was established in 1823 and is the oldest Christian cemetery in the state. Others buried in the cemetery include King Kaumualii, the last king of Kauai; Queen Keopuolani; and Hoapili Wahine (Kalakua), Maui's governor from 1840 to 1842.

By the time of his sister's death, Kamehameha III had backed down; authority was returned to the chiefs and a new Christian code of laws was enacted. In 1838, he appointed William Richards as his official "Chaplain, Teacher, and Translator." Richards quickly assumed great political power. Under his influence, Kamehameha III issued a decree of religious toleration and the June 7, 1839, Declaration of Rights.

The New Palace
In 1838, work had begun on a new palace in Lahaina for the king. The palace, called Hale Piula (house of the tin roof), would not be completed before the seat of government was moved to Honolulu in 1845. It ultimately was used as a courthouse.

Rise of the Whalers
Malo's prophesy about the large and unfamiliar fishes proved all too true. By the late 1840's, the

area had indeed been invaded—by whalers. The opening of lucrative new hunting grounds off Japan made Hawaii an ideal spot to resupply. Thousands of whalers traveled to Lahaina and Honolulu from Nantucket and New Bedford, making Hawaii the principal forward station of the American whaling fleet. Many whalers stopped in Lahaina twice a year: once in the spring, to resupply after their trip from New England before setting sail for the sea of Japan, and once in the fall, on their return from the North Pacific to resupply for a cruise of the equator.

They hunted many types of whales, including such species as the right, bowhead, fin, gray, humpback, and sperm whales. The sperm whales were both the most coveted and numerous. Scrimshaw artists wanted the large white teeth from its lower jaw, but the real money was to be made from the whales' oil. A single whale could produce three thousand gallons.

In 1834 Lahaina missionaries and whaling officers and captains worked together to build the first seamen's headquarters on the island. The building was intended to provide suitable reading rooms for visiting seamen and a place for the families of the ships' officers to visit with the missionaries. The two-story headquarters was built from coral blocks and field stones. The reading area, referred to as the Masters' Reading Room, was located on the second floor. Today, the building houses the Lahaina Restoration Foundation.

One of the whalers to visit Lahaina in 1843 was Herman Melville. Having served on several whaling vessels (two of which he deserted), Melville found himself stranded in Lahaina and looking for work. He stayed only briefly before heading to Honolulu, where he held a series of odd jobs. That August, he signed aboard the navy frigate *United States* and sailed back to America. When he later wrote of Lahaina in the appendix to his first novel, *Typee* (1846), he was highly critical of the administration there: "The ascendancy of a junto of ignorant and designing Methodist elders in the councils of a half-civilized king . . . was not precisely calculated to impart a healthy tone to the policy of the government."

For more than forty years, the whaling industry drove Lahaina's economy. In 1844, Lahaina hosted 326 whalers; two years later that figure increased to 400. Lahaina was home to 3,557 residents in 882 grass houses, 155 adobe houses, and 59 houses made of stone or wood. Its stores and businesses supplied the whalers with shipping-related goods and services, not to mention liquor and prostitutes. The local missionaries agreed with Henry T. Cheever, a parson who visited Lahaina in the early 1840's and called the area "one of the breathing holes of hell" and "a sight to make a missionary weep."

In the late 1850's, however, the American whaling industry entered a period of sharp decline brought on by the discovery of petroleum, a whale shortage in the Pacific, and the start of the Civil War. Petroleum was discovered in Pennsylvania in 1859, and kerosene soon replaced the whale oil used in lamps. People began using wax instead of spermaceti in candles. In 1861, when the Civil War began, the Union purchased forty whaling ships, only to load them with stone and sink them in the harbors of Savannah and Charleston in a strategic blockade effort. Confederate raiders further depleted the fleet by capturing other Yankee whaling ships. The *Shenandoah*, for instance, captured thirty-nine whalers. Finally, as the number of whales in the North Pacific declined from overhunting, whalers began frequenting the waters of the Arctic. In 1871, a group of thirty-three whaling ships hit ice off the northwest coast of Alaska and were abandoned. The two million-dollar loss crippled the fleet and ended the heyday of the American whalers.

Rise of the Planters

The new era at Lahaina would be ruled not by whalers, but by planters. With the California gold rush of 1849, Lahaina had become a port of supply for the American West Coast. The whaling season of 1847-1848 had been a poor one, and many Lahaina and Honolulu shop owners found themselves hopelessly overstocked. The gold rush opened up a new market for their goods. When the shop owners became wealthy from overseas trade and began looking to invest their money in real estate, the sugar boom was born.

The rise of the planters was made possible by reforms in laws governing real estate, reforms brought about by the influence of the missionaries and other *haoles* (foreigners). "By the end of the [1840's]," writes historian Gavan Daws, "the traditional land system, under which tenure was granted at the pleasure of the chiefs . . . , had been superseded by an arrangement that permitted Hawaiian commoners and foreigners alike to buy and sell land." The frenzy of land speculation triggered by these laws attracted missionaries as well as the shop owners. By 1886, foreigners had purchased two-thirds of all land sold by the government.

The planters' great difficulty was a shortage of labor. Hawaii's native population had been decimated by European diseases; the population dropped from a quarter million at the turn of the nineteenth century to less than sixty thousand by 1880. The planters believed that the remaining natives were not willing to engage in hard work. Those natives who had acquired small tracts through the land reform of the 1840's seemed content with subsistence farming. The planters turned instead to thousands of imported immigrant laborers from China, Japan, and Portugal. Many of these workers continued to live in the area after their contracts had expired, thus contributing to Lahaina's "melting pot" population. In 1909, the city's Chinese residents built the Wo Wing Temple, a Buddhist shrine that today also functions as a Chinese cultural center.

The Sugar Industry

The sugar plantations proved hugely successful. By 1898, 1.25 million acres were devoted to the crop in the Hawaiian Islands; these plantations were worth forty million dollars and exported five hundred million pounds of sugar a year. The planters had begun to exert their increased political power. They lobbied for a reciprocity treaty with the United States, which was passed by the U.S. Senate in March, 1875. In early 1893, they helped overthrow the Hawaiian monarchy itself and set up a new republic in the hope of being annexed by the United States, their largest trading partner. Annexation finally took place on July 7, 1898.

Present-day Lahaina and greater Maui still bear witness to the early period of the sugar industry. The smokestack of the Pioneer Mill, built in 1860 by James Campbell, is still visible from Lahaina. A restored 1890's sugar cane train now transports tourists from the mill to the Victorian-style train station at Lahaina. The route is the same as that used by the sugar mill until 1952.

With the ascendancy of the sugar industry, the decline of whaling, and the move of the government to Honolulu, Lahaina was gradually eclipsed by other Hawaiian cities. In 1962, Lahaina was designated a National Historic District, and the area soon began to attract thousands of visitors. Ironically, one of the main tourist attractions is a guided whale-watching cruise, which has led to heightened concern for the preservation of the very creatures that the residents and visitors to Lahaina once hunted and destroyed.

—*Kim M. Magon and Robert M. Salkin*

For Further Information:

Daw, Gavan. *Shoal of Time: A History of the Hawaiian Islands.* Honolulu: University Press of Hawaii, 1968. Provides a good overview of Lahaina's and Hawaii's history.

Judd, Walter F. *Palaces and Forts of the Hawaiian Kingdom: From Thatch to American Florentine.* Palo Alto, Calif.: Pacific Books, 1975. A more detailed discussion of Lahaina's historic architecture.

Kepler, Angela Kay. *Wonderful West Maui: A Guide to Lahaina, Kaanapali, Kapalua, and Iao Valley.* Honolulu: Mutual, 1992. A guidebook that includes illustrations and maps.

Simpson, MacKinnon. *Whale Song: The Story of Hawai'i and the Whales.* Honolulu: Beyond Words, 1989. The Lahaina whaling industry is discussed in this heavily illustrated book.

Sterling, Elspeth, comp. *Sites of Maui.* Honolulu: Bishop Museum Press, 1998. A history of Maui that describes its historic sites.

Pearl Harbor

Date: American rights granted in 1887; attack by Japanese air force on December 7, 1941

Relevant issues: Military history, World War II

Significance: This historic harbor was the site of the Japanese air attack of 1941 that led to the entry of the United States into World War II. The three-fingered inlet was an essential part of Hawaii's fishing and agriculture industries. It is the home of the Pacific Fleet and the location of the USS *Arizona* Memorial, a monument to the victims of the Pearl Harbor attack, run by the National Park Service in conjunction with the U.S. Navy.

Location: Ten miles west of Waikiki on the island of Oahu

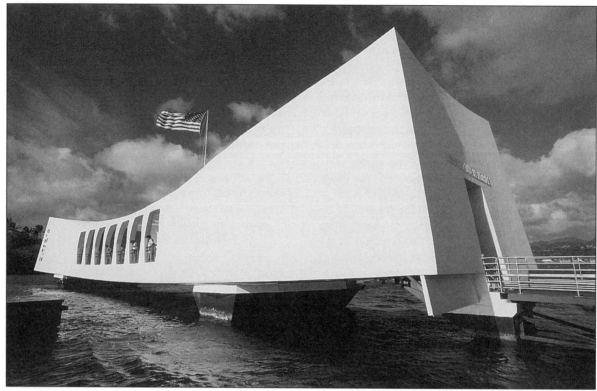

The USS Arizona *Memorial in Pearl Harbor.* (Digital Stock)

Site Office:
USS *Arizona* Memorial
1 Arizona Memorial Place
Honolulu, HI 96818
ph.: (808) 422-0561
Web site: www.nps.gov/usar/

To history buffs and Americans who were living in 1941, the words "Pearl Harbor" have become synomyous with President Franklin D. Roosevelt's "date which will live in infamy": December 7, 1941, when the Japanese took the sleepy island of Oahu by surprise one early Sunday morning and bombed Pearl Harbor in Hawaii. At the time, Hawaii was a territory of the United States, and Pearl Harbor was an American naval base. The base had been strengthened in 1940, in response to the Axis Pact, which established a coalition of states headed by Germany, Italy, and Japan. Victories in the Sino-Japanese War (1894-1895) and the Russo-Japanese War (1904-1905) had established Japan as a world power. Japan's aggression in Indochina and Thailand had led to extreme tension with the United States, and the rise of General Hideki Tojo to prime minister in October, 1941, marked the height of militarist power in Japan.

Japanese Preparations for War
U.S. political and military leaders had largely ignored intimations that the Japanese might attack the country at some point. President Franklin D. Roosevelt expected the United States to go to war with Germany eventually, but he believed the Japanese could be kept at bay through negotiations and small concessions. Most of the American public, as well, gave more thought to the situation in Europe than to that in Asia, and many Americans were determined that the country stay out of any conflict. There was not unanimous support for war among Japanese military leaders, either. Admiral Takijiro Onishi, for one, doubted the wisdom of going to war with the United States, and advised his fellow strategists to remain open to compromise. He was overruled, however, and Admiral Isoroku Yamamoto urged that Pearl Harbor be the target of the initial Japanese attack. The maneuver was sched-

uled for November 21, then delayed until December 7 to allow for more training time.

The Japanese military unit that struck Pearl Harbor was a task force called Kido Butai. Between 6:00 and 7:15 A.M. on December 7, the force's six aircraft carriers discharged 360 planes that made a coordinated attack in two phases. Their primary target was the U.S. Pacific Fleet—the battleships and aircraft carriers based at Pearl Harbor. The carriers were at sea that morning, but the warships were moored in their usual places at what was known as Battleship Row.

The Attack

The attack began about 7:55 A.M. A total of nineteen ships were wrecked. The USS *Arizona* suffered the worst damage and the heaviest casualties. An armor-piercing bomb exploded in its forward magazine, and the ship burst into flames and sank with more than 1,100 men trapped on it. In all, 2,403 Americans were killed in the attack, which was over by 9:15 A.M. Besides the ships, the bombers also struck military air stations and other installations, including Schofield Barracks, the U.S. Army's largest post at the time.

With Americans outraged, and lingering strains of isolationism gone, the U.S. Congress declared war on Japan, and Japan's allies Germany and Italy declared war on the United States. The attack also made many U.S. residents suspicious of anyone of Japanese descent, and led to the internment of many Japanese Americans in relocation camps. There also were charges of negligence against those responsible for Pearl Harbor's defense. A commission eventually absolved President Roosevelt, General Walter C. Short, and Admiral H. F. Kimmel of blame but censured the War Department and the Department of the Navy.

December 7, 1941, is often used by historians as a marker not only for the beginning of war for the United States but also as a historical, political, and social watershed, particularly for Hawaii. When the Japanese bombers attacked the harbor and surrounding environs, they shocked and devastated the islands and entirely changed the social and policital structure of the area. At this point, the military seized control of Hawaii, away from the few, mainly white landowners who had been progressively displacing the Hawaiian leaders since the first point of European contact in 1771. At 4:30 P.M.

on December 7, 1941, Governor Joseph P. Poindexter declared martial law and put Lieutenant General Walter C. Short in command. Martial law lasted until October, 1944.

History of the Harbor

The history of Pearl Harbor preceding 1941 should not be overlooked; the transformation of the harbor from an oyster-breeding site to a major military base reflected the changing economic, political, and social landscape of the islands. In some respects, the surprise of 1941 sped up a process of exploration, contact, and exploitation that had begun two centuries before.

When Europeans explored the Hawaiian Islands in the eighteenth century, they heard the locals speak of *Wai Momi*, or "river of pearls," at that time a day's horseback ride from downtown Honolulu. Sometimes called Harbor of Ewa after the river that flowed into it, this three-fingered loch had the Hawaiian name *Ke awa lau o Puuloa*, or "the leaf-shaped harbor of the Puuloa district." The harbor was surrounded and nourished by many small fishponds that dotted the shoreline.

Hawaiians used the harbor for their advanced fishing industry. According to legend, Chief Keaunui ordered his underlings to cut through the coral reef at the mouth of the inlet to allow his warrior canoes to enter. Fish used the passage as well, and large traps were built to capture them. The Hawaiian traps were said to be unique: funnel-shaped with a lead wall directing the fish to a walled-in pocket where they were caught. The traps were submerged at high tide and the fish were most likely removed with nets. The traps were also constructed to take advantage of natural ebb and flow of the tides and currents. The harbor was also home to a large number of oysters, whose pearls were of no apparent value or interest to the islanders.

Outside Intrusions

In 1793, George Vancouver conducted surveys of the northwest coast of America and Hawaii and brought the first cattle and sheep to the islands as gifts to King Kamehameha the Great in 1793 and 1794. Vancouver, under King George III of England, sent men to investigate the spacious bays of Oahu, which they found to be sandy and abundant with coral and oysters. Once King Kamehameha learned that the Europeans placed a significant value on pearls, he put the harbor under royal control and used the pearl sales to enrich the treasury.

During the first half of the nineteenth century, British, French, Russian, and American expeditions showed interest in Hawaii, and some white settlers established plantations and ranches there. The United States looked with disfavor on European interest in Hawaii; in 1842 President John Tyler declared that the Monroe Doctrine applied to the eastern Pacific islands, and specifically stated that European nations should not interfere with the Hawaiian monarchy. By the end of the century, the United States would take control of Hawaii.

The sugar industry was booming in Hawaii in the late 1800's and began to take its toll on the River of Pearls. As oysters thrive in water slightly less saline than normal ocean water, the mix of fresh water from the Ewa River and the extant water in the Pearl lochs made for a perfect mix. The surrounding lands were being cleared by Europeans, and the consequent devastation caused silt to flow into the waters. This silt, combined with the pollution from the sugar mills, caused the Hawaiian oyster crop to decline at a steady pace.

U.S. Involvement

It would be the agriculture industry, with its emphasis on sugar, that would bring the United States to Pearl Harbor in the late nineteenth century. The Americans convinced the Hawaiian rulers that eliminating tariffs on Hawaiian products entering the United States would cause the islands to prosper and told King Kalakaua that granting the United States the exclusive right to use Pearl Harbor would be a mutually beneficial arrangement. King Kalakaua reluctantly agreed, with the thought that in the long run his kingdom would benefit and prosper from the wealth of its agriculture. In 1887 the United States was granted the exclusive right to enter Pearl Harbor and to improve the site.

The Hawaiians had not passively ceded their lands and rights. In 1873, Major General J. M. Schofield (for whom the U.S. Army post is named) had arrived in Hawaii and reported that Pearl Harbor was a fine one with deep water extending inland, but that coral reefs blocked the entrance. Potential U.S. control of the harbor was discussed at that time, but met with great opposition from the Hawaiians. Their opinion was voiced in a poem in Honolulu newspaper *Nuhou*, and included the lines

> I am a messenger forbidding you
> To give away Puuloa (Pearl Harbor)
> Be not deceived by merchants,
> They are only enticing you.

Nevertheless, the Americans would persist, and it was with Schofield's recommendation and influence that the United States was granted rights in 1887. The resultant increased export of sugar to the United States caused the number of sugar plantations in Hawaii to increase tenfold from the 1870's; with the plantations came the importation of Asian peasants to work the fields, and the financial and political power fell into the hands of the few *haole* (white European) landowners.

While the agriculture industry flourished, the military, reliant on the U.S. government, was caught in a snare of legislation: It would be twenty years before Congress appropriated funds for dredging the coral from the harbor entrance. Although General Schofield had estimated a minimum cost of $250,000, the legislators authorized only $100,000. The delay can be explained, in part, by the wavering U.S. opinion of the value of Pearl Harbor as a naval base.

U.S. Military Expansion in the Pacific

In 1898, the Spanish-American War resulted in the United States gaining bases in the Philippines and Guam, causing the military to play close attention to Hawaii's strategic location. The United States annexed Hawaii the same year. In 1900, the first dredging at Pearl Harbor got under way; the first U.S. Navy small vessel to enter and anchor at Pearl Harbor was USS *Petral* on January 11, 1905.

Military posts along the shores of Pearl Harbor began to be established at the turn of the century. On July 6, 1901, land at Kuahua Island on the last loch was purchased and set up for ammunition storage. In 1904, the first permanent detachment of U.S. Marines arrived. In 1909 a contract was extended to the San Francisco Bridge Company for a dry dock, which collapsed four years into its construction. A new dock was begun two years later and was officially dedicated on August 21, 1919. Secretary of the Navy Josephus Daniels called it the "backbone of naval power in the Pacific." Naval aviation at Pearl Harbor began the same year: the USS *Chicago* arrived with four seaplanes and forty-nine officers under Lieutenant Commander R. D. Kirkpatrick. In 1922, thirty storage tanks for oil were built at Pearl Harbor for the Navy.

Pearl Harbor and the U.S. Navy

Pearl Harbor became the home of the Pacific Fleet and Schofield Barracks, the largest army post in the United States. After World War I, between fifteen thousand and twenty thousand men were stationed in Hawaii, with the dry dock at Pearl Harbor involving a payroll of sixty thousand dollars per month for almost ten years. After the 1941 attack, Pearl Harbor's facilities were repaired, and it became the most important U.S. base in the Pacific during World War II. After the war, the military continued to be a major power in Hawaii and its most significant source of income; coupled with tourism, it was to become a major Hawaiian industry, replacing agriculture.

It took more than twenty years after the Pearl Harbor attack for a memorial to be erected on the site. There was no lack of suggestions for memorials, but there were numerous funding problems. Finally, in the 1950's and early 1960's, a mix of federal, state (Hawaii became a state in 1959), and private funds came together; private funding sources included an appeal made on the television program *This Is Your Life* and a benefit concert by Elvis Presley. The USS *Arizona* Memorial was dedicated on Memorial Day of 1962, and was put under the jurisdiction of the U.S. Navy.

The USS *Arizona* Memorial is a simply executed white concrete structure designed by Alfred Preis, an Austrian, who was taken prisoner by Americans in Hawaii in 1941 and interned in the prisoner of war camp close by on Sand Island. The 184-foot-long memorial spans but does not touch the sunken battleship USS *Arizona*. The men who died on the ship lie interred in its hull. The memorial is supported by concrete pilings sunken into the harbor floor. The roofline dips at the center and rises to peaks at each end. Twenty-one open spaces puncture the sides and roof. While the structure is an engineered solution to the problem of weight distribution, it also serves as a fine metaphor for the nation's fall and rise during World War II. On October 10, 1980, the U.S. Navy turned the visitors'

center and the operation of the *Arizona* Memorial over to the National Park Service.

Modern Tourism

The memorial and visitors' center attract more than a million and a half visitors annually, and overcrowding is becoming a concern to the park service. Meanwhile, the participants in December 7, 1941, continue to haunt the harbor and add to the already serious pollution problem. Skeletons of the aircraft, the wreck of the USS *Utah*, and chunks of damaged ships litter the bottom. A toxic mixture of oil, lead, copper, and zinc leaks slowly from the debris, causing an ongoing ecological threat. While no one wants to tamper in this historical arena, it might be only a matter of time before measures must be taken.

Pearl Harbor is home port for twenty-two Navy surface ships and eighteen attack submarines. Budget cuts continue to threaten the jobs of many employed at Pearl Harbor. Although the military was the number-one industry in Hawaii between 1950 and 1970, tourism has now seized the top position. Nevertheless, the military remains an important part of Hawaii's economy and history. Pearl Harbor continues to employ thousands and attract tourists, many of whom have relatives buried in the USS *Arizona* Memorial. —*Sarah Bremser*

For Further Information:

Daws, Gavan. *Shoal of Time: A History of the Hawaiian Islands.* Honolulu: University of Hawaii Press, 1968. An excellent view of Hawaii's geological, historical, economic, and social background.

LaForte, Robert S., and Ronald E. Marcello, eds. *Remembering Pearl Harbor: Eyewitness Accounts by U.S. Military Men and Women.* Wilmington, Del.: Scholarly Resources, 1991. Firsthand observations of the attack.

Landauer, Lyndall Baker. *Pearl: The History of the United States Navy in Pearl Harbor.* South Lake Tahoe, Calif.: Flying Cloud Press, 1999. Examines the history of the U.S. Navy's presence in Pearl Harbor.

Murphy, William B. "Pearl Harbor Before 'Pearl Harbor.'" *Our Navy* (January, 1967). A description of Pearl Harbor's use and significance before World War II.

Slackman, Michael. *Remembering Pearl Harbor: The Story of the USS Arizona Memorial.* Honolulu: Arizona Memorial Museum Association, 1984. Provides a comprehensive overview of the memorial's construction.

Weintraub, Stanley. *Long Day's Journey into War.* New York: E. P. Dutton, 1991. Contains a good overview of the attack and provides extensive background on the major participants in World War II.

Other Historic Sites

Bowfin

Location: Honolulu, Honolulu County, Oahu
Relevant issues: Military history, naval history, World War II
Statement of significance: As the only World War II submarine now at Pearl Harbor, *Bowfin* (1943) represents the role of Pearl Harbor in the submarine war against Japan. It sank sixteen Japanese vessels and received eight battle stars, the Presidential Unit Citation, and the Navy Unit Commendation for its service in World War II.

Falls of Clyde

Location: Honolulu, Honolulu County, Oahu
Relevant issues: Naval history
Statement of significance: The world's only surviving four-masted, full-rigged ship, *Falls of Clyde* (1878) is the oldest surviving American tanker and the only surviving sailing oil tanker left afloat. Built during a shipbuilding boom inspired by increasing trade with the United States, the ship made several voyages to American ports while under the British flag. Sold to American owners in 1898, it gained American registry by a special act of Congress in 1900. Henceforth it was involved in the nationally important Hawaiian trans-Pacific sugar trade and later in transporting petroleum as a bulk cargo carrier.

Hickam Field

Location: Honolulu, Honolulu County, Oahu
Relevant issues: Aviation history, military history, World War II
Statement of significance: Established in 1935, this was Hawaii's largest and most important army airfield when World War II broke out, and in 1941 the only field in Hawaii large enough for B-17 bomber landings. In the attack on Pearl Harbor, Japanese bombing here and at other Oahu fields destroyed planes and gave Japanese forces the air superiority to proceed to attack Pearl Harbor warships.

Honokohau Settlement

Location: Honokohau, Hawaii County, Hawaii
Relevant issues: Asian American history
Statement of significance: Because of its ideal landing places for canoes and its fishponds, the Honokohau coastal area was important to historic as well as ancient Hawaiians. This site includes ancient house sites, temples, fishponds, a toboggan slide, tombs, and scattered petroglyphs. It is now part of Kaloko-Honokohau National Historical Park.

Huilua Fishpond

Location: Honolulu County, Oahu
Relevant issues: Asian American history, business and industry
Statement of significance: This is one of the last surviving fishponds out of an estimated ninety-seven such structures that once existed on coastal Oahu and one of the few ancient Hawaiian fishponds that were still operational well into the twentieth century. According to tradition, it was built by the native Hawaiians (specifically the Menehunes) for hatching and keeping fish.

Kalaupapa Leprosy Settlement

Location: Kalaupapa, Maui County, Molokai
Relevant issues: Health and medicine
Statement of significance: This is the location of Hawaii's well-known leprosarium where the Belgian priest Father Damien (1840-1889) ministered to the lepers and gained worldwide fame. It became a National Historical Park in 1980.

Kamakahonu

Location: Kailua Kona, Hawaii County, Hawaii
Relevant issues: Asian American history, political history

Statement of significance: Situated in the ahupuas of Lanihau at Kailua Kona, on Hawaii Island, this is where Kamehameha I, the unifier of the Hawaiian Islands, lived out the remaining years of his life and instituted some of the most constructive measures of his reign (1810-1819). The residential compound includes the Ahuena Heiau (personal temple) of the king. It was here, too, within a year of Kamehameha's death, that the first missionaries to the islands arrived in 1820.

Kaneohe Naval Air Station

Location: Kailua, Honolulu County, Oahu

Relevant issues: Aviation history, military history, World War II

Statement of significance: Kaneohe was bombed by the Japanese seven minutes earlier than Pearl Harbor; approximately one hour later the base came under a second attack and suffered great losses from both attacks that day. The Japanese goal was to destroy the American planes before they could take to the air and interfere with the bombing of Pearl Harbor. Hangar no. 1, the "parking" area, and the seaplane ramps remain.

Kaunolu Village Site

Location: Lanai City, Maui County, Lanai

Relevant issues: Asian American history

Statement of significance: Once a typical "vigorous" Hawaiian fishing community, this is the largest surviving example of a prehistoric Hawaiian village. These well-preserved ruins were abandoned in the 1880's.

Keauhou Holua Slide

Location: Keauhou, Hawaii County, Hawaii

Relevant issues: Asian American history, sports

Statement of significance: This is the largest and best-preserved holua (toboggan) slide, used in an extremely dangerous pastime restricted to chiefs. It served as the "Olympic Games" holua.

Loaloa Heiau

Location: Kaupo, Maui County, Maui

Relevant issues: Asian American history

Statement of significance: This is one of the few remaining intact examples of a large *luakini heiau* (state-level temple where human sacrifice was performed). It was once the center of an impor-tant cultural complex around Kaupo; oral tradition attributes the construction of the temple in about 1730 to Kekaulike, king of Maui, who lived at Kaupo and died in 1736.

Mauna Kea Adz Quarry

Location: Hilo, Hawaii County, Hawaii

Relevant issues: Asian American history, business and industry

Statement of significance: Located at an elevation of twelve thousand feet, this is the largest primitive quarry in the world, used by prehistoric Hawaiians to obtain basalt for stone implements. The archaeological complex contains religious shrines, trails, rockshelters, and petroglyphs.

Mookini Heiau

Location: Hawi, Hawaii County, Hawaii

Relevant issues: Asian American history, religion

Statement of significance: This is a massive *luakini* temple platform with an open, stone-paved court. It is one of the most important traditional sites in Hawaii through its association with the legendary Polynesian priest Paao who introduced new religious and social concepts to the islands about 1275. It is a unit of Lapakahi State Park.

Old Sugar Mill of Koloa

Location: Koloa, Kauai County, Kauai

Relevant issues: Business and industry

Statement of significance: Sugar cane had been grown by native Hawaiians, but the establishment in 1835 of the Ladd & Company sugar plantation, the first commercially successful such enterprise in the islands, marked the real foundation of what is now Hawaii's largest industry. Sugar long played a major role in Hawaiian economics and politics and was perhaps the dominant force in bringing about the annexation of the islands to the United States.

Palm Circle1

Location: Honolulu, Honolulu County, Oahu

Relevant issues: Military history, World War II

Statement of significance: This area, dubbed the "Pineapple Pentagon," housed the offices and headquarters of the commanding general and his staff, U.S. Army forces, Pacific Ocean Areas, during World War II. By 1944, this command was responsible for the supply and administration of all U.S. Army personnel in the Central and South Pacific, and from 1943 to 1945, carried out logistical planning for the invasion of the Gilberts, Marshalls, Mariannas, Guam, Palau, and Okinawa.

Puukohola Heiau

Location: Kawaihae, Hawaii County, Hawaii
Relevant issues: Asian American history, political history
Statement of significance: At this ancient *heiau*, in the summer of 1791, King Kamehameha the Great sacrificed Keoua, his chief rival for the kingship of the Hawaiian Islands. This event led to the unification of the Hawaiian Islands as a single kingdom under the rule of Kamehameha I.

South Point Complex

Location: Naalehu, Hawaii County, Hawaii
Relevant issues: Asian American history
Statement of significance: This group of sites provides the longest and most complete archaeological record of human occupation in the islands. Included in the complex is the earliest recorded occupation site (124 C.E.) in the state.

Wailua Complex of Heiaus

Location: Wailua, Kauai County, Kauai
Relevant issues: Asian American history
Statement of significance: This series of *heiaus* and sacred sites forms one of the most important complexes in the Hawaiian Islands. The sites typify a long period of Hawaiian prehistory as well as many aspects of Hawaiian aboriginal culture. The complex consists of a city of refuge, four important *heiaus*, royal birthstones, and a sacrificial rock.

Wheeler Field

Location: Schofield Barracks, Honolulu County, Oahu
Relevant issues: Aviation history, military history, World War II
Statement of significance: Bombing and strafing this site were important objectives of the Japanese force that attacked Oahu on December 7, 1941. The Japanese attack destroyed eighty-three aircraft and rendered this facility practically helpless. The 1941 flight line, hangars, and barracks building survive at what is today a U.S. Air Force facility.

Idaho

History of Idaho 384

Lemhi Pass, Tendoy 386

Nez Perce National Historical Park 388

Other Historic Sites 394

Boise, the state capitol. (Idaho Department of Commerce)

History of Idaho

Idaho's history is marked by its frontier origins. The state was settled later than neighboring Washington and Oregon, as pioneers passed through in the 1840's without stopping to settle until valuable gold strikes brought miners in significant numbers. The rough character of Idaho's early days was reflected in the violence of its first decades as a state, which came to a close only around the time of the U.S. entrance into World War I. This background is sometimes still apparent in extremist political groups, some of which are racist or anarchist.

Early History

Idaho was first inhabited by various American Indian tribes, such as the Nez Perce, Coeur d'Alene, Pend d'Oreille, Kutenai, Paiute, Shoshone, and Bannock. The origins of the indigenous inhabitants extend back around fourteen thousand years. Other ancient cultures flourished from eight thousand years ago until about the seventeenth century. By the eighteenth century, Shoshone bands (fragments of tribes) had obtained horses from European contacts, but these contacts decimated them by spreading smallpox among the Indians.

No whites are known to have explored Idaho before Meriwether Lewis and William Clark led their famous expedition through Lemhi Pass in Idaho in 1805. Traveling through the Bitterroot Mountains, the explorers built canoes with the assistance of the Shoshone and Nez Perce and floated down the Clearwater and Snake Rivers to the Columbia. Four years later, Canadian explorer David Thompson built Kullyspell House, known as the first non-native house in the Pacific Northwest, near Pend Oreille Lake. Decades later, in the 1830's, Forts Hall and Boise, site of the future state's capital, were founded.

Presettlement Decades

Missionaries, a constant feature of the early days of the Pacific Northwest, soon made their appearance in Idaho, bringing Christianity and—in their eyes—civilization to the native tribes. Henry Spalding arrived in 1836 and established the state's first school. He also created its first irrigation system and planted its first potatoes, both of which were to play significant roles in Idaho's later economic development.

The 1840's saw the arrival of the wagon trains headed west on the Oregon Trail. The steady stream of humanity became a flood in 1849, as twenty thousand forty-niners came through on their way to California's gold fields. Continuing heavy traffic led to the establishment of the U.S. military post Cantonment Loring near Fort Hall. There were still no settlers, however, even after French Canadians discovered gold on the Pend Oreille River in 1852, the year before a large piece of Oregon Territory broke off to form Washington Territory, of which Idaho was a part. The first permanent community had not even been founded when Oregon was admitted to the Union at the end of the decade. Mormon missionaries had established the Salmon River Mission (Fort Lemhi) in mid-decade, but it was not a success and was abandoned in 1858.

From Territory to State

Only in 1860, when much of the rest of the nation was gearing up for a bloody civil war, were roots for the first town put down, when Franklin, just over the Utah border, was founded by Mormons. The next several years, however, were to change Idaho's sparsely populated character, as major mining strikes were made in Pierce, Florence, Idaho City, and Silver City. Just two years after the first town was settled, the new community of Lewiston saw the region's first newspaper, the *Golden Age*. By 1863, the region east of Washington and Oregon was ready to take a giant step to statehood when it became a territory, with Lewiston as its capital.

This rapid invasion by European settlers was viewed with great alarm by the Native Americans. American Indian wars followed until the end of the 1870's, as Nez Perce, Bannock, and Sheepeater Indian wars followed in successive years. Thus, in 1877, after years of abuse by settlers, the Nez Perce resisted efforts to send them from Oregon to Lapwai Reservation in Idaho. In June, they

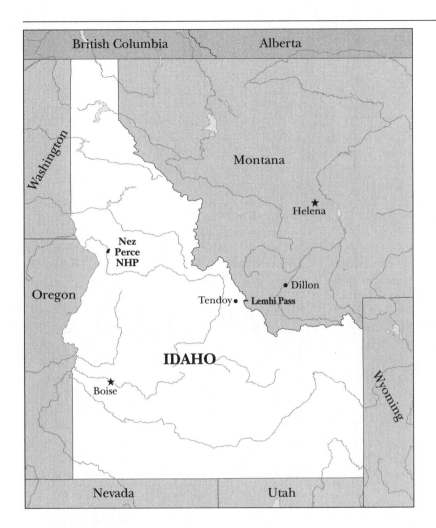

its appearance in 1866, as the first telegraph service reached the territory. A harbinger of modern social conflict arrived the next year, when the Owyhee Miners' League, Idaho's first labor union, made its appearance. Early in the following decade the first U.S. assay office and Idaho's first prison were built. Soon after, railroad service came to Franklin, and the way was open for even greater emigration fromthe restless east. By the next century these immigrants included English, Chinese, Czech, Dutch, French, French Canadian, German, Mexican, and Scandinavian settlers.

From the 1880's on, technological developments and their economic consequences followed with stunning speed for a region that was so recently an untamed wilderness. In the early 1880's electric light was introduced, and telephone service followed in 1883. The following year, an enormous silver strike, eventually recognized as the nation's largest, was registered in the Coeur d'Alene mining district, and more settlers arrived. By the close of the decade, Idaho was ready to trade its position as territory for the status of state. In 1889 a constitutional convention convened on Independence Day to institute a new frame of government. The next year Idaho was admitted to the Union.

crushed U.S. Army troops and settler volunteers at White Bird Canyon, in north-central Idaho. Forced to retreat after federal reinforcements arrived, the Nez Perce surrendered in Montana in October.

Other American Indians, in accordance with federal policy, were also settled on reservations provided by treaties. Conditions on reservations were in some cases so poor that rebellions took place. Thus, the Bannock Indians rebelled in 1878, when food on their reservation became inadequate and settlers objected to their foraging on cattle grazing land. However, they too were defeated by federal troops.

Economic Development and Statehood

In the meantime, other events were unfolding that foretold the new territory's social and economic future. The first wave of modern technology made

Government and Social Conflict

Government under the new state constitution, as in neighboring Washington, reflected the frontier distrust of power in the form of a powerful state governor. Accordingly, executive control was divided into a number of elective offices in which the secretary of state, state controller, state treasurer, attorney general, and superintendent of public instruction are separately elected rather than appointed by the governor. The governor is also denied the power of pardoning criminals. The state constitution underlines a commitment to liberal democracy. It opens with a declaration of the "inalienable rights of man" and a detailed enumeration of individual rights, the central idea of classical liberalism. Immediately following is the forthright statement that "All political power is inherent in the people," the key democratic idea of popular sovereignty. In keeping with a strong tradition of frontier democracy, voters have the rights of initiative, referendum, and recall.

While a framework for orderly government was in place, Idaho's rough-and-ready frontier origins could hardly disappear overnight. This became evident in the 1890's as serious violence broke out between union miners and mine owners. In 1892 the Coeur d'Alene mining area was the scene of dynamiting and shootings. More violence broke out when a new strike occurred in 1899. The strike was broken when the governor, Frank Steunenberg, called out federal troops.

Much bitterness remained, however. In 1905 former governor Steunenberg was murdered by a bomb. The perpetrator, a member of the Western Federation of Miners, an organization of the militant Marxist International Workers of the World (IWW), confessed but implicated three union officials. When a sensational trial was held in 1907, renowned defense attorney Clarence Darrow gained acquittals of two officials, and charges against the third were dropped. The prosecutor, William E. Borah, nevertheless won national fame and was elected six times to the U.S. Senate, where he became a stalwart foreign policy isolationist.

Two World Wars and Depression
Before World War I, the state's economy benefited from irrigation projects. A dam on the Snake River completed in 1906, for example, opened more than 100,000 acres of land for agriculture. The war created an agricultural boom when wartime food shortages brought demand for farm products. The end of the war, however, brought an economic downturn, whose effects were felt into the 1920's. Matters were worse in the Great Depression of the 1930's, when many banks collapsed. Federal spending helped to a degree through a highway construction program and employment in the Civilian Conservation Corps (CCC).

World War II brought renewed prosperity, as with the rest of the nation, with massive federal spending for war needs. Japanese who were relocated from western portions of Oregon and Washington, went to work in agriculture, where conscription had made labor scarce. Wartime industry made a lasting change in the economy, since in the postwar period manufacturing begun by defense needs continued, resulting in increased urbanization. By 1960, half of the population lived in cities or towns.

Postwar Economy and Society
As in neighboring states, postwar economic growth was also stimulated by development of cheap hydroelectric power. A series of dams was built in the 1950's, and projects continued in the 1960's. In 1976 one of the dams collapsed, and several rural communities were inundated, causing loss of life and considerable damage. In the 1970's, the state's prosperity brought rapid increase in population, which rose nearly one-third between 1970 and 1980.

By the 1990's, Idaho's economy was balanced between agriculture, mining, and nonagricultural industries. Various high-tech industries moved to the Boise area; food processing and wood products remained important. A tourist industry that, led by development of winter sports in Sun Valley, had grown up beginning in the 1950's was also important. Politically, the state was divided between conservationists and their opponents, and outsiders frequently noted the activity of unsavory fringe political groups, such as anarchists and neo-Nazis. Observers noted that the wise and efficient use of the state's natural resources would principally determine its future prosperity.

—*Charles F. Bahmueller*

Lemhi Pass, Tendoy

Date: Crossed by Lewis and Clark in 1805; designated a National Historic Landmark in 1960

Relevant issues: American Indian history, western expansion

Significance: Lemhi Pass was the highest point reached by Meriwether Lewis and William Clark on their epic journey across the American West. At this mountainous site, the Corps of Discovery first glimpsed the headwaters of the Columbia River and realized that a water passage across the continent was impossible.

Location: On the Idaho-Montana border, twelve miles east of Tendoy, Idaho

Site Office:

Beaverhead-Deerlodge National Forest
420 Barrett Street
Dillon, MT 59725
ph.: (406) 683-3900
Web site: www.fs.fed.us/r1/b-d/virtual-lemhi-pass.html

Rising 7,373 feet above sea level on the Continental Divide, lofty Lemhi Pass formed during the last Ice Age as a pair of alpine glaciers scoured in opposite directions, leaving a steep ridge between them. Long before the arrival of Lewis and Clark, Native Americans made use of this route through the otherwise impassable Beaverhead Mountains in the Bitterroot Range. Lemhi Pass anchored a well-worn American Indian trail across the Continental Divide: east for buffalo hunting along the headwaters of the Missouri River and west for the abundant salmon in the Salmon River and its tributaries. For the Shoshone and Nez Perce, the route was especially important for seasonal migrations between hunting areas, and the Blackfoot frequented the trail and pass so often that it was locally known as the "Blackfoot Road."

Lewis and Clark

Standing on the pass the morning of August 12, 1805, Meriwether Lewis and three expedition members became the first European Americans to cross the Continental Divide south of Alberta and north of New Mexico. Lemhi Pass and the divide formed the western boundary of the Louisiana Purchase and, until 1846, the far northwestern edge of the United States. As the explorers gazed at a seemingly endless sea of rugged mountains and deep valleys to the west, they also realized that the dream of Thomas Jefferson and so many others of a Northwest Passage—a water-only route across the continent—was impossible; there was no easy connection between the Missouri and Columbia Rivers, only a long and grueling overland portage.

Captain Lewis recorded the moment in his journal: "We proceeded on to the top of the dividing ridge from which I discovered immence ranges of

high mountains still to the West of us with their tops partially covered with snow." He descended the pass about three-fourths of a mile, which was much steeper here than on the opposite side, "to a handsome bold running Creek of cold Clear water. here I first tasted the water of the great Columbia river."

Later, upon returning to his tepee, Lewis received from a warrior a piece of roasted salmon, "which I eat with a very good relish. this was the first salmon I had seen and perfectly convinced me that we were on the waters of the Pacific Ocean." Despite the arduous task ahead of them, the corps was also elated by the knowledge that they could now trade for the fine Shoshone horses to assist in the portage. The expedition crossed Lemhi Pass numerous times before deeming the Salmon River route too rugged and striking out for their eventual successful crossing of the mountains of Idaho via Lolo Pass, 130 miles to the north.

The intrepid Indian guide for the corps, Sacagawea, was born west of the pass near Tendoy, Idaho. Sacagawea, a Lemhi Shoshone, was kidnapped as an eleven-year-old girl and later sold to a French fur trapper, Toussaint Charbonneau, who enlisted in the Corps of Discovery. Her knowledge of the area's geography and native residents was invaluable to the expedition. Sacagawea Memorial Camp—a small picnic area about two-tenths of a mile below and to the south of Lemhi Pass—was designated a special recreation area in 1932 and honors the memory of the expedition's incomparable young guide. A small spring bubbles near the picnic area, the spot where Meriwether Lewis may have paused for a drink on his ascent of the pass on August 12, 1805.

After Lewis and Clark

In the wake of Lewis and Clark, exploration and settlement pushed ever westward. Fur traders made use of Lemhi Pass as they traveled and trapped beaver along the plentiful streams and rivers of the northern Rockies. To them it was "North Pass," as distinguished from South Pass in Wyoming. In the 1860's, the region was seized by a gold rush. Freight wagon haulers and a stage line traversed Lemhi Pass during the area's mining boom. The Red Rock Stage Line connected Salmon City, Idaho, to Red Rock, Montana, the closest railhead in the region. For fifty years the wagons climbed and descended the precipitous pass until 1910, when they were replaced by the Gilmore and Pittsburgh Railroad over Bannock Pass, fifteen miles southeast of Lemhi Pass. The rutted and muddy route never regained its importance, and consequently remains largely as it was in 1805 when Lewis crossed it. Lemhi Pass is among the most pristine segments to be visited along Lewis and Clark's entire four thousand-mile route.

Just west of the pass in the Lemhi Valley, two small pioneer settlements were founded a few miles apart: Tendoy and Lemhi, Idaho. Both owe their names to a fierce, charismatic, and famous Indian chief, Tendoy. Born near Boise, Idaho, in 1834 of a Bannock father and a Shoshone (Sheepeater) mother, Tendoy distinguished himself in battle against bellicose neighboring tribes. Upon moving to the Lemhi Valley in 1863, he assumed leadership of the Lemhi band. Farsighted and realistic, Chief Tendoy realized the inevitability of European American settlement and guided the Lemhi through a series of treaties, failed agreements, forced relocation, and the establishment of a Lemhi reservation. Throughout, he skillfully negotiated and protected his people's interests. He died in May, 1907, received a hero's funeral, and is buried near Tendoy, Idaho.

—*Eric C. Ewert*

For Further Information:

Ambrose, Stephen E. *Undaunted Courage: Meriwether Lewis, Thomas Jefferson, and the Opening of the American West.* New York: Simon & Schuster, 1996. Traces the epic Lewis and Clark journey of discovery across the American West to the Pacific and back.

Conley, Cort. *Idaho for the Curious.* Cambridge, Idaho: Backeddy Books, 1982. A comprehensive guide to Idaho's human and natural geography, particularly detailing the state's historical development.

Crowder, David L. *Tendoy, Chief of the Lemhis.* Caldwell, Idaho: Caxton Printers, 1969. A thorough autobiography of the famed Shoshone-Bannock Native American Chief.

National Forest Service. *Lemhi Pass National Historic Landmark.* www.fs.fed.us/r1/b-d/virtual-lemhi-pass.html. Informative Web site includes map, photographs, road conditions, campground locations, weather information, and phone numbers.

Nez Perce National Historical Park

Date: Authorized as a National Historical Park on May 15, 1965

Relevant issues: American Indian history, military history

Significance: This National Historical Park does not focus on one location but rather comprises a unique cooperative arrangement of public and private lands administered by the National Park Service, state, tribal, local, or other federal agencies. The complete route of thirty-eight sites in four states includes locations of important encampments, missions, battles, trails, and other areas significant to Nez Perce and related U.S. history; the Idaho route alone comprises about four hundred miles of travel. The park sites' varying topographic and climatic features exemplify the wide diversity of Nez Perce country, which is largely still wilderness.

Location: Clearwater, Idaho, Lewis, and Nez Perce Counties in north-central Idaho, as well as southeastern Washington, northeastern Oregon, and western Montana

Site Office:
Superintendent
Nez Perce National Historical Park
P.O. Box 93
Spalding, ID 83551
ph.: (208) 843-2261
Web site: www.nps.gov/nepe/

The history of the Nez Perce Indians shows how the expansionist, commerce-based culture of the United States came into conflict with the nature-based, hunter culture of the Northwest's largest group of natives. The sheer novelty and might of the U.S. forces—religious, commercial, and military—complicated by the personalities of extraordinarily influential individuals on both sides, led to significant changes for the Nez Perce, including the near eradication of the economic, social, and spiritual bases of their culture.

Early History of the Nez Perce
Before the first visits by white men, the Nez Perce roamed a territory that stretched from the present Montana-Idaho border, across the Idaho panhan-

dle, and into southeastern Washington and north-eastern Oregon. By about 500 B.C.E., there were already villages of Nez Perce ancestral groups in parts of the southeastern Columbia River Plateau. As villages developed along the Clearwater, Salmon, Snake, and other rivers, the people added salmon to their diet of bison and the edible bulbs of camas lilies. By 1700 the Nez Perce population was about 4,500 and resided in 125 permanent villages that averaged 35 residents each. By about 1730 the Nez Perce had acquired horses, undoubtedly from Southwest Indians who had encountered the Spaniards, and eventually became expert horse breeders.

In about 1755 their Indian enemies—the confederated Blackfeet tribes—acquired British and French guns, putting the Nez Perce and their allies on the defensive. About a decade later, bison disappeared from the Nez Perce's hunting grounds, probably as a result of overhunting. Hunters now had to travel farther afield to find food. And in 1781 and 1782, the Nez Perce lost much of their population to smallpox, which had been introduced to other tribes by white traders.

First Encounters with Whites

The Nez Perce first encountered white men directly in 1805, when the Indians came to the aid of the bedraggled Lewis and Clark Expedition. The party had just emerged from a brutal portage through the Rocky Mountains. They spent two months with the Nez Perce, who provided food, made elkskin maps, and served as guides. Meriwether Lewis and William Clark's further friendly relations with the tribe in the spring of 1806 cemented a tradition of Nez Perce cooperation with whites.

In 1811 members of John Jacob Astor's Pacific Fur Company became the first white traders to enter Nez Perce country. Through white traders, the Nez Perce at last secured guns to defend themselves against the warring Plains tribes. In August, 1812, Donald McKenzie of the Astor group opened a post on the Clearwater River in the hope that the Indians would trap beaver for him. His expectations were untenable, and the post soon closed. The resulting tensions led to hostilities in 1813 and 1814—including the hanging of an Indian by one of the company's traders. Peace was reestablished, but only after the Nez Perce and whites had avoided each other for several years.

Eventually, mutual economic interests ameliorated the rancor be-

Chief Joseph, the leader of the Nez Perce in the 1870's. (National Archives)

tween the Nez Perce and the white traders. In 1816 McKenzie opened the Fort Nez Perce fur trading post on the Columbia River for the North West Company. He induced the Nez Perce and other tribes to make peace with each other and participate in his trapping brigades.

Trappers and Traders

In 1821 the British Hudson's Bay Company merged with the North West Company, and the company's expanded forays into beaver-rich Idaho brought trappers into frequent contact with the Nez Perce's buffalo-hunting bands. In 1818, however, the Americans and British had begun a joint occupancy of the Oregon Country, and the Nez Perce were most anxious to deal with Americans. The Americans simply offered better bargains than did the British. The Nez Perce rapidly became the most influential Indians on the Columbia Plateau and eventually assumed a pivotal role in the relations between the U.S. government and the Indians of the Pacific Northwest.

The Nez Perce's material success did not greatly affect integral aspects of their culture, such as their animistic beliefs, their gender roles, or their buffalo-hunting tradition. Yet the determined efforts of Presbyterian missionaries eventually led to deep and lasting changes. A series of lectures in 1829 and 1830 by Spokan and Kutenai youths who had studied at the Red River mission school extolled the benefits of Christianity, and in 1830 the Nez Perce sent two youths to the mission. Christian influences spread among the tribe, to the point that one group of Nez Perce would not join an American trapping brigade for a Sunday hunt.

Arrival of Missionaries

In a significant gesture, four Nez Perce warriors accompanied an American fur-trading group to St. Louis in 1831. There the Indians told William Clark, the superintendent of Indian Affairs, and the Roman Catholic bishop that the Nez Perce needed Bibles and Christian missionaries. The Indians likely sought increased social prestige and material enrichment more than spiritual benefits. Nonetheless, in 1835 the American Board of Commissioners for Foreign Missions sent Presbyterians Samuel Parker and Marcus Whitman to the Nez Perce. Whitman headed back east, but returned to the Nez Perce in 1836 with his wife and another

missionary couple, Henry and Eliza Spalding. The Whitmans then left to minister to the Cayuse, and the Spaldings remained with the Nez Perce.

This Christian crusade set the stage for the first significant rifts within the tribe since they had met white people. Anxious to keep the Nez Perce under his influence year-round, Spalding encouraged them to give up their annual buffalo hunts and farm instead. By May 1, 1837, the Indians were cultivating about fifteen acres of vegetables. Acceptance of the new lifestyle was not universal; some males objected to manual labor as being women's work, while others saw agriculture as a desecration of Mother Earth. The religious conversion was not total either, especially when material benefits and social status failed to accrue.

Even so, the Christian following was strong enough by 1840 to allow Spalding to baptize two leading tribesmen. One of these men was Tueka-kas, leader of the Nez Perce in the Wallowa Valley of present-day Oregon; Spalding named him Joseph. Spalding also baptized Joseph's son born in 1840, presumably the future Chief Joseph.

U.S. Government Intrusions

While the Presbyterian missionaries interfered substantially with Nez Perce culture, their efforts were subtle when compared with the government's attempts to control the Indians. In 1843 the federal government developed a set of laws directing the Indians to organize under a single high chief. This concept was completely alien to the Nez Perce, who operated with a number of headmen in charge of individual, small bands. Ultimately government officials selected the thirty-two-year-old grandson of the warrior chief Red Grizzly Bear, Ellis, who was one of the tribe's first Christian converts. The headmen mostly ignored this upstart, and antimissionary sentiments continued.

Meanwhile, the missionary movement expanded to include white settlers, including one thousand in covered wagons heading for Oregon's Willamette Valley. This incursion, combined with the murder in 1844 of the leading Wallawalla headman, who had relatives among the Nez Perce, further incited antiwhite sentiments. The Indians also became convinced that a measles epidemic was a plot by the missionaries to kill the natives and free the land for white settlers. The Cayuse killed the Whitmans and eleven other whites at their mission on November 28, 1847, and the Nez Perce looted the Spaldings' mission. These events drove the first generation of missionaries out of Nez Perce country.

White Encroachments on the Land

Removal of the missionaries did not mitigate the Nez Perce's problems. By 1848 the Indians faced the increasing threat of white encroachment into their homeland. Compounding the Indians' fears was uncertainty about the intentions behind the U.S. military's promotion of white settlement in the new Oregon Territory.

Despite the development of serious conflicts and confusion following the missionaries' departure, the Nez Perce continued the tradition of peace and cooperation that had served them well in the past. The government, aware of the Nez Perce's clout on the plateau, reciprocated by inviting some 250 tribesmen to a peace council on March 6, 1848, at Waiilatpu. Meanwhile, however, roving bands of American volunteers invaded Indian villages in pursuit of the Cayuse who had murdered the whites at the Whitman mission. Five Cayuse leaders were hanged for the crime in 1850.

In an opportunistic gesture that had serious long-term ramifications, a Nez Perce camp crier named Lawyer—a personable man who knew English and thus was able to ingratiate himself with the whites—accompanied several prowhite Nez Perce chiefs to see the new territorial governor in 1849. The Americans inferred that Lawyer was the main spokesman for the Nez Perce, and they treated him as chief when it came time to sign treaties in 1855 and 1863.

The Coming of the Railroad

When the Washington Territory was created in 1853, its first governor, a thirty-five-year-old military man named Isaac I. Stevens, also served as superintendent of Indian affairs. His goal was to run a railroad through Nez Perce country and over the Cascade Mountains to allow maximum movement of settlers into his territory. Stevens's entrance heralded a new era of tragedy and displacement for the Northwest Indians.

The government gave Stevens permission in 1854 to secure treaties from the tribes of the Northwest, including the Nez Perce. From May 29 to June 11, 1855, Stevens hosted the largest Indian council ever in the Northwest, with several thousand natives present. Conveniently for him, the anti-American Nez Perce were off hunting buffalo in Montana, and the pro-American headmen again chose the articulate, decidedly pro-American Lawyer to be their spokesman.

Dealing with Stevens was to be a lesson in American duplicity. It was not until June 4—well into the council—that Stevens finally got to the crux of the meeting: his plan to contain the Plateau Indians on two reservations, one in Yakima country, and one in Nez Perce country. Lawyer's arguments and Stevens's reassurances that most bands' ancestral homelands would be included in the reservation persuaded the Nez Perce to agree to occupy some five thousand square miles of territory. The 1855 treaty—the only one that the Nez Perce unanimously ratified—has remained the guiding treaty between the federal government and the Nez Perce ever since, although the United States subsequently appropriated more and more land for its white settlers.

Stevens promised the Nez Perce a one-year transition period, then promptly announced in the newspapers that the ceded lands were open for white settlement. This led to immediate conflicts between opportunistic settlers and the other Indian tribes who had also signed treaties with Stevens. The Nez Perce were sharply divided about their role in the matter. Ultimately, the desire to keep American troops out of Nez Perce homelands led them to reaffirm their pro-American stance.

Mounting Conflicts with Whites

As wanton acts of violence against Indians increased, including the hanging of a Nez Perce man, it became more difficult for the Nez Perce to maintain this stance. The tribe's antitreaty faction was becoming more alienated, and ultimately it challenged the authenticity of the treaty, insisting that Lawyer did not represent them and had sold their homelands without consent.

White settlement surged in 1860 with the discovery of gold on the Nez Perce reservation. Thousands of miners flooded the area, buying Lawyer's cooperation and bribing the Nez Perce with cash and the promise of new business. The newcomers built trails, wagon roads, ferries, saloons, stores, and log homes. By June, 1862, the eighteen thousand whites on the reservation far outnumbered the Nez Perce themselves. However, the indiscriminate miners moved into nontreaty territory as well, creating additional tensions there.

To formalize the de facto occupation of reservation lands by the whites, the federal government created a new treaty in 1863 (although it was not ratified by Congress until 1867) that left the Nez Perce with a mere 10 percent of the reservation designated in the 1855 treaty and furthermore divided that land into twenty-acre farms, one per family. Significantly, on June 9, 1863, Lawyer again signed for all the Nez Perce, despite the absence of the anti-American bands; the American commissioners could gloat that they had gotten six million acres for less than eight cents each.

Chief Joseph's Resistance

The Nez Perce who lived outside of the reservation boundaries, including the band led by Chief Joseph in Oregon's Wallowa Valley, would not tolerate Nez Perce complicity in the confiscation of their homelands. The outsiders officially parted company with their pro-American comrades, formalizing the split between "treaty" and "nontreaty" factions.

Furthering this division was a new government mandate that the Nez Perce reservation be administered by the Presbyterian church. The Catholics soon also established a presence among the Nez Perce. The missionaries sought to disengage the Indians from remaining "heathenish" practices. The nontreaty Nez Perce, meanwhile, turned increasingly to nativistic rituals that emphasized their own cultural history.

A number of territorial governors, Indian agents, and military commanders dealt with the Indians in the period between the spurious 1863 treaty and 1877, when war finally erupted between the nontreaty Nez Perce and the white settlers. Some of these government agents finally determined during the 1870's that the 1863 treaty was indeed invalid because only part of the tribe had signed it. Despite the government's understanding of the key legal issue—that one Nez Perce could not sell out another's land from beneath him—it was convinced that more money would set matters right.

Administrators dealing with the Nez Perce simply could not understand the cultural and religious traditions that made Chief Joseph and the non-treaty bands refuse to sell their lands. After another round of fruitless negotiations on November 13, 1876, the government directed the nontreaty Indians to move onto the reservation by April 1, 1877, or face military force. The nontreaty Nez Perce, no match for the U.S. Army, prepared for the inevitable move, selecting reservation lands that would most suit their needs.

The Beginning of War

The various nontreaty Nez Perce bands finally rendezvoused on June 2, 1877, two months after the original deadline for their move onto the reservation, and were due to arrive at the reservation on June 14. In the temporary absence of Joseph and other conciliatory headmen, however, some of the younger warriors decided to avenge the murder of the father of one of them by a white man. The young men never found the murderer, but they killed four other whites known for mistreating Indians. Other bands of Nez Perce raiders followed in the wake of the four warriors, settling scores with other settlers. These isolated murders were not sanctioned by the chiefs, but to all appearances, war had commenced.

General Oliver Otis Howard responded by ordering troops from Fort Lapwai to stop the Nez Perce at their new encampment on the Salmon River. The Nez Perce, hoping to reconcile with the aggrieved Americans, sent out a truce party to negotiate with Howard's forces. An advance guard of the U.S. troops led by Captain David Perry attacked anyway, and a bloody skirmish ensued. Though fewer than seventy Nez Perce had weapons—mostly bows and arrows or antiquated firearms—they killed a full third of Perry's ninety-nine troopers; the Indians had but three men wounded. This rout—though small in scale—was reminiscent of General George A. Custer's debacle a year earlier, and the nation's newspapers trumpeted "Chief Joseph's War." Both the press and Howard assumed that Joseph was behind all the trouble, even though he was but one of several chiefs leading the nontreaty Nez Perce. The violent turn of events left the Nez Perce little option but full flight, and panic swept the Northwest.

General Howard himself assembled a new army of some four hundred men to pursue the Indians, who had crossed the Salmon River on June 19. Howard's cumbersome militia did not begin to cross the Salmon River until July 1, and the Nez Perce then fooled him by recrossing the river far to the north. Howard lauded Joseph as a military genius, a notion that has persisted despite the fact that the nontreaty Nez Perce continued to form strategy by consensus among several chiefs.

Howard subsequently assembled a force of five hundred men and was again outmaneuvered by the Nez Perce. Yet the Seventh Infantry from Montana—unexpected by the Indians—charged into the Nez Perce camp in the Big Hole Valley. The Nez Perce left the infantry depleted and bloodied, but they themselves lost sixty to ninety people, among whom were twelve of their best warriors.

The Search for Allies

The weakened Nez Perce, running for their lives now, hoped to join the friendly Crow nation. They swept dramatically through Yellowstone National Park and continued to elude Howard and other troops sent to head them off in Montana. To the Nez Perce's dismay, however, the Crow were hostile, and the fleeing bands decided their only hope lay in reaching the Canadian border. Once in Canada, they could join Sitting Bull and his Hunkpapa Sioux.

The Nez Perce set up their last camp on the Snake Creek in Montana, only forty miles from the Canadian border. Troops led by Colonel Nelson A. Miles from Fort Keogh attacked the camp on September 30, 1877. After the Nez Perce killed fifty-three of Miles's men and lost twenty-two of their own people, a five-day siege ensued. The Indians were starving and freezing, however, and on October 5, Chief Joseph surrendered at last to Howard, who had belatedly arrived on the scene.

The Nez Perce had fought heroically during their 1,500-mile retreat. Their ranks numbered but 750, with barely 200 of them capable of fighting, yet throughout the summer they had defied some two thousand U.S. regulars and volunteers in four major battles, four serious skirmishes, and nearly a dozen other engagements. The nontreaty Nez Perce paid for this war with eight years of exile in Oklahoma. After repeated debates, Congress finally allowed the remaining 268 captives to return to the Northwest in 1885, sending some to the Nez Perce reservation and others to the Colville reservation in northeastern Washington. None, including Chief Joseph, were allowed to resettle in their original homelands.

Gradual Disintegration

Encouraged by the government and the Presbyterian missionaries, the tribe's traditional structure continued to break down. The chiefs were soon supplanted by more general councils. In addition, tensions between Christians and non-Christians on the reservation persisted. The federal government passed legislation in 1887 to further assimilate Indians by breaking up reservations into farms. This act ostensibly was to encourage the Nez Perce to prosper as farmers, but it also conveniently created "surplus" lands—a full 70 percent of the reservation—that the tribe was pressured to sell to the United States in 1893. By 1910 the reservation had about thirty thousand white residents and a more fifteen hundred Nez Perce.

It became obvious to the Nez Perce that a central leadership could help them deal with the federal government and its agents. On January 22, 1923, the Nez Perce approved the establishment of the Nez Perce Indian Home and Farm Association. Next, the tribe wrote a constitution, which the Bureau of Indian Affairs approved on October 27, 1927. With the institution in the late 1940's of the nine-member Nez Perce Tribal Executive Committee, the Indians achieved at last a leadership that could help them negotiate with outsiders and overcome their own divisiveness. It is this executive committee that has navigated for the Nez Perce the complex channels of pursuing claims against the federal government. The tribe—including those members who live off the reservation—has benefited from millions of dollars in government restitutions.

Creation of the National Historical Park

In a move to combine business with an new awareness of Nez Perce culture, the Indians and their non-Indian supporters promoted the idea of a Nez Perce National Historical Park. On May 15, 1965, Congress approved a unique entity comprising a total of twenty-four sites managed by the Nez Perce, the state of Idaho, the U.S. Forest Service, the Bureau of Indian Affairs, local governments, and private parties. In 1993 fourteen additional sites in Oregon, Washington, Idaho, and Montana were added.

The original twenty-four sites include various places associated with Nez Perce legends and daily living; battlefields where the Nez Perce met Howard's troops; the U.S. Army's Fort Lapwai; Donald McKenzie's trading post; the Spalding home; and several areas related to Lewis and Clark's activities in Nez Perce country. The additional sites include traditional Nez Perce campsites and wintering grounds; the grave of Chief Joseph; the Big Hole battlefield; and the Bear's Paw battleground, along the Snake Creek, where Chief Joseph finally surrendered.

—*Randall J. Van Vynckt*

For Further Information:

Haines, Francis. *The Nez Perces: Tribesman of the Columbia Plateau.* Norman: University of Oklahoma Press, 1955. A well-researched chronological account of the tribe.

Howard, Helen Addison. *Saga of Chief Joseph.* Lincoln: University of Nebraska Press, 1965. Focuses on the legendary war chief of the Nez Perce.

Josephy, Alvin M., Jr. *The Nez Perce Indians and the Opening of the Northwest.* New Haven, Conn.: Yale University Press, 1965. Offers an authoritative account of the Nez Perce's relations with white men from the very first peaceful encounters with Lewis and Clark through the tragic wars of the 1870's.

Nez Perce Country. Washington, D.C.: National Park Service, 1983. A wide-ranging introduction to the Nez Perce culture and landscape. This eminently readable and well-illustrated book includes an extensive history by scholar Alvin M. Josephy, Jr.

Stadius, Martin. *Dreamers: On the Trail of the Nez Perce.* Caldwell, Idaho: Caxton Press, 1999. A description and history of the Nez Perce National Historical Trail. Includes illustrations and maps.

Other Historic Sites

Assay Office

Location: Boise, Ada County

Relevant issues: Business and industry

Statement of significance: Built by the federal government in 1870-1871, the Boise Assay Office illustrates the importance of mining in the political, social, economic, and legal development of Idaho and the Far West. In operation from 1872 to 1933, it is one of the most significant public buildings remaining from Idaho's territorial days.

Bear River Massacre Site

Location: Southeastern Idaho

Relevant issues: American Indian history, military history

Statement of significance: On January 29, 1863, California Volunteers under the command of Colonel Patrick Edward Conner attacked a band of Northwestern Shoshone. The bloodiest encounter between Native American and white men to take place in the West in the years between 1848 and 1891, Bear River Massacre resulted in the deaths of almost three hundred Shoshone and fourteen soldiers.

Camas Meadows Battle Sites

Location: Kilgore, Clark County

Relevant issues: American Indian history, military history

Statement of significance: On August 19, 1877, the military force led by Major General Oliver Otis Howard which had been pursuing the Nez Perce since their departure from Clearwater was in a position to intercept them in their flight to Canada. Here, on August 20, a predawn raid by Nez Perce warriors succeeded in capturing most of Howard's pack mules, forcing the army to halt until more mules and supplies could be secured, which resulted in a time-consuming detour. The army's delay made it possible for the Nez Perce to escape into Yellowstone Park and Montana. Their remarkable journey toward Canada continued six weeks longer as a result of this raid.

Cataldo Mission

Location: Cataldo, Kootenai County

Relevant issues: American Indian history, religion

Statement of significance: The oldest extant mission church in the Pacific Northwest, Cataldo was used by Jesuit missionaries (1850 or 1853) in their efforts to convert the Coeur d'Alene Indians.

City of Rocks

Location: Almo, Cassia County
Relevant issues: Western expansion
Statement of significance: A popular stopping point on the California Trail named for its strange resemblance to a city skyline scattered across Graham and Circle Creeks and their basins and rising against a backdrop of wooded mountainsides, this complex provided westbound emigrants a refreshing contrast to the extensive sagebrush plains surrounding it. Thousands of emigrants camped here, leaving still-visible wagon rut tracks. The site is now a state park and a national reserve.

Experimental Breeder Reactor No. 1

Location: Arco, Butte County
Web site: www.inel.gov/resources/tours/ebr1.htm
Relevant issues: Science and technology
Statement of significance: On December 20, 1951, the EBR-I produced the first usable amounts of electricity created by nuclear means; in July, 1963, it was the first reactor to achieve a self-sustaining chain reaction using plutonium instead of uranium as the major component in the fuel. In addition, the EBR-I was the first reactor to demonstrate the feasibility of using liquid metal at high temperatures as a reactor coolant.

Fort Hall

Location: Fort Hall, Bannock County
Relevant issues: Western expansion
Statement of significance: Fort Hall is the most important trading post in the Snake River Valley and is known for its important association with overland migration on the Oregon-California Trails. In the 1860's and 1870's, it was a key road junction for the overland stage, mail, and freight lines to the towns and camps of the mining frontier in the Pacific Northwest.

Lolo Trail

Location: Lolo Hot Springs, Clearwater County
Relevant issues: Western expansion
Statement of significance: When, after reaching Lehmi Pass and crossing the Continental Divide, navigation of the Salmon River proved impossible, Meriwether Lewis and William Clark determined to use one of several trails over the mountains used by the Nez Perce in their annual journeys to the buffalo plains in the east. The Lolo Trail, used by the explorers to cross the Bitterroot Mountains in September, 1805, represents probably the most arduous single stretch of the entire route traveled by the expedition.

Weippe Prairie

Location: Weippe, Clearwater County
Relevant issues: American Indian history, western expansion
Statement of significance: On the morning of September 20, 1805, an advance party of the Lewis and Clark Expedition came out of the Bitterroot Mountains onto the southeastern corner of Weippe Prairie, the western terminus of the Lolo Trail and long a favored source of camas root for the Nez Perce Indians. Here, the expedition first met the Nez Perce, who had never before seen white men. The Nez Perce gave the explorers food as well as much-needed help and directions during the two-and-a-half-week period spent in their territory.

Illinois

History of Illinois 397
Cahokia. 399
Chicago Water Tower 403
Haymarket Square, Chicago. 408
Hull-House, Chicago. 414

Museum of Science and Industry and
    Midway Plaisance, Chicago 419
New Salem 425
Pullman. 429
Other Historic Sites 433

Chicago. (Corbis)

History of Illinois

Situated between the major waterways of the Mississippi River and Lake Michigan, and possessing unusually rich soil for agricultural purposes, Illinois has been an important area of human activity since the earliest days of habitation. The historical development of the region has been sharply divided among the urban northeast area, dominated by Chicago; the central area, a mixture of urban and rural cultures; and the rural southern area, which resembles its southern neighbors, Missouri and Kentucky, more than it does the rest of the state.

Early History

The earliest humans to inhabit the area were hunters and gatherers who roamed the southern part of the region ten thousand years ago. Over the next several thousand years, cultures developed that built permanent villages and depended primarily on the growing of corn. By the year 1300, the Mississippian culture, a highly developed society based on the raising of corn, squash, and beans, dominated central North America. This society, the largest Native American culture north of Mexico, built large, fortified cities and extensive earth-mound monuments. The largest of these monuments were found at Cahokia, the culture's religious center, located in southwestern Illinois.

By the time Europeans arrived in the New World, a large number of Native American peoples, belonging to the Algonquin language group, inhabited the region. Among these were the Kickapoo, Sauk, and Fox in the north; the Potawatomi, Ottawa, and Ojibwa near Lake Michigan; the Illinois, a confederation of five peoples, in the central prairies; and the Cahokia and Tamaroa in the south. These societies relied on agriculture and buffalo hunting for survival. By the end of the first third of the nineteenth century, all these peoples had sold, ceded, or been forced off their native lands and had settled in other areas.

Exploration and Settlement

The first Europeans to visit the Illinois area were led by the French explorers Louis Jolliet and Jacques Marquette in 1673 as they traveled south from Wisconsin along the Mississippi River as far as Arkansas. This expedition also explored the Illinois River on its return journey north. In 1680 the French explorers René-Robert Cavelier, Sieur de La Salle, and Henry de Tonti founded Fort Crevecoeur near the modern city of Peoria, followed two years later by Fort Saint Louis near the modern city of Ottawa. After a century of French settlement, the area became British territory at the end of the French and Indian War.

British policy was unfavorable to the economic development of the area, and settlements often lacked any form of government. Combined with violent encounters with Native Americans living in the area, these factors tended to discourage settlers. By 1773, the number of Europeans in Illinois had declined to about one thousand. The population also included a few hundred slaves.

During the American Revolution, American forces under George Rogers Clark captured British settlements at Kaskaskia and Cahokia in May of 1778, winning the region for the newly created United States. American control of the area was confirmed by the Treaty of Paris, which ended the war in 1783. At first a part of the state of Virginia, the region became part of the new Northwest Territory in 1787; part of the new Indiana Territory in 1800; a separate territory, including parts of modern Wisconsin and Minnesota, in 1809; and a state, with its modern borders, in 1818.

Conflict with Native Americans

Battles between European settlers and Native Americans began long before statehood. In 1730 French forces defeated Fox forces in east central Illinois. In 1803 the Kaskaskia ceded their lands to the United States. In 1812 Potawatomi forces killed fifty-two Americans and destroyed Fort Dearborn, a military establishment on the site of modern Chicago. The Kickapoo left their native lands in 1819, followed by the Ojibwa, Ottawa, and Potawatomi in 1829. The Illinois sold their land in 1832.

One of the most violent encounters between settlers and American Indians was the Black Hawk

of nearly all Native Americans to leave the area by 1837.

Slavery and the Civil War

At the time of statehood, slaves in Illinois were given the status of indentured servants, due to the fear that permitting slavery would block admission to the Union. In 1824 voters rejected a proposal to hold a constitutional convention for the purpose of making slavery legal. Increasing numbers of settlers from free states in the 1830's and 1840's led to a new state constitution in 1848, which abolished slavery and made it illegal to bring slaves into Illinois.

During the Civil War, most residents of the state were loyal to the Union and to President Abraham Lincoln, who was himself from Illinois. An attempt was made to unite southern Illinois, which was less sympathetic to the Union cause, to the Confederacy, but it ended in failure. About 250,000 residents of Illinois fought for the Union, including Ulysses S. Grant, one of its most capable generals.

The Rise of Chicago

During the early nineteenth century, about two-thirds of the population of Illinois lived in the southern part of the state. Although Jean Baptist Point du Sable, known as the father of Chicago, founded a trading post at the site in 1779, it remained a small settlement for nearly half a century. The opening of the Erie Canal in 1825, linking the Hudson River to Lake Erie, made transportation from eastern states to northern Illinois much easier. In 1837 Chicago had a population of 4,200 and was incorporated as a city.

The opening of the Illinois and Michigan Canal in 1848 linked Lake Michigan and the Illinois

War of 1832. Although some leaders of the Sauk and Fox had ceded their lands to the United States in 1804, others refused to leave. Black Hawk, a leader of these people, was driven into Iowa in 1831 but crossed back over the Mississippi River into Illinois the next year with about one thousand followers. Although at first Black Hawk was able to defeat the Illinois militia, lack of supplies forced him to retreat northward into Wisconsin, where most of his followers were killed. The destruction of Black Hawk's people, including women, children, and the elderly, was an important factor in the decision

River, providing Chicago with a waterway to the Mississippi River. By 1852 two railroad lines linked Chicago to eastern states. By 1856 it was the nation's most important railroad center.

The second half of the nineteenth century saw rapid economic growth in Chicago, with the city becoming dominant in iron and steel production, lumber distribution, slaughtering and meat packing, and marketing of produce. The Great Chicago Fire, lasting for two days in October, 1871, killed more than two hundred people, left ninety thousand homeless, and destroyed $200 million worth of property. Despite this disaster, Chicago continued to experience rapid growth. From 1850 to 1880 the population of the city grew from about thirty thousand to more than half a million.

The Twentieth Century

Although Illinois harbored a number of German and Irish immigrants in the 1840's, it was not until the turn of the century that large numbers of immigrants from other nations, including Poland, Hungary, Italy, Norway, Sweden, Austria, and Russia, arrived in the state. Chicago was the center of immigration, with more than three-fourths of its population in 1900 consisting of those born in other countries and their children.

The same period also saw a large increase in the number of African Americans in Illinois. From 1870 to 1910, the population of African Americans increased from 29,000 to more than 100,000. Prior to World War II, large numbers of European Jews immigrated to Illinois. In later years, increasing numbers of Asians and Latin Americans immigrated to the state.

The late nineteenth century and the early twentieth century brought Illinois a reputation for violence, particularly in Chicago, where the Haymarket Riot of 1886 resulted in numerous deaths in a confrontation between police and labor activists. Railroad worker strikes in Chicago in 1894 also led to violence. Elsewhere in the state, strikes by mine workers led to violence in 1898 and 1922. Race riots broke out in Springfield in 1908, in East St. Louis in 1917, and in Chicago in 1919. The 1920's saw an increase in violence against African Americans by the Ku Klux Klan. During the 1920's and 1930's, Chicago was a center of organized crime. Perhaps the most infamous event in the history of crime in Chicago occurred in 1929, when crime leader Al Capone had seven rivals killed in the Saint Valentine's Day Massacre.

Throughout the twentieth century, the Democratic and Republican parties struggled for control of Illinois. This fact, combined with the state's large number of electoral votes, made Illinois a key target of presidential election campaigns. In general, the city of Chicago has been strongly Democratic, the suburbs and farmlands of the north and central regions strongly Republican, and the southern region mixed.

After the economic recession of the 1970's, the electronic and computer technology industries in Illinois became an important part of the state's economy in the 1980's. Illinois also became a leader in nuclear-power production in the 1990's, when it had thirteen operating nuclear-power plants, more than any other state. These plants supplied more than half of the state's electricity.

—*Rose Secrest*

Cahokia

Date: Mounds built between 900 and 1300; town founded in 1699

Relevant issues: American Indian history, European settlement

Significance: The Cahokia Mounds were built by Mississippian Indians, who used the mounds as ceremonial centers. The largest and most famous of these structures is Monks Mound, which rises to a height of one hundred feet and has a base measuring eight thousand square feet. Sixty-eight of the estimated one hundred twenty mounds can still be viewed. The nearby town of Cahokia was founded in 1699 by French missionaries. It is the oldest permanent European settlement in Illinois and contains many historic French colonial buildings.

Location: The historic town is on the Mississippi River in southwestern Illinois, just off U.S. Interstate 255; the Cahokia Mounds State Historic and World Heritage Site is fifteen miles to the northeast, near Collinsville, extending just north of Route 40 and bordered on the east by U.S. Interstates 55 and 70, on the west by U.S. Interstate 255, and on the south by Routes 50 and 64

Site Offices:
Cahokia State Historic and World Heritage Site
P.O. Box 681
Collinsville, IL 62234
ph.: (618) 346-5160

Cahokia Chamber of Commerce
905 Falling Springs Road
Cahokia, IL 62206
ph.: (618) 332-1900

In southern Illinois, about fifteen miles east of St. Louis, Missouri, lie the Cahokia Mounds, the remains of what was once the largest prehistoric American city north of Mexico. Some authorities estimate that its population reached 20,000, although other scholars believe the population may have grown as large as 100,000. The people of ancient Cahokia, who are today referred to as Mississippians, were strong, successful, and peaceful. Their culture emerged between 850 and 900 C.E., out of an earlier, late Woodland culture that developed there around 500 C.E. The Mississippians are remembered most for the amazing ceremonial mounds they built, many of which still exist. Because their population had vanished long before Christopher Columbus found his way to America in 1492, their history at Cahokia was unknown until relatively recently.

Early Mound Builders
Cahokia's ceremonial mounds at one time numbered one hundred twenty and covered thousands of acres. They were built between 900 and 1300 C.E., along the Mississippi River. Today, the sixty-eight remaining mounds, which span an area of 2,200 acres, are preserved in an archaeological park. The remains of thousands of other mounds have been found nearby in Illinois.

It is said that early white settlers refused to farm near the mounds because they were afraid of disturbing an Indian god. Eventually, the settlers simply worked around the mounds, paying little attention to them until the late 1800's. Although many mounds have been carefully preserved, others are now located in the midst of local farms.

The site's earliest history was not even known until the early 1800's. The pioneers who came upon the mounds at first would not believe they were built by Indians. They thought instead that Vi-

kings, Phoenicians, or a lost tribe of Israel had built them. By the 1890's, people finally agreed that early Native Americans had indeed built the mounds.

Monks Mound
By far the most impressive mound is Monks Mound, or the Great Cahokia Mound. With a base measuring one thousand feet by eight hundred feet—broader than the Great Pyramid of Cheops in Egypt—and a height of one hundred feet, it is the largest prehistoric earthen structure in the New World. More than twenty-two million cubic feet of earth was moved just to build Monks Mound, a pyramidal structure with straight sides, almost in the shape of a parallelogram. On its south side, about thirty feet above the base, is a large terrace, which is now home to an orchard. On the other side, about sixty feet from the base, is a smaller, forested terrace. Atop the mound was a huge wooden palace, which measured 105 feet long by 48 feet wide by 50 feet high. According to one expert, construction of Monks Mound required the labor of thousands of Indians and was built in several stages. Named for Trappist missionaries who planted a garden there from 1809 to 1813, Monks Mound was originally home to the Mississippians' high chief, who lived on its flattened peak in the palace.

Smaller platform mounds were home to ceremonial buildings and the elite members of the population. The Mississippians also constructed conical and ridge-top mounds, which marked key locations and served as burial sites for the elite members of the population. In one smaller ridge-top mound known as Mound Seventy-two, archaeologists found a chief laid on a bed of twenty thousand shell beads, surrounded by copper, mica, arrowheads, and the remains of several people sacrificed to serve him in the next life. The victims included fifty-three young women, as well as four men with their heads and hands removed. The mound revealed more than two hundred other ceremonial and sacrificial burials, mostly of young women, in mass graves. Despite these findings, scholars believe that most Cahokians were buried in cemeteries.

Architectural Features
The mounds were arranged in neat rows around a

Tourists climb the steps of Monks Mound at Cahokia. (AP/Wide World Photos)

ceremonial plaza that featured stepped pyramid temples. Stone, shell, and wood tools were used to dig out the claylike earth that built the mounds. The Mississippians then carried this material in baskets on their backs. Other mounds included "wattle-and-daub" houses for the less elite members of the area. These structures were built from woven reed walls covered with mud plaster and were arranged in rows around central plazas. A fifteen-foot stockade encircled the city. There were also four or five large woodhenges, or circles of cedar posts spaced at twenty-foot intervals. These woodhenges, names for their similarity to England's Stonehenge, are thought to have been horizon calendars, which used shadows to mark the changing seasons and ceremonial periods. They were probably built around 1000 C.E.

Disappearance of the Mound Builders

Because the mound builders left no written language, there is much about them that may never be known. It is known, however, that at their peak around 1000 C.E., they were peacefully developing their own government, public works projects, science, art, and specialized labor force. Although the area was named by French missionaries for the Cahokia, a subtribe of the Illini, who lived near the mounds in the seventeenth century, its original population vanished between 1300 and 1500. By the standards of the time, the people of the area were very wealthy. Their success came in part from an abundant supply of corn, sunflowers, and squash. Their location along the Mississippi River also allowed them to create a vast trading network that reached as far south as the Gulf of Mexico and as far north as the Great Lakes.

Theories for the demise of the community vary. Some believe that the mound builders fell victim to war, disease, or a depletion of resources. The inhabitants might have become too reliant on lumber for fuel and building materials, causing them to remove too many trees from bluffs in the area. This would have allowed heavy rainfalls to wash over the soil and wipe out the crops. Other scholars claim that the cornfields gradually lost their fertility from overuse.

Later Inhabitants of the Region

Tamaroa Indians later inhabited the area, and European traders, merchants, and explorers soon visited it. In 1698 the French explorer Henry de Tonti led a group of missionaries to the region; in 1699 they returned to establish a mission there, just fifteen miles to the southwest of the mound site. It was the first permanent European settlement in what would become the state of Illinois.

Cahokia's Mission of the Holy Family was established by priests from Quebec's Seminary of Foreign Missions; these missionaries soon found themselves in a territorial conflict with Jesuits who were also working in the area. When several Jesuits entered the town and began constructing a Cahokia mission of their own, the Seminary of Foreign Missions sent a representative to France to reaffirm their sole authority there. The resulting June 7, 1701, decree gave them authority over Cahokia, but it gave the Jesuits jurisdiction over the rest of the Mississippi Valley. In 1703, the Jesuits established their own mission at Kaskaskia, sixty miles below Cahokia. Relations between the two towns would remain strained for more than a century.

Cahokia became a center of trade for the flat-bottomed boats that transported goods to and from New Orleans via the Mississippi River. This trade increased markedly in the early decades of the eighteenth century as a result of the "Mississippi Bubble," an ill-fated investment scheme initiated in 1717 by Scottish financier John Law. Law proposed to settle six thousand colonists and three thousand slaves in France's Mississippi Valley colonies. Although Law's Compagnie d'Occident soon went bankrupt, the scheme brought many colonists into the area and increased the demand for goods up and down the Mississippi.

British and American Rule
As a result of the French and Indian War, France ceded its Mississippi Valley colonies to Britain in November, 1762. The British took formal possession of the Cahokia area in 1765, by which point many of the French settlers has moved across the Mississippi to Spanish-controlled Missouri. In 1767, Captain Pittman, who served with the British forces in Illinois, wrote that "the village is long and straggling, about a half mile from north to south, with 45 dwellings."

In 1778, Virginia troops under Colonel George Rogers Clark gained possession of the area during the American Revolutionary War. The troops stayed until 1780, but, like the British, they had little impact on the town, which remained French in both its population and its character. By 1787, Cahokia's population had reached four hundred, almost all of whom were French.

The Colonial Legacy
Modern-day visitors to Cahokia can still see this French colonial legacy in the town's many historic buildings. One of the most famous is the St. Clair County Courthouse. The courthouse was originally built by Jean Roy Lapance as a residence, most probably in the late 1700's. Eventually, François Saucier married into the Lapance family and became the home's new owner. In 1793, he sold it to St. Clair County for one thousand dollars. As the oldest courthouse in Illinois, it remains a prime example of the structures built by the early French settlers. It is constructed of vertically arranged logs and is surrounded by extended eaves. Many of the French who came to Illinois were originally from the West Indies and had grown accustomed to using the eaves as protection against the hot sun and rains.

From 1793 until 1814, the building served as both courthouse and military center. Outside were a whipping post, stocks, a pillory, and other devices of punishment. In 1814, St. Clair's county seat was moved from Cahokia to Clinton Hills, which is now the city of Belleville, and François Vaudry bought the courthouse for $225. Over time the building would serve a variety of uses, including a warehouse, a residence, and even a saloon. Eventually, it was sold for exhibition at the World's Fair in St. Louis. Following the fair, the building was relocated to Jackson Park in Chicago. In 1939, the state of Illinois had the former courthouse restored and placed on its original site in Cahokia.

The courthouse is one of only a handful of vertical-log French structures still standing in Illinois. Another is the Church of the Holy Family, also located in Cahokia. Built in 1799 on the east side of what is today Illinois Route 3, it is the oldest church in the Mississippi Valley. Another vertical-log building stands just opposite the church; during the 1880's, it was home to François Saucier.

Another historical colonial building is the Jarrot Mansion, a two-story brick home built by Nicholas Jarrot between 1799 and 1806. In 1790, twenty-six-year-old Nicholas Jarrot came to America from France. He stopped first in Baltimore and New Orleans before settling in Cahokia, where he prospered from a successful trading business. (It was Jarrot who gave the large Cahokia mound to the Trappist order, resulting in the name "Monks Mound.") His mansion is a large, colonial-style house, thirty-eight by fifty feet, two stories high, with a basement and an attic. The massive structure also features walls ranging from sixteen inches to two feet thick. Many of the materials for the mansion were imported from France. Today, it is the oldest brick building still standing in Illinois. The Jarrots threw lavish parties at the mansion. A visitor during this period commented that so many balls were held there, he "often wondered how the ladies are enabled to support themselves under this violent exercise. . . . "

Because the house was located on a flood plain, it often took in water when the river was swollen. An earthquake damaged the structure further in the early 1810's. In recent years, the building has been used as a Catholic parochial school and a home for the nuns who teach there.

The End of Cahokia's Independence
Cahokia was virtually an independent city-state during the years immediately after the American Revolution. Whereas several of the surrounding towns succumbed to disorder and political corruption during this period, Cahokia, with its deep religious roots, governed itself with restraint and discipline. The difference between Cahokia and its neighbors soon grew to the point that Cahokians wished to remove themselves from the authority of the county government. Their desire was only quickened by the fact the county seat was in Kaskaskia, their longtime rival. In 1786, they officially petitioned the U.S. Congress to remove them from the authority of the Kaskaskians, whom they charged with "incapacity, spite, and partiality." In 1790, Cahokia was made a joint county seat with Kaskaskia and Prairie du Rocher, and in 1795 it was made sole seat of the newly drawn St. Clair County. As St. Clair County grew, so did Cahokia's prestige and authority; by 1809, St. Clair included all the territory in what are today the eighty northernmost counties of Illinois.

Cahokia would not enjoy this position of authority for long, however. When the political map was redrawn again in 1814, the seat of St. Clair County was moved to Clinton Hills (preserved Belleville). Furthermore, St. Louis and East St. Louis soon emerged as economic powers; because Cahokia was repeatedly flooded by the waters of the Mississippi, these cities attracted the settlers and businesses that Cahokia needed to grow. By 1914, the town was home to only forty-two dwellings, three less than Captain Pittman had counted in 1767. Descendants of the original French settlers continued to make up a large part of the local population. Thanks to industries that located to the area in the twentieth century, the town's population rose to approximately seventeen thousand by 1990.

Meanwhile, the nearby mounds had been all but forgotten. Farms, houses, and other buildings appeared on the land that covered the once-majestic structures. While some attempts at investigation and restoration began in the 1920's, it was not until 1982 that the United Nations Educational, Scientific, and Cultural Organization (UNESCO) named Cahokia one of its World Heritage Sites. Three years later, the state created the Illinois Historic Preservation Agency to protect such cultural sites. Over the course of the 1970's and 1980's, the state spent $1.3 million to remove an entire sixty-home subdivision from the site. An $8.2 million interpretive center was completed there in 1989. Despite these efforts, by 1993 less that 1 percent of the area had been excavated.   —*Kim M. Magon*

For Further Information:
Fowler, Melvin L. *The Cahokia Atlas.* Springfield: Illinois Historical Preservation Agency, 1989. A detailed, scholarly overview of archaeological knowledge about the mounds.

Gums, Bonnie L. *Archaeology at French Colonial Cahokia.* Springfield: Illinois Historical Preservation Agency, 1988. One of the best and most recent scholarly works on the town of Cahokia.

McDermott, John Francis, ed. *Old Cahokia: A Narrative and Document Illustrating the First Century of Its History.* St. Louis: St. Louis Historical Documents Foundation, 1949. Older, but still valuable.

Mink, Claudia G. *Cahokia: City of the Sun.* Collinsville, Ill.: Cahokia Mounds Museum Society, 1992. Quite informative and written for a general audience.

Young, Biloine W. *Cahokia, the Great Native American Metropolis.* Urbana: University of Illinois Press, 2000. An archaeological description of the mounds and ceramics at Cahokia and of the pre-Columbian history of Mississippian culture.

Chicago Water Tower

Date: Construction completed in 1869; designated a National Historic Landmark on December 6, 1971

The Chicago Water Tower. (American Stock Photography)

Relevant issues: Art and architecture, science and technology

Significance: This building, listed on the National Register of Historic Places, was designed by W. W. Boyington. It housed the 138-foot stand pipe necessary for the adjacent pumping station and survived the Great Chicago Fire of 1871; it is no longer in use as part of the waterworks of Chicago. The history of the Chicago Water Tower is featured in a program at the information center in the pumping station.

Location: 880 North Michigan Avenue (Michigan Avenue and East Pearson Street) in Chicago

Site Office:
Pumping Station
163 East Pearson Street
Chicago, IL 60611
ph.: (312) 280-5748

Dwarfed by the Sears Tower and John Hancock Center, two soaring examples of Chicago's present-day architectural flavor, the Chicago Water Tower is still one of Chicago's best-loved landmark towers. It stands at the top of Michigan Avenue, forcing the straight avenue to bend slightly in order to accommodate it. It is built of buff-colored Lemont limestone and is built in a fanciful neo-Gothic style, slightly reminiscent of a medieval European castle.

It is most famous for being the only municipal building in Chicago to survive the Great Chicago Fire of 1871. As the flames subsided on Tuesday, October 10, 1871, and gave way to a view of charred embers for miles around, the Chicago Water Tower provided a vital landmark for the survivors trying to find their way through the devastation. In subsequent years, the Water Tower has consolidated its role as the foremost Chicago landmark. It initially was seen as incorporating the "I will" mentality of the early Chicagoans: the determination of the city's population not to be defeated by the most devastating of all nineteenth century metropolitan fires, but to rebuild their thriving city bigger and better than before. Now, standing amid some of the finest architectural accomplishments of the twentieth century, it serves as a reminder of Chicago's nineteenth century history and of the city's beginnings.

Improving Chicago's Water Supply

In the pioneer days of the 1830's Chicagoans had to rely upon water taken from Lake Michigan, the Chicago River, and from a few wells in the city. This water was then transported through the streets in barrels sold to the citizens for ten cents a barrel. In

1839 a municipal water company was formed and a reservoir was built on the lakeshore near the present Michigan Avenue and Water Street. From here, with the help of a small steam-powered engine and an elementary network of wooden pipes which had been hollowed out of tree trunks, water was drawn from Lake Michigan and pumped to those within the city willing to pay for the service. However, the Chicago River also carried the city's sewage, including the effluent from the stockyards, tanneries, distilleries, and other industrial plants, into the lake. The inadequate separation of the city's clean water supply from its waste disposal led to a heavy annual death toll from cholera and typhoid.

In 1862 the water commissioners embarked upon plans to improve the water supply to the city's population of 330,000. The first move on the part of the water commissioners to address this problem was to lay a brick pipe five feet in diameter in the heavy blue clay sixty-six feet under the lake, letting it emerge two miles away from the shore where the water was clean. This in itself was hailed as an engineering feat and elicited intense interest elsewhere in the United States as well as in Europe, where plans of the construction were exhibited at the Paris Exposition in 1867. Others called it "Chicago's folly," predicting that it would never last. However, it was still in use in the early 1930's and proved to be the beginning of what in the early twentieth century became the world's largest water system and involved further famous engineering achievements, such as the subsequent reversal of the Chicago River: Through a system of locks the river was made to flow away from the lake, thus eliminating the potential for contaminating the fresh water supply with sewage.

The tunnel beneath the lake was started in 1864 and completed in December, 1866, but as it was only the first step of a three-part project, it was not until 1867 that Chicagoans were able to enjoy the fresh lake water it could supply. The three-part installation included the tunnel, the water tower, and a new pumping station. In order to draw the clean lake water through the newly constructed tunnel, a pumping station had to be constructed on the east side of the present Michigan Avenue. This housed the pumping engine which was capable of pumping eighteen million gallons of water in a day. Until then the maximum that had been pumped from the lake was 11,610,864 gallons, so that the new

supply was at the time considered far in excess of the city's current needs and that therefore the installation would prove to be a sound investment for the future of the quickly expanding city. The contract for the new engine was received by the Morgan Iron Works of New York in July, 1865, and by August, 1866, most of the machinery had been shipped to Chicago.

The final part in this new water supply system was a standpipe. In the proposed method of pumping water from the lake a vertical pipe was inserted into the horizontal one in order to relieve the pulsating pressure caused by the engine's pumping action. The design of the engine meant that water was pumped in regular bursts and the resulting pressure could prove too much for the network of pipes to bear. With the installation of a standpipe the excess water could simply escape from the horizontal pipe and rise up inside the vertical one, thus relieving the pressure.

In the Chicago installation it was determined that a standpipe 138 feet tall and 3 feet in diameter would be needed to relieve this pressure. Public officials believed the steel standpipe should be concealed by a building of "more than usual architectural beauty." Prominent Chicago architect W. W. Boyington was appointed by the Board of Public Works to design the Chicago Water Tower in which the standpipe would be housed.

The Architect

W. W. Boyington (1818-1898) was born in Southwick, Massachusetts, and came to Chicago in 1853. Buildings of his design included the Illinois State Penitentiary at Joliet and the Sherman House hotel in Chicago. For the Chicago Water Tower he chose a style known as Castellated Gothic, giving the construction the air of a medieval fortress or tower. The locally quarried buff-colored Lemont limestone was hewn in large rusticated blocks, further adding to the "fortress" feel of the building. The exterior of the tower is decorated with turrets and battlements. The actual shaft encompassing the standpipe is octagonal and rises 154 feet from the ground. At the top of the shaft there is an iron cupola. By March, 1867, the foundations had been laid and the tower was ready for the ceremonial laying of the cornerstone. This was done by the city's Masons and was preceded by an elaborate procession of members of various Masonic Lodges.

The parade began at Dearborn and Randolph Streets, moved north on Clark Street, and finally proceeded up Pine Street (now Michigan Avenue) to the site of the Chicago Water Tower. The ceremony, which culminated in the lowering of the stone and the ritual handing of the tools from the Principal Architect to the Grand Master and various other Masonic dignitaries was described vividly by a contemporary Chicago Republican reporter: "These officers tested the perfection of the stone by the square, level, and plumb. On their satisfactory report, the stone was consecrated with corn, wine and oil, the proper addresses being made by the representative officers; the Grand Master struck it three times with a gavel, and the ceremony was over." Upon completion in 1869, the Chicago Water Tower was architecturally the most imposing of the new waterworks buildings. When all the bills had been paid for it in 1870, the tower had cost $95,587.37 to construct.

The Great Chicago Fire

The tower was constructed entirely of stone, brick, and iron. The construction was proudly announced to be completely fireproof, and within less than two years this boast was put to a terrible test. On Sunday, October 8, 1871, the Great Chicago Fire broke out in the cowshed to the rear of 137 DeKoven Street—as legend has it, by Mrs. O'Leary's cow knocking over a lantern. The inferno lasted until the evening of Tuesday, October 10. During these two days flames swept across three and one-third square miles in the heart of the city, leaving nothing in their path except the Chicago Water Tower, the Mahlon D. Ogden residence at Dearborn and White (now Walton) Streets, and the cottage of a police officer at 2121 North Hudson. In the most destructive fire in U.S. history, eighteen thousand buildings—property valued at two hundred million dollars—turned to rubble, ninety thousand people were left homeless, and an estimated three hundred people died. The exact mortality has never been conclusively established, however, due to the difficulty of determining who fled the city and who perished without trace in the flames.

Several factors contributed to the fire's swift grasp of the city and its subsequent relentless destruction. The entire Great Lakes area had suffered a drought throughout the summer and fall of 1871, leaving the land dry and parched. Before the fire, Chicago was largely built of wood, with very few stone or brick buildings. This was typical of a nineteenth century booster town of the American West, of which Chicago was the supreme example. Many of its streets were dangerously overcrowded, leaving no space between the wooden buildings. In the light of these hazardous realities the city fire brigade was hopelessly inadequate—and was to be sorely put to the test.

Prior to the Great Chicago Fire there had been several smaller fires, which the municipal fire brigade had managed to bring under control. One fire in particular, however, had a crucial effect on the brigade. On Saturday, October 7, a planing mill on Canal Street, on the near west side between Jackson and Van Buren Streets caught fire. The entire fire department had to be called out and several pieces of its apparatus were put out of commission. When the fire was finally extinguished, more than half the firefighters were too tired to work any longer. No sooner had disaster been averted at the planing mill than the cowshed on DeKoven, also on the west side of the city, caught fire. The Great Chicago Fire started three-eighths of a mile west of the southern branch of the Chicago River. Before midnight it had crossed the river branch moving toward the northeast side of the city. Then it crossed the river itself, moving through the north side. By 3:30 A.M. on Monday the waterworks at Chicago Avenue and Pine Street (now Michigan Avenue) were blazing so fiercely that firefighters had to abandon them. The fire proceeded north as far as Fullerton Avenue, then the city limits. Rain extinguished the last smoldering embers of the fire, which by this stage had all but burnt itself out.

The ferocity of the fire lodged itself in the imagination of the city's population. Many eyewitness accounts spoke of walls of fire being blown across the city, causing new areas to be ignited in advance of the main body of the fire reaching those areas. It also is well documented, however, that the weather during the two days of the fire did not include strong winds. The phenomenon described by the eyewitnesses is that of so-called "fire devils," or convection heat, balls of flame hurled forward simply through the heat generated by the main body of the fire. Against such odds the wooden structures of the city were doomed. One famous testimony to the fire, a letter written by Mary L. Fales to her mother, speaks of burying the family's most treasured objects that were too heavy to carry in their escape. In the hope that they would be preserved both from the fire and from any subsequent looting, her husband buried her piano and some other things in their garden. When they returned to the charred remains of their house they discovered that the piano had "burned under the ground; nothing was left but the iron plates."

The devastation was on such a grand scale that of all the great U.S. metropolitan fires of the nineteenth century, Chicago's really caught the imagination, not only of Chicagoans but also of the nation as a whole. Within days after the fire the Chicago Relief and Aid Society had been organized and began accepting the generous donations which began to flood into Chicago from elsewhere in the country and later, when news spread, from Europe as well. As a result the city was able to start rebuilding immediately, and makeshift shelters were erected as a matter of priority. When the winter came, the city could proudly claim that none of the fire victims was homeless or without food.

Aftermath

The aftermath of the fire has contributed to the lore of the city as much as the fire itself. Due to the total destruction caused by the inferno, the fire in the long run provided Chicago's watershed—life in the city before and after the fire. If before the fire Chicago had been characterized by the booster spirit of the American West, afterward its population was motivated to start again and build a bigger and better city. The fire demonstrated that the booming city of Chicago was destined to become one of the foremost U.S. cities. Within days work began to clear the rubble and real estate speculation commenced. Soon land in the center of the city was more valuable laid to waste than it had been before the fire.

Although two hundred million dollars worth of property had been lost, new construction was far more costly. All this was financed not only through insurance claims, which were for the most part met, but by fresh entrepreneurial money which flooded into the city. Within three years after the fire, Chicago once more dominated its region. After 1871 Chicago became the fastest-growing city in the United States, attributable to its commercial strength in commodities trade, as well as to its fa-

vorable location at the crossroads of the transcontinental railway and the Great Lakes and other major waterways. The pride in the city's survival and resurrection is commemorated to this day in its flag and in the landmark status accorded to the Chicago Water Tower.

Decline of the Tower's Usefulness

Though the Water Tower survived the inferno the pumping station was destroyed and had to be rebuilt. By 1906 the pumping system that required a standpipe had become obsolete. Consequently, the Chicago Water Tower had a relatively short useful life and in 1918 faced demolition. Architectural tastes had changed and more people were inclined to agree with author Oscar Wilde, who is said to have called the Chicago Water Tower "a castellated monstrosity with pepper boxes stuck all over it." Furthermore, the tower stood in the path of the planned widening of Michigan Avenue as Pine Street had been renamed in 1917. The tower's proposed demolition, however, produced public outrage, and alternative plans to move the Chicago Water Tower and reconstruct it out of the way of the Michigan Avenue expansion proved impracticable. City officials relented and ordered that Michigan Avenue be bent a little to accommodate the tower. Other later attempts to have the tower demolished met with similar outrage, and efforts were made to secure a supply of limestone with which to keep the tower from falling into a state of disrepair.

In 1967, as a measure of the Chicago Water Tower's symbolic importance to twentieth century Chicago, at the one hundredth anniversary of the tower's construction, Mayor Richard J. Daley presented a piece of surplus stone from the tower to Robert E. Slater, president of the John Hancock Mutual Life Insurance Company. Slater promised the stone would be embedded in the John Hancock Center, which was then under construction.

Landmark Status

In 1971 the entire area of valuable publicly owned real estate known as the Water Tower District, comprising the Water Tower and its small park on North Michigan Avenue, the Chicago Avenue pumping station, Engine Company 98's fire station, and the ten-acre Seneca Park, was designated a city landmark. The Water Tower was placed safely out of reach of any further threats to its existence and its position in the hearts of Chicagoans was firmly established. The tower itself is not open to the public, but a tourist information center exists opposite the Tower on East Pearson Street at the site of the old pumping station. The one-hour long "Here's Chicago" show can be viewed here daily, giving the visitor a graphic idea of the early history of the city, the devastation of the Great Chicago Fire of 1871, and of the role of the Chicago Water Tower within that history.   —*Hilary Collier Sy-Quia*

For Further Information:

Angle, Paul M., ed. *The Great Chicago Fire.* Chicago: Chicago Historical Society, 1971. Another excellent source, with an introduction and notes by Angle. It is a compilation of eight eyewitness accounts given by men and women who lived through the horrors of October 8-10, 1871, and testified to the courage of the city's inhabitants.

Bales, Richard F. *Did the Cow Do It? A New Look at the Great Chicago Fire.* Springfield: Illinois State Historical Society, 1997. A history of Chicago and the fire in 1871 that examines its causes and outcome.

Lowe, D., ed. *The Great Chicago Fire in Eyewitness Accounts and Seventy Contemporary Photographs and Illustrations.* New York: Dover Press, 1979. Gives a vivid introduction to the scale and devastation of the Chicago fire of 1871.

Miller, Ross. *American Apocalypse: The Great Fire and the Myth of Chicago.* Chicago: University of Chicago Press, 1990. An excellent excerpt from this book was published in the Spring/Summer, 1990, edition of *Chicago History,* the Chicago Historical Society's magazine. It puts forward the thesis that the Great Fire was quickly given mythical proportions as part of the booster spirit on the back of which Chicago rose again so swiftly after the disaster.

Haymarket Square, Chicago

Date: Riot occurred on May 4, 1886; declared an Illinois State Historical Landmark in 1970; city of Chicago conferred historical landmark status to only the Haymarket Riot site in 1992

Relevant issues: Business and industry, disasters and tragedies, political history

Significance: Although no original structures from the Haymarket era exist in this one-block area of industrial lofts, offices, and parking lots, the base of a monument dedicated to the seven policemen who died as a result of the riot still stands at the northeast corner of Randolph Street and the Kennedy Expressway.

Location: A half mile west of Chicago's Loop; the original Haymarket Square public marketplace extended along West Randolph Street (150 North), between North Desplaines Street (640 West) and North Halsted Street (800 West), and the site of the 1886 Haymarket Riot was on Desplaines Street, about a half block north of Randolph

Site Office:
Illinois Labor History Society
28 East Jackson Boulevard
Chicago, IL 60604
ph.: (312) 663-4107

While labor historian William J. Adelman has said that "probably no event has had such a profound influence on the American labor movement or on the history of Chicago than what happened near Haymarket Square in 1886," it has only been relatively recently—March 25, 1992—that the Chicago City Council's Historical Landmark Committee passed an ordinance that officially granted landmark status to the site of the so-called Haymarket Riot. Today, the site is a rather unremarkable, if rough-edged, one-block stretch of parking lots and industrial and office lofts on Desplaines Street between Lake and Randolph Streets on Chicago's Near West Side. The city landmark designation finally came about through the twenty-two-year effort of the Illinois Labor History Society, though the former Haymarket Square area had been declared an Illinois State Historical Landmark in 1970.

The Haymarket Riot

The riot occurred on Tuesday night, May 4, 1886, when a bomb was thrown into a column of 176 armed policemen advancing on a crowd of several hundred workers, labor activists, and anarchists attending a city-sanctioned mass meeting half a block off Haymarket Square, then the largest pub-

The Haymarket Square Martyrs Monument in Forest Home Cemetery, dedicated to the labor activists who died in the melee or were executed for the bombing and to the rights of free speech and assembly. (Illinois Labor Historical Society)

sand workers up Michigan Avenue in Chicago—generally regarded around the world as the first May Day parade.

Initially, between 2,500 and 3,000 people showed up at the hastily planned meeting; attendance was deemed so small that it was held on a side street (Desplaines). The crowd had gathered in front of Crane's Alley, around a parked old delivery wagon that served as the speakers' platform. The first to speak was anarchist leader August Spies, editor of the socialist-worker *Arbeiter-Zeitung*, the largest German-language daily newspaper in the city; Spies had witnessed the McCormick police riot the day before. The second to mount the platform was Albert Parsons, anarchist and revolutionary labor leader; he retired to a nearby union hall immediately after addressing the crowd, which dwindled rapidly when a cold, windy rain began to fall. Mayor Carter Harrison, also present, left about this time, too, and advised police at the nearby Desplaines Street Station that everything was in order and that trouble was unlikely.

Just as final speaker Samuel Fielden, a labor leader and former Methodist preacher, was about to finish his speech, at 10:30 P.M., a police formation arrived from the station. Captain John Bonfield, long considered an enemy of working people and labor agitators, commanded the milling crowd to disband "immediately and peaceably." Suddenly, without warning, there was an ear-shattering explosion. Someone had thrown a dynamite bomb, probably from near the alley, into the middle of the police ranks. One policeman was killed instantly by the blast, and six others were mortally wounded. It was the first time such a bomb had ever been used in the United States.

Maddening confusion followed. The police immediately began firing wildly into the crowd and clubbing everyone in sight. At least four bystanders

lic gathering place in the city. The 7:30 P.M. Haymarket Protest Meeting (which actually began an hour later) had been called to denounce a police attack on locked-out workers at the McCormick Harvesting Works (now the International Harvester Company) on the south side of the city the previous afternoon; two workmen had been killed. The meeting had also been called to rally support for the eight-hour-day movement, which officially began May 1, 1886, with a march of eighty thou-

were killed by the police—the exact number is uncertain—and about two hundred people were injured; Fielden was shot in the knee shortly after leaving the speakers' wagon. Sixty policemen were wounded in the melee. Most of the police casualties were not inflicted by the bomb but by bullets fired by their panicked fellow officers.

Background to the Riot

What social forces sparked the explosion of the Haymarket bomb? In the latter half of the nineteenth century, Chicago was the fastest-growing city in the world, the country's foremost center of industrial capitalism. Wealthy businessmen viewed recent waves of Irish, German, and eastern European immigrants as cheap and easily exploited labor—which set the stage for ethnic, racial, and labor conflicts. The seeds of labor's "Great Upheaval" of the 1880's were planted in the great nationwide railroad strikes and riots of 1877, when unprecedented class violence left thirty workmen dead and over two hundred wounded. The strike's defeat taught workers that they needed more political and militant action in order to fight for their rights. Chicago labor historian Richard Schneirov has written,

> In this labor upsurge, working men and women from every trade, of every skill-level, and of all nationalities and races streamed into labor organizations by the tens of thousands, expressed insistent demands for shorter hours, higher wages and a permanent voice in determining their working conditions, and adopted new methods of labor solidarity to win these demands.

The business elite of Chicago felt understandably threatened, and a state bill was passed outlawing the right of workers to bear arms.

Who threw the dynamite bomb that set the struggle for an eight-hour day back a few decades and provoked a reign of terror over Chicago, then the national center of the often-overlapping radical labor, trade union, and anarchist movements? To this day, it has never been determined with any certainty, though a number of theories have been advanced by labor historians and Haymarket scholars. The Chicago police and city hall blamed the bomb throwing on anarchists or socialists; some union activists claimed it was the work of a police or

businessman agent provocateur who meant to bomb the workers in an effort to discredit the eight-hour movement. One theory, favored by the prosecution during the eventual trial, was that the bomb had been produced by Chicago anarchist leader Louis Lingg, one of the eight "Haymarket Martyrs" later convicted (this, however, has never been proven), and that it was thrown by Rudolph Schnaubelt, brother-in-law of Michael Schwab, another Haymarket Martyr. Schnaubelt, however, was twice arrested and twice released. In recent years, another strong possibility has emerged: minor German anarchist figure George Meng, acting on his own rather than as part of a conspiracy.

In any event, a wave of hysteria swept over Chicago in the weeks following the Haymarket Riot; freedom of speech and assembly were effectively suppressed. "Make the raids first and look up the law afterwards," State's Attorney Julius S. Grinnell instructed law officials. Police raided working-class neighborhoods, rounding up hundreds of known anarchists, socialists, and ethnic and labor leaders. The press, pulpit, business leaders, and eventually the public condemned labor unionism as an enemy of "law and order," a harbinger of violent anarchist revolt. Meeting halls, printing offices, and even private homes were invaded and ransacked (newspaper subscription lists were used for further arrests). Police beat and tortured conspiracy suspects while in jail.

Legal Aftermath

In all, thirty-one men were indicted for the crime of being accessories to the murder of policeman Mathias Degan, and for the general conspiracy to commit murder; the figure was finally reduced to eleven. Two agreed to turn state's witnesses, and one (Schnaubelt) left the country and was never found. The Haymarket Eight who actually stood trial included Spies, Parsons, Fielden, Schwab, Lingg, Adolph Fischer, George Engel, and Oscar Neebe. Only two—Spies and Fielden—were present at the meeting when the bomb was thrown. Parsons fled town for six weeks, but then freely turned himself in to face charges.

The trial, which lasted from June 21 to August 20, 1886, in the Cook County Courthouse, has been called a travesty and one of the most unjust in American history. It soon became clear that what took place in Judge Joseph E. Gary's courtroom was more than just a trial of eight men; a political philosophy was on trial. The handpicked (not randomly chosen) jury was inundated with anarchist writings and documents. The fact that the trial was about ideas, not deeds, was explicitly stated by Chief Prosecutor Grinnell in his summation to the jury: "Law is on trial. Anarchy is on trial. These men have been selected, picked out by the grand jury and indicted because they are the leaders. They are no more guilty than the thousands who follow them . . . convict these men, make examples of them, hang them and you save our institutions, our society."

Ideologically, Chicago anarchists believed in worker control over key industries; they saw government, business, and the police working in violation of constitutional principles. While state socialism, according to Parsons, called for government control of everything and sought to emancipate wage laborers by means of law, anarchists would have neither rulers or lawmakers; they sought the abolition of wage slavery "by the abrogation of law, by the abolition of all government." The Haymarket Eight did believe in the right of oppressed workers to defend themselves against police attack by means of bombs and "revolutionary violence"; but prominent newspapers and businessmen first talked of the idea of using terror tactics and dynamite against striking workers.

The weak case—charging eight men with murder, yet admitting that none had actually thrown the bomb—made it necessary for the prosecution to play up the fact that at least one of the men had some connection to bombs. They singled out Lingg because he was the only defendant known to have manufactured bombs and had already been dubbed "the Bomb-Maker."

The Verdict

As expected, the jury found all eight men guilty. Seven were sentenced to die by hanging. Neebe was given a fifteen-year prison term. Just before noon on Friday, November 11, 1887, despite an outpouring of worldwide protest and after all appeals had been exhausted, Spies, Engel, Fischer, and Parsons were executed in a courtyard between the Cook County Court House and the adjacent Cook County Jail. With nooses around their necks, Fischer cried out, "Hurrah for Anarchy! This is the happiest day of my life." Spies stated, "The time will come when our silence will be more powerful than the voices you strangle today." Lingg had committed suicide in his cell the day before by exploding a smuggled dynamite cap in his mouth, though some maintain he was murdered by the police. Schwab and Fielden had their sentences commuted to life imprisonment.

On June 26, 1893, a day after the Haymarket Martyrs Monument was dedicated in west suburban Waldheim (now Forest Home) Cemetery, where seven of the eight men are buried, prolabor Illinois governor John P. Altgeld granted amnesty to the three survivors, Neebe, Schwab, and Fielden. Altgeld attacked Judge Gary's ruling, as well as the police action; his pardon message noted that the men had not been proven guilty because the state "has never discovered who it was that threw the bomb which killed the policeman, and the evidence does not show any connection whatsoever between the defendants and the man who threw it." Characterized by the press as an alien, un-American anarchist, Altgeld sacrificed his promising political career by pardoning the three men and was not reelected in 1896.

Physical Remains of Haymarket Square

Except for the dilapidated base of the Haymarket Riot Monument, or Police Statue, dedicated in 1889 to the seven policemen killed in the riot and now located at the northeast corner of Randolph Street and the Kennedy Expressway (U.S. 90 and 94), little remains of the area once known as Haymarket Square or the nearby Desplaines Street riot site. Much of the area has either been burned down, razed for urban renewal, or sliced up by the highway. The Illinois Labor History Society (ILHS), however, is endeavoring to build a "Labor Park" in the area, which would include a monument to the Haymarket Martyrs.

The original Haymarket Square was not really a public square at all, but actually the section of Randolph Street between Desplaines and Halsted Streets (about two blocks). Once the biggest and busiest of five farmers' market areas in the city, the Haymarket was a hubbub of horse buggies, carts, and streetcars; truck farmers came from all over the countryside to sell food to the poor at dirt-cheap prices. Its proximity to north- and west-side working-class neighborhoods also made it a favorite gathering place for public meetings and workers' rallies; it could accommodate twenty thousand people.

The Haymarket Protest Meeting speaker's wagon was parked just a few feet north of Crane's Alley, on the east side of Desplaines, roughly halfway between Lake and Randolph. The alley lay just south of the Crane Plumbing Company factory complex, one of the largest in Chicago in 1886; the buildings have since either been burned or torn down. It has been theorized—with no certainty—that the bomb was thrown from the sidewalk on Desplaines, ten or fifteen feet south of Crane's Alley. The alley no longer exists, but there is a one-lane pathway between two parking lots in the same general area now. The bomb landed across the street, just north of the northwest corner of Randolph and Desplaines. The site is now home to one of the many parking lots in the area.

The Police Statue

The *Chicago Tribune* and the so-called Committee of Twenty-Five businessmen headed by factory owner R. T. Crane eventually raised over ten thousand dollars to erect a police statue. The winning design was submitted in 1888 by Charles F. Batcheider, a St. Paul, Minnesota, newspaper reporter who had once worked in Chicago. His design showed a sketch of a policeman with his arm raised, commanding peace. Recent Danish immigrant John Gelert was selected as the sculptor. He used as his model "robust patrolman" Thomas Birmingham. The committee, however, was horrified by the clay model; the figure looked too Irish. They wanted the policeman to look Protestant and Anglo-Saxon. According to historian William J. Adelman, "Gelert refused to change the figure, but he also used other models, since Birmingham was often drunk and unable to pose."

The statue, a life-size bronze figure dressed in characteristic nineteenth century police garb, was dedicated on Memorial Day, 1889, with about two thousand people present; 176 policemen took part in the ceremony, the same number that had formed the column three years earlier. The statue was unveiled by the seventeen-year-old son of Mathias Degan (the policeman instantly killed by the bomb blast), and Mayor DeWitt Cregier said, "May it stand here unblemished so long as the metropolis shall endure." A plaque listed the names of the seven dead policemen.

In 1900, the statue was defaced and began to be seen as a traffic hazard; streetcars had to swerve around it. So it was moved about a mile west, to Randolph and Ogden Streets in Union Park. In May, 1903, the crest of the city and state were stolen from the base. On May 4, 1927, the forty-first anniversary of the Haymarket tragedy, a streetcar jumped the tracks and smashed into the monument, knocking the statue off its base. In 1928, the statue was repaired and moved farther into Union Park, ending up on Jackson Boulevard. In 1957, the statue was moved to a special platform built for it during the construction of the Kennedy Expressway. The move was sponsored by the Haymarket Businessmen's Association, who hoped it would promote tourism in the area.

Modern Reevaluations of the Riot

During the social and political upheavals of the 1960's and 1970's, the monument became a symbol for police oppression and a frequent target for a newer wave of radical protesters. As William J. Adelman has noted, "With the coming of the Vietnam War, the Civil Rights Marches of the 1960's, police brutality during the Democratic Convention in Chicago in 1968, the 'Chicago Eight Conspiracy Trial' and Watergate, many people began to look again at the 'Haymarket Affair' and what it should have taught us."

On October 6, 1969, some members of the Youth International Party's Weathermen faction placed several sticks of dynamite between the bronze policeman's legs, toppling most of the statue and sending chunks onto the Kennedy Expressway; the blast also blew out a number of windows in nearby buildings. Mayor Richard J. Daley promised to replace it, and a WGN radio announcer helped raise the money—$5,500 from private individuals, police associations, and the city. Sculptor Mario Stampinato was hired to restore Gelert's statue, which was unveiled May 4, 1970.

On October 6, 1970, exactly one year after the first bombing, the police statue was bombed again; once again, Stampinato restored it. The statue was replaced for the second time in January, 1971. Mayor Daley ordered around-the-clock police security that cost the city $67,440 a year. In February, 1972, after the ILHS wrote a letter to the mayor suggesting that the statue be moved to "a more fitting and secure location," the statue was quietly removed from its base and placed in the lobby of the Central Police Headquarters at 11th and State Streets. In October, 1976, the statue was finally installed in the courtyard of the newly built Chicago Police Training Center, 1300 West Jackson Boulevard. No longer visible to the public, the statue can be viewed only by special arrangement. The plaque containing the names of the seven policemen killed in the Haymarket Riot had been left behind at the base; it was "liberated" in 1985 and is now reportedly enshrined at a community center in Nicaragua.

The ten-foot-high, stepped-stone pedestal still remains at the corner of Randolph and the Kennedy Expressway. The base is nearly forgotten, filth-ridden, and graffiti-scrawled, like some oddly leftover urban relic that never met the wrecking ball. Yet the original inscriptions are plainly visible. On the front, facing Randolph, it says, "In the name of the people of Illinois I command peace," the words supposedly spoken by Captain Bonfield as he urged the crowd to disperse. On the back, it says, "Dedicated by Chicago May 4th, 1889, to her Defenders in the riot of May 4th, 1886."

Ongoing Preservation Efforts

Since 1970, the ILHS—a private nonprofit group formed to encourage the preservation and study of labor history materials in Illinois—has campaigned to commemorate the site of the Haymarket Riot. On May 3, 1970, through the ILHS's efforts, a State Historical Landmark marker was placed on the corner of the Catholic Charities Building (southwest corner of Randolph and Desplaines) because the city of Chicago would not approve a spot on its property. The plaque was pulled off some months later, presumably by persons on the conservative right. The missing plaque's bolt holes are still visible on the Catholic Charities Building. That same year, the ILHS first recommended official city designation for the Haymarket area by presenting a petition to the Chicago Landmarks Commission, which must approve a site before the Chicago City Council votes on it. A report was written but nothing happened for many years. ILHS members made renewed bids for city designation throughout the 1970's and 1980's.

In November, 1985, as the Haymarket Centennial approached, plans were launched for a Labor Park in the former Haymarket Square area. The ILHS and the Haymarket Centennial Committee began a petition drive, requesting that the city purchase the parking lot at the northwest corner of Randolph and Desplaines, where the bomb supposedly landed. The park would include a monument dedicated to the Haymarket Martyrs, as well as to workers' struggle for an eight-hour day, the freedom of speech and assembly, the rights of ethnic minority groups, and the right of workers to have free democratic trade unions. It appears, however, that city funds for a park and a monument will not be forthcoming, and that the effort must be funded privately.

On March 25, 1992, the city of Chicago officially conferred landmark status on the site of the Haymarket Riot of 1886. The city council's Historical Landmark Committee approved the designation, assigning that status to the area of Desplaines Street between Lake and Randolph.

—*Jeff W. Huebner*

For Further Information:

Adelman, William J. *Haymarket Revisited.* Rev. ed. Chicago: Illinois Labor History Society, 1986. An excellent introductory and illustrated tour guidebook of labor history sites and ethnic neighborhoods connected with the Haymarket affair, by an ILHS cofounder. The cover and maps were designed by O. W. Neebe, grandson of one of the Haymarket Eight. Adelman has been accused of coopting the anarchist legacy through his left-labor slant.

Avrich, Paul. *The Haymarket Tragedy.* Princeton, N.J.: Princeton University Press, 1984. A thorough account of the tragedy by one of the major historians of the international anarchist movement.

Foner, Philip S., ed. *The Autobiographies of the Haymarket Martyrs.* New York: Humanities Press, 1969. A collection of autobiographical sketches of the Haymarket Eight (which originally appeared in the labor journal Knights of Labor between October 16, 1886, and October 8, 1887), along with comments by their attorney, W. P. Black. Includes a concise introduction by Foner.

Powers, Joe, and Mark Rogouin, eds. *The Day Will Come: Stories of the Haymarket Martyrs and the Men and Women Buried Alongside the Monument.* Chicago: Charles H. Kerr, 1994. A description of the Haymarket Square Riot of 1886 and a history of the labor movement in nineteenth century Chicago.

Roediger, Dave, and Franklin Rosemont, eds. *Haymarket Scrapbook*. Chicago: Charles H. Kerr, 1986. A profusely illustrated anthology by many of today's labor historians, focusing on the Haymarket affair, as well as its enduring influence in the United States and the world.

Hull-House, Chicago

Date: Founded in 1889

Relevant issues: Cultural history, education, social reform

Significance: This is the most renowned of American social settlement houses. Its founders attempted to alleviate the conditions of poverty in the surrounding neighborhood through cultural and educational programs, eventually becoming active in politics and labor movements while pioneering urban sociology and social work.

Location: Jane Addams' Hull-House Museum, which incorporates two of the original thirteen buildings of the Hull-House complex, is at the corner of Polk and Halsted Streets on the campus of the University of Illinois at Chicago

Site Office:

Jane Addams' Hull-House Museum
The University of Illinois at Chicago
800 South Halsted Street
Chicago, IL 60607-7017
ph.: (312) 413-5353
fax: (312) 413-2092

Hull-House, the museum, is a monument to progressive liberal ideas of the late nineteenth and early twentieth century United States. It can also be regarded as a memorial to Jane Addams, one of its founders and its most famous resident, and to the cult of personality that has developed around her. Hull-House, the social service agency, which since its decentralization in the 1960's has continued to serve the communities of Chicago, is a monument to the ideals as stated in Hull-House's original charter: to provide the neighborhood of poor immigrants of the area of Halsted and Polk Streets with a "center for a higher civic and social life, to initiate and maintain educational and philanthropic enterprises, and to investigate and improve the conditions in the industrial districts of Chicago."

Creation of Hull-House

Hull-House was founded in 1889. It was not a mission, a charity, or a shelter, as early observers tried to explain it. When its founders moved in, their stated purpose was to be neighbors to the poor, helping to improve their lot by understanding and experiencing their condition. Neither was Hull-House the first settlement of its kind. Having been inspired by Toynbee Hall, a university settlement in London's East End, Hull-House was part of a larger movement in the United States to establish settlements of college-educated women and men working among the poor to fight poverty and social injustice.

Hull-House is the most famous example of the settlement movement, largely because of the speeches, articles, and books written by Jane Addams, one of its founders. Through her lectures and publications, Hull-House rose to international prominence and Addams became a cult heroine, a role she encouraged. Yet it was only because of the prodding of Ellen Gates Starr, Addams's friend and cofounder of Hull-House, that the two women moved to Chicago to implement their plans. They moved to an apartment on Washington Place in 1889 to enlist support and to prepare for their "Toynbee Hall experiment."

By 1889, the mansion that Charles Hull, a real estate dealer, had built as a country home in 1856 was in disrepair, having narrowly escaped the Great Chicago Fire of 1871. An office, a saloon, and a storage room occupied the first floor, with rooms for rent on the second. Addams and Starr were able to sublet the entire second floor, with use of the reception room on the first. They moved in on September 18, and furnished the house with their own furniture, heirlooms, and art reproductions.

At first the two women's plans were vague. They began by inviting their neighbors to a reading in Italian of George Eliot's *Romola* (1862-1863); the need for more practical diversions soon became apparent. A kindergarten was suggested. Organized by Jenny Dow, the daughter of a prominent

Chicago family, the kindergarten had twenty-four children enrolled in the first year, with seventy more on the waiting list. Other activities quickly followed. Clubs for children and classes in sewing were organized. Art exhibitions and classes, arranged by Starr, brought neighbors in great numbers to Hull-House.

Hull-House attracted wealthy and influential supporters. Helen Culver, owner of the Hull mansion, eventually gave the property to Addams. Wealthy and dedicated women, such as Louise deKoven Bowen and Mary Rozet Smith, donated their time and money. Scholars Henry Demarest Lloyd, John Dewey, Albion Smith, and Charles Zueblin, clergymen Jenkin Lloyd Jones and Graham Taylor, architects Allen and Irving Pond, and numerous businessmen, lawyers, and labor leaders lent their support in a variety of ways.

Hull-House at Work

Hull-House offered accommodation for its teachers and supporters, so that they could live in the neighborhood they served. Early residents included Gerard Swope, the future president of General Electric; Charles Bond, the historian; and William Lyon Mackenzie King, who went on to become prime minister of Canada.

Yet it was the female residents who made it a renowned center for social research and reform. They went on to become active in a variety of government agencies, civic organizations, and educational institutions both within and outside of Hull-House. Julia Lathrop, who helped organize the first Juvenile Court and the Immigrants' Protective League and who became head of the Children's Bureau, came in 1890. In 1892, Florence Kelley moved in. She pushed the residents of Hull-House toward the reform movement. During her first year, she was appointed as a special agent for the State Bureau of Labor Statistics to investigate sweatshops in Chicago. Mary Kenney was a labor leader and founder of the Jane Club, a cooperative living arrangement for working women. Alzina Stevens became the first probation officer of the Juvenile Court. Grace Abbott became the director of the Immigrants' Protective League and succeeded Lathrop as head of the Children's Bureau. Alice Hamilton became the first female professor at Harvard Medical School. Sophonisba Breckinridge and Edith Abbott were professors at one of the first schools of social work, the Chicago School of Civics and Philanthropy.

Hull-House quickly became a community center for the neighborhood, a "think tank" and arena for progressive liberal ideas, and a center for social research. Classes and clubs continued; impractical college extension courses were supplanted by courses in English. In 1891, the Butler Art Gallery was established. In 1893, a coffeehouse and gymnasium were built, and the first public playground opened. In 1896, a rooming residence for men was added to the Butler Gallery, and the Jane Club was erected in 1898. A new coffeehouse and a theater were built in 1899.

The severe conditions of poverty that surrounded them on the Near West Side of Chicago, which included child labor, the sweatshop system, and municipal neglect, motivated the residents of Hull-House to become researchers and reformers. The Panic of 1893 and the ensuing depression further inspired activism. Reports filed by Florence Kelley in her role as special agent investigating labor conditions in the slums, led to the idea of a book modeled after Charles Booth's *Labour and Life of the People of London*. *Hull-House Maps and Papers* was a cooperative effort, led by Kelley, which detailed the nationalities and incomes of Nineteenth Ward inhabitants. It also included articles by Kelley and Alzina Stevens that exposed the sweatshop system and the deplorable conditions of child labor. While the book sold poorly, it helped to pioneer the developing field of urban sociology.

Neighborhood conditions also pushed Hull-House into politics. As a result of attempts to clean up the filthy streets and foul smell of the Hull-House area, Addams was appointed garbage inspector by Chicago's mayor. In 1896 and 1898, she and other residents tried to unseat the ward boss, John Powers, without success. The reporting of their experience gave Hull-House national prominence.

The Progressive Era

The "progressive era" began in 1900 and lasted until the start of World War I. Hull-House was at the forefront of progressive and reform movements. Residents helped implement the first important survey of Chicago's housing conditions in 1901. Other investigations included the licensing of mid-

Hull-House. (University of Illinois at Chicago, The University Library, Jane Addams Memorial Collection)

wives, infant mortality rates, children's reading habits, cocaine abuse, and juvenile delinquency.

The Hull-House group was active in local politics, helping to stimulate the development of public playgrounds and recreation centers. Addams and other Hull-House supporters served on the Chicago school board from 1905 to 1909. Nationally, Hull-House residents and graduates led the way in women's and labor movements, progressive education, Americanization of immigrants, and solving the root problems of juvenile delinquency.

Locally, Hull-House expanded its services to the community. The Labor Museum was opened in 1901; one of its purposes was to demonstrate to native-born Americans and, especially, to children of immigrants the importance of immigrant cultural resources. The Hull-House Players, a theater

troupe that was to achieve international recognition, began in 1900.

A succession of buildings was completed in the first decade of the twentieth century. These included the Hull-House Apartment Building in 1902; the Woman's Club Building in 1904; the Residents' Dining Hall in 1905; the Boys' Club Building in 1906; and the Mary Crane Nursery in 1907. The completed thirteen-building Hull-House Complex would remain until 1963.

Jane Addams's Memoirs

In 1910, Jane Addams published *Twenty Years at Hull-House*. Up to the publication of this book, the subjects of her writings tended to be social concerns. *Twenty Years at Hull-House*, however, was her autobiography. Much of it centers on Addams's early life and her reasons for founding Hull-House, her father, her schooling, a period of depression, subsequent trips to Europe in which she discovered Toynbee Hall, and eventually her decision to open a settlement in Chicago. According to Allen F. Davis, Addams's biographer, the book "is a conscious attempt to focus the reader's attention on Jane Addams." The story of Addams, not entirely factual, passed into popular mythology so completely that it was repeated, albeit more poetically, in a 1932 article by Edmund Wilson.

The book, which was a critical and commercial success, drove into the popular mind the notion that Jane Addams was Hull-House and vice versa. One review put it this way: "[*Twenty Years at Hull-House*] is an inspiring exhibit of what one brave and determined spirit has done and may still do in making rough ways smooth for sorely beset humanity." Yet Hull-House was not the effort of one brave and determined spirit, but of many. It was left to others to pioneer in such fields as art education for the masses (Starr), labor activism (Kenney), and urban sociology (Kelley). Addams was a founder and head resident of Hull-House. She was an excellent administrator and fund-raiser, and an effective crusader for Hull-House concerns—social justice, free thought, and Americanism. With *Twenty Years at Hull-House*, however, Addams also became a self-promoter.

A great deal of what Addams wrought through her involvement with Hull-House is profoundly good. However, the reality of Hull-House differed somewhat from the myth that grew up around Addams.

Opposition to Hull-House
Many immigrants openly resisted her and were hostile to her. In her thesis, *Pluralism and Progressives*, Rivka Shpak Lissak analyzes how many of the programs designed to "help" the new immigrant population were in fact attempts to assimilate them into the dominant Anglo-American culture. Organizations like the Immigrants' Protective League were meant to supplant established service agencies run by immigrants themselves. It is telling to note that no immigrant was elected to its executive board until 1920. Similarly, Hull-House's fight with the ward boss, who, while corrupt, represented immigrant concerns, was a well-resisted attempt to wrest control from lower- and lower-middle-class immigrant leaders and to replace them with Ameri-

canized immigrants with bourgeois values. Hull-House's cultural programs reflected a bias toward Anglo-Saxon art, music, and theater. The result was that the more ethnically oriented immigrants ignored the settlement, creating their own agencies, banks, schools, and community centers.

The fact that many immigrants were unimpressed with Addams and the Hull-House group did nothing to belie the myth that Addams was creating for herself. If she was not a heroine to the people she presumed to serve, she was to the rest of America. By admiring and praising Addams's work, many Americans could assuage their guilt over the conditions of poverty and quell their fears of new immigrant power. Addams was not to remain a heroine indefinitely, however.

In the years immediately following publication of her autobiography, Addams was at the height of her popularity. That popularity enabled her to become more involved in politics. She became a spokeswoman for woman suffrage, and in 1912 she seconded the nomination of Theodore Roosevelt as the presidential candidate of the Progressive Party ticket. She became leader of the Women's Peace Party and an advocate for pacifism when war broke out in 1914. She was a representative to the International Congress of Women at The Hague in 1915.

Decline of Addams's Reputation
Addams's star began to fall when she returned from The Hague and gave a speech at Carnegie Hall opposing the war. At the end of her speech, she related how she had been told that soldiers hated the bayonet charge and had to be given alcoholic beverages to induce them to it. That comment was but one small part of her talk, but it was the one that attracted the most press attention, disastrous for Addams. Addams had always spoken her mind, but up until then her mind and the public mind had been united. Now the public rebelled against her. They wanted to believe that soldiers fought because of duty and love of country. They would not accept that soldiers needed to be "doped" to engage in hand-to-hand combat. The public perceived Addams as impugning the bravery of soldiers everywhere, and she was attacked and vilified in the press.

In her further work for the cause of pacifism, Addams gave the public more reasons to mock and vilify her, especially after the United States entered the war, although Hull-House ended up doing much work for the war effort. When the war ended, the country did not return to the progressive ideals of peace, as even President Woodrow Wilson found out, but became obsessed with patriotism and rooting out radicals and Communists. Addams, once a heroine, was seen as the archenemy of America for her opposition to the war. In 1919, military intelligence worker Archibald Stevenson, testifying before a U.S. Senate subcommittee, produced a list of sixty-two persons whom he claimed held "dangerous, destructive, and anarchist sentiments." Jane Addams topped the list. She also was named in the Senate's Lusk Report as a Communist sympathizer; the report contained many false and exaggerated accusations against numerous persons who had been involved in the peace and reform movements. The "Red Scare" hysteria increased in the 1920's. Hull-House was labeled a seat of radical and communist movements.

Vindication of Jane Addams

Jane Addams spent less and less time in the United States, but managed to keep Hull-House solvent. In the 1920's, Hull-House continued its service to the community, which became increasingly settled by Mexicans, Italians, and Greeks, with a large number of African Americans to the south and west. While social work became a profession and the idealism of the progressive era subsided, the number of people using the settlement services actually increased.

In 1929, the stock market crashed, resulting in the Great Depression. Jane Addams came to be vindicated in the ensuing years; she won the Nobel Peace Prize in 1931 and saw her ideals reflected in the New Deal reforms of President Franklin D. Roosevelt's administration. Several of Roosevelt's appointees and advisers were Hull-House graduates. In 1935, the most remarkable era of Hull-House came to a close when Addams died of cancer.

After Addams

Addams had been Hull-House's chief administrator and fund-raiser, and there appeared to be no one qualified to take her place. Then Louise deKoven Bowen, who had been a chief financial supporter, became president of the board and began solving the problems of funding and finding a new head resident. The Jane Addams Memorial Fund provided partial support, and for the first time Hull-House sought money from the Chicago Community Fund, a group fund-raising venture. Rooms at Hull-House were let at higher rents, although this change involved having tenants who were not interested in Hull-House service. Adena Rich was the first head resident after Addams. Business continued much the same, but Rich initiated the Department of Naturalization and Citizenship and formed the Committee on International Relations and the Housing and Sanitation Committee. Hull-House residents also became involved with New Deal programs such as the Works Progress Administration, which provided sixty-six paid positions at the settlement.

Bowen and Rich were often at loggerheads over funding, staff, and programs, and Rich refused to become the head resident full-time. The difficulties led to Rich's resignation in 1939. The next head resident—who quickly changed her title to director—was Charlotte Carr, formerly director of New York's Emergency Relief Bureau. Carr, whose personal style was vastly different from Bowen's or Addams's, lasted only five years in the position.

Modern Concerns

In 1943, Russell Ward Ballard became director, and his tenure lasted until 1962, one year before Hull-House was taken over by the University of Illinois at Chicago. During Ballard's career, Hull-House emphasized programs for children and youth, and service to the neighborhood. He insisted on a multicultural staff, representative of the area's ethnic groups, which by 1950 included Italians, Greeks, Mexicans, Japanese, Lithuanians, Hungarians, blacks, and Puerto Ricans. Yet gang warfare and racism complicated his efforts to unify the neighborhood.

Ballard believed that delinquency grew out of poor housing and thought that people would be more interested in improving their own condition if they were involved personally in renovation. Hull-House helped to organize the Near West Side Planning Board for this purpose in 1949. From 1949 to 1961, the board struggled against poor funding, politics, and general apathy, yet cooperated with city officials on a plan for the clearing of fifty-five acres of dilapidated property around Hull-House.

In 1960, the city offered this area to the University of Illinois for its new Chicago campus—a slap in the face to those citizens who had worked hard to clear the land, which they believed to be allocated for new housing. An uproar of protest ensued, to no avail. On March 5, 1963, the board of trustees of Hull-House sold the original buildings to the city for $875,000. A new headquarters was established on the north side of Chicago, and Hull-House became a decentralized, rather than neighborhood-based, social service agency.

The Hull Mansion and the Residents' Dining Hall were restored by the university in the 1960's and became a National Historic Landmark in 1967. The mansion has been restored to look as it did when Jane Addams and Ellen Starr moved in, with rotating exhibits of the history of the settlement and its workers. The Residents' Dining Hall contains an exhibit on the history of the Hull-House neighborhood. —*Gregory J. Ledger*

For Further Information:

Addams, Jane. *Twenty Years at Hull-House.* New York: Macmillan, 1910. Reprint. Edited by Vicoria Bissel Brown. Boston: St. Martin's Press, 1999. The cofounder's account of the experiences and motivations that led her to establish a settlement in a poor Chicago neighborhood. This edition includes an introduction by Brown.

Bryan, Mary Lynn McCree, and Allen F. Davis, eds. *One Hundred Years at Hull House.* Bloomington: Indiana University Press, 1990. A collection of articles written by Hull-House residents, supporters, neighbors, and detractors, and gives the most complete coverage of the multifaceted story of Hull-House.

Davis, Allen F. *American Heroine: The Life and Legend of Jane Addams.* New York: Oxford University Press, 1973. Focuses on the mythology of Jane Addams, both that which was promoted by her, and that perpetuated in the popular mind.

Lissak, Rivka Shpak. *Pluralism and Progressives: Hull House and the New Immigrants, 1890-1919.* Chicago: University of Chicago Press, 1989. Focuses on the Hull-House ideology of the immigrant's place in society and its efforts, often thwarted, to be the culture broker and chief assimilator of new immigrants.

Museum of Science and Industry and Midway Plaisance, Chicago

Date: Opened in 1933
Relevant issues: Art and architecture, education, science and technology
Significance: The Museum of Science and Industry contains, in its almost twenty acres of floor space, an array of participatory exhibits relating to science and technology. The building, originally built in 1893 as the Palace of Fine Arts at the Columbian Exposition of 1893, was designed in the Greek classic style by Charles B. Atwood and reconstructed between 1929 and 1940. The Midway Plaisance, six hundred feet wide and a mile long, also originally part of the Columbian Exposition, is now a park area that serves as the southern gateway to the University of Chicago.
Location: The Museum of Science and Industry is at 57th Street and Lake Shore Drive; the Midway Plaisance lies between 59th and 60th Streets and extends from Stony Island to Cottage Grove, joining Jackson and Washington Parks
Site Office:
Museum of Science and Industry
57th Street and Lake Shore Drive
Chicago, IL 60637
ph.: (773) 684-1414
fax: (773) 684-7141
Web site: www.msichicago.org

By the last decade of the nineteenth century, the United States was ready to show the Old World the glories and accomplishments of the New, and what better occasion could there be for such an exposition than the four hundredth anniversary of Christopher Columbus's voyage of discovery?

Leading citizens in Chicago saw this as an opportunity to showcase their vibrant city of a million and a half people in the center of the nation. Chicago was then sixty years old, and only twenty-one years removed from the Great Fire that had both destroyed its mercantile heart and allowed it to start anew.

The Columbian Exposition

The Columbian Exposition of 1893, however, proved to be far more than a celebration of the past. It became a watershed, bringing together the nations of the world as no other event had done, glorifying the accomplishments of humanity and spotlighting futures that could be. This "White City" stood in sharp contrast to the reality of the burgeoning cities of the time and, while reflecting its era's prejudices, still marked great strides toward improved human understanding.

The concept of a "world's" fair originated in the nineteenth century, with the first such fair in London in 1851. The popularity of London's Crystal Palace led to other fairs, Chicago's being the fifteenth. The best known of the European fairs to that time was in Paris in 1889 and featured the Eiffel Tower. The United States had previously hosted a fair, in Philadelphia in 1876, to mark the nation's centennial.

A bill committing the U.S. government to provide financial support for the celebration was introduced in 1889 by Senator Shelby M. Cullom of Illinois. His failure to designate a site for the fair led to a battle among Chicago, New York, Washington, and St. Louis. Chicago boosted ample open parks and modern transportation facilities, and had also secured five million dollars to support the fair; in February, 1890, the city emerged triumphant (and with a new nickname—the "Windy City"—coined sneeringly by *New York Sun* editor Charles A. Dana in reference to the volume of claims made by the city's boosters). Chicago's rivals said a fair of the scope the city envisioned could never be built, but observers of the finished product considered it a triumph of concerted energy, ambition, and enthusiasm.

Chicago in 1893

Chicago at that time was a center of commerce, attracting innovation in industry and art. At the same time, it was a brawling, boisterous city, noted for corrupt government and a weakness for sin. By 1893, the city boasted 5 percent of the nation's millionaires; more than fifty separate rail lines run by thirty-two different railroads; the Union Stockyards; five hundred miles of street railroads; the world's first "skyscrapers" (a term coined by the *Chicago Tribune*), including the twenty-three-story Masonic Temple, built in 1891 and for years the tallest commercial building in the world; concert, lecture, and opera halls including the landmark Auditorium theater, office, and hotel complex; the nation's most famous settlement house, Hull-House; seven thousand saloons; almost one thousand brothels; vice districts with names like the Black Hole and Hell's Half Acre; a murder rate eight times that of Paris; and a mayor, Carter Henry Harrison, whose reelection in 1893 was taken as a sign that Chicago would be a "wide-open" city for the fair.

This "Black City" was as much an attraction for the visitors who came to Chicago as the "White City" of the fair. The planners had free rein to create the kind of world they had always dreamed of, and the contrasts between the real and the ideal were striking: Where the contemporary American metropolis was chaotic and disorganized, the exposition was planned and orderly; while the real city was private and commercial, the ideal was public and monumental; where Chicago was sooty and gray, the White City was clean and sparkling. One observer noted that "inside the exposition grounds all was glitter, gaiety and the celebration of progress; outside, sullen men shuffled the streets, slept in parks and bitterly faced a bleak future."

Funding the Exposition

Even before Congress finalized the choice of Chicago to host the fair, civic leaders had begun planning. The Chicago Exposition Company had raised the funds needed for its five million-dollar guarantee. To pick a site for the fair its directors turned to the renowned landscape architect Frederick Law Olmsted, who more than two decades earlier had been retained to plan a complex of parks south of the central city. Olmsted recommended Jackson Park, a flat, desolate, sandy stretch of land on Lake Michigan seven miles south of downtown. Olmsted and his partner, Henry Codman, planned to use the lake to complement the fair, dredging a system of navigable waterways and using the material removed to contour the site. The lagoon developed at that time, with its central island designed as a quiet retreat from the bustle of the fair's exhibit areas, remains a feature of Jackson Park.

The fair officials picked Chicago architects Daniel Burnham and John Wellborn Root as the fair's chief of construction and consulting architect, re-

A German U-boat on display outside the Museum of Science and Industry. (AP/Wide World Photos)

spectively. Working with Olmsted and Codman, they drew up preliminary plans for the fair in September, 1890. They recommended that the planners invite other architects to participate and, in January, 1991, the most noted architects in the country joined them for the first of a series of planning meetings that Augustus Saint-Gaudens, the fair's consulting sculptor, called "the greatest meeting of artists since the fifteenth century." While marred by Root's death on January 16 from pneumonia, the meetings produced the guidelines for the fair. They also produced a spirit of dedication and cooperation that resulted in an integration of architecture, sculpture, painting, and landscape never before seen.

Planning the Exposition's Buildings

Though Chicago had emerged as the leading center for modernist architecture after the Great Fire, and though Root had visualized a complex of designs and colors, the architects decided the major buildings of the exposition would be in the neoclassical style and the dominant color would be white. They grouped the "Great Buildings" in a "Court of Honor" around a basin, and while few

specific criteria were set, it was agreed they would have a uniform cornice height of sixty feet. In the end, the Great Buildings created a vision of celestial elegance, both by day and when lit at night. The lone use of color among them was the Transportation Building, designed by Dankmar Adler and Louis Sullivan in shades of red with an intricately etched, multitiered golden door.

The decision to look to the past for inspiration, and the impact of that decision on American public architecture after the fair, would prove a topic of heated discussion for decades. Edmund Mitchell, an Englishman who spent eight months at the fair, wrote that it was universally allowed that the "City of White Palaces in Chicago has never had a compeer as regards architectural magnificence"; at the other extreme, Louis Sullivan lamented the loss of a unique opportunity to showcase modernism, calling the fair an "appalling calamity" architecturally: The damage it wrought would last for a half century.

Work commenced toward an opening date of October 20, 1892, later changed to dedication ceremonies when the actual opening of the fair was postponed to May 1, 1893.

Workers were faced with a site of 533 acres in Jackson Park, plus the mile-long, six hundred-foot-wide wooded land of the Midway. Converting the main fair site—described as a treacherous morass that was liable to flooding, spotted with stunted, unshapely trees, and inadequate to bear the weight of ordinary structures—into a place of beauty required a massive effort. The work itself was an attraction for thousands of people who paid twenty-five cents each to watch the preparations.

Construction Begins

The transformation began in January, 1891. More than one million cubic yards of earth were dredged and more than sixty acres of waterways created. The areas where buildings would stand were raised several feet, and land where grass, flowers, and shrubbery would be planted was covered with loam. The lakefront was paved and a pier constructed. Seventeen miles of railroad track and an intricate network of streets were laid out. At the peak of construction, there were more than forty thousand workers.

Work went quickly, and despite delays caused by weather, materials shortages, and transportation problems, when the fair opened all but a few minor attractions on the main grounds were ready for the lines of people anxious to pay their fifty-cent admissions.

The exposition drew exhibits and buildings from forty-seven U.S. states and territories, fifty-one nations, and thirty-nine colonies. It was truly a World's Fair, unlike fairs held earlier in Europe, where rivalries led host countries to limit their invitations. The United States was still unencumbered by such geopolitical considerations.

The fourteen Great Buildings, with a total floor space of sixty-three million square feet, were surrounded by some two hundred smaller buildings. The Great Buildings cost eight million dollars, and the total cost of the fair, not including private exhibits, was twenty-eight million dollars. The builders used more than eighteen thousand tons of iron and steel and more than seventy-five million board feet of lumber.

The Fair Opens

The fair was a showcase for the use of electricity. The grounds required three times the lighting power then in use in Chicago and ten times that of the Paris fair held four years earlier. Water plants pumped sixty-four million gallons of water daily through twenty miles of water main, and the sewage system treated six million gallons per day, similar to the requirements of a city of 600,000.

Yet, despite these prodigious numbers, the fair was an illusion—a dream city with architecture and ornamentation meant to dazzle for a few months and then disappear, leaving behind only a gleaming memory. The Great Buildings and the statuary were built largely of staff, a mixture of plaster, cement, and a fiber such as hemp, that lasts at most a few years if painted regularly.

The Architecture of the Fair

Only one of the Great Buildings was permanent, the Palace of Fine Arts; as the showcase for an invaluable collection of paintings and statuary lent by the nations of the world, it needed greater resistance to the elements and the danger of fire and was therefore built chiefly of brick and cast iron. That building, designed by Charles B. Atwood of Kansas City, was considered by many the finest at the exposition. Poet Edgar Lee Masters years later wrote:

> Atwood with justice may be said to have won the architectural palm of the whole Fair. . . . Its projecting pediments, here and there supported by caryatids, reminded the beholder of the Temple of Victory on the Acropolis. The building as a whole was so much of a miracle that it did not pass with the closing of the Fair . . . and is now one of the genuine glories of Chicago.

Largest of the Great Buildings and, indeed, the largest roofed building ever constructed at that time, was the Manufactures and Liberal Arts Building, which which at 1,687 feet was longer than the Sears Tower is tall (1,454 feet) and had a width of 787 feet, greater than a Chicago city block (660 feet). Its floor space could have enclosed the U.S. Capitol, the Great Pyramid, Winchester Cathedral, Madison Square Garden, and St. Paul's Cathedral with room to spare, and it alone housed more exhibits than had been on display at the entire Philadelphia Centennial Exposition.

Among the smallest of the Great Buildings was the Woman's Building, which was considered undistinguished but which generated great interest because it was designed by a woman and highlighted the groundbreaking participation of women in the fair.

Dedication and Opening

The dedication ceremonies for the exposition had originally been planned for October 12, 1892, but were postponed so President Benjamin Harrison could attend an elaborate Columbus Day celebration in New York. While, as it turned out, Harrison was still unable to attend the Chicago festivities because of illness, the ceremony was a notable success. It started on October 20 with a civic parade that included a broad range of ethnic groups and ended on the grounds of the fair the next day with lavish ceremonies attended by between 100,000 and 500,000 people, who listened to hours of orations, invocations, hymns, and salutations.

Opening day six months later, May 1, 1893, was overcast, but the enthusiasm of onlookers was undampened. Dignitaries, including the Duke of Veragua, the sole living descendant of Columbus, and Spain's Infanta Eulalia, arrived in twenty-three carriages that passed through the Midway Plaisance to the Administration Building, where they mounted a platform constructed to hold three thousand people. After appropriate prayers and speeches, President Grover Cleveland turned a key activating a huge engine that unfurled flags and pumped water to fountains throughout the fair. Paid attendance that day was 128,965.

From opening day through the fair's closing at sunset on October 30, more than twenty-seven million people attended. At the time, based on the 1890 census, the entire population of the United States was only sixty-three million. The largest single day's attendance was more than three-quarters of a million on October 9, Chicago Day. The fair was open daily, a decision made after great debate with those who wanted it closed on Sunday. Those who fought the religious traditionalists argued that Sunday was the only day on which poorer people could see the fair and that they would benefit as much from its ennobling appeal to the imagination as from traditional Sunday observances.

Visiting the Fair

Visitors reached the fair by boat, by carriage, and by rail, either on the tracks of the Illinois Central Railroad or on the new elevated railroad powered by the innovation of an electrified third rail. When they arrived they found themselves in a clean, decorous island isolated from the troubles of labor unrest, anarchists, crime, and the Panic of 1893, which began with a stock market crash five days after the fair opened. The economic stimulation of the fair insulated Chicago from the effects of the panic, and only after its gates closed would the city feel its full impact.

Visitors rode the movable sidewalk, equipped with chairs, that ran the length of the Casino Pier. They wondered at the magnificence of the Peristyle, with its forty-eight columns representing the states and territories. They marveled at the Grand Basin, with its Columbian Fountain, the largest in the world, and the Statue of the Republic and the Court of Honor that surrounded it.

They listened to music from bands led by conductors such as John Philip Sousa; from symphony orchestras under the direction of Theodore Thomas, who established the Chicago Symphony Orchestra as the first permanent orchestra in the nation; from a 2,500-voice choir; and from native artists of participating nations. They tasted delicacies from around the world.

They examined the original contract made between Columbus and Queen Isabella and replicas of Columbus's three caravels and of the Monastery of La Rabida, where Columbus stayed before receiving an audience with the queen.

They saw a replica of a thousand-year-old viking ship, the largest cannon in the world, and the largest canary diamond in the United States. They saw the huge engines that pumped water throughout the fair grounds; Thomas Edison's new Kinetoscope, forerunner of the motion picture, and his updated phonograph; the most recent sewing machines; the latest in office equipment, including adding machines, cash registers, and typewriters; and the largest telescope in the world (later donated by Charles Yerkes to the University of Chicago's observatory in Williams Bay, Wisconsin). They saw too such oddities as models of the Liberty Bell made of oranges, lemons, and grapefruit, and a map of the United States done in pickles. They witnessed the first long-distance telephone call from the Midwest to the Atlantic seaboard; learned how cheese, glass, leather, and silk were made; and admired outstanding examples of livestock and produce. In all, there were more than sixty-five thousand exhibits, ranging from the sublime to the bizarre and highlighting the most up-to-date developments of the age.

Sideshows and Exhibits

The Midway Plaisance, named from the French word for pleasure, was the playground of the fair and the first ever such "sideshow," and the name "midway" has been used ever since to describe the central avenue at a carnival or amusement park. Here were housed restaurants, entertainments, rides, and exhibits from Ireland, Lapland, Germany, Austria, Hungary, Italy, Turkey, Algeria, Egypt, Hawaii, the South Seas, China, and Central Africa. The Midway was the home of Little Egypt and her controversial *danse du ventre*, or belly dance, and of champion boxer Gentleman Jim Corbett.

In the center of the Midway stood the crowning glory of the fair and the exposition's answer to Paris's Eiffel Tower. When planning this centerpiece, Burnham sought more than just size. "Something novel, original, daring and unique must be designed and built if American engineers are to retain their prestige and standing," he said. The solution was George Ferris's revolving wheel, which carried forty passengers in each of thirty-six cars to a height of 264 feet. During that summer, 1,750,000 people rode the Ferris Wheel.

The exposition was more than just exhibits. Held in conjunction with the fair, in the not-quite-finished home of the Art Institute of Chicago at the center of the city, was the World Congress Auxiliary. With the motto Not Matter, but Mind, the auxiliary convened in mid-May and continued until October 28 a series of meetings that examined every issue of the day. Some 700,000 people heard nearly 4,000 speakers deliver more than 6,000 presentations in programs organized by the 225 divisions of its principal departments: Women's Progress, the Public Press, Medicine and Surgery, Temperance, Moral and Social Reform, Commerce and Finance, Music, Literature, Education, Engineering, Art, Government, Science and Philosophy, Social and Economic Science, Labor, Religion, Sunday Rest, Public Health, and Agriculture.

These programs were surprisingly inclusive for the time. While African American and Native American involvement was minimal, women's issues received broad play and the World's Parlia-

ment of Religions brought together representatives of almost all the world's religions (the Anglicans were conspicuous by their absence, but an array of smaller sects were conspicuous by their presence). While the congresses did not necessarily reach conclusions, they succeeded in airing a wide range of views and defining the direction that many of these debates would take in ensuing years.

Closing of the Fair

As the fair approached its conclusion, attendance rose and plans proceeded for closing ceremonies as elaborate and festive as its dedication. Two days before they were to take place, however, a disgruntled office seeker shot Mayor Harrison at his home. The assassination turned the celebration funereal.

Less than three months after the fair closed, arsonists set fire to the Peristyle and other buildings on the lakefront, and in July, flames swept through the Court of Honor. Most of the buildings were torn down and salvaged for scrap. In 1896, *Scientific American* reported that among those still standing were was "the once beautiful German Building in dilapidation . . . [and] the sham convent of La Rabida [which became a cardiac hospital for children]. The Goddess of Liberty still occupies her lofty pedestal, with her cap gone and several of her fingers missing." Salvaged steel was returned to the furnaces; ornamentation was removed and sold as souvenirs; half a million square feet of glass panes went into greenhouses and cornices; and statues went to museums and universities.

The Museum of Science and Industry

Four of the buildings still exist intact, but only one remains in Jackson Park. The Maine Building was moved to a resort in Poland Springs, Maine; the Dutch House is in Brookline, Massachusetts; and the Norway Building is in Blue Mounds, Wisconsin. The fourth building, the Palace of Fine Arts, housed the Field Columbian Museum until that institution moved north to Grant Park in 1920 and became the Field Museum of Natural History. With the support of Julius Rosenwald, chairman of Sears, Roebuck and Company, the building was reconstructed between 1929 and 1940 to house the Museum of Science and Industry. (It was originally to be called the Rosenwald Industrial Museum, but

Rosenwald insisted that the name be changed so as to dedicate the museum to the public, and not to himself.) Limestone replaced staff; a new roof was built; a basement was dug; and two additional floors, 140 permanent Ionic columns, twenty-four caryatids, twelve figures above the door to the central pavilion, and a 120-foot-high central dome were added. In 1933, the museum's north and south courts and central dome were opened to the public.

Jackson Park was refashioned based on Olmstead's landscape design. The lagoons became small-craft harbors; the wooded island was developed for strolling and picnicking; and the Midway Plaisance was transformed into a tree-lined boulevard.

Legacy of the Fair

The Columbian Exposition had affirmed America's new position at the forefront of industry; it had brought together nations, individuals, and ideas in a spirit of cooperation; and, above all, its ideas and beauty inspired. It spurred the growth of the City Beautiful movement, of which Burnham became a driving force, frequently working with Olmstead and several of the architects of the Great Buildings. He completed plans for Washington, D.C., Cleveland, San Francisco, Manila and Baguio in the Philippines, and Chicago. The boulevards and landscaping in many American cities can be traced to his influence.

Scientific advances and industrial applications such as electric transit systems and the use of electric lighting for decoration were also a legacy of the fair.

Women's involvement in the fair, spearheaded by Bertha Honore Palmer as president of the Fair's Board of Lady Managers, greatly advanced the cause of suffrage and other issues. The extensive participation of foreign nations helped promote international cooperation and understanding, and numerous international business deals were reportedly struck by exhibitors impressed with each other's wares.

The exposition became a major part of thirteen novels and probably figured in the design of L. Frank Baum's Emerald City of Oz. Antonín Dvořák's New World Symphony was composed to be performed at the fair, but financial problems prevented its debut there. Katherine Lee Bates was moved by the exposition to write "America the Beautiful."

The *Chicago Tribune*, in its farewell to the fair, summed it up as

a little ideal world, a realization of Utopia, in which every night was beautiful and every day a festival, in which for the time all thoughts of the great world of toil, of injustice, of cruelty, and of oppression outside its gates disappeared, and in which this splendid fantasy of the artist and architect seemed to foreshadow some far away time when all the earth should be as pure, as beautiful and as joyous as the White City itself.

—*Richard Greb*

For Further Information:

Bertuca, David J. *The World's Columbian Exposition: A Centennial Bibliographic Guide*. Westport, Conn.: Greenwood Press, 1996.

Bolotin, Norman, and Christine Laing. *The World's Columbian Exposition*. Washington, D.C.: Preservation Press, 1992. Replete with pictures and description of the fair as it might have looked to a visitor.

Burg, David F. *Chicago's White City of 1893*. Lexington: University Press of Kentucky, 1976. Goes into great detail on the art and ideas of the fair, and quotes substantial portions of the speeches delivered at the ceremonies and the Congress Auxiliary

Masters, Edgar Lee. *The Tale of Chicago*. New York: G. P. Putnam's Sons, 1933. References to the fair in this book are interesting, especially for Masters's prose.

Muccigrosso, Robert. *Celebrating the New World*. Chicago: Ivan R. Dee, 1993. Looks at the fair in the context of the world of the 1890's.

New Salem

Date: Existed between 1829 and 1839
Relevant issues: Political history, western expansion
Significance: This Illinois State Historic Site is a re-creation of the original town that existed from 1829 to 1839. It primarily consists of reconstructed log homes as determined by survey

plans and interviews with town residents. The site had completely reverted to a prairie by the time that reconstruction started.

Location: In central Illinois, twenty miles northwest of the state capital, Springfield; about two hundred miles southwest of Chicago

Site Office:
New Salem State Historic Site
R.R. 1, Box 244A
Petersburg, IL 62675
ph.: (217) 632-4000
Web site: www.lincolnsnewsalem.com

New Salem is a reconstructed prairie town that owes its present existence to the fact that Abraham Lincoln lived there from 1831 to 1837, on his way to becoming the sixteenth U.S. president. The village existed for only a decade or so and in its prime was home to about twenty-five families. It lies on a bluff one hundred feet above the Sangamon River.

Origins of New Salem
The town originated in 1828 when the property was bought by John M. Camron. He and his uncle, James Rutledge, petitioned the General Assembly of Illinois in 1829 for permission to dam the Sangamon River in order to establish a saw and grist mill. The two were in business together and had tried unsuccessfully to dam the waters of Concord Creek a few miles away. Because that site did not work, they relocated to a new point on the Sangamon River and were successful at establishing the mill. It is this site that became New Salem.

The site seemed an appropriate place for a town. It lay on a bluff above a river and near a road connecting Springfield with Havana. It also lay in the center of a very promising agricultural area. Even the name of the river—Sangamon, an Indian word meaning the land of plenty to eat—reflected this promise.

On October 23, 1829, a surveyor, Reuben Harrison, laid out the town. Land sold for about ten dollars a lot, and by January, 1830, the first store was established by Samuel Hill and John McNeil. Later that same year Henry Onstot built his cooper shop, and William Clary started a ferry to make the mill and the town accessible from the eastern side of the river.

Potential for Growth
The town was well equipped for its size and had potential for growth. Among the people who settled in New Salem in 1831 were a doctor and a cobbler. The town also added a hotel/tavern and two stores, at one of which Abraham Lincoln worked as a clerk. In 1832 the new residents included another doctor, a hatter, a tanner, a wheelwright/woodworker, and a blacksmith. The town also had a carding mill and a school that also served as a church building.

In the early 1830's the basic needs of most of the settlers could be met in New Salem. The mill was a beacon to farmers who would come from miles away to have their grain ground and trade their goods. The grinding process took several hours, and to pass the time farmers and their families would picnic in the area of the mill and buy goods in the store while they waited for their grain. The town residents were able to buy goods they needed at the stores, employ the services of the skilled blacksmith and cobbler, and receive treatment, if needed, from the town doctors. The town also was a stagecoach stop and had a post office. New Salem seemed to be well on its way to becoming a thriving river town.

It was to this prosperous town that Abraham Lincoln came via the Sangamon River. To earn some money, he and a few other men had taken jobs to pole a flatboat loaded with farm goods from Springfield up the Sangamon River, then down the Illinois and Mississippi Rivers to New Orleans. At New Salem the heavily laden craft was caught on the mill dam and in danger of sinking. It was Lincoln who solved the problem by unloading the boat, draining out the water that had collected in it, and guiding it across the dam. The owner of the flatboat, Denton Offutt, was very impressed with the young Abraham Lincoln. He asked Lincoln to clerk in the new store he had decided to establish in New Salem later that year.

Abraham Lincoln in New Salem
In 1831, when Lincoln moved to New Salem, he had been in Illinois for only a little more than a year. Lincoln, his father, stepmother, and siblings had moved to Illinois from Indiana in 1830, enticed by the reports of good land. The Lincolns set up a new homestead near the banks of the Sangamon River a few miles from Decatur, Illinois.

The re-created nineteenth century village of New Salem. (Lincoln's New Salem National Historic Site)

In 1832 Lincoln also became a shopkeeper. Because he needed to earn a living, he bought a portion of a store from Rowan Herndon. William Berry owned the other half. In 1833 Lincoln and Berry bought out another store owner in New Salem and moved their store into a building across the street from the original one. This is what is today known as the second Berry-Lincoln store.

Lincoln and his partner had purchased the store and its goods on credit, and Lincoln was plagued with the debt from this business venture for years after the store failed and Berry died. Lincoln remained in New Salem and was named postmaster in 1833, a position he held until the post office was moved to Petersburg in 1836. As postmaster it is estimated that Lincoln earned between twenty-five and thirty dollars a year. This amount was based upon the gross receipts of the office.

Lincoln lived with his family for approximately a year to help establish the new homestead and then decided to set out on his own. He was twenty-two.

During the six years he lived in New Salem, Lincoln had a variety of occupations, often holding more than one job at a time. Offutt's store did not last very long, but Lincoln decided to stay in New Salem because the town held such promise. He also enjoyed the people there. After his rural upbringing, this was Lincoln's first contact with organized community life. In New Salem Lincoln voted in an election for the first time; he made lifelong friends there and learned how to deal with people of many different backgrounds.

A few months after arriving in New Salem, Lincoln announced his candidacy as a member of the Whig Party for the state legislature, but he was not elected. Later that same year, 1832, Lincoln volunteered to fight in the Black Hawk War and was chosen captain of his company. (The war was fought between Indians, under the direction of Chief Black Hawk, and settlers, over the issue of land.) Lincoln served for eighty days and returned to New Salem.

Lincoln the Surveyor

Another job Lincoln held while in New Salem was that of surveyor, which he started in January, 1834. When there was work, surveyors earned nearly three dollars a day. Because the land in Illinois was being settled so rapidly, surveyors were in demand. Lincoln secured a position as deputy surveyor to John Calhoun, the county surveyor, and borrowed books from Calhoun in order to learn the trade. Lincoln bought a horse on credit, and equipped with a few surveying tools, started his assignments in the northern part of what is now Menard County and the southern part of Mason County.

In addition to holding down his various jobs, Lincoln studied law, history, and literature, largely through extensive, independent reading, and was active in the New Salem Debating Society. He also is said to have been engaged to the local tavern owner's daughter, Ann Rutledge, who died before they could marry; however, many Lincoln scholars doubt that the two were romantically involved.

Lincoln ran for state representative again in 1834. This time he was elected, and he won a second term in 1836. Returning to New Salem when the legislature was not in session, he continued his law studies, and he was admitted to the bar on March 1, 1837. In April of that year he moved to Springfield, which had recently replaced Vandalia as the state capital, to practice law.

Failed Aspirations as a River Town

New Salem had been a rapidly developing town during Lincoln's residency. There was much excitement in the area when in the spring of 1832 the *Talisman*, a ninety-five-foot-long steamboat, was able to navigate the Sangamon River passing New Salem on its way to Springfield. Groups of local settlers followed the steamboat along the river banks. Most had never before seen such a large boat. Many people thought New Salem would become a thriving river town, just as St. Louis.

This, however, was not to be. The *Talisman* was able to navigate the Sangamon River successfully only with great difficulty. The Sangamon River did not run deep enough for large boats, and it was filled with sandbars and snags. The *Talisman*, in fact, was able to sail past New Salem on its way back to the Illinois River only after part of the mill dam was temporarily dismantled. No other large boats were able to navigate the Sangamon River to Springfield until 1961, and even then it was difficult.

Within a few years New Salem began its decline. In May, 1836, the post office was moved from New Salem to Petersburg, two miles away. Many of the residents sold their property and moved. The final blow came in February, 1839, when a new county, Menard, was created and Petersburg was named the county seat. Eventually the Bale family, who had owned and operated the saw and grist mill since 1832, owned the entire tract of land called New Salem.

New Salem in the Twentieth Century

In 1906 the sixty-acre tract of land was purchased by newspaper publisher William Randolph Hearst and given in trust to the Old Salem Chautauqua Association, a group which for years maintained an interest in the site. The Old Salem Lincoln League was formed in 1917 to continue to do research and expand public interest in New Salem. In 1919 the Chautauqua Association gave the site to the state of Illinois. Construction of several cabins began at the site, but they were later removed because they were not authentic reproductions of the town of New Salem.

The Illinois General Assembly appropriated fifty thousand dollars in 1931 for improvements at the site. The English Brothers, general contractors from Champaign, Illinois, started the reconstruction of twelve cabins on original foundations in late 1932. The Civilian Conservation Corps reconstructed several other buildings and added many of the public and service facilities for the site.

At the time of reconstruction there was scarcely any evidence of the buildings that stood on the spot almost a century earlier. Excavations revealed foundation outlines of buildings. Survey records and written accounts by original residents of the town aided in the reconstruction of many of the main structures of the town. When the pioneers moved from the town decades earlier, many of them dismantled their homes and took the homes along. Only one original building, the Henry Onstot Cooper Shop, which had been moved to Petersburg, two miles up the Sangamon River, still existed. It was returned to its original site in New Salem. Many of the furnishings in the buildings date from the period, and some were once the property of the original New Salem residents.

A Living Museum

New Salem today is a living museum serving as a memorial to the sixteenth U.S. president. It has been recreated in the way Lincoln saw it. Gardens have been replanted in the style in which many residents probably kept them in the 1830's. Outside the doctors' residences, for example, herb gardens have been planted. The doctors used herbs to treat ailments. Trees and other shrubs have been added to the site to complete its authenticity.

A replica of the *Talisman* operates, seasonally taking tourists for river rides. A visitors' center offers a laser-disc presentation of the history of New Salem. In the evenings of summer months, the "Great American People Show," a theatrical presentation depicting the life of Abraham Lincoln, is performed.

—Susen Taras

For Further Information:

Barton, William E. "Abraham Lincoln and New Salem." *The Journal of the Illinois State Historical Society* 19, no. 3-4 (1927). The text of an address delivered before the Mississippi Valley Historical Association and the Illinois State Historical Society on their journey to New Salem, May 8, 1926.

Chandler, Josephine Craven. "New Salem: Early Chapter in Lincoln's Life." *The Journal of the Illinois State Historical Society* 12, no. 4 (1930). A lengthy, detailed essay on Lincoln's life in New Salem.

Davis, James Edward. *Frontier Illinois*. Bloomington: Indiana University Press, 1998. A history of the trans-Appalachain frontier and Illinois history from 1778 to 1865.

Thomas, Benjamin P. *Lincoln's New Salem*. Springfield, Ill.: Abraham Lincoln Association, 1934. A comprehensive account of New Salem and its residents. It may be difficult to locate this book, but the search is well worth it.

Wilson, D. Ray. *Illinois Historical Tour Guide*. Carpentersville, Ill.: Crossroads Communications, 1991. Includes a thoughtful chapter on Springfield and the surrounding area, including New Salem.

Pullman

Date: Constructed between 1880 and 1888

Relevant issues: Business and industry, social reform

Significance: A National Historic Landmark, this residential neighborhood of Chicago, one-half mile square, was originally a company town constructed by and for the Pullman Palace Car Company. The architect was Solon Spenser Beman, and the landscape designer was Nathan F. Barrett. (Some structures that were originally part of the company town may be found outside the landmark district's borders—north of 111th Street in North Pullman and west of Cottage Grove Avenue in Roseland.)

Location: Chicago, fifteen miles south/southeast of the Chicago Loop; 111th Street (northern boundary) to 115th Street (southern boundary) and Cottage Grove Avenue (western boundary) to Ellis Avenue (eastern boundary)

Site Office:

Historic Pullman Foundation
11111 South Forrestville Avenue
Chicago, IL 60628
ph.: (773) 785-3828
Web site: www.pullmanil.org

A working-class neighborhood on the far southeast side of Chicago, Pullman began its existence in the 1880's as a company town, a home to the employees of the Pullman Palace Car Company, manufacturer of railway cars. There were two predominant opinions about the town: It was either a worthy social experiment or the ultimate in corporate paternalism. In the aftermath of a bitter strike by Pullman Company employees in 1894, however, observers generally agreed the experiment had been a failure.

Modern Preservation Efforts

The Pullman area has been well preserved; its appearance in the 1990's is remarkably similar to its appearance a century earlier. One can see the multifamily buildings that were constructed for occupancy by the rank-and-file Pullman Company employees and the grander, single-family dwellings that were home to the company's executives. Among the highlights are row houses on Champlain Street, including an attractive group with bay entries in the 11400 block. Numerous other original structures, including the Pullman Company administration buildings, the Green Stone Church, the Hotel Florence, and the Pullman Stables, also have been preserved.

George Pullman, founder of the Pullman Palace Car Company, conceived the company town when he decided to expand and consolidate the company's manufacturing and repair facilities in 1880. He had been in the railway car business since the 1850's, making the first significant improvements in railroad sleeping cars since these cars were introduced in the United States in 1836. His "Pioneer" sleeping car gained publicity when it was chosen to be part of the train that carried slain U.S. president Abraham Lincoln's body from Chicago to Springfield in 1865. The Pullman Palace Car Company was incorporated in 1867, and its sleeping, dining, and hotel cars became the standard of the day for luxurious travel. The company did not sell its cars to railroads, but rather leased them and managed all the cars' operations, including supplying the cooks, porters, and waiters who worked on them.

Origins of the Community

By 1879, the company's factory in Detroit and its three repair shops in other cities were insufficient to serve its thriving business. In 1880, George Pullman chose a four thousand-acre site a few miles south of Chicago, on the shore of Lake Calumet, as the location for his new manufacturing and repair facilities. He also decided the site would include homes, shopping areas, and recreational opportunities for workers. Many social reformers of the era decried the squalid conditions in which factory workers lived. The planned community of Pullman was one of the options put forth as a solution to this problem, but George Pullman's moves were driven by business considerations, not social reform. He believed that workers who lived in relative comfort and cleanliness were likely to be more productive and loyal, and less susceptible to alcoholism, absenteeism, and labor unrest, than those who lived in slum conditions. He also intended to charge rents high enough to make the town profitable.

The clock tower of the Pullman Palace Car Factory, which was partially destroyed by fire in 1998 and placed on the most endangered historic site list. (AP/Wide World Photos)

Architect Solon Spenser Beman and landscape designer Nathan F. Barrett were commissioned to plan the factory and the surrounding community. At this time, it was unusual for architects to work on industrial buildings, and it also was unusual to put an architect and landscape designer to work on an entire town. Ground was broken for the railway car factory in April, 1880, and work on the rest of the town proceeded quickly. The Pullman Company took numerous steps to minimize costs, hiring its own construction workers rather than using an outside labor force, and establishing its own carpentry shops and brickyards to produce materials. By January 1, 1881, the town was ready for its first residents: Lee Benson, a foreman from the Detroit factory, with his wife, child, and sister. The car works began operation in April of that year, and by the following month there were 350 residents of Pullman.

A Planned Community

From the beginning, the town won praise for its beauty and cleanliness. The housing stock ranged from tenement buildings, housing anywhere from 12 to 48 families, to detached homes that were reserved for Pullman Company executives. With the exception of sixty frame houses that were occupied by construction workers, all the residential buildings were brick with stone trimmings and slate roof. There were ample parks and playgrounds, while saloons and brothels were prohibited. The town's one and only bar was in the Queen Anne-style Hotel Florence. Other major public buildings included the Green Stone Church, the Pullman School, and the Arcade—the latter housing most of the town's retailers, its theater, library, post office, bank, and municipal and professional offices. In one respect, the town disappointed George Pullman; he had hoped to attract a wide range of industries, but most of the manufacturing companies that came to the town either were controlled by him or were suppliers to his company. For the most part, though, the town—at a cost of eight million dollars—was a source of great pride to the industrialist.

The town and the factories were administered by different agencies, but both were responsible to the Pullman Company. Certain features of the town did not sit well with workers. Rents were high; even after adjusting for the greater attractiveness and sanitation of the dwellings in Pullman, rental costs averaged 20 to 25 percent more than those in Chicago or other nearby communities. Also, workers were not allowed to buy homes in Pullman. George Pullman was adamantly opposed to subdividing the property, believing the special character and integrity of the model town would be compromised if this happened. When economic conditions were favorable, the company did not discourage employees from buying homes in surrounding communities. After the Panic of 1893 and subsequent depression, there was substantial discrimination against workers who did not rent homes in Pullman. Labor organization was prohibited in the town, and workers alleged that the company employed "spotters" to check for prounion and otherwise liberal tendencies among the citizenry. High utility rates and library fees were other sources of discontent among Pullman residents.

Political Status of the "Town"

Although referred to as a town, Pullman was not an independent municipality; politically, it was part of the village of Hyde Park, just south of Chicago. George Pullman and the Pullman Company, how-ever, were sufficiently powerful to keep the village government from interfering significantly in the administration of the town. While George Pullman had some disagreements with village trustees, he preferred their governance to rule by Chicago. When Hyde Park residents were to vote in 1887 on annexation to Chicago, George Pullman was able to have the company town's area excluded from consideration. A state court nullified the 1887 annexation vote, however, and set another referendum for 1889; this time the town of Pullman was included. George Pullman campaigned vigorously against annexation, and most company town residents voted against it, but the proannexation forces carried the day, with 62 percent of the vote.

With or without annexation, it probably would have been impossible to keep the town of Pullman isolated from the rest of Chicago—or the problems of the day. The once-rural region south of Chicago industrialized and grew rapidly during the 1880's and 1890's, and neighboring communities such as Kensington and Roseland often hosted prolabor speakers who would have been banned in Pullman. The factors that precipitated the Pullman Strike, however, did not come together until the Panic of 1893.

Town and Company

During 1893, the population of Pullman, and the Pullman Company's employment in the town, had peaked at 12,600 and 5,500 respectively. The company's total employment was much greater—14,500, including all the personnel who worked in the Pullman cars on various rail lines. In 1893, significant economic problems began to spread throughout the United States: 642 banks failed, 22,500 miles of railway went into receivership, and businesses laid off thousands of workers. The depression's effects on the Pullman Company were postponed a bit because the number of travelers visiting the Columbian Exposition in the spring of 1893 in Chicago created a huge demand for rail cars. This was only a temporary increase in business, however, and by the summer of that year the company was reducing its workforce and slashing wages for the employees who remained. Those who lived in the model town particularly resented the fact that their rents stayed the same while their wages were reduced and that there were decreasing housing options for them. Several of those who lived outside Pullman claimed they were threatened with firings if they did not move into the town. At the same time, company executives took no pay cuts.

The company's staunch antiunion posture had prevented effective labor organization up until this time. Some employees had joined the Knights of Labor in 1886 and had gone on strike briefly, demanding shorter working hours and higher wages, but the company had refused to negotiate and managed to break the union. The extent of the workers' grievances in 1893-1894 was such that the union movement finally managed to take hold. They were attracted to a relatively new and rapidly expanding organization, the American Railway Union, founded by Eugene Victor Debs. Since membership was open to employees of any company involved in the operation of railroads, although the Pullman Company owned and managed only a few miles of railway, its workers were eligible. With labor organizing forbidden in Pullman, the union signed up members in such neighboring areas as Grand Crossing and Kensington in the spring of 1894.

Union Strike

Union leaders cautioned Pullman Company employees against a strike, but the workers were not inclined to take this advice. In May, 1894, workers presented the company with demands for either a restoration of pay cuts or reduction in rents. George Pullman refused to consider either, and on the night of May 10 the union's grievance committee authorized a strike but did not set a date for it. The next morning, Pullman Company employees went to work, but there arose a rumor that the company would shut down operation at noon. The grievance committee called all workers out of the shops to give the action the status of a strike instead of a lockout.

The workers and the union were ill prepared for a strike; the union had no treasury to pay strike benefits to the workers, who had few resources of their own. Other unions and sympathetic groups provided the necessities of life for strikers and their families. The Pullman Strike dominated discussion at the American Railway Union's first convention in June, 1894. Convention delegates called for all union members to refuse to handle Pullman cars

or equipment—a move designed to deprive the company of a major source of revenue and lead it to a greater willingness to negotiate. For its part, however, Pullman Company was prepared to wait out the strike and at some point replace strikers with nonunion labor.

The Strike Becomes a National Issue

Still, the Pullman boycott made the local strike into a national issue, and set up a confrontation between the American Railway Union and the General Managers' Association, representing railroads. The boycott had some success; by the end of June, fifty thousand workers on all railway lines had walked out. Transportation in and around Chicago was particularly disrupted, and the delivery of mail also was a problem, setting the stage for federal government intervention. The union had offered crews for trains carrying mail, as long as those trains had no Pullman cars, but the railroads generally declined such an arrangement. Acting at the direction of Richard Olney, attorney general of the United States, a group of U.S. attorneys obtained an injunction from a Chicago circuit court prohibiting any action that could interfere with the movement of mail—including a prohibition of communications among union officers.

Union leaders chose to ignore the injunction. One of the next major occurrences in the boycott, however, apparently did not happen at the direction of union leadership, but was more or less spontaneous; a huge mob overran the Rock Island Railroad yards in Blue Island, southwest of Chicago, early in July. Some in the crowd were strikers, some sympathizers, some merely curious. Trains were no longer able to run over the lines, and the U.S. military was called in to disperse the crowd. Disturbances, including a fire at the Columbian Exposition grounds and destruction of railroad property, continued sporadically for several days, but the situation eventually calmed down and most of the troops left on July 19.

Failure of the Strike

Meanwhile, the strike and the boycott were losing steam, with little support forthcoming from other labor organizations. The strikers' resolve also was weakened by the arrests of Debs and other union leaders, ostensibly for violating the Olney injunction. In mid-July, Pullman Company officials posted a notice inviting strikers to reapply for work, although strike leaders and certain others would be ineligible for employment.

Bitterness remained in the Pullman area after the strike ended, although community leaders tried to put a brave face on the model town. Shortly after the strike ended, the chain of events that would dissolve the company town began; Illinois attorney general Maurice T. Maloney brought charges questioning the company's right to own and manage the town. An Illinois circuit court sided with the company, but in 1898 the Illinois Supreme Court reversed the lower court's finding. George Pullman had died the previous year. His successors were willing to abide by the court's decision, and dismantling of the model town began. Many houses were sold to Pullman Company employees. In retrospect, most observers pronounced the Pullman company town experiment a failure; one of the negative factors most frequently cited was the prohibition of home ownership.

During the twentieth century, the housing stock in Pullman deteriorated; built all at once, it aged all at once. In the 1960's, the Roseland Chamber of Commerce proposed destroying and rebuilding the entire area, a move that Pullman residents fought successfully. The area was declared a state historic landmark in 1969, a national one in 1971, and a city landmark in 1972. Residents began working together to preserve and renovate Pullman, establishing the Historic Pullman Foundation in 1973. In the 1990's the state of Illinois bought the Hotel Florence and company administration buildings for a proposed Pullman State Historic Site.

—*Trudy Ring*

For Further Information:
Buder, Stanley. *Pullman: An Experiment in Industrial Order and Community Planning, 1880-1930.* New York: Oxford University Press, 1979. Somewhat sympathetic to George Pullman. Combined with Lindsey's book below, provides a broad view of the company town and the labor problems.

Doty, Mrs. Duane. *The Town of Pullman: Its Growth with Brief Accounts of Its Industries.* Pullman, Ill.: T. P. Struhsacker, 1893. Reprint. Chicago: Pullman Civic Organization, 1974. A boosterish text written by the wife of a town official. Primarily a historical curiosity.

Lindsey, Almont. *The Pullman Strike: The Story of a Unique Experiment and of a Great Labor Upheaval.* Chicago: University of Chicago Press, 1942. Reprint. Chicago: Phoenix Books, 1964. An excellent and comprehensive study of the strike and of the conditions in Pullman and the nation leading up to it; the book is favorable to labor, but gives space to the company's stance.

Schneirov, Richard, Shelton Stromquist, and Nick Salvatore, eds. *The Pullman Strike and the Crisis of the 1890's: Essays on Labor and Politics.* Urbana: University of Illinois Press, 1999. A collection of academic essays detailing and analyzing the history and politics of the Pullman Strike.

Other Historic Sites

Abbott House

Location: Chicago, Cook County

Relevant issues: African American history, literary history

Statement of significance: From 1926 until his death, this house was the residence of Robert Sengstacke Abbott (1870-1940), the most successful black publisher of his era. Through his newspaper, the *Chicago Defender* (established 1905), Abbott encouraged southern blacks to leave the virulently racist South and seek a haven in the northern cities, particularly Chicago.

Bishop Hill Colony

Location: Bishop Hill, Henry County

Relevant issues: Social reform

Statement of significance: Founded in 1846 by religious dissidents who emigrated from Sweden to establish a new way of life on the Illinois prairie, the colony was run as a commune until its dissolution in 1861. Its archives, artifacts, and structures today are important documents for the study of immigration, ethnic heritage, and nineteenth century communitarian societies.

Charnley House

Location: Chicago, Cook County

Relevant issues: Art and architecture

Statement of significance: The Charnley House is important both nationally and internationally as one of the pivotal structures in the development of modernism in architecture. Its limestone and Roman brick walls are arranged with a strong sense of symmetry, but without any overt references to historical styles. Built in 1891-1892, it was one of the few major residential commissions of Louis Sullivan and was a benchmark in the architectural development of Frank Lloyd Wright, who was then a draftsman and designer in the office of Adler & Sullivan. The house remains close to its original condition, both inside and out. In 1995, in an effort to safeguard its future, Seymour H. Persky purchased it and donated it to the Society of Architectural Historians (SAH). Now serving as the national headquarters of the SAH, this seminal monument in architectural history is open to the public.

Crow Island School

Location: Winnetka, Cook County

Relevant issues: Education

Statement of significance: Constructed in 1940, Crow Island School was the model for the revolutionary Winnetka Plan, features of which are now familiar to most adult Americans. Built to embody the educational philosophy of Charleton Washburne, Winnetka's city school superintendent (1919-1943), the design incorporated progressive concepts: grade level zoning, child-scale furniture, self-contained classrooms, flexible spaces, classroom access to the outside—in short, the child-centered school. This approach gained broad public acceptance in large measure due to the reputations of its architects, Eliel and Eero Saarinen, and the architectural firm of Perkins, Wheeler, and Will, which spread the design nationwide through its many commissions.

Davis House

Location: Bloomington, McLean County

Relevant issues: Legal history

Statement of significance: From 1872 until his death, this two-story Italian Villa-style mansion was the residence of David Davis (1815-1886), associate justice (1862-1877) of the United States Supreme Court. Davis is best known for writing the majority opinion in *Ex parte Milligan*, which restricts the right of military courts to try civilians. In a case involving generally President Abraham Lincoln's controversial 1862 authorization of military arrest and trial, with suspension of *habeas corpus,* for draft resistance and other disloyal acts, and particularly a man sentenced to hang in Indiana, Davis wrote, "The Constitution of the United States is a law for rulers and people, equally in war and in peace."

Dawes House

Location: Evanston, Cook County

Relevant issues: Political history

Statement of significance: From 1909 until his death, this two-and-a-half-story brick mansion was the residence of Charles Gates Dawes (1865-1951), first Director of the Budget (1921) and vice president of the United States (1925-1929). In 1924, Dawes chaired an international committee that produced the Dawes Plan, which, though it did not solve the World War I reparations problem, did arrange a rational schedule of payments to be made by Germany. For his efforts, he received the Nobel Peace Prize (1925).

Deere Home and Shop

Location: Grand Detour, Ogle County

Relevant issues: Business and industry

Statement of significance: From 1836 to 1847, this was the home and shop of John Deere (1804-1886), a skilled blacksmith who invented and manufactured a steel plow that could scour the tough prairie soil cleanly, unlike other plows that became clogged with the dark, rich soil. Deere's farm implement thus made possible intensive cultivation of vast acres in Ohio, Indiana, and Illinois, bringing benefit to the entire United States.

Depriest House

Location: Chicago, Cook County

Relevant issues: African American history, political history

Statement of significance: From 1929 until his death, this was the residence of Oscar Stanton Depriest (1871-1951), the first African American to be elected to the House of Representatives from a northern state (1928). A Republican, Depriest lost his seat in 1934 to the first black Democrat to be elected to the U.S. Congress.

Du Sable Homesite

Location: Chicago, Cook County

Relevant issues: African American history, business and industry

Statement of significance: This is the site of the home of Jean Baptiste Pointe Du Sable (1745-1818), the black pioneer, fur trader, and independent entrepreneur whose establishment of a trading post at this location marked the beginning of the city of Chicago.

Grant Home

Location: Galena, Jo Daviess County

Relevant issues: Military history, political history

Statement of significance: In 1865, the citizens of Galena presented this two-story brick house to General Ulysses S. Grant (1822-1885), the victorious Union commander. Grant lived here until he became secretary of war in 1867 and again, briefly, following the end of his presidency and trip around the world.

Grosse Point Lighthouse

Location: 2601 Sheridan Road, Evanston, Cook County

Relevant issues: Naval history

Statement of significance: A coastal brick tower built on the Great Lakes, Grosse Point Light Station was the lead navigational marker in the waters of Lake Michigan just north of Chicago Harbor. The light safely guided lakeborne traffic through one of America's most commercially important and highly traveled corridors, a shipping route which connected the East Coast, Great Lakes, and Gulf Coast shipping interests. In recognition of the importance of this lighthouse to maritime navigation, Grosse Point Lighthouse was fitted with the first second-order Fresnel lens on the Great Lakes. Although the lighthouse was decommissioned by the Coast Guard in 1941, the second-order Fresnel lens remains in place in the lantern and all original buildings survive unaltered.

Illinois and Michigan Canal Locks and Towpath

Location: Northeastern Illinois

Relevant issues: Business and industry, naval history

Statement of significance: Begun in 1836 and completed in 1848, this canal linked Chicago to the Mississippi River, thus completing a continuous waterway to New York City and making Chicago a leading grain market and meat-packing center. Commercial use of the canal ended in 1933. It is now in Channahon State Park and is also recognized through the establishment of the Illinois and Michigan Canal National Heritage Corridor.

Kennicott Grove

Location: Glenview, Cook County

Relevant issues: Science and technology

Statement of significance: This was the home of Robert Kennicott (1835-1866), nineteenth century naturalist, explorer, and founder of the Chicago Academy of Sciences, whose career illustrates the development of scientific research in the Midwest.

Lincoln Home

Location: Springfield, Sangamon County

Relevant issues: Political history

Web site: www.nps.gov/liho/

Statement of significance: This was the residence of Abraham Lincoln (1809-1865), who lived here for most of the period from 1844 until 1861, an important era in his advancement from small-town lawyer to president of the United States.

Lincoln Tomb

Location: Springfield, Sangamon County

Relevant issues: Political history

Statement of significance: Dedicated in 1874, this is the final resting place of Lincoln, sixteenth president of the United States, his wife, and three of their four sons.

Lindsay House

Location: Springfield, Sangamon County

Relevant issues: Literary history

Statement of significance: For most of his life, this was the home of Vachel Lindsay (1879-1931), one of the major figures in the American poetic renaissance. Using evangelical rhythms to express his dreamlike conceptions, Lindsay created a style which was at once popular and unique. The house contains many of his drawings, writings, and possessions.

Lovejoy House

Location: East Peru Street, Princeton, Bureau County

Relevant issues: African American history, political history, social reform

Statement of significance: Owen Lovejoy (1811-1864), an influential abolitionist politician, lived here from 1838 until his death in 1864. He used this home to harbor fugitive slaves on their way north and several times he faced prosecution in the courts for his role in the Underground Railroad. Elected to Congress in 1856, he gained a national reputation through his congressional and party leadership and fiery antislavery speeches on the floor of the House.

Marshall Field Company Store

Location: Chicago, Cook County

Relevant issues: Business and industry

Statement of significance: This twelve-story granite building was designed to house the retail firm of Marshall Field, a pioneer of customer-service concepts.

Millikan House

Location: Chicago, Cook County

Relevant issues: Science and technology

Statement of significance: From 1907 to 1921, this three-story brick house was the residence of Robert A. Millikan (1868-1953), one of America's best-known twentieth century scientists. In 1923, Millikan received the Nobel Prize in Physics for his work in demonstrating the existence of electrons.

Montgomery Ward Company Complex

Location: Chicago, Cook County

Relevant issues: Business and industry

Statement of significance: Since 1909, this complex has served as national headquarters for the country's oldest mail-order firm. Founded in 1872 by Aaron Montgomery Ward (1843-1913), the company established the consumer trust which made a large-scale mail-order business possible and set a standard for the mail-order industry which other firms found it necessary to emulate in order to compete.

Nauvoo Historic District

Location: Nauvoo, Hancock County

Relevant issues: Religion

Statement of significance: For seven years, this was the principal city of the Mormons and the headquarters of their church. Originally known as Commerce, it was here that the Mormons began settling in 1839, following their flight from northwestern Missouri. Nauvoo, the largest city in the state, was abandoned by most of the Mormons in 1846 after their leader, Joseph Smith (1805-1844), had been killed by a mob and state authorities had grown increasingly hostile.

Old Main, Knox College

Location: Galesburg, Knox County

Relevant issues: Political history

Statement of significance: The oldest building on the campus of Knox College, Old Main is the best-preserved site associated with the Lincoln-Douglas Debates of 1858. The seven debates between Democratic senator Stephen A. Douglas and Republican challenger Abraham Lincoln keynoted the momentous issues of the sectional controversy which was carrying the nation toward disunion and civil war.

Old State Capitol

Location: Springfield, Sangamon County

Relevant issues: Political history

Statement of significance: From 1837 to 1876, this structure served as Illinois's fifth state capitol. Abraham Lincoln was a member of the first legislature which sat here (1840-1841). He made his noted "House Divided" speech here (1858), in accepting the Republican nomination for the U.S. Senate.

Old Stone Gate, Chicago Union Stockyards

Location: Chicago, Cook County

Relevant issues: Business and industry

Statement of significance: From about 1879 to 1971, this triple-arched, rough-faced limestone gate was the main entrance to the Chicago Union Stockyards. The Stockyards, founded in 1865 to consolidate the many scattered stockyards in Chicago into an efficient unit, symbolized Chicago's role as a major meat-packing center.

Riverside Historic District

Location: Riverside, Cook County

Relevant issues: Art and architecture, cultural history

Statement of significance: Designed in 1868-1869 by Frederick Law Olmsted and Calvert Vaux, Riverside was the first planned model community in the country, arranged so that open spaces and parkland would be a part of urban living.

Robie House

Location: Chicago, Cook County

Relevant issues: Art and architecture

Statement of significance: Designed and constructed from 1907 to 1909, the Robie House has won international acclaim for Frank Lloyd Wright's achievement in modern architecture. Designed in his Prairie style, the house utilizes an open plan.

Sears, Roebuck, and Company

Location: Chicago, Cook County

Relevant issues: Business and industry

Statement of significance: Constructed in 1905-1906, this complex has been symbolic of the company's dominance of the mail-order industry. Founded in 1893, Sears, Roebuck, and Company was the country's largest mail-order concern by 1900. The complex contains the printing plant that for many years produced the Sears Catalog, the company's principal selling instrument.

Wells-Barnett House

Location: Chicago, Cook County

Relevant issues: African American history, social reform, women's history

Statement of significance: From 1919 to 1929, this three-story brick building was the home of Ida B. Wells (1862-1931), African American teacher, journalist, and civil rights advocate. Almost single-handedly, Wells began the fight to awaken the world's conscience to the realities of lynching; in addition, she crusaded for the rights of black women.

Willard House

Location: Evanston, Cook County

Relevant issues: Social reform

Statement of significance: Constructed in 1865, this was the home of Frances Willard (1839-1898), who made the temperance movement a national force. She became president of the Women's Christian Temperance Union in 1879; her house is now the headquarters of that organization.

Williams House

Location: Chicago, Cook County

Relevant issues: African American history, health and medicine

Statement of significance: This was the home of Daniel Hale Williams (1858-1931), one of America's first black surgeons, among whose accomplishments are one of the first successful heart operations (1893) and the establishment of quality medical facilities for African Americans.

Wright Home and Studio

Location: Oak Park, Cook County

Relevant issues: Art and architecture

Statement of significance: Built and rebuilt by Frank Lloyd Wright (1867-1959), this is the place where he lived and practiced (1887-1909) in the "First Golden Age" of his long career.

Indiana

History of Indiana 439
Columbus 441
New Harmony 445

Vincennes 450
Other Historic Sites 454

The State Capitol Building in Indianapolis. (Jim West)

History of Indiana

Indiana's central position between earlier settled regions to the east and south and more recently settled regions to the north and west have made it an important area of commerce and transportation since the early years of the United States. Urban areas of the state, particularly in the northwest corner, which is located near the giant city of Chicago, have developed a multiethnic culture in sharp contrast to the white, western European, Protestant culture which dominates the rest of the state.

Early History

Several thousand years ago, early hunting, gathering, and crop-growing societies inhabited areas near the Ohio River. The oldest artifacts from this period have been discovered at Angel Mounds, a large archaeological site near Evansville. By the time Europeans arrived in the New World, the northern and central regions of the area were inhabited by the Miami Confederation, a group of Native Americans belonging to the Algonquin language group. The Miami, who depended largely on the growing of corn and the hunting of buffalo for survival, were organized into a confederation in order to protect their lands from the Iroquois, a large group of various Native American peoples living to the east. During the nineteenth century, the Miami ceded most of their land to the United States. Most of the Miami moved to Oklahoma, but some remained in Indiana.

French and British Settlement

During the seventeenth century, the Iroquois, who were generally hostile to the French, agreed to treaties which allowed the French to trade with the Miami. In 1679 the French explorer René-Robert Cavelier, Sieur de La Salle, led an expedition into the northern part of the region by traveling south from Michigan down the Saint Joseph River. At about the same time, traders from the British colonies along the Atlantic coast began to settle in the region along the Wabash River and the Ohio River.

In order to protect their access to the Wabash River, which led to the vital waterway of the Missis-

sippi River, the French built a series of forts in the area. The first was Fort Miami, built in 1704, followed by Fort Ouiatanon, built in 1719, and Fort Vincennes, built in 1732. The effort to win the region for France ended in failure in 1763, when the Treaty of Paris, which ended the French and Indian War, brought the area under British control. Although the British officially banned any further European settlement of the area, this prohibition was largely ignored. The area became part of the British province of Quebec in 1774.

American Settlement

During the American Revolution, American forces led by George Rogers Clark brought the region under the control of the newly created United States in 1779 in a surprise attack on British forces in Vincennes. The Peace of Paris, which ended the war in 1783, officially made the area part of the new nation. The first American settlement in the region was established in 1784 in Clarkville, across the Ohio River from Louisville, Kentucky.

The area was part of the Northwest Territory from 1787 to 1800, when the Indiana Territory, which included Michigan, Illinois, Wisconsin, and part of Minnesota, was created. The Michigan Territory was created in 1805, giving the region its modern northern border. In 1809 the Illinois Territory was created, giving the area its modern western border. Indiana became a state in 1816, with its first capital at Corydon.

Wars with Native Americans

Violent conflict with the Native Americans inhabiting the region began as soon as European settlers entered the area. The first phase of American Indian resistance ended in 1794 with the Battle of Fallen Timbers, near the border between Ohio and Indiana. About one thousand Americans led by Anthony Wayne defeated about two thousand Native Americans of the Northwest Indian Confederation, including members of the Miami, Potawatomi, Shawnee, Delaware, Ottawa, Ojibwa, and Iroquois, led by Shawnee chief Bluejacket. As a result of the battle, in 1795 Miami chief Little Turtle ceded much of his people's land to the United States in the Treaty of Fort Greenville.

The opening of this land to non-Indians led to a large increase in the number of settlers arriving from southern states. As a result, Indiana became culturally more southern than other states in the area and was inhabited primarily by Protestants of English, Scottish, Irish, and German ancestry. This rapid increase in the rate of European settlement led to an increase in the number of violent encounters with Native Americans.

The second phase of Native American resistance ended on November 7, 1811, at the Battle of Tippecanoe, near the modern city of Lafayette. During the battle, American forces led by William Henry Harrison defeated Shawnee forces led by Tenskwatawa. Although the two sides suffered equal losses, the battle was generally considered a decisive American victory, and it helped Harrison, a war hero, become president in 1840. Between 1820 and 1840 most Native Americans left the state.

Indianapolis

Settlement in Indiana in the first half of the nineteenth century was centered in the southern part of the state. The economy was based primarily on agriculture and transportation of goods along the Ohio River and the Wabash River. Indianapolis, a planned city designed to resemble Washington, D.C., was founded in 1821 in the center of the state and became the state capital in 1825. With the rise of railroads in the middle of the nineteenth century and the increase in motor-vehicle traffic in the twentieth century, Indianapolis became one of the largest cities in the world not located on a major waterway. It also went on to be served by more major highways than any other city in the United States.

Education and Industry

The first college in Indiana was founded in Vincennes in 1801. The first major institute of higher education, Indiana University, was founded

in Bloomington in 1820. This university went on to become one of the most respected in the United States, with a particularly well-regarded university press. Indiana later became the home of other outstanding universities, with the founding of the University of Notre Dame, near South Bend, in 1842, and Purdue University, in West Lafayette, in 1869.

The Civil War, in which many Indianans fought for the Union, brought a rapid increase in the growth of industry in the state, particularly in the northern region. Natural resources that contributed to this growth included limestone, found in the southern part of the state, and coal, found in the southwest area. The southern half of the state was also the site of the world's largest natural gas field in 1880's, but this resource was depleted by 1898.

Steel production became one of the state's most important industries, particularly with the founding of Gary, located near Chicago, in 1906. At about the same time, automobile manufacturing began in South Bend and Indianapolis. Certain cities specialized in the manufacturing of particular products. Elkhart became known for producing musical instruments in 1875, while Fort Wayne produces a large part of the world's diamond tools. Overall, Indiana is one of the top ten manufacturing states in the nation. Manufacturing accounts for about 40 percent of the state's income. Environmental destruction to the state's unique sand dunes along Lake Michigan, an indirect result of industrial growth, was slowed by the creation of Indiana Sand Dunes National Lakeshore in 1972.

The Twentieth Century
Although much of Indiana retains its character as an enclave of white, Anglo-Saxon, Protestant culture, the growth of the state's cities and the powerful influence of Chicago on the northwest region brought a mixture of ethnic groups to the area. World War I brought a steady flow of African Americans to the industrial centers of the state. By the late twentieth century, African Americans made up about 20 percent of the population of Indianapolis and about 70 percent of the population of Gary. Indianans of Polish ancestry constitute an important ethnic group in South Bend. Other ethnic groups in the state, particularly in northern cities, include Indianans whose ancestors arrived from Hungary, Belgium, and Italy. These groups give northern Indiana a higher percentage of Roman Catholics than the rest of the state, which is about two-thirds Protestant.

Politically, Indiana is generally conservative. The state spends less per capita on education, welfare, and health care than most other states. The amount of federal aid which the state receives per capita is one of the lowest in the nation. Change is slow to come to the state's political system, which still uses the state constitution of 1851. Although this constitution requires changes to be made in legislative districts based on population changes, this rule was disregarded from 1923 to 1963, giving the rural areas more political power than their dwindling population should have allowed. It was not until 1970 that voters approved a proposal to have the state legislature meet annually rather than every two years.

Despite this conservatism, the Republican party held only a slight advantage in the state after the

Civil War. Indiana counties are about one-third Republican, one-third Democratic, and one-third variable. Almost as many liberals and Democrats have been elected from the state as conservatives and Republicans. Indiana state politics are sometimes surprisingly innovative, as when Indianapolis merged with Marion County in 1969 to form a unique type of city/county government.

—*Rose Secrest*

Columbus

Date: Incorporated in 1837
Relevant issues: Art and architecture, business and industry
Significance: The capital of Bartholomew County, Columbus had a population of 31,802 in 1990. The principal employers are the Cummins Engine Company (diesel engines), Arvin Industries (automotive parts, metal laminates), and Cosco, Incorporated (furniture and housewares). The city is best known for its architecture.
Location: Forty-five miles south of Indianapolis and seventy-eight miles west of Cincinnati
Site Office:
Bartholomew County Historical Society
524 Third Street
Columbus, IN 47201
ph.: (812) 372-3541

The history of Columbus, Indiana, is similar to that of many other midwestern towns. The original village was founded during the westward drive of the nineteenth century. Columbus is organized according to the U.S. surveyors' grid plan, and its streets bear the names of the U.S. presidents. Given this rather typical profile, it may be surprising to learn that the American Institute of Architects rated Columbus sixth in the United States for the design quality and innovation of its buildings. Because of its citizens' dedication to architecture, Columbus is not only a typical midwestern town but also a historical place visited by thousands of tourists every year.

Early History
The area surrounding Columbus was covered with forests and inhabited by the Delaware Indians

when Generals John Tipton and Joseph Bartholomew arrived in 1813 to put down an Indian uprising. Soon after, some of the first white settlers, including Joseph Cox and his family, arrived from
Kentucky to live in the area. Official notice was
taken of the area a few years later when the question of a state capital arose; General Tipton and
General Bartholomew, impressed by the natural
beauty of the countryside, suggested the site that
would become Columbus. Although the capital
would ultimately be located in Indianapolis, the
state legislature conferred the status of county on
the Columbus area on January 12, 1821. When a
seat for the county was chosen, it seemed logical to
name it Tiptona after the general. When political
problems arose between Tipton and the new county
commissioners, the name was changed to Columbus and an angry Tipton left the town for good.

The citizens of Columbus petitioned for incorporation of the town in 1835, but they did not receive it until 1837. Columbus was not made a city
until 1864. By this time, however, the town and its
surroundings were already prospering. Settlers
were attracted to the fertile ground they found at
the meeting of the Driftwood, Flatrock, Hawcreek,
and Hawpatch Rivers. The early 1820's saw the
emergence of several gristmills, sawmills, woolen
mills, and distilleries, all of which encouraged the
flatboat trade with places as far south as New Orleans.

At first, education in Bartholomew County was
limited to meetings between students and teachers
in private homes. Then the Liberty School and
Meeting House was created in 1829. The public
school system was founded in 1851, and higher education was available at Hartsville College and the
Moravian Center for Young Ladies.

Arrival of the Railroad
The arrival of the first railroad in 1844 ushered in a
new era of prosperity for the region. Many lines
were built connecting Columbus to other parts of
Indiana. As a result of the increasing importance of
the area, the Kentucky Stock Bank was established
in 1853. Even the Civil War contributed to the success of the region. The nearby Camp Rendezvous
was a center for troops and supplies and thus fueled the local economy.

This economy was seriously damaged, though,
with the failure of the McEwan and Sons Bank in
1871. Its successor, Irwin's Bank, would become
the Irwin Union Trust Company, an important institution in Columbus to this day.

The first sign of modern industry was the Hoosier Boy Plow Company, which arrived in 1875.
Heavier industry came with Cummins, Arvin, and
Cosco, firms which now employ more than ten
thousand people.

Cummins Engine Company has played a large
part in transforming Columbus into the center of
art that it is. Through the joint efforts of Cummins
and J. Irwin Miller, the chairman of the board of
the Irwin Bank, and through the efforts of those
who have followed in their path, Columbus now
boasts of buildings designed by the Saarinens, I. M.
Pei, Cesar Pelli, and Harry Weese.

Unique Architecture
The town's architectural daring originated with
the decision by the community of the First Christian Church to hire modernist architect Eliel
Saarinen to build its new church. The community
thus made a daring choice for modernism, an ideo-
logical and cultural movement expressed in architecture through such elements as rectilinear design and the use of glass, steel, and concrete.
Despite the occasional harshness of modernist architecture, Saarinen's church emphasizes harmony. A founder and teacher at the Cranbrook
Academy of Art in Bloomfield Hills, Michigan,
Saarinen helped shape its humanistic interpretation of modernism. In fact, Saarinen was chosen
over Frank Lloyd Wright by the Columbus church
because of Saarinen's belief in adaptation rather
than domination. Because collaboration and personal expression were also important to Saarinen,
the church's design includes contributions from
his wife (the tapestry of the "Sermon on the
Mount") and from his son Eero who, with Charles
Eames, designed the furniture. The overwhelming
impression of the church, dedicated in 1942, is one
of power tempered by the warmth of a spiritual
community.

Soon afterward, J. Irwin Miller called upon Eero
Saarinen to design the new Irwin Union Bank, one
of the first banks ever to be built in glass with an
open plan. The influence of the Bauhaus movement, brought to Chicago by Ludwig Mies van der
Rohe, is clear in the bank's design. In 1957,
Saarinen worked again for the Millers to design

their home in Columbus. Balthazar Korab, who worked as an architect under Eero Saarinen, describes the house: "Subtle use of light, the white and marble and travertine contrasted with Girard's [the interior designer] rich, colorful textures and Kiley's [the landscape architect] formal landscaping makes this a serenely classical home." Thus, J. Irwin Miller's dedication to modernist architecture was already firmly established when he decided to seize upon an opportunity to bring modernism to the whole town.

Experiments in Education

Postwar prosperity required the building of new schools in Columbus. Miller suggested that these schools be designed by well-known and respected architects. To accomplish his goal, he enlisted the aid of the Cummins Engine Company, which agreed to pay the architect's fees provided that the community would choose from a list of top-notch architects drawn up by Cummins.

The first school to come out of this experiment was the Lillian C. Schmitt Elementary School, designed in 1957 by Harry Weese. The school is surprising in its discreetness. The low ceilings of its classrooms blend superbly with the surrounding residential neighborhood. Weese's contribution to Columbus's profile is indeed substantial. Along with the Schmitt school, he designed the Lincoln Center (1958), the Northside Middle School (1961), the Otter Creek Clubhouse (1964), and the First Baptist Church (1965), among other buildings.

Postmodern School Architecture

In his book *Columbus, Indiana*, Korab posits some postmodernist elements in Weese's work. Postmodernism in architecture relies, in part, on "quoting" from the history of architecture as well as from the surroundings of the building being designed. Weese's incipient postmodernism seems clear in the design of the Otter Creek Clubhouse, which is modernist in shape but, built of local timber, blends in with the surroundings. Another example of his postmodernist tendencies is the First Baptist Church, which has been described as romanesque. Whatever label one might apply, Weese's buildings continue, but expand, Saarinen's tradition of harmony and adaptation.

Several other schools were to come out of the Cummins program. Among the architects who par-

ticipated were John Carl Warnecke (Mabel McDowell Adult Education Center, 1960), Norman Fletcher (Parkside Elementary School, 1962), Edward Larrabee Barnes (W. D. Richards Elementary School, 1965), Gunmar Birkerts (Lincoln Elementary School, 1967), John M. Johansen (L. Frances Smith Elementary School, 1969), Eliot Noyes (Southside Elementary School 1969), Hardy Holzman Pfeiffer (Mount Healthy Elementary School, 1972), Mitchell-Giurgola (Columbus East High School, 1972), Paul Kennon and Truitt Garrison (Fodrea Community School, 1973), and Richard Meier (Clifty Creek Elementary School, 1982). The Fodrea School is particularly interesting; the parents and the students contributed to the design. This participation is but one indication of the involvement of Columbus's citizens in the aesthetic development of their town.

The list of impressive architecture goes far beyond the school system. Eero Saarinen made another important contribution to Columbus with his Northside Christian Church. Similar to the preparations for the Fodrea School, the preparations for this church involved communication between the architect and the church community. While he was working on the design, he wrote to the members, stating that he wanted to make a great building "so that as an architect when I face St. Peter I am able to say that out of the buildings I did during my lifetime, one of the best was this little church." Tragically, Saarinen died before his church was completed.

Other Architectural Projects

Aside from its commissioning of schools, Cummins Engine Company is responsible for several other architectural projects. Within the context of Cummins's own facilities there are the Walesboro plant, the Technical Center (designed by Harry Weese in 1968), and the company's new headquarters. Each of these buildings received thoughtful attention. When designing the corporate headquarters in the early 1980's, Kevin Roche took several issues into consideration: a desire to incorporate the landscape, a desire to adopt a monument from the past (the Cerealine Building), and a desire to keep the headquarters downtown to stimulate life at the center of town. In a small town with daring projects, such careful consideration protects Columbus from a feeling of artificiality.

Other famous architects have worked in Columbus. I. M. Pei lent his famous skills to the design of the Cleo Rogers Memorial Library in 1969. Roche convinced the U.S. Postal Service to depart from its standard design pattern so that he could create the Columbus Post Office with its colonnade in 1970. In 1971, Myron Goldsmith designed the headquarters for the local newspaper, the *Republic*. The building has glass walls that allow a view of the printing presses. In an article for the *Chicago Tribune* Blair Kamin described the experience of seeing it: "When the press runs, it resembles kinetic sculpture, great gobs of newsprint spinning through the yellow machine, emerging black and white." Perhaps one of the most outstanding buildings of the town, in both its design and its location, is the Commons-Courthouse complex created by Cesar Pelli in 1973; it is a combination shopping mall and community center, and it includes a motion-picture theater, a restaurant, an art gallery, and a playground. The whole provides an interesting but not shocking contrast to the Victorian buildings of downtown Columbus.

Attention to aesthetics has not been limited to new buildings in the history of Columbus. Renovation has also played an important part. The town decided that the older elements had to keep pace with the innovative architecture. Among the buildings that were restored are Franklin Square, the Visitors' Center, and the old Irwin Bank.

Sculpture

Modernist sculpture has also left its mark on Columbus. One of the outstanding examples is the *Large Arch* created by Henry Moore in 1971. The sculpture, which weighs five and one-half tons, is located in the same square as I. M. Pei's library. Jean Tinguely contributed *Chaos 1* to the Commons in 1974. It is described by Balthazar Korab as a "magical kinetic sculpture" and delighted the public immediately upon its unveiling. Other artists who have designed pieces for local buildings include Ivan Chermayeff, Harris Barron, Alexander Girard, Robert Indiana, and Constantino Nivola.

Amid overall admiration, a dissenting voice is to be heard from Blair Kamin. While respecting Columbus as a whole, he is critical of the town's more recent developments. For instance, he finds the City Hall (designed by Charles Bassett in 1981) out of touch with a relatively small community. According to Kamin, the design record is uneven. He attributes its unevenness to conservative clients who are hesitant to place their faith in rising architectural talents and to the declining influence of J. Irwin Miller.

Museums

It is important to note certain other features of modern-day Columbus that could be overshadowed by the impressive architecture. Several museums are located in the area, including a branch of the Indianapolis Museum of Art. The Bartholomew Historical Society operates a historical museum and sponsors tours of selected local homes. The town also supports an orchestra and a theater. Outdoor activities abound, and the town is only sixteen miles from Brown County State Park.

What is most remarkable about Columbus is that such a small town can contain so much impressive architecture without losing its own character. This distinctiveness comes from the residents' dedication to the project and to the fact that it extends to every facet of their community. Also, the plan has received excellent guidance and support. A sign that Columbus is keeping up with the changing face of architecture, postmodernism is gaining ground. Like its residents, the town is changing and growing.

—Kathleen M. Micham

For Further Information:

Akerson, Alan W. "Columbus, Indiana: An Architectural Treasure Trove." *St. Louis Globe-Democrat Sunday Magazine,* June 3, 1979. Older, but still worth consulting.

Bartholomew County Historical Society. *History of Bartholomew County—1888.* Columbus, Ind.: Bartholomew County Historical Society, 1976. A complete history of the town itself.

Columbus Area Visitors Center. *A Look at Architecture: Columbus, Indiana.* 7th ed. Columbus, Ind.: Author, 1998. An architectural guidebook.

Jeffery, David. "A Most Uncommon Town." *National Geographic,* September, 1978. Another older piece that is worth consulting.

Kamin, Blair. "Exploring Columbus." *Chicago Tribune,* November 30, 1993. One of the most up-to-date discussions of the town's recent architecture.

Korab, Balthazar. *Columbus, Indiana.* Kalamazoo, Mich.: Documan Press, 1989. One of the best, most beautifully illustrated books on the city's architecture. Korab worked as an architect under Eero Saarinen.

New Harmony

Date: Harmonie founded in 1814; sold and renamed New Harmony in 1825

Relevant issues: Religion, social reform

Significance: This is the site of two early nineteenth century utopian communities, Harmonie and New Harmony. The community consists of original residences of George Rapp's Harmonie Society and several buildings restored after Rapp and Robert Owen abandoned their experiments.

Location: On the banks of the Wabash River at the intersection of Routes 66 and 68, seven miles south of U.S. Interstate 64, north of the city of Evansville

Site Office:
Historic New Harmony
P.O. Box 579
Athenaeum/Visitors' Center
Corner of North and Arthur Streets
New Harmony, IN 47631
ph.: (800) 231-2168; (812) 682-4488, 464-9595
Web site: www.newharmony.org
e-mail: harmony@usi.edu

New Harmony, Indiana, is home to the restored remains of two utopian community experiments of the nineteenth century with radically different purposes. The early to mid-nineteenth century saw many forms of communitarian societies that attempted to reform society and its inhabitants' way of life for their benefit in this world or the next.

The founding inhabitants, the Harmonists (or Rappites or Swabians) followed their leader George Rapp from Württemburg, Germany, westward first to Butler County, Pennsylvania, and then to Harmonie, Indiana. In the millennialist spirit, Rapp sought to create a "harmonious" community that would be one of the first to receive Christ at the Second Coming. Robert Owen, a Scottish industrialist, then purchased Harmonie to create a moral model community and egalitarian society. He gathered a group of intellectuals who not only introduced a more practical vocation-based education to America but also introduced the first free public school. These two groups, despite their demise, have had a lasting influence on all of American society.

Father Rapp

The development of Harmonie initially began in the mind of George Rapp, a German "gentleman farmer" living in Württemburg, a hotbed of religious separatism. In the tradition of Martin Luther, Rapp became dissatisfied with the clerics who dictated theology to parishioners, disallowing independent thought. Rapp, nearly fifty years old, decided to move his followers to the United States. A well-read man, he had perused many travel accounts of the New World and found it attractive for the establishment of his society. Furthermore, his interpretation of the Book of Revelations required his community to sojourn in the wilderness in "a place prepared by God."

Physically, George Rapp was an imposing man. Standing six feet in height, he was well proportioned and had a full beard; he was referred to as Father Rapp by his followers. In 1803 Rapp, his son Johannes, and three other members traveled to the United States to purchase farmland. Left behind were his family and Frederick Reichart, a thirty-year-old architect adopted by Rapp. Reichart, who assumed the name of Rapp, managed business dealings in Germany, a function he would also perform in the New World. After months of searching, George Rapp and his followers purchased land near Pittsburgh in Butler County, Pennsylvania, and moved one thousand settlers then waiting in New York. In their petition to the 1804 U.S. Congress, these settlers described themselves as "tradesmen, farmers, and chiefly cultivators of the vine."

The settlement in Pennsylvania struggled not just because the poor soil limited the growth of the settlement but also because Father Rapp began to lose control over the society. Following Rapp was not easy; the society demanded celibacy, communal property, equality of work, self-denial, and separation from the outside world. Members dressed in gray in an older European style and retained their German language. All property came under the control of Rapp, who was accused by some of being greedy. Confession to a designated person in the household was to be regular. Discipline was rendered through public disapproval and ostracism. Further, as pacifists, members of the society did not serve in the military and readily paid the optional fine.

Celibacy, one of the most important and divisive membership requirements, had been adopted in 1807, two years after the founding of the colony in Pennsylvania. Marriage was generally forbidden, although it did occur. Those members who were married prior to joining the society where required to live celibately. Men and women slept on separate floors of the dormitories and houses. Legend holds that because Rapp's son Johannes took a wife who bore a child, Rapp castrated him. Johannes died in 1812 of an unknown cause. Whether true or not, the circulation of this story is itself illustrative of Rapp's loss of control. Because of this social disintegration and because the poor land around the settlement would not make expansion of cultivation profitable, Rapp decided to move the Harmonists further westward to Indiana in 1814.

Agricultural Success

The fertile land and isolation of western Indiana better suited the community. By 1820 Harmonie was the most prosperous settlement in Indiana, producing dark beer, wine, wool, cotton, silk, paper, coffee, tobacco, coarse and fine cloth, spices, crockery, and hats. Using the Wabash River as a connection to the Ohio River and then to the Mississippi, the community sent its goods to be sold in the markets of New Orleans. Consequently, these goods were purchased in twenty-two states and ten foreign countries. Such business transactions were the responsibility of Frederick Rapp, who insulated the Harmonists from the outside world.

The success of Harmonie in the wilderness was due, in part, to the careful planning that went into the community's creation. The first log houses were constructed on the periphery, with construction moving toward the center. As an architect, Frederick Rapp assisted in planning the town's grid design. Lining its streets were Lombardy poplars and, later, mulberry trees. The Harmonists, known for their gardening, planted flowers everywhere. Residential areas had public ovens and wells. The building designs were a combination of European and eastern American architecture. Because of the Harmonists' belief in equity, all houses were con-

structed on the same design. The large and airy brick dwellings varied in size, depending on their use either as dormitories or single-family units. Their entrances were secluded on the side of the house and not directly off the street. Common were "Christian Doors," six-paneled doors with the upper half forming a cross and the lower portion an open Bible. Public buildings included a granary, which could be used as a fort; a cotton mill, complete with steam engine; a brewery, which produced five hundred gallons per day; and a sawmill. Harmonie, like the other communities Rapp built, contained a labyrinth with a plain exterior and a more complicated and ornate interior that included small groves and a center grotto. The labyrinth was a metaphor for the crooked road of life; the world was not to be judged by outward appearances. By the time Rapp sold Harmonie to Robert Owen, 180 structures had been built.

Harmonie also prospered because of its insular self-sufficiency. Neighbors of the community, English, Irish, German, and Scots migrants from the hill regions of the Allegheny Mountains, believed the Harmonists to be stingy and mean with their finances. The society did not incur any labor or production costs and consequently often undercut local merchants and shopkeepers. Because the society owned the best section of the river for operating a mill, the community was legally required to grind the grain of the surrounding inhabitants. Its initial refusal resulted in a court case, a fine, and an order to process its neighbors' grain.

Internal and External Pressures

Despite its prosperity, by 1825 the Harmonist community was shaken by internal dissension and external animosity. The population was gradually aging and, because it was celibate, not replenishing itself. In 1817 another group from Germany arrived in Philadelphia to join the colony, but Frederick Rapp refused to pay for their passage, requiring many to sell themselves into indentured servitude. Newer members who arrived lacked the commitment to Rapp and his principles that the original settlers had shared. Further, while membership was not coercive, those wishing to leave the society could not regain their investment. Rapp often told his followers how to vote, a serious social offense in the West, where democratic principles carried great weight. The Harmonists' neighbors saw them

A drawing of the community of New Harmony shortly after its founding. (Library of Congress)

as slave labor. The community soon faced financial difficulties as well.

By the 1820's, banks in the West failed, causing the society to lose trade and profits. The society could have survived in isolation, but with no one to buy its goods, Rapp feared that idleness would tempt the community. As a further incentive to relocate, the Wabash River was unreliable for transporting goods because of its fluctuating water levels. Ultimately, Rapp decided to move the community back to Pennsylvania. Early in 1825, after lengthy negotiation, George Rapp sold Harmonie to Robert Owen, a Scotsman with his own utopian dream who had already founded a communitarian settlement in Scotland, New Lanark.

Enter Robert Owen

Robert Owen's purchase of the village, which he renamed New Harmony, was quite a steal. For $125,000 he acquired twenty thousand acres and all the improvements the Harmonists had made. Rapp had purchased the original undeveloped and uncleared land for $2.50 an acre, a total cost of $50,000. Owen paid for New Harmony in installments from capital supplied by his partners at New Lanark and through personal funds. The productive community in the wilderness required little ad-

aptation for Owen's intended utopian community. Owen realized he could never purchase such cheap land anywhere in Europe. He chose the location not only because of various reports of the settlement that he had heard but also because President James Monroe proposed a benevolent homeland for Native Americans somewhere in the West. Owen aspired to be the U.S. government agent for the Native American community and believed New Harmony would be a perfect headquarters.

Owen was a unique idealist and a reformer who shaped the notion of education and society in the future midwest. George Rapp had created the Harmonie Society to offer salvation to a few believers. Owen wanted to transform the world. He believed that society was the major shaper and corrupter of the human character. Individual property and religious belief led to inequalities of labor, to crime, and to poverty. Owen's solution to overcoming the evils was equal division of labor, equal participation (including for women) in community affairs, and a more vocational or practical education. Some of his communitarian ideas had already been tested on the inhabitants of New Lanark, his cotton manufacturing community in Scotland inherited from his father-in-law. The survival and prosperity of his new community relied on four elements of organization: the economic system of labor, the methodology of governance, the social organization, and the educational process.

Owen's Principles

Based on what Owen called the "Principles of United Production and Consumption," the community required individuals to work at only those essential activities necessary for survival. Work was the moral force of Owen's scheme. Actual monetary reward to the individual was unusual. Rather, individuals gave their skills to the community in exchange for a decent living. This communal concept attracted many who were poor or had large, young families, and not a few who were simply freeloaders. The large number of young children made for a small labor pool. In addition, those who entered the society wealthy could pay not to work. In 1825, the community had 812 residents of which only 137 were employed in the "professions," which included farmers. Problems arose in trying to reconcile payment with labor; for example, a credit for three hours of garden weeding might offset the debit of a pot of molasses and four pounds of corn meal.

The governance of the "society of cooperation" changed numerous times within the first year. The original constitution provided for the community, not Owen, to own the land after the first three years of operation. A council was elected to negotiate outside business. Throughout the community's history, however, Owen was in constant need of cash, causing several reorganizations. In one of his reorganizations, he leased land to some community members, the major lessor being William Maclure, who managed education.

Social Organization

The society's basic organization was built on a principle of equality (however, African Americans were discouraged from joining and were not given equal rights). Women, who had access to day care provided by the community, worked and possessed full voting and property rights. Society members wore the same clothes, ate the same food, and, when possible, lived in identical housing. They were to treat one another as brothers and sisters. The society was divided into work groups: agriculture, manufacturing, education, domestic economy, general economy, and commerce. Superintendents, or military police as they had been called at New Lanark, administered each division. Anyone who dissented from the society was permitted to leave, usually leasing uncleared property outside the central town.

Practical Education

The most unusual part of Owen's community was its view of what constituted a practical education. Owen's eldest son, Robert Dale Owen, had been educated in Switzerland according to the Pestalozzi principles, which emphasized an industrial and vocational education. Owen and his son gathered around them a group of intellectuals and educators who were to become pioneers and leaders in the fields of natural science and education. In the process of purchasing New Harmony, Owen had traveled the eastern United States extensively, professing his ideals. In Philadelphia, he met members of the Academy of Natural Sciences and its president, William Maclure. Maclure, enthusiastic over Owen's ideas, joined the communal society with several other members of the academy: Charles Alexander Lesueur, artist and naturalist; Gerard Troost, chemist and mineralogist; and Thomas Say, entomologist. Joining them were Joseph Neef, a Pestalozzian teacher, and Marie Fretageot, a Frenchwoman who ran an experimental boarding school in Philadelphia. This extraordinary group of individuals revolutionized the American educational system with their concept of free, public, and practical education. Arriving in New Harmony together on a flatboat called the Boatload of Knowledge, they were particularly excited about contributing their talents and knowledge to the community.

The First Vocational Boarding School

Neef organized the first public vocational boarding school. Financed by the community, it was open to anyone who wished to attend and incorporated practical education with apprenticeships. Maclure brought with him his own excellent natural sciences library and opened it to the public. The educational experiment was the most successful aspect of Owen's project. The rest of the society remained chronically in debt and never self-sufficient. Owen was continually reorganizing the governing structure of the society, reconfiguring the board of directors, and changing community representation. One such reorganization divided the society into three groups: the Agricultural and Pastoral Society, the Mechanic and Manufacturing Society, and the Education Society. Owen controlled and administered the first two divisions and gave Maclure sole control of the third. Although still in support of Owen's ideas, Maclure realized that Owen's debts would eventually destroy the experimental society and with it Maclure's school.

Withdrawal of Owen

Despite another reorganization, Owen withdrew his financial support from the community in the spring of 1827. He sold selected town buildings (the store, tavern, flour mill, and cotton mill) and tried to reclaim the land he had leased to Maclure. In that same year, Frederick Rapp demanded payment of forty thousand dollars worth of unpaid bonds for the property left by the Harmonists. Maclure paid the bonds in an attempt to entice Owen to deed him the land he leased. In dire financial straits, Owen sold New Lanark to pay off his debts and to support his wife and daughters, whom he had virtually abandoned in Scotland. In the final settlement, Owen's children, Robert Dale, William, David Dale, Nancy, and Richard, retained equal portions of New Harmony, each paying their father an annual fee of three hundred dollars.

Many of the Owenites remained at New Harmony and continued to work. The school, despite the fact that Maclure had left New Harmony, continued to be led by Marie Fretageot and later Maclure's brother and sister. With Robert Owen back in England, the remaining community managed to prosper. His children eventually settled in New Harmony themselves. Robert Dale Owen, his eldest son, had a lackluster career in the U.S. House of Representatives, where he sponsored the bill that created the Smithsonian Institution, and later he was appointed U.S. chargé d'affaires in Naples. Toward the end of his life he became a spiritual medium, ironic considering his father's distrust of religion. David Dale Owen became U.S. Geologist in 1839 and directed the U.S. Geological Survey. Richard Owen was a professor at Indiana University and in 1872 became the first president of Purdue University.

The Owen influence remained strong in New Harmony (some of his descendants still have ties there), and the community gradually grew and diversified. After the Civil War, it became known for its French grapes and wine. Until World War I, some farming implements were manufactured there as well. In the 1880's Dormitory Number Four became Thrall's Opera House.

Historic Preservation

The first attempts at historic preservation occurred under the auspices of the New Harmony Commission, established in 1937 by the state of Indiana. The commission, which purchased several key historic sites in the town, was disbanded in 1955. In the 1940's, New Harmony was visited by Jane Blaffer Owen, the wife of a descendant of Robert Owen and also the daughter of Humble Oil (now Exxon) founder Robert Lee Blaffer. She was taken with the town and began purchasing and renovating several buildings associated with New Harmony. In 1959 she founded the Robert Lee Blaffer Trust, which began construction of several new buildings, including the Roofless Church, designed by architect Philip Johnson and completed in 1960.

Over the next thirty years, additional renovation and development was carried out by a succession of private and state-run foundations, including a second New Harmony Commission, under the direction of urban planner Ralph G. Schwarz. Renovations included Dormitory Number Two, which had served alternately as a school, a telephone office, a newspaper plant, an inn, a tenement, and now a museum. Thrall's Opera House was also restored and now houses musical performances and conferences. New constructions included the New Harmony Inn, built in the simple architectural style of the Harmonists, and the award-winning Atheneum visitors' center, designed by architect Richard Meier. In 1975 a state park was created south of the town, and in 1991 the town's various historic commissions were unified under the auspices of the University of Southern Indiana.

—*Jenny Presnell*

For Further Information:

Menke, R. H. *Mary Fauntleroy and New Harmony: In Search of Community.* New Harmony, Ind.: Harmonie Haus, 1996. Includes a biography of Fauntleroy and historical documents. Addresses the community agenda of New Harmony.

Taylor, Anne. *Visions of Harmony: A Study in Nineteenth-Century Millenarianism.* Oxford, England: Clarendon Press, 1987. Somewhat scholarly. Despite Taylor's title, her examination of New Harmony concentrates more on Owen's experiment than the Harmonists. She also provides interesting discussions of Rapp and Owen.

Wilson, William E. *The Angel and the Serpent: The Story of New Harmony.* Bloomington: Indiana University Press, 1964. An excellent and highly readable account of the two utopian communities. Wilson examines not only the history of the area but also the folklore and beliefs of the two societies and their aftermath.

Young, Marguerite. *Angel in the Forest: A Fairy Tale of Two Utopias.* New York: Reynal and Hitchcock, 1945. An anecdotal account of the communities; Young's text is interesting to read but undocumented.

Vincennes

Date: French fort established in 1732

Relevant issues: European settlement, western expansion

Significance: A community dating to the early eighteenth century, Vincennes played an important role in the western campaign during the American Revolution. It includes the George Rogers Clark National Historical Park; Grouseland, the home of William Henry Harrison, a National Historic Landmark; the Indiana Territory State Historic Site; and the Fort Knox II Historic Park.

Location: In southwestern Indiana, on the Wabash River, via Indiana State Road 41/150 south from U.S. Interstate 70, or Indiana State Road 41 north from U.S. Interstate 64

Site Offices:

George Rogers Clark National Historical Park
401 South Second Street
Vincennes, IN 47591
ph.: (812) 882-1776
fax: (812) 882-7270
Web site: www.nps.gov/gero/

Grouseland (William Henry Harrison Home)
3 West Scott Street
Vincennes, IN 47591
ph.: (812) 882-2096

The city of Vincennes, on the Wabash River in southwestern Indiana, is one of the oldest communities in the Midwest. During its eventful early years, its inhabitants lived under the flags of three nations: France, Great Britain, and the United States. Its role in the American Revolutionary War led to the acquisition of a vast territory for the new republic, and it continued to play an important part in the development of the young country.

Establishment of Vincennes

The French first established a fort at Vincennes in 1732 as an outpost and center for the lucrative fur trade with the Indians. The post was named in honor of its founder, François-Marie Bissot, Sieur de Vincennes, who was burned at the stake by the Chickasaw Indians in 1736. The site drew settlers from Canada, Detroit, and other French outposts as far away as New Orleans. Today there are still many reminders of the French heritage in Vincennes. The Old Cathedral, 205 Church Street, served as the parish church to the Catholic French inhabitants. Now called the Basilica of St. Francis Xavier, it was begun in 1826, succeeding two prior log churches dating back to 1749. In its belfry hangs a bell brought from France in 1742. Four bishops are buried in its crypt, including Bishop Simon William Gabriel Bruté, who supervised its construction. Bruté's fine collection of books dating to the fifteenth century is in the Old Cathedral Library, located in the courtyard behind the cathedral.

Next to the cathedral is the Old French Cemetery, in use since 1750 (although the oldest marker is dated 1800). The Old French House, 509 North First Street, was built between 1786 and 1814 by Michel Brouillet, a French-Canadian fur trader. Behind the house is the French-Indian Heritage Museum, which displays artifacts from prehistoric through French colonial times.

George Rogers Clark and the Revolutionary War

With the end of the French and Indian War in 1763, all of the North American continent claimed by the French was ceded to Great Britain. Vincennes was far off the beaten paths, however, and it was the late 1770's before the British actually claimed their post on the Wabash, renaming the garrison Fort Sackville. The inhabitants were asked to swear allegiance to Great Britain, and as a matter of expediency, most of them did.

The war between Great Britain and the colonies on the eastern seaboard soon forced the issue of political allegiance. The British began encouraging their Indian allies to raid the American settlers moving into the Kentucky country. These allies then retreated to the safety of the wilderness and their British protectors north of the Ohio River. During the winter of 1777-1778, a tall, auburn-haired Kentuckian named George Rogers Clark went to Governor Patrick Henry in Williamsburg with an audacious proposal: He wanted to attack the British outposts north of the Ohio one by one, with the ultimate goal of capturing Fort Detroit. Clark left Virginia with public orders to raise a company of 350 men to defend Kentucky; his secret orders permitted him to launch a campaign across the Ohio.

Early in 1778 Clark marched 150 Virginia volunteers to western Pennsylvania; from there they floated down the Ohio to Corn Island, across from the present site of Louisville, Kentucky. Here the volunteers were drilled and joined by more men from Kentucky and Tennessee. In June they set out, floating down the Ohio to the abandoned Fort Massac, where they hid their boats and marched north across southwestern Illinois. On the evening of July 4 they reached Kaskaskia, which surrendered without resistance. Clark told the French inhabitants of the alliance between France and the new United States and promised them religious freedom if they chose to support the American cause. The Kaskaskians readily agreed and helped convince the residents of Cahokia to join them.

Clark also won a powerful ally in the Jesuit priest who ministered to the far-flung inhabitants of the region, Father Pierre Gibault. Gibault volunteered to go himself to Vincennes, where he won the support of the French. Clark sent Captain Leonard Helm to Vincennes to command the French militia at Fort Sackville. All three towns had been won without firing a shot.

However, the British were not willing to let their outposts go without a fight. When Lieutenant Governor Henry Hamilton learned of Clark's activities he put together a large force of British, French, and Indian soldiers and headed south from Detroit, reaching Vincennes in December of 1778. Captain Helm's militia was vastly outnumbered.

He was forced to surrender, and the Union Jack again flew above Fort Sackville.

Francis Vigo

Another important ally won over by Clark was Francis Vigo, an Italian-born trader based in Spanish St. Louis. Vigo had loaned Clark money for supplies and had provided the Americans with goods from his own stock. Unaware of the capture of Vincennes, Vigo arrived there shortly afterward and was taken prisoner. He managed to keep the extent of his relationship with Clark from Hamilton and was released after promising he would take no action against the British on his way back to St. Louis. Vigo kept his promise strictly. He returned directly to St. Louis. Then he hurried to Kaskaskia to inform Clark of the situation at Vincennes.

Among the crucial pieces of information Vigo provided Clark was the news that Hamilton was remaining in Vincennes for the winter but had released his French soldiers and Indian allies. Hamilton planned to regroup in the spring and attack Clark at Kaskaskia. Clark saw he must seize the advantage of Hamilton's reduced garrison. He recruited about seventy-five French volunteers to join one hundred of his own men for an overland march. It was February and the worst possible time for such a venture. The flat plains of Illinois were inundated with ice-covered water from the swollen rivers. The weather was cold and continuously rainy. Under such conditions, however, Hamilton would never expect an attack. On February 5 Clark and his men left Kaskaskia for Vincennes, two hundred miles away.

Invasion and Victory

For days the men slogged through water, sometimes so deep they had to carry guns and powder over their heads. The men were tired, cold, and hungry. Occasionally they had to stop to build canoes in order to cross the flooded plains. Nearly two weeks later they reached the Embarrass River, just west of the Wabash, where they could hear the guns of Fort Sackville. After some scouting revealed that the British still suspected nothing, they crept closer. On the evening of February 23 they quietly entered the town of Vincennes. Clark had sent a letter to the French inhabitants warning them not to interfere, and the invaders met no resistance. Clark deployed his men around the fort, using several ruses to make it appear that his force was much larger than it was.

Although Hamilton had heard rumors of American forces in the area, he had not taken them seriously. Even after hearing gunfire, he did not realize he was under attack. At last the garrison pulled itself together, but Hamilton saw that he had lost the support of the French and had little hope of relief. The exchange of fire continued throughout the next day, with intermittent messages between Clark and Hamilton arguing over terms. When Clark ordered a group of captured British-allied Indians to be killed in plain view of the fort, Hamilton was finally convinced that Clark was serious in his warning that no quarter would be given if the fort were stormed. On February 25 Hamilton surrendered. Fort Sackville was renamed Fort Patrick Henry.

George Rogers Clark National Historical Park, on the site of Fort Sackville overlooking the Wabash River, was established to memorialize Clark's contribution. The centerpiece of the park is the George Rogers Clark Memorial, a classically styled structure containing a statue of Clark by Hermon A. MacNeil and seven murals by Ezra Winter depicting the western campaign. The memorial was dedicated by President Franklin D. Roosevelt in 1936.

A bronze statue of George Rogers Clark by Hermon A. MacNeil inside the memorial in Vincennes to this legendary soldier. (National Park Service)

Organization of the Northwest Territory

Although Clark was unable to achieve his ultimate goal of seizing Fort Detroit, the conquest of Fort Sackville and the other outposts above the Ohio gave the United States a crucial claim on the region during the treaty negotiations ending the Revolutionary War. In 1787 Congress organized the newly won land into the Northwest Territory, now known as the Old Northwest. Out of it would come the states of Ohio, Indiana, Illinois, Michigan, and Wisconsin, and part of Minnesota.

Vincennes was named the capital of the Indiana Territory, created from the Old Northwest Territory when Ohio became a state, and served as the seat of the Indiana Territory General Assembly from 1800 to 1813. A modest two-story frame building was the territory's first capital building; it has been moved to its current location at First and Harrison Streets, where it is part of the Indiana Territory State Historic Site. Also at the site is a recreation of the *Western Sun* print shop. The territory's first newspaper, the *Indiana Gazette*, was printed in the original building by Elihu Stout in 1804. The press was destroyed by a fire in 1806. The next year the paper reappeared as a weekly publication, the *Western Sun*.

William Henry Harrison's Governorship

The first governor of the Indiana Territory was William Henry Harrison, later ninth president of the United States; appointed territorial governor by President John Adams, he served from 1800 to

1812. Harrison's home, Grouseland, is operated as a National Historic Landmark by the Daughters of the American Revolution. The Federal-style house, at the corner of Park and Scott Streets, was built between 1802 and 1804. Harrison lived there until 1812. The house has been restored and furnished with Harrison family furniture.

Indian affairs occupied much of Harrison's time as governor. He was aggressive in obtaining land concessions from the Native American tribes still living in the territory and stirred up resentment among the tribes. Realizing that Harrison was playing one tribe off against the other, the great Shawnee leader Tecumseh and his brother, the Prophet, began to urge the formation of an Indian confederation to oppose white encroachment. Both came to Vincennes to meet with Harrison at Grouseland on several occasions. Harrison recognized the danger to white settlement presented by the intelligent and eloquent Tecumseh and made plans to attack early in 1811. On September 26 he led one thousand men north from Fort Knox to engage Tecumseh's followers. They reached the Prophet's town near the Tippecanoe River in early November; Tecumseh was not present, and Harrison's men defeated an attack by the Prophet's warriors on November 7 in the Battle of Tippecanoe.

The fort from which Harrison led his troops was the second of three Vincennes garrisons named for Henry Knox, the first U.S. secretary of war. It was located three miles north of the village and used from 1803 to 1813; one of its commanders was Captain Zachary Taylor, later the twelfth president of the United States. The Indiana Historical Society now operates the Fort Knox II Historical Park, a forty-four-acre park on the site.

Vincennes University

In 1801 the Jefferson Academy was founded in Vincennes; its name was changed when the first General Assembly of Indiana Territory chartered it as Vincennes University in 1806. Vincennes University is the oldest comprehensive junior college in the United States. Its charter provided for the free education of Indian students and encouraged the inclusion of women. The first building was completed in 1811. Competition from Indiana University in Bloomington lost Vincennes University its state support; instead Vincennes created a

place for itself as an outstanding junior college. The original campus southeast of the current site was sold by the trustees in 1839. The school moved to the corner of Fifth and Busseron Streets, then moved again in 1953 to the eighty-five-acre site it occupies today near the Wabash River.

As a boy Abraham Lincoln passed through Vincennes when his family moved from Indiana to Illinois in 1830. Later, Lincoln's law practice often brought him back to Vincennes, where he was sometimes a guest of friends and clients. The Lincoln Memorial Bridge, which crosses the Wabash from Vigo Street, commemorates that association with the sixteenth president. A monument to Lincoln was erected on the Illinois side of the bridge in 1938; a bronze statue of the young Lincoln stands before a stone bas-relief of the Lincoln family crossing the Wabash into Illinois.

Architecture of Vincennes

Vincennes also offers a number of architecturally and historically significant houses and commercial buildings. The Old State Bank, 114 North Second Street, the oldest surviving bank structure in the state, was built between 1836 and 1838 as the Vincennes branch of the State Bank of Indiana. It is now an Indiana Territory State Historic Site, restored and operated by the Daughters of the American Revolution. Across the street is the Ellis Mansion, a two-story brick structure built by Judge Abner T. Ellis in 1830. In addition to his legal duties, Ellis was the first president of the Ohio and Mississippi Railroad, which later became the Baltimore and Ohio. Abraham Lincoln was his attorney and a frequent guest in the house.

The Baty Place, 617 North Second Street, served as the first hospital in Indiana. It was built by Samuel Judah, a pioneer lawyer, about 1840. Dr. Jean Isidore Baty, a French physician, lived in the house from 1848 to 1865 and built a three-story addition to serve as a hospital. The Bonner-Allen Mansion is the home of the oldest continuously operating family business in the state. The house was built for David S. Bonner in 1842 and purchased by Cyrus M. Allen, a lawyer and railroad contractor, in 1845. Allen was a personal friend of Abraham Lincoln, and a plaque marks the bedroom Lincoln used when a guest. The Gardner family purchased the home in 1915. In 1816 Andrew Gardner started a cabinet and coffin-making shop; a sixth-generation Gardner now operates the Gardner Funeral Home in the mansion at 505 Main Street.

In 1842 a merchant named Adam Gimbel arrived in Vincennes and began a mercantile store. His sons continued his business, founding the Gimbel Brothers department stores in Milwaukee, Philadelphia, Pittsburgh, and New York. The second Gimbel store was located in the building at 200 Main Street, constructed in 1875.

—*Elizabeth Brice*

For Further Information:

Day, Richard. *Vincennes.* Dover, N.H.: Arcadia, 1998. Offers a pictorial history of Vincennes from picture postcards and rare photographs.

Derleth, August. *Vincennes: Portal to the West.* Englewood Cliffs, N.J.: Prentice-Hall, 1968. Provides a thorough and detailed account of the city's origin and history up to the War of 1812, focusing on Clark's campaign and including William Henry Harrison's dealings with the Indians.

Taylor, Robert M., Jr., Errol Wayne Stevens, Mary Ann Ponder, and Paul Brockman. *Indiana: A New Historical Guide.* Indianapolis: Indiana Historical Society, 1992. An excellent city guide to Vincennes attractions. It is geographically arranged and could serve for a self-guided walking or auto tour.

Other Historic Sites

Angel Mounds

Location: Evansville, Vanderburgh County

Relevant issues: American Indian history

Statement of significance: Covering a hundred-acre area, this site is the northeastern-most extension of the Mississippian culture, which flourished in the period 1000-1600 C.E. The mounds now form a state park.

Butler Fieldhouse

Location: Indianapolis, Marion County

Relevant issues: Sports

Statement of significance: This is the oldest of the major college basketball fieldhouses and still the largest at a private institution. Its large size helped transform college basketball in the late 1920's and 1930's. It was long the location of the Indiana State High School Tournament, one of the most active and well-known such tournaments in the country.

Cannelton Cotton Mills

Location: Cannelton, Perry County

Relevant issues: Business and industry

Statement of significance: Begun in 1849, this is one of the most impressive pre-Civil War mills in the Midwest. Situated on the bluffs above the Ohio River, the mill operated for over one hundred years, manufacturing thread and cloth. It was one of the first American mill buildings which strove to wed utility and aesthetics. Innovative in design, using steam instead of water power and Southern cotton as raw material, the manufactory never reached its goal as a major industrial center in spite of the fact that it was constructed as a challenge to the textile industry of New England.

Coffin House

Location: Fountain City, Wayne County

Relevant issues: African American history

Web site: www.waynet.wayne.in.us/nonprofit/coffin.htm

Statement of significance: From 1827 to 1847, this two-story brick house served as the "Union Depot of the Underground Railroad"; its owner, Levi Coffin (1789-1877), a successful businessman, is believed to have helped as many as two thousand runaway slaves on their flight to freedom during this period. After emancipation occurred during the Civil War, Coffin devoted much of the remainder of his life to improving the lot of freedmen.

Debs Home

Location: Terre Haute, Vigo County

Relevant issues: Political history, social reform

Statement of significance: From 1890 until his death, this two-story frame building was the home of Eugene Victor Debs (1855-1926), the founder of industrial unionism in the United States and the Socialist Party's presidential candidate in five presidential elections (1900-1920, except 1916).

Harrison Home

Location: Indianapolis, Marion County

Relevant issues: Political history

Statement of significance: From 1875 until his death, this was the residence of Benjamin Harrison (1833-1901), twenty-third president of the United States (1889-1893). Harrison accepted the Republican Party's nomination for the presidency in this home in 1888.

Indianapolis Motor Speedway

Location: Speedway, Marion County

Relevant issues: Sports

Statement of significance: Constructed in 1909, this is the only reasonably intact early twentieth century high-speed auto race course in the country and the oldest continuously operated automobile race course anywhere. It has long been the premier auto racing site in the United States: Since 1911, it has been the site of the Indianapolis 500, one of the largest single-day spectator sporting events in the world. The Speedway has also made significant contributions to automobile design, performance, technology, and safety.

Lincoln Boyhood Home

Location: Lincoln City, Spencer County

Relevant issues: Political history

Statement of significance: The family of Abraham Lincoln (1809-1865) lived in southern Indiana from 1816 to 1830, a period in which he grew to manhood and received his early instruction in reading the law. The traditional gravesite of Lincoln's mother and the site of the Lincoln cabin are here.

Madam C. J. Walker Manufacturing Company

Location: Indianapolis, Marion County

Relevant issues: African American history, business and industry, women's history

Statement of significance: This building (1927) was the hub of the beauty industry initiated and developed by Madam C. J. Walker (1867-1919), the first black woman to open the field of cosmetology as a new and lucrative industry for black women. For years, the Walker Company was the most successful black business in the United States. Besides being the national headquarters and manufacturing site where approximately three thousand women were employed, the Walker Company also served as a community cultural center, housing a ballroom and theater. The Walker Theater is one of the few remaining examples of Africanized architecture popularized in the 1920's and 1930's.

Riley House

Location: Indianapolis, Marion County

Relevant issues: Literary history

Statement of significance: From 1893 until his death, this two-story Victorian style brick building was the home of James Whitcomb Riley (1849-1916), the "Hoosier poet." Riley wrote in the American vernacular on homespun subjects; his residence contains memorabilia of his life and career.

Studebaker House

Location: South Bend, St. Joseph County

Relevant issues: Business and industry

Statement of significance: From 1889 until his death, this was the residence of Clement Studebaker (1831-1901), blacksmith and wagonmaker. In 1852, he cofounded the company which by the 1890's would become the largest producer of horse-drawn vehicles in the world; Studebaker Brothers Manufacturing Company also has the distinction of being the only wagon-manufacturing firm in the country to convert successfully to automobile manufacture.

Tippecanoe Battlefield

Location: Lafayette, Tippecanoe County

Relevant issues: American Indian history, military history

Statement of significance: In response to the efforts of Shawnee chief Tecumseh and his brother, the Prophet, to unite the Indian nations of the northwest and southwest territories to resist American expansion, Indiana Territory governor William Henry Harrison led a force of about one thousand men to the Shawnee settlement at the Great Clearing, where Tippecanoe Creek flows into the Wabash. On November 7, 1811, Harrison's army defeated the Shawnee led by the Prophet and sacked their village, in the process destroying all hope that Tecumseh had for an Indian confederacy. The American victory here was also an important cause of the second war with Britain (1812-1815).

Wallace Circus Winter Headquarters

Location: Peru, Miami County

Relevant issues: Cultural history

Statement of significance: Used by Benjamin ("Ben") E. Wallace and his successors, the American Circus Corporation and the Ringlings, the complex contains several rare examples of structures associated with the heyday of the American circus which date from an era of prosperity in the business, the 1920's.

Wallace Study

Location: Crawfordsville, Montgomery County

Relevant issues: Civil War, literary history, military history

Statement of significance: From 1898 until his death, this was the study of Lew Wallace (1827-1905), American general, diplomat, and author. During the Civil War, Wallace played an important part in the victory at Fort Donelson and the Battle of Monocacy, Maryland; after the war's end, he served on the military tribunal that tried and convicted the conspirators in Abraham Lincoln's assassination. During Reconstruction, he was an influential Radical Republican. His novel *Ben-Hur* was published in 1880.

Webster House

Location: Marion, Grant County

Relevant issues: Art and architecture, cultural history

Statement of significance: This was the home of Marie Webster (1859-1956), a master of quilting and a noted advocate of this artistic craft. Webster did not begin quilting until she was fifty years old; her first quilt, based on the traditional Rose of Sharon pattern, displayed Webster's creative talent, resulting in a stunning three-dimensional effect. In 1911 and 1912, Webster's unique designs were featured in *Ladies' Home Journal*. The popularity of these designs led to the publication in 1915 of her book *Quilts: Their History and How to Make Them.*

West Baden Springs Hotel

Location: West Baden Springs, Orange County

Relevant issues: Art and architecture

Web site: wbs@historiclandmarks.org

Statement of significance: The focus of the community that dubbed itself the "Wiesbaden" (West Baden) or "Carlsbad" of America because of its mineral water springs, the hotel (1902) is a major feat of engineering, with an immense covered steel and glass dome, two hundred feet in diameter, which was the largest in the world when built.